THE
FILM STUDIES READER

THE
FILM STUDIES
READER

Edited by

Joanne Hollows
Senior Lecturer in Media and Cultural Studies,
Nottingham Trent University

Peter Hutchings
Senior Lecturer in Film Studies, University of Northumbria

and

Mark Jancovich
Director of the Institute of Film Studies, University of Nottingham

A member of the Hodder Headline Group
LONDON
Co-published in the United States of America by
Oxford University Press Inc., New York

First published in Great Britain in 2000 by
Arnold, a member of the Hodder Headline Group,
338 Euston Road, London NW1 3BH

http://www.arnoldpublishers.com

Co-published in the United States of America by
Oxford University Press Inc.,
198 Madison Avenue, New York, NY10016

The advice and information in this book are believed to be true and
accurate at the date of going to press, but neither the author[s] nor the publisher
can accept any legal responsibility or liability for any errors or omissions.

British Library Cataloguing in Publication Data
A catalogue record for this book is available from the British Library

Library of Congress Cataloging-in-Publication Data
A catalog record for this book is available from the Library of Congress

ISBN 0 340 69278 2 (hb)
ISBN 0 340 69279 0 (pb)

4 5 6 7 8 9 10

Production Editor: Wendy Rooke
Production Controller: Priya Gohil
Cover Design: Terry Griffiths

Typeset in10/12pt Times by Saxon Graphics Ltd, Derby
Printed and bound in Great Britain by MPG Books Ltd, Bodmin, Cornwall

What do you think about this book? Or any other Arnold title?
Please send your comments to feedback.arnold@hodder.co.uk

CONTENTS

PREFACE

Cinema has existed for more than a hundred years; it has been analysed, theorised about and studied for nearly as long. This book is an introduction to the key approaches that have been developed for the study of film. It offers a wide range of examples of the work of those critics and theorists whose activities have helped to shape this particular area of intellectual endeavour. By encountering critics 'in their own words', so to speak, it is hoped that a clearer sense will be gained of the kinds of ideas and debates that have proved so important and influential for our understanding of the cinematic medium.

The book is organized into nine sections, each dealing with a key approach in film studies. In many places, we have edited the selections in order to include as diverse a sample as possible. While there is no simple chronology to the organization of the book, we have attempted to organize the extracts so that students gain a sense of key debates both within, and between, approaches. In order to guide the reader through these extracts, each section has a brief introduction, which aims to contextualize and explain the significance of each extract. We have also tried to draw connections between different sections of the book. Not only do we refer the reader forward or backward to places where specific ideas are discussed in more detail, we have also tried, in the process, to provide some sense of the relationships *between* the ideas in each section.

We are well aware that the extracts we have chosen would not have been everybody's choice. However, these are the selections that make sense to us and have helped to shape our own understanding of the field. We hope that the book offers readers an accessible entry into the field of film studies. We also hope that it will help to illuminate what it is about cinema that has proved so fascinating for generations of scholars and critics.

ACKNOWLEDGEMENTS

Arthouse, Inc. for the excerpts from Andrew Sarris, 'Notes on the *Auteur* Theory in 1962', *Film Culture* 27 (1962/63); Blackwell Publishers for the excerpts from *Hollywood in the Information Age* by Janet Wasko, Copyright © 1994; and the excerpts from 'Utopian Possibilities' in *Women and Soap Opera* by Christine Geraghty (1991); Richard Maltby and Blackwell Publishers for the excerpts from *Hollywood Cinema: An Introduction* by Richard Maltby (1995); the British Film Institute for the excerpts from Thorold Dickinson, 'The Filmwright and the Audience', *Sight and Sound* 19 (1950); the excerpts from Howard Koch, 'A Playright Looks at the "Filmwright"', *Sight and Sound* 19 (1950); the excerpts from *Men, Women and Chainsaws* by Carol Clover (1992); the excerpts from *Stars* by Richard Dyer (1979); the excerpts from Maria LaPlace, 'Producing and Consuming the Woman's Film' in *Home Is Where the Heart Is* edited by Christine Gledhill (1987); the excerpts from Chapter 3 of *Sex, Class and Realism* by John Hill (1986); the excerpts from Chapter 3 of *Genre* by Steve Neale (1980); the excerpts from François Truffaut, 'A Certain Tendency of the French Cinema', *Cahiers du Cinema in English* 31 (1966); the excerpts from 'Critical Method: Auteur and Genre' in *Theories of Film* by Andrew Tudor (1974); and for the excerpts from *Signs and Meaning in the Cinema* by Peter Wollen (1972); Nicholas Garnham and Carfax Ltd for the excerpts from Garnham, 'Concepts of Culture: Public Policy and the Cultural Industries', *Cultural Studies* 1 (1987); Marie Gillespie and Carfax Ltd for the excerpts from Gillespie, 'Technology and Tradition: Audio-visual Culture among South Asian Families in West London', *Cultural Studies* 3 (1989); The Continuum Publishing Company for the excerpts from *Dialectic of Enlightenment* by Theodor W. Adorno and Max Horkheimer, Copyright © 1972 by Herder & Herder; Pam Cook for the excerpts from Pam Cook and Claire Johnston, 'The Place of Woman in the Cinema of Raoul Walsh' in *Raoul Walsh*, edited by Phil Hardy (1974); Indiana University Press for the excerpts from *Signs and Meaning in the Cinema* by Peter Wollen (1972); Jim Kitses for the excerpts from his book *Horizons West* (1969) (special thanks to Jim Kitses for giving permission to edit his chapter to meet the aims of the book); The Johns Hopkins University Press for the excerpts from Tom Gunning, 'Cinema of Attractions', *Wide Angle* 3 (1986), Copyright © 1986 by Ohio University: Athens Center for Film and Video; Macmillan Press Ltd for the excerpts from *Heavenly Bodies* by Richard Dyer (1986); *Movie* for the excerpts from Ian Cameron 'Films, directors and critics', *Movie* 2 (1962); Oxford University Press for the excerpts from Jean-Luc Comolli and Paul Narboni, 'Cinema/Ideology/Criticism', *Screen* 12 (1971); the excerpts from Christian Metz, 'The Imaginary Signifier', *Screen* 16 (1975); and for the excerpt from Peter Kramer, 'Postclassical Hollywood' in *The*

Oxford Guide to Film Studies edited by John Hill and Pamela Church (1998); Steven Cohan and Oxford University Press for the excerpts from Cohan, 'Cary Grant in the fifties', *Screen* 33 (1992); Colin MacCabe and Oxford University Press for the excerpts from MacCabe, 'Realism and the Cinema', *Screen* 15 (1974); Laura Mulvey and Oxford University Press for the excerpts from Mulvey, 'Visual Pleasure and Narrative Cinema', *Screen* 16 (1975); Barbara Klinger and Oxford University Press for the excerpts from Klinger, 'Film History Interminable: Recovering the Past in Reception Studies', *Screen* 38 (1997); Robert Stam, Louise Spence and Oxford University Press for the excerpts from Stam and Spence, 'Colonialism, Racism and Representation', *Screen* 24 (1983); Jane Gaines and Oxford University Press for the excerpts from Gaines, 'White Privilege and Looking Relations: Race and Gender in Feminist Film Theory', *Screen* 29 (1988); Princeton University Press for the excerpts from *Men, Women and Chainsaws* by Carol Clover, Copyright © 1992 by Princeton University Press; Routledge, Inc. for the excerpts from Eileen R. Meehan, ' "Holy Commodity Fetish, Batman!" ': The Political Economy of a Commercial Intertext from *The Many Lives of Batman* edited by Roberta Pearson and William Uricchio, Copyright © 1991; for the excerpts from Janet Staiger, 'Taboos and Totems: cultural meanings of "The Silence of the Lambs" ' in *Film Theory Goes to the Movies* edited by Jim Collins, Hilary Radnor and Ava Preacher Collins, Copyright © 1993; and for the excerpts from *Femmes Fatales* by Mary Ann Doane, Copyright © 1991; Jackie Stacey and Taylor & Francis Books Ltd for the excerpts from Stacey, 'Feminine Fascinations' in *Stardom* edited by Christine Gledhill (1991); Iain Chambers and Taylor & Francis Books Ltd for the excerpts from *Border Dialogues* by Iain Chambers (1990); Charlotte Brunsdon and Taylor & Francis Books Ltd for the excerpts from *Screen Tastes* by Charlotte Brunsdon (1997); Robyn Wiegman and Taylor & Francis Books Ltd for Wiegman, 'Feminism, "The Boyz", and Other Matters Regarding the Male' in *Screening the Male* edited by Steven Cohan and Ina Rae Hark (1993); Tamsin Wilton and Taylor & Francis Books Ltd for the excerpts from Wilton, 'On Not Being Lady Macbeth: Some (Troubled) Thoughts on Lesbian Spectatorship' in *Immortal, Invisible: Lesbians and the Moving Image* edited by Tamsin Wilton (1995); University of California Press for the excerpts from Dayan, 'The Tutor-Code of Classical Cinema', *Film Quarterly* 28 (1974), Copyright © 1974 by the Regents of the University of California; James Naremore and the University of California Press for the excerpts from Naremore, 'American Film Noir: The History of an Idea', *Film Quarterly* 49 (1995/96), Copyright © 1996 by the Regents of the University of California; University of Minnesota Press for the excerpts from *Making Things Perfectly Queer* by Alexander Doty (1993); University of Texas Press for the excerpts from *Hollywood in the Information Age* by Janet Wasko, Copyright © 1994; Verso for the excerpts from *Dialectic of Enlightenment* by Theodor W. Adorno and Max Horkheimer (1972); Robin Wood for the excerpts from his book *Personal Views* (1976).

Every effort has been made to trace copyright holders of material reproduced in this book. Any rights not acknowledged here will be acknowledged in subsequent printings if notice is given to the publisher.

SECTION ONE

POLITICAL ECONOMY AND MASS CULTURE THEORY

While most of the approaches discussed in the later sections of this book are concerned with the aesthetic and political significance of film texts, mass culture theorists and political economists focus on the ways in which films are the product of industrial and economic processes that shape their form, content and the ways in which they are consumed by audiences. For these critics, the films we get to see are the product of film industries which are formed in relation to other industries and to wider political and economic systems. To take the film text as the starting-point for analysis therefore ignores important questions about how the structure and practices of film industries 'determine what films can be made by whom and what films can be viewed and by what audiences' (Garnham 1990: 171). Using these approaches, it becomes clear that film industries are in the business of producing not only films but also audiences for these films. However, despite common interests between mass culture theory and more contemporary work on the political economy, the latter has also been highly critical of many of the assumptions of the former.

Mass culture theory has a long history. From the 1930s to 1950s, it became a key framework for critics who were trying to make sense of new cultural forms such as cinema and radio. For these critics, mass culture was the product of industrialization, a process through which the production and consumption of culture had become economic activities, governed by commercial interests. These conditions of production based on the search for economies of scale, mass culture critics argued, resulted in standardized and homogeneous cultural forms which, in turn, created standardized responses in their audiences. Moreover, for these critics, the rise of mass culture, and the mass audience that it produced, were part of a process of cultural decline. Whereas older cultural forms such as music were taken over by the cultural industry, cinema was seen as a result of this insidious mass culture: from its earliest moments, cinema was a product of 'technology' and mechanical reproduction, and from an early stage it was based on a system of industrial production and mass distribution.

However, for critics such as Theodor Adorno and Max Horkheimer (see extract 1), mass culture did not just present a threat to aesthetic standards, it was also politically dangerous. The nature of these threats needs to be understood in relation to three contextual factors. First, Adorno and Horkheimer's critique of mass culture was shaped by their experiences in their native Germany during the 1920s and 1930s, where they reacted not only against what they saw as a process of Americanization and a growing 'cult of technology', but also against the rise of Fascism (Huyssen 1975). Their critique of mass culture is, in part, an attempt to make sense of Fascism and the conditions under which it could take hold. Second, Adorno and Horkheimer brought the values of a European avant-garde aesthetic to the products of the culture industry, which they encountered when they were forced to flee Germany and move to America. 'Clinging to their old-world prejudices like cultural life-preservers', it is perhaps unsurprising that they related the political dangers of mass culture to what they saw as its aesthetic poverty (Davis 1990: 47). Finally, their critique of the culture industry needs to be understood in relation to their wider theoretical project which was an attempt to explain why capitalism, despite Marx's predictions, had not collapsed. For these critics, the culture industry was related to a process in which scientific rationality no longer promised to liberate humanity but had become integrated within the capitalist economy and transformed into a new, and more powerful, mechanism of domination.

In the first extract, Adorno and Horkheimer explain how cinema is aesthetically impoverished because it is the product of a culture industry based on a system of mass reproduction and distribution. Films, they argue, are standardized products, and any differences between them are pseudo-individual, or illusory, differences. However, they also claim that mass cultural forms are politically dangerous because they leave audiences with no room for individual interpretation and so help to reproduce the capitalist economic system. Standardized films 'prescribe every reaction', and the mass audience created by the film industry reacts *en masse*. In the process, the audience learns to defer to authority and to conform and, in this way, film is implicated in creating the preconditions for a totalitarian society.

In *Dialectic of Enlightenment*, from which extract 1 is taken, Adorno and Horkheimer therefore present a 'pessimistic thesis' about the fate of culture under twentieth-century capitalism. For them, the only source of political optimism is found in avant-garde art, which transcends the all-encompassing control of the culture industry because it refuses to become a commodity and so maintains both its aesthetic and political freedom. Whereas mass culture reconciled its audience to the system, avant-garde art showed its audience the contradictions within the system. Unlike the masses who passively consumed the product of the culture industry, the audience for avant-garde art were 'enlightened outsiders' who struggled to make meanings from art forms that refused to let themselves be easily consumed.

For Adorno and Horkheimer, there is no position from which good cinema could exist: cinema is part of the culture industry and therefore its aesthetics have one ideological purpose: to reproduce the spectator as a consumer. Furthermore, cinema was a product of technologies of mass reproduction and distribution and was therefore already implicated in the maintenance of ideological and economic domination. In this way, Adorno and Horkheimer could see little scope for a radical film-making practice. As a result, Adorno and Horkheimer's theoretical framework largely precluded the possibility of making political and aesthetic distinctions within cinema (although Adorno would modify his position in the mid-1960s to argue that low-tech films which courted imperfection might provide the basis for an avant-garde film-making practice: see Adorno 1975.)

In contrast, while Dwight Macdonald draws on many of Adorno and Horkheimer's insights in the second extract, he does so from his position as a film critic. His analysis is an attempt to think about the uses of mass culture theory for making a critically informed distinction between standardised and formulaic cinema and that which might have aesthetic and, therefore, political merits. Like Adorno and Horkheimer, Macdonald establishes a relationship between mass culture and modes of political domination. However, like the work of many other US radicals in the 1950s, Macdonald's writing is shaped by a growing disenchantment with Stalin's Russia, and his fears about the effects of mass culture on American political life are related to fears about totalitarianism in the USSR, where mass culture was 'worse and more pervasive' than in the US because it exploited people politically rather than commercially (Macdonald 1963: 29).

Like many other mass culture critics, Macdonald argued that cultural distinctions between, and within, nations were being eroded by 'masscult' (for Macdonald, culture was too good a term for this new bastardized form), a form that was 'fabricated by technicians hired by business men' (Macdonald 1963: 14). Masscult, he argued, respected quantity, not quality, repetition, not innovation. Just as Adorno and Horkheimer drew attention to standardization, so Macdonald notes how Hollywood film establishes formulas which reproduce previous successes: different 'genres' simply represented what Adorno and Horkheimer had called 'pseudo-individualized' differences between films. Furthermore, Macdonald again believed that the audience response to Hollywood film was standardized: popular films had a 'built-in reaction' which trained people to defer to authority.

However, while Macdonald shared Adorno and Horkheimer's belief that the avant-garde represented the only hope for art in the modern world, he drew on the distinction between the avant-garde and mass culture to distinguish between good and bad films. Macdonald did acknowledge that Hollywood was capable of producing some great movies, but these were seen as the product of an exceptional genius or 'auteur' such as Orson Welles and Ernst Lubitsch. Macdonald therefore largely equates 'good' cinema with the 'art' cinema produced by European directors such as Bergman, Truffaut and Bunuel. These directors, he claimed, produced work of individual genius for a minority audience, a community of individuals able to understand the codes and conventions of cinema. Bad commercial cinema, he argued, was the product of an industrial system staffed by technicians and consumed by a mass audience who were conditioned to want predigested entertainment. In this way, he not only distinguished art cinema from masscult, but sought to legitimate some films as art by seeing them as the product of a creative genius or auteur, a strategy which would be an important move in establishing film studies as a discipline (see Section Two).

Mass culture theory has been subject to numerous criticisms, not least from within cultural studies. For example, Stuart Hall has questioned the way in which mass culture criticism presents the products of the culture industry as 'purely manipulative and debased' and consumed by people who are 'cultural dopes', either 'debased by these activities or living in a permanent state of false consciousness' (Hall 1981: 231). Indeed, it has been argued that 'the masses' are not so much a product of the activities of the culture industry and more a product of the discourses of mass culture theory: as Raymond Williams (1963) argues, there are no such thing as 'masses', only ways of seeing people as masses. However, while contemporary political economists have tended to refute the idea of the cinema audience as a passive mass, they have also stressed that an 'active' audience is not necessarily a 'free' audience. The structure, organization and practices of the cultural industries still shape what is produced and distributed and made available for audiences to consume.

Many political economists have also challenged the ways in which the opposition between art and mass culture structures mass culture criticism. For example, Nicholas Garnham challenges this idea that 'art' can exist in a state of splendid isolation 'outside' economic relations: indeed, 'art' has a political economy. He also stresses that the values of the high cultural tradition which mass culture critics legitimate are 'far from being universal ... closely linked to the structural inequality of access to society's resources' (Garnham 1977: 347). For Garnham, the notion of legitimate culture that is mobilized by mass culture critics underpins contemporary forms of patronage. State funding for cultural production is predominantly used to support traditional high culture or the 'legitimate' branches of newer cultural forms – for example, art films and art-house cinemas. In this way, alternatives to the market tend to serve the existing tastes and habits of the middle class and ignore the popular audience (Garnham 1987).

Political economists of cinema demonstrate how questions about the power relations within which cultural production takes place are still pertinent today. While political economists have been critical of film studies' tendency to ignore the ways in which the economics of film production and distribution shape the films that we get to see, they have also been critical of mass culture critics such as Adorno and Horkheimer who characterize the culture industry as having both monolithic and non-contradictory effects. Is standardization really an automatic result of the processes and practices of the film industry, and to what extent are films produced for, and do they in turn produce, a mass audience? While the cultural industries are capital-intensive and hierarchical organizations, whose aims are, like any other industry, to make a profit, they also face specific problems, as Garnham makes clear in the third extract. People only have a limited amount of time and money to spend on cultural pursuits. Furthermore, it is difficult for the cultural industries to pin down the 'use values' of specific cultural products.

For example, while the film industry knows that there is a market for films, it still has to predict which films people are prepared to pay to watch. As a result, the film industry must offer what Garnham calls a 'cultural repertoire' of products: it cannot guarantee which film will be a success, so it has to offer a range of films in order to spread risks. However, the industry also has to match the costs of production to the spending power and size of the audience. The need to produce large audiences exerts a dual pressure to limit diversity and innovation, while still requiring some degree of diversity and innovation in order to continue to attract audiences.

For Garnham (1990), distribution also exerts considerable control within the contemporary film industry. Film distribution is controlled by the major studios, and although these studios are directly involved in the production of a small number of films, the majority of films are produced by independents. However, most independent producers are dependent on the majors not only for distribution but also, in many cases, for film finance, which is given on terms that favour the majors. In the contemporary film industry it is distribution, rather than production, which gives the most opportunities to maximise efficiency and profit. As Garnham argues, 'because of the limit on productivity in production, there ... is always a premium on expanding the audience to the maximum possible for each unit of production' (1990: 185). Therefore, distributors generally aim to maximise audience size and recoup their costs as quickly as possible.

The significance of these issues can be seen in the final extracts. In extract 5, for example, Janet Wasko provides a political economy of contemporary Hollywood, in which she examines how new technologies such as video and cable have opened up new channels of distribution which, in turn, have opened up new sources of profit for the majors. The attempt to maximise audience size by distributors also puts an increased emphasis on promotion within the film industry's practices. While these new technologies promised more diversity of product and more choice for consumers, they have often resulted in attempts to maximize the audience for a smaller number of films.

In extract 4, Eileen Meehan demonstrates how promotion was central to the success of the blockbuster *Batman* (1989). As Meehan demonstrates '*Batman* is best understood as a multimedia, multimarket sales campaign' (1991: 61). The case of *Batman* demonstrates the ways in which what Wasko calls 'corporate synergy' and 'cultural synergy' characterize contemporary Hollywood. Corporate synergy refers to 'a strategy of diversifying into directly related technologies and areas of entertainment and using the opportunities that this provides for extending the exposure of ... [materials] and artists' (Negus 1992: 5). For Wasko, this results in a form of cultural synergy in which 'similar ideas, values, and expressions are reproduced' across different media.

A political economy of cinema is therefore necessary if we are to understand why and how certain films get produced and distributed; the industrial processes and practices that structure the form and content of these film texts; and how audiences select and interpret them. Furthermore, political economy offers film studies an understanding of how power relations and structural inequalities underpin film production and consumption. While the content of films is not a simple reflection of the economics of the film industry, as Meehan demonstrates, the relations of cultural production do profoundly shape the formal properties of the film text. As Garnham puts it, 'the budget available and the given structure of the division of labour affects what you can say and how you can say it' (Garnham 1990: 15).

Nonetheless, despite the insistence on understanding the complex relations between production, distribution, the film text and consumption, political economy has only made a limited contribution to the understanding of consumption. While political economists deal with key questions about how audiences are created for films and questions about access to the products of the cultural industries, the activities of audiences themselves are seen as relatively insignificant. Certainly, audiences are relatively powerless in relation to the cultural industries in determining what gets produced and distributed. However, control over what is produced does not necessarily equate with control over how films are consumed and how their meanings might be transformed within the contexts of lived culture (see Section Eight).

References

Adorno, T. (1975). 'Culture Industry Reconsidered'. *New German Critique* **6**(4): 12–19.

—— and Horkheimer, M. (1979). *The Dialectic of Enlightenment*. London: Verso.

Davis, M. (1990). *City of Quartz: Excavating the Future in Postmodern Los Angeles*. London: Verso.

Garnham, N. (1977). 'Towards a Political Economy of Culture'. *New Universities Quarterly* **1**(1): 341–57.

—— (1987). 'Concepts of Culture: Public Policy and the Cultural Industries'. *Cultural Studies* **1**(1): 23–37.

—— (1990). *Capitalism and Communication: Global Culture and the Economics of Information*. London: Sage.

Hall, S. (1981). 'Notes on Deconstructing "The Popular" '. In R. Samuel (ed.), *People's History and Socialist Theory*. London: Routledge, 227–40.

Huyssen, A. (1975). 'Introduction to Adorno'. *New German Critique* **6**(4): 3–11.

MacDonald, D. (1957). 'A Theory of Mass Culture'. In B. Rosenberg and D. Manning White (eds), *Mass Culture: The Popular Arts in America*. New York: Free Press, 59–73.

—— (1963). *Against the American Grain*. London: Gollancz.

Meehan, E. R. (1991). ' "Holy Commodity Fetish, Batman!" ': The Political Economy of a Commercial Intertext'. In R. E. Pearson and W. Uricchio (eds), *The Many Lives of Batman: Critical Approaches to a Superhero and His Media*. New York: Routledge, 47–65.

Negus, K. (1992). *Producing Pop*. London: Arnold.

Wasko, J. (1994). *Hollywood in the Information Age*. Cambridge: Polity.

Williams, R. (1963). *Culture and Society*. Harmondsworth: Penguin.

1 The culture industry: enlightenment as mass deception

Theodor W. Adorno and Max Horkheimer

The sociological theory that the loss of the support of objectively established religion, the dissolution of the last remnants of precapitalism, together with technological and social differentiation or specialization, have led to cultural chaos is disproved every day; for culture now impresses the same stamp on everything. Films, radio and magazines make up a system which is uniform as a whole and in every part. Even the aesthetic activities of political opposites are one in their enthusiastic obedience to the rhythm of the iron system. [...] Under monopoly all mass culture is identical, and the lines of its artificial framework begin to show through. The people at the top are no longer so interested in concealing monopoly: as its violence becomes more open, so its power grows. Movies and radio need no longer pretend to be art. The truth that they are just business is made into an ideology in order to justify the rubbish they deliberately produce. They call themselves industries; and when their directors' incomes are published, any doubt about the social utility of the finished products is removed.

Interested parties explain the culture industry in technological terms. It is alleged that because millions participate in it, certain reproduction processes are necessary that inevitably require identical needs in innumerable places to be satisfied with identical goods. The technical contrast between the few production centers and the large number of widely dispersed consumption points is said to demand organization and planning by management. Furthermore, it is claimed that standards were based in the first place on consumers' needs, and for that reason were accepted with so little resistance. The result is the circle of manipulation and retroactive need in which the unity of the system grows ever stronger. No mention is made of the fact that the basis on which technology acquires power over society is the power of those whose economic hold over society is greatest. A technological rationale is the rationale of domination itself. It is the coercive nature of society alienated from itself. Automobiles, bombs, and movies keep the whole thing together until their leveling element shows its strength in the very wrong which it furthered. It has made the technology of the culture industry no more than the achievement of standardization and mass production, sacrificing whatever involved a distinction between the logic of the work and that of the social system. This is the result not of a law of movement in technology as such but of its function in today's economy. The need which might resist central control has already been suppressed by the control of the individual consciousness. The step from the telephone to the radio has clearly distinguished the roles. The former still allowed the subscriber to play the role of subject, and was liberal. The latter is democratic: it turns all participants into listeners and authoritatively subjects them to broadcast programs which are all exactly the same. No machinery of rejoinder has been devised, and private broadcasters are denied any freedom. They are confined to the apocryphal field of the 'amateur', and also have to accept organization from above. But any trace of spontaneity from the public in official broadcasting is controlled and absorbed by talent scouts, studio competitions and official programs of every kind selected by professionals. Talented performers belong to the industry long before it displays them; otherwise they would not be so eager to fit in. The attitude of the public, which ostensibly and actually favors the system of the culture industry, is a part of the system and not an excuse for it. If one branch of art follows the same formula as one with a very different medium and content; if the dramatic intrigue of broadcast soap operas becomes no more than useful material for showing how to master technical problems at both ends of the scale of musical experience – real jazz or a cheap imitation; or if a movement from a Beethoven symphony is crudely 'adapted' for a film soundtrack in the same way as a Tolstoy novel is garbled in a film script: then the claim that this is done to satisfy the spontaneous wishes of the public is no more than hot air. We are closer to the facts if we explain these phenomena as inherent in the technical and personnel apparatus which, down to its last cog, itself forms part of the economic mechanism of selection. In addition there is the agreement – or at least the determination – of all executive authorities not to produce or sanction anything that in any way differs from their own rules, their own ideas about consumers, or above all themselves.

In our age the objective social tendency is incarnate in the hidden subjective purposes of company directors, the foremost among whom are in the most powerful sectors of industry – steel, petroleum, electricity, and chemicals. Culture monopolies are weak and dependent in comparison. They cannot afford to neglect their appeasement of the real holders of power if their sphere of activity in mass society [...] is not to undergo a series of purges. The dependence of the most powerful broadcasting company on the electrical industry, or of the motion picture industry on the banks, is characteristic of the whole sphere, whose individual branches are themselves economically interwoven. All are in such close contact that the extreme concentration of mental forces allows demarcation lines between different firms and technical branches to be ignored. The ruthless unity in the culture industry is evidence of what will happen in politics. Marked differentiations such as those of A and B films, or of stories in magazines in different price ranges, depend not so much on subject matter as on classifying, organizing, and labelling consumers. Something is provided for all so that none may escape; the distinctions are emphasized and extended. The public is catered for with a hierarchical range of mass-produced products of varying quality, thus advancing the rule of complete quantification. Everybody must behave (as if spontaneously) in accordance with his previously determined and indexed level, and choose the category of mass product turned out for his type. Consumers appear as statistics on research organization charts, and are divided by income groups into red, green, and blue areas; the technique is that used for any type of propaganda.

How formalized the procedure is can be seen when the mechanically differentiated products prove to be all alike in the end. That the difference between the Chrysler range and General Motors products is basically illusory strikes every child with a keen interest in varieties. What connoisseurs discuss as good or bad points serve only to perpetuate the semblance of competition and range of choice. The same applies to the Warner Brothers and Metro Goldwyn Mayer productions. But even the differences between the more expensive and cheaper models put out by the same firm steadily diminish: for automobiles, there are such differences as the number of cylinders, cubic capacity, details of patented gadgets; and for films there are the number of stars, the extravagant use of technology, labor, and equipment, and the introduction of the latest psychological formulas. The universal criterion of merit is the amount of 'conspicuous production', of blatant cash investment. The varying budgets in the culture industry do not bear the slightest relation to factual values, to the meaning of the products themselves. [...]

Not only are the hit songs, stars, and soap operas cyclically recurrent and rigidly invariable types, but the specific content of the entertainment itself is derived from them and only appears to change. The details are interchangeable. The short interval sequence which was effective in a hit song, the hero's momentary fall from grace (which he accepts as good sport), the rough treatment which the beloved gets from the male star, the latter's rugged defiance of the spoilt heiress, are, like all the other details, ready-made clichés to be slotted in anywhere; they never do anything more than fulfill the purpose allotted them in the overall plan. Their whole *raison d'être* is to confirm it by being its constituent parts. As soon as the film begins, it is quite clear how it will end, and who will be rewarded, punished, or forgotten. In light music, once the trained ear has heard the first notes of the hit song, it can guess what is coming and feel flattered when it does come. The average length of the short story has to be rigidly adhered to. Even gags, effects, and jokes are calculated like the setting in which they are placed. They are the responsibility of special experts and their narrow range makes it easy for them to be apportioned in the office. The development of the culture industry has led to the predominance of the effect, the obvious touch, and the technical detail over the work itself – which once expressed an idea, but was liquidated together with the idea. [...]

The whole world is made to pass through the filter of the culture industry. The old experience of the movie-goer, who sees the world outside as an extension of the film he has just left (because the latter is intent upon reproducing the world of everyday perceptions), is now the producer's guideline. The more intensely and flawlessly his techniques duplicate empirical objects, the easier it is today for the illusion to prevail that the outside world is the straightforward continuation of that presented on the screen. This purpose has been furthered by mechanical reproduction since the lightning takeover by the sound film.

Real life is becoming indistinguishable from the movies. The sound film, far surpassing the theater of illusion, leaves no room for imagination or reflection on the part of the audience, who is unable to respond within the structure of the film, yet deviate from its precise detail without losing the thread of the story; hence the film forces its victims to equate it directly with reality. The stunting of the mass-media consumer's powers of imagination and spontaneity does not have to be traced back to any psychological mechanisms; he must ascribe the loss of those attributes to the objective nature of the products themselves, especially to the most characteristic of them, the sound film. They are so designed that quickness, powers of observation, and experience are undeniably needed to apprehend them at all; yet sustained thought is out of the question if the spectator is not to miss the relentless rush of facts. Even though the effort required for his response is semi-automatic, no scope is left for the imagination. Those who are so absorbed by the world of the movie – by its images, gestures, and words – that they are unable to supply what really makes it a world, do not have to dwell on particular points of its mechanics during a screening. All the other films and products of the entertainment industry which they have seen have taught them what to expect; they react automatically. The might of industrial society is lodged in men's minds. The entertainments manufacturers know that their products will be consumed with alertness even when the customer is distraught, for each of them is a model of the huge economic machinery which has always sustained the masses, whether at work or at leisure – which is akin to work. From every sound film and every broadcast programme the social effect can be inferred which is exclusive to none but is shared by all alike. The culture industry as a whole has molded men as a type unfailingly reproduced in every product. All the agents of this process, from the producer to the women's clubs, take good care that the simple reproduction of this mental state is not nuanced or extended in any way. [...]

The consumers are the workers and employees, the farmers and lower middle class. Capitalist production so confines them, body and soul, that they fall helpless victims to what is offered them. As naturally as the ruled always took the morality imposed upon them more seriously than did the rulers themselves, the deceived masses are today captivated by the myth of success even more than the successful are. Immovably, they insist on the very ideology which enslaves them. The misplaced love of the common people for the wrong which is done them is a greater force than the cunning of the authorities. It is stronger even than the rigorism of the Hays Office, just as in certain great times in history it has inflamed greater forces that were turned against it, namely, the terror of the tribunals. It calls for Mickey Rooney in preference to the tragic Garbo, for Donald Duck instead of Betty Boop. The industry submits to the vote which it has itself inspired. What is a loss for the firm which cannot fully exploit a contract with a declining star is a legitimate expense for the system as a whole. By craftily sanctioning the demand for rubbish it inaugurates total harmony. The connoisseur and the expert are despised for their pretentious claim to know better than the others, even though culture is democratic and distributes its privileges to all. In view of the ideological truce, the conformism of the buyers and the effrontery of the producers who supply them prevail. The result is a constant reproduction of the same thing.

A constant sameness governs the relationship to the past as well. What is new about the phase of mass culture compared with the late liberal stage is the exclusion of the new. The machine rotates on the same spot. While determining consumption it excludes the untried as a risk. The movie-makers distrust any manuscript which is not reassuringly backed by a bestseller. Yet for this very reason there is never-ending talk of ideas, novelty, and surprise, of what is taken for granted but has never existed. Tempo and dynamics serve this trend. Nothing remains as of old; everything has to run incessantly, to keep moving. For only the universal triumph of the rhythm of mechanical production and reproduction promises that nothing changes, and nothing unsuitable will appear. Any additions to the well-proven culture inventory are too much of a speculation. The ossified forms – such as the sketch, short story, problem film, or hit song – are the standardized average of late liberal taste, dictated with threats from above. The people at the top in the culture agencies, who work in harmony as only one manager can with another, whether he comes from the rag trade or from college, have long since reorganized and rationalized the objective spirit. One might think that an omnipresent authority had sifted the material and drawn up an official catalogue of cultural commodities to provide a smooth supply of available mass-produced lines [...]

Amusement and all the elements of the culture industry existed long before the latter came into existence. Now they are taken over from above and brought up to date. The culture industry can pride itself on having energetically executed the previously clumsy transposition of art into the sphere of consumption, on making this a principle, on divesting amusement of its obtrusive naïvetés and improving the type of commodities. The more absolute it became, the more ruthless it was in forcing every outsider either into bankruptcy or into a syndicate [...]

Amusement under late capitalism is the prolongation of work. It is sought after as an escape from the mechanized work process, and to recruit strength in order to be able to cope with it again. But at the same time mechanization has such power over a man's leisure and happiness, and so profoundly determines the manufacture of amusement goods, that his experiences are inevitably after-images of the work process itself. The ostensible content is merely a faded foreground; what sinks in is the automatic succession of standardized operations. What happens at work, in the factory, or in the office can only be escaped from by approximation to it in one's leisure time. All amusement suffers from this incurable malady. Pleasure hardens into boredom because, if it is to remain pleasure, it must not demand any effort and therefore moves rigorously in the worn grooves of association. No independent thinking must be expected from the audience: the product prescribes every reaction: not by its natural structure (which collapses under reflection), but by signals. Any logical connection calling for mental effort is painstakingly avoided. As far as possible, developments must follow from the immediately preceding situation and never from the idea of the whole. For the attentive movie-goer any individual scene will give him the whole thing. [...]

The stronger the positions of the culture industry become, the more summarily it can deal with consumers' needs, producing them, controlling them, disciplining them, and even withdrawing amusement: no limits are set to cultural progress of this kind. But the tendency is immanent in the principle of amusement itself, which is enlightened in a bourgeois sense. If the need for amusement was in large measure the creation of industry, which used the subject as a means of recommending the work to the masses – the oleograph by the dainty morsel it depicted, or the cake mix by a picture of a cake – amusement always reveals the influence of business, the sales talk, the quack's spiel. But the original affinity of business and amusement is shown in the latter's specific significance: to defend society. To be pleased means to say Yes. It is possible only by insulation from the totality of the social process, by desensitization and, from the first, by senselessly sacrificing the inescapable claim of every work, however inane, within its limits to reflect the whole. Pleasure always means not to think about anything, to forget suffering even where it is shown. Basically it is helplessness. It is flight; not, as is asserted, flight from a wretched reality, but from the last remaining thought of resistance. [...]

In the culture industry the individual is an illusion not merely because of the standardization of the means of production. He is tolerated only so long as his complete identification with the generality is unquestioned. Pseudo individuality is rife: from the standardized jazz improvization to the exceptional film star whose hair curls over her eye to demonstrate her originality. What is individual is no more than the generality's power to stamp the accidental detail so firmly that it is accepted as such. The defiant reserve or elegant appearance of the individual on show is mass-produced like Yale locks, whose only difference can be measured in fractions of millimeters. The peculiarity of the self is a monopoly commodity determined by society; it is falsely represented as natural. It is no more than the moustache, the French accent, the deep voice of the woman of the world, the Lubitsch touch: finger prints on identity cards which are otherwise exactly the same, and into which the lives and faces of every single person are transformed by the power of the generality. Pseudo-individuality is the prerequisite for comprehending tragedy and removing its poison: only because individuals have ceased to be themselves and are now merely centres where the general tendencies meet, is it possible to receive them again, whole and entire, into the generality. In this way mass culture discloses the fictitious character of the 'individual' in the bourgeois era [...]

2   A theory of mass culture

Dwight Macdonald

For about a century, Western culture has really been two cultures: the traditional kind – let us call it 'High Culture' – that is chronicled in the textbooks, and a 'Mass Culture' manufactured wholesale for the market. [...]

It is sometimes called 'Popular Culture',[1] but I think 'Mass Culture' a more accurate term, since its distinctive mark is that it is solely and directly an article for mass consumption, like chewing gum. A work of High Culture is occasionally popular, after all, though this is increasingly rare. [...]

The nature of mass culture

The historical reasons for the growth of Mass Culture since the early 1800's are well known. Political democracy and popular education broke down the old upper-class monopoly of culture. Business enterprise found a profitable market in the cultural demands of the newly awakened masses, and the advance of technology made possible the cheap production of books, periodicals, pictures, music, and furniture, in sufficient quantities to satisfy this market. Modern technology also created new media such as the movies and television which are specially well adapted to mass manufacture and distribution.

The phenomenon is thus peculiar to modern times and differs radically from what was hitherto known as art or culture. It is true that Mass Culture began as, and to some extent still is, a parasitic, a cancerous growth on High Culture. As Clement Greenberg pointed out in 'Avant-Garde and *Kitsch*' (*Partisan Review*, Fall, 1939):

'The precondition of *kitsch* (a German term for "Mass Culture") is the availability close at hand of a fully matured cultural tradition, whose discoveries, acquisitions, and perfected self-conscious *kitsch* can take advantage of for its own ends.'[...] *Kitsch* 'mines' High Culture the way improvident frontiersmen mine the soil, extracting its riches and putting nothing back. Also, as *kitsch* develops, it begins to draw on its own past, and some of it evolves so far away from High Culture as to appear quite disconnected from it.

It is also true that Mass Culture is to some extent a continuation of the old Folk Art which until the Industrial Revolution was the culture of the common people, but here, too, the differences are more striking than the similarities. Folk Art grew from below. It was a spontaneous, autochthonous expression of the people, shaped by themselves, pretty much without the benefit of High Culture, to suit their own needs. Mass Culture is imposed from above. It is fabricated by technicians hired by businessmen; its audiences are passive consumers, their participation limited to the choice between buying and not buying. The Lords of *kitsch*, in short, exploit the cultural needs of the masses in order to make a profit and/or to maintain their class rule – in Communist countries, only the second purpose obtains. (It is very different to *satisfy* popular tastes, as Robert Burns' poetry did, and to *exploit* them, as Hollywood does.) Folk Art was the people's own institution, their private little garden walled off from the great formal park of their masters' High Culture. But Mass Culture breaks down the wall, integrating the masses into a debased form of High Culture and thus becoming an instrument of political domination. If one had no other data to go on, the nature of Mass Culture would reveal capitalism to be an exploitative class society and not the harmonious commonwealth it is sometimes alleged to be. The same goes even more strongly for Soviet Communism and *its* special kind of Mass Culture.

Mass culture: USSR

'Everybody' knows that America is a land of Mass Culture, but it is not so generally recognized that so is the Soviet Union. Certainly not by the Communist leaders, one of whom has contemptuously observed that the American people need not fear the peace-loving Soviet state which has absolutely no desire to deprive them of their Coca-Cola and comic books. Yet the fact is that the USSR is even more a land of Mass Culture than is the USA. This is less easily recognizable because their Mass Culture is *in form* just the opposite of ours, being one of propaganda and pedagogy rather than of entertainment. None the less, it has the essential quality of Mass, as against High or Folk, Culture: it is manufactured for mass consumption by technicians employed by the ruling class and is not an expression of either the individual artist or the common people themselves. Like our own, it exploits rather than satisfies the cultural needs of the masses, though for political rather than commercial reasons. Its quality is even lower [...]

Gresham's law in culture

The separation of Folk Art and High Culture in fairly watertight compartments corresponded to the sharp line once drawn between the common people and the aristocracy. The eruption of the masses onto the political stage has broken down this compartmentation, with disastrous cultural results. Whereas Folk Art had its own special quality, Mass Culture is at best a vulgarized reflection of High Culture. And whereas High Culture could formerly ignore the mob and seek to please only the *cognoscenti*, it must now complete with Mass Culture or be merged into it.

The problem is acute in the United States and not just because a prolific Mass Culture exists here. If there were a clearly defined cultural élite, then the masses could have their *kitsch* and the *élite* could have its High Culture, with everybody happy. But the boundary line is blurred. A statistically significant part of the population, I venture to guess, is chronically confronted with a choice between going to the movies or to a concert, between reading Tolstoy or a detective story, between looking at old masters or at a TV show; i.e., the pattern of their cultural lives is 'open' to the point of being porous. Good art competes with *kitsch*, serious ideas compete with commercialized formulae – and the advantage lies all on one side. There seems to be a Gresham's Law in cultural as well as monetary circulation: bad stuff drives out the good, since it is more easily understood and enjoyed. It is this facility of access which at once sells *kitsch* on a wide market and also prevents it from achieving quality.[2] Clement Greenberg writes that the special aesthetic quality of *kitsch* is that it 'predigests art for the spectator and spares him effort, provides him with a shortcut to the pleasures of art that detours what is necessarily difficult in genuine art' because it includes the spectator's reactions in the work of art itself instead of forcing him to make his own responses. [...]

When to this ease of consumption is added *kitsch's* ease of production because of its standardized nature, its prolific growth is easy to understand. It threatens High Culture by its sheer pervasiveness, its brutal, overwhelming *quantity*. The upper classes, who begin by using it to make money from the crude tastes of the masses and to dominate them politically, end by finding their own culture attacked and even threatened with destruction by the instrument they have thoughtlessly employed. [...]

Homogenized culture

Like nineteenth-century capitalism, Mass Culture is a dynamic, revolutionary force, breaking down the old barriers of class, tradition, taste, and dissolving all cultural distinctions. It mixes and scrambles everything together, producing what might be called homogenized culture, after another American achievement, the homogenization process that distributes the globules of cream evenly throughout the milk instead of allowing them to float separately on top. It thus destroys all values, since value judgments imply discrimination. Mass Culture is very, very democratic: it absolutely refuses to discriminate against, or between, anything or anybody. All is grist to its mill, and all comes out finely ground indeed. [...]

Academicism and Avantgardism

Until about 1930, High Culture tried to defend itself against the encroachments of Mass Culture in two opposite ways: Academicism, or an attempt to compete by imitation; and Avantgardism, or a withdrawal from competition.

Academicism is *kitsch* for the *élite*: spurious High Culture that is outwardly the real thing but actually as much a manufactured article as the cheaper cultural goods produced for the masses. It is recognized at the time for what it is only by the Avantgardists. [...]

The significance of the Avantgarde movement (by which I mean poets such as Rimbaud, novelists such as Joyce, composers such as Stravinsky, and painters such as Picasso) is that it simply refused to compete. Rejecting Academicism – and thus, at a second remove, also Mass Culture – it made a desperate attempt to fence off some area where the serious artist could still function. It created a new compartmentation of culture, on the basis of an intellectual rather than a social *élite*. The attempt was remarkably successful: to it we owe almost everything that is living in the art of the last fifty or so years. In fact, the High Culture of our times is pretty much identical with Avantgardism. [...]

A merger has been arranged

In this new period, the competitors, as often happens in the business world, are merging. Mass Culture takes on the color of both varieties of the old High Culture, Academic and Avantgarde, while these latter are increasingly watered down with Mass elements. There is slowly emerging a tepid, flaccid Middlebrow Culture that threatens to engulf everything in its spreading ooze. [...]

This is not a raising of the level of Mass Culture, as might appear at first, but rather a corruption of High Culture. [...] consider the relationship of Hollywood and Broadway. In the twenties, the two were sharply differentiated, movies being produced for the masses of the hinterland, theatre for an upper-class New York audience. The theatre was High Culture, mostly of the Academic variety (Theatre Guild) but with some spark of Avantgarde fire (the 'little' or 'experimental' theatre movement). The movies were definitely Mass Culture, mostly very bad but with some leaven of Avantgardism (Griffith, Stroheim) and Folk Art (Chaplin and other comedians). With the sound film, Broadway and Hollywood drew closer together. Plays are now produced mainly to sell the movie rights, with many being directly financed by the film companies. The merger has standardized the theatre to such an extent that even the early Theatre Guild seems vital in retrospect, while hardly a trace of the 'experimental' theatre is left. And what have the movies gained? They are more sophisticated, the acting is subtler, the sets in better taste. But they too have become standardized: they are never as awful as they often were in the old days, but they are never as good either. They are better entertainment and worse art. The cinema of the twenties occasionally gave us the fresh charm of Folk Art or the imaginative intensity of Avantgardism. The coming of sound, and with it Broadway, degraded the camera to a recording instrument for an alien art form, the spoken play. The silent film had at least the *theoretical possibility*, even within the limits of Mass Culture, of being artistically significant. The sound film, within those limits, does not.

Division of labour

[...] Art workers are as alienated from their brainwork as the industrial worker is from his handwork. The results are as bad qualitatively as they are impressive quantitatively. The only great films to come out of Hollywood, for example, were made before industrial elephantiasis had reduced the director to one of a number of technicians all operating at about the same level of authority. Our two greatest directors, Griffith and Stroheim, were artists, not specialists; they did everything themselves, dominated everything personally: the scenario, the actors, the camera work, and above all the cutting (or *montage*). Unity is essential in art; it cannot be achieved by a production line of specialists, however competent. There have been successful collective creations (Greek temples, Gothic churches, perhaps the *Illiad*) but their creators were part of a tradition which was strong enough to impose unity on their work. We have no such tradition today, and so art – as against *kitsch* – will result only when a single brain and sensibility is in full command. In the movies, only the director can even theoretically be in such a position; he was so in the pre-1930 cinema of this country, Germany, and the Soviet Union. [...]

The problem of the masses

Conservatives such as Ortega y Gasset and T.S. Eliot argue that since 'the revolt of the masses' has led to the horrors of totalitarianism (and of California roadside architecture), the only hope is to rebuild the old class walls and bring the masses once more under aristocratic control. They think of the popular as synonymous with cheap and vulgar. Marxian radicals and liberals, on the other hand, see the masses as intrinsically healthy but as the dupes and victims of cultural exploitation by the Lords of *kitsch* – in the style of Rousseau's 'noble savage' idea. If only the masses were offered good stuff instead of *kitsch*, how they would eat it up! How the level of Mass Culture would rise! Both these diagnoses seem to me fallacious: they assume that Mass Culture is (in the conservative view) or could be (in the liberal view) an expression of *people*, like Folk Art, whereas actually it is an expression of *masses*, a very different thing.

There are theoretical reasons why Mass Culture is not and can never be any good. I take it as axiomatic that culture can only be produced by and for human beings. But in so far as people are organized (more strictly, disorganized) as masses, they lose their human identity and quality. For the masses are in historical time what a crowd is in space: a large quantity of people unable to express themselves as human beings because they are related to one another neither as individuals nor as members of communities – indeed, they are not related to *each other* at all, but only to something distant, abstract, nonhuman: a football game or bargain sale in the case of a crowd, a system of industrial production, a party or a State in the case of the masses. The mass man is a solitary atom, uniform with and undifferentiated from thousands and millions of other atoms who go to make up 'the lonely crowd,' as David Riesman well calls American society. A folk or a people, however, is a community, i.e., a group of individuals linked to each other by common interests, work, traditions, values, and sentiments; something like a family, each of whose members has a special place and function as an individual while at the same time sharing the group's interests (family budget) sentiments (family quarrels), and culture (family jokes). The scale is small enough so that it 'makes a difference' what the individual does, a first condition for human – as against mass-existence. He is at once more important as an individual than in mass society and at the same time more closely integrated into the community, his creativity nourished by a rich combination of individualism and communalism. (The great culture-bearing *élites* of the past have been communities of this kind.) In contrast, a mass society, like a crowd, is so undifferentiated and loosely structured that its atoms, in so far as human values go, tend to cohere only along the line of the least common denominator; its morality sinks to that of its most brutal and primitive members, its taste to that of the least sensitive and most ignorant. And in addition to everything else, the scale is simply too big, there are just *too many people*.

Yet ths collective monstrosity, 'the masses', 'the public', is taken as a human norm by the scientific and artistic technicians of our Mass Culture. They at once degraded the public by treating it as an object, to be handled with the lack of ceremony and the objectivity of medical students dissecting a corpse, and at the same time flatter it, pander to its level of taste and ideas [...] But the *plebs* have their dialectical revenge: complete indifference to their human *quality* means complete prostration before their statistical *quantity*, so that a movie magnate who cynically 'gives the public what it wants' – i.e., assumes it wants trash – sweats with terror if box-office returns drop 10 per cent.

The future of high culture: dark

The conservative proposal to save culture by restoring the old class lines has a more solid historical base than the Marxian hope for a new democratic, classless cultures for, with the possible (and important) exception of Periclean Athens, all the great cultures of the past were *élite* cultures. Politically, however, it is without meaning in a world dominated by the two great mass nations, USA and USSR and becoming more industrialized, more massified all the time. The only practical thing along those lines would be to revive the *cultural élite* which the Avantgarde created. As I have already noted, the Avantgarde is now dying, partly from internal causes, partly suffocated by the competing Mass Culture, where it is not being absorbed into it. Of course this process has not reached 100 per cent, and doubtless never will unless the country goes either Fascist or Communist. There are still islands above the flood for those determined enough to reach them, and to stay on them: as Faulkner has shown, a writer can even use Hollywood instead of being used by it, if his purpose is firm enough. But the homogenization of High and Mass Culture has gone far and is going farther all the time, and there seems little reason to expect a revival of Avantgardism, that is, of a successful countermovement to Mass Culture. Particularly not in the country, where the blurring of class lines, the absence of a stable cultural tradition, and the greater facilities for manufacturing and marketing *kitsch* all work in the other direction. The result is that our intelligentsia is remarkably small, weak, and disintegrated [...]

The future of mass culture: darker

If the conservative proposal to save our culture via the aristocratic Avantgarde seems historically unlikely, what of the democratic-liberal proposal? Is there a reasonable prospect of raising the level of Mass Culture? In his recent book, *The Great Audience*, Gilbert Seldes argues there is. He blames the present sad state of our Mass Culture on the stupidity of the Lords of *kitsch*, who underestimate the mental age of the public; the arrogance of the intellectuals, who make the same mistake and so snobbishly refuse to work for such mass media as radio, TV and movies; and the passivity of the public itself, which doesn't insist on better Mass Cultural products. This diagnosis seems to me superficial in that it blames everything on subjective, moral factors: stupidity, perversity, failure of will. My own feeling is that, as in the case of the alleged responsibility of the German (or Russian) people for the horrors of Nazism (or Soviet Communism), it is unjust to blame social groups for this result. Human beings have been caught up in the inexorable workings of a mechanism that forces them, with a pressure only heroes can resist (and one cannot *demand* that anybody be a hero, though one can *hope* for it), into its own pattern. I see Mass Culture as a reciprocating engine, and who is to say, once it has been set in motion, whether the stroke or the counterstroke is 'responsible' for its continued action?

The Lords of *kitsch* sell culture to the masses. It is a debased, trivial culture that voids both the deep realities (sex, death, failure, tragedy) and also the simple, spontaneous pleasures, since the realities would be too real and the pleasures too *lively* to induce what Mr. Seldes calls 'the mood of consent,' i.e., a narcotized acceptance of Mass Culture and of the commodities it sells as a substitute for the unsettling and unpredictable (hence unsalable) joy, tragedy, wit, change, originality and beauty of real life. The masses, debauched by several generations of this sort of thing, in turn come to demand trivial and comfortable cultural products. Which came first, the chicken or the egg, the mass demand or its satisfaction (and further stimulation) is a question as academic as it is unanswerable. The engine is reciprocating and shows no signs of running down.

Indeed, far from Mass Culture getting better, we will be lucky if it doesn't get worse. [...] Since Mass Culture is not an art form but a manufactured commodity, it tends always downward, toward cheapness – and so standardization – of production. [...] The only time Mass Culture is good is at the very beginning, before the 'formula' has hardened, before the money boys and efficiency experts and audience-reaction analysts have moved in. Then for a while it may have the quality of real Folk Art. But the Folk artist today lacks the cultural roots and the intellectual toughness (both of which the Avantgarde artist has relatively more of) to resist for long the pressures of Mass Culture. His taste can easily be corrupted, his sense of his own special talent and limitations obscured, as in what happened to Disney between the gay, inventive early Mickey Mouse and Silly Symphony cartoons and the vulgar pretentiousness of *Fantasia* and heavy-handed sentimentality of *Snow White* [...] Whatever virtues the Folk artist has, and they are many, staying power is not one of them. And staying power is the essential virtue of one who would hold his own against the spreading ooze of Mass Culture.

Notes

1 As I did myself in 'A Theory of Popular Culture' (*Politics*, February 1944) parts of which have been used or adapted in the present article.
2 The success of *Reader's Digest* illustrates the law. Here is a magazine that has achieved a fantastic circulation – some fifteen millions, much of which is accounted for by its foreign editions, thus showing that *kitsch* by no means appeals only to Americans – simply by reducing to even lower terms the already superficial formulae of other periodicals. By treating a theme in two pages which they treat in six, the *Digest* becomes three times as 'readable' and three times as superficial.

3 Concepts of culture: public policy and the cultural industries

Nicholas Garnham

[...] An analysis of culture structured around the concept of the cultural industries, on the other hand, directs our attention precisely at the dominant private market sector. It sees culture, defined as the production and circulation of symbolic meaning, as a material process of production and exchange, part of, and in significant ways determined by, the wider economic processes of society with which it shares many common features.

Thus, as a descriptive term, 'cultural industries' refers to those institutions in our society which employ the characteristic modes of production and organization of industrial corporations to produce and disseminate symbols in the form of cultural goods and services, generally although not exclusively, as commodities. These include newspapers, periodical and book publishing, record companies, music publishers, commercial sports organizations, etc. In all these cultural processes, we characteristically find at some point the use of capital-intensive, technological means of mass production and/or distribution, highly developed divisions of labour and hierarchical modes of managerial organization, with the goal, if not of profit maximization, at least of efficiency. I refer to this as a descriptive use of the term 'cultural industries' because it describes characteristics common to the cultural process in all industrial societies, whether capitalist or socialist. Within the descriptive usage we need to note a further distinction made by Adorno, who originally coined the term, between those cultural industries which employ industrial technology and modes of organization to produce and distribute cultural goods or services which are themselves produced by largely traditional or pre-industrial means (e.g. books and records) and those where the cultural form itself is industrial (e.g. newspapers, films and TV programmes). We need to remember this distinction because the two forms tend to give rise to different relations of production and types of economic organization.

But the term 'cultural industries' can also be used analytically to focus upon the effects on the cultural process within the capitalist mode of production of cultural goods and services produced and distributed as commodities by labour, which is itself a commodity.

A key point here is that the cultural sector operates as an integrated economic whole because industries and companies within it compete:
1 for a limited pool of disposable consumer income;
2 for a limited pool of advertising revenue;
3 for a limited amount of consumption time;
4 for skilled labour. [...]

The structure and dynamics of the cultural industries

The particular economic nature of the cultural industries can be explained in terms of the general tendencies of commodity production within the capitalist mode of production as modified by the special characteristics of the cultural commodity. Thus we find competition driving the search for profits via increased productivity, but it takes specific forms.

There is a contradiction at the heart of the cultural commodity. On the one hand, there is a very marked drive towards expanding the market share or the form this takes in the cultural sector, audiences. This is explained by the fact that in general, because one of the use-values of culture is novelty or difference, there is a constant need to create new products which are all in a sense prototypes. That is to say, the cultural commodity resists that homogenization process which is one of the material results of the abstract equivalence of exchange to which the commodity form aspires. This drive for novelty within cultural production means that in general the costs of reproduction are marginal in relation to the costs of production (the cost of each record pressing is infinitesimal compared to the cost of recording, for instance). Thus the marginal returns from each extra sale tend to grow, leading in turn to a powerful thrust towards audience maximization as the preferred profit maximization strategy.

On the other hand, the cultural commodity is not destroyed in the process of consumption. My reading of a book or watching of a film does not make it any less available to you. Moreover, the products of the past live on and can be relatively easily and cheaply reproduced anew. Thus it has been difficult to establish the scarcity on which price is based. And thus cultural goods (and some services, such as broadcasting, for technical reasons) tend towards the condition of a public good. Indeed, one can observe a marked tendency, where they are not *de jure* so treated, for consumers to so treat them *de facto* through high levels of piracy, as is now the case with records, video cassettes and books. (It should be noted that this in its turn relates to another contradiction in the cultural sphere, on which I shall comment shortly, between the producers of cultural hardware and software. It is the development of a market in cheap reproduction technology that makes piracy so difficult to control.) In contradiction, then, to the drive to maximize audiences, a number of strategies have had to be developed for artificially limiting access in order to create scarcity.

The drive to audience maximization leads to the observed tendency towards a high level of concentration, internationalization and cross-media ownership in the cultural industries. The strategies to limit access have taken a variety of forms:

1 Monopoly or oligopolistic controls over distribution channels, sometimes, as in broadcasting, linked to the state. One often finds here a close relationship between commercial interests and those of state control.
2 An attempt to concentrate the accumulation process on the provision of cultural hardware – e.g. radio and television receivers, hi-fi, VCRs, etc. – with the programmes, as in the early days of British broadcasting, as necessary loss-leaders. The rationale for the introduction of cable in the UK is an example of this.
3 The creation of the audience as a commodity for sale to advertisers, where the cultural software merely acts as a free lunch. This has proved itself the most successful solution; both the increased proportion of advertising to sales revenue in the press and periodicals market, culminating in the growth of free newspapers and magazines, and the steady expansion of wholly advertising-financed broadcasting services, are indications of this.

4 The creation of commodities, of which news is the classic example, which require constant reconsumption.

Audiences, cultural repertoire and distribution

The third key characteristic of the cultural commodity lies in the nature of its use-values. These have proved difficult if not impossible to pin down in any precise terms, and demand for them appears to be similarly volatile. As I have already remarked, culture is above all the sphere for the expression of difference. Indeed, some analysts would claim that cultural goods are pure positional goods, their use-value being as markers of social and individual difference. While this aspect of culture merits much deeper and more extended analysis, it is only necessary here to draw one key conclusion, namely that demand for any single cultural product is impossible to predict. Thus the cultural industries, if they are to establish a stable market, are forced to create a relationship with an audience or public to whom they offer not a simple cultural good, but a cultural repertoire across which the risks can be spread. For instance, in the record industry only 1 in 9 singles and 1 in 16 LPs makes a profit, and 3 per cent of the output can account for up to 50 per cent of turnover. Similarly, in films the top 10 films out of 119 in the UK market in 1979 took 32 per cent of the box-office receipts and the top 40 took 80 per cent.

Thus the drive to audience maximization, the need to create artificial scarcity by controlling access and the need for a repertoire bring us to the central point in this analysis. *It is cultural distribution, not cultural production, that is the key locus of power and profit*. It is access to distribution which is the key to cultural plurality. The cultural process is as much, if not more, about creating audiences or publics as it is about producing cultural artefacts and performances. Indeed, that is why that stress upon the cultural producers that I noted earlier is so damaging.

We need to recognize the importance, within the cultural industries and within the cultural process in general, of the function which I shall call, for want of a better word, editorial: the function not just of creating a cultural repertoire matched to a given audience or audiences but at the same time of matching the cost of production of that repertoire to the spending powers of that audience. These functions may be filled by somebody or some institution referred to variously as a publisher, a television channel controller, a film distributor, etc. It is a vital function totally ignored by many cultural analysts, a function as creative as writing a novel or directing a film. It is a function, moreover, which will exist centrally within the cultural process of any geographically dispersed society with complex division of labour.

Taking these various factors into account, we are now in a position to understand why our dominant cultural processes and their modes of organization are the way they are. The newspaper and the television and radio schedule are montages of elements to appeal to as wide a range of readers, viewers and listeners as possible. The high levels of concentration in the international film, record and publishing industries are responses to the problem of repertoire. The dominance of broadcast television stems from its huge efficiency as a distribution medium, with its associated economies of scale.

For this reason, the notion that the new technologies of cable and VCR are fragmenting the market rather than shifting the locus of oligopolistic power needs to be treated with caution, since there are strict limits to how far such fragmentation can go economically.

The hierarchy of cultural industries

As I have noted, power in the cultural sector clusters around distribution, the channel of access to audiences. It is here that we typically find the highest levels of capital intensity, ownership concentration and multi-nationalization, the operation of classic industrial labour processes and relations of production with related forms of trade-union organization. These characteristics are exhibited to their highest degree in the manufacture of the hardware of cultural distribution, especially domestic hardware. This is a sub-sector increasingly dominated by a few Japanese corporations such as Matsushita, Sony, Sanyo, Toshiba and Hitachi, together with Eastman Kodak, Philips and RCA. The major UK firm of this type is Thorn-EMI.

Then there are the major controllers of channels of software distribution, often closely linked to specific modes of reproduction, such as record pressing or newspaper printing. In non-print media there is again a high level of concentration and internationalization, and US firms dominate, owing to the large size of the domestic US market. [...]

The increasing tendency in this field, as an extension of the principle of repertoire, is the formation of multi-media conglomerates [...] who own interests across a number of media, thus enabling them both to exploit the same product, be it a film, a book or a piece of music, across several media, and also to expand the principles of risk-spreading not only across a range of consumer choice in one medium but also across consumers' entire range of cultural choice. The development of such centres of cultural powers also, of course, raises barriers to entry.

Around these centres of power cluster groups of satellites. These satellites can be either small companies, for instance independent production companies in relation to Channel Four, or individual cultural workers such as freelance journalists, writers, actors and film directors. In these satellite sectors we find high levels of insecurity, low levels of profitability, low levels of unionization and, where they exist, weak trade-union organizations. Often labour is not waged at all, but labour power is rented out for a royalty.

The existence of this dependent satellite sector fulfils a very important function for the cultural industries because it enables them to shift much of the cost and risk of cultural research and development off their own shoulders and on to this exploited sector, some of which is then indeed supported from the public purse. It also enables them to maintain a consistently high turnover of creative cultural labour without running the risk of labour unrest, or bearing the cost of redundancy or pension payments. Their cup brimmeth over when, as is often the case, the workers themselves willingly don this yoke in the name of freedom.

The market and culture

[...] I think it is crucial to separate the concept of the market from the concept of the capitalist mode of production, that is to say from a given structure of ownership and from the special features derived from labour as a market commodity. In terms of this relationship between consumers, distributors and producers of cultural goods and services, the market has much to recommend it, provided that consumers enter that market with equal endowments and that concentration of ownership power is reduced, controlled or removed. However, we must be clear that removal of the power vested in private or unaccountable public ownership will not remove the need for the function I have described as editorial, whether such a function is exercised individually or collectively. It also has to be stressed that even within the capitalist mode of production the market has, at crucial historical junctures, acted as a liberating cultural force. One thinks of the creation of both the novel and the newspaper by the rising bourgeoisie in the eighteenth century and of working men's clubs and the working-class seaside holiday in the late nineteenth century.

Indeed, the cultural market, as it has developed in the last 150 years in the UK as a substitute for patronage in all its forms, cannot be read either as a destruction of high culture by vulgar commercialism or as a suppression of authentic working-class culture, but should be read as a complex hegemonic dialectic of liberation and control [...]

What analysis of the cultural industries does bring home to us is the need to take the question of the scarcity and thus of the allocation of cultural resources seriously, together with the question of audiences – who they are, how they are formed and how they can best be served. For it needs to be said that the only alternative to the market which we have constructed, with the partial exception of broadcasting, has tended either simply to subsidize the existing tastes and habits of the better-off or to create a new form of public culture which has no popular audience; cultural workers create for the only audience they know, namely the cultural bureaucrats who pay the bill and upon whom they become psychologically dependent even while reviling them. [...]

---

4 'Holy commodity fetish, Batman!': the political economy of a commercial intertext

Eileen R. Meehan

Batman took the United States by storm in the spring and summer of 1989. Tee shirts, posters, keychains, jewelry, buttons, books, watches, magazines, trading cards, audiotaped books, videogames, records, cups, and numerous other items flooded malls across the United States with images of Batman, his new logo, and his old enemy the Joker.[1] Presaged by a much pirated trailer, *Batman* the film drew unprecedented crowds to theatre chains, of which the two largest (United Artist Theater Circuits and American Multi-Cinema) distributed four to five million brochures for mail order Bat-materials.[2] *Batman*'s premiere on the big screen was

matched by appearances on the small screen. Film clips were packaged as advertisements and free promotional materials for the interview and movie review
circuits on both broadcast and cable television; Prince's 'Batdance' video played in
heavy rotation on MTV. Over radio, 'Batdance' and other cuts from Prince's
Batman album got strong play on rock stations and 'crossed over' for similarly
strong play on black radio stations. Subsequently, retail outlets filled with Bat-
costumes and Joker make-up kits for Halloween; Ertl Batmobiles and ToyBiz
Batcaves and Batwings were being deployed for Christmas shoppers. In the
specialty stores serving comics fandom, the *Advance Comics Special Batlist*
offered 214 items ranging from $576 to $2 in price.[3] And in grocery stores, special
Bat-displays offered children a choice between Batman coloring books, Batman
trace-and-color books, and Batman magic plates. It would seem that Batman and
his paraphernalia transcend age, gender, and race. [...]

If the prevalence of Bat-paraphernalia in the stores and the ubiquity of the Bat-
logo on the streets are indicators, then indeed *Batman* has struck a chord deep in the
American psyche. Certainly the temptation to speculate on the larger significance of
Batman is strong given the irony of this dark, yet ultimately hopeful, film being
released at a time when the mythic Gotham of the *Dark Knight's Return* and the
mythos of the American Imperium both seem to crack under the strains of social
injustice and personal irresponsibility.

This speculation, however tempting, is not quite fair to us or to the film. Such
speculation requires an assumptive leap that reduces consciousness, culture, and
media to reflections of each other. It assumes that the American psyche can be read
off the film, which reflects American culture which determines how we see the
world and how the film is constructed. This old and much criticized error retains its
emotional force, despite the articulation of more careful theories about media texts
and intertexts, about reception and reinterpretation of those materials by active
viewers [...]. In this essay, however, I will argue that another dimension must be
added to our analyses of media generally and of *Batman* specifically. Namely,
economics must be considered if we are fully to understand the texts and intertexts
of American mass culture. Most cultural production in the United States is done by
private,   for-profit   corporations.   These   corporations   comprise   the
entertainment/information sector of the American economy and encompass the
industries of publishing, television, film, music, cable, and radio. Significantly,
American capitalism organizes the creation of cultural artifacts as a process of mass
production carried out by profit-oriented businesses operating in an industrial
context. Profit, not culture, drives show business: no business means no show.

For much of American culture, corporate imperatives operate as the primary
constraints shaping the narratives and iconography of the text as well as the manufacture and licensing of the intertextual materials necessary for a 'mania' to sweep
the country. This is not a claim that evil moguls force us to buy Bat-chains: such
reductionism is as vulgar and untenable as the assumptive leap from a film to the
national psyche. Rather, the claim here is that mass-produced culture is a business,
governed by corporate drives for profit, market control, and transindustrial integration. While movies may (and do) flop, the decision to create a movie is a business
decision about the potential profitability of a cinematic product. Further, as
film studios have been either acquired by companies outside the industry or have

themselves acquired companies in other entertainment/information industries, decisions about movies are increasingly focused on the potential profitability of a wide range of products. The film per se becomes only one component in a product line that extends beyond the theater, even beyond our contact with mass media, to penetrate the markets for toys, bedding, trinkets, cups and the other minutiae comprising one's everyday life inside a commoditized, consumerized culture.

To understand *Batman*, then, requires that our analyses of the text and intertext, and of fandom and other audiences, be supplemented by an economic analysis of corporate structure, market structures, and interpenetrating industries. These conditions of production select, frame, and shape both *Batman* as a commercial text and the product line that constitutes its commercial intertext. We begin, then, with *Batman*'s owner, Warner Communications Incorporated (WCI).

WCI: structures and industries

To see how [...] structure constrains content, we will trace the ways that WCI's external business pressures and internal markets shaped *Batman* as text and intertext. After sketching the emerging structure of Time-Warner, we will examine conditions at WCI from 1982 to 1989 and analyse the commercial intertext as a response to economic conditions.

WCI is now half of the newly merged, transindustrial Time-Warner. The combined holdings of Time and WCI in book publishing, cable channels, song publishing, cable systems, recorded music, television production, magazine/comics publishing, film production, television stations, and licensing make Time-Warner the predominant media conglomerate in the world. The Time-Warner merger signals a further concentration in the ownership of outlets, distribution systems, and content production across multiple media industries by a single company.[4]

Significantly, the major difference between the independent WCI and the new Time-Warner is a difference in size, not in kind. Prior to the 1989 merger, WCI had assumed the aggressive, expansionist pose typical of the 1970s and 1980s.[5] By the 1980s the company had joint ventures with American Express in cable operations, satellite distribution, pay cable channels, and basic cable channels (QUBE; Warner Amex Satellite; Showtime and The Movie Channel; MTV Networks comprised by MTV, NIK, and VH1). These rounded out WCI's wholly owned operations in film and television production, recorded music, cartoons and comic books, magazines, books, video cassettes, and licensing of characters. But WCI had pushed beyond these interests to purchase [...] non-media firms. Throughout this expansion, revenues from WCI's core media companies remained strong.

However, the economic burdens of expansion almost capsized WCI [...]. Despite its prodigious losses in 1983, WCI's film and television production units earned revenues of $109 million while the publishing division enjoyed $43.3 million in revenues. By reconcentrating operations in its profitable media operations, WCI began rebuilding profits, with earnings spiralling up to $693 million by October 1986.[6] With these revenues, WCI was poised for another round of acquisitions in December 1986.

This time, however, WCI focused its efforts more narrowly, absorbing and investing in companies that operated in the entertainment/information industries.

Beginning with investment as a white knight in the Cannon Group (film production, home video, European theatre chains),[7] WCI went on to acquire such firms as Lorimar Telepictures (film and television production, home video, television stations, television series including *Dallas* and *Alf*, licensing,[8] and Cinema Venture a theatre chain co-owned by Gulf and Western),[9] and Chappell Music Publishing[10] before the culminating merger with Time Inc.

In economic terms, the initial diversification helped trigger a crisis that forced WCI to shed its non-media acquisitions and to sell off some of its profitable media operations. Because of continued profitability in film, television, publishing, and music, WCI soon found itself poised for reexpansion. However, this time WCI adopted a more restrained approach to expansion, emphasizing acquisition of media companies to achieve further integration in industries where it was already strong. The merger with Time marks an intensification in the extent to which operations in different media industries are subordinated under WCI (now Time-Warner)'s aegis. WCI's recovery and retrenchment transformed the Warner of 1982, a diversified conglomerate with strong media interests, into the pre-merger Warner of 1989, a highly concentrated and integrated media conglomerate.

Financing recovery: recycling

While WCI's retrenchment required that its media companies remained profitable, WCI's reemergence as a major media conglomerate and its subsequent expansion required increases in revenues and profits. This fostered greater cost efficiencies in film production as more profit was required from each project, whether directly from box office revenues or indirectly by repackaging sections of the film for recycling through WCI's non-film outlets. For instance, film soundtracks became much more important as a source of possible revenues since WCI could repackage soundtracks as records and music videos. [...] repackaging and recycling have the immediate effect of encouraging media conglomerates both to mine their stock of owned materials for new spin-offs and to view every project as a multimedia product line. WCI and Prince seem to have pioneered an intensified recycling of content.

[...] the Bat-project began with a tried and true product that was already earning revenues for WCI: Batman, the only 'normal' adult in DC Comics stable of superheroes. When DC was acquired by WCI in 1971, it was evidently viewed by the chair of WCI's publishing division (William Sarnoff) as a source of licensing revenues and movie materials.[11] However, both licensing and book sales were decreasing across the comics industry due to problems in distribution, an exodus of production personnel, and a perceptible drop in the quality of narratives, portrayals of characters, and artwork. Compounding this was the phenomena of underground comix (*sic*) with their explicit portrayals of drugs, sex, violence, political corruption, and the ills of capitalism. [...]

To compete in its own industry, then, DC and its comics had to be reorganized. From 1976 to 1981, DC struggled to rebuild revenues, achieving profitability with one-third of its revenues from comics sales, one-third from licensing and one-third from other sources. Obviously movies helped, as *Superman* proved a box office smash in 1978 to be followed by three sequels (1979, 1988, and 1987) and one spin-off (*Supergirl* in 1984) all distributed by WCI. After six months of negotiating, DC granted rights for a Batman film to independent producers Peter Gruber and Jon Peters, whose films have all been released through WCI. With WCI's decision to bankroll as well as distribute the film, *Batman* achieved the status of an in-house blockbuster production on which vast sums would be lavished. Hence, it is notable that the film's director, Tim Burton, enjoyed a track record with WCI, having directed *PeeWee's Big Adventure* at a cost of $7 million with box office revenues of $40 million as well directing Michael Keaton in *Beetlejuice* at a cost of $13 million with box office revenues of $80 million. [...] With WCI risking $30 million with *Batman* in 1988, some assurances were necessary; hence the selection of producers, directors, and stars with solid track records at the box office. But WCI had other ways to build assurances given its internal markets, and the decision to release the film on Batman's fiftieth birthday.

Internal markets and Batman

The mid-1980s marked the beginning of a process in which WCI both tested the waters and began building towards the release of *Batman*.[12] By issuing *The Dark Knight Returns* in comic form, WCI essentially test marketed a dark reinterpretation of Batman with an adult readership whose experience with the character would include the camp crusader of the 1960s. [...]

The *Dark Knight*'s success prompted DC's repackaging of classic superheroes in a 48-page anthology *Action Comics Weekly*, selling at $1.50 per issue and the Warner Books publication of *Batman: Year One*. Also, circulation figures for the Batman comic began rising as the Dark Knight's success rubbed off on the younger, less dystopian version of the character. The process of building an audience for the Batman film was thus started. [...]

Be that as it may, filming started in 1988 with the revenues from *Beetlejuice* safely in hand. Negative reactions from fans to casting decisions made the first page of the *Wall Street Journal*[13] with claims by the *Journal* that WCI would modify content in order to ensure fan attendance. From WCI's use of its publishing division, WCI already had market measures that fans and the general public were willing to buy a darker interpretation of a lone vigilante. Just as important, WCI had information on the identity of fans from an industry survey funded by DC's main rival, Marvel, which described the average reader as a 20-year-old male spending $10 a week on comics. As a male-oriented action film, *Batman* would rely on the public personae of Jack Nicholson and Michael Keaton to widen the audience. Similarly, WCI would rely on the film to feed its internal markets in both the short and long run.

The $30 million sunk into *Batman* is not entirely the cost of a single film. Rather, it includes the root costs of a film series. The construction of sets, development of props, total investment, and plot presume that sequels will be shot. In the long run, WCI's investment in plant for *Batman* can be spread out across two or four other films. While revenues per sequel can be expected to decrease as the number of Bat-movies increase, the major cost of sets for each sequel was largely included in WCI's original $30 million budget. [...] Over the long run, then, WCI's $30 million investment in *Batman* has built the basic infrastructure necessary for manufacturing a line of films, albums, sheet music, comics, and novelizations.

In the short run, this investment served as the seed money for a line of Bat-media to be distributed through WCI's non-film media outlets. The script for the film was adapted to both novel and comic book forms. The novel retells the film with only minor differences; the comic's visuals reproduce the shots of the film with slight variation in plot and pictorials. Thus both the plot and the movie's visuals were broken out to earn income. Similarly, the soundtrack was broken out as two products: an album by Prince[14] with songs from the soundtrack and songs inspired by the film (with the album going double platinum) plus an orchestral album by Danny Elfman which surpassed the usual sales for orchestral scores with sales around 150,000. [...] In a departure from previous practice, Prince's video of his album's lead song, 'Batdance', featured no footage from the film. Instead, 'Batdance' broke out dialogue from the film, using the actors' lines as the basis for rap elements in Prince's funk sound.[15] The video played with Prince's usual themes of sexuality, androgyny, and punishment. 'Batdance' was frequently featured on MTV, the music channel targeted primarily to middle class whites from youth to middle age.[16] The use of a rap-funk style secured airplay on radio stations targeted to black audiences. This was a rather significant extension of Prince's audience, which WCI had pegged as white females in their late 20s to middle 30s. The crossover had the effect of cultivating black audiences and Batlogos began to crop up on black male performers featured on MTV's rap segments. But if rap elements generalized 'Batdance's appeal, Prince's performance in the video replayed the themes that endeared him to his longtime fans and made *Purple Rain* a hit at the box office and in the record store. In this way, the decision to showcase Prince as a musical guest on the film's soundtrack promoted the film to an audience atypical of comic fans (white women); the style of Prince's musical performance promoted *Batman* in terms of black culture to black youth despite the minimal role of black actors (including Billy Dee Williams) in the film. All this had the effect of widening the pool of potential ticket-buyers for *Batman*.

This also earned revenues for WCI. Both albums represented extra income from an integral part of *Batman*: musical score and dialogue. Similarly, the sheet music from the film score and from Prince's songs inspired by the film provided fodder for WCI's song publishing operation. This had recently expanded to become the largest song publisher in the world with WCI's acquisition of Chappell, thereby also enlarging WCI's need for music to publish. [...]

The relative swiftness of those ... sequels is suggested by WCI's video cassette release of *Batman* on November 15, 1989, less than six months after the film's premiere. Taking the trade press by surprise, this decision should serve to hasten *Batman* into the tertiary distribution circuits of pay cable and home video, cutting short the film's booking in second-run theaters. This promises to feed product to WCI's home video operations as well as Time-Warner's HBO/Cinemax pay channels and WCI's pay-per-view channels on QUBE [...]

WCI's use of the Batman product line to feed its internal markets for media products indicates how media conglomerates bring together media industries that were once distinct and separate. The interpenetration of the music, film, print, and video industries does not arise in response to demand from movie goers, record buyers, or comics subscribers. Rather, this interpenetration is orchestrated by the conglomerate in its search for more profitable and cost-efficient ways to manufacture culture.

But internal markets, corporate structure, and interpenetrating industries are not the total sum of economic structures that constrain cultural production. External markets are also important in show business. Earning profits from shows means working in two very different external markets. The first is the market for licensing, a closed market in which a limited number of corporations secure exclusive rights over copyrighted materials. The second is an open market where real people go to movies, listen to favorite songs, read murder mysteries, change channels, and rent videos. After feeding internal markets, media conglomerates sometimes turn to external markets and negotiate licensing agreements with firms whose concerns lie outside the pale of the licensor's operations. By granting exclusive use of copyrighted materials for use in the manufacture of particular product categories (e.g., toys figures, keychains, etc.), the licensor guarantees a secondary source of income from images, logos, and characters from the original media product. [...]

External markets and Bat-mania

The extent to which WCI could make *Batman* a 'must see' film depended on promotion, comprised by advertising and licensing. While the former is a cost, the latter is a source of revenues. However, the $10 million WCI spent on advertising would not be a complete loss even if the film did poorly at the box office. Under US tax law, advertising is an ordinary cost of doing business and deductible as such. When advertising is accompanied by licensing in a promotional campaign, the producing company has the opportunity of earning revenues from licenses to toy companies, clothes manufacturers, fast food chains, etc., even if the film flops. Licensing is increasingly used, then, to augment revenues and licensed products are used to augment advertising for the film.

Because of WCI's cartoon properties, licensing has always played a role in the company's revenues. For *Batman*, WCI licenses two different properties: *Batman* the movie or Batman of comics and television fame. Potential licensees could opt for the film's logo or the traditional logo; for the Dark Knight or the Dynamic Duo; for Keaton's body armor or Adam West's costume; for Nicholson's Joker or DC's Joker, Riddler, Penguin, and Catwoman. This mix-or-match approach gave WCI's 100 licensed manufacturers considerable latitude in devising merchandising campaigns to cash in both on WCI's and campaign for the film and on Batman's anniversary. Manufacturers could license images appropriate to their targeted consumers [...]

The last market: show

In this last market, the 'show' in show business finally becomes important as the show itself finally earns revenues directly from people through ticket sales. However, this market has some distinctive features, which differentiate it from other media markets; but it is similar to most consumer markets in advanced capitalist economies since the market for movies depends on advertising to stimulate consumption of products selected by an oligopoly of producers.[17] Like most consumer markets, the market for films is not driven by demand; WCI was not picketed by millions of moviegoers demanding a Bat-film. Quite the opposite: once WCI decided to go ahead with the Bat-project, the company needed to test market the new Bat-image and to convince people that we wanted to see this particular film of *Batman*. So, while we count in this market, we count as consumers who must be enticed to buy a ticket, thus renting a seat for one viewing of a particular film selected from all movies currently playing. Obvious though this process is, it has some rather subtle consequences: in the market where people consume shows, all shows compete against each other regardless of the manufacturer's identity. So if WCI releases five films, each movie competes with the other four films by WCI as well as with all the other films released into the marketplace.

As a result, it is in the interest of film producers to control the number of releases per year, artificially decreasing the number of films available in order to decrease competition between films.[18] By limiting our choices to a handful of films and by consolidating release dates into two 'seasons' – summer and Christmas – the major film studios create a business cycle that alternates forced choices between a limited number of 'hot films' with stretches of doldrums. This industry-generated business cycle sets up conditions of production that favor the funding and distribution of relatively few films by each major studio. By limiting releases, a studio decreases the amount of competition between its releases. Since every studio follows this policy, the effect is a decrease in competition over all films in each season. To argument each season's line-up, a studio will selectively contract with semi-independent producers for a limited number of additional films. Willingness to accept such product varies inversely with the amount of a studio's own product that it has slated for release. Further, releases within a season are staggered so that most studio product (and the more favored semi-independent product) shares its opening date with no other major release. Such favored films are proceeded by massive advertising campaigns in an attempt to pack the house for the film's premiere. Taken together, these components create a market in which even 'failures' earn a minimum box office, like the $8 million earned by the WCI flop *Supergirl*. This potential for failure regardless of advertising, business cycle, etc., is rooted in the market itself, as we will discuss later.

This decreased competition among films regardless of studio has decreased competition among studios for screens and ticket-buyers. It also has the effect of channeling money from multiple projects into one or two projects, so that major theatrical releases become increasingly expensive with production costs running into millions of dollars, before millions more are spent for advertising. In fact, the enormous cost of a film can be an impetus for news coverage, hence gaining free advertising providing one reason to see the film. For *Batman*, the press reported figures ranging from $30–40 million plus another $10 million for promotion.[19] The sheer size of production costs may well be the source of studios' willingness to pay similarly high costs for promotion. The $10 million figure for *Batman* represents an attempt to hype the film as a 'must see', to fill theaters across the nation for the film's premiere performances. By releasing *Batman* after most major films had opened, including the sequels (*Indiana Jones and the Last Crusade, Star Trek VI*), and by hyping that release through the radio, television, cable, print, and film industries, WCI tried to ensure that its early revenues would be as high as possible. Even if word-of-mouth damned the movie, the early revenues could carry the film into a respectable slot on *Variety*'s chart of money-makers.

All this joins together to create a market for theatrical release films that stresses high production costs, limited seasons, limited number of releases, slightly staggered releases within a season, and extensive pre-release advertising, as film companies try to cope with the vagaries of this last market.

Where people are the prime purchasers, revenues can not be completely shielded from the direct responses of consumers. Word-of-mouth can break a film designed as a blockbuster, or elevate an obscure movie to the status of a cult film or even a sleeper. Thus, expensive films may be box office bonanzas or big-time disasters. Where some media revenues are protected by the habits of subscription, film remains in direct relationship with an open, unstructured market of potential ticket-buyers. This encourages film producers to cultivate 'brand loyalties' in an attempt to establish purchasing habits so that consumers routinely select a particular genre, personnel (actor or director), recurring characters, and continuing stories. For consumers, the decision turns on projected satisfaction: we can not know if the film is worth the price until after viewing it. Thus word-of-mouth and published reviews may shape our willingness to pay. Similarly, genre, personnel, recurring characters, or continuing stories can be used to make quick decisions based on past experience when selecting from a season's releases. Sequels and stars can be used to manage demand just as pre-release advertising can be used to inflate revenues from premieres before word-of-mouth makes its rounds. For WCI, building a Bat-series required both extensive pre-release advertising to produce a 'hit' premiere as well as a sufficiently solid foundation to earn a steady income after the hype subsided. By holding the film until June 23–24, WCI could count on post-premiere drops in attendance for the early releases. After that, the summer-long success of *Batman* at the box office would depend on the film itself, its ability to resonate with our experiences and visions, and to tap into the conflicting ideologies through which we make sense of social life.

From cultural economics to economic culture

[...] The economic logics of profit and cost efficiency suggest that *Batman* is best understood as multimedia, multimarket sales campaign. Yet, although that campaign's primary purpose is to earn revenues and decrease production costs, it also 'sells' ideologies – visions of the good, the true, the beautiful. Herein lies the contradiction of capitalist media: to understand our mass media, we must be able to understand them as always and simultaneously text and commodity, intertext and product line. This contradiction is well captured in the phrase 'show business'. In our fascination with the highly visible show, let us not overlook the less visible business that ultimately shapes, constructs, recycles, breaks out, and distributes the show for a profit. No business means no show and doing business means constructing shows according to business needs. These are the ground rules, recoverable through critical analysis, from which we can safely approach the analysis of a commodified culture and the products of show business. One might well exclaim: 'Holy commodity fetish, Batman!'

Notes

1   The author would like to thank Tim Emmerson for research assistance and Alfred Babbit for word processing this text.

2   Jim Robbins, 'Orders for Batstuff Bring 2% to Exhibs [*sic*]; Brochure System Cheered', *Variety*, 5 July 1989, p. 8.

3   *Advance Comics* is a catalogue listing comic books and fan materials that are scheduled to be distributed to specialty stores in two months time. Resembling a black-and-white comic book, issues include an order form.

4   For a complete listing of Time's and Warner's holdings, consult *Standard and Poor's Corporation Descriptions*, New York; 1989 and *Who Owns Whom: 1989 North America*, Dun & Bradstreet International: England.

5   *Standard and Poor's Corporation Descriptions*, Standard and Poor Corporation, New York, 1980–1989.

6   Geraldine Fabrikant, 'How Warner Got Back Its Glitter', *New York Times*, 14 Dec. 1983, section 3, p. 1.

7   'Warner Pact Helps Rescue Cannon', *New York Times*, 24 Dec. 1986, p. 2.

8   Geraldine Fabrikant, 'Warner and Lorimar in "Early" Talks', *New York Times*, 8 Mar. 1988, Section 4, p. 1; Richard Gold, 'WCI to Appeal N.Y. Court Ruling Against Its Merger with Lorimar', *Variety*, 5 Oct. 1988, p. 3; 'Warner Merges with Lorimar', *New York Times*, 12 Jan. 1989, p. D19.

9   Laura Landro, 'Warner Is Cleared to Buy 50% Stake in Cinema Venture', *Wall Street Journal*, 14 Dec. 1988, p. B6.

10 'Purchase of Chappell Music From Investors Is Completed', *Wall Street Journal*, 8 Oct. 1987, p. 16.

11 Philip S. Gritis, 'Turning Superheroes into Super Sales', *New York Times*, 6 Jan 1985, p. 6.

12 Information on *The Dark Knight Returns*, on circulation, demographics and Robin is taken from: Georgia Dullea, 'Holy Bomb Blast! The Real Robin Fights On'; New York Times, 10 Nov. 1988, p.23; Alexandra Peers, 'Given His Costume, It's a Wonder He Didn't Die of Embarrassment', *Wall Street Journal*, 26 Oct. 1988, p. B1; Lisa H. Towle, 'What's New in the Comic Book Business', New York Times, 31 Jan. 1988, p. 21; 'Growing Up into Graphic Novels' and 'America Is Taking Comic Books Seriously', *New York Times*, 31 July 1988, p. 7.

13 Kathleen A. Hughes, 'Batman Fans Fear the Joke's on Them In Hollywood Epic', *Wall Street Journal*, 29 Nov. 1988, pp. 1 and 8.

14 Kevin Zimmerman, 'Soundtracks: Not Too Much Noise in '89', *Variety*, Jan. 3, 1990, pp. 49–57.

15 Nelson George, 'Prince Is Back on Wings of "Batdance" ', *Billboard*, 24 June 1989.

16 From the start, MTV was targeted for white audiences, 14–34, with an average income of $30,000: Jack Loftus, 'Warner Amex Preps All-Music Cable Channel', *Variety*, 4 March 1981, p. 1; (Young adults 14–34, stress on 14–24 year olds) Sally Bedell, 'All Rock Cable-TV Service Is A Hit', *New York Times*, 2 August 1982 p. 15; Ed Levine, 'TV Rocks with Music', *New York Times*, 8 May 1983, pp. 42, 55–56, and 61.

17 Thomas Guback, 'Capital, Labor Power, and the Identity of Film', paper presented at the Conference on Culture and Communication, Philadelphia, March 1983.

18 This market structure arises from two conditions. The first condition was the divorcement of film production and film exhibition required by the decision rendered in U.S. v. Paramount Pictures (334 U.S. 131, 142, 161). This decision resulted in the studios' divesting themselves of their theatre chains, which freed the studios from the necessity of producing 'B' movies simply to fill screens. Such production became less attractive

partly due to the availability of 'free' entertainment from broadcasters, which eroded the guaranteed audience that had once existed for any film (cf., Thomas Guback, 'Theatrical Film', in Benjamin M. Compaine, *Who Owns the Media?* (New York: Harmony Books, 1979, pp. 179–250 and Wasko, pp. 103–147). Currently, WCI and other conglomerates with interests in film studios are reintegrating film production and exhibition, while also pursuing further intergration of film as an industry with the once distinct industries of television, cable, recorded music, book publishing, etc. Reintegration may encourage the production of more film product for the screen, since that product can also be recycled across the entire array of distribution channels, including pay cable and videocassette rental. Reintegration may also encourage the current practice of playing a single title on multiple screens at cineplexes, followed by shortened runs at independent theatres and a quick turnaround to cable and rental. The precise dynamics have yet to be worked out by the relevant companies.

19 The $30 million figure is the most widely reported, generally with $10 million given for advertising costs. The $40 million figure tends to be cited without a separate figure for advertising.

---

5 Hooray for Hollywood: moving into the twenty-first century

Janet Wasko

Yes, there have been changes

One cannot deny that there were some pretty dramatic changes in the distribution and exhibition of Hollywood films and other entertainment products during the 1980s. While the introduction of new technologies was responsible for some of these changes, the political-economic context in which these innovations were introduced is crucial. Indeed, deregulation and globalization tendencies have set the stage for Hollywood in this era as much as technological development, and it seems clear from this study that these various factors can scarcely be separated.

New technologies – new outlets

Audiences of the 1990s experience mass-mediated culture differently to earlier generations. VCRs have made viewing time more flexible and convenient, and cable has provided a range of new programming possibilities with special interest channels catering to smaller audiences. In addition, there is the potential for consumers to participate in media production themselves via relatively inexpensive video equipment.

Undoubtedly, the technologies introduced by a variety of large corporations in the 1970s and 1980s provided the film industry with some wonderful new distribution outlets. Despite claims of unfair competition and piracy, the Hollywood majors are indeed benefitting from a variety of outlets. We have seen how home video has become an enormously profitable market for Hollywood companies, and cable continues to provide additional revenue for film distributors. In addition, the large Hollywood companies' involvement in these new technologies via ownership of cable channels and systems, video companies, etc., has meant even further profits.

Diversified revenues

For some time now, the Hollywood majors have not depended solely on revenues from theatrical exhibition. But these latest distribution outlets have meant that revenues are even further diversified, which adds even more power to the majors' operations. Quite simply, there are many more markets for their products. Hollywood executive Frank Rothman observed: 'When television started in the 1950s, there was a strong view that that was the end of Hollywood. When cable came, we thought that would kill our sales to networks. None of these things happened. Every time the market expands, the combination is greater than before.'[1]

Realignments in the television industry have meant adjustments in markets for the majors. Yet these changes, in many instances, have led to even more business for the majors. Even though the studios have sold fewer movies to the major networks, independent stations have been more interested in Hollywood films, as well as syndicated TV programming.

With so many more markets, it has also been possible for some smaller companies to survive or find new life, at least for a while. For instance, Republic Pictures was able to profit in the 1980s from the new outlets for film release (especially videocassettes), as well as from television production. Under new ownership in 1987, Republic capitalized on its library by 'squeezing every possible dollar out of its films' and keeping costs down for production of made-for-TV movies. By the end of the decade, Republic had tripled its sales from these various sources.[2]

Spreading the risks

For the film industry, then, more outlets have translated into less risk.

Video and cable release of films have provided extra benefits for films which did well in theatres, and given 'legs' to films which did not do well in theatrical release. Furthermore, globalization tendencies have opened new markets, to further reduce the risk of producing big budget films.

As Asu Aksoy and Kevin Robins point out,

> The ability to coordinate and exploit different media outlets means that major production companies can now spread risks over increasingly segmented audiences.
>
> If part of the success of the Hollywood majors can be explained by the rationalization of production costs, we would argue that what has made them the dominant powers in the film business has been the ability to get their films (whatever their production cost) to a worldwide audience. And it was this ability – that is to say, control over the distribution side of the business – that allowed the majors to continue their dominance even after the Paramount Decree.[3]

New trends in film financing

As a result of new distribution technologies, there have been some claims that film production is less risky as there is an increased need for product. However, with the average negative cost for a Hollywood film reported to be well over $25 million and advertising costs rising, the majors, at least, argue that there is even more risk.

While many of the majors rely on in-house productions, independents look for financing sources in many locations. And new distribution outlets have led to a wider range of pre-buy or pre-licensing deals. This is not necessarily new, as TV networks, foreign distribution outlets and other sources have been involved in such deals in the past. But important new sources are pay cable and home video companies, and sometimes these new players also become directly involved in production. Examples include HBO's production program [...] Other income sources are represented by the expanding market for entertainment-related merchandise.[4] [...]

New sources of funds have also come from new owners of distribution and production companies. With an increased need for product, the Hollywood companies have become attractive to those wanting to (and now able to) expand their communications empires. Examples include Turner's and Paretti's brief flings with MGM, Murdoch's takeover of Fox, the Sony and Matsushita purchases of Columbia and MCA, and the struggle over Paramount in 1993–4. It is not surprising that these corporations were interested in Hollywood investments. The value of the libraries of the major studios alone represent a sizable asset. For instance, in 1987 MCA's 3,000 films were valued at $1.5 billion.[5]

Meanwhile, Hollywood companies developed their own devices for raising funds. Disney has been quite successful raising production funding through public offerings such as Silver Screen Partners. Meanwhile, Twentieth Century Fox raised $63 million through limited partnership funds called American Entertainment Partners, formed by Shearson Lehman Brothers. Other financial innovations will no doubt follow, as the majors seek others to carry the risk of blockbuster filmmaking.

Hooray for success

Hollywood in the 1980s represented more than just a dream factory – it was an industry that brought home the bacon. New distribution outlets (as well as enhanced advertising campaigns) brought a new level of popularity to movies, and Hollywood reaped the benefits.

Aksoy and Robins observe: 'With the emergence of competition from television and cable channels, film companies are now extending these cascading strategies and playing on the time of release across different media.' Enormous profits were made with wildly successful blockbusters, such as *Batman, Terminator 2, Jurassic Park*, and countless others. But even further rewards came from distributing American cultural products throughout the world. More than once the US film industry received praise for its success in foreign markets, representing one of the strongest net export industries in the country. More and more global markets provided revenue for the expansion by Hollywood companies abroad, thus representing an enterprise which the USA seemed destined to control through the turn of the century.

Continuity in the 1990s

The More Things Change, the More They Remain the Same
(Dennis Stanfill, former Fox chairman)

But even though there have been these dramatic developments in the production, distribution and exhibition of filmed entertainment, what has actually changed about the film industry? After having looked more closely at Hollywood in the 1970s and 1980s, it is possible to conclude that there is a good deal of continuity as well as change.

More commodities

While there are new means of producing and distributing filmed entertainment, Hollywood's creative efforts are still aimed at creating commodities. In other words, the potential of video, cable and satellite technologies have been developed with profit, rather than expanded communication and/or enlightenment, in mind. In other words, the film industry's primary motivation has to do with profits, not necessarily with film. As a few of the Hollywood executives confessed in the early 1980s, they do not care whether or not their products are exhibited in theatres or in the home, as long as they get paid their 'fair share'. But it may also be true that the corporations that represent Hollywood may not necessarily be as locked into films as one might think. As Thomas Guback points out, 'the ultimate product of the motion picture business is profit; motion pictures are but means to that end.'[6]

It is important to note that despite these motivations, the introduction of new technological wonders by corporate innovators does not always succeed. Despite the power of large corporations, there are still examples of failure and misjudgment, sometimes leading to huge losses, as with other commodities. Among the examples covered in this study are the early attempts by Hollywood to enter broadcasting, the introduction of videodiscs, and a pay-per-transaction arrangement for video retailing.

The point, however, is that the development of technologies that have vast potential for enlightenment and understanding has been controlled by the business sector of our society, and by a relatively small set of players within that sector.

More films?

One would think with these new outlets for films on a global scale, more production would follow logically. Well, at least for a while in the mid-1980s, film production blossomed. 1985 was the busiest filming period for Hollywood in 12 years, while film production reportedly was up 50 per cent in 1986. Yet the total domestic theatrical releases by all companies increased only 4 per cent to 472 titles in 1986. Since then, the number of domestic film releases has varied: 466 in 1988, 472 in 1989, 379 in 1990 and 424 in 1991.[7]

Indeed, at the beginning of the 1990s, the majors even released fewer films than in previous years. The distributors blame the situation on megasalaries for stars and high distribution costs (advertising and prints), which continued to rise during the decade.[8] But these increasing costs can be associated directly with the blockbuster mentality that pervades the industry as well as the inflated costs associated with the major studios' operations.[9]

That's entertainment!

As Erik Barnouw suggests [...] technologies are often envisioned as new possibilities for enlightenment and democracy. However, their actual development may be something else.

Once again, the new technologies discussed in this volume have evolved as forms of entertainment. Yes, there are informational programs on cable and even pay cable. Yes, there are documentary videos and informational programs available on videocassettes. But the *dominant* use of these new media forms is entertainment. No, nothing against a good laugh, a good cry, a mindless romp through outer space. The point, again, is that we were promised so much more.

Many popular writers and social scientists, and more than a few government inquiries, have argued that there may be serious consequences of such a preoccupation with being passively entertained, rather than being creative and informed.[10] It also might be noted that since this phenomenon has occurred with the introduction of most new communication technologies, as Barnouw suggests, we might look to the social setting in which these technological developments occur, rather than the technologies themselves. This view was echoed by an industry visionary, Bob Stein of the Voyager Company, when asked about the future of laser technology:

> Technologies don't grow up in a vacuum, they grow up – in this case – under moribund imperialist life in the late 20th century.... The same crap that is coming out of Hollywood is going to come out of these technologies by and large. If things don't change radically socially, then we're going to be using one tiny-tiny bit of the potential of the technology.[11]

Some may hold out for new creative possibilities that may be provided by some new entertainment technologies, promoting alternatives to the passive experiences presented by the culture industry. For instance, after observing his children exploring and playing with computers, James Monaco expressed hope that 'there will be millions more like them who will take their rightful place with the priests of sounds and images and experience the joy of creation as often as the dubious pleasure of consumption'.[12] Yet, the 'joy' of consumption still may be overpowering to many viewers, especially when surrounded by appealing and/or subversive commercial pitches to accept a more passive, pay-per society mentality.

More channels for advertising

Many of the discussions of the new communications technologies connected to the information revolution seem to avoid the issue of advertising via these new outlets. While more consumer choice or diversity is praised, the possibilities of new technologies as more exact marketing devices are less often acknowledged. [...] the latest distribution outlets for Hollywood films have incorporated more deliberate and extensive advertising and marketing campaigns than in the past. While these trends might have intensified without new communication outlets, the new technologies have nevertheless assisted in the further commercialization of our culture.

Property is property

Another concept that has changed little throughout these developments is the notion of culture as property. In other words, the introduction of cable, home video, or satellite communication has not altered the accepted perception of cultural or creative expression which is owned rather than shared. The Disney culture may be international, reaching beyond national and cultural boundaries, but it is *owned* by the Disney company.

The notion of culture as property is illustrated quite well with the issue of piracy, a problem which has accelerated with some of the new communication technologies discussed in this book, and especially in relation to video technology. Again, the entertainment industry has turned to the state to protect its interests (i.e. profits) by enforcing the notion of culture as property, a value which automatically accompanies the development of these new technologies in capitalist societies.

We also are reminded from this discussion that technologies may be changing some of the ways in which we experience entertainment and information in the 1990s, but the relations of production remain the same. There has been no revolution in social relations.[13]

Uneven distribution

The boom in new distribution outlets and markets has been enormously lucrative for the film industry and its leaders. During a decade when the gap between the poor and the rich in the USA became even more glaring, many of the Hollywood majors reported record profits and the corporate heads of the largest companies were rewarded for their success, often with profit incentives and stock options.

A survey by the *Los Angeles Times* in 1984 indicated that 'more than 100 stars, directors, producers, writers, agents and studio executives have built fortunes of $50 million or more in the last few years'.[14] The salaries of Hollywood stars continue to skyrocket,[15] while executive salaries and compensations have reached all-time highs. Steven J. Ross (Time Warner) topped Forbes' list of best paid chief executives, receiving combined compensation of $302 million in 1990. Martin S. Davis of Paramount made the list for the second year, as did Michael D. Eisner of Disney.[16] At the end of 1992, Eisner made an astounding move, cashing in over $90 million in stock options, prompting other executives to do the same in order to avoid potential tax hikes by the Clinton administration during 1993. Again, what has changed about these tales of the wealthy becoming wealthier? Not a lot.

Meanwhile, Hollywood unions were losing members and strength, suffering from the proliferation of non-union films and runaway production, and giving in to concessions demanded by prosperous (and some would argue, greedy) studios.[17]

Another question of distribution relates to how much new technology is really needed, at what cost and to whom. When asked his opinion of HDTV, one might have expected Ted Turner – head of Turner Entertainment, which has benefited from many of the recent technological changes – to wax eloquent on the advantages of this specific technology. His response, however, was surprising (again, typical for Turner):

> Over half the people on earth don't have enough to eat and probably a third of the people don't have any TV at all. It's gonna be mega-billions to convert over to that, and I think there are a lot more things that can be done with that money before the rich world pigs out on high-density color TV. We oughta supply people that don't have electricity with electricity before we do that.[18]

Of course, that would provide a larger audience for Turner's expanding regular-TV audience, but nevertheless, his thoughts remind us that constant technological change is not always automatically necessary for real human progress.

Myth-busting

[...]

Myth 1: competition – concentration versus independence

Despite the claim that the new technologies introduced in the 1970s and 1980s would foster competition, this has not been the case, as much of the evidence in this study has indicated.

With the enhanced need for product or software, the Hollywood majors were poised and ready to supply it. While the majors already received income from diverse resources, new distribution outlets meant even further diversification. Despite the initial skirmishes and claims of foul play, the majors were well positioned (or made the necessary adjustments) to maintain their prominence, not only in the traditional film industry, but in the larger culture industry. They were able and willing to build alliances with other companies – outside the traditional film industry or even with new 'competitors' – as well as developing interdependencies between old and new technologies. In addition, they have benefitted from relaxed government regulation, thus merging into large synergistic corporations that control huge chunks of popular cultural production, not only in the USA but around the world.

The majors' strength might be contrasted to a typical independent filmmaker who only produces films, and thus is unable to capitalize on or draw strength from these diversified revenues. And, if there was one observation that prevailed in Hollywood at the beginning of the 1990s, it was the difficulties faced by independents. The majors' entry into exhibition further exacerbated the situation. As one independent observed, 'You have all these screens, but they're showing the same eight movies over and over again, as opposed to giving (smaller) films a chance to find their audience.'[19]

So the majors rule the entertainment roost. If there is any doubt about concentration in the traditional film industry, recall that the top five or six distribution companies regularly receive nearly 90 percent of domestic (North American) theatrical film rentals and still dominate the distribution of motion pictures to home video and cable markets. Indeed, the notion of competition in the traditional film industry is a legendary myth, and remains so as Hollywood looks toward the twenty-first century.

Myth 2: industrial conflict

Throughout this book, there have been references to 'the film industry'. And in many of the developments during the last decades, 'the film industry' has been pitted against other entertainment or communications industries – broadcasting, cable, and home video. This is the rhetoric of the industries themselves and the government representatives who regulate or deregulate them. Yet, there are several reasons why this terminology is misleading, especially for those who seek to understand the impact of these activities on our culture.

Increasingly, the same products are seen in all these supposedly-separate industries. [...] Furthermore, the giant communications corporations are involved in many, if not all, of these activities. [...] all of the Hollywood majors have subsidiaries which deal with film, television, music, cable, and home video. Most of the larger companies also are involved in publishing, theme parks, and merchandising. Thus, how is it possible to separate the interests of these corporations into specific 'industries'? [...] As Aksoy and Robins conclude:

> The major Hollywood companies are being turned into image empires with tentacles reaching down, not only to movies and TV programmes, but also to books, records, and even hardware. The feature film business no longer exists in its own right, but is increasingly becoming part of an integrated, global image business, central to the broader media strategies of entertainment companies and conglomerates. However, the major studios are the fundamental building blocks of the emerging entertainment megacompanies.[20]

Certainly there are differences in the characteristics of various distribution outlets for entertainment, necessitating some differences in industry structures and policies. Indeed, there are differences in the essences of these various media, as Marshall McLuhan and Harold Innis showed us in their work.

Yet these differences are breaking down and it might behoove us to think in terms of *transindustrial* activities, emphasizing the overlapping strategies of a relatively few corporations producing and distributing entertainment and cultural products. Again, we might also revisit the notion of a *culture industry*, as depicted by the Frankfurt School theorists in the 1930s. One need not argue that the effects of the culture industry are uniform or overpowering (as the Frankfurt School assumed) to accept that there are shared interests and activities among these various business sectors, and to resist the notion that there is constant industrial conflict, as many industry and government representatives would contend. Further, it is possible, without sinking to economic reductionism, to accept the terminology popular with the corporations themselves, as they stress the notion of 'synergy' between their various operations. But this brings us to the question of diversity, the next myth of the information age.

Myth 3: diversity or more of the same?

A common theme in past discussions of new technologies is the enhanced diversity offered the consumer, with terms such as 'television of abundance' and 'technologies of freedom'.[21] Yet, the more common observation these days is that the range of programming has not been enhanced with new distribution outlets. *Channels* magazine observed in 1987, it is more like 'old wine in many new bottles'. As British communications scholar Graham Murdock has argued:

> It is possible to greatly increase the number of channels and the number of goods in circulation without significantly extending diversity. More does not necessarily mean different. It can also mean more of the same thing distributed in a variety of ways.... Diversity is not multiplicity.[22]

After a decade of new cable channels and home video options, it is no longer an academic exercise to predict less true diversity. Articles in the popular press, editorial cartoons, public opinion polls, and even writers of popular songs (e.g. Bruce Springsteen) reflect the disillusionment with the promises of more diversity through new entertainment technologies. For instance, in early 1992 an Associated Press survey reported that 40 percent of people in the USA believed that cable and video rentals made it easier to find programs they wanted to see, while one-third of those polled said that cable and VCRs made no difference and 20 percent claimed that choices had become even worse.[23]

As we have seen in this study, the new distribution outlets which have been introduced over the last few decades have provided us (for a price) with at least the outlets (or conduits) for cultural diversity. We are no longer prisoners of the 'tyranny' of watching or listening to the same sources, at the same time. Yet, by looking at the narrow range of producers and the typical duplication of programming, it is possible to argue that similar ideas, values and expressions are reproduced in these different outlets. In other words, a form of *cultural synergy* has coincided with the corporate synergy stressed by the megacorporations which produce and distribute cultural products. The economic logic is compelling, as once a character or story is created and developed (and, of course, owned), there are advantages in moving it into different formats. For instance, it is not unusual to find films made into television programs, because the same companies that often produce and distribute major films also produce prime-time programming. With a popular film, there is no need to make a pilot, which can cost around $2.2 million per hour. And, while some films do not transfer into successful television fare, they still have the advantage of being recognized immediately by audiences.[24] Roger Rabbit, the movie, becomes Roger Rabbit, the cartoon, becomes Roger Rabbit, the video, etc. The production savings and promotional value of different outlets seems obvious. But the result is less diversity from channel to channel (or conduit to conduit).

The notion of cultural synergy implies that characters, stories and ideas are made into products for different outlets. However, what often occurs is that we see the same products on different outlets, or, in other words, we experience *recycled culture*. While cable offers many more channels than previous systems, much of the programming includes recycled TV shows, movies, or documentaries. While video-cassette versions of films provide the opportunity to see a movie in the comfort of our homes, the film still is recycled from another outlet, and will be recycled again for network television, again for syndicated television, etc. While many fans enjoy seeing their favorite TV programmes, movies, etc. over and over again, and can even 'own' their own copies, it seems disturbing that our culture may not be actually evolving, but merely recycling. At the very least, there is much less diversity than promised when new distribution outlets display the same programming as previous outlets.

[...]

Notes

1 John Micklethwait, 'The Entertainment Industry: Raising the Stakes', *The Economist*, July 1983.

2 Michael Barrier, 'The Republic for Which He Stands', *Nation's Business*, May 1991, pp. 54–7; Robert Wrubel, 'The Ghost of Glitz Past'. *Financial World*, 9 January 1990, pp. 56–7.

3 Asu Aksoy and Kevin Robins, 'Hollywood for the 21st Century: Global Competition for Critical Mass in Image Markets', *Cambridge Journal of Economics* 16, no. 1, 1992, pp. 1–22.

4 A recent example of the value of these new income sources was the film *Terminator 2*, which sold rights to video, cable, and television to raise production funds, as well as expecting $20 million in licensed merchandise. See 'Conan, the Humanitarian,' *Time*, 6 July 1991, p. 57.

5 Lawrence Cohn, 'New Economy of Scale in Hollywood', *Variety*, 14 January 1987.

6 Thomas H. Guback, 'The Structure and Policies of the Theatrical Exhibition Business in the United States', paper presented at the Conference on Culture and Communication, Philadelphia, Penn., 1986.

7 Tom Bierbaum, 'Don't Scrap Breadth for Depth ...', *Variety*, 16 March 1988, p. 93; *1991 International Motion Picture Almanac*, New York: Quigley Publishing, 1991, p. 26A; 'Production Update', *Variety*, 6 January 1992, p. 10; *1993 International Motion Picture Almanac*, New York: Quigley Publishing, 1993, p. 19A.

8 Average US marketing costs (prints and advertising) for new features was over $12 million, as reported in *1993 International Motion Picture Almanac*, p. 19A.

9 See, for instance, Steven Bach, *Final Cut: Dreams and Disaster in the Making of Heaven's Gate*, New York: New American Library, 1985. Also, interesting insights into the majors' typical distribution of film revenues was revealed in the suit filed by Art Buchwald against Paramount Pictures in 1992.

10 For instance, see Neil Postman, *Amusing Ourselves to Death*, New York: Viking Press, 1985; Herbert I. Schiller, *Culture, Inc.*, New York: Oxford University Press, 1990.

11 Frank Spotnitz, 'What's Next?', *American Film*, January/February 1989, p. 33.

12 James Monaco, 'Into the 90s', *American Film*, January/February, 1989, pp. 24–7.

13 A point emphasized by Sarah Douglas and Thomas H. Guback in 'Production and Technology in the Communication/Information Revolution', *Media, Culture and Society* 6, no. 3, July 1984, pp. 233–45.

14 Cited in Marc Cooper, 'Concession Stand', *American Film*, December 1987, p. 37.

15 Examples are the salaries for *A Few Good Men:* Jack Nicholson received $500,000 for his relatively small role, while Tom Cruise got $12.5 million for the film. Meanwhile, Arnold Schwarzenegger was reported to have received a $15 million jet, in addition to his salary, for appearing in *Terminator 2*. See Alan Citron, 'The Hollywood that Can't Say No', *Los Angeles Times*, 13 December 1992, p. D1:4.

16 Steve Kichen et al., 'Corporate America's Most Powerful People,' *Forbes*, 27 May 1991, pp. 214–89.

17 See Cooper, 'Concession Stand'.

18 Greg Dawson, 'Ted Turner', *American Film*, January/February 1989, pp. 38–9.

19 Spotnitz, 'What's Next?', p. 30.
20 Aksoy and Robins, 'Hollywood for the 21st Century'.
21 Sloan Commission on Cable Communication, *On the Cable: The Television of Abundance*, New York: McGraw-Hill, 1971: Ithiel de sola Pool, *Technologies of Freedom*, Cambridge, Mass.: Belknap Press, 1983.
22 Graham Murdock, 'Programming: Needs and Answers', paper presented at New Dimensions in Television meeting, Venice, Italy, 15 March 1981.
23 'Watering TV's Soup', *Register-Guard*, 23 February 1992.
24 Leo Bogart suggested the notion of cultural synergy in 'The American Media System and Its Commercial Culture,' Occasional Paper No. 8, Gannett Foundation Media Center, March 1991, p. 5: 'The underlying principle is that the transfer of symbolic messages across media boundaries permits a "synergy" that makes the whole larger and more profitable than the sum of its separate parts.' Also see Richard Mahler, 'Movie Spinoffs on TV', *American Film*, June 1990, p. 13, and Schiller, *Culture, Inc.*

SECTION TWO
FILM AND AUTHORSHIP

From the early 1950s to the late 1960s, French, British and American critics argued for the importance of looking at cinema (especially Hollywood cinema) in terms of authorship. For a while, authorship study, in its various forms, represented the cutting edge of film criticism. It was state-of-the-art, a new and sometimes controversial approach that managed to enthuse some while irritating others. In retrospect, now that some of the fuss associated with it has died away, a number of authorship's claims seem eminently reasonable; others are more problematic.

The main point made in most authorship work, possibly the only point, is that as far as cinema is concerned the author is (or should be) the film director. Of all the potential candidates for the authorial role – including the screenwriter, the producer, the cinematographer – the director is presented as the figure who most obviously controls a film's visuals and thereby most embodies that which is 'cinematic'. Moreover, this author-director is seen as expressing himself (given the sexual division of labour in the film business, most author-directors turn out to be male) via the cinematic medium in a way that makes him comparable with artists working in other, more traditional art forms. An author's films are linked together as products of a single artistic sensibility; they are an expression of the author's personal vision. In order fully to appreciate the author, one needs to view as many of his films as possible and look for connections between them. The most likely place to find such authors is, surprisingly, in the apparently inhospitable terrain provided by Hollywood. Indeed much of authorship study can be seen as driven by the need to rescue Hollywood cinema, or at least parts of it, from the critical oblivion to which it had been relegated by earlier work on mass culture (see Section One).

Objections to authorship study raised both during the period of authorship's critical ascendancy and since usually relate to the inappropriateness of such an approach when applied to an understanding of American film. Film production in general, it has been pointed out, and Hollywood production in particular, is a collaborative process involving a large number of people working in clearly defined roles. In the classical Hollywood studio system, this specialization of labour and the production-line process associated with it ensured that, with the exception of a few individuals who managed to negotiate privileged positions for themselves within the industry, opportunities for any individual to exert a totalizing authorial control over any film were extremely limited.

Authorship study was also criticized for its conception of the artist within Hollywood. For those who perceived Hollywood as simply a capitalist machine churning out entertainment product, the idea that this institution might have a cultural or artistic dimension was scandalous. Even for those critics who wanted to think positively of Hollywood in terms of mass and popular culture, the figure of the author-director was also troubling but for different reasons. While authorship study did offer a way of taking Hollywood seriously, it was felt that the focus on talented, exceptional individuals working within – and often against or despite of – the Hollywood system hindered an investigation into how this system itself could produce work of significance and merit, work which required a different set of evaluative criteria from those deployed for other art forms. As Alan Lovell put it, 'This implicit acceptance of the dominance of the traditional arts was strengthened by the use of the *auteur* theory which used the common critical tool of traditional artistic criticism (the author expressing the personal vision)' (Lovell 1975: 5). Even the critic André Bazin, sometimes unfairly thought of as the 'father' of French authorship criticism, wrote of the need to address what he called 'the genius of the system' when thinking about Hollywood (Bazin 1985: 258).

Perhaps the best way of assessing authorship as an approach to film is via an account of its historical development, for as the authorship debates move from one group of critics to another group, from one country and one language to another, important changes and revisions occur. While it is tempting to see this process as a linear one – with the enthusiastic and impressionistic outpourings of 1950s French cinephiles turned into something more systematic by British and American critics in the early 1960s, and then made very systematic indeed after an encounter with structuralism in the late 1960s – the reality is more fragmented than this scenario might suggest. What a review of film authorship literature in the 1950s and 1960s reveals instead are clusters of activity, with the relations between these clusters characterized as much by rupture and discontinuity as they are by a developmental cohesion. Certainly some ideas are passed on, but others – often interesting ones – are dropped; there are significant changes in terminology and also substantial (although harder to quantify) shifts in tone.

It was the French film journal *Cahiers du Cinéma* which first made authorship an important critical issue in film culture, with its discussions of and support for what it called 'la politique des auteurs', auteur policy. However, there was some critical activity in this area before *Cahiers*' intervention – Alexandre Astruc's 'The Birth of a New Avant-Garde: La Caméra-Stylo' is an often quoted example, understandably so, given the way that it obviously lays part of the foundation for subsequent French film criticism (Astruc 1968). The Thorold Dickinson piece reprinted here (along with Howard Koch's response) is less well known but is still interesting both in the way it anticipates Truffaut's important 1954 article 'A Certain Tendency of the French Cinema' and in the way it suggests an approach to questions of film authorship that is in certain respects different from the approach set out by Truffaut.

Both Dickinson and Truffaut focus on the issue of adaptation and what distinguishes a 'literary' film from a 'cinematic' film. They agree that what is required for the development of a cinematic (as opposed to a literary) aesthetic is the raising of the status of the film director over the screen-writer. They even come up with new terms for the director – Dickinson offers 'filmwright' (which was probably too theatrical a term ever to catch on with the cinephiles) and Truffaut the more provocative 'auteur'. However, they are speaking from very different positions. At the time of his article, Dickinson was a British film director with an established reputation who was concerned to raise the status of the directing profession gener-ally. The Truffaut of 'A Certain Tendency ...', by way of a contrast, was a young film critic, some years away from himself becoming a film director, who wanted to identify particular directors of cinematic merit.

The difference between the views of the film-makers and the critics are clarified by Howard Koch's response to what Dickinson has to say. Koch was a successful Hollywood screenwriter whose grievance was that screenwriting was not valued highly enough. Interestingly, he sees the director as part of a management structure and as a profession which already has enough power. Koch's ideal director is William Wyler, someone respectful of the script and, perhaps unsurprisingly, a film-maker whose reputation with the later auteurists was never especially high (although, as ever, André Bazin (1997) would go his own way in producing an appreciation of Wyler's work). The Dickinson–Koch exchange offers itself as a cross-Atlantic, intra-industrial squabble which reveals different professions jockeying for influence and recognition and confirms, if such confirmation is required, that commercial film production is far from being the one-dimensional, monolithic institution imagined by some critics. Importantly, it is precisely this sense of voices and perspectives emanating from within the industry (or, to be more precise in this case, two industries – British and American) and its professional contexts which is often lost in subsequent authorship debates.

Cahiers du Cinéma in the 1950s was the home for a certain kind of cinephilia which for the critics involved manifested itself in obsessive and extensive cinema-going along with the production of provocative articles which sought to communicate and reflect upon this experience. Many of these articles feel rushed, as if dashed off between film screenings (which some probably were). The fact that *Cahiers'* auteurist writing never resolved itself into a coolly theorized account of film production was arguably one consequence of this cinephile intensity. The term used by the auteurists themselves to describe their approach was accordingly prag-matic – la politique des auteurs, auteur policy. (For examples of *Cahiers* work in this period, see Hillier 1985.)

Truffaut's article 'A Certain Tendency of the French Cinema' typifies the *Cahiers* auteurist approach in its concern to identify that which is 'cine-matic' – i.e. that which fully exploits the visual resources of cinema and which is best seen as the property of the director or auteur, the one who controls a film's visuals or *mise-en-scène*. In the article, Truffaut attacks what he terms the 'tradition of quality', a type of French film which he sees as too dependent on screenwriters – Aurenche and Bost in this case – and therefore too 'literary' and insufficiently cinematic. Truffaut also makes what would become the standard *Cahiers* distinction between auteurs and *metteurs-en-scène*, the former 'men of cinema' in Truffaut's words, the latter directors incapable of imposing a personal signature on their films.

At the same time, Truffaut's focus on French cinema and its traditions does not sit easily with the more usual auteurist preoccupation with Hollywood. Truffaut's attack on a writer-centred cinema is not readily transferable to the Hollywood studio system, where – as we have already seen in the Koch article – the screenwriter was rarely a powerful figure. In much of the auteurist writing of the 1950s and 1960s – French, British and American – the issue demanding attention is the presence of the auteur within Hollywood, while authorship in European cinema is taken for granted. It often seems to be the case that European directors such as Federico Fellini and Ingmar Bergman are perceived as being so obviously authors that their authorship is simply not problematic. Establishing Howard Hawks and Alfred Hitchcock (to name two of *Cahiers*' favourite directors) as authors, on the other hand, takes a lot of work from critics. The assumption apparent here that European cinema in some way provides a non-industrial arena for the artist's free expression is clearly a misleading one, as is demonstrated by Truffaut's forceful construction of an authorship problematic within the context of French cinema and French film history.

Ian Cameron in 'Films, Directors and Critics' and Andrew Sarris in 'Notes on the Auteur Theory in 1962' both shift the focus back to Hollywood. Each is concerned to distance himself from what are perceived as some of the excesses of French auteurism while still holding onto the idea of the director as the key creative personality in film production. Cameron's article first appeared in the second issue of the film periodical *Movie*, the main British voice of authorship study throughout the 1960s. Characteristically for this publication, the article's claims that certain directors are significant artists is based on a detailed analysis of movies. Like Truffaut, Cameron values films in which the full resources of cinema – especially those to do with *mise-en-scène* – are successfully mobilized and coordinated by the director in order to produce a particular effect or effects, and is critical (mildly so compared to Truffaut) of those films which lack a coherence of effect, where what is said in dialogue and the visual presentation of this do not cohere into a meaningful whole.

More ambitiously, and more controversially, Sarris introduces the word 'theory' into the authorship debate. His article sets out in a more abstract and discursive way than *Movie* what Sarris sees as the constitutive principles of auteurism, with a particular stress on finding the personal in Hollywood films. At the same time, and despite the presentation of this as 'theory', the critical language used by Sarris is a very subjective one and, as is so often the case with authorship writing in this period, relies on and presupposes an extensive cinephile involvement with film to find the

signatures of interesting auteurs. The article is then less a theoretical statement and more an expression of Sarris' own critical beliefs – concluding,
appropriately, with a cinephile's revelatory encounter with an obscure
Raoul Walsh movie – as well as being a polemic designed to provoke
debate. Sarris himself, obviously bemused by the hostile reception his
ideas received in certain quarters, later described the article as 'modest,
tentative, experimental ... certainly not intended as the last word on the
subject' (Sarris 1968: 26).

An interesting feature of Sarris' article is that in the movement from la
politique des auteurs to auteur theory the word 'auteur' remains untranslated. As Sarris himself pointed out in his book *The American Cinema*:

> Strictly speaking, 'auteur' means 'author', and should be so translated when the
> reference is to literary personalities. When Truffaut writes of Gide or Giraudoux,
> and refers to them incidentally as 'auteurs', there is no special point being made,
> and 'author' is both an adequate and accurate translation. It is another matter
> entirely when Truffaut describes Hitchcock and Hawks as 'auteurs'. 'Author' is
> neither adequate nor accurate as a translation into English mainly because of
> the inherent literary bias of the Anglo-American cultural Establishment. (Sarris
> 1968: 27)

Leaving 'auteur' untranslated renders it, for English speakers at least, a
foreign term, so that to say a particular director is an auteur is in effect to
say that he or she is like an author but not an author in the traditional sense
of that term. A certain ambiguity becomes apparent here, as the English-
speaking auteurist's attempts to rise the status of cinema to other art forms
seems to be problematized by the very term which is used to define the
attempt.

The next significant intervention into film authorship debates was
provided by Peter Wollen, who in his 1969 book *Signs and Meanings in the
Cinema* offered 'auteur-structuralism' as a solution to what he saw as the
overly impressionistic earlier auteurist writings. Wollen argues that what
links an author's work together is a series of structuring oppositions – in
Hawks's case between his comedies and the action films, in Ford's case
shifting oppositions within the films themselves. The critic, whose role is
more central and explicit here than previously, has to work to identify these
structures (of which the auteur himself may well be unaware) and thereby
produce a sense of the auteur which has a material basis in the films themselves rather than in the inevitably unquantifiable personality of the
director concerned.

Wollen's approach certainly avoids the danger of personality cults
endemic in auteurist writing, and it clarifies the role of the critic, who is no
longer the rapt spectator bearing witness to an author's presence in films
but instead the practical analyser of film texts. There are problems with
Wollen's auteurism, however. For one thing, it is not clear how distinctive
and specific a structure has to be before it becomes author-specific; the
oppositions that Wollen identifies in Ford's work, for example, are virtually
indistinguishable from those used by other critics to define the Western

genre. In addition, Wollen's considered refusal to engage with something as imponderable as the artist's personality means that any idea of the director as creative agent becomes marginal to the auteur-structuralist project. Wollen's acknowledgement that there will be elements in any auteur film which do not necessarily pertain to a defined auteur-structure draws our attention to some of the contextual, industry-specific constraints upon a director. In calling these elements 'noise', however, Wollen renders them a problem which a critic has to negotiate, rather than potentially meaningful and significant in their own right. Ultimately, the privilege accorded the author-structure over competing elements has an arbitrary quality to it: it seems to exist as a prior condition to Wollen's analysis rather than as a product of it.

Robin Wood was a contributor to *Movie*, and his 1965 book *Hitchcock's Films* was a milestone in British auteurist writing. In his response to Wollen (taken from Wood's book *Personal Views*), Wood combines the traditional *Movie* detailed formal analysis with what might be termed here a situated auteurism, one which, while maintaining a focus on the author-director as key creative voice, also seeks to locate this author in relation to particular collaborative contexts, in this case Hawks's collaborations with different screenwriters. In his important work on Hitchcock from the 1970s onwards, Wood has explored further the relation of the director to genre, stars, narrative structures and ideology, in each case identifying elements which pre-exist the director and which are meaningful without reference to him but into which the director intervenes in order to produce significant work (see in particular Wood 1989, which contains both the 1965 material on Hitchcock and Wood's later work on the director and film authorship).

In the 1970s, the sort of approach represented by Wood's work on Hawks – one firmly committed to a sense of the individual artist, no matter how much the activities of that artist might be moulded and limited by different contextual and institutional pressures – became distinctly unfashionable in certain circles. The introduction of semiotics and psycho-analysis into film studies shifted the intellectual agenda towards a consideration of the ways in which cinema as an institution worked to construct particular forms of spectatorship and subjectivity (see Sections Three, Four, Six and Seven). Seen from such a perspective, any notion of the author-director as creative agent was deeply problematic.

Yet authorship as a way of thinking about film has prevailed: auteurist assumptions underpin much journalistic film criticism, director studies are a regular feature of academic publishing, and even non-auteurist studies of film often fall back on notions of authorship in the way they group and assess films. To a certain extent, this can be seen as the product of an intensive investment in the figure of the author by both the industry and the critical establishment. On another level, however, it does register a certain truth about film production – namely that directors fulfil a particular privileged function within the film-making process and have done so for a long time. Clearly it is important to think through the question of what creative agency means in the cinema, and perhaps the best way of doing this is to explore in detail the industrial, collaborative and hierarchical systems of interaction and decision-making which constitute the production process. What do directors actually do? What is it about the director's function that is so significant, and how does it relate to other functions of the production process? And most importantly, is the centrality accorded to the director in much film criticism justified by his or her position within the industry?

Generally the issue of the industry has not been explored at any length within authorship study. Instead, authorship in film emerged from cinephilia, a particularly intense relation to film which has always been the property of the few (critics/cinephiles) rather than the many (audiences). Even in contemporary cinema, where the name of the director is frequently used in the marketing of a film, it is not at all clear that audiences care that much about the director as author (as opposed to director as brand name). When seen from this perspective, the very idea of the author or auteur has often had a cultish or elitist quality attached to it. Indeed, the division between auteurs – those who can transcend or subvert the Hollywood system – and the less valuable *metteurs-en-scène* – those who in a sense embody the system – can on a certain level be seen as reiterating some of the anxieties about Hollywood expressed in earlier mass culture work.

The main historical benefit of authorship study has probably been its development of ways of engaging with films in terms of a cinematic aesthetic (as opposed, say, to a more literary approach apparent in some pre-auteurist criticism). However, it does seem that so far as further development of this area is concerned, a move away from the private realm of the cinephile and a clearer sense of the industrial functions of direction would be helpful. Ultimately, any claims for a director as 'author' should rest as much on the material circumstances of film production as they do on critical reception.

References

Astruc, A. (1968). 'The Birth of a New Avant-Garde: La Caméra-Stylo'. Originally published in 1948, reprinted in P. Graham (ed.), *The New Wave*. London: Secker & Warburg, 17–23.

Bazin, A. (1985). 'On the Politique des Auteurs'. Originally published in April 1957, reprinted in J. Hillier (ed.), *Cahiers du Cinéma – The 1950s: Neo-Realism, Hollywood, New Wave*. Cambridge, MA: Harvard University Press, 248–59.

—— (1997). 'William Wyler, or the Jansenist of Directing'. In B. Cardullo (ed.), *Bazin at Work*. New York and London: Routledge, 1–22.

Cameron, I. (1962). 'Films, Directors and Critics'. *Movie* **2**: 4–7.

Dickinson, T. (1950). 'The Filmwright and the Audience'. *Sight and Sound* **19**(1): 20–5.

Hillier, J. (ed.) (1985). *Cahiers du Cinéma – The 1950s: Neo-Realism, Hollywood, New Wave*. Cambridge, MA: Harvard University Press.

Koch, H. (1950). 'A Playwright Looks at the "Filmwright" '. *Sight and Sound* **19**(5): 210–14.

Lovell, A. (1975). *Don Siegel: American Cinema*. London: BFI.

Sarris, A. (1962–3). 'Notes on the Auteur Theory in 1962'. *Film Culture* **27**: 1–8.

—— (1968). *The American Cinema: Directors and Directions, 1929–68*. New York: E. P. Dutton.

Truffaut, F. (1966). 'A Certain Tendency of the French Cinema'. Originally published in French in 1954; published in English translation in *Cahiers du Cinéma in English* **1**: 30–40.

Wollen, P. (1969). *Signs and Meanings in the Cinema*. London: Secker & Warburg.

Wood, R. (1976). *Personal Views*. London: Gordon Fraser.

—— (1989). *Hitchcock's Films Revisited*. London: Faber & Faber.

6   The filmwright and the audience

Thorold Dickinson

[...] Within the film industry too many craftsmen live too close to their own particular work. They pursue technique and polish, they comb and shine every hair into
place, they light and compose every shot like an academy picture, every day's work
looks too beautiful and striking, and yet when the whole film is assembled it can be
as dead as a doornail. The vital spark is missing. There are so many departments in
sound film, and so many more in the colour film, that nowadays there is a genuine
tendency to believe that one man can no longer govern the job. My contention is that
we must find and encourage the one man who *can* govern the job. For excepting
those film makers who hunt in pairs, the sound film is as much a one-man job as any
other art.

It is generally assumed by laymen that the controlling influence is the director's.
Yet eighty per cent. of story films are subject to that influence at only one stage in
their making. Directors in Hollywood are regarded not as creative artists but as interpreters of the created screen-play, which has often been invented by a committee of
writers. Roger Manvell, in his Pelican book on *Film*, quotes a letter from Frank
Capra to the *New York Times* of April 2nd, 1939, in which he says:—

'There are only half a dozen directors in Hollywood who are allowed to shoot as
they please and who have any supervision over their editing. I would say that 80 per
cent. of the directors to-day shoot scenes exactly as they are told to shoot them
without any changes whatsoever, and that 90 per cent. of them have no voice in the
story or in the editing. Truly a sad situation for a medium that is supposed to be the
director's medium. All of us realise that situation and some of us are trying to do
something about it by insisting on producer-director set-ups, but we don't get any
too much encouragement along this line. Our only hope is that the success of these
producer-director set-ups will give others the guts to insist upon doing likewise.'

In 1939, then, the method behind ninety per cent. of American films was mass-
production and the individual approach was a luxury. The good director was occasionally given a small concession by the boss. William Wyler has told us that Samuel
Goldwyn made an exception in allowing him to work on the screenplay of *The Best
Years of Our Lives* and to supervise the first editing of the film. Subsequently
Goldwyn took charge of the editing and lengthened Wyler's version by thirty-five
minutes.

The custom in European production has been to allow the director a much
stronger position than in America. But this has largely persisted because of the
shortage of experienced producers. The term *producer* has been loosely used to
indicate the impresario who raises the money and initiates the production.
Nowadays many of these men have gained experience beyond business organisation and like to take a hand in the artistic control as well. But their influence still
remains largely economic; they begin by learning that the popular audience
follows the star players, they therefore offer the stars contracts, choose their

subjects to fit the capacity of their contract players and influence the shaping of their films with like purpose.

Another increasing influence in current production is the screenwriter's. Here we tread on more delicate ground, as anyone who has met a screenwriter will know. There are two categories of writers in films, the rare one who creates original stories and the normal one who adapts other people's works into film terms. The latter is always unhappy because he is despised for being a mere adapter and at the same time blackguarded heavily if he dare draw on his own ideas in an attempt to make an inappropriate subject more filmic. He is then accused of tampering with a classic.

The creative writer seldom has the patience to master the elements of cinema to the full. But if he has any experience in writing dialogue, he can ensure that his intentions are carried out by failing to render his story in visuals and by taking the easier course of telling the story in dialogue only. Here he is enthusiastically supported by the narrow-minded among the economists. It takes far longer and costs far more to visualise a story on the screen than to grind it out in endless talk. There is no doubt that a writer is more interested in the speaking of his dialogue, which is a direct expression of his talent, than he is in any interpretation which the director may give to his descriptions of visual action. This is particularly so in cases where that interpretation may be subsequently influenced by producer and editor and possibly diverted from its original purpose and emphasis by the undue application of sound effects and music: undoubtedly the screenwriter is frustrated in every element of his work except in the direct use of his dialogue. And inevitably in self-defence he likes to compare himself with the playwright and to adopt the same attitude towards the film director as the dramatist towards the stage producer, who is the interpreter of the written play, or the composer to the conductor, who again is the interpreter of his music.

Before pursuing this question of influence further, let us exorcise from our minds this misconceived parallel of theatre and film by supplanting it with the truer analogy of ballet. The successful ballet is initiated by an impresario. Though he may not have written the original scenario (which can be the work of a layman to ballet), the dominant mind in the creation of the ballet is the choreographer. An interpretive mind can later reproduce the original choreography, but even with the eventual development of a ballet script or alphabet like Nijinsky's, the first production of a ballet must always be the work of the original choreographer because of the need to complete the theories of the choreography in the practice of rehearsal. The designer of the costumes and settings can only complete his work after studying the demands of the choreography. The function of the impresario is to bend his business management to the best interests of the creative work of his colleagues, and he must possess either sufficient funds to fulfil all their demands or sufficient character to curb them without unduly frustrating them. Impresarios who transcend that function are as rare as diamonds.

Here in ballet exists a close parallel to the proper organisation of a film. Good ideas for films are hard to come by and they may come from anywhere. In a true film the choreographer of the chosen idea is the film director. Jean Benoit-Lévy in his book, *The Art of the Motion Picture*, suggests that he should be called the *author* of the film, and I recently saw the director so described on a Russian documentary film. I would like to introduce the term 'filmwright' as a proper title for the creator of films. Because film direction is by nature physically as well as mentally exhausting, the preparatory function of choreographer may be shared by more than one person, particularly in the matter of dialogue writing, which is a gift as special as direction. Hence, while the best silent films were written and directed by the same person, in sound films it is customary for a writer to collaborate to supply dialogue where necessary, and to indicate the visual interpretation of characterisation without which the dialogue would be meaningless. [...]

To my mind progress in sound films, which the articulate audience should look for and encourage, lies in freeing the medium from the humdrum, matter-of-fact, so called straightforward use of sound. Straightbackward is an apter term to use. The current practice of using sound to give geographical perspective to the scene is theatrical and uncinematic. We welcome the exceptions, however timid in their departure from convention. How bald and obvious *Brief Encounter* would have been, told objectively; how grateful one is for its selective style, subjective to the experience of one character. How intolerable is the American practice of laying music through a film to drown the audience's restlessness at dull moments which only the bare demands of the plot can justify! But music as part of the drama, as commentator and interpreter to point the emotional colour of the scene while restraint elsewhere is called for, such use of music is a proper element in the scheme of a film.

In remembering the horse of form, we must not forget the cart of content. The artist has to have something to film before he can experiment with the way to film it. I have said that many of the films which are critically admired are failures financially. New and better films must be about new and better ideas as well as being better expressions of the old ideas. Toscanini and all the resources of the Scala at Milan could not turn *The Desert Song* into grand opera. And what is more important, they would feel insulted if one asked them to.

The film of personalities, the gossip film, is the standard film of to-day. The sound film of ideas, equivalent to Eisenstein's 'intellectual cinema' of the silent period, is a new field for experiment which we have scarcely glimpsed as yet, except in the case of a few mildly dramatic documentaries. And those were exciting enough. No filmwright will dare to venture into that field unless the audience dares him to be daring. It has become a joint responsibility.

---

7   A playwright looks at the 'filmwright'

Howard Koch

[...] There is no doubt that the average run-of-the-mill picture of our day is shamefully verbose, using dialogue as a crutch to limp through its hackneyed formula plot. But the fault goes much deeper than the wordy proclivities of so-called dialogue writers. If Hollywood has one sin above all others, it is the persuasion of too many of its film makers in all categories that the audiences will not 'understand' the implication of what they see on the screen unless it is spelt out in words. This is a form of contempt for people which, unfortunately, is present in many aspects of our national life besides our cinema. The word is used not only to explain the deed, but often, alas, as its substitute. [...]

The important question remains – who conceives this experience in its essential dramatic terms? It seems incontrovertible to me that the writer is the primary creative source. He puts down on paper the significant symbol, visual as well as auditory, through which character is revealed in a progressive series of definitive tensions. It is the writer's imagination that first previews – however inchoately and incompletely – the substance of what eventually appears on the screen.

Now what is the province of the director who is clearly not in authority and, in most cases, not even in evidence during the initial creative process? Unless, of course, he is Cecil B. De Mille dictating what he wants in the script to a roomful of glorified clerks. But this is concoction rather than creation, and the resulting epic is a painful reminder of the method by which it was achieved.

Nevertheless, the director's role can be creative in quite a different way, depending on his capacities for developing and enriching the originally conceived story. Whenever I try to imagine motion picture direction on its highest and most creative level, I invariably think of William Wyler. Besides his sensitive appraisal of dramatic values and his abundant technical resources, he displays an unswerving allegiance to the true line of every story he is putting on film. Because he measures every facet of his production in terms of its relationship to the whole – the thing – he achieves an unfailing unity.

In the preparation period he never tells a writer what to write – he has too much respect for the creative process – but he is relentless in pushing the writer to a fuller realisation of the story he set out to tell. Once on the set Wyler further enriches the action that was preconceived in the script by his meticulous attention to every detail of the production.

I would like to mention one personal example, because it illustrates so precisely what I consider the ideal creative junction of writer and director. In my script of *The Letter*, made some years ago at Warner Brothers, I had used the tropical moonlight with its hard shadows as an atmospheric reminder to Leslie of the lover she had killed on such a moonlight night at the opening of the picture. When I went down on the set, I found that Wyler, in collaboration with the set designer and the cameraman, was merging my image of the past with a portent of Leslie's future. When she tried to shut out the moonlight and its anguishing memories, it crept through venetian blinds or lattice work to cast bars at her feet. When *The Letter* appeared on the screen, it was basically a transference of my dramatisation of the Somerset Maugham story. But the picture was better than my screen-play because the production had enormously enriched its value.

However, this is not an average experience in Hollywood, because Wyler is not an average director. I think it is fair to say that any writer who finds in his produced film an approximation of the dramatic values he has written into the screen play is extraordinarily lucky. This is not to claim that all members of the Screen Writers' Guild are competent playwrights – that would be too much to expect in any art or craft – but I have justifiable reason to assert that those who *are* qualified find them-selves at the mercies of the directors, stars, and executive heads of the studios. In our present set-up, any of these can, and often do, alter the original content in whatever way they see fit. The playwright must thread his precarious way through all sorts of hazards, such as the constant fear of many studio executives that the picture will be 'over the audience's head', the avarice of some stars for showy and wordy scenes, and the unfounded notion on the part of many directors that they can change a scene at will without affecting the whole structure. All these 'creative' privileges often weigh more heavily than the unity of the writer's basic conception. In my opinion, Mr. Dickinson's suggestion does not add protection to the creator, but tends to divest him further of what little authority over his work he now enjoys.

For the average American director is an instrument of the star system by which business men operate as artistic arbiters over someone else's work. Whereas the writer is treated as an outsider and often as a necessary evil, the director is consid-ered part of the company: Significantly he even sits in the sacrosanct executive dining room. The screen play is not considered a thing in itself, but rather a flexible chart for something much more synthetic that will emerge from the set. This is not what Mr. Dickinson means, of course, but these are the facts of life, at least in Hollywood. I am afraid that his proposal of further extending the director's province would only serve to give artistic sanction to what is primarily and illogically a busi-ness arrangement.

In my mind there is one solution – and only one. The screen play must be given the same centrality and protection accorded the stage play under the Dramatist's Guild Contract. The screen writer must thereby assume his primary responsibility – and he should be weeded out if he is unfitted to assume it – as his fellow authors writing for the theatre. Instead of the salaried status of a studio employee, he should be willing to rent his screen play on a royalty basis to a qualified producer and director. As in the theatre, they would be close collaborators with the author on every aspect of their mutual enterprise and less dependent on the peculiar exigencies of the front-office, star-system set-up.

This view is antithetical to Mr. Dickinson's stated position. He asks us flatly to exorcise from our minds the 'misconceived parallel of theatre and the film', and, by extension, that of the screen playwright and the stage playwright. For the life of me, I don't see why the parallel is not very close, inasmuch as the play, in both cases, is conceived and written in terms of visual action and dialogue which actors perform under the guidance of a director. One is spatially mobile and recorded on film; the other is performed in a confined area within view of its audience. Outside of the technical and stylistic differences, the basic dramatic requirements are the same.

I also disagree with the sharp distinction Mr. Dickinson makes between writers who 'adapt' stories already in existence and those who 'create' original stories. In this instance, the words 'adapt' and 'create' are his. In actual practice, the screen writer, in the great majority of cases, must so completely re-conceive his material in terms of the film medium that the creative quotient is extremely high. Often the content, by its nature, can only be satisfactorily transferred to the screen by what amounts to a new story with merely a thematic relationship to the original. It is true there are occasional assignments where the screen writer's work amounts to an adaptation, or more accurately, a collaboration with the original author – as in the case of a story by Steinbeck, who develops his material in the objective terms of dramatic continuity. But these are rare exceptions.

On the other hand the so-called original screen story is a sad and amorphous literary form. Since the studios regard them as unproved and highly suspect, these sporadic efforts are scarcely ever accepted as the basis of an important picture. Nor do most of them merit any better consideration. The writers are well aware of the low esteem (and low price) in which the studios hold 'originals'. Consequently, they turn them out with as little mental activity as possible, usually in the hope that some 'gimmick' contained in the naked outline might bring them a quick buck at Republic or Monogram.

I have to admit that my own guild – The Screen Writers – observes Mr Dickinson's distinction in this respect, by giving the 'originals' two special classifications in their Academy Award list. Conscientious voters in these dubious categories are embarrassed to find themselves scraping the bottom of the barrel and usually settling for the lesser literary evil. As a minority in the matter, I have to voice my suspicion that the unspoken purpose of these fine distinctions is to increase the number of writers' Oscars. I am opposed equally to the method and the result. I see no added dignity accruing to screen writers or any other film maker by multiplicity of Oscars – a trend that is bringing the whole award system to the verge of the ridiculous. I think it will be a hopeful indication of an improved status when the writers petition the Motion Picture Academy that only one writing award be given – for the best screen play – and I, for one, will not be concerned whether that screen play is based on material from a published work, an item from a newspaper, or an anecdote overheard in a barber shop. [...]

---

8   A certain tendency of the French Cinema

François Truffaut

[...] After having sounded out directing by making two forgotten shorts, Jean Aurenche became a specialist in adaptation. In 1936, he was credited, with Anouilh, with the dialogue for *Vous N'Avez Rien A Déclarer* and *Les Dégourdis De La Onzième*.

At the same time Pierre Bost was publishing excellent little novels at the NRF.

Aurenche and Bost worked together for the first time while adapting and writing dialogue for *Douce*, directed by Claude Autant-Lara.

Today, no one is ignorant any longer of the fact that Aurenche and Bost rehabilitated adaptation by upsetting old preconceptions of being faithful to the letter and substituting for it the contrary idea of being faithful to the spirit – to the point that this audacious aphorism has been written: 'An honest adaptation is a betrayal' (Carlo Rim, 'Traveling And Sex-Appeal').

In adaptation there exists filmable scenes and unfilmable scenes, and that instead of omitting the latter (as was done not long ago) it is necessary to invent *equivalent* scenes, that is to say, scenes as the novel's author would have written them for the cinema.

'Invention without betrayal' is the watchword Aurenche and Bost like to cite, forgetting that one can also betray by omission.

The system of Aurenche and Bost is so seductive, even in the enunciation of its principles, that nobody even dreamed of verifying its functioning close-at-hand. I propose to do a little of this here. [...]

They will tell me, 'Let us admit that Aurenche and Bost are unfaithful, but do you also deny the existence of their talent ...?' Talent, to be sure, is not a function of fidelity, but I consider an adaptation of value only when written by a *man of the cinema*. Aurenche and Bost are essentially literary men and I reproach them here for being contemptuous of the cinema by underestimating it. They behave, *vis-à-vis* the scenario, as if they thought to reeducate a delinquent by finding him a job: they always believe they've 'done the maximum' for it by embellishing it with subtleties, out of that science of nuances that make up the slender merit of modern novels. It is, moreover, only the smallest caprice on the part of the exegetists of our art that they believe to honor the cinema by using literary jargon. (Haven't Sartre and Camus been talked about for Pagliero's work, and phenomenology for Allégret's?)

The truth is, Aurenche and Bost have made the works they adapt insipid, for *equivalence* is always with us, whether in the form of treason or timidity. Here is a brief example: in *Le Diable Au Corps*, as Radiguet wrote it, Francois meets Marthe on a train platform with Marthe jumping from the train while it is still moving; in the film, they meet in the school which has been transformed into a hospital. What is the point of this *equivalence*? It's a decoy for the anti-militarist elements added to the work, in concert with Claude Autant-Lara.

Well, it is evident that Radiguet's idea was one of *mise en scène*, whereas the scene invented by Aurenche and Bost is *literary*. One could, believe me, multiply these examples infinitely. [...]

Secrets are only kept for a time, formulas are divulged, new scientific knowledge is the object of communications to the Academy of Sciences and since, if we will believe Aurenche and Bost, adaptation is an exact science, one of these days they really could apprise us in the name of what criterion, by virtue of what system, by what mysterious and internal geometry of the work, they abridge, add, multiply, devise and 'rectify' these masterpieces.

Now that this idea is uttered, the idea that these equivalences are only timid astuteness to the end of getting around the difficulty, of resolving on the soundtrack problems that concern the image, plundering in order to no longer obtain anything on the screen but scholarly framing, complicated lighting effects, 'polished' photography, the whole keeping the 'Tradition of Quality' quite alive – it is time to come to an examination of the ensemble of these films adapted, with dialogue, by Aurenche and Bost, and to research the permanent nature of certain themes that will explain, without justifying, the constant *unfaithfulness* of two scenarists to works taken by them as 'pretext' and 'occasion.'

In a two-line résumé, here is the way scenarios treated by Aurenche and Bost appear:

La Symphonie Pastorale: He is a pastor, he is married. He loves and has no right to.

Le Diable Au Corps: They make the gestures of love and have no right to.

Dieu A Besoin Des Hommes: He officiates, gives benedictions, gives extreme unction and has no right to.

Jeux Interdits: They bury the dead and have no right to.

Le Blé En Herbe: They love each other and have no right to.

You will say to me that the book also tells the same story, which I do not deny. Only, I notice that Gide also wrote *La Porte Etroite*, Radiguet *Le Bal Du Comte d'Orgel*, Colette *La Vagabonde* and that each one of these novels did not tempt Delannoy or Autant-Lara.

Let us notice also that these scenarios, about which I don't believe it useful to speak here, fit into the sense of my thesis: *Au Delà Des Grilles*, *Le Château De Verre*, *L'Auberge Rouge*....

One sees how competent the promoters of the 'Tradition of Quality' are in choosing only subjects that favor the misunderstandings on which the whole system rests.

Under the cover of literature – and, of course, of quality – they give the public its habitual dose of smut, non-conformity and facile audacity. [...]

There are scarcely more than seven or eight scenarists working regularly for the French cinema. Each one of these scenarists has but one story to tell, and, since each only aspires to the success of the 'two greats', it is not exaggerating to say that the hundred-odd French films made each year tell the same story: it's always a question of a victim, generally a cuckold. (The cuckold would be the only sympathetic character in the film if he weren't always infinitely grotesque: Blier-Vilbert, etc. ...) The knavery of his kin and the hatred among the members of his family lead the 'hero' to his doom; the injustice of life, and for local color, the wickedness of the world (the curés, the concierges, the neighbors, the passers-by, the rich, the poor, the soldiers, etc. ...)

For distraction, during the long winter nights, look for titles of French films that do not fit into this framework and, while you're at it, find among these films those in which this line or its equivalent does not figure, spoken by the most abject couple in the film: 'It's always they that have the money (or the luck, or love, or happiness). It's too unjust, in the end.'

This school which aspires to realism destroys it at the moment of finally grabbing it, so careful is the school to lock these beings in a closed world, barricaded by formulas, plays on words, maxims, instead of letting us see them for ourselves, with our own eyes. The artist cannot always dominate his work. He must be, sometimes, God and, sometimes, his creature. You know that modern play in which the principal character, normally constituted when the curtain rises on him, finds himself crippled at the end of the play, the loss of each of his members punctuating the changes of acts. Curious epoch when the least flash-in-the-pan performer uses Kafkaesque words to qualify his domestic avatars. This form of cinema comes straight from modern literature – half-Kafka, half-Bovary!

A film is no longer made in France that the authors do not believe they are re-making Madame Bovary.

For the first time in French literature, an author adopted a distant, exterior attitude in relation to his subject, the subject becoming like an insect under the entomologist's microscope. But if, when starting this enterprise, Flaubert could have said. 'I will roll them all in the same mud – and be right' (which today's authors would voluntarily make their exergue), he could declare afterwards 'I am Madame Bovary' and I doubt that the same authors could take up that line and be sincere! [...]

The object of these notes is limited to an examination of a certain form of cinema, from the point of view of the scenarios and scenarists only. But it is appropriate, I think, to make it clear that the *metteurs-en-scène* are and wish to be responsible for the scenarios and dialogues they illustrate.

Scenarists' films, I wrote above, and certainly it isn't Aurenche and Bost who will contradict me. When they hand in their scenario, the film is done; the *metteur-en-scène*, in their eyes, is the gentleman who adds the pictures to it and it's true, alas! I spoke of the mania for adding funerals everywhere. And, for all that, death is always juggled away. Let us remember Nana's admirable death, or that of Emma Bovary, presented by Renoir; in *La Pastorale*, death is only a make-up job and an exercise for the camera man: compare the close-ups of Michèle Morgan in *La Pastorale*, Dominique Blanchar in *Le Secret De Mayerling* and Madeleine Sologne in *L'Eternel Retour*: it's the same face! Everything happens *after* death.

Let us cite, lastly, that declaration by Delannoy that we dedicate, with perfidy, to the French scenarists: 'When it happens that authors of talent, whether in the spirit of gain or out of weakness, one day let themselves go to "write for the cinema", they do it with the feeling of lowering themselves. They deliver themselves rather to a curious temptation towards mediocrity, so careful are they to not compromise their talent and certain that, to write for the cinema, one must make oneself understood by the lowliest' ('*La Symphonie Pastorale* ou L'Amour Du Métier', *Revue Verger*, November 1947).

I must, without further ado, denounce a sophism that will not fail to be thrown at me in the guise of argument: 'This dialogue is spoken by abject people and it is in order to better point out their nastiness that we give them this hard language. It is our way of being moralists.'

To which I answer: it is inexact to say that these lines are spoken by the most abject characters. To be sure, in the films of 'psychological realism' there are nothing but vile beings, but so inordinate is the authors' desire to be superior to their characters that those who, perchance, are not infamous are, at best, infinitely grotesque.

Well, as for these abject characters, who deliver these abject lines – I know a handful of men in France who would be INCAPABLE of conceiving them, several cinéastes whose world-view is at least as valuable as that of Aurenche and Bost, Sigurd and Jeanson. I mean Jean Renoir, Robert Bresson, Jean Cocteau, Jacques Becker, Abel Gance, Max Ophuls, Jacques Tati, Roger Leenhardt; these are, nevertheless, French cinéastes and it happens – curious coincidence – that they are *auteurs* who often write their dialogue and some of them themselves invent the stories they direct. [...]

[...] 'But why,' they will say to me, 'why couldn't one have the same admiration for all those cinéastes who strive to work in the bosom of this 'Tradition of Quality' that you make sport of so lightly? Why not admire Yves Allégret as much as Becker, Jean Delannoy as much as Bresson, Claude Autant-Lara as much as Renoir?'

Well – I do not believe in the peaceful coexistence of the 'Tradition of Quality' and an '*auteur's* cinema'.

Basically, Yves Allégret and Delannoy are only caricatures of Clouzot, of Bresson.

It is not the desire to create a scandal that leads me to depreciate a cinema so praised elsewhere. I rest convinced that the exaggeratedly prolonged existence of *psychological realism* is the cause of the lack of public comprehension when faced with such new works as *Le Carrosse D'Or (The Golden Coach), Casque D'or*, not to mention *Les Dames Du Bois De Boulogne* and *Orphée*.

Long live audacity, to be sure, still it must be revealed as it is. In terms of this year, 1953, if I had to draw up a balance-sheet of the French cinema's audacities, there would be no place in it for either the vomiting in *Les Orgueilleux* (*The Proud And The Beautiful*) or Claude Laydu's refusal to be sprinkled with holy water in *Le Bon Dieu Sans Confession* or the homosexual relationships of the characters in *Le Salaire De La Peur* (*The Wages Of Fear*), but rather the gait of *Hulot*, the maid's soliloquies in *La Rue De L'Estrapade*, the *mise-en-scène* of *Le Carrosse D'Or*, the direction of the actors in *Madame de* (*The Earrings Of Madame De*), and also Abel Gance's studies in polyvision. You will have understood that these audacities are those of *men of the cinema* and no longer of scenarists, directors and littérateurs.

For example, I take it as significant that the most brilliant scenarists and *metteur-en-scène* of the 'Tradition of Quality' have met with failure when they approach comedy: Ferry-Clouzot *Miguette Et Sa Mère*, Sigurd-Boyer *Tous Les Chemins Mènent A Rome*, Scipion-Pagliero *La Rose Rouge*, Laudenbach-Delannoy *La Route Napoléon*, Auranche–Bost–Autant-Lara *L'Auberge Rouge* or, if you like, *Occupe-toi d'Amélie*.

Whoever has tried, one day, to write a scenario wouldn't be able to deny that comedy is by far the most difficult genre, the one that demands the most work, the most talent, also the most humility. [...]

The dominant trait of psychological realism is its anti-bourgeois will. But what are Aurenche and Bost, Sigurd, Jeanson, Autant-Lara, Allégret, if not bourgeois, and what are the fifty thousand new readers, who do not fail to see each film from a novel, if not bourgeois?

What then is the value of an anti-bourgeois cinema made by the bourgeois for the bourgeois? Workers, you know very well, do not appreciate this form of cinema at all even when it aims at relating to them. They refused to recognize themselves in the dockers of *Un Homme Marche Dans La Ville*, or in the sailors of *Les Amants De Brasmort*. Perhaps it is necessary to send the children out on the stairway landing in order to make love, but their parents don't like to hear it said, above all at the cinema, even with 'benevolence'. If the public likes to mix with low company under the alibi of literature, it also likes to do it under the alibi of society. It is instructive to consider the programming of films in Paris, by neighborhoods. One comes to realize that the public at large perhaps prefers little naive foreign films that show it men 'as they should be' and not in the way that Aurenche and Bost believe them to be. [...]

It is always good to conclude, that gives everyone pleasure. It is remarkable that the 'great' *metteurs-en-scène* and the 'great' scenarists have, for a long time, all made minor films, and the talent they have put into them hasn't been sufficient to enable one to distinguish them from others (those who don't put in talent). It is also remarkable that they all came to 'Quality' at the same time, as if they were giving themselves a good address. And then, a producer – even a director – earns more money making *Le Blé En Herbe* than by making *Le Plombier Amoureux*. The 'courageous' films are revealed to be very profitable. The proof: someone like Ralph Habib abruptly renounces demi-pornography, makes *Les Compagnes De La Nuit* and refers to Cayatte. Well, what's keeping the André Tabets, Companeer, the Jean Guittons, the Pierre Vérys, the Jean Lavirons, the Ciampis, the Grangiers, from making, from one day to the next, intellectual films, from adapting masterpieces (there are still a few left) and, of course, adding funerals, here, there and everywhere?

Well, on that day we will be in the 'Tradition of Quality' up to the neck and the French cinema, with rivalry among 'psychological realism', 'violence', 'strictness', 'ambiguity', will no longer be anything but one vast funeral that will be able to leave the studio in Billancourt and enter the cemetery directly – it seems to have been placed next door expressly, in order to get more quickly from the producer to the grave-digger.

Only, by dint of repeating to the public that it identified with the 'heroes' of the films, it might well end by believing it, and on the day that it understands that this fine big cuckold whose misadventures it is solicited to sympathize with (a little) and to laugh at (a lot), is not, as had been thought, a cousin or neighbor down the hall but ITSELF, that abject family ITS family, that scoffed-at religion ITS religion – well, on that day it may show itself to be ungrateful to a cinema that will have labored so hard to show it life as one sees it on the fourth floor in Saint-German-desPrés.

To be sure, I must recognize it, a great deal of emotion and taking-sides are the controlling factors in the deliberately pessimistic examination I have undertaken of a certain tendency of the French cinema. I am assured that this famous 'school of psychological realism' had to exist in order that, in turn, *The Diary Of A Country Priest, Le Carrosse D'Or, Orpheus, Casque D'Or, Mr Hulot's Holiday* might exist.

But our authors who wanted to educate the public should understand that perhaps they have strayed from the primary paths in order to become involved with the more subtle paths of psychology: they have passed on to that sixth grade so dear to Jouhandeau, but it isn't necessary to repeat a grade indefinitely!

9 Films, directors and critics

Ian Cameron

[...] The assumption which underlies all the writing in *Movie* is that the director is the author of a film, the person who gives it any distinctive quality it may have. There are quite large exceptions, with which I shall deal later. On the whole we accept this cinema of directors, although without going to the farthest-out extremes of *la politique des auteurs* which makes it difficult to think of a bad director making a good film and almost impossible to think of a good director making a bad one. One's aesthetic must be sufficiently flexible to cope with the fact that Joseph Pevney, having made dozens of stinkers, can suddenly come up with an admirable western in *The Plunderers*, or that Minnelli, after years of doing wonders often with unpromising material, could produce anything as flat-footed as *The Bells Are Ringing*.

Everyone accepts the cinema of directors for France, Italy, Japan, India, Argentina, Sweden and Poland – everywhere, in fact, that the Art is easily identifiable. Critics will talk happily about a Bergman film, or a Mizoguchi film, or even a Carol Reed film. It is only over American movies that the trouble starts, and reviews are likely to end with a desultory 'George Cukor directed efficiently'. The reasons are easy enough to find. Hollywood pictures are not so much custom-built as manufactured. The responsibility for them is shared, and the final quality is no more the fault of the director than of such parties as the producer, the set designer, the cameraman or the hairdresser. Only by a happy accident can anything good escape from this industrial complex. The good American film comes to be regarded as the cinematic equivalent of a mutant.

Now there are qualities superimposed on most big studio films (these days there are very few of them indeed) that depend not on the director but on the studio: the look of colour films is particularly prone to this sort of control. An extreme example is Fox films in the late forties and early fifties which are almost immediately identifiable by their photography and music, particularly if these are by the leading exponents – photographers Joseph la Shelle and Joe MacDonald and composers Leigh Harline and David Raksin. However, these qualities are rather peripheral, and one common accusation of this sort, that Gregg Toland effectively directed the films he photographed so remarkably, has been disposed of by Andrew Sarris in *Film Culture*: 'Subtract Gregg Toland from Welles and you still have a mountain; subtract Toland from Wyler and you have a molehill.'

The closer one looks at Hollywood films, the less they seem to be accidents. There is a correlation between the quality of the films and the names of their directors. When one notices that such masterpieces as *Scarface, Bringing Up Baby* and *Gentlemen Prefer Blondes* were all directed by the same man, one begins to wonder whether the merits of these otherwise dissimilar films might not be explained by this man's talent. On a slightly closer look, one finds that he was also responsible for such generally admired movies as *Twentieth Century, Sergeant York, Red River* and *Monkey Business*, not to mention *Rio Bravo*, a film which gained little attention on its release and is now accepted as a masterpiece, even by *Sight and Sound*, which greeted its appearance with a singular lack of enthusiasm.

Hawks is just beginning to be accepted in Britain and the US. Raoul Walsh, on the other hand, is virtually unknown. Yet if one looks at Walsh's films (or some of them – he has made 200 since he started directing in 1913), one can identify the same talent and highly sympathetic personality behind a British cheapie of 1937, *Jump for Glory*, a 1945 racecourse movie, *Salty O'Rourke*, and more recent works like *Blackbeard the Pirate* (1952), *The Lawless Breed* (1952), *Battle Cry* (1955), *Esther and the King* (1960) and *Marines Let's Go* (1961). The similarity of these movies made in three different countries over a period of 25 years by a director whose name does not spell prestige, who will thus not have an exceptional degree of freedom, should leave no doubt that, provided he has any talent, it is the director, rather than anyone else, who determines what finally appears on the screen.

Part of the neglect of American directors comes from the simple fact that it is easier to accept foreign films as Art: a status word to indicate that the film is worth the critic's serious attention. In foreign language movies, one of the biggest obstacles has been limited: the dialogue. Even if they are bad, subtitles provide a shock-absorber between the dialogue and the audience. Everyone knows that laughable subtitles do not necessarily indicate defects in the original language. But two lines of ill-written dialogue in an American picture will put the critics on their guard. Almost invariably it is duff dialogue that alienates them, not unconvincing motivation, or false movements of actors or pointless camerawork. [...] When a *Sight and Sound* critic does manage to work up some enthusiasm for an American film, it is usually self-limiting: 'very good ... of its kind.' So we are treated to dimly remembered sections of John Russell Taylor's childhood erotic fantasies about Maria Montez and Veronica Lake as a picture of the forties. Reviews of American films tend to link them together in remarkably ill-assorted pairs. One would be amazed at the current review of *The Man Who Shot Liberty Valance* and *Guns in the Afternoon* (both 'so consciously old-fashioned and nostalgic that, appearing in 1962, they seem almost esoteric') if one had not already been treated to such unlikely joint reviews as *Exodus* plus *The Guns of Navarone* and *Psycho* plus *The Apartment*. If the writers of these pieces were literacy critics, which, barring a certain illiteracy, they very nearly are, one imagines that they would happily review *Tender Is the Night, Miss Loneli-hearts* and *Manhattan Transfer* together entirely in terms of American *mal-de-siècle* in the twenties. Any other qualities would be written off in a well-chosen sentence: 'Mr. Dos Passos's narrative technique of intertwining a number of almost unconnected stories does not make for easy comprehension.' *Sight and Sound* has just produced the most accurate piece of unconscious self-criticism in its most recent and most desperate attempt to be hip: a column in which the glad hand of John Russell Taylor is hidden behind the name of Arkadin. 'Why,' he opens brightly, 'don't we take horror films more seriously? Well, not seriously seriously ...'

The worst sufferer from restricted admiration has been Hitchcock. *Psycho* was passed over as one big laugh. As a joke it could not possibly be anything else. *Psycho*'s joke-content is very large, but that doesn't mean it is only joke. Example: the scene of Janet Leigh and Anthony Perkins getting acquainted is both an ingeniously extended double entendre on stuffing birds and a very real and touching picture of two people, isolated from others by their actions, voluntary or otherwise, trying to talk to each other.

The great weakness of *la politique des auteurs* is its rigidity: its adherents tend to be, as they say, totally committed to a cinema of directors. There are, however, quite a few films whose authors are not their directors. The various film versions of Paddy Chayefsky's works are all primarily Chayefsky movies rather than Delbert Mann, or John Cromwell or even Richard Brooks movies. Given a weak director the effective author of a film can be its photographer (Lucien Ballard, *Al Capone*), composer (Jerome Moross, *The Big Country*), producer (Arthur Freed, *Light in the Piazza*) or star (John Wayne, *The Comancheros*). None of those films was more than moderately good. Occasionally, though, something really remarkable can come from an efficient director with magnificent collaborators. Such a film was Michael Curtiz's *Casablanca*, which contained Humphrey Bogart, Ingrid Bergman, Paul Henreid, Claude Rains, Sidney Greenstreet, Conrad Veidt, Peter Lorre and Marcel Dalio, and was somehow missed from John Russell Taylor's knee-high panorama of the forties. More recently we have had *The Sins of Rachel Cade*, which, although directed by the excellent Gordon Douglas, was above all an Angie Dickinson movie, being entirely shaped by her personality and deriving all its power, which was considerable, from her performance.

Many films have also an iconographical interest, which is something quite apart from any aesthetic merits they may have. This interest comes from their relationship either to conditions external to their making (things as diverse as the discovery of the H bomb or current trends in automobile design, which influenced the design of the submarine in *Voyage to the Bottom of the Sea*) or to other films. Joseph Newman's *Spin of a Coin (The George Raft Story)* is fascinating because of its similarity to other period gangster movies: the sequences are built in the same way towards a climax of slaughter – only in this case the burst of gunfire is replaced by equally staccato laughter, for instance, as Al Capone (played by Neville Brand, who was Capone in Karlson's *The Scarface Mob*) tells Georgie (Ray Danton, whose performance is an extension of his previous *Legs Diamond* in Boetticher's film) how much he liked his performance as Capone in *Scarface*, the climatic scene of which has been reconstructed for us. This sort of kick is also available even more lavishly in Vincente Minnelli's amazing new *Two Weeks In Another Town*, where faded movie star Kirk Douglas sits in a viewing theatre watching a film he has previously made with the director for whom he is now working in the dubbing room. The film is *The Bad and the Beautiful*, which Minnelli made ten years ago with Douglas, as well as the same writer, producer and composer (Charles Schnee, John Houseman and David Raksin). In another Joseph Newman movie, *The Big Bankroll (Arnold Rothstein, King of the Roaring Twenties)*, it is assumed that the audience has seen the earlier movies which found it necessary to explain how boot-legging and protection worked. *The Big Bankroll* (in spite of 26 missing minutes in the British version one of the very best of its kind) builds on the knowledge it assumes to tell the story of Arnold Rothstein, who turned the mechanics of corruption to his own ends.

A few films are interesting for a related reason: the picture of their audience which they provide. The best example is Delmer Daves, who makes movies for stenographers and provides them with just what they wish to see. His pictures may be trivial, dishonest, immoral – Daves' movies have every fault in the book except bad production values – but they do provide a picture of the girl Daves is aiming his films at (very successfully, it seems). However irritating one may find Suzanne Pleshette in *Lovers Must Learn (Rome Adventure)*, one has to admit that her performance is brilliantly pitched at just the right level of gush.

While one can appreciate films for their iconographical significance or as a critique of their audience, any merit they may have still comes from the director, much more than from any other source. Although finally our belief in the cinema of directors can only be justified though continuous application of our ideas in *Movie*, I want to conclude this article with an extended example of the part played by the

director, based on three films, two of them well-liked, more or less, British offerings, J. Lee Thompson's *The Guns of Navarone* and David Lean's *Bridge on the
River Kwai*, the third a much less respected American film, Don Siegel's *Hell Is
for Heroes*.

All three contain the simple moral that war is futile and degrading; all three use
one of the basic war film stories: the strategic action of considerable importance
which devolves on a very few men. *Navarone* sets out with the obvious intention of
telling a rattling good yarn about the way our chaps heroically battled against almost
impossible obstacles to knock out the Jerry guns. Even this it almost fails to do by
disastrously overplaying its suspense potential in a lengthy sequence of spurious
thrills as the team crawl up a crumbling cardboard cliff so early in the movie that
everyone will need to survive to justify their billing on the credits. However, its
worst sin is stopping off at least twice in the course of the narrative for dialogue
meditations on the nastiness of war, which the audience is meant to accept and
which would in themselves be perfectly sympathetic, if slightly superfluous, in a
film that refused to present war as enjoyable. But here their effect is completely viti-
ated by the rest of the action, and in context they seem almost hypocritical. I have a
feeling that the failure is not inherent in the script but comes from the lack of any
firm control in the direction. Even the one moment which could hardly help having
some force, the shooting of Gia Scala as a collaborator, in the film has none. Here
admittedly the script does side-step by letting Irene Papas, who is Greek and only a
secondary character, forestall Peck and Niven in shooting her, when they are both
more directly affected by the responsibility for her death. But even allowing for this,
the lack of conviction is total.

Hell Is for Heroes is based on a story by Robert Pirosh which could easily have
been turned into the sort of plug for the gallantry of the American fighting man
which William Wellman made 13 years ago from a Pirosh story in *Battleground*. I
am not concerned here with the central theme in the film which is embodied in the
Steve McQueen character, the psychopath who makes an ideal soldier but goes to
pieces outside the field of combat. Two sequences are particularly relevant to my
purpose here as they could easily have degenerated to the same level as *Kwai* and
Navarone. In the first, three soldiers set out at night on a manoeuvre to trick the
enemy into thinking that they are sending out large patrols and therefore have the
front well-manned. The idea is to take empty ammunition tins out into no-man's
land, fill them with stones and rattle them by remote control from their position by
means of lengths of telephone wire. The noise of these would be picked up by the
enemy's ground microphones and all hell would be let loose to greet the ghost
patrol. Siegel does not tell us what they are doing until their mission is almost
completed. We take the episode seriously, which is right because it is serious and no
less dangerous than a real patrol. If he had shown us beforehand exactly what they
were doing, the episode would have been invested for us in the safety of our cinema
seats with a feeling of fun, of fooling the enemy. Never once in the film do we get
this feeling.

The last sequence for once does sum up the whole film by its picture of the contribution an individual can make to the action. In serious trouble after leading an
abortive attack on the crucial pillbox, which has resulted in the death of his two
companions, McQueen takes it upon himself to put the pillbox out of action. He

manages by a suicidal charge to get close enough to lob a satchel charge into the mouth of the box. Inevitably he is shot. Seeing the charge thrown out of the pillbox, he staggers forward, grabs it and rolls into the mouth of the box with it as it explodes. A flame-thrower is played on the mouth of the pillbox to make sure it is out of action. The last shot of the film is a longshot of a general advance beginning along the section of the front around the pillbox. The advance is obviously going to be very costly. The camera zooms into the mouth of the pillbox and the end title is superimposed. The zoom in from the general view to the detail emphasises the smallness of the gain from McQueen's death. One pillbox has been put out of action, and as the advance continues that pillbox ceases to have any significance. It is left behind a dead, almost abstract object. Unlike *Navarone*, there is no conflict between the intended content and the form which expresses it.

Contrast with the last shot of *Hell Is for Heroes* the end of *Bridge on the River Kwai*. James Donald stands surveying the wreckage after the destruction of the bridge. 'Madness, madness,' he says, and the camera soars back away from him in a mood of triumph which is taken up by the martial music on the soundtrack. In the contradiction between the sentiments expressed by the dialogue and the meaning contained in the treatment, critics have noticed only the former. *Bridge on the River Kwai's* anti-war content is widely accepted to be impeccable. But *Hell Is for Heroes*, where the ideas are expressed by the whole form of the film, can pass nearly unnoticed and even be described as equivocal in its attitude to war. The lack of perception which results in this sort of fuzzy thinking is the best argument for a detailed criticism.

10 Notes on the *auteur* theory in 1962

Andrew Sarris

[...] First of all, the *auteur* theory, at least as I understand it and now intend to express it, claims neither the gift of prophecy nor the option of extracinematic perception. Directors, even *auteurs*, do not always run true to form, and the critic can never assume that a bad director will always make a bad film. No, not always, but almost always, and that is the point. What is a bad director, but a director who has made many bad films? What is the problem then? Simply this: the badness of a director is not necessarily considered the badness of a film. If Joseph Pevney directed Garbo, Cherkassov, Olivier, Belmondo, and Harriet Andersson in *The Cherry Orchard*, the resulting spectacle might not be entirely devoid of merit with so many subsidiary *auteurs* to cover up for Joe. In fact, with this cast and this literary property, a Lumet might be safer than a Welles. The realities of casting apply to directors as well as actors, but the *auteur* theory would demand the gamble with Welles, if he were willing.

Marlon Brando has shown us that a film can be made without a director. Indeed, *One-Eyed Jacks* is more entertaining than many films with directors. A director-conscious critic would find it difficult to say anything good or bad about direction which is non-existent. One can talk here about photography, editing, acting, but not direction. The film even has personality, but like *The Longest Day* and *Mutiny on the Bounty*, it is a cipher directorially. Obviously, the *auteur* theory cannot possibly cover every vagrant charm of the cinema. Nevertheless, the first premise of the *auteur* theory is the technical competence of a director as a criterion of value. A badly directed or undirected film has no importance in a critical scale of values, but one can make interesting conversation about the subject, the script, the acting, the color, the photography, the editing, the music, the costumes, the décor etc. That is the nature of the medium. You always get more for your money than mere art. Now by the *auteur* theory, if a director has no technical competence, no elementary flair for the cinema, he is automatically cast out from the pantheon of directors. A great director has to be at least a good director. This is true in any art. What constitutes directorial talent is more difficult to define abstractly. There is less disagreement, however, on this first level of the *auteur* theory than there will be later.

The second premise of the *auteur* theory is the distinguishable personality of the director as a criterion of value. Over a group of films, a director must exhibit certain recurring characteristics of style which serve as his signature. The way a film looks and moves should have some relationship to the way a director thinks and feels. This is an area where American directors are generally superior to foreign directors. Because so much of the American cinema is commissioned, a director is forced to express his personality through the visual treatment of material rather than through the literary content of the material. A Cukor who works with all sorts of projects has a more developed abstract style than a Bergman who is free to develop his own scripts. Not that Bergman lacks personality, but his work has declined with the depletion of his ideas largely because his technique never equaled his sensibility. Joseph L. Mankiewicz and Billy Wilder are other examples of writer-directors without adequate technical mastery. By contrast, Douglas Sirk and Otto Preminger have moved up the scale because their miscellaneous projects reveal a stylistic consistency.

The third and ultimate premise of the *auteur* theory is concerned with interior meaning, the ultimate glory of the cinema as an art. Interior meaning is extrapolated from the tension between a director's personality and his material. This conception of interior meaning comes close to what Astruc defines as *mise-en-scène*, but not quite. It is not quite the vision of the world a director projects, nor quite his attitude toward life. It is ambiguous in any literary sense because part of it is imbedded in the stuff of the cinema and cannot be rendered in non-cinematic terms. Truffaut has called it the temperature of the director on the set, and that is a close approximation of its professional aspect. Dare I come out and say what I think it to be is an élan of the soul?

Lest I seem unduly mystical, let me hasten to add that all I mean by soul is that intangible difference between one personality and another, all other things being equal. Sometimes, this difference is expressed by no more than a beat's hesitation in the rhythm of a film. In one sequence of *La Règle du Jeu*, Renoir gallops up the stairs, turns to his right with a lurching movement, stops in hop-like uncertainty when his name is called by a coquettish maid, and then, with marvelous post-reflex continuity, resumes his bearishly shambling journey to the heroine's boudoir. If I could describe the musical grace note of that momentary suspension, and I can't, I might be able to provide a more precise definition of the *auteur* theory. As it is, all I can do is point at the specific beauties of interior meaning on the screen, and later catalogue the moments of recognition.

The three premises of the *auteur* theory may be visualized as three concentric circles, the outer circle as technique, the middle circle personal style, and the inner circle interior meaning. The corresponding roles of the director may be designated as those of a technician, a stylist and an *auteur*. There is no prescribed course by which a director passes through the three circles. Godard once remarked that Visconti had evolved from a *metteur-en-scene* to an *auteur* while Rossellini had evolved from an *auteur* to a *metteur-en-scene*. From opposite directions, they emerged with comparable status. Minnelli began and remained in the second circle as a stylist; Bunuel was an *auteur* even before he had assembled the technique of the first circle. Technique is simply the ability to put a film together with some clarity and coherence. Nowadays it is possible to become a director without knowing too much about the technical side, even the crucial functions of photography and editing. An expert production crew could probably cover up for a chimpanzee in the director's chair. How do you tell the genuine director from the quasi-chimpanzee? After a given number of films, a pattern is established.

In fact, the *auteur* theory itself is a pattern theory in constant flux. I would never endorse a Ptolemaic constellation of directors in a fixed orbit. At the moment, my list of *auteurs* runs something like this through the first twenty: Ophuls, Renoir, Mizoguchi, Hitchcock, Chaplin, Ford, Welles, Dreyer, Rossellini, Murnau, Griffith, Sternberg, Eisenstein, Stroheim, Bunuel, Bresson, Hawks, Lang, Flaherty, Vigo. This list is somewhat weighted toward seniority and established reputations. In time, some of these *auteurs* will rise, some will fall, and some will be displaced by either new directors or rediscovered ancients. Again, the exact order is less important than the specific definitions of these and as many as two hundred other potential *auteurs*. I would hardly expect any other critic in the world to fully endorse this list, especially on faith. Only after thousands of films have been revaluated, will any personal pantheon have a reasonably objective validity. The task of validating the *auteur* theory is an enormous one, and the end will never be in sight. Meanwhile, the *auteur* habit of collecting random films in directorial bundles will serve posterity with at least a tentative classification.

Although the *auteur* theory emphasizes the body of a director's work rather than isolated masterpieces, it is expected of great directors that they make great films every so often. The only possible exception to this rule I can think of is Abel Gance, whose greatness is largely a function of his aspiration. Even with Gance, *La Roue* is as close to being a great film as any single work of Flaherty's. Not that single works matter that much. As Renoir has observed, a director spends his life on variations of the same film.

Two recent omnibus films – *Boccaccio 70* and *The Seven Capital Sins* – unwittingly reinforced the *auteur* theory by confirming the relative standing of the many directors involved. If I had not seen either film, I would have anticipated that the order of merit in *Boccaccio 70* would be Visconti, Fellini and De Sica, and in *The*

Seven Capital Sins, Godard, Chabrol, Demy, Vadim, De Broca, Molinaro. (Dhomme, Ionesco's stage director and an unknown quantity in advance, turned out to be the worst of the lot.) There might be some argument about the relative badness of De Broca and Molinaro, but otherwise, the directors ran true to form by almost any objective criterion of value. However, the main point here is that even in these frothy, ultra-commercial servings of entertainment, the contribution of each director had less in common stylistically with the work of other directors on the project than with his own previous work.

Sometimes a great deal of corn must be husked to yield a few kernels of internal meaning. I recently saw *Every Night at Eight*, one of the many maddeningly routine films Raoul Walsh has directed in his long career. This 1935 effort featured George Raft, Alice Faye, Frances Langford and Patsy Kelly in one of those familiar plots about radio shows of the period. The film keeps moving along in the pleasantly unpretentious manner one would expect of Walsh until one incongruously intense scene with George Raft thrashing about in his sleep, revealing his inner fears in mumbling dream talk. The girl he loves comes into the room in the midst of his unconscious avowals of feeling, and listens sympathetically. This unusual scene was later amplified in *High Sierra* with Humphrey Bogart and Ida Lupino. The point is that one of the screen's most virile directors employed an essentially feminine narrative device to dramatize the emotional vulnerability of his heroes. If I had not been aware of Walsh in *Every Night at Eight*, the crucial link to *High Sierra* would have passed unnoticed. Such are the joys of the *auteur* theory.

11 The *auteur* theory

Peter Wollen

[...] The *auteur* theory grew up rather haphazardly; it was never elaborated in programmatic terms, in a manifesto or collective statement. As a result, it could be interpreted and applied on rather broad lines; different critics developed somewhat different methods within a loose framework of common attitudes. This looseness and diffuseness of the theory has allowed flagrant misunderstandings to take root, particularly among critics in Britain and the United States. Ignorance has been compounded by a vein of hostility to foreign ideas and a taste for travesty and caricature. However, the fruitfulness of the *auteur* approach has been such that it has made headway even on the most unfavourable terrain. For instance, a recent straw poll of British critics, conducted in conjunction with a Don Siegel Retrospective at the National Film Theatre, revealed that, among American directors most admired, a group consisting of Budd Boetticher, Samuel Fuller and Howard Hawks ran immediately behind Ford, Hitchcock and Welles, who topped the poll, but ahead of Billy Wilder, Josef Von Sternberg and Preston Sturges.

Of course, some individual directors have always been recognised as outstanding: Charles Chaplin, John Ford, Orson Welles. The *auteur* theory does not limit itself to acclaiming the director as the main author of a film. It implies an operation of decipherment; it reveals authors where none had been seen before. For years, the model of an author in the cinema was that of the European director, with open artistic aspirations and full control over his films. This model still lingers on; it lies behind the existential distinction between art films and popular films. Directors who built their reputations in Europe were dismissed after they crossed the Atlantic, reduced to anonymity. American Hitchcock was contrasted unfavourably with English Hitchcock, American Renoir with French Renoir, American Fritz Lang with German Fritz Lang. The *auteur* theory has led to the revaluation of the second, Hollywood careers of these and other European directors; without it, masterpieces such as *Scarlet Street* or *Vertigo* would never have been perceived. Conversely, the *auteur* theory has been sceptical when offered an American director whose salvation has been exile to Europe. It is difficult now to argue that *Brute Force* has ever been excelled by Jules Dassin or that Joseph Losey's recent work is markedly superior to, say, *The Prowler*.

In time, owing to the diffuseness of the original theory, two main schools of *auteur* critics grew up: those who insisted on revealing a core of meanings, of thematic motifs, and those who stressed style and *mise-en-scène*. There is an important distinction here [...] The work of the *auteur* has a semantic dimension, it is not purely formal; the work of the *metteur-en-scène*, on the other hand, does not go beyond the realm of performance, of transposing into the special complex of cinematic codes and channels a pre-existing text: a scenario, a book or a play. As we shall see, the meaning of the films of an *auteur* is constructed *a posteriori*; the meaning – semantic, rather than stylistic or expressive – of the films of a *metteur-en-scène* exists *a priori*. In concrete cases, of course, this distinction is not always clear-cut. There is controversy over whether some directors should be seen as *auteurs* or *metteurs-en-scène*. For example, though it is possible to make intuitive ascriptions, there have been no really persuasive accounts as yet of Raoul Walsh or William Wyler as *auteurs*, to take two very different directors. Opinions might differ about Don Siegel or George Cukor. Because of the difficulty of fixing the distinction in these concrete cases, it has often become blurred; indeed, some French critics have tended to value the *metteur-en-scène* above the *auteur*. MacMahonism sprang up, with its cult of Walsh, Lang, Losey and Preminger, its fascination with violence and its notorious text: 'Charlton Heston is an axiom of the cinema.' What André Bazin called 'aesthetic cults of personality' began to be formed. Minor directors were acclaimed before they had, in any real sense, been identified and defined.

Yet the *auteur* theory has survived despite all the hallucinating critical extravaganzas which it has fathered. It has survived because it is indispensable. Geoffrey Nowell-Smith has summed up the *auteur* theory as it is normally presented today:

> One essential corollary of the theory as it has been developed is the discovery that the defining characteristics of an author's work are not necessarily those which are most readily apparent. The purpose of criticism thus becomes to uncover behind the superficial

contrasts of subject and treatment a hard core of basic and often recondite motifs. The pattern formed by these motifs ... is what gives an author's work its particular structure, both defining it internally and distinguishing one body of work from another.

It is this 'structural approach', as Nowell-Smith calls it, which is indispensable for the critic.

The test case for the *auteur* theory is provided by the work of Howard Hawks. Why Hawks, rather than, say, Frank Borzage or King Vidor? Firstly, Hawks is a director who has worked for years within the Hollywood system. His first film, *Road to Glory*, was made in 1926. Yet throughout his long career he has only once received general critical acclaim, for his wartime film, *Sergeant York*, which closer inspection reveals to be eccentric and atypical of the main *corpus* of Hawks's films. Secondly, Hawks has worked in almost every genre. He has made westerns (*Rio Bravo*), gangsters (*Scarface*), war films (*Air Force*), thrillers (*The Big Sleep*), science fiction (*The Thing from Another World*), musicals (*Gentlemen Prefer Blondes*), comedies (*Bringing Up Baby*), even a Biblical epic (*Land of the Pharaohs*). Yet all of these films (except perhaps *Land of the Pharaohs*, which he himself was not happy about) exhibit the same thematic preoccupations, the same recurring motifs and incidents, the same visual style and tempo. In the same way that Roland Barthes constructed a species of *homo racinianus*, the critic can construct a *homo hawksianus*, the protagonist of Hawksian values in the problematic Hawksian world.

Hawks achieved this by reducing the genres to two basic types: the adventure drama and the crazy comedy. These two types express inverse views of the world, the positive and negative poles of the Hawksian vision. [...]

Whereas the dramas show the mastery of man over nature, over woman, over the animal and childish; the comedies show his humiliation, his regression. The heroes become victims; society, instead of being excluded and despised, breaks in with irruptions of monstrous farce. It could well be argued that Hawks's outlook, the alternative world which he constructs in the cinema, the Hawksian heterocosm, is not one imbued with particular intellectual subtlety or sophistication. This does not detract from its force. Hawks first attracted attention because he was regarded naïvely as an action director. Later, the thematic content [...] was detected and revealed. Beyond the stylemes, semantemes were found to exist; the films were anchored in an objective stratum of meaning, a plerematic stratum, as the Danish linguist Hjelmslev would put it. Thus the stylistic expressiveness of Hawks's films was shown to be not purely contingent, but grounded in significance.

Something further needs to be said about the theoretical basis of the kind of schematic exposition of Hawks's work which I have outlined. The 'structural approach' which underlies it, the definition of a core of repeated motifs, has evident affinities with methods which have been developed for the study of folklore and mythology. In the work of Olrik and others, it was noted that in different folk-tales the same motifs reappeared time and time again. It became possible to build up a lexicon of these motifs. Eventually Propp showed how a whole cycle of Russian fairy-tales could be analysed into variations of a very limited set of basic motifs (or moves, as he called them). Underlying the different, individual tales was an archi-tale, of which they were all variants. One important point needs to be made about this type of structural analysis. There is a danger, as Lévi-Strauss has pointed out, that by simply noting and mapping resemblances, all the texts which are studied (whether Russian fairy-tales or American movies) will be reduced to one, abstract and impoverished. There must be a moment of synthesis as well as a moment of analysis: otherwise, the method is formalist, rather than truly structuralist. Structuralist criticism cannot rest at the perception of resemblances or repetitions (redundancies, in fact), but must also comprehend a system of differences and oppositions. In this way, texts can be studied not only in their universality (what they all have in common) but also in their singularity (what differentiates them from each other). This means of course that the test of a structural analysis lies not in the orthodox canon of a director's work, where resemblances are clustered, but in films which at first sight may seem eccentricities.

In the films of Howard Hawks a systematic series of oppositions can be seen very near the surface, in the contrast between the adventure dramas and the crazy comedies. If we take the adventure dramas alone it would seem that Hawks's work is flaccid, lacking in dynamism; it is only when we consider the crazy comedies that it becomes rich, begins to ferment: alongside every dramatic hero we are aware of a phantom, stripped of mastery, humiliated, inverted. With other directors, the system of oppositions is much more complex: instead of there being two broad strata of films there are a whole series of shifting variations. In these cases, we need to analyse the roles of the protagonists themselves, rather than simply the worlds in which they operate. The protagonists of fairy-tales or myths, as Lévi-Strauss has pointed out, can be dissolved into bundles of differential elements, pairs of opposites. Thus the difference between the prince and the goose-girl can be reduced to two antinomic pairs: one natural, male versus female, and the other cultural, high versus low. We can proceed with the same kind of operation in the study of films, though, as we shall see, we shall find them more complex than fairy tales.

It is instructive, for example, to consider three films of John Ford and compare their heroes: Wyatt Earp in *My Darling Clementine*, Ethan Edwards in *The Searchers* and Tom Doniphon in *The Man Who Shot Liberty Valance*. They all act within the recognisable Ford world, governed by a set of oppositions, but their *loci* within that world are very different. The relevant pairs of opposites overlap; different pairs are foregrounded in different movies. The most relevant are garden versus wilderness, ploughshare versus sabre, settler versus nomad, European versus Indian, civilised versus savage, book versus gun, married versus unmarried, East versus West. These antinomies can often be broken down further. The East, for instance, can be defined either as Boston or Washington and, in *The Last Hurrah*, Boston itself is broken down into the antipodes of Irish immigrants versus Plymouth Club, themselves bundles of such differential elements as Celtic versus Anglo-Saxon, poor versus rich, Catholic versus Protestant, Democrat versus Republican, and so on. At first sight, it might seem that the oppositions listed above overlap to the extent that they become practically synonymous, but this is by no means the case. As we shall see, part of the development of Ford's career has been the shift from an identity between civilised versus savage and European versus Indian to their separation and final reversal, so that in *Cheyenne Autumn* it is the Europeans who are savage, the victims who are heroes.

The master antinomy in Ford's films is that between the wilderness and the garden. As Henry Nash Smith has demonstrated, in his magisterial book *Virgin Land*, the contrast between the image of America as a desert and as a garden is one which has dominated American thought and literature, recurring in countless novels, tracts, political speeches and magazine stories. In Ford's films it is crystallised in a number of striking images. *The Man Who Shot Liberty Valance*, for instance, contains the image of the cactus rose, which encapsulates the antinomy between desert and garden which pervades the whole film. Compare with this the famous scene in *My Darling Clementine*, after Wyatt Earp has gone to the barber (who civilises the unkempt), where the scent of honeysuckle is twice remarked upon: an artificial perfume, cultural rather than natural. This moment marks the turning-point in Wyatt Earp's transition from wandering cowboy, nomadic, savage, bent on personal revenge, unmarried, to married man, settled, civilised, the sheriff who administers the law.

Earp, in *My Darling Clementine*, is structurally the most simple of the three protagonists I have mentioned: his progress is an uncomplicated passage from nature to culture, from the wilderness left in the past to the garden anticipated in the future. Ethan Edwards, in *The Searchers*, is more complex. He must be defined not in terms of past versus future or wilderness versus garden compounded in himself, but in relation to two other protagonists: Scar, the Indian chief, and the family of homesteaders. Ethan Edwards, unlike Earp, remains a nomad throughout the film. At the start, he rides in from the desert to enter the log-house; at the end, with perfect symmetry, he leaves the house again to return to the desert, to vagrancy. In many respects, he is similar to Scar; he is a wanderer, a savage, outside the law: he scalps his enemy. But, like the homesteaders, of course, he is a European, the mortal foe of the Indian. Thus Edwards is ambiguous; the antinomies invade the personality of the protagonist himself. The oppositions tear Edwards in two; he is a tragic hero. His companion, Martin Pawley, however, is able to resolve the duality; for him, the period of nomadism is only an episode, which has meaning as the restitution of the family, a necessary link between his old home and his new home.

Ethan Edwards's wandering is, like that of many other Ford protagonists, a quest, a search. A number of Ford films are built round the theme of the quest for the Promised Land, an American re-enactment of the Biblical exodus, the journey through the desert to the land of milk and honey, the New Jerusalem. This theme is built on the combination of the two pairs: wilderness versus garden and nomad versus settler; the first pair precedes the second in time. Thus, in *Wagonmaster*, the Mormons cross the desert in search of their future home; in *How Green Was My Valley* and *The Informer*, the protagonists want to cross the Atlantic to a future home in the United States. But, during Ford's career, the situation of home is reversed in time. In *Cheyenne Autumn* the Indians journey in search of the home they once had in the past; in *The Quiet Man*, the American Sean Thornton returns to his ancestral home in Ireland. Ethan Edwards's journey is a kind of parody of this theme: his object is not constructive, to found a home, but destructive, to find and scalp Scar. Nevertheless, the weight of the film remains orientated to the future: Scar has burned down the home of the settlers, but it is replaced and we are confident that the homesteader's wife, Mrs Jorgensen, is right when she says: 'Some day this country's going to be a fine place to live.' The wilderness will, in the end, be turned into a garden.

The Man Who Shot Liberty Valance has many similarities with *The Searchers*. We may note three: the wilderness becomes a garden – this is made quite explicit, for Senator Stoddart has wrung from Washington the funds necessary to build a dam which will irrigate the desert and bring real roses, not cactus roses; Tom Doniphon shoots Liberty Valance as Ethan Edwards scalped Scar; a log-home is burned to the ground. But the differences are equally clear: the log-home is burned after the death of Liberty Valance; it is destroyed by Doniphon himself; it is his own home. The burning marks the realisation that he will never enter the Promised Land, that to him it means nothing; that he has doomed himself to be a creature of the past, insignificant in the world of the future. By shooting Liberty Valance he has destroyed the only world in which he himself can exist, the world of the gun rather than the book; it is as though Ethan Edwards had perceived that by scalping Scar, he was in reality committing suicide. It might be mentioned too that, in *The Man Who Shot Liberty Valance*, the woman who loves Doniphon marries Senator Stoddart. Doniphon when he destroys his log-house (his last words before doing so are 'Home, sweet home!') also destroys the possibility of marriage.

The themes of *The Man Who Shot Liberty Valance* can be expressed in another way. Ransom Stoddart represents rational-legal authority, Tom Doniphon represents charismatic authority. Doniphon abandons his charisma and cedes it, under what amount to false pretences, to Stoddart. In this way charismatic and rational-legal authority are combined in the person of Stoddart and stability thus assured. In *The Searchers* this transfer does not take place; the two kinds of authority remain separated. In *My Darling Clementine* they are combined naturally in Wyatt Earp, without any transfer being necessary. In many of Ford's late films – *The Quiet Man, Cheyenne Autumn, Donovan's Reef* – the accent is placed on traditional authority. The island of Ailakaowa, in *Donovan's Reef*, a kind of Valhalla for the homeless heroes of *The Man Who Shot Liberty Valance*, is actually a monarchy, though complete with the Boston girl, wooden church and saloon, made familiar by *My Darling Clementine*. In fact, the character of Chihuahua, Doc Holliday's girl in *My Darling Clementine*, is split into two: Miss Lafleur and Lelani, the native princess. One represents the saloon entertainer, the other the non-American in opposition to the respectable Bostonians, Amelia Sarah Dedham and Clementine Carter. In a broad sense, this is a part of a general movement which can be detected in Ford's work to equate the Irish, Indians and Polynesians as traditional communities, set in the past, counterposed to the march forward to the American future, as it has turned out in reality, but assimilating the values of the American future as it was once dreamed.

It would be possible, I have no doubt, to elaborate on Ford's career, as defined by pairs of contrasts and similarities, in very great detail, though – as always with film criticism – the impossibility of quotation is a severe handicap. My own view is that Ford's work is much richer than that of Hawks and that this is revealed by a structural analysis; it is the richness of the shifting relations between antinomies in Ford's work that makes him a great artist, beyond being simply an undoubted *auteur*.

Moreover, the *auteur* theory enables us to reveal a whole complex of meaning in films such as *Donovan's Reef*, which a recent filmography sums up as just 'a couple of Navy men who have retired to a South Sea island now spend most of their time raising hell'. Similarly, it throws a completely new light on a film like *Wings of Eagles*, which revolves, like *The Searchers*, round the vagrancy versus home antinomy, with the difference that when the hero does come home, after flying round the world, he trips over a child's toy, falls down the stairs and is completely paralysed so that he cannot move at all, not even his toes. This is the macabre *reductio ad absurdum* of the settled.

Perhaps it would be true to say that it is the lesser *auteurs* who can be defined, as Nowell-Smith put it, by a core of basic motifs which remain constant, without variation. The great directors must be defined in terms of shifting relations, in their singularity as well as their uniformity. Renoir once remarked that a director spends his whole life making one film; this film, which it is the task of the critic to construct, consists not only of the typical features of its variants, which are merely its redundancies, but of the principle of variation which governs it, that is its esoteric structure, which can only manifest itself or 'seep to the surface', in Lévi-Strauss's phrase, 'through the repetition process'. Thus Renoir's 'film' is in reality a 'kind of permutation group, the two variants placed at the far ends being in a symmetrical, though inverted, relationship to each other'. In practice, we will not find perfect symmetry, though as we have seen, in the case of Ford, some antinomies are completely reversed. Instead, there will be a kind of torsion within the permutation group, within the matrix, a kind of exploration of certain possibilities, in which some antinomies are foregrounded, discarded or even inverted, whereas others remain stable and constant. The important thing to stress, however, is that it is only the analysis of the whole *corpus* which permits the moment of synthesis when the critic returns to the individual film.

Of course, the director does not have full control over his work; this explains why the *auteur* theory involves a kind of decipherment, decryptment. A great many features of films analysed have to be dismissed as indecipherable because of 'noise' from the producer, the cameraman or even the actors. This concept of 'noise' needs further elaboration. It is often said that a film is the result of a multiplicity of factors, the sum total of a number of different contributions. The contribution of the director – the 'directorial factor', as it were – is only one of these, though perhaps the one which carries the most weight. I do not need to emphasise that this view is quite the contrary of the *auteur* theory and has nothing in common with it at all. What the *auteur* theory does is to take a group of films – the work of one director – and analyse their structure. Everything irrelevant to this, everything non-pertinent, is considered logically secondary, contingent, to be discarded. Of course, it is possible to approach films by studying some other feature; by an effort of critical ascesis we could see films, as Von Sternberg sometimes urged, as abstract light-show or as histrionic feasts. Sometimes these separate texts – those of the cameraman or the actors – may force themselves into prominence so that the film becomes an indecipherable palimpsest. This does not mean, of course, that it ceases to exist or to sway us or please us or intrigue us; it simply means that it is inaccessible to criticism. We can merely record our momentary and subjective impressions.

12 Hawks de-Wollenized

Robin Wood

[...] We can now return to the claims for the 'structuralist' method that I suggested were implicit in the work of Wollen [...] Firstly, any sense we may receive of 'scientific' objectivity is manifestly illusory: Wollen's account of Hawks reveals as strong a personal bias as one will find in the most admittedly 'subjective' criticism, the more dangerous for being concealed beneath an appearance of detached analytical method. As much as any other critic, Wollen sets his own personal value-system against the artist's in order to criticize the latter, as when he describes the Hawksian view of life as 'desolate and barren' (Hawks clearly does not find it so – witness the joyousness and serenity of *Rio Bravo*), or sees the comedies as 'the agonized exposure of the underlying tensions of the heroic dramas' (a description of *Bringing up Baby* and *Monkey Business* that will startle most viewers responsive to the *tone* of a film). Wollen's account reveals, one may say, a strong, unadmitted, and largely unconscious animus against Hawks expressing itself as distortion and parody. The grounds for that animus are not difficult to deduce. Wollen is nothing if not an intellectual, and the positive values implicit everywhere in his work are those associated with intellectual activity: one may suppose him to set very high, perhaps supreme, value on the pursuit of knowledge. This does not mean, of course, that he can only do justice to artists who share such values (his account of Ford, while open to some of the same basic objections, is in a different class from his work on Hawks). But in confronting Hawks he is faced with a value-system not merely different from his own but diametrically opposed to it – a value-system centred on a commitment to the intuitive, the physical, the 'primitive', and that shows no interest in concepts such as 'progress'. He responds with unconscious parody.

A film Wollen scarcely mentions, but which seems to me central in that it is the one film in the canon that presents the definitive Hawks villain, seems significant here: *The Thing from Another World*. The villain is the 'Thing' itself: an extra-terrestrial vegetable of extreme intellectual development, entirely devoid of emotion; it is also asexual, reproducing itself by dropping seeds from the palms of its hands. The leader of the scientific expedition, Dr Carrington – who elsewhere in the film expresses the belief (roughly paraphrasing Bertrand Russell) that the only purpose of and justification for human existence is the pursuit of knowledge – regards it as an unequivocal advance on the human race: 'No pleasure, no pain, no emotions ... Our superior, gentlemen, our superior in every way.' Against the Thing is set the 'camaraderie' of the group, and all that goes with it – human affection, mutual respect, sexual attraction. Peter Wollen is not exactly a 'Supercarrot' (his writing, in fact, always seems to carry a strong emotional charge, a sense of excitement and personal pressure, that is either its weakness or its saving grace, depending on the point of view); but the Thing represents no more grotesque a parody of the values his criticism asserts than the account he offers parodies Hawks.

It remains to consider the status and value of the 'structuralist' method, as exemplified here. I have indicated that I have myself found it very useful; I must add that its evaluative validity seems to me precisely nil, its utility strictly contingent upon other procedures (and ultimately on one's sense of values). [...] It is a tool, one among many, to be picked up and discarded at one's convenience, useful but not indispensable.

But perhaps this evades the ultimate question: the question of precisely what is to be evaluated. Are we interested in works of art, or in the abstractions that can be made from an artist's work? My answer is that for me art is concrete and specific: it is *Rio Bravo* in all its local detail, each little alive bit of business worked out between Hawks and his actors – not the 'Homo hawksianus' or the 'Hawksian heterocosm'. I believe that a film's excellence is (in the overwhelming majority of cases) ultimately attributable to its director, but not at all in a simple 'great artist reveals his view of the world' way. The term Wollen uses for anything that distracts our attention from the recurrent structural motifs, prevents our perceiving the structure in its abstract purity, is 'noise', by which he appears to mean, primarily, the interference of producers or studio heads. Yet the distinction this suggests appears damagingly simplistic – damagingly, that is, in relation to any adequate sense of the complexities of 'realized' art within a collaborative medium. The opposition structure/'noise' allows no means – to take the most obvious example – of discussing the intricacies of Hawks's collaborations with particular writers, though something of the quality of individual films clearly derives from this. One can trace through his work, for instance, a Ben Hecht – Charles Lederer weave and a Jules Furthman – William Faulkner – Leigh Brackett weave. Without being exhaustive, the former gives us *Scarface* (Hecht), *His Girl Friday* (Lederer, from a Hecht–MacArthur play), *Monkey Business* (Hecht and Lederer), *I was a Male War Bride, The Thing* and *Gentlemen Prefer Blondes* (Lederer); the latter gives us *Only Angels Have Wings* (Furthman), *To Have and Have Not* (Furthman and Faulkner), *The Big Sleep* (Furthman, Faulkner and Brackett), *Rio Bravo* (Furthman and Brackett), *Hatari!, El Dorado* and *Rio Lobo* (Brackett). The two 'weaves' continually cross through Hawks's work, but never combine: there are no Hecht/Furthman screenplays, for instance, though each was involved in at least six Hawks scripts. While the impossibility of making clear-cut thematic distinctions between the weaves testifies to the pervasive and unifying presence of Hawks, each weave emphasizes and highlights characteristics the other plays down. The resulting richness cannot be adequately represented by means of a single schematic structure. Beyond that, there may be all kinds of complex forces working on a given film, a multitude of determinants with the director at its centre. It is far from inconceivable that a director's finest work may be his least typical, the one that least corresponds to any total structure or 'heterocosm', a work in which circumstances (script, subject, actors, working conditions, *genre*) held in check his weaknesses and excesses. A work of art can transcend the personality, values, world-view of the artist; the greatness of a given film may be the product of an intricate interaction in which collaborators, circumstances of production, studio pressures, might all play their part.

Wollen, of course, would be the last critic to fall for the 'Romantic' fallacy of equating the quality of a work of art with the artist's direct self-expression: he finds the significance of an *oeuvre* in the gradual, inadvertent revelation of a structure of 'recondite' motifs of which the artist himself may remain unaware. One can grant the intellectual excitement of the search for such a structure; one can see that it may reveal interesting features in failed or inferior films (*Wings of Eagles, Donovan's Reef*) – though I personally cannot see that it reveals such films as, after all, successful works of art; most importantly, it can draw attention to some of the possible sources of a successful work's vitality. It constitutes, in other words, a potentially valuable preliminary to full understanding.

Mistaken for a valid method of evaluation, it leads Wollen to some very curious decisions. Hawks's interest lies, apparently, in the 'structural' opposition between the adventure films and the comedies. Hence: 'If we take the adventure dramas alone it would seem that Hawks's work is flaccid, lacking in dynamism.' So what becomes of one's response to actual films, to the experience of sitting in front of one? Presumably, we endure flaccid, undynamic works like *Only Angels Have Wings, To Have and Have Not, Rio Bravo*, feeling nothing but boredom and exasperation, until we have seen *Bringing up Baby* and *Monkey Business* (also, I take it, of little interest in themselves). *Then*, however, 'alongside every dramatic hero we are aware of a phantom, stripped of mastery, humiliated, inverted', and what was previously flaccid somehow ceases to be. It will seem to most people a very curious process, whereby we can only enjoy one film if we are thinking of another one while we watch it. In fact, an examination of *Rio Bravo* will show, I think, that the major tensions of Hawks's 'world' are successfully and coherently contained within it: there is no need to place the comedies, or anything else, beside it for it to 'become rich' and 'begin to ferment'.

Wollen's method rides roughshod over the internal delicacies and complexities of a work of art – the local significances that arise from the fusion of context and concrete realization. It is difficult to grasp, ultimately, what his valuation of Hawks actually is, or what it is based on. His structural analysis reduces the films to a scheme that, while it is assumed to convey Hawks's significance, appears trite, trivial and uninteresting; yet Hawks is included in Wollen's 'Pantheon' of ten Hollywood directors at the end of the book (omitted from the second edition). I can see no justification for this high assessment in his text. As an antidote, and for the basis on which a serious case for Hawks might be built, the reader might look up an altogether more unassuming and less influential article by John Belton, reprinted in *Focus on Howard Hawks* (Prentice-Hall): it seems to me the best thing on Hawks I have read, searching out significance not in a simplified abstraction but in the concrete detail of the films.

To point to a constructive alternative – or at least counter-balance – to Wollen's parody, and to exemplify what I mean by the significance of concrete detail, without a sensitivity to which we cannot began to 'read' a work of art, I shall end by indicating two brief moments in *Rio Bravo*. Neither of them is accountable for in the terms of Wollen's structural analysis, though a more just and rational sense of the Hawksian value-system's finer aspects would certainly relate them to the concerns of the whole film and of Hawks's work in general. The first is the moment when Chance and Dude, patrolling the street at night, encounter the Burdett man set to watch the jail. Dude watches from across the street; Chance stands silently over the man (who begins to shuffle awkwardly) then speaks the words 'Good evening', as only John Wayne can. The man mutters and moves away; Dude smiles admiringly.

The incident establishes Chance's authority as essentially *moral*: the authority of the man who acts from inner principle over the hired mercenary. It also acts as an object-lesson for Dude: implicit in Chance's authority is the personal integrity and self-respect that Dude, in his lapse into alcoholic degradation, has forfeited and must strive to regain. He is separated from Chance by the street (and by the editing), a pupil-onlooker. Thus a mini-scene with only two words spoken encapsulates the film's leading moral and dramatic concerns.

The second moment, which occurs at the end of the 'blood-in-the-beer' scene, again takes up the theme of authority and can be seen as both development and qualification of the first, hence exemplifying the complexity of attitude achievable without pretension or explicitness in a fictional narrative. The scene ends with Chance reminding Dude – now provisionally reinstated by virtue of his very un-alcoholic aliveness of perception and action – that he has still to deal with the man who taunted him by flinging a coin into the spittoon. Dude compels the man (by moral authority backed by the *possibility* of force) to retrieve it personally, with his bare hand. His comment is a succinct, 'That's all for *me*, Chance.' The comment clearly refers the spectator back to an incident earlier in the scene when Chance, as a punishment, struck a man savagely across the face with a gun-barrel. The moral centre of *Rio Bravo* is the developing comparison between the two men, the 'infallible' leader, always refusing help yet constantly dependent on it, the extremely fallible, more human and responsive deputy. Dude's remark emerges as a criticism of Chance, a pointing of the human limitations and dangers that the role of infallible leader carries with it. The criticism is less one of physical violence *per se* than of motivation and role: Chance metes out punishment to an inferior, Dude demands his human rights through the enactment of a precise justice. Dude's participation in the song, in the democratic equality of individuals, and Chance's exclusion from their circle, are already implicit in that moment – the sort of moment one imagines developing, in a Hawks movie, out of the director's collaborative involvement with writers and actors, out of his sense of each actor's nature and what he can give. The life of a film is in its detail.

SECTION THREE
GENRE CRITICISM

Genre criticism emerged as a distinct approach within film studies in the late 1960s and early 1970s. For some critics, like Kitses (see extract 13), it was a way of developing auteur theory, but even in these cases the issue of genre raised questions that would begin to displace the focus on authorship. To put it another way, the study of genre introduced a series of theories which began seriously to challenge the notion of the author as the source of a film's meaning. It began to shift the focus of critical attention to cultural systems and structures that not only pre-date the individual author, but also could be said to be constitutive of individuals (see Section Four).

The concept of film genres pre-dates the emergence of genre criticism, however. The notion that films could be divided into categories such as the musical, the western, the thriller, etc., categories that were recognized both by the industry and the audience, is not a new one. In mass culture theory, for example, genre was an important concept, but it was also one that was simply seen to be proof of the standardized nature of popular films (see Section One).

For the mass culture theorists, and many others, genres were seen as formulas, in which all the films of a particular genre repeated a fixed and familiar pattern. As Macdonald wrote, 'imagine a Western in which the hero loses the climactic gun fight or an office romance in which the mousey stenographer loses out to the predatory blonde' (1963: 28). A similar position was also held by many *auteur* critics, for whom genres were often seen as the very materials that the individual director must transcend or subvert in order to distinguish themselves from the mass and so be defined as an *auteur* (see Section Two).

In the first extract in this section, however, Kitses clearly tries to rework this position. On the one hand, he tries to present the western not as material against which *auteurs* have to work, but rather as a resource upon which they can draw. In other words, a genre can be significant and meaningful in and of itself, regardless of the intervention of an auteur. As Kitses has put it: 'Rather than an empty vessel breathed into by the filmmaker, the genre [the western] is a vital structure through which flow a myriad of themes and concepts' (1969: 26).

Kitses therefore tries to specify the cultural meanings of the western, meanings which pre-date the intervention of a specific director, and like other genre critics he is influenced in this endeavour by the theories of semiotics and structuralism, theories which had a major impact on the humanities in the late 1960s and early 1970s.

These theories were developed in relation to the work of a Swiss linguist, Ferdinand de Saussure (1974). For Saussure, linguistic units were called signs and were made up of two components the signifier and the signified. Hence, a sign (such as a word) is made up of the material elements which he called the signifier (the ink marking on a page or the sound waves in the air) and the signified (the meanings which a culture attaches to those material markings or sound waves). Saussure argues not only that the relationship between the signifier and signified is an arbitrary one – there is no reason why the letters CAT should be tied to the concept of a small furry animal – but also that the concept or signified does not simply refer to some pre-existing object in the world. Saussure is not denying that cats exist, but rather that reality is not made up of a series of discrete objects that we simply name through language. On the contrary, he argues, it is language that cuts reality up into objects and classes of objects. The meaning of a word derives not from its reference to an object in the world but from its place within the system of language. The word 'cat' is defined through its relationship to other words within our language.

This leads Saussure to make a distinction between three sets of terms: the diachronic and the synchronic; langue and parole; and the paradigmatic and the syntagmatic. The first of these distinguishes between two ways of studying a language. The diachronic concerns the historical development of language over time, in which, for example, one tracks the changing meaning of a word. The synchronic, on the other hand, involves the study of a language at a specific moment in time, and so permits the analysis of the structures and relationships which compose that language at any given moment.

This system or structure of language is what Saussure refers to as 'langue', and he distinguishes it from the individual speech act, or 'parole'. For Saussure, then, the study of language requires us to acknowledge that any specific speech act is only meaningful to the extent that it obeys a system of words and grammars which pre-date it, and which the individual speaker is not at liberty to change. We cannot make a word mean anything that we want, and as a result our individual speech acts are only meaningful to the extent that they work within a linguistic system that pre-dates us. For this reason, it is often claimed that it is not the individual speech act that is the source of meaning but the system of language. It is not the author that produces meaning, but the linguistic system.

Saussure's third distinction therefore does not simply concern the meaning of individual words, but also acknowledges the significance of grammar. The paradigmatic concerns the relationships of similarity and difference between words that are interchangeable with one another, while the syntagmatic concerns the procedures for their combination. Sentences, for example, have syntax, or a pattern of combination. The simplest version of this is probably that of subject, verb and object: that is, the subject of the sentence (the thing that performs an action), the verb (the action that is performed) and the object (the thing on which the subject acts).

These ideas were applied to the study of myths by the French anthropologist Claude Lévi-Strauss (1968). For Lévi-Strauss, myths should not simply be seen as stories which are untrue or false, but rather as particular ways of making sense of the world. A culture's stories tell us about how that culture thinks, and allows us to analyse it. Lévi-Strauss drew on Saussure in at least two ways. First, he rejected the notion that myths were simply inaccurate representations of the world, and second, he suggested that one should study a myth by identifying the structure of relationships of which it is composed. Taking the Oedipus myth, for example, Lévi-Strauss did not simply study the linear chain of events that constitute its story, but identified a series of recurring and related oppositions. Thus, he claimed one could find a continual concern with the question of origins so that the myth can be seen as a very complex way of thinking about where we come from (birth) and where we are going to (death).

In a similar way, then, Kitses suggests that we should not see a genre as a fixed and familiar formula in which all the films of that genre are the same, but rather that we need to focus on the structure of oppositions which underpin the genre, and which constitute its meaning. He identifies a series of oppositions which structure the western as a genre, and argues that the western is therefore centrally about the conflict between the wilderness and civilization. As such, it is argued, the western genre is 'no less than a national world-view', a story of origins which tackles 'the grave problem of [the American nation's] identity'. As a result, unlike earlier genre critics, Kitses refuses to see all films of a genre as the same. If he argues that the western exists to think through the problem of American identity, he firmly refuses to accept that one can 'freeze the genre once and for all in a definitive model of the "classical" Western', and he stresses that it is 'a loose, shifting and variegated genre with many roots and branches'.

Nonetheless, and despite Kitses' innovations, his attempt to identify the structure of oppositions that underpinned the genre has problems, as Tudor argues in extract 14. For Tudor, genre criticism has been based on a fundamentally problematic search for factor X: that which defines a particular genre. This search not only seeks to identify what all films of a genre *must* share, but also implicitly what films from another genre *cannot* share. As a result, genre theories often end up with definitions that either seem to include films that had never previously been associated with a specific genre, or to exclude films that had. Indeed, even Kitses' definition has this problem. Numerous films can be seen as operating around the opposition between the wilderness and civilization (many science fiction films, for example, and even melodramas such as *All that Heaven Allows* (1955)), and the logical tendency within genre criticism has therefore been to argue that such cases are in some sense *really* westerns. Furthermore, Lévi-Strauss' own work identifies the opposition between nature and culture, which are synonymous with Kitses' opposition between wilderness and civilization, as the fundamental oppositions which underpinned *all* myths, not oppositions which allowed one to distinguish one category of myth from another.

For Tudor, the pursuit of factor X is inherently doomed to failure, and is even based on a fundamentally flawed methodology. Not only does it return to the presumption that all films of a genre are in some sense essentially the same as one another, and different from the films of other genres, but it is also based on an 'empiricist dilemma':

> They are *defining* a 'Western' on the basis of analysing a body of films which cannot possibly be said to be 'Westerns' until after the analysis ... To take a *genre* such as a 'Western', analyse it, and list its principle characteristics, is to beg the question that we must first isolate the body of films which are 'Westerns'. But they can only be isolated on the basis of the 'principle characteristics' which can only be discovered *from the films themselves* after they have been isolated.

Tudor therefore rejects the notion of trying to identify factor X and instead suggests that we simply accept that 'Genre is what we collectively believe it to be'.

Tudor argues that instead of trying to isolate a factor that is shared by all films of a genre (a factor which simply may not exist), it is more useful to study the films that have been commonly understood to belong to a genre, and to analyse the similarities and differences between them. In his book *Monsters and Mad Scientists* (1989), for example, he studies different types of horror films and the ways in which the genre has changed over time. He is able to identify tendencies, patterns and distinctions within the genre, rather than simply engaging in the essentialist pursuit of some Factor X. For Tudor, the interesting question is not the ways in which all films are the same, but rather how and why they differ.

Nonetheless, the pursuit of factor X has continued to be one of the main forms of genre criticism. In extract 15, for example, Steve Neale attempts to provide an account of genre from within the terms of *Screen* theory (see Sections Six and Seven). However, for all the sophistication here, Neale still continues to view genres as ways of organizing the relationship between repetition and difference. He does stress that difference is essential to genre, and he even argues that 'the notion that "all westerns (or all gangster films, or war films, or whatever) are the same" is not just an unwarranted generalization, it is profoundly wrong'. However, he also argues that this is simply because 'if each text within a genre were, literally, the same there would not be enough difference to generate either meaning or pleasure'. In this way, the differences between films become little more than the 'pseudo-individualism' of mass culture theory (see Section One). They are largely illusory, and function to permit a more fundamental repetition.

For Neale, then, films of a specific genre may have to appear to be different – people are not going to pay repeatedly to see the same film over and over again – but at some fundamental level the films of a genre still repeat certain ideological functions. For example, he argues that horror movies function to reproduce and support masculinity. All horror movies, it is suggested, essentially work around masculine anxieties so that it is 'women's sexuality ... which constitutes the real problem that the horror film exists to explore' (Neale 1980: 61).

Indeed, the notion that genres are inherently associated with the psychic needs or socially defined interests of specific genders became increasingly important to work on genre, and also to the ways in which genres were ranked and valued. Genres such as the romance or the musical, for example, have been dismissed by some critics, for whom their association with feminine tastes was sufficient proof of their lack of aesthetic value. More recently, critics such as Barbara Creed (1993) have criticized genres such as horror for their presumed sexism. For Creed, all horror films are based on a masculine fear of the maternal, that which they must distance themselves from and repress in order to achieve masculinity.

At times, this work is deeply problematic. The horror genre, for example, has been frequently derided specifically through an association with feminine rather than masculine tastes, and hence the gendering of genres is often more complex than is often acknowledged (see for example the discussion of the Gothic in Jancovich 1992). However, there is also much to be gained from studying the ways in which gender is bound up with the processes through which certain genres are valued over others. Also, while one needs to avoid the suggestion that gendered tastes are either natural or inevitable, it is certainly true that the taste for specific genres is heavily gendered.

In extract 16, then, Christine Geraghty examines the woman's film. These films were produced by Hollywood with the explicit intention of addressing a female audience, and have frequently been discussed as though they were a genre. Indeed, in the chapter from which this extract is taken, Geraghty compares it to the television soap opera and to romantic fiction in order to analyse both the ways in which these genres are frequently dismissed as less worthy than other genres and the ways in which they 'appeal to women' (Geraghty 1991: 107). Interestingly, Geraghty herself is uncertain about the appropriateness of the term 'genre' for these forms, and while she does, at times, refer to them as genres, she also uses other terms such as 'formats' to describe them.

This problem is also relevant to the final extract in which James Naremore discusses film noir, a category which has been discussed as a genre, but which has also been variously called a style, a movement, a period and a mood. As Naremore suggests, one of the reasons for this uncertainty is specifically that the term 'film noir', like all genre terms, is inherently indefinable. Drawing on Michel Foucault's critique of the function of the 'author', Naremore suggests that a genre is less a matter of a pre-existing factor X which unites a group of films than of the critical task of linking a group of films together. Genre criticism frequently works towards what Tudor called 'genre imperialism', in which the desire to link films becomes the desire to identify 'a point where contradictions are resolved, where incompatible elements are at last tied together or organised around a fundamental and organising contradiction' (Foucault quoted in Naremore). In other words, genre criticism often involves not only an

attempted identification of relationships between films but also an assertion that these relationships are the most significant features of these films.

Naremore argues that film noir was more a product of certain conditions
of reception within postwar France than of some inherent property of the
films themselves. Indeed, he demonstrates not only that different critics
have defined the term 'film noir' in ways that are often incompatible with
one another (hence the debate over whether film noir refers to a style, a
genre, a mood or a period) but that this term has never even had a stable
object to which it refers, so that the films that are said to constitute the
category of film noir are always changing.

None of this should lead us to conclude that the study of genre is not a
valuable one. It remains true that most, if not all, people still use genre
categories. If Tudor's 'neurotic critics' were wrong to believe that genres
had specific essences, his 'untroubled spectators' continue to use genre
definitions to define their own tastes and the tastes of others, and this
aspect of genre has rarely been studied. There is therefore a great deal of
work to be done on how people understand terms such as 'western',
'musical' or 'horror film', and how these terms effect the reception of genre
films.

References

Creed, B. (1993). *The Monstrous Feminine: Film, Feminism and Psychoanalysis*.
London: Routledge.
Foucault, M. (1984). 'What Is an Author?', In P. Rabinow (ed.), *The Foucault Reader*.
Harmondsworth: Penguin, 101–20.
Geraghty, C. (1991). *Women and Soap Opera*. Oxford: Polity.
Grant, B. K. (ed.) (1995). *The Film Genre Reader II*. Austin: University of Texas
Press.
Jancovich, M. (1992). *Horror*. London: Batsford.
Kitses, J. (1969). *Horizons West*. London: Thames & Hudson/British Film Institute.
Lévi-Strauss, C. (1968). *Structural Anthropology*. Harmondsworth: Penguin.
Macdonald, D. (1963). 'Masscult and Midcult'. In *Against the American Grain*.
London: Gollancz, 3–75.
Naremore, J. (1995–6). 'American Film Noir: The History of an Idea'. *Film Quarterly*
49(2): 12–28.
Neale, S. (1980). *Genre*. London: British Film Institute.
—— (1990). 'Questions of Genre'. *Screen* **31**(1): 45–66.
Saussure, F. de (1974). *A Course in General Linguistics*. London: Fontana/Collins.
Tudor, A. (1973). *Theories of Film*. London: Secker & Warburg.
—— 1989: *Monsters and Mad Scientists: A Cultural History of the Horror Movie*.
Oxford: Blackwell.

13 Authorship and genre: notes on the western

Jim Kitses

The most popular and enduring of Hollywood forms, the western has yet received scant critical attention. Especially in recent years, it has been the director rather than the form that has occupied critical energies. Rightly so, up to a point, and much of this book springs from the desire to rescue three talented men from the neglect forced upon them. The gains resulting from the emergence of *auteur* theory have been remarkable: the beginnings of a systematic critical approach; the foundation for a subject with its own body of knowledge; the great task of re-evaluation of the American cinema under way.

But I should make clear what I mean here by *auteur* theory. In my view the term describes a basic principle and a method, no more and no less: the idea of personal authorship in the cinema and – of key importance – the concomitant responsibility to honour all of a director's works by a systematic examination in order to trace characteristic themes, structures and formal qualities. In this light the idea of the *auteur* does not seem to me to solve all our problems so much as to crystallize them. Can we speak defensibly of a director who transcends his forms? Of genre as part of the industrial complex that the film-maker must dominate? At their most simplistic *auteur* critics have insisted that there is only good work and bad, authors and others. Years ago André Bazin warned fellow critics of *Cahiers du Cinéma* about the dangers of a cult of the personality latent in a narrow approach. In my view if we are to avoid this pitfall and build a body of film scholarship that is both vigorous and educationally valid, we must begin to explore the inner workings of genre. It is the belief that *auteur* theory must confront this problem that has led me to structure this book in the way that I have. In place of the reactionary notion that Hollywood directors function like the charismatic heroes of their films, I have wanted to advance the idea of an American *tradition*, of which the western seems to me an admirable and central model. However, I have not tried to catalogue the history of the genre or to chart the ebb and flow of its recent usage. In lieu of these more general approaches, I here embark on a survey of what I take to be the constituent elements of the form before going on to examine in some detail the contributions of three of its finest champions in the post-war era.

First of all, the western is American history. Needless to say, this does not mean that the films are historically accurate or that they cannot be made by Italians. More simply, the statement means that American frontier life provides the milieu and *mores* of the western, its wild bunch of cowboys, its straggling towns and mountain scenery. Of course westward expansion was to continue for over a century, the frontier throughout that period a constantly shifting belt of settlement. However, Hollywood's West has typically been, from about 1865 to 1890 or so, a brief final instant in the process. This twilight era was a momentous one: within just its span we can count a number of frontiers in the sudden rash of mining camps, the building of the railways, the Indian Wars, the cattle drives, the coming of the farmer. Together with the last days of the Civil War and the exploits of the badmen, here is the raw material of the western.

At the heart of this material, and crucial to an understanding of the gifts the form holds out to its practitioners, is an ambiguous, mercurial concept: the idea of the West. From time immemorial the West had beckoned to statesmen and poets, existing as both a direction and a place, an imperialist theme and a pastoral Utopia. Great empires developed ever westward: from Greece to Rome, from Rome to Britain, from Britain to America. It was in the West as well that the fabled lands lay, the Elysian fields, Atlantis, El Dorado. As every American schoolboy knows, it was in sailing on his passage to India, moving ever westward to realize the riches of the East, that Columbus chanced on the New World. Hand in hand with the hope of fragrant spices and marvellous tapestries went the ever-beckoning dream of life eternal: surely somewhere, there where the sun slept, was the fountain of youth.

As America began to be settled and moved into its expansionist phases, this apocalyptic and materialist vision found new expression. In his seminal study *Virgin Land*, Henry Nash Smith has traced how the West as symbol has functioned in America's history and consciousness. Is the West a Garden of natural dignity and innocence offering refuge from the decadence of civilization? Or is it a treacherous Desert stubbornly resisting the gradual sweep of agrarian progress and community values? Dominating America's intellectual life in the nineteenth century, these warring ideas were most clearly at work in attitudes surrounding figures like Daniel Boone, Kit Carson and Buffalo Bill Cody, who were variously seen as rough innocents ever in flight from society's artifice, and as enlightened pathfinders for the new nation. A folk-hero manufactured in his own time, Cody himself succumbed towards the end of his life to the play of these concepts that so gripped the imagination of his countrymen: 'I stood between savagery and civilization most all my early days.'

Refracted through and pervading the genre, this ideological tension has meant that a wide range of variation is possible in the basic elements of the form. The plains and mountains of western landscape can be an inspiring and civilizing environment, a moral universe productive of the western hero, a man with a code. But this view, popularized by Robert Warshow in his famous essay, 'The Westerner', is one-sided. Equally the terrain can be barren and savage, surroundings so demanding that men are rendered morally ambiguous, or wholly brutalized. In the same way, the community in the western can be seen as a positive force, a movement of refinement, order and local democracy into the wilds, or as a harbinger of corruption in the form of Eastern values which threaten frontier ways. This analysis over-simplifies in isolating the attitudes: a conceptually complex structure that draws on both images is the typical one. If Eastern figures such as bankers, lawyers and journalists are often either drunkards or corrupt, their female counterparts generally carry virtues and graces which the West clearly lacks. And if Nature's harmonies produce the upright hero, they also harbour the animalistic Indian. Thus central to the form we have a philosophical dialectic, an ambiguous cluster of meanings and attitudes that provide the traditional thematic structure of the genre. This shifting ideological play can be described through a series of antinomies, so:

THE WILDERNESS	CIVILIZATION
The individual	*The community*
freedom	restriction
honour	institutions
self-knowledge	illusion
integrity	compromise
self-interest	social responsibility
solipsism	democracy
Nature	*Culture*
purity	corruption
experience	knowledge
empiricism	legalism
pragmatism	idealism
brutalization	refinement
savagery	humanity
The West	*The East*
America	Europe
the frontier	America
equality	class
agrarianism	industrialism
tradition	change
the past	the future

In scanning this grid, if we compare the tops and tails of each sub-section, we can see the ambivalence at work at its outer limits: the West, for example, rapidly moves from being the spearhead of manifest destiny to the retreat of ritual. What we are dealing with here, of course, is no less than a national world-view: underlying the whole complex is the grave problem of identity that has special meaning for Americans. The isolation of a vast unexplored continent, the slow growth of social forms, the impact of an unremitting New England Puritanism obsessed with the cosmic struggle of good and evil, of the elect and the damned, the clash of allegiances to Mother Country and New World, these factors are the crucible in which American consciousness was formed. The thrust of contradictions, everywhere apparent in American life and culture, is clearest in the great literary heritage of the romantic novel that springs from Fenimore Cooper and moves through Hawthorne and Melville, Mark Twain and Henry James, Fitzgerald and Faulkner, Hemingway and Mailer. As Richard Chase has underlined in his *The American Novel and Its Tradition*, this form in American hands has always tended to explore rather than to order, to reflect on rather than to moralize about, the irreconcilables that it confronts; and where contradictions are resolved the mode is often that of melodrama or the pastoral. For failing to find a moral tone and a style of close social observation – in short, for failing to be *English* – the American novel has often had its knuckles rapped. As with literature, so with the film: the prejudice that even now persists in many quarters of criticism and education with reference to the Hollywood cinema (paramountly in America itself) flows from a similar lack of understanding.

The ideology that I have been discussing inevitably filters through many of Hollywood's genres: the western has no monopoly here. But what gives the form a particular thrust and centrality is its historical setting; its being placed at exactly that moment when options are still open, the dream of a primitivistic individualism, the ambivalence of at once beneficent and threatening horizons, still tenable. For the film-maker who is preoccupied with these motifs, the western has offered a remarkably expressive canvas. Nowhere, of course, is the freedom that it bestows for personal expression more evident than in the cinema of John Ford.

It would be presumptuous to do more than refer here to this distinguished body of work, the crucial silent period of which remains almost wholly inaccessible. Yet Ford's career, a full-scale scrutiny of which must be a priority, stands as unassailable proof of how the historical dimensions of the form can be orchestrated to produce the most personal kind of art. As Andrew Sarris has pointed out, 'no American director has ranged so far across the landscape of the American past'. But the journey has been a long and deeply private one through green valleys of hope on to bitter sands of despair. The peak comes in the forties where Ford's works are bright monuments to his vision of the trek of the faithful to the Promised Land, the populist hope of an ideal community, a dream affectionately etched in *The Grapes of Wrath, My Darling Clementine, Wagonmaster*. But as the years slip by the darker side of Ford's romanticism comes to the foreground, and twenty years after the war – in *The Man Who Shot Liberty Valance, Two Rode Together, Cheyenne Autumn* – we find a regret for the past, a bitterness at the larger role of Washington, and a desolation over the neglect of older values. The trooping of the colours has a different meaning now. As Peter Wollen has described in his chapter on *auteur* theory in *Signs and Meaning in the Cinema*, the progression can be traced in the transposition of civilized and savage elements. The Indians of *Drums Along the Mohawk* and *Stagecoach*, devilish marauders that threaten the hardy pioneers, suffer a sea-change as Ford's hopes wane, until with *Cheyenne Autumn* they are a civilized, tragic people at the mercy of a savage community. The ringing of the changes is discernible in the choice of star as well, the movement from the quiet idealism of the early Fonda through the rough pragmatism of the Wayne *persona* to the cynical self-interest of James Stewart. As Ford grows older the American dream sours, and we are left with nostalgia for the Desert.

Imperious as he is, Ford is not the western; nor is the western history. For if we stand back from the western, we are less aware of historical (or representational) elements than of form and *archetype*. This may sound platitudinous: for years critics have spoken confidently of the balletic movement of the genre, of pattern and variation, of myth. This last, ever in the air when the form is discussed, clouds the issues completely. We can speak of the genre's celebration of America, of the contrasting images of Garden and Desert, as national myth. We can speak of the parade of mythology that is mass culture, of which the western is clearly a part. We can invoke Greek and medieval myth, referring to the western hero as a latter-day knight, a contemporary Achilles. Or we can simply speak of the myth of the western, a journalistic usage which evidently implies that life is not like that. However, in strict classical terms of definition myth has to do with the activity of gods, and as such the western has no myth. Rather, it incorporates elements of *displaced* (or corrupted) myth on a scale that can render them considerably more prominent than in most art.

It is not surprising that little advance is made upon the clichés, no analysis undertaken that interprets how these elements are at work within a particular film or director's career. What are the archetypal elements we sense within the genre and how do they function? As Northrop Frye has shown in his monumental *The Anatomy of Criticism*, for centuries this immensely tangled ground has remained almost wholly unexplored in literature itself. The primitive state of film criticism inevitably reveals a yawning abyss in this direction.

Certain facts are clear. Ultimately the western derives from the long and fertile tradition of Wild West literature that had dominated the mass taste of nineteenth-century America. Fenimore Cooper is again the germinal figure here: Nash Smith has traced how the roots of the formula, the adventures of an isolated, aged trapper/hunter (reminiscent of Daniel Boone) who rescues genteel heroines from the Indians, were in the *Leatherstocking Tales* which began to emerge in the 1820s. These works, fundamentally in the tradition of the sentimental novel, soon gave way to a rush of pulp literature in succeeding decades culminating in the famous series edited by Erastus Beadle which had astonishing sales for its time. Specialists in the adventure tale, the romance, the sea story, turned to the West for their setting to cash in on the huge market. As the appetite for violence and spectacle grew, variations followed, the younger hunter that had succeeded Cooper's hero losing his pristine nature and giving way to a morally ambiguous figure with a dark past, a Deadwood Dick who is finally redeemed by a woman's love. The genre, much of it sub-literary, became increasingly hungry for innovation as the century wore on, its Amazon heroines perhaps only the most spectacular sign of a desperation at its declining hold on the imagination. As the actual drama of the frontier finally came to a close, marked by Frederick C. Turner's historic address before the American Historical Association in 1893 where he advanced his thesis on free land and its continual recession westward as the key factor in America's development, the vogue for the dime novel waned, its hero now frozen in the figure of the American cowboy.

In 1900 the Wild Bunch held up and robbed a Union Pacific railway train in Wyoming; in 1903 Edwin S. Porter made *The Great Train Robbery* in New Jersey. The chronology of these events, often commented on, seems less important than their geography: it had been the East as well from which Beadle westerns such as *Seth Jones; or, The Captives of the Frontier* had flowed. The cinema was born, its novel visual apparatus at the ready, the heir to a venerable tradition of reworking history (the immediate past) in tune with ancient classical rhythms. In general, of course, the early silent cinema everywhere drew on and experimented with traditional and folkloric patterns for the forms it required. What seems remarkable about the western, however, is that the core of a formulaic lineage already existed. The heart of this legacy was romantic narrative, tales which insisted on the idealization of characters who wielded near-magical powers. Recurrent confrontations between the personified forces of good and evil, testimony to the grip of the New England Calvinist ethic, had soon focused the tales in the direction of morality play. However, in any case, the structure was an impure one which had interpolated melodramatic patterns of corruption and redemption, the revenge motif borrowed from the stage towards the end of the century, and humour in the Davy Crockett and Eastern cracker-barrel traditions. The physical action and spectacle of the Wild West shows, an offshoot of the penny-dreadful vogue, was to be another factor.

This complex inheritance meant that from the outset the western could be many things. In their anecdotal *The Western* George N. Fenin and William K. Everson have chronicled the proliferating, overlapping growth of early days: Bronco Billy Anderson's robust action melodramas, Thomas H. Ince's darker tales, W.S. Hart's more 'authentic' romances, the antics of the virtuous Tom Mix, the Cruze and Ford epics of the twenties, the stunts and flamboyance of Ken Maynard and Hoot Gibson, the flood of 'B' movies, revenge sagas, serials, and so on. Experiment seems always to have been varied and development dynamic, the pendulum swinging back and forth between opposing poles of emphasis on drama and history, plots and spectacle, romance and 'realism', seriousness and comedy. At any point where audience response was felt the action could freeze, the industrial machine moving into high gear to produce a cycle and, in effect, establish a minor tradition within the form. Whatever 'worked' was produced, the singing westerns of the thirties perhaps only the most prominent example of this policy of eclectic enterprise.

For many students of the western Gene Autry and Roy Rogers have seemed an embarrassing aberration. However, such a view presupposes that there is such an animal as *the* western, a precise model rather than a loose, shifting and variegated genre with many roots and branches. The word 'genre' itself, although a helpful one, is a mixed blessing: for many the term carries literary overtones of technical *rules*. Nor is 'form' any better; the western is many *forms*. Only a pluralist vision makes sense of our experience of the genre and begins to explain its amazing vigour and adaptability, the way it moves closer and further from our own world, brightening or darkening with each succeeding decade. Yet over the years critics have ever tried to freeze the genre once and for all in a definitive model of the 'classical' western. Certainly it must be admitted that works such as *Shane* and *My Darling Clementine* weld together in remarkable balance historical reconstruction and national themes with personal drama and archetypal elements. In his essay, 'The Evolution of the Western', Bazin declared *Stagecoach* the summit of the form, an example of 'classic maturity', before going on to see in Anthony Mann's early small westerns the path of further progress. Although there is a certain logic in searching for films at the centre of the spectrum, I suspect it is a false one and can see little value in it. Wherever definitions of *the* genre movie have been advanced they have become the weapons of generalization. Insisting on the purity of his classical elements, Bazin dismisses 'super-westerns' (*Shane, High Noon, Duel in the Sun*) because of their introduction of interests 'not endemic'. Warshow's position is similar, although his conception of the form is narrower, a particular kind of moral and physical texture embodied in his famous but inadequate view of the hero as 'the last gentleman'. Elsewhere Mann's films have been faulted for their neurotic qualities, strange and powerful works such as *Rancho Notorious* have been refused entry because they are somehow 'not westerns'. This impulse may well be informed by a fear that unless the form is defined precisely (which inevitably excludes) it will disappear, wraith-like, from under our eyes. The call has echoed out over the lonely landscape of critical endeavour: what *is* the western?

The model we must hold before us is of a varied and flexible structure, a thematically fertile and ambiguous world of historical material shot through with archetypal elements which are themselves ever in flux. [...]

14 Critical method . . . genre

Andrew Tudor

[...] *Auteur* at least originated in film criticism in the recent past; *genre* had a lengthy pedigree in literary criticism long before the advent of the cinema. Hence the meaning and uses of the term vary considerably and it is very difficult to identify even a tenuous school of thought on the subject. For years it provided a crudely useful way of delineating the American cinema. The literature abounds with references to the 'Western', the 'Gangster' movie, or the 'Horror' film, all of which are loosely thought of as *genre*. On occasions it becomes almost the end point of the critical process to fit a film into such a category, much as it once made a film 'intelligible' to fit it into, say, the French 'nouvelle vague'. To call a film a 'Western' is thought of as somehow saying something interesting or important about it. To fit it into a class of films about which we presumably have some *general* knowledge. To say a film is a 'Western' is immediately to say that it shares some indefinable 'X' with other films we call 'Westerns'. In addition, it provides us with a body of films to which our film can be usefully compared; sometimes, the *only* body of films. The most extreme, and clearly ridiculous, application might be to argue that it is *necessarily* more illuminating to compare, say, *The Man Who Shot Liberty Valance* with a Roy Rogers short than with *The Last Hurrah*. Not that the first comparison might not be instructive; merely that it is not necessarily the case. Extreme *genre* imperialism leads in this direction.

Now almost everyone uses terms like 'Western'; the neurotic critic as much as the undisturbed cinemagoer. The difference, and the source of difficulty, lies in the way the critic seeks to use the term. What is normally a thumb-nail classification for everyday purposes is now being asked to carry rather more weight. The fact that there is a special term, *genre*, for these categories suggests that the critic's conception of 'Western' is more complex than is the case in everyday discourse; if not, why the special term? But in quite what way critical usage is more complex is not entirely clear. In some cases it involves the idea that if a film is a 'Western' it somehow draws on a tradition, in particular, on a set of conventions. That is, 'Westerns' have in common certain themes, certain typical actions, certain characteristic mannerisms; to experience a 'Western' is to operate within this previously defined world. Jim Kitses tries to isolate characteristics in this way, by defining *genre* in terms of such attributes: '... a varied and flexible structure, a thematically fertile and ambiguous world of historical material shot through with archetypal elements which are themselves even in flux.'[1] But other usages, such as 'Horror' films, might also mean films displaying certain themes, actions, and so on, or, just as often, films that have in common the *intention* to horrify. Instead of defining the *genre* by attributes it is defined by intentions. [...]

Both these uses display serious problems. The second, and for all practical purposes least important, suffers from the notorious difficulties of isolating intentions. In the first and more common case the special *genre* term is frequently entirely redundant. Imagine a definition of a 'Western' as a film set in Western America between 1860 and 1900 and involving as its central theme the contrast between Garden and Desert. Any film fulfilling these requirements is a Western, and a Western is *only* a film fulfilling these requirements. By multiplying such categories it is possible to divide all films into groups, though not necessarily mutually exclusive groups. The usefulness of this (and classification can only be justified by its use) depends on what it is meant to achieve. But what *is* certain is that just as the critic determines the criteria on which the classification is based, so he also determines the name given to the resultant groups of films. Our group might just as well be called 'type 1482/9a' as 'Westerns'.

Evidently there are areas in which such individually defined categories might be of some use. A sort of bibliographic classification of the history of film, for instance, or even an abstract exploration of the cyclical recurrence of certain themes. The films would be simply defined in terms of the presence or absence of the themes in question. But this is not the way in which the term is usually employed. On the contrary, most writers tend to assume that there is some body of films we can safely call the 'Western' and then move on to the real work – the analysis of the crucial characteristics of the already recognized *genre*. Hence Kitses' set of thematic antinomies and four sorts of *genre* conventions. [...] These writers, and almost all writers using the term *genre*, are caught in a dilemma. They are *defining* a 'Western' on the basis of analysing a body of films which cannot possibly be said to be 'Westerns' until after the analysis. If Kitses' themes and conventions are the *defining* characteristic of the 'Western' then this is the previously discussed case of arbitrary definition – the category becomes redundant. But these themes and conventions are arrived at by analysing films *already distinguished from other films by virtue of being 'Westerns'*. To take a *genre* such as a 'Western', analyse it, and list its principle characteristics, is to beg the question that we must first isolate the body of films which are 'Westerns'. But they can only be isolated on the basis of the 'principal characteristics' which can only be discovered *from the films themselves* after they have been isolated. That is, we are caught in a circle which first requires that the films are isolated, for which purposes a criterion is necessary, but the criterion is, in turn, meant to emerge from the empirically established common characteristics of the films. This 'empiricist dilemma' has two solutions. One is to classify films according to *a priori* chosen criteria depending on the critical purpose. This leads back to the earlier position in which the special *genre* term is redundant. The second is to lean on a common cultural consensus as to what constitutes a 'Western', and then go on to analyse it in detail.

This latter is clearly the root of most uses of *genre*. It is this usage that leads to, for example, the notion of *conventions* in a *genre*. The 'Western', it is said, has certain crucial established conventions – ritualistic gun-fights, black/white clothing corresponding to good/bad distinctions, revenge themes, certain patterns of clothing, typed villains, and many, many more. [...]

In short, to talk about the 'Western' is (arbitrary definitions apart) to appeal to a common set of meanings in our culture. From a very early age most of us have built up a picture of a 'Western'. We feel that we know a 'Western' when we see one, though the edges may be rather blurred. Thus in calling a film a 'Western' the critic is implying more than the simple statement, 'This film is a member of a class of films ("Westerns") having in common x, y, z'. He is also suggesting that such a film would be universally recognized as such in our culture. In other words, the crucial factors which distinguished a *genre* are not *only* characteristics inherent to the films themselves; they also depend on the particular culture within which we are operating. And unless there is world consensus on the subject (which is an empirical question) there is no basis for assuming that a 'Western' will be conceived in the same way in every culture. The way in which the *genre* term is applied can quite conceivably vary from case to case. *Genre* notions – except the special case of arbitrary definition – are not critic's classifications made for special purposes; they are sets of cultural conventions. *Genre* is what we collectively believe it to be.

It is for precisely this reason that *genre* notions are so potentially interesting. But more for the exploration of the psychological and sociological interplay between film-maker, film, and audience, than for the immediate purposes of film criticism. (Given that it is not entirely possible to draw a clear line between the two, this is really an argument for using a concept in one area rather than another.) Until we have a clear, if speculative, notion of the connotations of a *genre* class, it is difficult to see how the critic, already besieged by imponderables, could usefully use the term, certainly not as a special term at the root of his analysis. To use the concept in any stronger sense it becomes necessary to establish clearly what film-makers mean when they conceive themselves as making a 'Western'; what limits such a choice may impose on them; in effect, what relationship exists between *auteur* and *genre*. But specific answers to such questions must needs tap the conceptions held by particular film-makers and industries. To methodically analyse the way in which a film-maker utilizes a *genre* for his own purposes (at present a popular critical pursuit) requires that we clearly establish the principal components of *his* conception of the *genre*. But this is not all. The notion that someone utilizes a *genre* suggests something about audience response. It implies that any given film works in such-and-such a way *because* the audience has certain expectations of the *genre*. We can only meaningfully talk of, for instance, an *auteur* breaking the rules of a *genre* if we know what these rules are. And, of course, such rule-breaking has no consequence unless the audience knows as well. [...]

This is not to suggest that *genre* terms are totally useless. It is merely that to employ them requires a much more methodical understanding of the workings of film. And this in turn requires that we specify a set of sociological and psychological context assumptions and construct explicit *genre* models within them. If we imagine a general model of the workings of film language, *genre* directs our attention to sub-languages within it. Less centrally, however, the *genre* concept is indispensable in more strictly social and psychological terms as a way of formulating the interplay between culture, audience, films, and film-makers. For example, there is a class of films thought of by a relatively highly-educated, middle-class, group of filmgoers as 'art-movies'. Now for present purposes *genre* is a conception existing in the culture of any particular group or society; it is not a way in which a critic classifies films for methodological purposes, but the much looser way in which an audience classifies its films. On this meaning of the term 'art-movies' is a *genre*. If a culture includes such *genre* notions then, over a period of time, and in a complicated way, certain conventions become established as to what can be expected from an 'art-movie' as compared to some other category. The critics (the 'posh' critics in this case) are mediating factors in such developments. But once such conventions develop they can in turn affect a film-maker's conception of what he is doing. Hence we get a commercial playing up of the 'art-movie' category. [...] It has become so much a part of our cultural patterning that film criticism has tended to use it as if it were possible to assume common agreement in all the respects on which research would be necessary in the 'art-movie' case. It may be that there is such common agreement on the 'Western'; but it does not follow that this would be true of all *genre* categories. Anyway, it is not at all clear that there is *that* much consensus on the 'Western'. [...]

In sum, then, *genre* terms seem best immediately employed in the analysis of the relation between groups of films, the cultures in which they are made, and the cultures in which they are exhibited. That is, it is a term which can be usefully employed in relation to a body of knowledge and theory about the social and psychological context of film. Any assertion we might make about the use a director makes of *genre* conventions – Peckinpah uses the contrast between our expectations and actual images to reinforce the 'end of an era' element in *Ride the High Country* and *The Wild Bunch* – assumes, wrongly, the existence of this body of knowledge. To labour the point, it assumes (1) we know what Peckinpah thinks; (2) we know what the audience thinks (a) about the films in question, and (b) about 'Westerns'; (3) Peckinpah knows the answer to (2(b)) and it is the same as our answer, etc. Most uses of *genre* effectively *invent* answers to such questions by implicitly claiming to tap some archetypal characteristic of the *genre*, some universal human response.

Notes

1   Jim Kitses, *Horizons West* (Thames and Hudson/British Film Institute, 1970), p. 19.

15 Extract from *Genre*

Steve Neale

In the preceding chapters it has been argued that genres constitute specific variations of the interplay of codes, discursive structures and drives involved in the whole of mainstream cinema. On the other hand, the point was made that genres cannot, in fact, be systematically characterised and differentiated one from another solely on the basis of such instances, taken in isolation as if they constituted specific generic essences. Time and time again it emerged that generic specificity is extremely difficult to pin down in general statements that are anything other than rudimentary and banal, such as: the narrative setting of the western is that of the American frontier; the gangster film involves the depiction of organised crime in the context of industrial capitalism; the melodrama centres its narrative structure on the vicissitudes of heterosexual love, etc. The apparent contradiction here is an important one, since it is symptomatic of the very nature of the genres themselves as systemic processes and, also, it is indicative of their function to produce regularised variety. The appearance of the contradiction is due, in other words, to the fact that genres are instances of repetition and difference.

Repetition and difference have firstly to be understood in their relationship to desire, pleasure and *jouissance*, i.e. as modalities of the process of the subject. Desire is always a function of both repetition and difference. It is founded in the difference between on the one hand the initial experience of pleasure, the mark established by that experience and which functions as its signifier(s), and on the other, future attempts to repeat the experience, future repetitions of the signifier(s). Desire is hence also founded on the urge to repeat and the impossibility of ever being able to do so. The reproduction of the signifier allows satisfaction, but it is a satisfaction marked by the gap between signifier and experience. The existence of the gap is the reason for the inexhaustibility of desire, but it also allows whatever satisfaction is attainable to be renewed. Hence pleasure lies both in the repetition of the signifier(s) and in the limited but nonetheless fundamental difference underpinning and separating such instances of repetition. The subject is maintained in an oscillation that thus rarely threatens either its pleasure or its existence. That threat only occurs in moments of *jouissance*: the possibility of 'total' pleasure, the extinction of desire, of death. Or, as Paul Willemen explains:

> The term *jouissance* is an untranslatable term used by some psychoanalysts to suggest a 'beyond pleasure', intimately linking desire and death with the death drive as the dominant partner. Pleasure is located in the moment of homeostasis between tension and its release, in the zero between before and after. But whereas pleasure is founded on the (quasi) repeatability of such moments, i.e. the possibility to annul the moment of annulation of tension, *jouissance* relates to the freezing of such a zero, to the representation of annulation which is not reversable (i.e. death).[1]

Hence Roland Barthes' distinction:

> Text of pleasure: the text that contents, fills, grants euphoria; the text that comes from culture and does not break with it, is linked to a *comfortable* practice of reading. Text of bliss (jouissance): the text that imposes a state of loss, the text that discomforts (perhaps to the point of boredom), unsettles the reader's historical, cultural, psychological assumptions, the consistency of his tastes, values, memories, brings to a crisis his relation with language.[2]

The mainstream narrative is nothing if not a 'text of pleasure': a text that regulates the subject's desire for pleasure, that functions, therefore, according to a precise economy of difference (the movement of desire, the subject ceaselessly in process) and of repetition (the containment of that movement, its repletion, the subject ceaselessly closed through the recuperation of difference in figures of tightly bound symmetry). [...]

The spectator, then, is maintained as subject in an economy of narration through the articulation or desire. The mainstream narrative text operates as a binding of desire in the figuration of coherence, a coherence that is specified anew in each individual text through its own particular textual system (each film consists of its difference from any other). This system engages specific versions of the figures, functions and logics allowed by the economy of the mainstream system (in this respect, each film is an instance of repetition of this system itself, the same as any other mainstream film).

Genres intervene between the two instances of process, of subject regulation: that of the mainstream narrative and that of the individual text. Genres thus establish a regulation of the variety of mainstream narrative across a series of individual texts, organising and systematising the difference that each text represents, filling in the gap between text and system. For example, genres can be directly related to the textual economy of the mainstream narrative in that they systematise its regime of difference and repetition, specifying its rhythm of oscillation between the two. In this way genres function to move the subject from text to text and from text to narrative system, binding these instances together into a constant coherence, the coherence of the cinematic institution. In doing so, genres themselves are marked by a similar economy of repetition and difference. If the nature of that economy can perhaps best be characterised as one of repetition and limited difference, it should, however, be stressed that the element of difference is not only real but fundamental. The notion that 'all westerns (or all gangster films, or all war films, or whatever) are the same' is not just an unwarranted generalisation, it is profoundly wrong: if each text within a genre were, literally, the same, there would simply not be enough difference to generate either meaning or pleasure. Hence there would be no audience. Difference is absolutely essential to the economy of genre. As Jacques Lacan stressed, 'Repetition demands the new'. Moreover, repetition and difference are themselves not separable, either as 'entities', so to speak, or, even, as tendencies: they function as a relation. There is hence not repetition *and* difference, but repetition *in* difference. Bearing in mind the nature of the economy of genre, an economy of variation rather than of rupture, a better formulation as far as genre is concerned would be: difference *in* repetition.

The mechanism which produces this element of difference in each instance of repetition at the level of the individual text has been outlined by Yuri Lotman as follows:

> Repetition means the same as equivalence, which emerges as the basis of an incomplete sameness, where there is one level (or more) at which the elements are the same together with one (or more) at which they aren't. Equivalence cannot be reduced to a dead uniformity; which is precisely why it includes dissimilarity. Similar levels organise dissimilar ones in that they establish relations of similarity within them, while simultaneously dissimilar levels work in the opposite direction, pointing up difference within similarity.[3]

The same kind of mechanism is at work on the level of genre itself, where it is similarly the case that what is involved is not simply a single system but rather a combination of several systems, so that any instance of repetition is always subject to the modifications that that combination produces. For instance, this proposition has a number of consequences for the notions of iconography. Visual signifiers are usually held to constitute 'icons' (i.e. signifiers of a particular genre) if they are subject to regular occurrences, i.e. repetitions. Their function is generally considered to be the establishment of a stable framework of signs in relation to which difference and variation can be both produced on the one hand and read and understood on the other. However, once it is established that repetition always involves an element of difference, that difference and variation are properties not only of the elements outside the framework so to speak, but also of the framework itself, then the nature and function of iconography have to be re-thought, if, indeed, the term is to be retained at all. Iconography would consist not of individual visual signifiers, repeated identically across a series of generic texts, nor even of the relations between them, conceived as the function of a single system, but rather of the 'rules' governing both the successive appearances of those signifiers and the transformations to which they are subject. Its function would consist in the provision of that which systematises both repetition and difference at the level of the visual image.

At the root of the presence of difference in repetition, and at the root of the mechanisms which govern its manifestation, is the fact of the existence of process. It is this, above all, that is responsible not only for the double-edged nature of iconography, but for the double-edged nature of genres themselves, one in which a rule-bound element and an element of transgression are both equally important. It is process, therefore, that accounts for the contradiction outlined at the beginning of this chapter. It accounts, on the one hand, for the fact that genres appear to constitute clearly defined systems and, on the other, for the fact that they are rarely, if ever, susceptible to detailed analysis as such. As Jean-Louis Leutrat noted in his analysis of the western genre:

> Genre being the locus par excellence of repetition and difference, it is necessary to disengage both the constant and the variable elements. This operation requires a prior diachronic investigation, as variation manifests itself in the course of a historical development. By the same token, it is impossible to give a definition of a genre. All one can do is remain on the level of observation and note some facts. One can confirm the existence of the genre when one has disengaged a series of 'works related to each other by means of a structure that establishes a continuity and which is manifested in a historical series'.[4]

Genres, then, are not systems: they are processes of systematisation. It is only as such that they can perform the role allotted them by the cinematic institution. It is only as such that they can function to provide, simultaneously, both regulation and variety.

Notes

1 Paul Willemen, 'Notes Towards the Construction of Readings of Tourneur' in *Jacques Tourneur*, (eds.) P. Willemen and C. Johnston (Edinburgh, 1975), p. 35.
2 Roland Barthes, *The Pleasure of the Text* (London, 1976), p. 14.
3 Yuri Lotman, *La Structure du Texte Artistique* (Paris, 1973), p. 131.
4 Jean-Louis Leutrat, *Le Western* (Paris, 1973), p. 22. The final sentence is a quote from Hans-Robert Jauss' article in *Poétique*, no. **1**, p. 82.

16 The woman's film

Christine Geraghty

[...] Women's fiction is usually and rightly in a sense labelled as 'escapist' or 'fantasy'. It is associated with an allegedly self-indulgent desire to move away from reality and to retreat into another world created by the fiction. It is as if women are taking time out and in doing so are laying both themselves and their source of escape open to criticism. Janice Radway describes the act of romance reading as a means of the reader absenting herself from the demands of her work in the home; 'reading in this sense,' she suggests 'connotes a free space where they [romance readers] feel liberated from the need to perform duties that they otherwise willingly accept as their own'.[1] Although little work has been done on analysing film audiences for the woman's picture of the 1930s and 1940s, it seems likely that the woman's film gave female audiences a socially acceptable reason for getting out of the home and escaping into the unobserved dark of the cinema. [...]

This creation of another space by the act of enjoying women's fiction is reinforced within the fictions themselves by the organisation of their narratives around utopian possibilities. The most common criticism of fiction aimed at women is paradoxically either that it is too happily escapist or that it is too depressing. On the one hand, the romance is seen as a fantasy, offering a happy ending in which no one could really believe while on the other, the unhappy ending of many woman's films led to the derogatory nicknames of 'weepies' or 'four handkerchief pictures'. In both cases, the absorption of the female reader, bound up in the emotional life of fictional heroines, is the subject of derogatory comment. [...] Women's fiction thus tends to be seen as excessive both in the unreality of the world it creates and in the emotional response it demands from the reader. The importance of the other worlds which are at the heart of women's fiction is that they offer models of both happiness and grief and the opportunity thereby to rehearse the extremes of emotional feeling; they establish utopias in which emotional needs are imaginatively fulfilled or, more frighteningly, distopias in which the values of women's fiction are undermined and destroyed. If this is recognised it becomes possible to see why 'escapist' may be a proper term for much women's fiction and that its derogatory connotations are ill placed. [...]

The woman's film

Feminist writing on romance has clearly taken up the challenge of the epithet 'escapist' and has reworked it sympathetically, though not uncritically, to analyse the appeal of the romance. The other world created by women's fiction is not always so harmonious, however, and in the woman's films of the 1930s and 1940s critics have found a rather different appeal being made to a female audience. Rather more than with the romance, there have been problems as to how to define a woman's film and to fit any proposed definition into the broader perspective of melodrama. At one level, the definition requires simply (although the implications are far from simple) the presence of a central woman protagonist. Pam Cook argues that 'the woman's picture is differentiated from the rest of cinema by virtue of its construction of a "female point-of-view" which motivates and dominates the narrative, and its specific address to a female audience'.[2] Maria LaPlace, in her exemplary analysis of the film, *Now Voyager*, refers to the industrial situation which led the Hollywood studio system in the 1930s and 1940s to produce so many woman's films and points out that gender-differentiated surveys conducted by the Hollywood studios concluded that women audiences preferred female stars. LaPlace thus concurs with Cook on the importance of the central female figure in the woman's film and adds other criteria familiar from our study of soap opera: 'the woman's film is distinguished by its female protagonist, female point of view and its narrative which most often revolves around the traditional realms of women's experience: the familial, the domestic, the romantic.'[3] Mary Ann Doane refines her definition more specifically to the assumption of a female audience as the premise on which the films are made, commenting on: 'the nomenclature by means of which certain films of the 1940s are situated as "women's pictures" – a label which stipulates that the films are in some sense the "possession" of women and that their terms of address are dictated by the anticipated presence of the female spectator.'[4]

A broad definition based on a female protagonist and an address to a female audience is thus a possibility, but it covers a multitude of films and behind its wide front lurks a confusing number of sub-genres including the maternal melodrama,[5] the 'gaslight' genre[6] and what LaPlace calls 'the "heroine's text", a story of a woman's personal triumph over adversity'.[7] The central female protagonist in such films may be the successful career woman (*Imitation of Life*), the grieving, self-sacrificing mother (*Stella Dallas*), the emerging individual (*Now Voyager*) or the self-abnegating woman who demands nothing (*Letter from an Unknown Woman*). We need to recognise that not only does the woman's film, unlike the more orderly romance, allow for a number of narratives, it is also criss-crossed by other genres – melodrama, film noir and horror among them. There is indeed a certain confusion between how far it is necessary to distinguish between a woman's film and melodrama and how precisely individual films of the period can be placed. Christine Gledhill suggests that this uncertainty can be traced to the films themselves: 'confusion – or contest – is suggested by the range of permutations produced in the 1930s between patriarchal melodrama and women's fiction, offering such sub-genres as maternal sacrifice, fallen woman and romantic melodramas alongside women's pictures.'[8]

What seems to hold such films together as a group is the underwriting of the importance of domestic values and the acknowledgement of the critical role of women in determining the nature of emotional relationships. In creating a world in which female strengths can be valued, the woman's film, like the romance, sets up the possibility of a different kind of society but unlike the romance it goes on to dramatise the high cost paid by the heroines who seek to make such a world. The conventionally unhappy endings of these films seem to be the counter weight to the equally conventional happy endings of the romance. In one way or another, the different variants of the woman's film mark out the precariousness of the romance's utopia.

Two rather different instances of the genre can be cited here. The first is the cycle of films which Doane calls 'the paranoid woman's film'[9] – films like *Rebecca*,

Secret Beyond the Door and *Suspicion* – in which the newly married wife comes to believe that her husband is a (potential) killer who is likely to turn on her. Far from setting women's desire in the utopian world of the romance, this variant of the woman's picture presents a world of shadowy terrors in which the woman's viewpoint is distorted by paranoia and fear. The heroine is isolated and confused, her helplessness reinforced by her inability to make sense of the world in which she finds herself. In such films, women's desire is marked as illness and 'the woman's ability to see is frequently questioned; she may be ... blinded by desire (*Spellbound*), or lost in a world of shadows and uncertainty (*Rebecca, Suspicion*). Her desire is often presented as a symptom, resulting in mental and physical illness.'[10] Doane points out that in the most paranoid of these women's films, the strict separation of the public and domestic, male and female space is breached; 'the paradigmatic woman's space – the home – is yoked to dread, and a crisis of vision.'[11] The woman's fear that her husband is going to kill her manifests itself in the dark corners, hidden rooms, twisting staircases and blind windows of the home of which she is notionally the mistress. This gothic version of the woman's film allows a happy ending only through the heroine's active acquiescence in suffering, making herself the potential victim in order to allow the 'misreading' of her husband's nature to be revealed, accused of madness herself in trying to cure her husband's madness. In such woman's films, female values struggle to survive and the transformation of the hero, if it is achieved at all, is a fragile and precarious victory.

The other strand of the woman's film offers a more positive heroine even if her strength is not always recognised by the other male characters. In films such as *Imitation of Life*, *Now Voyager*, *Stella Dallas* and *Letter from an Unknown Woman*, the heroines learn how to survive, to bring up children and to express their emotions without the support of the hero. Even in those films where the woman is unable to mould the world to her desires, her capacity to act on her own decisions is critical. The unhappy endings of *Stella Dallas* and *Letter from an Unknown Woman*, for instance, in which the woman loses or gives up her child, still acknowledge the stoical strength of the heroines and their capacity to feel emotion which the men in the films cannot match and which they undervalue because they cannot understand it. The audience is invited to recognise female worth even if in these films it cannot transform the world and the woman can only forlornly gaze into a society which is incapable of responding to her needs. In other films, the heroines are more successful in establishing an order which accommodates and sustains them. In *Now Voyager*, the heroine, Charlotte, transforms the gothic mansion of her mother's house into an ideal world in which 'peace and contentment' are the norm. LaPlace describes it as a domestic utopia and comments that 'the space has been transformed into one of laughter, light, music and gaiety'.[12] In Stahl's *Imitation of Life*, the heroine, her financial security threatened by the death of her husband, establishes a business which enables her to be financially independent and live luxuriously in the home which she has paid for. At the end of both films, the heroines specifically reject the hero's offer of romance and thereby refuse him the role of head of the household. Other relationships, particularly that between mother and daughter, are given value and indeed take precedence over that between the hero and heroine so that both films end with the woman's rejection of a central relationship with the man in favour of a domestic harmony which she controls.

Critical analysis of what the woman's film offers its female audience has been less unified than work on the romance's appeal. Conclusions vary considerably, in part because critics frequently argue a general position on the basis of an analysis of particular films and, as we have seen, the films themselves differ quite considerably in their narrative organisation and themes. Maria LaPlace, in her analysis of the discourses which sustain *Now Voyager*, suggests that the film's use of women's wider culture has created despite itself 'a symbolic system in which women can try to make sense of their lives and even create imaginative spaces for resistance'.[13] Doane, looking specifically at the gothic paranoid sub-group, argues that by transmuting women's desire into metaphors of illness and paranoia, the woman's film works effectively 'to deny the woman the space of a reading ... it functions quite precisely to immobilise.'[14] Williams, on the other hand, in her discussion of *Stella Dallas*, questions this assumption that the female audience automatically identifies with the heroine and asserts that 'melodrama does not reconcile its audience to an inevitable suffering. Rather than raging against a fate that the audience has learnt to accept, the female hero often accepts a fate that the audience at least partially questions.'[15] As we shall see, when we consider the way in which these films organise their utopian possibilities, the imagined world of the woman's film is a more complex and difficult one than that offered by the romance.

Notes

1 Janice A. Radway, *Reading the Romance Women: Patriarchy and Popular Literature* (University of North Carolina Press Chapel Hill NC. 1984). p. 93.
2 Pam Cook, 'Melodrama and the Women's Picture', in Sue Aspinall and Robert Murphy (eds), *Gainsborough Melodrama* (British Film Institute, London, 1983), p. 14.
3 Maria LaPlace, 'Producing and Consuming the Woman's Film Discursive Struggle in *Now Voyager*', in Christine Gledhill (ed.), *Home Is Where the Heart Is* (British Film Institute, London, 1987), p. 138.
4 Mary Ann Doane, 'The "Woman's Film": Possession and Address', in Mary Ann Doane, Patricia Mellencamp and Linda Williams (eds), *Revision: Essays in Feminist Film Criticism* (American Film Institute, USA, 1984), p. 68.
5 See E. Ann Kaplan, 'Mothering, Feminism and Representation: The Maternal in Melodrama and the Woman's Film 1910–40' and Christian Viviani, 'Who Is Without Sin? The Maternal Melodrama in American Film, 1930–39,' both in Gledhill, *Home Is Where the Heart Is*.
6 See Doane, 'The "Woman's Film" '.
7 LaPlace, 'Producing and Consuming the Woman's Film', p. 151.
8 Christine Gledhill, 'The Melodramatic Field: An Investigation', in Gledhill, *Home Is Where the Heart Is*, p. 36.
9 Doane, 'The "Woman's Film" ' p. 69.
10 Cook, 'Melodrama and the Women's Picture', p. 20.
11 Doane, 'The "Woman's Film" ' p. 70.
12 LaPlace, 'Producing and Consuming the Woman's Film', p. 164.
13 Ibid., p. 165.
14 Doane, 'The "Woman's Film" ', p. 80.
15 Linda Williams, ' "Something Else Besides a Mother": *Stella Dallas* and the Maternal Melodrama', in Gledhill, *Home Is Where the Heart Is*, p. 320.

17 American film noir: the history of an idea

James Naremore

Only that which has no history is definable.

– FRIEDRICH NIETZSCHE

The past is not dead. It isn't even past.

– WILLIAM FAULKNER

It has always been easier to recognize a film noir than to define the term. One can easily imagine a large video store where examples of such films would be shelved somewhere between Gothic horror and dystopian science fiction: in the center would be *Double Indemnity*, and at either margin *Cat People* and *Invasion of the Body Snatchers*. But this arrangement would leave out important titles. There is in fact no completely satisfactory way to organize the category, and nobody is sure whether the films in question constitute a period, a genre, a cycle, a style, or simply a 'phenomenon.'[1]

Whatever noir 'is', the standard histories say it originated in America, emerging out of a synthesis of hard-boiled fiction and German Expressionism. The term is also associated with certain visual and narrative traits, which some commentators have tried to localize in the period between 1941 and 1958. Others contend that noir began much earlier and never went away.[2] One of the most comprehensive (but far from complete) references, Alain Silver and Elizabeth Ward's *Film Noir: An Encyclopedia of the American Style* begins in 1927 and ends in the present, listing over 500 motion pictures of various stylistic and generic descriptions.[3]

Encyclopedic surveys of the Silver and Ward type can be educational and enter-taining, but they also have a kinship with Jorge Luis Borges's fictional work of Chinese scholarship, *The Celestial Emporium of Benevolent Knowledge*, which contains a whimsical taxonomy of the animal kingdom: those belonging to the Emperor; mermaids; stray dogs; those painted with a fine camel's-hair brush; those resembling flies from a distance; others; etc. Unfortunately, nothing links together all the things discussed as noir – not the theme of crime, not a cinemato-graphic technique, not even a resistance to Aristotelian narratives or happy endings. Little wonder that no writer has been able to find the category's neces-sary and sufficient characteristics, and that many generalizations in the critical literature are open to question. If noir is American in origin, why does it have a French name? (The two Frenchmen who supposedly coined the term, writing separate essays in 1946, were referring to an international style.) More intrigu-ingly, if the heyday of noir was 1941–58, why did the term not enjoy widespread use until the 1970s? A plausible case could indeed be made that, far from dying out with the old studio system, noir is almost entirely a creation of postmodern culture – a belated reading of classic Hollywood that was popularized by cinéastes of the French New Wave, appropriated by reviewers, academics, and film-makers, and then recycled on TV.

At any rate, a term that was born in specialist periodicals and revival theaters has now become a major signifier of sleekly commodified artistic ambition. Almost 20 per cent of the titles currently on the National Film Preservation List at the Library of Congress are associated with noir, as are most of the early volumes in the British Film Institute 'Film Classics' series. Meanwhile, 'neo noirs' are produced by Hollywood with increasing regularity and prominence. Consider the last three American winners of the Grand Prize at Cannes: *Wild at Heart* (1991), *Barton Fink* (1992), and *Pulp Fiction* (1994). Consider also such big-budget television productions as 'Twin Peaks,' 'Wild Palms' (marketed to ABC as 'TV noir'), and 'Fallen Angels'.

Some of these instances might be described as 'pastiche', but pastiche of what? The classical model is notoriously difficult to pin down, in part because it was named by critics rather than film-makers, who did not speak of film noir until well after it was established as a feature of academic writing. Nowadays, the term is ubiquitous, appearing in reviews and promotions of many things besides movies. If we want to understand it, or to make sense of genres or art-historical categories in general, we need to recognize that film noir belongs to the history of ideas as much as to the history of cinema; it has less to do with a group of artifacts than with a discourse – a loose, evolving system of arguments and readings, helping to shape commercial strategies and aesthetic ideologies.

It seems odd that film theorists did not arrive at this conclusion long ago. After all, the Name of the Genre (or Mood, or Generic Tendency, or whatever) functions in much the same way as the Name of the Author. Michel Foucault has pointed out that the 'author function' is tied to the 'institutional system that encompasses, determines, and articulates the universe of discourses'.[4] The author, Foucault says, is chiefly a means of textual *classification*, allowing us to establish 'a relationship of homogeneity, filiation, authentification of some texts by the use of others' (147). At bottom, these relationships are psychological 'projections,' governed by the belief that there must be 'a point where contradictions are resolved, where incompatible elements are at last tied together or organized around a fundamental and originating contradiction' (151).

Could we not say exactly the same things about the 'genre function'? And could we not ask of it many of the same questions that Foucault asks of authorship: What are the modes of existence of this discourse? Where has it been used, how can it circulate, and who can appropriate it (160)? In the case of film noir, one of the most amorphous yet important categories in film history, these questions seem particularly apt. As a start toward answering them, the following pages offer a commentary on early writings about noir. Instead of looking for the essential features of a group of films, I shall try to explain a paradox: film noir is both an important cinematic legacy and an idea we have projected onto the past.

Noir is born: Paris, 1946–59

[...] We can never say when the first film noir was made, but everyone agrees that significant *writings* on American noir began to appear in French film journals in August, 1946. [...] The term was used in discussions of five Hollywood features made during the war, all of which had just been exhibited in succession on Paris movie screens: *The Maltese Falcon*; *Double Indemnity*; *Laura*; *Murder, My Sweet*;

and – somewhat surprisingly, in light of the fact that it disappears from most subsequent writings – *The Lost Weekend*. Another picture released in Paris that summer, *Woman in the Window*, described by one French reviewer as a 'bourgeois tragedy', was later to become a noir classic.[5] The forthcoming MGM production of *The Postman Always Rings Twice* was mentioned alongside the initial group of five, and *Citizen Kane*, which was also mentioned, was placed in a class by itself. Critical discussion centred mainly on the first four thrillers – which, even though they were not exactly alike (*The Maltese Falcon* does not have a first-person narrator or flashbacks, and *Laura* is not based on a hard-boiled novel), seemed to belong together. These films would become the prototypical members of an emergent category, and they would have an unusual influence on French thinking for over a decade.

In one sense the French invented film noir, and they did so because local conditions predisposed them to view Hollywood in certain ways. As R. Barton Palmer has observed, France possessed a sophisticated film culture consisting of theatres, journals, and 'ciné-clubs' where movies were treated as art rather than as commercial entertainment.[6] Equally important, the decade after the liberation saw a resurgence of Americanism among directors and critics, many of whom sought to refashion the French art cinema along the more 'authentic' lines of Hollywood genre movies. A *nouvelle vague* would eventually grow out of this dialectic between America and Europe, and the so-called film noir – which was visibly indebted to European modernism – became the most important category in French criticism. [...]

Reviewers in the United States had already seen a vague connection between the pictures [...] but they made no attempt to invent a new term.[7] [...] French writers, on the other hand, were fascinated with the noir metaphor [...] Over the next decade, as the category expanded and became the subject of retrospectives and catalogues raisonnés, French critics often praised noir for its dynamism, its cruelty, and its irrationality; but they also searched the dark Hollywood streets for what Chartier called 'accents of rebellion' against the 'fatality of evil'. [...][8]

French discussion of American film noir was conditioned by the prevailing and sometimes conflicting trends in Left Bank intellectual culture. The importance of existentialism to the period has long been recognized; what needs to be emphasized is that French existentalism was intertwined with a residual surrealism, which was crucial for the reception of any art described as noir. [...] The surrealists were [...] attracted to the cinema of the 'social fantastic', to stories about doomed erotic love, and to Hollywood thrillers with Sadeian titles. Among their particular favorites were movies about gangsterism and murder, partly because such pictures depicted violent, antisocial behavior, and partly because they bestowed an aura of the marvelous upon ordinary urban decor. [...] Not surprisingly, such films were admired and discussed in *L'Age du cinéma*, a surrealist publication of 1951, and in *Positif*, which maintained strong connections to surrealism throughout the 1950s and 60s. They were also given their first important study in a book that was profoundly surrealist in its ideological aims: Raymond Borde and Etienne Chaumeton's *Panorama du film noir américain* (1955), which has been described as a 'benchmark' for all later work on the topic.[9] [...]

Throughout, an 'objective' tone serves as a mask for the celebration of kinky irrationality. Borde and Chaumeton have surprisingly little to say about visual style (the

French were generally unimpressed by what Bazin called 'plastics' or expressionist imagery); in fact they emphasize that the dark atmosphere of Hollywood crime movies is *'nothing in itself'* and ought not to be adopted for its own sake (180). On the other hand, they place great emphasis on the theme of death, and on the 'essential' affective qualities of noir, which they list in the form of five adjectives typical of surrealism: 'oneiric, bizarre, erotic, ambivalent, and cruel' (3).[10] [...]

But according to Borde and Chaumeton, there are also noir narratives and characters; and at this level film noir becomes a full-fledged outlaw genre, systematically reversing Hollywood's foundational myths. True films of the type, Borde and Chaumeton insist, not only take place 'inside the criminal milieu,' but also represent 'the point of view of criminals' (7). Such films are 'moral' in an approximately surrealist sense: instead of incorruptible legal agents, they give us shady private eyes, crooked policemen, murderous plainclothes detectives, or lying district attorneys. [...]

It follows that the ideal noir hero is the opposite of John Wayne. Psychologically, he is passive, masochistic, morbidly curious; physically, he is 'often mature, almost old, not very handsome. Humphrey Bogart is the type' (10). By the same logic, the noir heroine is no Doris Day. Borde and Chaumeton never allude to the Marquis de Sade's Juliette, one of the most famous sexual terrorists in French literature,[11] but the character they describe resembles her in every respect save the fact that she is 'fatal even to herself' (10). Beautiful, adept with firearms, and 'probably frigid', this new woman contributes to a distinctive noir eroticism, 'which is usually no more than the eroticization of violence' (10).[12] [...]

Above all, Borde and Chaumeton are intrigued by the way film noir has 'revived the theme of violence' (10). [...] 'In this incoherent brutality', Borde and Chaumeton remark, 'there is the feeling of a dream' (12). Indeed the narratives themselves are often situated on the margins of dreams, as if to intensify the surrealist atmosphere of violent confusion or disequilibrium that Borde and Chaumeton regard as the very basis of noir. 'All the components of noir style,' they write, are designed to 'disorient the spectator' (14). [...] French discussion of noir was also affected by existentialist literature and philosophy, which placed emphasis on different matters. Existentialism was despairingly humanist rather than perversely anarchic, and it had a different attitude toward violence; thus if the surrealists saw the Hollywood thriller as a theater of cruelty, the existentialists saw it as an absurdist novel. For critics who were influenced by existentialism, film noir was especially attractive because it depicted a world of obsessive return, dark corners, and *huis clos*. [...]

In the years before and after the war, when the French themselves were entrapped by history, several themes of French existential philosophy had been elaborated through readings of such novelists as Hammett, Chandler, and Cain, who were often bracketed with Wright, Hemingway, Dos Passos, and Faulkner; indeed the French 'discovered' several of these talents, just as they later discovered the Hollywood auteurs. [...]

This passion for literary toughness has an interesting relation to the social and political climate after the war. [...] The left had been in disarray in the West since the Nazi–Soviet pact, and the situation in France was complicated by the fact that the country had recently emerged from what the French themselves described as *les années noires* – a time of torture, compromise, and collaboration.[13] Faced with a choice between capitalism and Stalinism, many French artists tried to achieve 'freedom' through individualized styles of resistance. For them, prewar American novels offered a model – especially novels depicting a violent, corrupt world in which ambiguous personal action is the only redemptive gesture. [...] Sartre claimed that modern life had become 'fantastic', as if it were made up of a 'labyrinth of hallways, doors, and stairways that lead nowhere, innumerable signposts that dot routes and signify nothing'.[14]

Bazin's style of existentialism is everywhere apparent in his 1957 eulogy for Humphrey Bogart, written only two years before his own death. According to Bazin, Bogart was important because 'the *raison d'être* of his existence was in some sense to survive', and because the alcoholic lines on his face revealed 'the corpse on reprieve within each of us' (Hillier, 98). Jean Gabin, the star of prewar French films noirs, seemed romantic by comparison; Bogart was a man '*defined* by fate', and because he was associated with 'the *noir* crime film whose ambiguous hero he was to epitomize', he became the quintessential 'actor/myth of the postwar period' (Hillier, 99). Bazin argued that Bogart's portrayal of Sam Spade was theoretically equivalent to the almost simultaneous release of *Citizen Kane*: 'It must be the case', he wrote, 'that there is some secret harmony in the coincidence of these events: the end of the prewar period, the arrival of a certain novelistic style of cinematographic *écriture*, and, through Bogart, the triumph of interiorization and ambiguity' (Hillier, 100).

The 'ambiguity' of which Bazin speaks is quite different from the disorientation or inversion of moral norms valued by the surrealists. It has more to do with ethical complexity, and with the cinema's ability to capture what Bazin elsewhere calls the 'structure of reality' in all its phenomenological uncertainty. Likewise, Bazin's 'interiorization' has little to do with the Freudian subconscious. It suggests instead a radical isolation or individuality that forces the subject to create identity out of existential choice. Bazin apparently believes that the 'secret harmony' linking Bogart and Welles is a byproduct of what French literary critic Claude-Edmonde Magny (in a book heavily influenced by Sartre) had called 'the age of the American novel'.[15] On a more general level, however, the themes of isolation, uncertainty, and ambiguity must have exerted a strong appeal to anyone who was wary of collective politics and inclined to treat social issues in terms of personal ethics.

During this period, younger critics at *Cahiers* began to project Bazin's ideas onto films noirs, which became existential, depoliticized allegories of the white male condition. The favored existential hero, however, was not Bogart but Nicholas Ray, who directed *They Live by Night, In a Lonely Place*, and *On Dangerous Ground*. [...]

At this juncture, 'film noir' and 'auteur' began to work in tandem, expressing the same values from different angles. (It is no accident that the two terms would enter the English language at the same moment.) Film noir was a collective style operating within and against the Hollywood system; and the auteur was an individual stylist who achieved freedom over the studio through existential choice. [...]

In 1959, Godard's *Breathless* was released, and Truffaut's *Shoot the Piano Player* soon followed. Both films were [...] littered with references to Bogart, *Gun Crazy, On Dangerous Ground*, etc.;[16] and both made film noir available as a 'pretext' for directors who wanted to assert their personalities. [...] The first age of film noir had come to an end.

Darkness everywhere

The discourse on noir was initiated by two generations of Parisian intellectuals who announced the death of the form soon after they discovered it. [...] Eventually, French critical terminology migrated to Britain and America, where it exerted considerable influence and acquired new interpreters. By the 1990s, it had become what Dennis Hopper describes as 'every director's favorite genre'.[17]

A complete history of noir in America would take into account such things as New York film culture in the East Village during the late 1950s, or the Bogart cult that developed at the Brattle Theater in Cambridge, Mass., in the early 1960s. It would look closely at the role of alternative criticism and college film societies in the late 1960s and early 1970s. On a more general level, it would consider the Vietnam war (a structuring absence in Paul Schrader's 'Notes on *Film Noir*'); the rise of academic film theory; the vast changes in the economics and censorship of Hollywood; and the increasing dissolution of discursive boundaries between high and commercial art.

Today, the 'original' films noirs still circulate alongside new ones. The noir mediascape in the late twentieth century spreads across virtually every national boundary and every form of communication, including museum retrospectives, college courses, parodies, remakes, summertime blockbusters, mass-market paperbacks, experimental literature and painting, made-for-TV films (there is a significant B-movie industry known in the trade as 'cable noir'), and soft-core 'erotic thrillers' that go directly to video stores. Why has noir become so important? The answer is beyond the scope of an essay, but it seems obvious that the idea of film noir has been useful to the movie industry, providing artistic cachet and spectacular opportunities for both the 'New Hollywood' auteurs of the 1970s and the sex-and-violence specialists of the 1980s. The more interesting question is whether a category developed by critics to influence what Borde and Chaumeton called 'the occidental and American public of the 1950s' (5) can function in the same way for us. [...]

Quite obviously, a concept that was generated ex post facto has become part of a worldwide mass memory; a dream image of bygone glamour, it represses as much history as it recalls, usually in the service of cinephilia and commodification. Not every recent instance of film noir [...] can be explained in this way, and it would be naïve to assume that the classic films noirs were ever free of show business and the consumer economy. Nevertheless, the term now plays a central role in the vocabulary of ludic, commercialized postmodernism.[18] Depending on how it is used, it can describe a dead period, a nostalgia for something that never existed, or perhaps even a vital tradition. One thing is clear: the last film noir is no easier to name than the first. [...]

Notes

1 Film noir is described as a genre by, among others, Robin Buss, *French Film Noir* (London: Marion Boyars, 1994); Charles Higham and Joel Greenburg, *Hollywood in the Forties* (New York: A. S. Barnes, 1968); Foster Hirsch, *The Dark Side of the Screen* (New York: A. S. Barnes, 1981); Alain Silver and Elizabeth Ward, eds., *Film Noir: An Encyclopedia of the American Style* (Woodstock, N.Y.: Overlook Press, rev. ed., 1992); and Jon Tuska, *Dark Cinema: American Film Noir in Cultural Perspective* (Westport, CT: Greenwood Press, 1984). Noir is a movement or period characterized by 'tone and

mood' in Paul Schrader, 'Notes on *Film Noir*', in *Film Genre Reader*, ed. Barry Keith Grant (Austin, TX: University of Texas Press, 1986), pp. 167–82; a set of 'patterns of nonconformity' within the classical Hollywood style in David Bordwell, Janet Staiger, and Kristin Thompson, *The Clasical Hollywood Cinema* (New York: Columbia University Press, 1985); a series in Raymond Borde and Eugene Chaumeton, *Panorama du film noir américain, 1941–1953* (Paris: Editions du Minuit, 1955); a motif and tone in Raymond Durgnat, 'Paint It Black: The Family Tree of Film Noir', *Cinema* nos. 6–7 (1970), pp. 49–56; a visual style in J. A. Place and L. S. Peterson, 'Some Visual Motifs of *Film Noir*', *Film Comment*, vol. 10, no. 1 (1974), pp. 13–18; a canon in J. P. Telotte, *Voices in the Dark: The Narrative Patterns of Film Noir* (Urbana, IL: University of Illinois Press, 1989); a phenomenon in Frank Krutnik, *In a Lonely Street: Film Noir, Genre, Masculinity* (London: Rutgers, 1991); and a transgeneric phenomenon in R. Barton Palmer, *Hollywood's Dark Cinema: The American Film Noir* (New York: Twayne, 1994). For an argument similar to Palmer's, see John Belton, 'Film Noir's Knights of the Road', *Bright Lights Film Journal* 12 (Spring 1994), pp. 5–15.

2 The dates 1941–1958 seem to have been first proposed by Schrader, who used *The Maltese Falcon* and *Touch of Evil* to mark the beginning and end of the noir period. Schrader's position is accepted by Place and Peterson, and by a few writers in E. Ann Kaplan, ed., *Women in Film Noir* (London: BFI, 1980). Several other books on film noir implicity endorse this periodization, even when they do not set fixed dates; see, for example, Telotte and Krutnik. Most recent discussions treat film noir as a genre that begins somewhere in the late 30s or early 40s and continues to the present day; see Palmer, and many of the essayists in Joan Copjec, ed., *Shades of Noir* (London: Verso, 1993). In the Copjec volume, there are skeptical voices; see especially Marc Vernet, '*Film Noir* on the Edge of Doom', pp. 1–31, who questions many of the standard historical and stylistic assumptions.

3 The Silver and Ward encyclopedia omits a number of titles that might logically be called film noir, but as Marc Vernet has noted, one of the beauties of the category is that 'there is always an unknown film to be added to the list'. For a larger filmography, see Spencer Selby, *Dark City: The Film Noir* (Jefferson, N. C.: McFarland, 1984).

4 'What Is an Author?', in V. Harari, ed., *Textual Strategies* (Ithaca, N.Y.: Cornell University Press, 1979), p. 153. All further references are noted in the text.

5 Jacques Bourgeois, 'La Tragédie policier', *Revue du cinéma* 2 (1946), pp. 70–72.

6 Palmer is almost the only writer on film noir to have recognized that movies have different meanings for different audiences. My survey of French criticism differs from his in substantial ways, but I recommend his excellent survey of writings on noir in *Hollywood's Dark Cinema*, pp. 1–31.

7 One exception to this rule was Siegfried Kracauer, writing in the same month that the French coined the term film noir ('Hollywood's Terror Films: Do They Reflect an American State of Mind?', *Commentary* 2 (August 1946), pp. 132–36). Kracauer had recently completed *From Caligari to Hitler*, his book about German expressionist cinema, and he used the same arguments to discuss a recent spate of American 'terror films', including *Shadow of a Doubt, The Stranger, The Dark Corner, The Spiral Staircase*, and *The Lost Weekend.* His essay is discussed briefly in Telotte. pp. 4–5, and extensively in Edward Dimendberg, *Film Noir and Urban Space*, Ph.D. Diss., University of California at Santa Cruz, 1992, pp. 116–63.

8 Jean Pierre Chartier, 'Les Américains font des films "noirs" ', *Revue du cinéma* 2 (1946), p. 67 (my translation). Hereafter noted in text. *Cahiers du Cinéma: The 1950s*, ed. Jim Hillier (Cambridge, MA: Harvard University Press, 1985), trans. Liz Heron, p. 37.

9 Silver and Ward, p. 372.

10 *Onirique, insolite, erotique, ambivalent, et cruel.* I have translated *insolite* as 'bizarre',

but there is no good English equivalent. It connotes the Gothic, somewhat like the Freudian *unheimlich*, but with a more shocking or horrific effect. Judging from its frequency, *insolite* is the most important adjective in the *Panorama*.

11 Compare Sharon Stone's comments to a reporter about the role she played in *Basic Instinct* (1992): 'I never thought the character really cared about sex at all. That's why it was so easy for her to use her sexuality – it had no value.' *Parade Magazine* (January 30, 1994), p. 10.

12 Quoted by Roy Hoopes, *Cain: The Biography of James M. Cain* (New York: Holt, Rinehart and Winston, 1982), p. xiii.

13 For a detailed account of the politics of French intellectuals in the period, see Tony Judt, *Past Imperfect: French Intellectuals, 1944–1956* (Berkeley, CA: University of California Press, 1992).

14 Quoted by Dana Polan, *Power and Paranoia: History, Narrative, and the American Cinema, 1940–1950* (New York: Columbia University Press, 1986), p. 252.

15 Claude-Edmonde Magny, *The Age of the American Novel: The Film Aesthetic of Fiction Between the Two Wars*, trans. Eleanor Hochman (New York: Ungar, 1972). This book, published in France in the 1950s, helped to transmit Sartre's ideas about the novel into French film theory.

16 For a listing of allusions to films noirs in *Breathless*, and for a useful survey of the French intellectual background, see Dudley Andrew, '*Breathless*: Old As New', in *Breathless*, ed. Dudley Andrew (Rutgers, N.J.: Rutgers University Press, 1987), pp. 3–20.

17 Quoted by Leighton Grist, 'Moving Targets and Black Widows: Film Noir in Modern Hollywood', in *The Book of Film Noir*, ed. Ian Cameron (New York: Continuum, 1993), p. 267.

18 Fredric Jameson, *Postmodernism: Or, the Cultural Logic of Late Capitalism* (Durham, N.C.: Duke University Press, 1991). See also Marcia Landy and Lucy Fischer, '*Dead Again* or A-Live Again: Postmodern or Postmortem?' *Cinema Journal*, vol. 33, no. 4 (Summer 1994), pp. 3–22.

SECTION FOUR
STAR STUDIES

Like genres such as the western, the star was not a category invented by critics, but one that was central both to the industrial organization of film production and to the consumption of films by audiences. Indeed, stars are used by the industry because of their appeal to a significant section of the film-going public, and as star studies emerged in the mid- to late 1970s, it did so as an attempt to analyse and explain this appeal. In the process, star studies rejected earlier approaches to stars and developed ideas derived from semiotics and structuralism, which had been introduced into film studies, in part, through the study of genre (see Section Three). However, while genre criticism had concentrated on the analysis of myth, the focus on the star led star studies to concentrate on the analysis of ideology and particularly the concept of individualism.

One of the key works in the development of star studies was Richard Dyer's *Stars*, from which extracts 18 and 19 have been taken. In his work, Dyer takes issue with the concept of charisma, which is often associated with stars. Charisma is usually seen as some natural quality that is possessed by a person, a quality that makes them unique, fascinating and attractive. It is that magical and indefinable 'star quality', which is so often used to explain their appeal to audiences. Dyer draws on the work of Max Weber to argue that, rather than simply some quality peculiar to the individual, charisma needs to be understood as a product of the ways in which an individual's 'image' relates to certain social issues or dilemmas.

For Dyer, the object of star studies should be the star 'image', or rather the meanings that are associated with a particular star. Star studies shifts the focus of concern away from the 'real' individual to the ways in which the meaning of star images are constructed, a shift that deploys structuralist notions of myth and ideology. For example, Dyer draws on the concept of myth developed by Claude Lévi-Strauss (see Section Three). For Lévi-Strauss (1968), myths not only tell us how a culture thinks, but are also attempts to imaginatively resolve some social contradiction or conflict. In a similar way, Dyer argues that stars such as Marilyn Monroe appealed to audiences because their images worked in relation to, and resolved, certain social concerns. In Monroe's case, he argues that she was fascinating to audiences because she was able to be both sexy and innocent, positions that had previously been seen as socially incompatible for women. In other words, Monroe was able to be overtly sexual without being threatening to men, and she was able to do so at a time of important shifts in the social organization of sexuality and sexual behaviour.

However, it is also important to note that here Dyer is referring not to Monroe the individual but rather to a star image which is constructed through a series of texts: photographs, trailers, interviews, news reports, etc. Indeed, he suggests that this star image is all we can ever have access to, and that even those texts that purport to uncover the *real* Marilyn are simply texts themselves. The star image is therefore a series of signs and texts that can be studied as such.

In extract 18, Dyer discusses these points through an account of the various media texts through which the star image is constructed. The star image is often said to be constructed 'intertextually', by which critics mean that it is the product of a range of texts. Certainly, a star's films may, in particular cases, have a central role in the construction of that star's image, but in other cases a star's films may be relatively unimportant to, or even contradict, the meanings constructed through, for example, gossip columns or news media.

In extract 19, however, Dyer tries to show how star's images work within films. His point is that a star's image is always complex – that it is made up of numerous aspects and elements – and hence that it can be used in films in a variety of different ways. He therefore distinguishes between the star's image and the narrative character which they play in a particular film, and claims that these two can either fit together perfectly or, clash violently or, more usually, that the film will try to emphasize certain aspects of the star image, and to play down other aspects.

Extract 20, also from Dyer, emphasises another aspect of the ideological significance of stars. Here Dyer is drawing on the theory of ideology developed by Marxists such as the French philosopher Louis Althusser. For Althusser (1971), ideology is a process through which individuals are constituted as social subjects. It is the process through which we come to see ourselves as unique and autonomous individuals. Althusser suggests that our sense of self is not something inherent to us as individuals, but conversely that our sense of self is a product of the ways in which we are placed and positioned, from infancy onwards, by various social discourses and institutions.

To understand this process, it is helpful to think back to the theories of semiotics and structuralism that were discussed in the previous section on genre, where it was argued that meaning is not the product of the speaker but rather of the rules of language that the speaker must obey. In other words, all our thoughts and feelings are structured by and through language, to the extent that, in a sense, 'it is not we who speak language but language which speaks us'. Another way of thinking about this is to look at the syntax of a sentence, a syntax which divides the world into the subject (the thing that performs an action), the verb (the action that is performed) and the object (the thing on which the subject acts). In the sentence 'I hit the wall', for example, the word 'I' is a position within the structure of language. To speak, we are obliged to position ourselves within, or rather to be positioned by, a particular linguistic order; to fit into a pre-existing position.

Althusser argues that society itself constructs positions of subjectivity, 'I' positions, in a manner comparable with that of language; and that in order to be a social subject, we must occupy these positions. However, rather than seeing ourselves as simple effects of the social order, we come to see these positions as somehow natural and inherent to us. For example, the culture in which one lives will determine one's tastes for food. What might be seen as a delicacy in one culture is seen as disgusting in another. Yet these tastes are experienced not as socially constructed and learned, but rather as deeply personal and even physiological. They are experienced as though they are natural to us as individuals.

It is this process which Althusser refers to as 'interpellation', a term which simply means 'to be hailed or addressed'. For Althusser, then, individuals are addressed by language and by culture, and so inserted or positioned within them. These processes are considered to be ideological because they result in us experiencing the social world as the effect of individual decision and action, rather than as a structure which positions subjects within it. In other words, we see the existing social order not as the cause of our actions, but rather as the effect of them. This can mean, for example, that social inequality is experienced as the effect of individual action or inaction rather than as a structural feature of the social order. In other words, that which is social is made to appear natural.

In extract 20, Dyer argues that stars function in relation to ideology in so far as they relate to notions of individualism. However, he does not suggest that they straightforwardly affirm individualism as an ideology. On the contrary, he argues that while they 'express the particular notion we hold of the person, the "individual" ', they 'do so complexly, variously ... they articulate both the promise and the difficulty that the notion of individuality presents to all of us who live by it.' The appeal of star images is that they operate as exemplary individuals who articulate both the ideals and the traumas of individualism. They are fascinating to us because they embody broader social processes.

This also accounts for the continual fascination with trying to uncover the 'real', private self of the star behind the social artifice of public accounts. For Dyer, this search for the authentic person will always be doomed to failure. However, it demonstrates the way in which ideologies of individualism depend upon the notion of a private personal self that exists outside of the social order, while also illustrating the ways in which stars do not necessarily simply reproduce ideologies of individualism, but can also express its tensions and contradictions.

In extract 21, Maria LaPlace provides a detailed case study in the analysis of a star image. It analyses the way in which Bette Davis's image was constructed through the industry's promotional strategies and more general publicity, as well as through the films that she made and through various criticisms and commentaries on her. However, this extract also shows that the construction of this image was not a seamless process, but also involved conflicts between Davis and the studios, conflicts that feed back into her image in various ways. For example, Davis's much-publicized disagreements with the studios were often taken to define her as a strong and independent woman, and to present her as more than just a star but also as a serious and professional actor.

In extract 22, Steve Cohan offers an analysis of Cary Grant's star image in the 1950s, in which he draws upon the work of Judith Butler (1990). Here he uses more contemporary theories of performance and masquerade (see Section Seven) to analyse the construction of Grant's image in relation to issues of masculinity and sexuality. Like earlier approaches, however, this work stresses that contemporary concepts of individuality are often related to concepts of gender and sexuality, and that these are socially produced, rather than being either natural or inherent qualities of an individual person.

In analysing Grant's star image, Cohan does not simply explain its meanings within the 1950s, but also deconstructs this meaning. He provides a 'queer reading' of Grant's star image (see Section Nine), in which he demonstrates its contradictions and instabilities. In other words, while Grant's image was constructed in terms of heterosexuality, it is continually haunted by that from which it sought to distance itself – homosexuality. In so doing, Cohan also demonstrates that a star image is not simply constructed through the texts that circulate about it but also in relation to other discourses and debates. Cohan therefore positions Grant's star image in relation to a series of discourses around masculinity and male sexuality within the period.

Finally, in extract 23, Jackie Stacey raises questions about the audience. As early as *Stars* (1979), Dyer had stressed that star images were polysemic: that they would be interpreted differently due to the cultural competences and dispositions of different audiences. However, most star studies have concentrated on the construction of star images through the texts of promotion, publicity, films and criticism, or have simply provided a reading of star images and their meanings.

Stacey's research is based on questionnaires and letters she received from British women who were asked to recount their memories of female stars of the 1940s and 1950s (see Stacey 1994). Her work clearly demonstrates how star images signify not only in the range of written, visual and cinematic texts in which they circulate but also in the ways in which they are appropriated by audiences and integrated into their cultural practices. Stacey offers an understanding of the different pleasures that female audiences gained from star images during the period. She also shows how star images may act as a cultural resource through which audiences may negotiate what it means to be a woman. On the one hand, Stacey argues that cinematic images of female stars reproduce a visual image of feminine beauty: for example, by 'copying' stars, female audiences attempt to increase the similarity between themselves and a star 'through the typical work of femininity: the production of oneself as both subject and object in accordance with cultural ideals of femininity' (1994: 168). On the other hand, Stacey also shows how female stars might be used as a resource to resist and negotiate dominant definitions of femininity. For example, she notes that in the UK 'American feminine ideals are clearly remembered as transgressing restrictive British femininity and thus employed as strategies of resistance' (1994: 204). Not only were women invited to choose between different notions of feminine beauty, but also 'the production of a feminine self in relation to Americanness signified "autonomy", "individuality", and "resistance" ' (238).

Like earlier versions of Star studies, Stacey considers the appeal of stars, but, unlike earlier approaches, she pays far more attention to the ways in which star images were appropriated by specific historically, socially and geographically situated audiences. Rather than simply concentrating on the construction of the star image as text, she acknowledges that star images mean different things to different audiences in different contexts, and what is appealing and attractive to one set of viewers may well be, for that very reason, unappealing and unattractive to others. It does seem that this turn to the study of audience is necessary if star studies are to engage fully with the intricacies and complexities of 'star appeal'.

References

Althusser, L. (1971). Ideology and Ideological State Apparatuses. In *Lenin and Philosophy*. New York: Monthly Review Press, 127–86.

Butler, J. (1990). *Gender Trouble: Feminism and the Subversion of Identity*. New York: Routledge.

Cohan, S. (1992). Cary Grant in the Fifties: Indiscretions of the Bachelor's masquerade. *Screen* **33**(4): 394–412.

—— (1998). *Masked Men: Masculinity and the Movies in the Fifties*. Bloomington: Indiana University Press.

Dyer, R. (1979). *Stars*. London: British Film Institute.

—— (1986). *Heavenly Bodies: Film Stars and Society*. London: Macmillan/British Film Institute.

Laplace, M. (1987). 'Producing and Consuming the Woman's Film: Discursive Struggle in *Now Voyager*'. In C. Gledhill (ed.), *Home Is Where the Heart Is: Studies in Melodrama and the Women's Film*. London: British Film Institute, 138–66.

Lévi-Strauss, C. (1968). *Structural Anthropology*. Harmondsworth: Penguin.

Stacey, J. (1991). 'Feminine Fascinations'. In C. Gledhill (ed.), *Stardom: Industry of Desire*. London: Routledge, 141–163.

—— (1994). *Stargazing: Hollywood Cinema and Female Spectatorship*. London: Routledge.

18 Stars as images

Richard Dyer

Stars embody social types, but star images are always more complex and specific than types. Types are, as it were, the ground on which a particular star's image is constructed. This image is found across a range of media texts. I want in this section to discuss the nature of the different categories into which these texts fall [...] A star image is made out of media texts that can be grouped together as *promotion, publicity, films* and *commentaries/criticism.*

Promotion

This refers to texts which were produced as part of the deliberate creation/manufacture of a particular image or image-context for a particular star. It includes (i) material concerned directly with the star in question – studio announcements, press hand-outs (including potted biographies), fan club publications (which were largely controlled by the studios), pin-ups, fashion pictures, ads in which stars endorse a given merchandise, public appearances (e.g. at premieres, as recorded on film or in the press); and (ii) material promoting the star in a particular film – hoardings, magazine ads, trailers, etc. Thomas B. Harris has described this in some detail in 'The Building of Popular Images'.

Promotion is probably the most straightforward of all the texts which construct a star image, in that it is the most deliberate, direct, intentioned and self-conscious (which is not to say that it is by any means entirely any of those things).

Promotion can get things wrong. Early promotion may not push the aspects of the performer which were subsequently to make them a star (e.g. both Davis and Monroe were promoted as routine pin-up starlets to begin with). However, this is more the exception than the rule, and either way promotion can be taken as an indicator of the studio's (or its promotion department's), agent's or star's conception of a given star image. [...]

Publicity

This is theoretically distinct from promotion in that it is not, or does not appear to be, *deliberate* image-making. It is 'what the press finds out', 'what the star lets slip in an interview', and is found in the press and magazines (not only the strictly film ones), radio and television interviews, and the gossip columns. In practice, much of this too was controlled by the studios or the star's agent, but it did not appear to be, and in certain cases (e.g. Ingrid Bergman's 'illegitimate' child by Roberto Rossellini) it clearly was not. The only cases where one can be fairly certain of genuine publicity are the scandals: Fatty Arbuckle's rape case, Ingrid Bergman's child, the murder of Lana Turner's gigolo boy-friend, Robert Mitchum's dope charge, Judy Garland's drunken break-downs, Elizabeth Taylor's 'breaking up' of Debbie Reynolds' marriage with Eddie Fisher. Scandals can harm a career (Arbuckle permanently,

Bergman temporarily) or alternatively give it a new lease of life (Turner, Mitchum, Taylor). An unnamed publicity man is quoted by Hollis Alpert to suggest a link between scandal and success and glamour:

> The stars are losing their glamour. It's next to impossible to get Burt Lancaster into columns these days. He's too serious. The public prefers its stars to behave a little crazy. Look what that dope party did for Bob Mitchum! Look how Deborah Kerr's divorce troubles sent her price way up! Who wants to form a fan club for a businessman? (*The Dreams and the Dreamers*, p.39)

The importance of publicity is that, in its apparent or actual escape from the image that Hollywood is trying to promote, it seems more 'authentic'. It is thus often taken to give a privileged access to the real person of the star. It is also the place where one can read tensions between the star-as-person and her/his image, tensions which at another level become themselves crucial to the image (e.g. Marilyn Monroe's attempts to be considered something other than a dumb blonde sex object, Robert Redford's 'loner' shunning of the attention his star status attracts).

Films

Inevitably, the films have a distinct and privileged place in a star's image. It is after all *film* stars that we are considering – their celebrity is defined by the fact of their appearing in films. However, the star is also a phenomenon of cinema (which as a business could make money from stars in additional ways to having them make films e.g. in advertising, the fan industry, personal appearances) and of general social meanings, and there are instances of stars whose films may actually be less important than other aspects of their career. Brigitte Bardot is a case in point, and Zsa Zsa Gabor is a film star whose films only a dedicated buff could name. The deaths of Montgomery Clift, James Dean, Marilyn Monroe and Judy Garland (and the premature retirement of Greta Garbo) may be as significant as the films they made, while Lana Turner's later films were largely a mere illustration of her life. It may be as pin-ups that Betty Grable and Rita Hayworth are really important, and as recording stars that Frank Sinatra and Bing Crosby really matter. While in general films are the most important of the texts, one should bear these points in mind when, as here, the focus is the star's total image rather than [...] the role of that image in the films.

Particularly important is the notion of the *vehicle*. Films were often built around star images. Stories might be written expressly to feature a given star, or books might be bought for production with a star in mind. Sometimes alterations to the story might be effected in order to preserve the star's image. This is what is implied by the term star 'vehicle' (a term actually used by Hollywood itself).

The vehicle might provide a) a character of the type associated with the star (e.g. Monroe's 'dumb blonde' roles, Garbo's melancholic romantic roles), b) a situation, setting or generic context associated with the star (e.g. Garbo in relationships with married men, Wayne in Westerns; as Colin McArthur has noted of stars of gangster films, they 'seem to gather within themselves the qualities of the genre ... so that the violence, suffering and *Angst* of the films is restated in their faces, physical presence, movement and speech.' *Underworld USA*, p. 24); or c) opportunities for the star to do her/his thing (most obviously in the case of musical stars; e.g. a wistful solo number for Judy Garland, an extended ballet sequence for Gene Kelly, but also, for instance, opportunities to display Monroe's body and wiggle walk, scenes of action in Wayne's films). Vehicles are important as much for what conventions they set up as for how they develop them, for their ingredients as for their realisation. In certain respects, a set of star vehicles is rather like a film genre such as the Western, the musical, the gangster film. As with genres proper, one can discern across a star's vehicles continuities of iconography (e.g. how they are dressed, made-up and coiffed, performance mannerisms, the settings with which they are associated), visual style (e.g. how they are lit, photographed, placed within the frame) and structure (e.g. their role in the plot, their function in the film's symbolic pattern). [...] Of course, not all films made by a star are vehicles, but looking at their films in terms of vehicles draws attention to those films that do not 'fit', that constitute inflections, exceptions to, subversions of the vehicle pattern and the star image. [...]

One needs also to consider the star's *filmic presentation*, the specific ways in which the star appears, performs, is used in individual films. [...]

Criticism and commentaries

This refers to what was said or written about the star in terms of appreciation or intepretation by critics and writers. It includes contemporary and subsequent writings (including obituaries and other material written after a star's death or retirement), and is found in film reviews, books on films and indeed in almost any kind of writing dealing, fictitiously or otherwise, with the contemporary scene. To this can be added film, radio and television profiles of stars. These always appear after the initial promotion and film-making of a star, although they may act back on subsequent promotion and film activity (e.g. the response of critics to Davis in *Of Human Bondage* legitimated her demand for 'strong' roles; the intellectuals' 'discovery' of Monroe is discernible in the increasingly self-reflexive nature of her last films). We need to distinguish between criticism and commentaries that did that, and those that have been elaborated after the star's active involvement in film-making. The latter may suggest an intepretation of the star at odds with the star's contemporary image (e.g. to-day's cult of Humphrey Bogart and Monroe – do we see more worldly wisdom in him, more tragic consciousness in her?).

Criticism and commentaries are oddly situated in the star's image. They are media products, part of the cinematic machine, yet it is commonly held that they are to be placed on the side of the audience – the consumers of media texts – rather than that of the industry – the producers of media texts. Critics and commentators are often taken to express rather than to construct the response to a star, and indeed on occasion they may well be expressing a widely held, pre-existing sentiment or view about a star. More frequently, however, they contribute to the shaping of 'public opinion' about a star (and the relationship of what the media call 'public opinion' to the opinion of the public must always remain problematic). Despite this, critics and commentators do not operate in the same space as those who construct the image in promotion and films. This gap between on the one hand promotional and filmic construction of the star image (which is further complicated by the highly ambivalent way publicity relates to promotion and films) and on the other the role of criticism and commentaries in that construction is a real one, and accounts for both the complexity, contradictoriness and 'polysemy' (see next section) of the star image and also for the capacity of critical opinion to contribute to shifts in careers such as those of Davis and Monroe noted above. [...]

It is misleading to think of the texts combining cumulatively into a sum total that constitutes the image, or alternatively simply as being moments in a star's image's career* that appear one after the other – although those emphases are important. The image is a *complex totality* and it does have a *chronological dimension*. What we need to understand that totality in its temporality is the concept of a *structured polysemy*.

By *polysemy* is meant the multiple but finite meanings and effects that a star image signifies. In looking at Jane Fonda's image, I shall not be trying to say what she meant for the 'average person' at various points in her career, but rather what the range of things was that she could be read as meaning by different audience members. In other words, to look at her image in terms of the multiplicity of its meanings. This does not mean that these are endless. The possibilities of meaning are limited in part by what the text makes available.

This polysemy is *structured*. In some cases, the various elements of signification may *reinforce* one another. John Wayne's image draws together his bigness, his association with the West, his support for right-wing politics, his male independence of, yet courtliness towards, women – the elements are mutually reinforcing, legitimating a certain way of being a man in American society. In other cases, the elements may be to some degree *in opposition or contradiction*, in which case the star's image is characterised by attempts to negotiate, reconcile or mask the difference between the elements, or else simply hold them in tension. At an extreme – for example the later part of Marilyn Monroe's career – the contradictions threaten to fragment the image altogether. [...]

Images also have a *temporal dimension*. Structured polysemy does not imply stasis; images develop or change over time.

---

* This phrase is used throughout to emphasise the fact that we are talking about a film-star as a media text, not as a real person.

---

19 Stars and 'character'

Richard Dyer

What then is involved in studying a film text in terms of a star and the character she or he plays?

We may note first of all the points at which the star is effective in the construction of character. These can be considered from two points of view: the fact of a star being in the film, and their performance in it. [...] As regards the fact that a given star is in the film, audience foreknowledge, the star's name and her/his appearance (including the sound of his/her voice and dress styles associated with her/him) all already signify that condensation of attitudes and values which is the star's image. Perhaps this is most blatantly demonstrated by Marlene Dietrich's appearances in *Around the World in Eighty Days* (1956) and *Touch of Evil* (1958). The former is, with its string of cameo appearances by stars, testimony enough to how much a star's mere presence in a film can signal character. When Dietrich tells Quinlan/Orson Welles his sombre fortune, towards the end of *Touch of Evil*, it is enough that it is her telling it for it to take on a mysterious and faintly erotic authority. The Dietrich example is particularly interesting, in that the enigmatic-exotic-erotic complex which her image signifies and which is irresistibly read into her appearances is sustained principally by vague memories of the Sternberg films, glamour photographs and her cabaret act, and not by the substance of her films or interviews. Her face, her name even, carries the 'mystique', no matter what films she makes or what she says.

The star image is used in the construction of a character in a film in three different ways:

Selective use

The film may, through its deployment of the other signs of character and the rhetoric of film, bring out certain features of the star's image and ignore others. In other words, from the structured polysemy of the star's image certain meanings are selected in accord with the overriding conception of the character in the film.

This selective use of a star's image is problematic for a film, in that it cannot guarantee that the particular aspects of a star's image it selects will be those that interest the audience. To attempt to ensure this, a film must use the various signifying elements of the cinema to foreground and minimise the image's traits appropriately. For us it is not enough simply to say that such-and-such a film uses such-and-such an aspect of a star's image: we have to show *how*. Let me take a conveniently narrow example, the use of one signifying element, lighting, in relation to Robert Redford. We might begin by considering the way he is lit in *The Way We Were* [...] as compared to in *All the President's Men*. In the first named, Redford is primarily the film's erotic/romantic focus and he is accordingly glamorously lit, with light from behind that both creates the warm glow of classic Hollywood glamour photography and also makes his already fair, all-American hair still more golden. [...]

All the President's Men on the other hand is entirely concerned with his political side and accordingly not at all with the erotic/romantic. He is lit in standard 'high-key' lighting which, as J. A. Place and L. S. Peterson note, was developed in the 1940s 'to give what was considered an impression of reality, in which the character's face is attractively modelled' (p.327). As Woodward, Redford is not filmed in any mock *cinéma verité* lighting; he is still the 'attractively modelled' classic film hero, but without the glamorous, erotic/romantic emphases of *The Way We Were* [...] It would be interesting to extend this analysis of the lighting to *The Candidate*, where the Redford character is simultaneously political for himself and erotic/romantic for the political machine that takes him up.

Perfect fit

In certain cases, all the aspects of a star's image fit with all the traits of a character. That is, all the various signs of character, including those achieved through the use of stars, accord. (Probably some aspects of the star's image will not be especially important, but they will not be incompatible either.) There are cases of this working with already known characters – Clark Gable as Rhett Butler in *Gone With the Wind*, Gérard Phillipe as Julien Sorel in *Le rouge et le noir* – and one would expect it to be the case with films not based on previous material but written and developed expressly for a given star.

For example, John Wayne. While most Wayne films simply use, and celebrate, his relaxed, masculine, Westerner/leader qualities, certain have also brought in his awkwardness with women and his 'authoritarian self-sufficiency' (Leo Braudy): *Red River, Rio Bravo, The Searchers, The Man Who Shot Liberty Valance*. Equally a film like *The Sands of Iwo Jima*, by eliminating women from the scene and setting the narrative within an accepted authoritarian social structure, capitalises on the Wayne image without having to criticise it. As Lawrence Alloway observes in *Violent America*:

> His authority, physically massive, more at ease with men than women on the screen, makes him a natural for action pictures with teaching situations. (p.37)

(such as *The Sands of Iwo Jima*). 'A natural' here indicates the perfect fit between image and character. [...]

Problematic fit

Although good cases can certainly be made for both a selective use of a star image and perfect fits between star images and film characters, it seems to me that the powerfully, inescapably present, always-already-signifying nature of star images more often than not creates problems in the construction of character. As Leo Braudy observes:

> Without an awareness of the aesthetic weight of a film star's accumulated image, a director can easily make mistakes that destroy the unity of his [*sic*] film. (op. cit., p. 210)

[...] The contradictory and polysemic nature of the images makes it hard either to delimit a few aspects or to fully articulate the whole thing with the character as constructed by the other signs in the film. [...] In certain cases, the contradiction may be at all points, such that one can conceptualise the problem in terms of a clash between two complex sign clusters, the star as image and the character as otherwise constructed. A prime example of this, in my view, is Monroe as Lorelei in *Gentlemen Prefer Blondes*. Everything about Anita Loos' character (in best-selling novel and smash hit Broadway musical and in Carol Channing's widely seen and known about interpretation of her in the latter) as well as the script of the film (e.g. what Jane Russell/Dorothy says about Lorelei), other performances and casting (e.g. the obvious manipulability of 'wet' Gus/Tommy Noonan and 'dirty old man' Piggy/Charles Coburn, the suspicion of 'straight man' Malone/Elliott Reid) and the structure of the film (Dorothy and Lorelei as polar opposites, in name, hair colour, interests in men and money; the basic hermeneutic of the Lorelei plot being whether or not Gus will realise Lorelei's true intentions); all of this constructs Lorelei as a cynical gold-digger, who fully understands how to use her sex appeal to trap rich men and is motivated above all by cupidity. Her dialogue as written is self-aware and witty, signalling (to us and to herself) amusement at what she is doing even while she is playing the *fausse-naive*. The weight of the Monroe image on the other hand is on innocence. She is certainly aware of her sexuality, but she is guiltless about it and it is moreover presented primarily in terms of narcissism – i.e. sexuality for herself rather than for men. At this stage in her image's development, her motivations were taken to be 'spiritual', either in the magic, 'little-girl' aspirations to be a movie star or in the 'pretentious' interests in Acting and Art. There is thus a quite massive disjunction between Monroe-as-image and Lorelei-as-character. They only touch at three points: the extraordinary impact of their physicality, a certain infantile manner and a habit of uttering witticisms. Yet even these points need to be qualified. Lorelei is quite definitely in control of her physicality whereas Monroe (at this stage in her image) was equally clearly not; Lorelei pretends to be infantile, Monroe was by and large taken to be so; Lorelei's wit expresses an intelligent but cynical appraisal of the situation, whereas Monroe's remarks to the press (known as Monroeisms) were regarded far more, at this point, as wisdom on a par with that 'out of the mouths of babes and sucklings' (i.e. wise by chance rather than by design).

As a result of this disjunction (and one would need to demonstrate through close analysis the full complexity of the two image clusters we are talking of, Monroe's and Lorelei's), the character of Monroe-as-Lorelei becomes contradictory to the point of incoherence. This is not a question of Lorelei/Monroe being one thing one moment and another the next, but of her being simultaneously polar opposites. Thus, for instance, when Lorelei/Monroe says to Piggy that she had expected him to be older, him 'being a diamond miner and all', the lines as written and situated (in particular by Russell/Dorothy, straight-woman and confidante, thus in some measure privileged with respect to the truth of narrative and characters) indicate her manipulative propensities, but, because they emanate from Monroe's mouth, they also at the same time indicate innocent pleasure in being sexy.

Where there is such disjuncture, analysis will be concerned to specify how, and with what particular ideological significance. At the same time we also need to ask to what degree it 'shows' as a disjuncture. Various possibilities suggest themselves in this regard:

1) The disjuncture may indeed be glaring (as I find it in *Gentlemen Prefer Blondes*). Such disjunctures need not only be evident after analysis; we are after all speaking of a familiar enough idea, miscasting.
2) The star may be thought to rejig the contradictions so as to make them more reconcilable. (Thus Maurice Zolotow – 'In her characterization of Lorelei Lee, Marilyn put together a sympathetic portrait of a girl who mingles tenderness of heart with a greed for status symbols'; *Marilyn Monroe*, p.143)
3) The placing of the audience in relation to the characters, through the hierarchy of discourses, may deny the truth of the star's image *vis-à-vis* the character. For example, it might be argued that the fact that in *Niagara* we see Monroe/Rose

with her lover kissing passionately behind the Falls makes it impossible to read any legitimacy into her behaviour with her husband. (It seems likely that this can only happen when the audience is unaware of the star's image, or when the film is deliberately having a joke at the expense of the star's image, as with the utterly evil doings of Henry Fonda in *Once Upon a Time in the West*.)

4) The star's image is so powerful that all signs may be read in terms of it. From this perspective, all Lorelei's manipulative lines and actions would be read as genuine and innocent. [...]

What analysis is concerned to do is both to discover the nature of the fit between star image and character, and, where the fit is not perfect or selective, to work out where the contradictions are articulated (at what level(s) of signification of character) and to attempt to see what possible sources of 'masking' or 'pseudo-unification' the film offers (such as the irresistible unifying force of a star image).

20 Living stars

Richard Dyer

[...] Stars articulate what it is to be a human being in contemporary society; that is, they express the particular notion we hold of the person, of the 'individual'. They do so complexly, variously – they are not straightforward affirmations of individualism. On the contrary, they articulate both the promise and the difficulty that the notion of individuality presents for all of us who live by it.

'The individual' is a way of thinking and feeling about the discrete human person, including oneself, as a separate and coherent entity. The individual is thought of as separate in the sense that she or he has an existence apart from anything else – the individual is not just the sum of his or her social roles or actions. He or she may only be perceived through these things, may even be thought to be formed by them, yet there is, in this concept of the person, an irreducible core of being, the entity that is perceived within the roles and actions, the entity upon which social forces act. This irreducible core is coherent in that it is supposed to consist of certain peculiar, unique qualities that remain constant and give sense to the person's actions and reactions. However much the person's circumstances and behaviour may change, 'inside' they are still the same individual; even if 'inside' she or he has changed, it is through an evolution that has not altered the fundamental reality of that irreducible core that makes her or him a unique individual.

At its most optimistic, the social world is seen in this conception to emanate from the individual, and each person is seen to 'make' his or her own life. However, this is not necessary to the concept. What is central is the idea of the separable, coherent quality, located 'inside' in consciousness and variously termed 'the self', 'the soul', 'the subject' and so on. This is counterposed to 'society', something seen as logically distinct from the individuals who compose it, and very often as inimical to them. If in ideas of 'triumphant individualism' individuals are seen to determine society, in ideas of 'alienation' individuals are seen as cut adrift from and dominated, battered by the anonymity of society. Both views retain the notion of the individual as separate, irreducible, unique.

It is probably true to say that there has never been a period in which this concept of the individual was held unproblematically throughout society. The notion of the individual has always been accompanied by the gravest doubts as to its tenability. It is common, for instance, to characterise Enlightenment philosophy as one of the most shiningly optimistic assertions of individuality; yet two of its most sparkling works, Hume's *An Essay on Human Understanding* and Diderot's *Rameau's Nephew*, fundamentally undercut any straightforward belief in the existence of the coherent, stable, inner individual; Hume by arguing that all we can know as our self is a series of sensations and experiences with no necessary unity or connection, Diderot by focusing on the vital, theatrical, disjointed character of Rameau's nephew, so much more 'real' than Diderot, the narrator's stodgily maintained coherent self.

If the major trend of thought since the Renaissance, from philosophical rumination to common sense, has affirmed the concept of the individual, there has been an almost equally strong counter-tradition of ideas that have severely dented our confidence in ourselves: Marxism, with its insistence that social being determines consciousness and not vice versa, and, in its economist variant, with its vision of economic forces propelling human events forward; psychoanalysis, with its radical splitting of consciousness into fragmentary, contradictory parts; behaviourism, with its view of human beings controlled by instinctual appetites beyond consciousness; linguistics and models of communication in which it is not we who speak language, but language which speaks us. Major social and political developments have been understood in terms of the threat they pose to the individual: industrialisation can be seen to have set the pace for a whole society in which people are reduced to being cogs in a machine; totalitarianism would seem to be the triumph, easily achieved, of society over the individual; the development of mass communications, and especially the concomitant notion of mass society, sees the individual swallowed up in the sameness produced by centralised, manipulative media which reduce everything to the lowest common denominator. A major trajectory of twentieth-century high literature has examined the disintegration of the person as stable ego, from the fluid, shifting self of Woolf and Proust to the minimal self of Beckett and Sarraute. 'Common sense' is no less full of tags acknowledging this bruised sense of self: the sense of forces shaping our lives beyond our control, of our doing things for reasons that we don't understand, of our not recognising ourself in actions we took yesterday (to say nothing of years ago), of not seeing ourselves in photographs of ourselves, of feeling strange when we recognise the routinised nature of our lives – none of this is uncommon.

Yet the idea of the individual continues to be a major moving force in our culture. Capitalism justifies itself on the basis of the freedom (separateness) of anyone to make money, sell their labour how they will, to be able to express opinions and get them heard (regardless of wealth or social position). The openness of society is assumed by the way that we are addressed as individuals – as consumers (each freely choosing to buy, or watch, what we want), as legal subjects (free and responsible before the law), as political subjects (able to make up our mind who is to run society). Thus even while the notion of the individual is assailed on all sides, it is a necessary fiction for the reproduction of the kind of society we live in.

Stars articulate these ideas of personhood, in large measure shoring up the notion of the individual but also at times registering the doubts and anxieties attendant on it. In part, the fact that the star is not just a screen image but a flesh and blood person is liable to work to express the notion of the individual. A series of shots of a star whose image has changed – say, Elizabeth Taylor – at various points in her career could work to fragment her, to present her as nothing but a series of disconnected looks; but in practice it works to confirm that beneath all these different looks there is an irreducible core that gives all those looks a unity, namely Elizabeth Taylor. Despite the elaboration of roles, social types, attitudes and values suggested by any one of these looks, one flesh and blood person is embodying them all. We know that Elizabeth Taylor exists apart from all these looks, and this knowledge alone is sufficient to suggest that there is a coherence behind them all.

It can be enough just to know that there was one such person, but generally our sense of that one person is more vivid and important than all the roles and looks s/he assumes. People often say that they do not rate such and such a star because he or she is always the same. In this view, the trouble with, say, Gary Cooper or Doris Day, is that they are always Gary Cooper and Doris Day. But if you like Cooper or Day, then precisely what you value about them is that they are always 'themselves' – no matter how different their roles, they bear witness to the continuousness of their own selves.

This coherent continuousness within becomes what the star 'really is'. Much of the construction of the star encourages us to think this. Key moments in films are close-ups, separated out from the action and interaction of a scene, and not seen by other characters but only by us, thus disclosing for us the star's face, the intimate, transparent window to the soul. Star biographies are devoted to the notion of showing us the star as he or she really is. Blurbs, introductions, every page assures us that we are being taken 'behind the scenes', 'beneath the surface', 'beyond the image', there where the truth resides. Or again, there is a rhetoric of sincerity or authenticity, two qualities greatly prized in stars because they guarantee, respectively, that the star really means what he or she says, and that the star really is what she or he appears to be. Whether caught in the unmediated moment of the close-up, uncovered by the biographer's display of ruthless uncovering, or present in the star's indubitable sincerity and authenticity, we have a privileged reality to hang on to, the reality of the star's private self.

The private self is further represented through a set of oppositions that stem from the division of the world into private and public spaces, a way of organising space that in turn relates to the idea of the separability of the individual and society:

private	public
individual	society
sincere	insincere

country	city
small town	large town
folk	urban
community	mass
physical	mental
body	brain
naturalness	artifice
sexual intercourse	social intercourse
racial	ethnic

When stars function in terms of their assertion of the irreducible core of inner individual reality, it is generally through their associations with the values of the left-hand column. Stars like Clark Gable, Gary Cooper, John Wayne, Paul Newman, Robert Redford, Steve McQueen, James Caan establish their male action-hero image either through appearing in Westerns, a genre importantly concerned with nature and the small town as centres of authentic human behaviour, and/or through vivid action sequences, in war films, jungle adventures, chase films, that pit the man directly, physically against material forces. It is interesting that with more recent examples of this type – Clint Eastwood, Harrison Ford – there has been a tendency either to give their films a send-up or tongue-in-cheek flavour (Eastwood's chimp films, Ford as Indiana Jones) or else a hard, desolate, alienated quality (Eastwood in *Joe Kidd*, Ford in *Blade Runner*), as if the values of masculine physicality are harder to maintain straight-facedly and unproblematically in an age of microchips and a large scale growth (in the USA) of women in traditionally male occupations.

The private self is not always represented as good, safe or positive. There is an alternative tradition of representing the inner reality of men, especially, which stretches back at least as far as the romantic movement. Here the dark, turbulent forces of nature are used as metaphors for the man's inner self: Valentino in *The Son of the Sheik*, the young Laurence Olivier as Heathcliff in *Wuthering Heights* and as Maxim de Winter in *Rebecca*. In the forties and fifties the popularisation of psycho-analysis added new terms to the private:public opposition. Thus:

private	public
subconscious	conscious
Id	Ego

and in the still more recent Lacan inflection:

| imaginary | symbolic |

These have been particularly important in the subsequent development of male stars, where the romantic styles of brooding, introspective, mean-but-vulnerable masculinity have been given Oedipal, psychosexual, paranoid or other crypto-psychoanalytical inflections with stars like Montgomery Clift, James Dean, Marlon Brando, Anthony Perkins, Jack Nicholson, Richard Gere. Recent black male stars such as Jim Brown, Richard Roundtree and Billy Dee Williams are interesting in that their fiercely attractive intensity seems closer to the 'dangerous' romantic tradition proper; at the same time they also draw on the old stereotype of the black man as brute, only now portraying this as attractive rather than terrifying; and they are almost entirely untouched by the psychoanalytical project of rationalising and systematising and naming the life of the emotions and sensations. All these male stars work variations on the male inner self as negative, dangerous, neurotic, violent, but always upholding that as the reality of the man, what he is really like.

The stars analysed in the rest of this book also have strong links with the left-hand, 'private' column. Monroe was understood above all through her sexuality – it was her embodiment of current ideas of sexuality that made her seem real, alive, vital. Robeson was understood primarily through his racial identity, through attempts to see and, especially, hear him as the very essence of the Negro folk. Both were represented insistently through their bodies – Monroe's body was sexuality, Robeson's was the nobility of the black race. Garland too belongs with the left-hand column, initially through her roles as country or small-town girl, later through the way her body registered both her problems and her defiance of them. All the descriptions of her from her later period begin by describing the state of her body and speculating from that on what drugs, drink, work and temperament have done to it, and yet how it continues to be animated and vital. Not only are Monroe, Robeson, Garland stars who are thought to be genuine, who reveal their inner selves, but the final touchstone of that genuineness is the human body itself. Stars not only bespeak our society's investment in the private as the real, but also often tell us how the private is understood to be the recovery of the natural 'given' of human life, our bodies. Yet as the chapters that follow argue, what we actually come up against at this point is far from straightforwadly natural; it is particular, and even rather peculiar, ways of making sense of the body. The very notions of sexuality and race, so apparently rooted in the body, are historically and culturally specific ideas about the body, and it is these that Monroe and Robeson, especially, enact, thereby further endowing them with authenticity.

What is at stake in most of the examples discussed so far is the degree to which, and manner in which, what the star really is can be located in some inner, private, essential core. This is how the star phenomenon reproduces the overriding ideology of the person in contemporary society. But the star phenomenon cannot help being also about the person in public. Stars, after all, are always inescapably people in public. If the magic, with many stars, is that they seem to be their private selves in public, still they can also be about the business of being in public, the way in which the public self is endlessly produced and remade in presentation. Those stars that seem to emphasise this are often considered 'mannered', and the term is right, for they bring to the fore manners, the stuff of public life. When such stars are affirmative of manners and public life they are often, significantly enough, European or with strong European connections – stars to whom terms like suave, gracious, debonair, sophisticated, charming accrue, such as Fred Astaire, Margaret Sullavan, Cary Grant, David Niven, Deborah Kerr, Grace Kelly, Audrey Hepburn, Rex Harrison, Roger Moore. These are people who have mastered the public world, in the sense not so much of being authentically themselves in it nor even of being sincere, as of performing in the world precisely, with poise and correctness. They get the manners right. [...]

Many of the women stars of screwball comedy – Katharine Hepburn, Carole Lombard, Rosalind Russell, and more recently Barbra Streisand – have the uncomfortable, sharp quality of people who do survive and succeed in the public world, do keep up appearances, but edgily, always seen to be in the difficult process of doing so. Bette Davis's career has played variations on this representation of public performance. Many of her films of the thirties and forties exploit her mannered style to suggest how much her success or survival depends upon an ability to manipulate manners, her own and those of people around her, to get her own way (*Jezebel, The Little Foxes*), to cover her tracks out of courage (*Dark Victory*) or guilt (*The Letter*), to maintain a public presence at all costs for a greater good than her own (*The Private Life of Elizabeth and Essex*), to achieve femininity (*Now Voyager*) and so on. If being in public for Davis in these films is hypertense, registered in her rapid pupil movements, clenching and unclenching fists, still in the thirties and forties she is enacting the excitement, the buzz of public life, of being a person in public. Later films become something like the tragedy of it. *All About Eve* details the cost of keeping up appearances, maintaining an image. *Whatever Happened to Baby Jane?* evokes the impossibility of achieving again the public role that made her character feel good. Yet the end of *Baby Jane* affirms the public self as a greater reality than the private self cooped up in the dark Gothic mansion – we learn that it is Crawford not Davis who is the baddie; away from the house, on the beach, surrounded by people, the ageing Jane can become the public self she really is, Baby Jane. Davis's career thus runs the gamut of the possibilities of the private individual up against public society; from, in the earlier films, triumphant individualism, the person who makes their social world, albeit agitatedly, albeit at times malignantly, to, in the later films, something like alienation, the person who is all but defeated by the demands of public life, who only hangs on by the skin of their teeth – until the up-tempo happy ending.

The private/public, individual/society dichotomy can be embodied by stars in various ways; the emphasis can fall at either end of the spectrum, although it more usually falls at the private, authentic, sincere end. Mostly too there is a sense of 'really' in play – people/stars are really themselves in private or perhaps in public but at any rate somewhere. However, it is one of the ironies of the whole star phenomenon that all these assertions of the reality of the inner self or of public life take place in one of the aspects of modern life that is most associated with the invasion and destruction of the inner self and corruptibility of public life, namely the mass media. Stars might even seem to be the ultimate example of media hype, foisted on us by the media's constant need to manipulate our attention. We all know how the studios build up star images, how stars happen to turn up on chat shows just when their latest picture is released, how many of the stories printed about stars are but titillating fictions; we all know we are being sold stars. And yet those privileged moments, those biographies, those qualities of sincerity and authenticity, those images of the private and the natural can work for us. We may go either way. As an example, consider the reactions at the time to John Travolta in *Saturday Night Fever*. I haven't done an audience survey, but people seemed to be fairly evenly divided. For those not taken with him, the incredible build-up to the film, the way you knew what his image was before you saw the film, the coy but blatant emphasis on his sex appeal in the film, the gaudy artifice of the disco scene, all merely confirmed him as one great phoney put-on on the mass public. But for those for whom he and the film did work, there were the close-ups revealing the troubled pain behind the macho image, the intriguing off-screen stories about his relationship with an older woman, the spontaneity (= sincerity) of his smile, the setting of the film in a naturalistically portrayed ethnic subculture. A star's image can work either way, and in part we make it work according to how much it speaks to us in terms we can understand about things that are important to us.

Nonetheless, the fact that we know that hype and the hard sell do characterise the media, that they are supreme instances of manipulation, insincerity, inauthenticity, mass public life, means that the whole star phenomenon is profoundly unstable. Stars cannot be *made* to work as affirmations of private or public life. In some cases, the sheer multiplicity of the images, the amount of hype, the different stories told become overwhelmingly contradictory. Is it possible still to have any sense of Valentino or Monroe, their persons, apart from all the things they have been made to mean? [...]

---

21 Stars and the star system: the case of Bette Davis

Maria LaPlace

[...] In the woman's film the star-system and the female stars who are associated with the genre have an especially important function for it is in the articulation of the patriarchal dichotomies of private/public and domestic/social that the conventions of the star-system mesh with those of women's fiction, consumerism and the woman's film itself to form a powerful constellation of forces addressing and engaging the female spectator on a variety of levels.

The star-system exists as both a marketing tool in the selling of films and as an institution which solicits the psychic mechanisms of identification. It does so in a variety of ways, one of the most important being the 'dramatisation of the private realm', with particular emphasis on the 'spectacle of consumption' (de Cordova, 1982 and Dyer, 1979).[1]

More precisely, the star is an actress/actor whose private life takes on as much significance as her/his acting of roles. The discourse of the star goes beyond professional considerations of competence, artistry, career; the star's private life is a major arena of discourse. Who the star is as a 'real person' plays a large part in the circuit of cinema-related texts: fan magazines, gossip columns, articles in main-stream magazines and the 'news' section of newspapers, star biographies and general books on Hollywood, newsreels, radio programmes.

Thus, any single viewing of the star in a film is imbued with an accumulation of significance made up not only of former roles, but of everything the spectator knows about the star as a 'real person'. This 'personal knowledge' of the star becomes a means to identify with her/him and possibly to emulate his/her personality and lifestyle.

What is particularly interesting is how much of this material is not only directed at women but is also written by them: most of the fan magazine articles I have seen are authored by women, and the three top Hollywood gossip columnists were women: Hedda Hopper, Louella Parsons and Sheilah Graham. Fan magazines have always been weighted towards articles about women stars, featuring descriptions of their home lives, clothes, entertaining and romantic relationships. Additionally, there are beauty advice columns, home decorating tips, fashion spreads, advice to the lovelorn (often 'written' by a woman star) and even recipes. This is a realm of discourse clearly marked as female, even when male stars are being discussed, and its themes, preoccupations and conventions are very similar to those of the woman's film and women's fiction.

On one level, the star-system can be taken as part of the larger effort of consumer capitalism to create and win a female market/audience. But on another level this construct cannot contain its effects, just as consumerism and advertising cannot. Certain ideas and pleasures are introduced into the realm of the public and legitimated with unpredictable consequences. The discourse of the star and the star-system can offer a validation of the values of the personal and the domestic (love, feelings, relationships), which stands in contrast to masculinist values of dominance, 'honour' and competition. And it offers a representation of female power in the social world which contests the confinement of women to the family: the female star is visibly a woman whose work earns her large amounts of money and public acclaim. The latter is especially powerful in films which call on the subversive significations of their stars in narratives in which there is a particular heightening of discursive contradictions, as in the case of Bette Davis in *Now, Voyager*.

From 1938–43, Bette Davis was one of the ten top-grossing stars in Hollywood and the most popular and critically acclaimed female star. She appeared almost exclusively in the woman's film and was popularly thought to appeal mainly to women spectators. What was Davis's fascination for female spectators?

In *Stars* (BFI, 1979), Richard Dyer maintains that stars become identified with or are constructed along the lines of various social types and cultural stereotypes. Certain of these can function for (rather than against) the groups they represent, especially in the case of social outgroups (women, gays, racial and ethnic minorities) and have the potential to be 'subversive or oppositional ... to dominant ideology' (p. 38). For women one such stereotype is the Independent Woman. In cinema the Independent Woman falls into two categories: one is the 'good' strong woman, noble, generous, sympathetic; the other is 'evil', aggressive, domineering, sexual, 'neurotic'. Both convey strength and take action.

Davis's film roles are almost all one or the other Independent Woman. Some of her most famous early roles are the latter type – 'bitches' Dyer calls them: *Of Human Bondage* (1934), *Dangerous* (1935, Oscar for Davis), *Jezebel* (1938, Oscar for Davis), and *The Little Foxes* (1939). In this incarnation, Davis plays 'headstrong' women, snappy, sharp-witted, wilful, selfish and sexy, who often come to a bad end (or turn noble and sacrifice themselves). In the years just preceding *Now, Voyager*, there were a growing number of 'good' women; courageous, intelligent, competent, who persevere with dignity in the face of difficulties: *Marked Woman* (1937, actually a combination of the two types), *The Sisters* (1939), *Dark Victory* (1939), and *All This and Heaven, Too* (1941).

What links these roles is Davis's performance style. Characterised by a high level of intensity, energy and charged emotionality, it conveys a specific 'personality' that interacts with each film role. The Davis style consists in a deliberate, clipped vocal inflection; darting eye movements and penetrating stares; a swinging, striding walk; gestures such as clenching fists and sudden, intense drags on cigarettes; and quick shifts in mood and register. These connote assertiveness, intelligence, internal emotional conflict and strength. Her performances are 'bravura' – they call attention to their own skill and display pleasure in it. It is a 'powerful' performance style and adds an extra dimension of transgressive excess to the Independent Woman film roles.

As forceful in constructing a star image as film roles and performance style is the publicity material written *about* the star: commentary, biography and gossip. Since it appears not to be deliberate image-making, it appears '... more authentic. It is thus privileged or rather taken to give privileged access to the "real person" of the star' (Dyer, p. 69). This drama of the star's personal life is a central feature of the workings of the star-system, serving as a kind of anchor to identification, drawing the spectator 'close' to this 'person' and encouraging empathy, which can be brought into play in the reading of a film.

In looking at a variety of articles on Davis, written from 1934–42, I am struck by how similar they are to the themes and forms of women's fiction (see below, pp. 151–154), especially the fan magazine features, and how much they differ from what Dyer describes as the major motifs of the discourse of stardom – an elaborate lifestyle featuring large homes, swimming pools and limousines; leisure activities such as sports, hobbies and parties and, especially for female stars, notions of charm, sex appeal and glamour.

By contrast, the Davis 'story' is of a plucky, resourceful, 'self-made' woman, whose success is due not to beauty, but to personal qualities of talent, determination, and down-to-earth self-awareness. The product of a fatherless, mother-supported, lower-middle-class family, Davis, like the heroines of women's fiction, meets and surmounts adversity because she knows who she is and what she wants:

> She's not your ordinary blue-eyed blonde, this Davis girl. She's ambitious, courageous, un-complaining with a distinct mind of her own ... willing to work for what she gets out of life; the world is too full of women – and men – who think it owes them a living. ('Bette from Boston', *Silver Screen*, in Martin Levin (ed.), *Hollywood and the Great Fan Magazines.*)

Thus, the image is strongly marked by attributes of strength and independence, constructed in another way through the depiction of Davis as anti-glamour and anti-consumerism, eschewing all the trappings of stardom:

> Davis dislikes equally the stuffed shirts and glamour girls of Hollywood and makes no effort to please them ... Her social circle is made up of non-professionals, including her sister; her closest approach to a hobby is her interest in dogs. Informality is her keynote ... she no longer dyes her hair and she never diets. ('Bette Davis', *Life*, 8 January 1939.)

Work is the privileged aspect of the Davis image; she is portrayed as completely dedicated to her career. The qualities of strength, independence and devotion to career find their most forceful representation in the widely reported stories of Davis's 1936 lawsuit against Warner Bros. The first actor to try to break the infamous seven-year contract, Davis stressed in her suit that she wanted control over her work, contending that the studio's choice of material jeopardised her career. The press reports are sympathetic to her position. *Life*'s cover story on Davis, written three years after the trial, begins with a lengthy account of the suit – an index of its centrality to her image – and states that she was a better judge of material than her employers and that, though she lost her case in court, she won the battle for better parts. They add, 'if Davis had won her case, other stars would have rebelled also and she would have become the Joan of Arc of a cinema revolution.'[2] Davis, then, came to signify rebellion against authority and a willingness to fight for herself and her autonomy as an artist.

Attempts are made to contain this relatively unconventional 'femininity'. One method is to explain her 'eccentricities' in terms of the regional stereotype of Davis's native New England, the Yankee. Yankees are thought to be particularly strong-minded, self-reliant, self-disciplined and ascetic, devoted to the Puritan value of hard work. (Interestingly, two other similarly unconventional Independent Woman stars, Katharine Hepburn and Rosalind Russell, are also New Englanders.)

Another is to claim that she is a great artist and not just a mere movie star: hence she is justified in deviating from feminine norms. It is acceptable that finding time to spend with her husband is difficult 'with Bette working pretty consistently most of the time'[3] and that she says 'I'm not very domestic',[4] because she is 'the ablest US-born movie star',[5] 'Dramatic Actress No. 1',[6] and 'the screen's finest actress and Hollywood's most regular person'.[7] A different approach calls Davis's sexuality into question and this strategy has a double edge. On the one hand, questions are raised about Davis's desirability to and desire for men (and the Yankee stereotype is recruited here, with references to Davis's 'New England conscience'). On the other hand, her image's transgressiveness is reinforced in more positive ways for women. Thus, while doubt is cast on whether she is sexually passionate in her marriages – Davis divorced and remarried during this period – a more companionate and egalitarian idea of marriage (much like that of nineteenth-century women's fiction) emerges, and passion is shifted to the realm of work and creativity. Two quotes are exemplary here:

> Another indication of how satisfactory she finds her professional life was an opinion of marriage, 'Domesticity is all right if it's not carried too far.' ... Characteristic was the reason Harmon Nelson divorced the screen's most celebrated impersonator of vixens ... she studied her parts in bed. ('Bette Davis', *Life*, 8 January 1939)
>
> Bette said she wasn't going to miss all the fun of a partnership marriage because she was a movie star. They had a plan of living which would prevent either of them from feeling dominated or cheated of independence. Ham paid his way, Bette paid hers. They had separate expense accounts and shared household expenses. ('That Marital Vacation', *Modern Screen*, 1938, in Martin Levin (ed.), *Hollywood and the Great Fan Magazines*.

The emphasis on economic independence and mutuality and the idea that a woman popularly thought to be neither beautiful nor sexy could become a major film star on the basis of her talent, persistence and appeal to female spectators, contradict the dominant patriarchal discourses on the achievement of female stardom – the myths of (passive) 'discovery' due to beauty and of 'sleeping one's way to the top'.

Thus, Davis's image in 1942 could offer a certain kind of ego ideal for women: a woman who is intelligent, articulate, self-possessed, dedicated to her profession and an artist, willing to fight for herself; a woman whose satisfaction and success are not based on passivity, romance or male approval; a woman with (a relative amount of) power. As an historical construction of 'woman', it enters into the circuit of female discourses and discursive struggle.

In the first part of *Now, Voyager*, and particularly in its promotion, consumerist discourse attempts to use the Davis image as a commodity. The film was sold as a Davis vehicle, exploiting spectator knowledge of her previous roles and personal life as major marketing tools. Thus, exhibitors are exhorted to 'remind your fans that Bette Davis has given them some of their most dramatic film entertainments' and the Press Book lists them at length. However, the roles stressed are the 'bitch' roles, with *Now, Voyager* presented, inaccurately, as a completely new departure: 'Recent releases seemed to indicate she was reaching new heights of insolence and selfish-ness ... the change in character in *Now, Voyager* is sudden, complete and probably healthy'. The Press Book differentiates between these roles and the 'real' Bette Davis. She is not 'a neurotic, hyperthyroid young woman with a tragic outlook on life' but rather 'a lady whose chief enthusiasms are her New England farm, her horses and practical jokes'. The 'real' Bette 'is from New England and therefore knows what an inhibition is'.

The Press Book attempts to link the representation of the 'real' Davis with her character in *Now, Voyager*, Charlotte Vale. Like certain elements of the Davis image, Charlotte is a New Englander from Boston, inhibited and unglamorous; during the course of the film she is physically transformed and her sexuality is freed. The Press Book's strategy is to use the name of the actress and the character interchangeably, implying that it is Davis who is being glamorised: 'Bette is unattractive to begin with but beautiful before the film is well underway.' This blurring of actress and role reinforces the recruitment of the Davis image to promote a consumerist discourse on female beauty and grooming. By enlisting the strong, sensible and poised elements of the Davis image in the form of her supposed beauty advice to women, with a covert playing on her reputation as unglamorous and uninterested in fashion, the impression is given that Davis, as well as Charlotte Vale, has changed in appearance and has learned to value these skills.

However, as the film progresses the contradictoriness (for female audiences) of consumerism and the Davis image are activated as they intersect with the major structuring discourse of women's fiction and are thereby pulled into the circuit of women's culture, underscoring the contradictions of the woman's film as a genre. [...]

Notes

1   Richard de Cordova, 'The Emergence of the Star System and the Bourgeoisification of the American Cinema', *Star Signs* (British Film Institute Education, 1982); Richard Dyer, *Stars* (British Film Institute, 1979).
2   'Bette Davis', *Life*, 8 January 1939.
3   'Bette from Boston', *Silver Screen*, 1935, in Martin Levin (ed.), *Hollywood and the Great Fan Magazines* (New York: Arbor House, 1970).

4 Ibid.
5 'Bette Davis', *Life*, 8 January 1939.
6 'That Marital Vacation', *Modern Screen*, 1939, in *Hollywood and the Great Fan Magazines*, op. cit.
7 'The Man Bette Davis Married', *Photoplay-Movie Mirror*, 1941, in *Hollywood and the Great Fan Magazines*, op. cit.

22 Cary Grant in the fifties: indiscretions of the bachelor's masquerade

Steven Cohan

While the male stars who most dominate our cultural memories of the 1950s are the sexual rebels – Brando, Dean, Presley – one of the most popular leading men at the time was Cary Grant, a Hollywood star since the thirties who returned to box-office prominence at the end of the decade with the great successes of *An Affair to Remember* (1957), *Indiscreet* (1958), *North by Northwest* (1959) and *Operation Petticoat* (1959). Grant's renewed popularity in the late fifties is notable for two reasons. The first major star to achieve independence from the studios in the forties, Grant financially owned and thus controlled much of his screen output during the fifties. He was consequently able to preserve the star image from his prewar films in a way that other actors of his generation did not. As Peter Biskind has pointed out, during the 1950s Cooper, Cagney, Wayne, Bogart, Stewart all played psychotic or neurotic variations of their older screen images.[1] Cary Grant, on the other hand, not only seemed to hold the clock still, but his star persona acquired even more glamour and appeal during this decade as 'an authentic American hero' (in William Rothman's phrase[2]), or 'a national monument' (in Stanley Cavell's[3]). Thus in 1958, when *Photoplay* included Grant, dubbed 'Hollywood's epitome of romance', in a pictorial spread featuring a number of male stars in swimming pools, it did not at all seem surprising – or inappropriate – to find the fifty-four-year-old actor placed alongside such younger heartthrobs as Tony Curtis, Rock Hudson, George Nader, Hugh O'Brian and Mark Damon.[4]

Despite his legendary career as a leading man in the fifties, though, Cary Grant was surely something of a paradoxical romantic hero for the period. Grant's biographers Charles Higham and Roy Moseley explicitly call his fifties screen image a 'mask', by which they mean, with reference to his 'sexual problems', 'his false image, so carefully sustained, of unequivocal masculinity and strong emotional security'.[5] While successfully personifying a screen image of eternal youthfulness, Americanness, heterosexual attractiveness, and sartorial elegance, Grant was actually middle-aged, British, bisexual, and a secret crossdresser (apparently wearing women's nylon panties underneath his expensively tailored grey flannel suits[6]). 'Cary Grant' was nonetheless so paradigmatic of romantic masculinity in the late fifties that Billy Wilder could simply have Tony Curtis imitate the star's well-known speaking style and audiences at *Some Like It Hot* (1959) immediately recognized this joke as a reference to Hollywood's exemplary leading man. 'Where did you get that phoney accent?' Jack Lemmon asks Curtis after watching the latter pose as a bachelor oil heir to catch Marilyn Monroe's attention: 'Nobody talks like that'. Of course, everyone watching Wilder's film knew who *did* speak that way – though audiences at the time were divided as to whether the point of the joke was tribute, satire, or just plain gossip.

More than a simple reference to a famous cultural icon of romantic seduction, this allusion to Grant in *Some Like It Hot* represents his celebrated persona as a *fabrication*, a construction of masculinity out of voice, clothes, bearing – all, as the Wilder film plays it out, taken from someone else to cover up a fundamental failure of male sexuality. 'I'm harmless', Tony Curtis confesses to Marilyn Monroe in Cary Grant's voice: and while the male's disguise in this scene is nothing but a decoy for his own heterosexual aggression (the pretence of impotence lures Monroe into making all the moves in Curtis's seduction of her), Wilder's reference to Grant recognizes something of a disturbing underside to the star's male screen image. Most obviously, it implies that this famous screen persona of charm and elegance is actually covering up the great fear which preoccupied fifties American culture when it came to thinking about masculinity: impotence, which the culture equated with emasculation, particularly in light of the two Kinsey reports in 1948 (on men) and 1953 (on women), and their widely circulated claim that female sexuality peaked late in life while male sexual performance petered out much earlier in the game.[7]

The reference to 'Cary Grant' in *Some Like It Hot* goes even further than that, however. For far from simply making a joke about the apparent sexual durability of a legendary Hollywood leading man (and at his own expense, too) it also means to ask what lies behind the star's deceptively transparent but also enduring romantic style, suggesting that his consummate masculinity is a masquerade. Grant's successful manipulation of signs (voice, bearing, looks), Tony Curtis parodically shows – when he plays a man who disguises himself as a woman and then, while still pretending to be her, also passes himself off as a generic version of 'Cary Grant' – continues to produce this quintessential leading man for the benefit of American movies. What lies underneath that masquerade of romantic masculinity, the Wilder film suggests – if only indirectly as the effect of this joke – is a potential subversion of the stable, binarized gender terms by which American culture in the fifties represented masculinity as an automatic, unchanging, and natural relation between male sexuality and male identity. This consummate American lover, the film teases, may therefore be harmless but he is irresistible all the same – and possibly for that very reason.

To be sure, with its naughty implication of castration, the value placed on the star image of 'Cary Grant' by *Some Like It Hot* in 1959 appears to reverse the more attractive and progressive screen persona Andrew Britton sees in Grant's thirties films, particularly the screwball comedies which crystallized his star image. Those comedies, Britton argues, singling out *The Awful Truth* (1937), *Bringing up Baby*

(1938) and *Holiday* (1938), are remarkable for 'the extent to which characteristics assigned by those [traditional gender] roles to women can be presented as being desirable and attractive in a man'. The comic plots of 'male chastisement' in those films established Grant's star image around a bisexual premise of 'male femininity' which leads a Grant character to renounce the phallus and find 'an experience of release and pleasure' in his symbolic castration. In this way, Britton concludes, the screwball comedies 'use Grant to formulate a type of masculinity which is valuable and attractive by virtue of the sharing of gender characteristics with women.'[8]

Two decades later, in the frequent reminders in his fifties films of the longevity of his career and the celebrated familiarity of his face, Grant's mature screen persona still evoked those screwball comedies and their revisionist organization of male and female sexual identities. This is one reason why Billy Wilder's citation of Grant's star image in *Some Like It Hot* did not appear at all farfetched or forced at the time of its release but perfectly in tune with the crossdressing premise of that farce. Even more telling, that film's representation of the star through the related tropes of disguise, bachelorhood, and emasculation begins to suggest something of the popular actor's historical significance as a movie star for postwar US audiences.

To start with, in one way or another many of Grant's films during this period lead the character he plays to undertake some form of disguise, however flimsy the pretence, innocent the motivation, and transparent the mask. Grant masquerades in some of his earlier films, to be sure: in *Bringing Up Baby*, for example, he has to hide his identity from Katharine Hepburn's aunt; and in *Mr Lucky* (1943) his character first adopts the name of a dead Greek crony in order to avoid the draft and then he goes on to double his masquerade by trying to con a socialite (Laraine Day). But such disguises become even more of a routine feature in his postwar films. For a variety of reasons, most of them rather farfetched in order to emphasize the selfconsciousness of his role-playing, Grant poses as a teenager in *The Bachelor and the Bobby Soxer* (1947); as a bride in *I was a Male War Bride* (1949); as an adolescent and child in *Monkey Business* (1952); as a businessman from Oregon in *To Catch a Thief* (1955); as a married man in *Indiscreet* (1958); as a spy in *North by Northwest*: and these various impersonations culminate in the multiple masks his character wears before Audrey Hepburn in *Charade*, his last straight romantic leading role in 1963. Although the narrative explanations offered for his disguises differ in motivation and tone from film to film, depending on the genre (farce, romantic comedy, thriller), these roles keep grounding the sexual appeal of Grant's masculinity in a masquerade of one sort or another. The significance of masquerade in Grant's postwar films has a great deal to do with the growing disparity between his age and the romantic roles he continued to play: however, rather than achieving, as *Some Like it Hot* implies, the concealment of male lack – the diminishment in sexual capacity that, Kinsey showed, accompanies a man's maturity – the masquerading in these films encourages impersonation and play, in this way renewing the mobile screen persona of the earlier screwball comedies.

I am well aware that, following Joan Riviere's by now famous case study, the term 'masquerade' has had a specific psychoanalytic purchase for an understanding of *femininity* as an adventure in selfconscious self-representation, with the feminine mask used, according to Riviere's account, to cover up the female's theft of the phallus.[9] This context has dominated the question of masquerade in film studies, not least because of several important articles published by *Screen* which applied Riviere's comments to film in order to theorize female spectatorship and subjectivity.[10] In my own use of the term here, though, I am more interested in picking up the performative rather than the phallocentric implications of the masquerade, using it in accordance with Judith Butler's discussion of gender as 'performative – that is, constituting the identity it is purported to be', an effect achieved by treating expressions of gender as if they were their causes as well as their results.[11] A masquerade of this sort does not conceal a deep, dark secret so much as define an identity in terms of opposing planes in order to establish the impression of dimensionality: an outside in relation to an inside, surface to depth, performance to authenticity. What the mask – one specific cultural form of which is the Hollywood star whose screen personality is, not accidentally, termed a *persona* – signifies is the mark or playing out of those differences.

That Grant's star image became inseparable from the values of gender mobility and sexual play celebrated by the screwball comedies may help to explain why his screen persona could successfully move back and forth between apparently rigid binaries (not only feminine/masculine, as Britton shows, but also British/American, youthful/ageing, genteel/common) in a way uncharacteristic of other major stars of the studio era. As Bruce Babington and Peter William Evans note,

> Where among Screwball stars William Powell, say, was one-dimensionally debonair, Ray Milland bland, Don Ameche plebeian and suspiciously Latin, Henry Fonda the soul of uprightness, and Gary Cooper a prodigy of plainspeaking (though in some of these cases they played against type), Grant is marvellously protean, the multifarious embodiment of all these qualities and more.[12]

The protean quality of his screen persona, however, did more than create an effect of multidimensionality, integrating those various qualities under a single name. Rather, the fluidity with which Grant moved between binarized terms like masculine/feminine, British/American, genteel/common, allowed him to personify them as a contradiction: on the one hand representing gentility and bearing without, as did many comic actors of lesser rank, appearing effete; and on the other hand, trading upon his undeniable good looks as a screen lover without, as did many other foreign leading men, sacrificing his ability to connote the combination of virility and middle-class Americanness that ranked him alongside stars like Wayne, Stewart, Cooper, and Bogart. As a consequence, the performance style that produced 'Cary Grant' could be at once civilized and anarchic, subtle and broad, verbal and physical, elitist and popular, suggesting how his signature characteristics as a Hollywood star always implicitly ran the risk of putting him across that line which, for the American popular imagination of the 1950s in particular, polarized virility against effeminacy in an effort to authenticate a standardized version of masculinity.

In most of his postwar films, furthermore, the middle-aged Grant plays a bachelor playboy. The casting of Grant in this type of part is not all that remarkable, of course, since the genre of romantic comedy served as his most comfortable and reliable vehicle: so with a few exceptions (*Mr Blandings Builds His Dream House* [1948], *Monkey Business, Room for One More* [1952]), the characters he played were generally single and sought after. To fifties audiences, the bachelor playboy – that 'big dame hunter', as Robert Q. Lewis calls Cary Grant/Nicky Ferrante in *An Affair to Remember* – was more than just a romantic male role in movie comedies; he was also a highly potent cultural figure, the glamorized 'bum' who encoded some of the most deeply felt and conflicting anxieties about male sexual identity. The cultural resonance of the bachelor, particularly when linked to masquerade in the movies, provided the crucial context for reading 'Cary Grant' as the exemplary romantic star during this period.

In its various representations of the domestic and feminized space of the postwar suburban home, fifties USA repeatedly enacted what it read as a symbolic castration of the white middle-class American male; yet the culture also equated *any* form of deviation from that norm with emasculation. 'In the 1950s ...', Barbara Ehrenreich reports

> there was a firm expectation (or as we would now say, 'role') that required men to grow up, marry and support their wives. To do anything else was less than grown up, and the man who wilfully deviated was judged to be somehow 'less than a man'. This expectation was supported by an enormous weight of expert opinion, moral sentiment and public bias, both within popular culture and the elite centers of academic wisdom.

At the same time, Ehrenreich continues, 'in the fifties "conformity" became the code word for male discontent'.[13]

With the Man in Grey Flannel paradoxically epitomizing the white middle-class male's success and his *malaise* (heart disease, stress, alcoholism, impotence, boredom), the burning question in the pages of both the popular press and the academic journals was, as one feature article in *Look* magazine put it: 'How did the American male get into this pit of subjection, where even his masculinity is in doubt?' This was not an idle rhetorical question by any means, for as the article took pains to explain:

> Scientists who study human behavior fear that the American male is now dominated by the American female. These scientists worry that in the years since the end of World War II, he has changed radically and dangerously; that he is no longer the masculine, strong-minded man who pioneered the continent and built America's greatness.... And the experts pin most of the blame for his new plight squarely on women....[14]

To be sure, it was widely agreed in the culture that 'Today's breadwinner must be a part-time nursemaid, kitchen helper, handyman and mechanic',[15] but these multiple requirements seemed to tax American men beyond their limits. In an effort to rescue them from the barbecue pits of suburban subjection, the *Woman's Home Companion* admonished its readers:

> But remember that a man in a gray flannel suit is also a man and that for two or three years he was away from you in one or another war. For two or three years he lived as undomesti- cated men do live: without the bills and taxes perhaps, living among other men and not inhibiting man's natural impulse to obscene language and obscene storytelling, seeing men die and perhaps expecting to die himself, free in the sense that he often had no idea what the next day would bring. And free, if he wished, to lie on his bunk evenings, to think and dream.
>
> There are certain deep and perfectly normal masculine drives that were 'permitted' during a war as they are not permitted in a suburban back yard. They are an inborn attrac-

tion to violence and obscenity and polygamy, an inborn love of change, an inborn need to be different from the others and rebel against them, a strong need for the occasional company of men only and an occasional need for solitude and privacy.

Certainly all men do not feel these drives to the same degree. And certainly these drives shouldn't all be permitted in that clean, green, happy back yard. But if they are always and completely inhibited – the man in the gray flannel suit will stop being a man.[16]

I have quoted these remarks in full because they indicate the extent to which the fifties idealization of the domesticated married male was in large measure a consequence of demobilization, with social authority being transferred from the American male's platoon commander to his wife. Since the social regulation delegated to women amounted to a symbolic castration, a diminution of the mythic American male spirit as personified by the folk heroes of the nineteenth century, the culture's understanding of masculinity was always in conflict, torn between an abiding concern with upholding the middle-class breadwinning ethic as the true index of manliness, and a deepseated worry that the domestic and corporate spaces in which the male exercised his power sapped him of his natural virility and national character.

The bachelor playboy, hailed by Hugh Hefner as the rebel refusing to serve the dictates of women by succumbing to the institution of marriage, was the admired antithesis of the domesticated suburban husband who wore a grey flannel suit and repressed his irresistible urge to scratch a seven-year itch. According to Ehrenreich, the success of *Playboy* magazine in the early fifties owed much to the way it packaged 'male rebellion' as an alternative representation of masculinity that could compete with the stifling ethic of the male breadwinner. From this perspective, the infamous centrefold nude in every issue was crucial because it confirmed the heterosexuality of the *Playboy* reader, guarding against any suspicions about why he preferred to remain single.[17] More than its centrefolds, though, the real genius of Hefner's magazine showed through in its addressing the bachelor playboy as a consumer, locating his heterosexual desires in his bachelor pad, that fantasy playpen of seduction and technology most famously exemplified by Rock Hudson's apartment in *Pillow Talk* (1959). Here he could safely fulfil those 'perfectly normal masculine drives that were "permitted" during a war as they are not permitted in a suburban back yard'. In serving this function, the primary economic and cultural importance of *Playboy* magazine was therefore its address a male consumer as part of the postwar effort to enlarge the leisure time market by overtly including men, who were pitched the desirability of the latest high-fidelity stereo equipment, stylish clothing, appealing aftershaves, virile liquors, exotic vacations, controversial books, hip music, all with the aim of intensifying *their* sexual attractiveness to women as single men.[18]

As far as the dominant cultural reading of the bachelor playboy was concerned, then, he cut quite an ambiguous figure. His single status and independence from marital obligations and domestic spaces represented a fundamental 'immaturity', 'irresponsibility', 'insecurity', and 'latent homosexuality' that simultaneously needed correction (to promote a man's maturity) *and* expression (to preserve his heterosexual masculinity). Consequently, when American romantic sex comedies of this period draw on the cultural currency of the bachelor playboy, particularly his conventional strategy of seducing women with the pose of being unmasculine or powerless in her hands, what they put at issue in this peculiarly American battle of the sexes is not male sexual desire so much as male sexual identity. Fifties American culture generally made gender and sexuality comparable, focusing on sexual identity as its primary means of remaining silent on questions of sexual desire and orientation. For this reason gender issues in movies of this period – most apparently in the transformation of Tennessee Williams's plays onto the screen, but also in the sex comedies that waged a war of genders around the site of the virginal female body – always appear to encode problems of sexuality too, particularly when dealing with men, their social identities, and their desires.

Film after film in the sex comedy genre begins by valorizing the bachelor playboy for his 'natural' – which is actually to say 'undomesticated' – virility, only to critique him for his immaturity in resisting marriage out of fear of losing his manliness.[19] Tuned to perfection in the Rock Hudson–Doris Day pairings in *Pillow Talk* and *Lover Come Back* (1961), this genre typically leads the bachelor playboy to appreciate the 'tender trap' of institutionalized heterosexual union; and then, in his climactic disavowal of 'sexual freedom', to internalize what was considered the woman's driving desire: monogamous companionship and security. 'Don't worry', Grant's Philip Adams tells Ingrid Bergman's Anna Kalman at the end of *Indiscreet*, 'you'll *like* being married, you will, you'll see'.

At the same time, the playboy bachelor of fifties sex comedies always has the potential to subvert the culture's rather orthodox understanding of a masculine identity as something natural, spontaneous, and unchanging. Films of this genre typically take the bachelor playboy's sexual virility for granted as the motivating drive behind the formation of the heterosexual couple. However, when, as their comic premise, the films also make the male star conceal his identity as part of his campaign to seduce the female star, they end up by calling his virility into question, because the disguise implicates his heterosexuality as well as his masculinity in his masquerade. To trick the female star he feigns some form of male lack (effeminacy or impotence, both of which encode suggestions of homosexuality), turning his virility inside out to impersonate a feminized masculinity. This disguise then circumstantially leads a medical authority (a doctor, a psychiatrist) to draw the same erroneous conclusion. So, for example, in *Pillow Talk* a doctor thinks Rock Hudson may be pregnant, and in *That Touch of Mink* (1962), a psychiatrist assumes that Cary Grant is Gig Young's lover.

As Babington and Evans remark, in the light of later knowledge about Hudson's sexuality, 'there is a particular irony about a great heterosexual icon of the cinema whose fabrication includes even the nature of his sexuality', even though it may not have been intentional.[20] Consequently, as in the comparable case of Grant, though the implications of the male star's various layers of masquerade were surely not lost on the people making the films – and may well be apparent to contemporary audiences – they did not necessarily contribute to the reception of these films at the time of their release. On the contrary, the narrative closure always safeguards the male star from any implication of sexual transgression; and so does the pairing of the star with a more effeminate and neurotic buddy (Tony Randall, Gig Young) who is sometimes a rival, sometimes a confidante, and whose function regardless is to authenticate the virility and normality of the lead. But even so, that the questioning of a male star's sexual identity became fundamental to the sex comedy genre as its central comic situation shows how much the bachelor's masquerade can unsettle the conventional sexual binaries which the genre's closure tries to uphold through the romantic couple. For the very premise of the bachelor's masquerade is grounded in audience recognition that any form of sexual identity amounts to a masquerade, a construction involving performance, theatricality, and disguise – of the very sort epitomized by the Hollywood star system itself.

Although the Hudson-Day comedies may push the bachelor's masquerade much more obviously towards this pattern of first interrogating and then recuperating a phallocentric virility, Grant's postwar films, with their particular glossing of his bachelorhood through a masquerade, generally have a similar effect. His most popular roles of this era equated the attractiveness of his brand of male sexual identity with the performance of a masquerade of some sort, giving that original screen persona of the screwball comedies a different inflection, one more specifically responsive to the crisis of masculinity dominating the fifties representation of gender in US popular culture. Thus, even when the character he plays may appear to capitulate to the traditional organization of sexual difference around simplistic gendered binaries, in order to be made legible as a star image 'Cary Grant' turns out to dominate the film text with a more unconventional representation of male sexual identity as a masquerade. This point seems to me to be the important conclusion to be drawn from his postwar success as a screen lover [...]

Notes

1 Peter Biskind, *Seeing is Believing. How Hollywood Taught Us to Stop Worrying and Love the Fifties* (New York: Pantheon, 1983), p. 252.
2 William Rothman, '*North by Northwest*: Hitchcock's monuments to the Hitchcock film', in *The 'I' Of The Camera: Essays In Film Criticism, History, and Aesthetics* (Cambridge: Cambridge University Press, 1988), p. 177.
3 Stanley Cavell, '*North by Northwest*', *Critical Inquiry*, vol. 7, no. 4 (1981), p. 769.
4 '6 ways to rope in that summer romance', *Photoplay*, September 1958, p. 95. Cary Grant's advice, by the way, was: 'Don't show jealousy, but diplomacy'.
5 Charles Higham and Roy Moseley, *Cary Grant: The Lonely Heart* (New York: Avon, 1990), p. 248.
6 'They were easy to drip dry when one was traveling', Grant reportedly told reporter Joe Hyams in explanation: see Higham and Moseley, *Cary Grant*, p. 281.
7 That the problem of impotence was crucial to an understanding of the social and sexual pressures faced by American men was a theme stressed in popular accounts of American manliness, as in some of the magazine articles cited below: and it also appeared in academic discussions, as in sociologist Helen Mayer Hacker's discussion of impotence in 'The new burdens of masculinity', *Marriage and Family Living*, vol. 19, no. 3 (1957), pp. 228–9.
8 Andrew Britton, 'Cary Grant: comedy and male desire', *Cine-Action!*, no. 7 (1986), pp. 37, 38, 43.
9 Joan Riviere, 'Womanliness as a masquerade', reprinted in Victor Burgin, James Donald, and Cora Kaplan (eds). *Formations of Fantasy* (New York: Methuen, 1986), pp. 35–44.
10 See Mary Ann Doane, 'Film and the masquerade: theorizing the female spectator', *Screen*, vol. 23, nos 3–4 (1982), pp. 74–88; and John Fletcher, 'Versions of masquerade', *Screen*, vol. 29, no. 3 (1988), pp. 43–69. For a more recent critique of both Riviere's

formulation and its application by psychoanalytic film theorists, see Chris Holmlund, 'Masculinity as multiple masquerade: the "mature" Stallone and the Stallone clone', in Steven Cohan and Ina Rae Hark (eds), *Screening the Male: Exploring Masculinities in Hollywood Cinema* (London: Routledge, forthcoming 1992).

11 Judith Butler, *Gender Trouble: Feminism and the Subversion of Identity* (New York: Routledge, 1990), p. 25.

12 Bruce Babington and Peter William Evans, *Affairs to Remember: The Hollywood Comedy of the Sexes* (Manchester: Manchester University Press, 1989), p. 22.

13 Barbara Ehrenreich, *The Hearts of Men: American Dreams and the Flight from Commitment* (New York: Anchor Press, 1983), pp. 11–12, 30.

14 J. Robert Moskin, 'The American male: why do women dominate him?' *Look*, 4 February 1958, pp. 80, 77.

15 William Attwood, 'The American male: why does he work so hard?' *Look*, 4 March 1958, p. 73.

16 Louis Lyndon, 'Uncertain hero: the paradox of the American male', *Woman's Home Companion*, November 1956, p. 107.

17 Ehrenreich, *The Hearts of Men*, pp. 42–51.

18 For an account of the magazine's development in this direction as it was occurring, see Martin Ryan, 'Portrait of *Playboy*', *Studies in Public Communication*, no. 1 (1957), pp. 11–21.

19 For a discussion of the sexual warfare characteristic of fifties American comedy, see Frank Krutnik, 'The faint aroma of performing seals: the "nervous" romance and the comedy of the sexes'. *Velvet Light Trap*, no. 26 (1990), pp. 59–62.

20 Babington and Evans, *Affairs to Remember*, p. 205.

23 Feminine fascinations: forms of identification in star–audience relations

Jackie Stacey

Cinematic identificatory fantasies

Devotion and worship

> I wanted to write and tell you of my devotion to my favourite star Doris Day. I thought she was fantastic, and joined her fan club, collected all the photos and info I could. I saw Calamity Jane 45 times in a fortnight and still watch all her films avidly. My sisters all thought I was mad going silly on a woman, but I just thought she was wonderful, they were mad about Elvis, but my devotion was to Doris Day. (V.M.)

Some letters do not even mention the self, but simply offer evidence of devotion to a female star. However, this is unusual; most letters I received framed their comments on stars in relation to their own identities. In this first group, many of the letters speak of the pleasure produced by some kind of difference from the star, the distance produced by this difference providing a source of fascination. Stars are frequently written about as out of reach, and belonging to a different world or plane of existence:

> Film stars ... seemed very special people, glamorous, handsome and way above us ordinary mortals. (J.T.)
> I'll never forget the first time I saw her, it was in *My Gal Sal* in 1942, and her name was Rita Hayworth. I couldn't take my eyes off her, she was the most perfect woman I had ever seen. The old cliché 'screen goddess' was used about many stars, but those are truly the only words that define that divine creature ... I was stunned and amazed that any human being could be that lovely. (V.H.)
> Stars were fabulous creatures to be worshipped from afar, every film of one's favourite gobbled up as soon as it came out. (P.K.)

These statements represent the star as something different and unattainable. Religious signifiers here indicate the special status and meaning of the stars, as well as suggesting the intensity of the devotion felt by the spectator. They also reinforce the 'otherness' of the stars who are not considered part of the mortal world of the spectator. The last example, however, does introduce the star into the mortal world by a metaphor of ingestion reminiscent of the act of communion. Worship of stars as goddesses involves a denial of self found in some forms of religious devotion. The spectator is only present in these quotes as a worshipper, or through their adoration of the star. There is no reference to the identity of the spectator or suggestion of closing the gap between star and fan by becoming more like a star; these are simply declarations of appreciation from afar. The boundaries between self and ideal are quite fixed and stable in these examples, and the emphasis is very strongly on the ideal rather than he spectator. Even in the last statement, where the self is implicit in that the star is to be gobbled up, the star none the less remains the subject of the sentence.

The desire to become

In other examples, the relationship between star and audience is also articulated through the recognition of an immutable difference between star and spectator: 'Bette Davis was the epitome of what we would like to be, but knew we never could!' (N.T.). Yet here the desire to move across that difference and become more like the star is expressed, even if this is accompanied by the impossibility of its fulfilment.[1] The distance between the spectator and her ideal seems to produce a kind of longing which offers fantasies of transformed identities.

These desires to become more like the stars occur on several levels. Many of them are predictably articulated in relation to appearance:

> I finally kept with Joan Crawford – every typist's dream of how they'd like to look. (M.R.). And of course her [Betty Grable's] clothes – how could a young girl not want to look like that? (S.W.)
> Although I wished to look like a different star each week depending what film I saw, I think my favourite was Rita Hayworth, I always imagined, if I could look like her I could toss my red hair into the wind ... and meet the man of my dreams ... (R.A.)

Clearly, stars serve a normative function to the extent that they are often read as role models, contributing to the construction of the ideals of feminine attractiveness circulating in culture at any one time. The age difference between the star and the younger fans is central here: stars provide ideals of femininity for adolescent women in the audience, preoccupied with attaining adult femininity. Part of this kind of identification involves recognising desirable qualities in the ideal and wanting to move towards it:

> Doris Day ... seemed to epitomise the kind of person who, with luck, I as a child could aspire to be. (B.C.)
> I loved to watch Deanna Durbin. I used to put myself in her place. She lived in a typical girl's dream. (J.G.)

These examples demonstrate not simply the desire to overcome the gap between spectator and star, but a fantasy of possible movement between the two identities, from the spectator to the star.

Pleasure in feminine power

However, the difference between the female star and the female spectator is a source of fascination not only with ideals of physical beauty, but also with the stars' personalities and behaviour, which are often admired or envied by spectators. These identifications demonstrate the contradictory pleasures offered by Hollywood stars, on the one hand reproducing normative models of feminine glamour, whilst on the other hand offering women fantasies of resistance. For example, some female stars represented images of power and confidence. These were frequent favourites because they offered spectators fantasies of power outside their own experience.

> We liked stars who were most different to ourselves and Katharine Hepburn, with her self-assured romps through any situation was one of them. We were youngsters at the time, and were anything but self confident, and totally lacking in sophistication, so, naturally, Bette Davis took the other pedestal. She who could be a real 'bitch', without turning a hair, and quelled her leading men with a raised eyebrow and sneer at the corners of her mouth ... (N.T.)
> Bette Davis ... was great, I loved how she walked across the room in her films, she seemed to have a lot of confidence and she had a look of her own, as I think a lot of female stars had at that time ... (E.M.)

Powerful female stars often play characters in punishing patriarchal narratives, where the woman is either killed off, or married, or both, but these spectators do not seem to select this aspect of their films to write about. Instead, the qualities of confidence and power are remembered as offering pleasure to female spectators in something they lack and desire.

Identification and escapism

This movement from spectator to star is part of the pleasure of escapism articulated in many of the letters. Instead of the difference between the spectator and the star being recognised and maintained, the difference provides the possibility for the spectator to leave her world temporarily and become part of the star's world:[2]

> It made no difference to me if the film was ushered in by a spangled globe, the Liberty Lady or that roaring lion, I was no longer in my seat but right up there fleeing for my life

from chasing gangsters, skimming effortlessly over silver ice, or singing high and sweet like a lark. (D.H.)

I was only a girl, but I could be transported from the austerity and gloom of that time to that other world on the silver screen. (J.T.)

Joan Crawford – could evoke such pathos, and suffer such martyrdom ... making you live each part. (M.B.)

In these examples, the movement from self to other is more fluid than in the previous categories, and this fluidity provides the well-known pleasure of the cinema: 'losing oneself' in the film. Here, in contrast to the distinction between self and ideal maintained in the processes of spectatorship discussed above, the spectator's identity merges with the star in the film, or the character she is portraying.

In this first section I have discussed processes of spectatorship which involve negotiating the difference between the star and the spectator in various ways: beginning with the denial of self, in favour of praising the screen goddesses, and moving on to the desire to become like the star, but realising the impossibility of such desires, and ending with the pleasure in overcoming the difference and merging with the ideal on the screen.

Extra-cinematic identificatory practices

Now I want to move on to discuss representations which concern what I shall call 'identificatory practices' of spectatorship. These nearly all relate to forms of identification which take place outside the cinematic context. These practices also involve the audience engaging in some kind of practice of transformation of the self to become more like the star they admire, or to involve others in the recognition of their similarity with the star.

Pretending

... there was a massive open-cast coal site just at the tip of our estate – there were 9 of us girls – and we would go to the site after school, and play on the mounds of soil removed from the site. The mounds were known to us as 'Beverley Hills' and we all had lots of fun there. Each of us had our own spot where the soil was made into a round – and that was our mansion. We played there for hours – visiting one mansion after another and each being our own favourite film star ... (M.W.)

I really loved the pictures, they were my life, I used to pretend I was related to Betty Grable because my name was Betty, and I used to get quite upset when the other children didn't believe me. (B.C.)

Pretending to be particular film stars involves an imaginary practice, but one where the spectator involved knows that it is a game. This is rather different from the processes of escapism in the cinema discussed above whereby the spectator feels completely absorbed in the star's world and which thus involves a temporary collapsing of the self into the star identity. The first example given above is also different in that it involves a physical as well as an imaginary transformation. Furthermore pretending does not simply involve the privatised imagination of the individual spectator, as in the process of escapism, but also involves the participation of other spectators in the collective fantasy games. This kind of representation of the relationship between star and fan is based more on similarity than difference, since the fan takes on the identity of the star in a temporary game of make-believe, and the difference between them is made invisible, despite the recognition of the whole process as one of pretending.

Resembling

> Bette Davis – her eyes were fabulous and the way she walked arrogantly ... I have dark eyes, in those days I had very large dark eyebrows ... and my Dad used to say ... 'Don't you roll those Bette Davis eyes at me young lady ...' ... Now Doris Day, that's a different thing – we share the same birthday ... (P.O.)

There are numerous points of recognition of similarities between the spectator and the star. These are not based on pretending to be something one is not, but rather selecting something which establishes a link between the star and the self based on a pre-existing part of the spectator's identity which bears a resemblance to the star. This does not necessarily involve any kind of transformation, but rather a highlighting of star qualities in the individual spectator. The significance of particular features, such as 'Bette Davis eyes', seems to exceed physical likeness, to suggest a certain kind of femininity, in this case a rebellious one which represented a challenge to the father's authority.

Imitating

Unlike the above process of recognising a resemblance to a star, many spectators wrote about practices which involved transforming themselves to be more like the star. This is different from the fantasy of becoming the star whilst viewing a film, or even expressing the desire to become more like the star generally, since it involves an actual imitation of a star or of her particular characteristics in a particular film. In other words this identificatory practice involves a form of pretending or play-acting, and yet it is also different from pretending, since pretending is represented as a process involving the whole star persona, whereas imitation is used here to indicate a partial taking-on of part of a star's identity.

Several letters gave examples of imitating singing and dancing of favourite stars after the film performance:

> We used to go home and do concerts based on the songs and dances we had seen in the films, and one of my friends had an auntie who was a mine of information on the words of songs from films ... (B.F.)
> The films we saw made us sing and sometimes act our way home on the bus ... (J.T.)
> My favourite female star was Betty Grable. The songs she sang in the film, I would try to remember, I would sing and dance all the way home ... (P.G.)

The imitation of stars was not limited to singing and dancing, but was clearly a pleasure in terms of replicating gestures, speech and star personalities: 'I had my favourites of course ... One week I would tigerishly pace about like Joan Crawford, another week I tried speaking in the staccato tones of Bette Davis and puffing a cigarette at the same time' (D.H.).

Copying

Although imitation and copying are very closely linked as practices, I want to use them here differently to distinguish between audiences *imitating* behaviour and activities, and copying appearances. As the attempted replication of appearance, then, *copying* relates back to the desire to look like stars discussed above. However it is not simply expressed as an unfulfillable desire or pleasurable fantasy, as in the earlier examples, it is also a practice which transforms the spectators' physical appearance.

Copying is the most common form of identificatory practice outside the cinema. Perhaps this is not surprising given the centrality of physical appearance to femininity in general in this culture, and to female Hollywood stars in particular. The 'visual pleasure' offered by the glamour and sexual appeal of Hollywood stars has been thoroughly criticised by feminists elsewhere.[3] Here I am interested in how women audiences related to these ideals of femininity as presented by Hollywood stars on the screen, and particularly in how identification extends beyond individualised fantasies into practices aimed at the transformation of identity.

> I was a very keen fan of Bette Davis and can remember seeing her in *Dark Victory* ... That film had such an impact on me. I can remember coming home and looking in the mirror fanatically trying to comb my hair so that I could look like her. I idolised her ... thought she was a wonderful actress. (V.C.)

This process involves an intersection of self and other, subject and object. The impact of the film on the spectator was to produce a desire to resemble physically the ideal. In front of a reflection of herself, the spectator attempts to close the gap between her image and her ideal image, by trying to produce a new image, more like her ideal. In this instance, her hair is the focus of this desired transformation. Indeed hairstyle is one of the most frequently recurring aspects of the star's appearance which the spectators try to copy:

> My friends and I would try and copy the hair styles of the stars, sometimes we got it right, and other times we just gave up, as we hadn't the looks of the stars or the money to dress the way they did. (E.M.)
> Now Doris Day ... I was told many times around that I looked like her, so I had my hair cut in a D.A. style. Jane Wyman was a favourite at one stage and I had hair cut like hers, it was called a tulip ... Now Marilyn Monroe was younger and by this time I had changed my image, my hair was almost white blonde and longer and I copied her hairstyle, as people said I looked like her. (P.O.)

These forms of copying involve some kind of self-transformation to produce an appearance more similar to Hollywood stars. Some spectators clearly have a stronger feeling of their success than others; the first example includes a sense of defeat whilst the last seems to be able to achieve several desired likenesses, especially bearing in mind this respondent is the one who had 'Bette Davis eyes'. The difference then between the star and the spectator is transformable into similarity through the typical work of femininity: the production of oneself simultaneously as subject and object in accordance with cultural ideals of femininity.

Copying and consumption

Copying the hairstyles of famous film stars can be seen as a form of cultural production and consumption. It involves the production of a new self-image through the pleasure taken in a star image. In this last section I want to consider an extension of the identificatory practice of copying where it intersects with the consumption of cultural products in addition to the star image. The construction of women as cinema spectators overlaps here with their construction as consumers.

To some extent copying the hairstyles of the stars overlaps with this. However I have separated hairstyles from other aspects of this process, since changing hairstyles does not necessarily involve the actual purchasing of other products to transform the identity of the spectator, although it may do. The purchasing of items such as clothing and cosmetics in relation to particular stars brings into particularly sharp focus the relationship between the cinema industries and other forms of capitalist industry. Stars are consumable feminine images which female spectators then reproduce through other forms of consumption.

> and I bought clothes like hers [Doris Day] ... dresses, soft wool, no sleeves, but short jackets, boxy type little hats, half hats we used to call them and low heeled court shoes to match your outfit, kitten heels they were called ... as people said I looked like her [Marilyn Monroe] I even bought a suit after seeing her in *Niagara*. (P.O.)
>
> It was fun trying to copy one's favourite stars with their clothes, hats and even make-up, especially the eyebrows. Hats were very much in vogue at that time and shops used to sell models similar to the styles the stars were wearing. I was very much into hats myself and tried in my way (on a low budget) to copy some of them. Naturally I bought a Deanna Durbin model hat and a Rita Hayworth one. (V.C.)
>
> I'd like to name Deanna Durbin as one of my favourite stars. Her beautiful singing voice, natural personality and sparkling eyes made her films so enjoyable, and one always knew she would wear boleros; in one film she wore six different ones. I still like wearing boleros – so you can tell what a lasting effect the clothes we saw on the screen made on us. (J.D., member of the Deanna Durbin Society)

Stars are thus identified with particular commodities which are part of the reproduction of feminine identities. The female spectators in these examples produce particular images of femininity which remind them of their favourite stars. In so doing they produce a new feminine identity, one which combines an aspect of the star with their own appearance. This is different from imitation, which is more of a temporary reproduction of a particular kind of behaviour which resembles the star. It transforms the spectators' previous appearance, and in doing so offers the spectator the pleasure of close association with her ideal.

> As teenagers and young girls we did not have the vast variety of clothing and choices of make-up that is available today, so hairstyles and make-up were studied with great interest and copied ... I seem to remember buying a small booklet by Max Factor with pictures of the stars, M.G.M. mostly, with all the details of their make-up and how to apply it ... (E.H.)
>
> Their make-up was faultless and their fashion of the forties platform shoes, half hats with rows of curls showing at the back under the hat ... We used to call the shoes 'Carmen Miranda' shoes ... I felt like a film star using Lux Toilet soap, advertised as the stars' soap. (V.B.)

Through the use of cosmetic products, then, as well as through the purchasing and use of clothing, spectators take on a part of the stars identity and make it part of their own. The self and the ideal combine to produce another feminine identity, closer to the ideal. This is the direct opposite of the process of identification I began with in the first section, in which the spectator's own identity remained relatively marginal to the description of the pleasure taken in female Hollywood stars. In this final process, the star becomes more marginal and is only relevant in so far as the star identity relates to the spectator's own identity. As has been noted by other commentators, these latter practices demonstrate the importance of understanding Hollywood stars and their audiences in relation to other cultural industries of the 1940s and 1950s.[4]

Notes

1 For a discussion of the representation of desire between women produced by their differences, see Jackie Stacey, 'Desperately seeking difference', in *Screen*, 28, 1 (1987), 48–61.
2 For a discussion of the pleasurable feelings escapism offers to the cinema audience, see Richard Dyer, 'Entertainment and utopia', *Movie*, 24 (Spring 1977), 2–13.
3 See Laura Mulvey, *Visual and Other Pleasures* (London, Macmillan, 1989), and E. Ann Kaplan, *Women and Film: Both Sides of the Camera* (London, Methuen, 1983).
4 Angela Partington, 'Melodrama's gendered audience', in Sarah Franklin, Celia Lury and Jackie Stacey, eds, *Off Centre: Feminism and Cultural Studies* (London, Unwin Hyman, forthcoming).

SECTION FIVE

THE HISTORICAL POETICS OF THE CINEMA

Historical poetics is a very eclectic and diverse approach. However, according to David Bordwell (1988), its most prominent spokesperson, it draws on Russian formalism, an approach to the study of literature which emerged in pre-revolutionary Russia and which involved the application of Saussurean linguistics to the study of 'literary language' (see e.g. Bennett 1979). The Russian formalists were concerned to identify the 'literariness' of literature, or that which defined it as a specific form of language, and to do so they drew on Saussure's notion of the 'arbitrariness' of language (see Section Three). In other words, they argued that despite the fact that language does not simply name a reality that exists outside it, and that it is therefore utterly conventional in nature, most uses of language specifically depend on the repression of this arbitrariness. They therefore claim that most of the time language is seen as 'transparent'; that is, as though it were a neutral 'reflection' of reality.

By contrast, they argued, literary language was precisely that which did not present language as transparent but rather emphasized its formal and conventional nature. It was a use of language that forced its reader to become aware of its existence as a linguistic object, and also, in the process, made the reader see the world differently. Literary language was that which defamiliarized language, or 'made it strange'. However, while the aesthetic strategies through which it achieves these effects are inevitably shocking and defamiliarizing when they first appear, they also, equally inevitably, become familiar, accepted and established so that new techniques have to be developed to defamiliarize and displace them.

From this work, historical poetics took the concept of the 'aesthetic norm'. For the Russian formalists, literary language did not just defamiliarize 'ordinary' language, but also those earlier aesthetic forms that had become accepted, dominant, and hence no longer challenged perceptions or made things strange. The 'aesthetic norm' refers to these accepted, dominant and unchallenging aesthetic forms.

One of the most significant and important aspects of historical poetics, however, is that, unlike earlier approaches, it has not simply assumed that the norms of film-making are known entities against which one can easily identify radical innovations. Instead, it has always been deeply committed to the detailed study of these norms. This approach marks a major advance on, say, certain varieties of *auteur* theory, for which the majority of films were not seen as worthy of study. On the contrary, these *auteur* theorists presupposed that the character of most films was already known, and that it was the ways in which individual directors transcended or subverted this character that should be the object of study.

Certainly, historical poetics does suggest that the defamiliarization of these norms is more significant aesthetically than the norms themselves, but it also acknowledges that the meaning and even the presence of any defamiliarization can only be determined on the basis of a properly researched examination of the norms in relation to which it works. As a result, more than any other approach, historical poetics has provided film studies with detailed historical scholarship into an extraordinary range of aspects of film-making, including camera-work, the use of music and sound, lighting practices, the use of colour film processes, editing, set design, and censorship practices.

It is also important that, in the study of these features, historical poetics sees the aesthetic norm in terms of tendencies rather than rules. In other words, the aesthetic norm does not concern claims about how a film *must* behave but instead relates to guidelines about how films are expected to behave under 'normal' circumstances. Breaks from the norm are therefore not only seen as permissible but also quite common. The point is rather that the meanings of such deviations are defined in relation to the norm. For example, it is normal practice for film-makers to hold the camera steady. Even in shots where the camera moves, it is normal practice to make the movement as smooth as possible. However, this does not mean that filmmakers cannot, or do not, use unsteady or shaky shots. It is simply that the meaning of these shots is defined by their divergence from what is expected to be normal practice. For example, they are often used to suggest earthquakes, explosions, the 'subjective point of view' of a particular character within the film, or to create a sense of documentary realism.

As a result, Bordwell has claimed that, unlike other approaches to the study of film, historical poetics is not an 'interpretative school'. This claim is highly contested, but Bordwell's contention is that historical poetics is directed more by scholarly research than is the case with other approaches; and that it does not seek to interpret the meaning of texts, but to identify the principles according to which they are made, and the circumstances under which these principles came into being.

The first three extracts in this section therefore concern the analysis of the three main periods within the history of cinema as defined by historical poetics: early cinema; the classical period of Hollywood cinema; and the post-classical or 'New' Hollywood. These extracts, in different ways, seek to discuss the specific aesthetic norm of each period, or rather the specific principles that governed film-making. In his work on early cinema, for example, Tom Gunning refutes the notion that early cinema should be seen as a primitive forerunner of the classical period, but instead suggests that it embodied a series of different norms and principles which were later displaced by the classical period.

In the extract on the classical period, Richard Maltby discusses Bordwell, Staiger and Thompson's groundbreaking work, *The Classical Hollywood Cinema* (1985). He not only takes issue with some of the assumptions in this work but also discusses the ways in which changing conceptions of its audience began to transform this system and produce a new set of norms.

Indeed, there is considerable disagreement about the scope of the term 'Classical Hollywood cinema'. While Bordwell seems to suggest that it dates from about 1917 to the present day, other figures within historical poetics have tried to identify a series of transformation from the late 1940s onwards which have given rise to what is either called the 'new' Hollywood or post-classical Hollywood. It is this particular period that Peter Krämer discusses in extract 26. Here Krämer not only provides an account of the problems of periodization, and of the numerous ways in which this period has been conceived, but also offers his own suggestions for how historical poetics might go about analysing the norms or principles which govern this period.

These pieces reveal some of the problems with historical poetics. First, there is the basic lack of clarity about the meaning of the term 'aesthetic norm'. For example, the word 'aesthetic' is used to refer both to the practice of defamiliarization *and* to the norms that are defamiliarized. Perhaps more problematically, it remains unclear whether the 'aesthetic norm' is supposed to constitute an 'ideal type' to which few films, if any, actually conform but in relation to which most films operate, or a general tendency to which most films conform and from which only a few, special films deviate.

On the one hand, it is suggested that the aesthetic norm is only a guideline, a rule of thumb, rather than a fixed formula that most films follow. In this sense, the term 'norm' is not used to define what is common practice, but rather that which is taken to be the standard against which other cases are judged, even if no films actually conform to it. In a similar way, for example, some people claim that the norm of the nuclear family in our culture is a construct to which, by definition, few if any conform, but which is none the less ideologically powerful as an expectation about how people *should* live under 'normal' circumstances. According to this use of the term 'norm', it is unclear how one can create a special category of films that defamiliarize. If hardly any films conform to the aesthetic norm, then most films would have to be defined as a defamiliarization of it. However, Bordwell and others often use the term 'aesthetic norm' and 'ordinary film' interchangeably, as though in fact the majority of films *do* conform to the aesthetic norm and only certain films can be seen to deviate from it, and hence to defamiliarize it.

Indeed, as some critics have pointed out, the concept of the aesthetic norm seems almost impossibly elastic, 'so that the similarities between, say, *The Crowd*, *The Band Wagon* and *Touch of Evil* overwhelm their more distinctive qualities' (Jenkins 1995: 104). While Jenkins makes a spirited defence of historical poetics, he shows that this sense of elasticity is also related to another fundamental problem, the actual conception of history within historical poetics. It is not simply that there is a disagreement over whether or not the classical norms are still in place today; there is something very unsettling about a *historical* account of cinema which suggests that nothing fundamental has changed in 80 out of 100 years of cinema.

Indeed, despite their reliance on Russian formalism, it is rarely acknowledged that most examples of historical poetics seem to have reversed two basic tenets of this earlier approach. First, Russian formalism was basically a historical model of permanent literary revolution in which one literary avant-garde after another challenges and then displaces the literary establishment, before themselves becoming a new establishment which needs, in turn, to be challenged and displaced. By contrast, historical poetics is a model of permanent cinematic counter-revolution in which challenge after challenge is incorporated and neutralized, so ensuring the stability and continuity of aesthetic norms.

Furthermore, the Russian formalists presented the aesthetic norm as being the literary establishment, and the popular (or 'lower branch') as the soil from which challenges emerged. Historical poetics, on the other hand, seems to have reversed this model of cultural politics so that it is the popular cinema of Hollywood which is defined as the aesthetic norm, and the art cinema from which challenges tend to emerge.

This shift in cultural politics also raises another problem: that of the audiences for films. For example, the focus on the principles by which films are constructed has often lead historical poetics to privilege production-based, rather than consumption-based, approaches to film. To put it another way, it has often seen the meaning of films as being determined by their production, rather than their consumption (see Section Eight). Thus, while Jenkins claims that 'Norms are seen as a shared framework of understanding between artists and consumers, both of which groups are situated in relation to formal systems and aesthetic institutions' (1995: 108), this often leads to an approach to reception in which audiences are little more than the 'implied readers' of post-formalist critics such as Roman Ingarden (1973a; 1973b) and Wolfgang Iser (1974; 1978). In this model, the spectator is not a concrete social subject but simply a position determined by the film, the hypothetical addressee who performs the actions demanded by the text: 'Spectators draw upon norms and expectations from their previous film-viewing experience to make sense of the perceptual challenges posed by a new film narrative' (Jenkins 1995: 108). This often tends towards a universalized and ideal reader who is often specifically opposed to the vast majority of filmgoers. As Jeffrey Sconce has argued, this position frequently divides the filmgoing public into ' "skilled" and "unskilled" audiences' (1995: 392).

There are, however, other approaches to the study of audiences within historical poetics. One is concerned with the production strategies of film industries. This work largely focuses on how industries have understood their audiences as markets and have tried to organize those markets and their production strategies accordingly. This work is to some extent represented by the latter sections of the Maltby extract (25), and it is of the utmost importance. However, it still does not address what the cinema has meant to actual audiences. On the contrary, it is concerned with the industries' beliefs about these audiences. Moreover, as Peter Krämer has pointed out, these beliefs should not be taken at face value as an accurate reflection of the audience, and there are often very good reasons for arguing that film industries have often been very wrong in their assumptions about their audiences (Krämer 1999).

Another major approach to the audience from within historical poetics has come to be known as historical reception studies. This work takes a number of different forms, and has drawn on a number of different intellectual traditions (for an alternative approach, see extract 41 in Section Eight). Within historical poetics, however, the figure most directly associated with historical reception studies is Janet Staiger, whose work on *The Silence of the Lambs* (1991) is extract 27 in the current section. For Staiger, meanings do not reside in a text, waiting to be discovered by the reader. Meanings are instead the product of specific historical events. These events are also the product of specific historical conditions. In other words, readers make meanings from texts on the basis of the specific assumptions and knowledges that they bring to their encounter with the text. To study these events historically, Staiger turns to 'reviews, news articles, letters to papers, advertisements, illustrations, and publicity which circulated in the major mass media'. These texts are then analysed to identify the tropes and discourses on which they draw in an attempt to identify the historical processes and structures that constitute specific events of reading (see also Section Eight).

It was argued earlier that one of the strengths of historical poetics has been the detailed historical scholarship that it has provided on a range of different aspects of film history. For example, in Douglas Gomery's monumental study, *Shared Pleasures: A History of Movie Exhibition in the United States*, he reminds us that film history needs to be seen as more than the study of films texts, or even of their production and interpretation. As he argues in his account of the rise of the national theatre chains in the 1910s and 1920s, one company, Balaban and Katz, built its empire and became the most successful and imitated exhibitor in the country, but not because of the movies they showed. As Gomery puts it: 'Remarkably, one of the variables that did *not* count in Balaban and Katz's rise to power and control was the movies themselves. Indeed the company grew and prospered despite having little access to Hollywood's top films' (Gomery 1992: 43). Instead they succeeded through a concentration on other aspects of the cinema-going experience, and so 'differentiated its corporate product through five important factors – location, the theatre building, service, stage shows and air conditioning' (p. 43). During the period of classical Hollywood and even today the meaning of cinema-going is about more than the watching of films, and film history should therefore be about far more than the analysis of films, their production and even the ways in which they are interpreted by audiences.

References

Allen, R. C. and Gomery, D. (1985). *Film History: Theory and Practice*. New York: McGraw-Hill.

Bennett, T. (1979). *Formalism and Marxism*. London: Methuen.

Bordwell, D. (1988). 'Historical Poetics of the Cinema'. In B. Palmer (ed.), *The Cinematic Text: Methods and Approaches*. Atlanta: University of Georgia Press, 369–98.

—— Staiger, J. and Thompson, K. (1985). *The Classical Hollywood Cinema: Film Style and Mode of Production to 1960*. New York: Columbia University Press.

Gomery, D. (1992). *Shared Pleasures: The History of Movie Exhibition in America*. London: British Film Institute.

Gunning, T. (1990). 'The Cinema of Attractions: Early Film, its Spectator and the Avant-Garde'. In T. Elsaesser (ed.), *Early Cinema: Space, Frame, Narrative*. London: British Film Institute, 56–62.

Ingarden, R. (1973a). *Cognition and the Literary Work of Art*. Evanston, IL: Northwestern University Press.

—— (1973b). *The Literary Work of Art: An Investigation on the Borderlines of Ontology*. Evanston, IL: Northwestern University Press.

Iser, W. (1974). *The Implied Reader: Patterns of Communication in Prose Fiction from Bunyan to Beckett*. Baltimore: Johns Hopkins University Press.

—— (1978). *The Act of Reading: A Theory of Aesthetic Response*. Baltimore: Johns Hopkins University Press.

Jenkins, H. (1995). 'Historical Poetics'. In J. Hollows and M. Jancovich (eds), *Approaches to Popular Film*. Manchester: Manchester University Press, 99–122.

Klinger, B. (1994). *Melodrama and Meaning: History, Culture, and the Films of Douglas Sirk*. Bloomington: Indiana University Press.

Krämer, P. (1998). 'Post-Classical Hollywood'. In J. Hill and P. C. Gibson (eds), *The Oxford Guide to Film Studies*. Oxford: Oxford University Press, 289–309.

—— (1999). 'A Powerful Cinema-Going Force? Hollywood and Female Audiences since the 1960s'. In M. Stokes and R. Maltby (eds), *Identifying Hollywood's Audiences: Cultural Identity and the Movies*. London: British Film Institute.

Maltby, R. with Craven, I. (1995). *Hollywood Cinema: An Introduction*. Oxford: Blackwell.

Sconce, J. (1995). 'Trashing the Academy: Taste, Excess and an Emerging Politics of Cinematic Style'. *Screen* **36**(4): 371–393.

Staiger, J. (1993). 'Taboos and Totems: Cultural Meanings of *The Silence of the Lambs*'. In J. Collins *et al*. (eds), *Film Theory Goes to the Movies*. New York: Routledge, 142–54.

The cinema of attractions: early film, its spectator and the avant-garde

Tom Gunning

Writing in 1922, flushed with the excitement of seeing Abel Gance's *La Roue*, Fernand Léger tried to define something of the radical possibilities of the cinema. The potential of the new art did not lie in 'imitating the movements of nature' or in 'the mistaken path' of its resemblance to theatre. Its unique power was a 'matter of *making images seen*'.[1] It is precisely this harnessing of visibility, this act of showing and exhibition, which I feel cinema before 1906 displays most intensely. Its inspiration for the avant-garde of the early decades of this century needs to be re-explored.

Writings by the early modernists (Futurists, Dadaists and Surrealists) on the cinema follow a pattern similar to Léger: enthusiasm for this new medium and its possibilities, and disappointment at the way it has already developed, its enslavement to traditional art forms, particularly theatre and literature. This fascination with the *potential* of a medium (and the accompanying fantasy of rescuing the cinema from its enslavement to alien and passé forms) can be understood from a number of viewpoints. I want to use it to illuminate a topic I have also approached before, the strangely heterogeneous relation that film before 1906 (or so) bears to the films that follow, and the way a taking account of this heterogeneity signals a new conception of film history and film form. My work in this area has been pursued in collaboration with André Gaudreault.[2]

The history of early cinema, like the history of cinema generally, has been written and theorized under the hegemony of narrative films. Early film-makers like Smith, Méliès and Porter have been studied primarily from the viewpoint of their contribution to film as a storytelling medium, particularly the evolution of narrative editing. Although such approaches are not totally misguided, they are one-sided and potentially distort both the work of these film-makers and the actual forces shaping cinema before 1906. A few observations will indicate the way that early cinema was not dominated by the narrative impulse that later asserted its sway over the medium. First there is the extremely important role that actuality film plays in early film production. Investigation of the films copyrighted in the US shows that actuality films outnumbered fictional films until 1906.[3] The Lumière tradition of 'placing the world within one's reach' through travel films and topicals did not disappear with the exit of the Cinématographe from film production. But even within non-actuality filming – what has sometimes been referred to as the 'Méliès tradition' – the role narrative plays is quite different from in traditional narrative film. Méliès himself declared in discussing his working method:

> As for the scenario, the 'fable,' or 'tale,' I only consider it at the end. I can state that the scenario constructed in this manner has *no importance*, since I use it merely as a pretext for the 'stage effects,' the 'tricks,' or for a nicely arranged tableau.[4]

Whatever differences one might find between Lumière and Méliès, they should not represent the opposition between narrative and non-narrative film-making, at least as it is understood today. Rather, one can unite them in a conception that sees cinema less as a way of telling stories than as a way of presenting a series of views to an audience, fascinating because of their illusory power (whether the realistic illusion of motion offered to the first audiences by Lumière, or the magical illusion concocted by Méliès), and exoticism. In other words, I believe that the relation to the spectator set up by the films of both Lumière and Méliès (and many other film-makers before 1906) had a common basis, and one that differs from the primary spectator relations set up by narrative film after 1906. I will call this earlier conception of cinema, 'the cinema of attractions'. I believe that this conception dominates cinema until about 1906–7. Although different from the fascination in storytelling exploited by the cinema from the time of Griffith, it is not necessarily opposed to it. In fact the cinema of attractions does not disappear with the dominance of narrative, but rather goes underground, both into certain avant-garde practices and as a component of narrative films, more evident in some genres (e.g. the musical) than in others.

What precisely is the cinema of attractions? First, it is a cinema that bases itself on the quality that Léger celebrated: its ability to *show* something. Contrasted to the voyeuristic aspect of narrative cinema analysed by Christian Metz,[5] this is an exhibitionist cinema. An aspect of early cinema which I have written about in other articles is emblematic of this different relationship the cinema of attractions constructs with its spectator: the recurring look at the camera by actors. This action, which is later perceived as spoiling the realistic illusions of the cinema, is here undertaken with brio, establishing contact with the audience. From comedians smirking at the camera, to the constant bowing and gesturing of the conjurors in magic films, this is a cinema that displays its visibility, willing to rupture a self-enclosed fictional world for a chance to solicit the attention of the spectator.

Exhibitionism becomes literal in the series of erotic films which play an important role in early film production (the same Pathé catalogue would advertise the Passion Play along with 'scènes grivoises d'un caractère piquant', erotic films often including full nudity), also driven underground in later years. As Noïl Burch has shown in his film *Correction Please: How We Got into Pictures* (1979), a film like *The Bride Retires* (France, 1902) reveals a fundamental conflict between this exhibitionistic tendency of early film and the creation of a fictional diegesis. A woman undresses for bed while her new husband peers at her from behind a screen. However, it is to the camera and the audience that the bride addresses her erotic striptease, winking at us as she faces us, smiling in erotic display. [...]

Modes of exhibition in early cinema also reflect this lack of concern with creating a self-sufficient narrative world upon the screen. As Charles Musser has shown,[6] the early showmen exhibitors exerted a great deal of control over the shows they presented, actually re-editing the films they had purchased and supplying a series of offscreen supplements, such as sound effects and spoken commentary. Perhaps most extreme is the Hale's Tours, the largest chain of theatres exclusively showing films before 1906. Not only did the films consist of non-narrative sequences taken from moving vehicles (usually trains), but the theatre itself was arranged as a train car with a conductor who took tickets, and sound effects simulating the click-clack of wheels and hiss of air brakes.[7] Such viewing experiences relate more to the attractions of the fairground than to the traditions of the legitimate theatre. The relation between films and the emergence of the great amusement parks, such as Coney

Island, at the turn of the century provides rich ground for rethinking the roots of early cinema.

Nor should we ever forget that in the earliest years of exhibition the cinema itself was an attraction. Early audiences went to exhibitions to see machines demonstrated (the newest technological wonder, following in the wake of such widely exhibited machines and marvels as X-rays or, earlier, the phonograph), rather than to view films. It was the Cinématographe, the Biograph or the Vitascope that were advertised on the variety bills in which they premièred, not *Le Déjeuner de bébé* or *The Black Diamond Express*. [...]

To summarise, the cinema of attractions directly solicits spectator attention, inciting visual curiosity, and supplying pleasure through an exciting spectacle – a unique event, whether fictional or documentary, that is of interest in itself. The attraction to be displayed may also be of a cinematic nature, such as the early close-ups just described, or trick films in which a cinematic manipulation (slow motion, reverse motion, substitution, multiple exposure) provides the film's novelty. Fictional situations tend to be restricted to gags, vaudeville numbers or recreations of shocking or curious incidents (executions, current events). It is the direct address of the audience, in which an attraction is offered to the spectator by a cinema showman, that defines this approach to film making. Theatrical display dominates over narrative absorption, emphasizing the direct stimulation of shock or surprise at the expense of unfolding a story or creating a diegetic universe. The cinema of attractions expends little energy creating characters with psychological motivations or individual personality. Making use of both fictional and non-fictional attractions, its energy moves outward towards an acknowledged spectator rather than inward towards the character-based situations essential to classical narrative.

The term 'attractions' comes, of course, from the young Sergei Mikhailovich Eisenstein and his attempt to find a new model and mode of analysis for the theatre. [...] I pick up this term partly to underscore the relation to the spectator that this later avant-garde practice shares with early cinema: that of exhibitionist confrontation rather than diegetic absorption. Of course the 'experimentally regulated and mathematically calculated' montage of attractions demanded by Eisenstein differs enormously from these early films (as any conscious and oppositional mode of practice will from a popular one).[8] However, it is important to realize the context from which Eisenstein selected the term. Then, as now, the 'attraction' was a term of the fairground [...]

The source is significant. The enthusiasm of the early avant-garde for film was at least partly an enthusiasm for a mass culture that was emerging at the beginning of the century, offering a new sort of stimulus for an audience not acculturated to the traditional arts. It is important to take this enthusiasm for popular art as something more than a simple gesture to *épater les bourgeois*. The enormous development of the entertainment industry since the 1910s and its growing acceptance by middle-class culture (and the accommodation that made this acceptance possible) have made it difficult to understand the liberation popular entertainment offered at the beginning of the century.

[...] Dealing with early cinema within the context of archive and academy, we risk missing its vital relation to vaudeville, its primary place of exhibition until around 1905. Film appeared as one attraction on the vaudeville programme, surrounded by a mass of unrelated acts in a non-narrative and even nearly illogical succession of performances. Even when presented in the nickelodeons that were emerging at the end of this period, these short films always appeared in a variety format, trick films sandwiched in with farces, actualities, 'illustrated songs', and, quite frequently, cheap vaudeville acts. It was precisely this non-narrative variety that placed this form of entertainment under attack by reform groups in the early 1910s. The Russell Sage Survey of popular entertainments found vaudeville 'depends upon an artificial rather than a natural human and developing interest, these acts having no necessary and as a rule, no actual connection'.[9] In other words, no narrative. A night at the variety theatre was like a ride on a streetcar or an active day in a crowded city, according to this middle-class reform group, stimulating an unhealthy nervousness. It was precisely such artificial stimulus that [...] Eisenstein wished to borrow from the popular arts and inject into the theatre, organizing popular energy for radical purpose.

What happened to the cinema of attractions? The period from 1907 to about 1913 represents the true *narrativization* of the cinema, culminating in the appearance of feature films which radically revised the variety format. Film clearly took the legitimate theatre as its model, producing famous players in famous plays. The transformation of filmic discourse that D. W. Griffith typifies bound cinematics signifiers to the narration of stories and the creation of a self-enclosed diegetic universe. The look at the camera becomes taboo and the devices of cinema are transformed from playful 'tricks' [...] to elements of dramatic expression, entries into the psychology of character and the world of fiction.

However, it would be too easy to see this as a Cain and Abel story, with narrative strangling the nascent possibilities of a young iconoclastic form of entertainment. Just as the variety format in some sense survived in the movie palaces of the 20s (with newsreel, cartoon, sing-along, orchestra performance and sometimes vaudeville acts subordinated to, but still coexisting with, the narrative *feature* of the evening), the system of attraction remains an essential part of popular film-making. [...]

As Laura Mulvey has shown in a very different context, the dialectic between spectacle and narrative has fuelled much of the classical cinema.[10] Donald Crafton in his study of slapstick comedy, 'The pie and the chase', has shown the way slapstick did a balancing act between the pure spectacle of gag and the development of narrative.[11] Likewise, the traditional spectacle film proved true to its name by highlighting moments of pure visual stimulation along with narrative. The 1924 version of *Ben Hur* was in fact shown at a Boston theatre with a timetable announcing the moment of its prime attractions:

8.35   *The Star of Bethlehem*
8.40   *Jerusalem Restored*
8.59   *Fall of the House of Hur*
10.29 *The Last Supper*
10.50 *Reunion*[12]

The Hollywood advertising policy of enumerating the features of a film, each emblazoned with the command, 'See!' shows this primal power of the attraction running beneath the armature of narrative regulation.

We seem far from the avant-garde premises with which this discussion of early cinema began. But it is important for the radical heterogeneity which I find in early cinema not to be conceived as a truly oppositional programme, one irreconcilable with the growth of narrative cinema. This view is too sentimental and too ahistorical. [...] Clearly in some sense recent spectacle cinema has reaffirmed its roots in stimulus and carnival rides, in what might be called the Spielberg-Lucas-Coppola cinema of effects.

But effects are tamed attractions. Marinetti and Eisenstein understood that they were tapping into a source of energy that would need focusing and intensification to fulfil its revolutionary possibilities. [...] Every change in film history implies a change in its address to the spectator, and each period constructs its spectator in a new way. Now in a period of American avant-garde cinema in which the tradition of contemplative subjectivity has perhaps run its (often glorious) course, it is possible that this earlier carnival of the cinema, and the methods of popular entertainment, still provide an unexhausted resource – a Coney Island of the avant-garde, whose never dominant but always sensed current can be traced from Méliès through Keaton, through *Un Chien andalou* (1928), and Jack Smith.

Notes

1 Fernand Léger, 'A Critical Essay on the Plastic Qualities of Abel Gance's Film *The Wheel*', in Edward Fry (ed.), *Functions of Painting*, trans. Alexandra Anderson (New York: Viking Press, 1973), p. 21.
2 See my articles 'The Non-Continuous Style of Early Film', in Roger Holman (ed.), *Cinema 1900–1906* (Brussels: FIAF, 1982), and 'An Unseen Energy Swallows Space: The Space in Early Film and Its Relation to American Avant Garde Film' in John L. Fell (ed.), *Film Before Griffith* (Berkeley: University of California Press, 1983), pp. 355–66, and our collaborative paper delivered by A. Gaudreault at the conference at Cerisy on Film History (August 1985) 'Le Cinéma des premiers temps: un défi à l'histoire du cinéma?' I would also like to note the importance of my discussions with Adam Simon and our hope to investigate further the history and archaeology of the film spectator.
3 Robert C. Allen, *Vaudeville and Film, 1895–1915: A Study in Media Interaction* (New York: Arno Press, 1980), pp. 159, 212–13.
4 Méliès, 'Importance du scénario', in Georges Sadoul, *Georges Méliès* (Paris: Seghers, 1961), p. 118 (my translation).
5 Metz, *The Imaginary Signifier: Psychoanalysis and the Cinema*, trans. Celia Britton, Annwyl Williams, Ben Brewster and Alfred Guzzetti (Bloomington: Indiana University Press, 1982), particularly pp. 58–80, 91–7.
6 Musser, 'American Vitagraph 1897–1901', *Cinema Journal*, vol. 22. no. 3. Spring 1983, p. 10.
7 Raymond Fielding, 'Hale's tours: Ultrarealism in the pre-1910 Motion Picture', in Fell, *Film Before Griffith*, pp. 116–30.
8 'The Montage of Attractions', in S.M. Eisenstein, *Writings 1922–1934*, ed. Richard Taylor (London: BFI, 1988), p. 35.
9 Michael Davis, *The Exploitation of Pleasure* (New York: Russell Sage Foundation, Dept. of Child Hygiene, Pamphlet, 1911).
10 'Visual Pleasure and Narrative Cinema', in Laura Mulvey, *Visual and Other Pleasures* (London: Macmillan, 1989).
11 Paper delivered at the FIAF Conference on Slapstick, May 1985, New York City.
12 Nicholas Vardac, *From Stage to Screen: Theatrical Method from Garrick to Griffith* (New York: Benjamin Blom, 1968), p. 232.

25 The Classical Hollywood Cinema

Richard Maltby

If Hollywood is not a place it is also not a time. Since the 1960s Hollywood has persistently been described as not being 'what it was,' and a succession of both journalistic and critical works have talked of *The Fifty-year Decline of Hollywood, Hollywood in Transition, The New Hollywood*, or *Hollywood and After*.[1] But as well as changing, Hollywood has also remained the same, at least in the sense of remaining in the same business of entertaining its audience, of producing the maximum pleasure for the maximum number for the maximum profit. If we are to take Hollywood seriously and understand its business, the first thing we must do is to 'describe the way American films *work*'.[2] The most important and influential critical work written on Hollywood in the last twenty years is *The Classical Hollywood Cinema: Film Style and Mode of Production to 1960*, by David Bordwell, Janet Staiger, and Kristin Thompson. In it, they delineate the formal features of what they call the 'Classical Hollywood' style, and trace its evolution, along with the organizational history of Hollywood's production practices. By 1917, the authors argue, the essential features of the classical style were in place. Since then, these features – the way that a movie organizes narrative time and space, the continuity script, the management structure, and the division of labor in production – have remained fundamentally unchanged. It is this historical continuity that enables us to make generalizations about Hollywood over a period that spans most of this century.

Published in 1985, *The Classical Hollywood Cinema* set new standards for historical research in film studies, and also gave a new precision to ideas of 'the classical' in relation to Hollywood. The French critic André Bazin [...] first described Hollywood as 'a classical art', arguing that it should be admired for 'the richness of its ever-vigorous tradition, and its fertility when it comes into contact with new elements'. He also suggested that the genius of the Hollywood system should be analysed via a sociological approach to its production, since a crucial element of that system was the way in which it 'has been able, in an extraordinarily competent way, to show American society just as it wanted to see itself'.[3] The idea of a classical cinema has remained in play as part of most critical accounts of Hollywood, although it has most frequently been invoked as a background against which exceptional works could be defined and distinguished. Bordwell, Staiger, and Thompson investigated the formal organization of the 'ordinary film', basing their account of Classical style on an analysis of a randomly selected sample of Hollywood movies. Their analysis of style thus addressed what Bazin had suggested was most admirable about Hollywood, with a precision that had been largely absent from previous descriptions of 'classic narrative film' or 'classic realism.' The idea of 'the classical' implies the observance of rules of composition and aesthetic organization that produce unity, balance, and order in the resulting artwork. 'Classical' works conform. They are bound by rules that set strict limits on innovation. The authors of *The Classical Hollywood Cinema* regard the style they describe as classical because 'the principles which Hollywood claims as its own rely on notions of decorum, proportion, formal harmony, respect for tradition, mimesis, self-effacing craftsmanship, and cool control of the perceiver's response – canons which critics in any medium usually call "classical" '.[4]

[...] Hollywood functions according to what we have called a commercial aesthetic, one that is essentially opportunist in its economic motivation. This argument sits uneasily with the stylistically determined view of a movie's organization implicit in the idea of classicism. The assumption that Hollywood movies are determined, in the last instance, by their existence as commercial commodities is central to our understanding of what Hollywood is. Bordwell, Staiger, and Thompson conclude that, although economic factors have strongly affected the development of the classical style, in their final analysis 'stylistic factors can explain the most specific and interesting aspects of Hollywood filmmaking'. For them, a set of formal conventions of narrative construction, spectacle, verisimilitude, and continuity 'constituted Hollywood's very definition of a movie itself'.[5] From our critical perspective [...] these investigations of Hollywood's formal conventions can address one of the two sets of questions we can ask about the way movies work: the way in which Hollywood is, in David Bordwell's phrase, 'an excessively obvious cinema'.[6] But there is another set of questions, dealing with the relationships that exist between movies and their audiences, that needs to take into account other considerations than those examined in *The Classical Hollywood Cinema*. A history of Hollywood's stylistic evolution cannot fully acknowledge the sociological approach that Bazin argued for, or describe the wider external pressures and forces at work in the Hollywood system. [...]

Answers to questions about what Hollywood is for must be sought not only in its movies but also in the social, cultural, and institutional contexts that surround it. The approach that we have called 'consumerist criticism' aims to answer these questions, by examining Hollywood's commercial aesthetics. At one level, we are concerned with what viewers use movies for: 'to learn how to dress or how to speak more elegantly or how to make a grand entrance or even what kind of coffee maker we wish to purchase, or to take off from the movie into a romantic fantasy or a trip.'[7] At another level, we examine how Hollywood movies are organized to deliver pleasure to their audiences. Take something as obvious as Hollywood's happy endings. The authors of *The Classical Hollywood Cinema* found that 60 per cent of the movies they analysed 'ended with a display of the united romantic couple – the cliché happy ending, often with a "clinch" – and many more could be said to end happily.'[8] In contrast to a strictly formal analysis that sees classical movies as driven by the logical progression of their narratives, Rick Altman has pointed out that the similarity of Hollywood happy endings suggests that classical narrative 'reasons backward'. A movie's beginning, he argues, must be 'retrofitted' so that it appears to lead logically to the predetermined happy ending. 'The end is made to *appear* as a function of the beginning in order better to disguise the fact that the beginning is actually a function of the ending.'[9] More generally, movies are engineered to produce a sequence of audience responses, 'thrilling us when we should be thrilled', as a writer in the *Nickelodeon* put it in 1910, 'making us laugh or cry at the appointed times, and leaving us, at the end of the film, in a beatific frame of mind'.[10] Screenwriting manuals and practicing screenwriters alike emphasize that scripts are engineered to maintain a level of engagement on the part of the audience. John Sayles describes the concise discussions he had with the producers of *Piranha* (1978):

> They said, 'You're going to rewrite *Piranha*. Make sure you keep the main idea, the idea of piranhas being loose in North American waters.' I said, 'Okay, how often do you want an attack? About every fifteen minutes?' They said, 'Yeah, but it doesn't have to be an attack. Maybe just the threat of an attack – but some sort of action sequence about that often to keep the energy going.' I said, 'Anything else?' They said, 'Keep it fun.'[11]

As a final level of its inquiry, consumerist criticism examines the institutional and ideological constraints on Hollywood. Movies, we argue, have happy endings because part of their cultural function is to affirm and maintain the culture of which they are part. That cultural function was, for instance, inscribed in the industry's Production Code, which regulated the content and treatment of every Hollywood movie between 1931 and 1968. The fact that 85 per cent of Hollywood movies feature heterosexual romance as their main plot device needs to be seen in the context of this regulatory framework. And if, as we suggest, the movie theater is a site in which cultural and ideological anxieties can be aired in the relative safety of a well-regulated fiction, we might well ask why we need quite so much reassurance that heterosexual romance is supposed to end happily. [...] The set of questions that consumerist criticism addresses indicates that the Hollywood of our inquiry is different from that uncovered by *The Classical Hollywood Cinema*. At a practical level, however, this disagreement is a matter of emphasis, and the two kinds of analysis complement each other.

One further question about classical Hollywood has to do with whether it still exists. Bordwell, Staiger and Thompson end their book in 1960, a date that they acknowledge is 'somewhat arbitrary'.[12] By then, classical Hollywood's mode of production, the vertically integrated company operating a studio, had come to an end, but the style it produced persisted. Although the style altered after 1960, it had also altered before, and the style of the new Hollywood of the 1970s can best be explained, they suggest, by the same process of stylistic assimilation that had operated throughout Hollywood's history: 'As the "old" Hollywood had incorporated and refunctionalized devices from German Expressionism and Soviet montage, the "New" Hollywood has selectively borrowed from the international art cinema.'[13] [...] Classical Hollywood cinema is taken to be a period of Hollywood's history, and refers to the style, the mode of production, and the industrial organization under which movies were made from the early 1920s to the late 1950s.

Hollywood and its audiences

[...]Although Hollywood's goal of entertainment has remained constant, the audience it has sought to entertain has changed as many times in the 80 years of Hollywood's existence as have the ways of producing and packaging movies.[14] Since 1950, moviegoing has been a minority activity. In 1946, one third of the American public went to a movie every week. By 1983, fewer than a quarter went once a month, but that group accounted for 85 per cent of all movie admissions.[15] As significantly, the industry's idea of its audience has changed. In the late 1920s, the industry estimated that between three-quarters and four-fifths of its audience were women.[16] Although the reliability of this estimate is open to question, for most of the 1930s and 1940s there was a widespread assumption among production and distribution personnel that the large majority of movie audiences in the US and Europe were female. At a story conference during the production of *Snow White* in 1936, Walt Disney argued that the dream sequence in which Snow White sings 'Some Day My Prince Will Come' would appeal particularly to the female audience. 'After all,' he said, '80 per cent of our audience are women.'[17] In 1939 a sociologist reported that 'it is really that solid average citizen's wife who commands the respectful attention of the industry'.[18]

From about 1955, however, the industry's conception of its audience shifted. In the mid-1960s, American-International Pictures (AIP), an independent company specializing in 'exploitation' pictures (its first major success was in 1957 with *I Was a Teenage Werewolf*), codified the strategy behind its production and distribution policy in what it called 'the Peter Pan Syndrome': younger children would watch anything older children would watch, and girls would watch anything boys would watch, but not vice versa; therefore, 'to catch your greatest audience you zero in on the 19-year-old male'.[19] The industry began to pursue the teenage audience because they were 'the best picture-goers in the country at this time – the most consistent, the best equipped with leisure time and allowance money, the most gregariously inclined, and to be sure the most romantic'. This led to what Thomas Doherty has called 'a progressive "juvenilization" of movie content and the movie audience that is today the operative reality of the American motion picture business'.[20]

Because of its professed commitment to providing universal entertainment for an undifferentiated audience, the industry made relatively few systematic attempts to inquire into the composition or preferences of that audience in the studio period. In the late 1960s, however, Hollywood's relation to its audience underwent a substantial revision when the industry trade association, the Motion Picture Association of America, established a ratings system, classifying certain movies as unsuitable for sections of the potential audience. Censor boards in many foreign countries had long prohibited children from attending some movies, but American distributors had always resisted proposals for similar schemes in their domestic market. Instead they preferred to use the Production Code as a system of regulation to ensure that all Hollywood movies would only offer entertainment that would prove harmless to all their audiences. [...] By the mid-1960s, however, shifts in American cultural values had undermined the credibility of the Production Code, and it was abandoned in 1968. The industry's decision to introduce a ratings system was immediately provoked by two decisions of the US Supreme Court, upholding the rights of local governments to prevent children being exposed to books or movies considered suitable only for adults. In the wake of these decisions the industry faced a flood of state and municipal legislation establishing local schemes for film classification, and the introduction of a ratings system was an attempt to outmaneuver that legislation.[21]

The Code and Ratings Administration (CARA) divided movies into four categories: G, suitable for general admission; M, allowing unrestricted admission, but suggesting that parents should decide whether the movie was suitable for children under 16; R, restricting attendance by requiring children under 16 to be accompanied by an adult; and X, restricting attendance to those over 16. Since 1968, the system has been modified several times. In 1970 the M category became GP, when the age restriction was raised to 17; in 1972 GP was renamed PG (for parental guidance suggested); and CARA itself was renamed the Classification and Rating Administration in 1977, abandoning any reference to the existence of a Code governing movie production as well as the practice of vetting scripts in advance of production. In 1983, CARA added another category, PG-13, providing a 'strong caution' to parents of children under 13. In 1990, CARA renamed the X category NC-17 in an attempt to create a category for art movies restricted to the over-17s, since X had become generally understood as referring to pornography. The ratings system has imposed few actual limitations on attendance, but it has required producers to conceive of their audiences differently, engineering their movies to achieve a particular rating – a requirement often built into a movie's finance agreements. Distributors will not handle X-rated movies, and movies such as *Dressed to Kill* (1980) and *Angel Heart* (1987) have been re-edited to qualify for an R. The G rating has been almost equally firmly avoided. Of 336 films rated in 1981, only seven were rated G, and it has been common industry practice to insert swearing, nudity, or violence to ensure a PG or R rating.[22]

In a further move away from the commercial assumptions underlying the operation of the studio system, the industry started to make more use of market research in attempts to target movies more effectively at particular audiences at the same time as the ratings system was introduced. By the late 1980s, marketing strategists in the major companies were reconsidering the assumption that their movies should appeal primarily to teenage boys, in recognition of the 'greying of the movie-going audience'. In 1984, only 15 per cent of the audience was over 40. In 1990, the over-40s made up 24 per cent of the audience, providing a more viable target market. Fox production chief Roger Birnbaum suggested that these changes in audience composition meant that 'a studio can develop a slate of pictures that doesn't just cater to one demographic'. In a return to much earlier assumptions, he reported that 'the demographic on women, today, is very strong'.[23]

However, Hollywood's notion of its audience has always had to remain very generalized, because of the size of a movie's market. Hollywood movies have always been made for an international audience, and since the early 1920s, between a third and half of Hollywood's earnings have come from audiences outside the United States. Much of the cultural power of Hollywood and other artifacts of American mass culture has lain in the fact that they were designed 'for universal exhibition'.[24] [...] we describe these values as Utopian. As our description of its immaterial geography suggests, Hollywood itself is a Utopia, a nowhere that has also been America to most of the rest of the world for much of this century. For the citizens of Manchester, Melbourne, and Mombassa, Westerns have provided the most recognizable American landscape. The most familiar American cityscapes may even have been shot on a studio backlot. Hollywood has exported an image of the United States that has become so much a part of everyday life in even distant and scarcely westernized areas as to seem, paradoxically, less an *American* product and more a part of an international mass culture in which we all share. At the center of this empire, Americans can become too possessive of their cultural capital. In a recent history of the American musical, Rick Altman claims that however much non-American critics may understand 'the context and meaning' of a movie such as *Singin' in the Rain* (1952), they will inevitably lack the familiarity with American culture that equips them to translate the movie's 'raw thematic material into ... the culture's master themes'.[25] Altman argues that:

> The culture's master themes are not actually *in* the text, yet the text is produced in such a way as to evoke them for a particular interpretive community. Perception of the relationship is a more important cultural phenomenon than any actual relationship that might exist. It is through the spectator's knowledge and perception that culture and cinema interact in a reciprocal relationship.[26]

While not questioning Altman's general proposition about the relationship between cinema and culture, we would point out that because Hollywood movies have never been made only for an American audience, they have also been part of the other cultures they have visited. An Austrian audience watching *The Sound of Music* (1965) or an Australian audience watching *The Sundowners* (1960) saw their national histories Americanized. In movies like these, audiences outside the United States have viewed their own cultural pasts through a filter in which their domestic environment has been represented as exotic, while the 'domestic market' addressed by the movie has not been theirs but that of North America. In such circumstances, it is hardly surprising that Hollywood should have become an imaginative home to many of its foreign audiences. In a 1989 article about the effect of new communications technologies on cultural identity, David Morley and Kevin Robins suggested that 'American culture repositions frontiers – social, cultural, psychic, linguistic, geographical America is now within'.[27] But for much of the world, American popular culture had become part of their cultural identity by 1926, when a State Department official observed: 'If it were not for the barrier we have established, there is no doubt that the American movies would be bringing us a flood of the immigrants. As it is, in vast instances, the desire to come to this country is thwarted, and the longing to emigrate is changed into a desire to imitate.'[28] Two years later, a film industry representative declared that motion pictures 'color the minds of those who see them. They are demonstrably the greatest single factors in the Americanization of the world and as such fairly may be called the most important and significant of America's exported products.'[29] Less enthusiastically, the *Daily Express* complained that British cinemagoers 'talk America, think America, and dream America. We have several million people, mostly women, who to all intent and purpose are temporary American citizens.'[30] They were, of course, not American citizens at all, but citizens of Hollywood's imagined Utopian community. But for many people who visit the familiar foreign territory of Hollywood in the movies and in their imagination, Hollywood is what they imagine America to be.

Our discussions of Hollywood's audience and of classical Hollywood will have already alerted you to our concern with questions of history. [However,] we need to understand Hollywood from a range of historical perspectives. Hollywood has at least three separate but overlapping histories. The history of production, the story of the studios and their stars, has preoccupied the majority of movie historians. Much less notice tends to be taken of movie reception, but Hollywood's audience has a history, too, and that history – the history of the box office – has had a determining influence on the history of production. Thirdly, Hollywood has a critical history: a history of the changes in what critics have understood Hollywood to be. Most critical histories of Hollywood are descriptive, charting its high and low points, although different critics, of course, describe that history differently. [...]

These three overlapping accounts of Hollywood are narratives of continuity as well as change. All are in competition with Hollywood's history of itself, projected in fan magazines, star biographies, and 'exposés', as well as in movies about Hollywood. Much of what passes for Hollywood's history has been written as if it were itself a Hollywood story and as if the history of entertainment were under an obligation to be entertaining. *Singin' in the Rain*, for instance, provides us with a history of Hollywood's introduction of sound, during the course of which Cosmo Brown (Donald O'Connor) discovers the principles of sound dubbing by standing in front of Kathy Selden (Debbie Reynolds) and moving his mouth while she sings; a much more entertaining version of history than a mundane account of the development of multiple channel recording and post-synchronization would be. The most common explanation for the introduction of sound, that it was a last desperate gamble by an almost bankrupt Warner Bros., is likewise a Hollywood fantasy, discredited by research that has shown that the major companies' transition to sound was a much more orderly and considered process.[31] Nevertheless, it is still widely reproduced, because its story of the kids from the ghetto making good with an invention the big studios had turned down fits in with the mythological history of Hollywood, the *Singin' in the Rain* history of the place, which proposes that the history of Hollywood must conform to the conventions of its own narratives. This Hollywood was the invention of press and publicity agents. It served as a disguise for the American film industry, the means by which public attention was diverted away from the routine, mechanical, standardized aspects of the industry's central operations toward its more attractive, glamorous periphery. That disguise has worked almost as well for many of Hollywood's critics and historians as it did for the readers of its fan magazines in the 1930s, since all the pressures of the industry act against the displacement of Hollywood as 'Metropolis of Make-Believe' by a more prosaic description of the economic forces and business practices involved in selling entertainment. [...]

Notes

1 Ezra Goodman, *The Fifty-year Decline of Hollywood* (New York: Simon and Schuster, 1961); Richard Dyer McCann, *Hollywood in Transition* (Boston: Houghton Mifflin, 1962); Jim Hillier, *The New Hollywood* (London: Studio Vista, 1993); Jerzy Toeplitz, *Hollywood and After: The Changing Face of Movies in America* (London: Allen and Unwin, 1974).
2 Thomas Elsaesser, 'Why Hollywood?', *Monogram* 1 (1971), p. 6.
3 André Bazin, 'La Politique des auteurs', in Peter Graham, ed., *The New Wave* (London: Secker and Warburg, 1968), pp. 143–4, 154.
4 David Bordwell, Janet Staiger, and Kristin Thompson, *The Classical Hollywood Cinema: Film Style and Mode of Production to 1960* (London: Routledge and Kegan Paul, 1985), p. 4.
5 Bordwell et al., p. 367.

6 Bordwell et al., p. 3. Part One of *The Classical Hollywood Cinema* provides an analysis of the formal properties of classical Hollywood style.

7 Kael, p. 101.

8 David Bordwell, *Narration in the Fiction Film* (London: Methuen, 1985), p. 159.

9 Rick Altman, 'Dickens, Griffith, and Film Theory Today', in Jane Gaines, ed., *Classical Hollywood Narrative: The Paradigm Wars* (Durham, NC: Duke University Press, 1992), p. 32.

10 H. Kent Webster, 'Little Stories of Great Films', *Nickelodeon* 3:1 (January 1, 1910), p. 13, quoted in Bordwell et al., p. 195.

11 Quoted in Hillier, p. 44.

12 Bordwell et al., p. 10.

13 Bordwell et al., p. 373.

14 Contemporary Hollywood makes made-for-TV movies and television mini-series, for instance, but most critical and historical accounts have ignored them, limiting their discussion of Hollywood's output to feature-length motion pictures.

15 Bruce A. Austin, *Immediate Seating: A Look at Movie Audiences* (Belmont, CA: Wadsworth, 1989), pp. 44, 90.

16 In 1929, the industry's trade association suggested that 75 per cent of its audience were women. Two years earlier, *Moving Picture World* had suggested women had an 83 per cent majority in the audience. In 1928, an *Exhibitors Herald* article asserted that 'Woman has, in the last ten years at least, become the objective in the [theater] manager's planning, because it has become an established fact that women fans constitute the major percentage of patronage or at least cast the final vote in determining the majority patronage.' *The Film in National Life: Being the Report of an Enquiry Conducted by the Commission on Educational and Cultural Films into the Service which the Cinematograph may Render to Education and Social Progress* (London: Allen and Unwin, 1932), p. 35. This report led to the establishment of the British Film Institute; Beth Brown, 'Making Movies for Women', *Moving Picture World* (March 26, 1927), p. 34, quoted in Gaylyn Studlar, 'The Perils of Pleasure? Fan Magazine Discourse as Women's Commodified Culture in the 1920s', *Wide Angle* 13:1 (January 1991), p. 7; Jeanne Allen, 'The Film Viewer as Consumer', *Quarterly Review of Film Studies* 5:4 (Fall 1980), p. 486.

17 Walt Disney, Disney studio story conference, December 8, 1936, quoted in Robin Allen, 'European Influences on the Animated Feature Films of Walt Disney', PhD thesis, University of Exeter, 1992.

18 Margaret Thorp, *America at the Movies* (London: Faber, 1946), p. 17.

19 Robin Bean and David Austen, 'U.S.A. Confidential', *Films and Filming* 215 (November 1968), pp. 21–2. Quoted in Thomas Doherty, *Teenagers and Teenpix: The Juvenilization of American Movies in the 1950s* (Boston: Unwin Hyman, 1988), p. 157.

20 William R. Weaver, 'AIP Heads Set Sight on Teenage Patron', *Motion Picture Herald* (May 25, 1957), p. 20. Quoted in Doherty, p. 156; Doherty, p. 3.

21 Douglas Ayer, Roy E. Bates, and Peter J. Herman, 'Self-Censorship in the Movie Industry: An Historical Perspective on Law and Social Change', *Wisconsin Law Review* 3 (1970), pp. 791–838; Austin, pp. 106–16.

22 Aljean Harmetz, 'Rating the Ratings', in *Rolling Breaks and Other Movie Business* (New York: Knopf, 1983), p. 96; Georgia Jeffries, 'The Problem with G', *American Film* (June 1978), p. 51.

23 Quoted in Hillier, p. 31.

24 From 1913, the British Board of Film Censors categorized movies as being suitable either for exhibition to adult audiences, or 'for universal exhibition'.

25 Rick Altman, *The American Film Musical* (Bloomington: Indiana University Press, 1989), p. 340.

26 Altman, *American Film Musical*, p. 340.
27 David Morley and Kevin Robins, 'Spaces of Identity: Communications Technologies and the Reconfiguration of Europe', *Screen* 30:4 (Autumn 1989), p. 21.
28 James True, *Printer's Ink* (February 4, 1926), quoted in Charles Eckert, 'The Carole Lombard in Macy's Window', *Quarterly Review of Film Studies* 3 (Winter 1978), pp. 4–5.
29 'Certain Factors and Considerations Affecting the European Market,' internal MPPDA memo, October 25, 1928, Motion Picture Association of America Archive, New York (hereafter MPA).
30 Quoted in Jeffrey Richards, *The Age of the Dream Palace: Cinema and Society in Britain 1930–1939* (London: Routledge and Kegan Paul, 1984), p. 63.
31 Douglas Gomery, 'The Coming of Sound: Technological Change in the American Film Industry', in Tino Balio, ed., *The American Film Industry*, revised edn (Madison: University of Wisconsin Press, 1985), pp. 229–51.

26 Post-classical Hollywood

Peter Krämer

Critical responses to developments in the New Hollywood: movie brats, neo-classicism, and postmodernism

When 'New Hollywood' became firmly established as a critical term in film studies in the mid-1970s, Hollywood itself was in the midst of an aesthetic, cultural, and industrial reorientation, which was signalled most dramatically by the unprecedented box-office successes of *Jaws* (USA, 1975) and *Star Wars* (USA, 1977). In subsequent years critics described Hollywood's reorientation in the second half of the 1970s in terms of the films' increasing emphasis on special effects and cinematic spectacle (Neale 1980), their return to a psychologically and politically regressive outlook (Wood 1985, 1986, ch. 8; Britton 1986) and the film industry's increasingly narrow focus on 'blockbusters', that is heavily promoted big-budget films (Monaco 1979, chs. 1–3). In retrospect, the original New Hollywood of the years 1967–75 came to be seen as a brief and exceptional period in American film history in which artistically ambitious and politically progressive filmmaking had been commercially viable, competing successfully for a while with conservative film cycles (Maltby 1983, ch. 10; Ray 1985, chs. 8–9; Ryan and Kellner 1988, chs. 1–3). Auteurist critics have continued to explore and evaluate the achievements of the small group of directors who had been at the centre of Hollywood's short-lived artistic renaissance (Pye and Myles 1979; Kolker 1980, 1988). Other critics, however, have concentrated on a general outline and critique of the aesthetic and commercial logic underpinning Hollywood's operations since the 1960s, best exemplified by *Jaws* and subsequent films by George Lucas and Steven Spielberg

(Monaco 1979; Thompson 1981; Biskind 1990; Schatz 1993; Wyatt 1994). These critics emphasize the incorporation of Hollywood studios into giant industrial conglomerates since the mid-1960s, the proliferation of delivery systems for films gaining momentum with the successful introduction of pay-cable and home video in the mid-1970s, and the multi-media marketing of movies, which connects their theatrical release with the launching of a whole product line of popular cultural arte-facts (ranging from pop songs to computer games), while also using a film's theatrical exposure as the key to ancillary markets such as video and pay-cable, where the bulk of film revenues have been generated since the mid-1980s. Confusingly, this second group of critics frequently employs the term 'New Hollywood' to refer to the much longer period they are dealing with, and, in partic-ular, to the years after 1975. Thus, in different critical contexts 'New Hollywood' may refer to the period 1967–75 as well as to the post-1975 period, to the aesthetic and political progressivism of the liberal cycles of the earlier period as well as to the regressiveness of the blockbusters of the later period (Tasker 1996).

As if that was not confusing enough, critical discourses about the New Hollywood often revolve around the very same issues that concerned critics writing about Hollywood's transitional period between the late 1940s and the mid-1960s. For example, European influences, stylistic innovations, taboo subject-matter, new cinematic conceptions of heroism and masculinity, and critical awareness of social realities had already been hotly debated with respect to key Hollywood films and cycles of the late 1940s and the 1950s, long before they became identified with the Hollywood renaissance after 1967. Juvenilization, the technological renewal of the cinematic experience, the trend towards big event pictures, and the displacement of narrative by spectacle had all been the subject of critical debates in the 1950s, long before the new breed of blockbusters in the 1970s and 1980s provoked strong crit-ical reactions along these lines. Such continuities in critical debates and in Hollywood's aesthetic and commercial logic often go unacknowledged. Consequently, recent critical discourses about the New Hollywood (in both its restricted and its general meaning) have tended to exaggerate its newness, instead of situating the New Hollywood in relation to long-term trends in the post-war period.

To complicate matters further, since the 1980s critics have made concerted efforts to apply the concepts of modernism and postmodernism to developments in post-war American cinema. These concepts are used both to demarcate historical periods and to characterize particular film cycles. They may be used primarily with refer-ence to aesthetic issues, or more generally with reference to the totality of a cultural formation, comprising cultural artefacts as well as media industries, forms of social organization, and ideologies. In the light of the wide-ranging and varying applica-tions of these concepts in film criticism, it is difficult to map them onto the estab-lished periodizations of post-war Hollywood which take the concept of classicism as their starting-point. For example, studies of the emergence and development of postmodern culture in the United States tend to refer broadly to the post-war period, identifying the 1960s as a decade of crucial cultural transformations in the arts, yet locating the key examples of postmodern cinema such as *Blade Runner* (USA, 1982), *Blue Velvet* (USA, 1984), and *Batman* (USA, 1989) in more recent years (Denzin 1991; Jameson 1991; Corrigan 1991). In this view, then, despite the late appearance of exemplary postmodern films, the whole period since the Second

World War is overshadowed by postmodernism. In sharp contrast, an analysis using a narrow Bazinian definition of Hollywood classicism, which sees the year 1939 as a crucial historical turning-point, would identify *Citizen Kane* as the beginning of a modernist trend in American cinema which gained momentum with the self-consciously artistic New Movie of the 1950s and the experiments of the New American Cinema in the early 1960s, and culminated in the artistic renaissance of the New Hollywood between 1967 and 1975. Alternatively, using *Monogram*'s definition of classicism as the dominant Hollywood aesthetic betwen the 1910s and the mid-1960s, only the sustained attack on the fundamental principles of Hollywood storytelling in the liberal cycles of the New Hollywood qualifies as a genuinely modernist intervention into mainstream American cinema. In both cases, the post-1975 period may be characterized either as a turn towards postmodernism or as a return to the principles of classicism. [...]

Since the mid-1970s, then, critical debates about the New Hollywood have been characterized by a confusing proliferation of contradictory and shifting definitions of the term, and by different attempts to conceptualize the development of mainstream American cinema in the post-war era with reference to modernism and postmodernism. Yvonne Tasker's (1996) review of these debates indicates that, while there is still no agreement about proper definitions and mappings, there is perhaps a general direction in which these definitions and mappings develop. The original association of the term 'New Hollywood' with the artistic renaissance of the late 1960s and early 1970s has largely been displaced by its identification with the post-1975 period. Furthermore, the critical analysis of the stylistic and thematic innovations introduced by a new generation of auteurs has given way to a concern with the corporate strategies of media conglomerates, with blockbusters and multi-media marketing, and with new forms of film consumption. Indeed, Tasker suggests that changes in the wider cultural and media landscape may be the best way to separate New Hollywood from classical American cinema and to situate it in relation to postmodernism: 'The newness of the new Hollywood stems from the rapidly changing entertainment world in which it exists. In this context an analysis of film style in the new Hollywood might be most usefully approached through an awareness of the interaction between film and other media and the proliferation of cultural commodities, rather than exclusively in terms of a relationship to the cinematic past' (1996: 226–7). Hence, New Hollywood may be defined not so much in terms of stylistic and thematic changes in filmmaking, clearly separating the contemporary period from a previous modernist moment in American film history as well as from Hollywood's classicism, but in terms of a postmodern multi-media world which undermines the very notion of 'film as a distinct medium' (Tasker 1996: 226). Postmodern New Hollywood, then, is American filmmaking in the age of a fully integrated multi-media culture which originated in the 1960s and consolidated itself in the 1970s and 1980s.

The historical poetics of classicism and post-classicism

In her discussion of the New Hollywood, Yvonne Tasker employs the term 'post-classical' to refer primarily and specifically to stylistic changes in mainstream

American filmmaking since the 1960s (1996: 220–1). She refers to Bordwell, Staiger, and Thompson's monumental study *The Classical Hollywood Cinema* (1985) as the most comprehensive account of the normative stylistic system, which the innovations of post-classicism need to be defined against. In doing so, Tasker follows the model of other recent critics such as Justin Wyatt (1994: 7–8, 15–16, 60–4), Henry Jenkins (1995: 113–17), and Richard Maltby and Ian Craven (1995: 217–21), all of whom have identified significant departures from classical story-telling, as described in *The Classical Hollywood Cinema*, in certain film cycles since 1960, although they acknowledge that the majority of American films stay firmly within the classical tradition. While the term 'post-classical' may also be used more loosely to refer to other aspects of contemporary American cinema (Rowe 1995; Neale and Smith, forthcoming), its value as a critical tool would seem to depend on its precise application to the form of stylistic analysis exemplified by Bordwell, Staiger, and Thompson's study.

Bordwell has called this form of analysis 'historical poetics of the cinema', and defined it as 'the study of how, in determinate circumstances, films are put together, serve specific functions, and achieve specific effects' (1989: 266–7). While histor-ical poetics proceeds from the stylistic analysis of individual films and sees any film as 'the result of deliberate and founding choices' made by filmmakers, '[t]he poetician aims to analyze the conceptual and empirical factors – norms, traditions, habits – that govern a practice and its products' (269). To establish the norms and traditions governing a mode of film practice such as classical Hollywood, it is necessary to analyse a large number of films and to ensure that these films consti-tute a representative sample of the vast corpus they are meant to exemplify. The idiosyncracies of individual films are thus discussed systematically in relation to the norms embodied in a larger body of texts. Similarly, the use of particular devices in any given film is analysed in relation to the stylistic system of the film as a whole. Furthermore, film analysis is typically complemented by an investigation into the concrete work procedures of filmmaking and the system of production which organizes them. This investigation can make use of a variety of sources ranging from written codifications of rules and norms (e.g. manuals) to interviews with participants. Finally, historical poetics aims to identify stylistic developments within particular film practices, by tracing the diffusion of new stylistic devices such as, for example, zooms, split screens, and freeze frames across the overall corpus of films, and by identifying changes in the normative stylistic system which, in any given film, assigns individual devices a particular function, in Hollywood usually for the purpose of storytelling.

An example of a systemic stylistic change in classical Hollywood filmmaking would be the introduction of aimless protagonists, the loosening of causal connec-tions between narrative events, the foregrounding of stylistic devices in their own right, which serves to demonstrate the filmmakers' artistic presence and intentions, and the refusal of unambiguous narrative closure, which invites audiences to specu-late about the film's significance. According to Bordwell, these are some of the key narrational strategies of European art cinema that were absorbed by the filmmakers of the New Hollywood in the late 1960s. While *Monogram* had argued that this absorption constituted a decisive break in the development of mainstream American filmmaking, Bordwell writes: 'these new films do not constitute a sharply distinct style, but can better be explained by that process of stylistic assimilation we have seen at work throughout Hollywood's history' (Bordwell, Staiger, and Thompson 1985: 373). Bordwell uses the penultimate chapter of *The Classical Hollywood Cinema*, entitled 'Since 1960: The Persistence of a Mode of Film Practice', to argue, in effect, that all stylistic innovations in American filmmaking in recent decades 'remain within classical boundaries' (377), and that the date 1960 is a fairly arbitrary cut-off point for their study, which is by no means meant to indicate the end of the classical epoch. By analysing narrational strategies in a sample of recent Hollywood films and their codification in contemporary script-writing manuals in comparison with practices in early American feature filmmaking in the mid-1910s, Kristin Thompson (1995) has also argued forcefully for the overall continuity of the classical Hollywood up to the present.

Bordwell, Staiger, and Thompson's work has been criticized (much like *Screen*'s concept of the classical text) for its tendency to play down or erase the differences between individual Hollywood films and between particular œuvres, cycles, and periods, and to describe the basic tenets of classical Hollywood style in such general terms that any form of mainstream filmmaking would appear to fit into this model (Britton 1988–9; Williams 1994). Henry Jenkins (1995), however, argues that *The Classical Hollywood Cinema* and its underlying methodology allow for a more dynamic account of stylistic differences and developments than they are sometimes given credit for. At the centre of Bordwell, Staiger, and Thompson's study and of the project of historical poetics in general are, after all, processes of stylistic change, brought about, for example, by the introduction of new technologies such as synchronized sound or by the encounter with alternative stylistic systems such as European art cinema. Jenkins finds the description and explanation of such stylistic changes offered by Bordwell, Staiger, and Thompson 'essentially correct', although he would prefer to shift the critical focus of the investigation from the ultimate assimilation of new stylistic elements into the established system, to the early stages of that process, that is the 'periods of transition and experimentation before the system can fully stabilize itself around these changes' (1995: 114, 104). During these usually very brief periods, new stylistic elements are perceived by filmmakers and audiences alike as a disruption of the normative stylistic system or as a welcome novelty. The force of this perception is easily underestimated when such innovations are analysed in retrospect from a position which has already witnessed their complete assimilation.

While numerous examples of the process of defamiliarization and assimilation can be found in Hollywood between the 1910s and the 1940s, Jenkins suggests that the post-war period is characterized by the dramatic intensification of stylistic change: 'Since the breakdown of the studio system, Hollywood has entered a period of prolonged and consistent formal experimentation and institutional flux with a media-savvy audience demanding ... aesthetic novelty and difference. As a result, stylistic changes which might have unfolded over several decades under the studio system have occurred in a matter of a few years in contemporary Hollywood' (114). It is this increased speed and intensity of stylistic change which the concept of post-classicism is meant to describe. While Jenkins's examples are mainly from the 1960s, 1970s, and 1980s (the movie brats, 'high-concept' films, MTV aesthetics), his analysis would also seem to apply to the immediate post-war period, during which critics, and presumably American filmmakers and audiences as well, responded very strongly to a wide variety of stylistic developments which included: the increasing use of long takes, deep-focus cinematography and staging in depth; the move towards quasi-documentary; the self-conscious artistry of the New Movie; the wide-screen revolution; and the big picture.

Some of these developments in the post-war period have been covered in *The Classical Hollywood Cinema*. Yet, in general, critical debates about developments in post-war American cinema have dealt with stylistic change only in a cursory, abstract, and unspecific fashion, quickly moving from observations about individual film examples to claims about fundamental shifts in the overall aesthetic and industrial system. In this situation, the conceptual debate about Old Hollywood and New Hollywood, modernism and post-modernism, classicism and post-classicism, is perhaps less urgent and productive than the kind of careful, systematic, and complex stylistic analysis which historical poetics demands.

References

Biskind, Peter (1990), 'Blockbuster: The Last Crusade', in Mark Crispin Miller (ed.), *Seeing through Movies* (New York: Pantheon).

Bordwell, David (1989), *Making Meaning: Inference and Rhetoric in the Interpretation of Cinema* (Cambridge, Mass.: Harvard University Press).

—— Janet Staiger, and Kristin Thompson (1985), *The Classical Hollywood Cinema: Film Style and Mode of Production to 1960* (London: Routledge & Kegan Paul).

Britton, Andrew (1986), 'Blissing Out: The Politics of Reaganite Entertainment', *Movie*, **31–2**: 1–42.

—— (1988–9), 'The Philosophy of the Pigeonhole: Wisconsin Formalism and "The Classical Style" ', *CineAction*, **15**: 47–63.

Cameron, Ian *et al.* (1975), 'The Return of the Movie', *Movie*, **20**: 1–25.

Carroll, Noel (1982), 'The Future of Allusion: Hollywood in the Seventies (and Beyond)', *October*, **20**: 51–81.

Corrigan, Timothy (1991), *A Cinema without Walls: Movies and Culture after Vietnam* (London: Routledge).

Denzin, Norman K. (1991), *Images of Postmodern Society: Social Theory and Contemporary Cinema* (London: Sage).

Hillier, Jim (1993), *The New Hollywood* (London: Studio Vista).

Jameson, Fredric (1991), *Postmodernism; or, The Cultural Logic of Late Capitalism* (Durham, NC: Duke University Press).

Jenkins, Henry (1995), 'Historical Poetics', in Joanne Hollows and Mark Jancovich (eds.), *Approaches to Popular Film* (Manchester: Manchester University Press).

Kolker, Robert Phillip (1980), *A Cinema of Loneliness: Penn, Kubrick, Coppola, Scorsese, Altman* (New York: Oxford University Press).

—— (1988), *A Cinema of Loneliness: Penn, Kubrick, Scorsese, Spielberg, Altman*, 2nd edn. (New York: Oxford University Press).

Madsen, Axel (1975), *The New Hollywood: American Movies in the 1970s* (New York: Thomas Y. Crowell).

Maltby, Richard (1983), *Harmless Entertainment: Hollywood and the Ideology of Consensus* (Metuchen, NJ: Scarecrow).

—— with Ian Craven (1995), *Hollywood Cinema: An Introduction* (Oxford: Blackwell).

Modleski, Tania (1991), *Feminism without Women: Culture and Criticism in a Postfeminist Age* (London: Routledge).

Monaco, James (1979), *American Film Now: The People, the Power, the Money, the Movies* (New York: Plume).

Neale, Steve (1976), 'New Hollywood Cinema', *Screen* **17**/2: 117–22.

—— (1980), 'Hollywood Strikes Back: Special Effects in Recent American Cinema', *Screen*, **21**/3: 101–5.

—— and Murray Smith (eds.) (1998), *Contemporary American Cinema* (London: Routledge).

Pye, Michael, and Lynda Myles (1979), *The Movie Brats: How the Film Generation Took over Hollywood* (New York: Holt, Rinehart, & Winston).

Ray, Robert B. (1985), *A Certain Tendency of the Hollywood Cinema 1930–1980* (Princeton: Princeton University Press).

Rowe, Kathleen (1995), 'Melodrama and Men in Post-Classical Romantic Comedy', in Pat Kirkham and Janet Thumim (eds.), *Me Jane: Masculinity, Movies and Women* (London: Lawrence & Wishart).

Ryan, Michael, and Douglas Kellner (1988), *Camera Politica: The Politics and Ideology of Contemporary Hollywood Film* (Bloomington: Indiana University Press).

Schatz, Thomas (1983), *Old Hollywood/New Hollywood: Ritual, Art, Industry* (Ann Arbor, Mich.: UMI Research Press).

—— (1988), *The Genius of the System* (New York: Pantheon).

—— (1993), 'The New Hollywood', in Jim Collins, Hilary Radnor, and Ava Preacher Collins (eds.), *Film Theory Goes to the Movies* (New York: Routledge).

—— (1956), *The Public Arts* (New York: Simon & Schuster).

Tasker, Yvonne (1996), 'Approaches to the New Hollywood', in James Curran, David Morley, and Valerie Walkerdine (eds.), *Cultural Studies and Communications* (London: Arnold).

Thompson, Kristin (1995), 'Narrative Structure in Early Classical Cinema', paper presented to Celebrating 1895: An International Conference on Film before 1920, National Museum of Photography, Film, and Television, Bradford, June 1995.

Thomson, David (1981), *Overexposures: The Crisis in American Filmmaking* (New York: William Morrow).

Time (1967/1971), 'The Shock of Freedom in Films', in Arthur F. McClure (ed.), *The Movies: An American Idiom* (Rutherford: Fairleigh Dickinson University Press).

Williams, Christopher (1994), 'After the Classic, the Classical and Ideology: The Differences of Realism', *Screen*, **35**/3: 275–92.

Wood, Robin (1985), '1980s Hollywood: Dominant Tendencies', *CineAction*, **1**: 1–5.

—— (1986), *Hollywood from Vietnam to Reagan* (New York: Columbia University Press).

Wyatt, Justin (1994), *High Concept: Movies and Marketing in Hollywood* (Austin: University of Texas Press).

27 Taboos and totems: cultural meanings of *the silence of the lambs*

Janet Staiger

By the fifth week of the release of *Silence of the Lambs* (1991), the debates over the film had solidified into a set of propositions: 1) that whether or not Jonathan Demme had intended to create a homophobic film, the character of the serial murderer had attributes associated with stereotypes of gay men; 2) that in a time of paranoia over AIDS and increased violence directed toward gays in the United States, even suggesting connections between homosexuals and serial murderers was irresponsible; but 3) that the character of Clarice Starling played by Jodie Foster was a positive image of a woman working in a patriarchal society and, thus, empowering for women viewers. The diversion in views produced a consequent division: two non-dominant groups, some gay men and some feminists (both straight and lesbian), found themselves at odds over evaluating the film.

The controversy further escalated when several activists 'outed' Jodie Foster. [...] Foster's outing produced in the most vitriolic counter-analysis the claim that Foster was being outed because she was a strong woman and that she was being 'offer[ed] up [by gay activists] as a sacrifice in the furtherance of gay visibility'.[1] Although other women were not so strong in their condemnation of Foster's outing, all thirteen of those women whose views of the movie, *Silence of the Lambs*, I had available to me expressed praise for the film. [...]

Whether Foster is or is not a lesbian or bisexual 'in real life' is not the point of this essay. Whether the character she plays in *Silence of the Lambs* is or is not a lesbian is also not at issue here. What I shall be pursuing instead is the ultimate *stitching* together of gay and woman that became the 'climax' of the discussion. I shall argue that this possibility, while not inevitable, is grounded in its reception context and process. What I shall be doing here is what I call historical reception studies. This research attempts to illuminate the cultural meanings of texts in specific times and social circumstances to specific viewers, and it attempts to contribute to discussions about the spectorial effects of films by moving beyond text-centered analyses.

Because I wish to give you an application of this rather than an extended theoretical argument, I will simply lay out several hypotheses informing my research:

1) Immanent meaning in a text is denied.
2) 'Free readers' do not exist either.
3) Instead, contexts of social formations and constructed identities of the self in relation to historical conditions explain the interpretation strategies and affective responses of readers. Thus, receptions need to be related to specific historical conditions as *events*.
4) Furthermore, because the historical context's discursive formation is contradictory and heterogeneous, *no* reading is unified.

5) The best means currently available for analyzing cultural meanings exist in post-structuralist and ideological textual analyses. These methods, of necessity, draw upon multiple theoretical frameworks and perspectives such as deconstructionism, psychoanalysis, cognitive psychology, linguistics, anthropology, cultural studies Marxism, and feminist, ethnic and minority, lesbian and gay studies. They do so with a clear understanding that the connections and differences among the frameworks and perspectives must be theorized.

Consequently, historical reception studies work combines contemporary critical and cultural studies to understand why distinct interpretive and affective experiences circulate historically in specific social formations. In a case study, the following steps might occur:

1) An object of analysis is determined. This object is an *event*, not a text: that is, it is a set of interpretations or affective experiences produced by individuals from an encounter with a text or set of texts within a social situation. It is not an analysis of the text except in so far as to consider what textually might be facilitating the reading.
2) Traces of that event are located. Here I shall be using primarily traces in the form of printed prose and images, but when available, oral accounts would be very good sites of additional evidence. The print and images include about twenty reviews, news articles, letters to papers, advertisements, illustrations, and publicity which circulated in the major mass media.
3) The traces are analyzed textually and culturally. That is, as new historians elucidate causal processes to explain conjunctions called 'events' and then characterize the social significance of these events in relation to specific groups of people, so too does this research. Furthermore, the analyses avoid categorizing receptions into preferred, negotiated, or resistant readings. Rather the processes of interpretation are described since more richness in explanation can be achieved than by reducing readings to three specific generalizations.
4) Finally, the range of readings is considered not only by what seems possible at that moment but also by what the readings did not consider. That is, structuring absences are as important as well.

My project will be to work toward explicating the event of the 'sacrificial' outing of Jodie Foster. I shall argue that, although this event might be explained simply through contemporary U.S. stereotypes of lesbians – i.e., a strong woman must be a lesbian – or even because of informal oral communication circulated by gays and lesbians about Foster's sexual preferences, the possibility of making such an inference was facilitated by the critical response *Silence of the Lambs* received. [...]

In this initial study of the event, three specific reading strategies occur.[2] These are: 1) the construction of binary oppositions with deployments of high and low, good and bad attributions; 2) the use of metaphor and analogy; and 3), most pertinent to the event, the hybridization or grafting of incompatible terms together. This practice is activated from the prior two strategies and even finds its motivation from one of the dominant metaphors in the discourse.

Taboos

Perhaps because many writers have gone to film school or because thinking in oppositions so colors our everyday lives, reviewers of *Silence of the Lambs* often structured their plot analyses around a central binary opposition. The most obvious opposition was one between Hannibal 'The Cannibal' Lecter and Jame 'Buffalo Bill' Gumb. One reviewer notices that Lecter is upper class and witty while Gumb is a 'working-class lout'.[3] The reviewer even emphasizes how this sets up an audience to sympathize with the 'good' Lecter and to find disgusting the 'bad' Gumb. [...]

Important to this evaluation is that Lecter's victims are bureaucrats and authority figures, such as the census taker whose liver he ate with a nice Chianti. Meanwhile, Gumb goes after young, overweight women. Additionally, of course, Gumb is played as effeminate – something remarked upon by several reviewers who also acknowledged the gay community's concern about the film.

Binary oppositions are commonly deployed in ways such that the two terms in the opposition are not equal. [...] The hierarchization of binary oppositions functions analogically to legitimate Lecter's cannibalism. Thus, the class attributions, choice of victims, and socialized behavior patterns are read not merely as oppositions but ones with values attached which reinforced each other. [...]

Can we explain the spectator's acceptance of this transgression beyond the functioning of the textual array of values attached to the binary oppositions? Freud writes in *Totem and Taboo* that taboos are occasionally breached only to reassert the boundaries authenticating them. One instance of such a breach is the ritual eating of something considered taboo. Such a thing might even be the plant or animal which the tribe considers to be its totem. Totems stand as symbols for the group.

But according to Freud, they are also causal explanations. The totem is the tribe's origin, the 'father' of the tribe. Thus, Freud links the ritual eating of totems to the Oedipal story and argues that what has been established as out-of-bounds (e.g., killing one's father) is in the ritual the symbolic consumption of the totem's character. [...] Lecter, of course, foregoes the more oblique symbolism: he actually eats members of the tribe but for the same purpose.[4] Lecter's ingestion of his own kind, authorized as the incorporation of the bodies of authority figures and legitimated through socially originated hierarchies of binary oppositions, provides both textual and contextual determinations for spectators to accept, and even find pleasure in, his destruction of boundaries.

Consequently, and as part of the weirdly disconcerting pleasure of the event, the reviewers make all sorts of jokes about accepting the broken taboo as if they too wish to participate in the ritual. These jokes occur in the form of puns, doubly validating as they are by puns being a lawful disruption of traditional meanings. [...] Notice that all of these wisecracks are made apologically, because they do, indeed, open fissures in social categorizing. Headlines are particularly susceptible to word play, and the discursive motif continues there. Examples include: 'Overcooked Lambs', 'Skin Deep: Jonathan Demme's Chatter of the Hams', and 'Gluttons for Punishment'.[5]

Thus, a very powerful and significant binary opposition between Lecter and Gumb is constructed and circulated by viewers of the film. A second structuring binary opposition is proposed by Denby and J. Hoberman who point out that Clarice Starling has several fathers with which to contend.[6] Hoberman expands the comparison: Crawford, the FBI agent, is her daytime dad who is rational; Lecter, her night-time father, is a 'charismatic suitor'.[7] This reading of the film as an incest story is transformed in other reviews. As one writer suggests, *Silence of the Lambs* can be seen as about Starling who is 'changing, trying to formulate an identity'.[8] [...]

Psychoanalytical discourse is widespread, and Hoberman, among others, is familiar with it. Thus, the historical discourse of psychoanalysis may be abetting his reading the film as an Oedipal crisis for Starling, one that ends 'happily.' Starling is permitted to join the FBI; Lecter rewards her with unfettered independence from threats by him. Furthermore, and most significantly, Starling kills Gumb, symbol of aberrant sexual behavior, thus overtly denying homoeroticism while permitting it to exist in the apparently heterosexual Crawford-Starling pair.

Thus, one way some reviewers seem to have read the film is Starling-as-Masquerading-Woman who accedes into patriarchy. However, another way exists to understand parts of the interpretive reception of *Silence of the Lambs*. To explore that I need to draw out further the second interpretive strategy: the functions of metaphor and analogy.

Totems

We can assume that some reviewers of the movie read the original novel which is thus part of the potential context for interpreting the film. The novel employs a rather hackneyed device: the various characters are linked to animals, with a theme of natural preying.[9] [...]

The animal motif as metaphor and category for social cognition, perhaps set up by having read the novel, perhaps from Starling's name itself – or from the title of the film – perhaps from habit, permeates reception discourse about *Silence of the Lambs*. Lecter is a 'cobra'[10] who lives in a 'snake pit of an asylum'.[11] He makes 'hissing, vile, intimate remarks to women'.[12]

The initiation theme crisscrosses with this motif. Starling is described as 'mole-like' for her penetration of the killers' habitats. [...] But Starling is not always, or usually, the one doing the preying. 'Lecter plays cat and mouse with Clarice.'[13] For viewers, Starling can become the totem animal with whom she identifies: *she* is the 'lamb in wolves' territory'.[14] [...]

Social discourses are never uniform nor logical even as they try to map hierarchies across semantic categories. In the reception of *Silence of the Lambs*. Lecter's meaning is mobile; some times on the top, other times on the bottom. This inversion is most obvious when he is positioned not to counsel but to threaten Starling. [...] Some men reviewers took Starling to be a woman-victim. Could readers perceive Starling as a woman in danger?

In a discussion of the representation of the naked female body, Margaret R. Miles points out that by the 15th century, a common visual motif is the positioning of a woman in a frontal pose with the figure of Adam, her lover, standing behind her.[15] Or, Adam is transformed into the Figure of Death and the woman dances with him. Or in even more threatening and troubling images. Death copulates with the woman in sadomasochistic brutalism. These images are reminiscent of representations of vampirism, a later connection of animals, eating, sexuality, and death. Miles argues that their significance is the patriarchal connection of woman with sin, sex, and death. [...]

Hauntingly, then, another theme in the critical reception of the film is the ambiguous threat of Lecter to Starling as woman-victim. When they discussed it, many reviewers did take the threat to be sexual in some way. [...] This reading, however, does not mean that Starling is necessarily being read psychically as female, with the sexuality as heterosexual – in fact it would be repressed polymorphous sexuality – but it does open the space for such a reception. This opens for discussion another feature in the array of interpretations.

Minotaurs and moths

Women who discussed the film in the public discourse that I surveyed liked *Silence of the Lambs* and seemed especially to sympathize with Starling. Julie Salamon describes Starling as 'an attractive woman of unexceptional size doing what used to be thought of as a man's job. [...] She is a rare heroine, a woman who goes about her work the way men do in movies, without seeming less a woman.'[16] Amy Taubin praises the movies as a 'feminist film' which 'suggests that [sexuality and sexual role] fantasies can be exumed and examined, and that their meanings can be shifted.' Taubin goes on to invert traditional mythology: after describing Starling's discussions with Lecter as 'the meeting of Oedipus and the Sphinx,' she claims that the pleasure of the film is 'the two-hour spectacle of a woman solving the perverse riddles of patriarchy – all by herself'.[17]

Again, Starling is being placed in the narrative position traditionally given to a male. However, in Taubin's scenario, Lecter is not the patriarchal father. Rather, Lecter must fit in the slot of the Sphinx, the monstrous hybrid with the upper torso of a woman and the lower torso an amalgamation of animal body parts. Although symptomatically its gender is unknown, the Sphinx has traditionally been associated with the 'maternal'. Interestingly, however, no other reviewer surveyed suggested that Lecter had any feminine traits, perhaps because by contrast he seemed masculine compared with Gumb.[18]

Another monstrous hybrid is also mentioned in the reviews. Hoberman retitles the movie 'Nancy Drew Meets the Minotaur'. The Minotaur is a double inversion of the Sphinx, for its lower body is that of a human male while its head is that of a bull.[19] Thus, the human body halves that define the two beasts are reversed as well as the genders. Furthermore, the Minotaur is absolutely knowable as male since the lower portion of its body is entirely visible – the area legitimated by medical discourse as that which defines and describes sexual difference.[20] This Minotaur association is reinforced through the labyrinth metaphors mentioned earlier.

The third reading strategy is hybridization, the grafting together of irreconcilables. The associations with these particular mythical beasts are some evidence of this. Note, in particular, that what is grotesque is not the blurring of boundaries or even their transgression, which is the case for Lecter's cannibalism in which he ingests another and takes on its attributes. Rather what is disturbing is the all-too-apparent, the *see-able*, combination of disparate semantical categories: human/animal. Again, Hoberman's discourse is particularly insightful. About

Gumb, he writes, '[Buffalo Bill] is a jarring billboard of discordant signs – a figure stitched together like the Frankenstein monster.'[21]

Hoberman's vocabulary, then, gives us the thread to another pattern of interpretation motivated by the text and mobilized by the historical context. Gumb received his nickname because he skins his victims and sews those skins together to make himself an outfit. Literally stripping the women of their outer raiment, Gumb tries to fashion himself into the woman he desires to be. All of the reviewers decide he is the ultimate monster.

Working from Kristeva's thoughts about the abject, Barbara Creed has recently argued that the horror to be confronted in some films is not just the phallic mother but, finally, the archaic mother of the imaginary, pre-Oedipal experience.[22] The monstrous horror is into the castrated female but the maternal authority which threatens the 'obliteration of the self'.

Many of the reviewers observe that Gumb's behavior is readable as effeminate, leading to the inference, despite lines of dialogue, that he is homosexual. [...] Gumb's is by cultural categories feminized.

Also reinforcing this threat of the engulfing maternal monster is Gumb's totem: the death's-head moth, so named because the markings on its back resemble those of a skull. It is this animal which he wishes to imitate in its transformation into beauty; it is this totem which he shoves down his victims' throats. [...] The death's-head moth functions symbolically to write 'Gumb' on the bodies of women. According to the movie plot, Gumb did this as well to forecast his forthcoming transformation and new link to the identity 'woman'. Holding the moth in their mouths, the women's interiors are now exteriorized – their skins gone but their bodies the cocoon for a new beauty.

This association of moth, maternity, and monster is strongly prepared for extra-textually, so the fact that viewers responded to it is not surprising. For *Silence of the Lambs*, the moth was a major motif in the advertising campaign through the posters of it covering Starling's mouth.[23] But the ad's image does not have the moth *in* Starling's throat. It would not be visible. It covers her mouth, hiding an orifice. In this film, and in symptomatic displacement, inversions have existed all over the interpretational landscape. Outsides become insides both in Lecter's cannibalism and Gumb's scripting his forthcoming transformation.

Furthermore, the moth is *stitched* across her mouth. Starling is figured and readable as a hybrid monster as well. If she is easily thought of as an individual in search of her identity, she, like Gumb, can be associated with the moth. She is interpretable as part of his clan. But this stitching is across the mouth, leaving Starling, like that of so many victims, silenced.

Recall that readers have also equated Starling with the lambs she tried to save from slaughter. After death, lambs have two functions: they can be eaten; their hides can be worn. In both cases, the sacrifice is incorporated by the killer – internally via swallowing and externally via masquerading as an other. [...] Starling *is* a woman, she may not be a '*normal*' woman. We thus have a complete quadrant of gender and sexual preferences available in the film: Lecter: heterosexual male; female victims: (heterosexual) females; Gumb: homosexual male; Starling: homosexual female. Reading Starling as a lesbian, however, is not a direct result of textual evidence but an inference from the interpretive strategies and the discursive context of the film.

[...]

As I have indicated, Foster might well have come under attack simply because of stereotypes of the strong woman as a lesbian as well as informal oral communication about her, but motifs in the advertising and film, combined with reading strategies by its viewers, reinforced the credibility of the accusation by those who chose to out her. Starling's gender is ambiguous. She is easily read as a 'son' in a patriarchal identity crisis; she is easily read as 'unfeminine', tracking archaic mothers in their lairs; she is easily read as a hybrid – a moth-person. And within a structural square of oppositions and inversions, her position is the most 'other': not heterosexual, not male. She could be the lamb sacrificed in punishment for the film's expressed homophobia and repressed polymorphous sexuality.

[...]

In closing I wish to underline what I have been doing theoretically. This study is an attempt to indicate how contemporary theoretical frameworks can be useful in determining the cultural meanings (with the plural emphasized) of a specific text. What I have not done is to try to unify the text or the readings by asserting that one reading or set of oppositions or displacements is more viable than another. I have tried to provide the *range* of readings and to give an initial account of what might explain that range.

Additionally, my *primary* evidence for the cultural meanings of the events was not derived from a textual reading of the film. It came from public discourse. From that discourse, mediated though it is, I determined what textual, extratextual, and social determinants might account for the readings in my sample. [...]

Determining the cultural meaning of a text is full of assumptions and pitfalls. Interpreting interpretations is viciously circular. Additionally, the discourse I used in public and therefore already suspect. It is by no means representative of its culture – although I would be willing to argue that it has some relation to it as well as an effect on it. Given these (and other) problems, however, I still believe that research of this sort is helpful in a project of trying to understanding how individuals interpret the world and how they use discourse to shape, or reshape, that world. [...]

Notes

1 Leslie Larson, 'Foster Freeze', [Letter to] *Village Voice* (April 2, 1991) [n.p. – from *Silence of the Lambs* clipping file, Academy of Motion Picture Arts and Sciences Margaret Herrick Library – hereafter SLfile]. Background, descriptions, and debates preceding this can be found in David J. Fox, 'Gays Decry Benefit Screening of "Lambs" ', *Los Angeles Times* (February 4, 1991) [n.p. SLfile]; Michael Musto, 'La Dolce Musto', *Village Voice* (February 12, 1991) [n.p. SLfile]; Amy Taubin, 'Demme's Monde', *Village Voice* (February 19, 1991), pp. 64, 76–77; Lisa Kennedy, ed., 'Writers on the *Lamb*', *Village Voice* (March 5, 1991), pp. 49, 56; Michelangelo Signorile, '*Lamb* Chops', [Letter to] *Village Voice*, (March 12, 1991) [n.p. SLfile]; [Letters to] *Village Voice* (March 19, 1991) [n.p. SLfile]; Elaine Dutka, ' "Silence" Fuels a Loud and Angry Debate', *Los Angeles Times* (March 20, 1991) [n.p. SL file]; and Michael Bronski, 'Reel Politic', *Z Magazine* 4:5 (May, 1991), pp. 80–84.

2 If I were explaining something else about the reception of *Silence of the Lambs*, other features and practices in the discourse might be pertinent.

3   Henry Sheehan, 'Overcooked Lambs', *Los Angeles Reader* (February 15, 1991), pp. 29–30. These footnotes contain only the sources which I quote from; other reviews were part of my sample.

4   Sigmund Freud, *Totem and Taboo: Resemblances Between the Psychic Lives of Savages and Neurotics* [1918], trans. A.A. Brill (New York: Vintage Books, 1946). 'The cannibalism of primitive races derives its more sublime motivation in a similar manner. By absorbing parts of the body of a person through the act of eating we also come to possess the properties which belonged to that person' (p. 107).

5   Sheehan, 'Overcooked Lambs', p. 29; John Powers, 'Skin Deep: Jonathan Demme's Chatter of the Hams', *L.A. Weekly* (February 15–21, 1991), p. 27: Stanley Kauffmann, 'Gluttons for Punishment', *New Republic* (February 18, 1991), p. 48.

6   J. Hoberman, 'Skin Flick', *Village Voice* (February 19, 1991), p. 61.

7   As Hoberman notices, in the original novel, Starling's relation with her mother is a dominant theme. In the film, her mother's death and its meaning to Starling are repressed, with the film concentrating on Starling's need to deal with her father's death.

8   Terrence Rafferty, 'Moth and Flame', *New Yorker* (February 25, 1991), pp. 87–88.

9   Thomas Harris, *The Silence of the Lambs* (New York: St. Martin's, 1988).

10 Rafferty, 'Moth and Flame'.

11 Peter Travers, 'Snapshots from Hell: The Silence of the Lambs', *Rolling Stone* (March 7, 1991), pp. 87–88.

12 Denby, 'Something Wilder'.

13 Powers, 'Skin Deep'.

14 Smith, 'Hollywood Horror'.

15 Margaret R. Miles, *Carnal Knowing: Female Nakedness and Religious Meaning in the Christian West* (New York: Vintage Books, 1989).

16 Salamon, 'Weirdo Killer'.

17 Amy Taubin, in Kennedy, ed., 'Writers'.

18 Reviewers did at times discuss him not only as monstrous but as alien or an extraterrestrial.

19 In *Alice Doesn't: Feminism, Semiotics, Cinema* (Bloomington: Indiana University Press, 1984), Teresa de Lauretis's analysis of narrativity and gender uses the Oedipal myth with its stories of meeting the Sphinx and the Minotaur tale as part of her argument about patriarchy's construction of desire. This odd coincidence is not particularly troublesome to explain since the equation is widely known through feminist discourse, and Taubin and Hoberman both are familiar with that discourse. We do not need to assume anything more than common social and discursive networks provoked this conjunction of terms.

20 Arnold I. Davidson, 'Sex and the Emergence of Sexuality', *Critical Inquiry* 14:1 (Autumn, 1987), pp. 16–48, writes that it was through psychiatry that a split was made between anatomical sex and psychological sex. Medicalization takes over, investigating for visual evidence of gender both externally and internally.

21 Hoberman, 'Skin Flick'.

22 Barbara Creed, 'Horror and the Monstrous-Feminine: An Imaginary Abjection', *Screen* 27:1 (January–February, 1986), pp. 44–70.

23 It was derived from the novel but appears even during publicity generated while the film was in production. Its potency is obvious from the fact that the ad campaign recently won an award for the best movie poster of the year. Eithne Johnson informs me that the posters used Dali's 'punning' picture of women to create the skull. Furthermore, moths and butterflies have a long-standing association with the vagina. No reviewer, however, made note of either.

SECTION SIX

SCREEN THEORY I: FROM MARXISM TO PSYCHOANALYSIS

Screen theory emerged during the early to mid-1970s, and was probably more central to the establishment of film studies as a discipline within higher education than any other approach. This is not to imply that it was solely responsible for this process, or that its influence was uncontested, but simply that, for a crucial and critical period, *Screen* theory had a certain dominance as a way of thinking about cinema.

Screen theory is named after the journal *Screen*, which became well known for its championing of French structuralist and poststructuralist theory. Most particularly, the work associated with the journal drew on what has become known as Althusserian or structuralist Marxism and on Lacanian psychoanalysis, two theoretical movements that sought to rethink the work of Marx and Freud in the light of Saussurean linguistics.

As we have already seen in Section Four, structuralist Marxism reworked the concept of ideology to claim that it was not a matter of explicit ideas, but rather of the process through which we are constructed as individuals. To put it another way, structuralist Marxists argued that society positions us within itself so that we come to see our identities and our actions as the product of our own individual will, rather than as the effect of social structures (see Sections Four and Six).

This led *Screen* theory to take issue with the 'taken for granted' or 'common sense', and to seek to 'deconstruct' social life. In relation to film, for example, it sought to 'defamiliarize' our relationship to film texts, and was particularly critical of the concept of realism 'Realism', for *Screen* theorists, was not a positive attribute in a film, but was instead one of the primary mechanisms through which cinema functioned to reproduce the dominant ideology. The problem with realism, they argued, was that it presupposed an objective social world that had meaning independent of any subjective perception of it. Indeed, it assumed a model of representation which Saussurean linguistics challenged: that signs simply named a world that pre-data them. Furthermore, realism also positioned spectators outside the fictional action, and so reproduced their sense of themselves as independent and autonomous beings.

To put this another way, *Screen* theorists argued that realism did not simply present the world as it was, but rather reproduced the structures of bourgeois individualism. As we have seen, for structuralism, subjects may perceive themselves as independent and autonomous individuals, but are in fact simply functions of the structures of language and culture (see Section Three). Indeed, as we have also seen the very structure of language divides the world into subjects (things that act), verbs (actions that are performed) and objects (those things that are acted on). It is for this reason that we refer to the subjective (the perception of an object as it is perceived by a particular individual) and the objective (the object as it actually is, independent of the perceptions of particular individuals).

There were, therefore, supposed to be two ideological functions of 'realism'. First, realism was said to reproduce the notion that there was an objective view of the world, or rather that the world could have a meaning outside of particular ideological perspectives. Second, it was claimed to reproduce 'subjectivity', the sense of identity and completeness through which individuals mistakenly see themselves as the cause of their actions, rather than as the effects of social structures.

In the first case, it was argued that, while films may acknowledge that there are conflicting interpretations within their narratives, they present their fictional worlds as though there were an objective 'truth' that could be identified. For example, while some shots within a film are clearly marked as 'subjective' perceptions by characters within the film, others will present themselves as revealing the 'truth'. A character may say they are innocent of a crime, for example, but earlier we have been shown the image of them committing the offence. In this case, we are normally expected to believe the evidence of our eyes, rather than the words of the character, unless the image of them committing the act has been clearly marked as unreliable in some way – as the subjective perception of another character, for example.

For *Screen* theory, the problem with this aspect of realism is that it inevitably presents one interpretation as though it were an uncontested truth. It asserts that there is a position of truth that can be identified outside of language or culture. In other words, it creates a hierarchy of interpretations, in which one interpretation is privileged over others and, by extension, in which certain interpretations are subordinated or marginalized. This is perhaps clearer if we take a particular example. In a film about the Second World War, say *Saving Private Ryan* (1998), the American forces are clearly presented as fighting for a good cause, and the German army are clearly presented as a force who are fighting for a bad cause. This is not presented as an interpretation within the film; on the contrary, it is taken for granted as being the truth. Whether or not we disagree with this position, however, it is nonetheless possible to accept that it is not an objective and irrefutable 'truth', but itself an interpretation which the film presents *as though it were* a 'truth'. If America had been defeated, we would probably be watching films that presented the Germans as fighting for a good cause, and the Americans as a force that was fighting for a bad cause. Indeed, it might be added that in both cases, despite apparent ideological differences, both narratives define the 'truth' as being defined by the experiences of the individual soldiers, rather than being concerned with the broader historical processes through which those experiences are produced. Reality is defined as what individuals experience rather than the social processes that produce that 'reality'.

Screen theorists therefore refer to the 'discourse' of a film, by which they mean the position from which it is told and the assumptions that are taken for granted by this position. However, this is sometimes also referred to as the 'metadiscourse', by which they mean that although a film may present many discourses or interpretations within itself, it will privilege one discourse or interpretation as the truth, as the discourse which corrects and explains all the other discourses that are presented within it.

For these reasons, *Screen* theorists also claim that realism cannot deal with social contradiction. As they point out, realism is often directly related to narrative and it therefore structures the social world as though it were 'subject-centred'. In other words, realist narratives present the world as the story of a subject, and usually an individual subject. Indeed, classic realist novels were often specifically named after their central characters: *Robinson Crusoe*, *Tom Jones*, *Emma*, *Jane Eyre*, and *David Copperfield*. As such, it is argued, they cannot help presenting the social world as though it were simply the effect of individuals and individual actions, rather than a structure or system that is the cause of individual identity and action. Conflicts within narratives, they argue, become conflicts between individuals, rather than social conflicts that are rooted in social contradictions.

Indeed, the structure of narrative is also supposed to require a narrative resolution in which conflicts are resolved, and this requirement prevents narratives from handling inherent social contradictions. Inequality, for example, is a structural feature of the capitalist system that cannot be dispensed with from within the terms of that system. Film narratives dealing with inequality, therefore, have to structure their problems in such a way that they can be resolved within the terms of the existing social system. For example, the problem is often shifted from one of structural inequality to one of personal social mobility in which the individual characters, through their own efforts, escape their social situation. In this way, such narratives fail to tackle the systematic inequality within capitalism and may in effect provide a defence of capitalism in which it is suggested that the poor are simply unworthy. In *Boyz N the Hood* (1991), for example, despite its social concern with inequality in Los Angeles, the need for a narrative resolution requires an individualist solution – Tre and his girl-friend escape the 'hood' and get away to college.

However, realism is supposed to be subject-centred not only in terms of its narrative organization, but also in the ways in which it addresses the spectator. As we have seen, structuralism claimed that the subject is constructed in and through language. To operate within the social world, we must allow ourselves to be positioned by it. For example, to speak a language we must occupy certain positions that are structured by that language. One such set of structures is the position of addresser and addressee: that is, the person who speaks and the person to whom that speech is directed. However, just as the addresser is a particular position from which one speaks, so the addressee is also a position. It is not simply anyone who hears a particular speech act, but rather the intended or implied listener. We have all been in positions in which we ask, 'Are you talking to me?', in which we identify some discrepancy between our identities and the person to whom a particular speaker seems to be addressing their words. The words seem to be addressed to someone who is different from us, or rather we are unwilling to position ourselves as the point of address. When we ask 'Are you talking to me?', we are also sometimes saying, 'Who the hell do you think I am?'

Although the position of addresser and addressee are more clear with spoken language, it is also true that any film will have an assumed addressee, and these are usually referred to in *Screen* theory as 'spectators'. Indeed, one of the effects of realist narrative is that it positions the spectator in such a way that it reproduces the dominant ideology by reproducing the forms of 'subjectivity' on which that ideology depends. In other words, it is claimed, the film addresses itself to a hypothetical spectator, a particular position from which the film becomes meaningful, and in so doing the film's viewers are forced to adopt this position. This process is referred to as 'the positioning of the subject within ideology'.

Seen in this way, the realist narrative is supposed to reproduce the notion of an autonomous subject who exists independently of an objective exterior world. Indeed, the meaning of this world is presented as clear, simple and non-contradictory, as presenting no problems of interpretation for the spectator. The address of the film constructs a spectator that not only sees him- or herself as the cause of the film's meaning rather than as its effect but also as being in full self-control. In other words, the narrative closure of realist texts represses conflicts and contradictions both within society and within subjectivity itself. All subjects are riven with contradictory desires and impulses, but in order to function as individuals, we need to repress these contradictions and to act as though we were unitary, coherent subjects.

It is this concern with contradiction to which Lacanian psychoanalysis was meant to provide a contribution. Indeed, Lacanian psychoanalysis emphasises that contradiction is the inevitable price of subjectivity itself – or, to put it another way, that the desire for a coherent and autonomous self is fundamentally impossible to satisfy. Like other thinkers who were influenced by structuralism, Lacan argues that there can be no sense of self outside of language. The child is born without a sense of self, and only acquires one through its positioning within 'the symbolic order' (language and culture). However, from the start, this sense of self brings with it a profound sense of self-division. As Robert Allen and Douglas Gomery have put it, 'We are defined in terms of social and linguistic relationships: "the son of ...," "I," "Mary Smith". The young child has no choice but to submit to society and the web of language which at the same time ensnares and defines him or her' (Allen and Gomery 1985:167). As a result, we can only identify ourselves with reference to pre-existing linguistic terms, and there is always a gap between 'the subject of enunciation' (the self that speaks) and 'the subject of the enounced' (the self of which we speak). In other words, any sense of self always entails a division because to have a sense of self, one must be both the subject and the object (the self that perceives and the self that is perceived).

For Lacanian psychoanalysis, then, human subjects are driven by the unconscious desire for a sense of wholeness and completion but it is a wholeness and completion that can never be attained. Thus, *Screen* theorists distinguished between the 'imaginary' and the 'symbolic'. Describing an early stage of child development, Lacan claims that the young child initially lacks any sense of its body as a unitary object, and that it is therefore literally uncoordinated. However, this state is overcome by the process through which the child learns to see itself as a unitary and coherent whole through its identification with the image of other bodies. The imaginary is therefore about identification with an image, and gives a sense of wholeness and completions, while the symbolic, as we have already seen, always involves the recognition that we are defined by pre-existing terms that determine us. It threatens to destroy that illusion associated with the imaginary by forcing us to recognize that our identities are the effect of the social and linguistic order rather than the cause of them.

All this theoretical work, however, lead back to a fairly familiar series of oppositions. Indeed, almost all mainstream films were dismissed as realist narratives, and a clear preference was stated for the avant-garde, which was seen as emphasizing its formal features and hence as breaking with the ideological mechanisms of realism. In this way, *Screen* theory seemed to repeat oppositions between 'high' and 'low' culture that go back at least as far as mass culture theory. For example, mass culture theorists had distinguished between the simple and easy pleasures of mass culture with its supposedly 'built-in reactions' and the complexity and difficulty of the avant-garde which required an active audience (see Section One).

In a similar way, *Screen* theory drew on Barthes's distinction between the open and the closed text, the writerly and the readerly text, or the text of 'jouissance' and the text of pleasure. The closed, readerly text or the text of pleasure is therefore the one that is supposed to require little effort from its reader. It is 'the text that contents, fills, grants euphoria; the text that comes from culture and does not break with it [and] is linked to a *comfortable* practice of reading'. In contrast, the open, writerly text, or the text of jouissance, is supposed to be the text that requires an active reader who does not simply consume the text but 'writes' it in their act of reading. It is 'the text that imposes a state of loss, the text that discomforts (perhaps to the point of boredom), unsettles the reader's historical, cultural, psychological assumptions, the consistency of his tastes, values, memories, [and] brings to a crisis his relation with language' (Barthes 1975: 14).

While this position did present the majority of popular films and even some types of art film as inherently ideological, it did permit a space for some radical films within popular cinema. Comolli and Narboni, for example (extract 28), describe the various ways in which films were supposed to operate ideologically, before moving on to discuss what has become known as the 'category e' film. This type of film, it is suggested, conformed to the Althusserian notion of art, which was positioned between ideology and science (by which Althusser and his followers meant Althusserian Marxism itself). For Althusserian theory, while art did not offer a scientific view of society, as did Althusserian theory, it could be distinguished from ideology, and therefore from more straightforwardly ideological films, because it did not present ideology straight, but rather allowed us to 'see' the ideology. It took ideology and allowed us to see it not as a transparent reflection of reality, but rather as ideology. Instead of smoothing over its contradictions, it revealed problems and tensions.

However, it was never clear how this came about. These types of film tended to be associated with certain directors, but *Screen* theory's anti-individualism made it difficult for critics to suggest individual intention as the cause. The fact that most of these directors were hardly Marxists also led to problems. Often it had to be implied that the films' critical features were present despite the intentions of the directors. Furthermore, it is arguably possible to deconstruct any film, to reveal its contradictions and tensions; and as a result it is difficult to tell whether one film is presenting its ideology straight, is simply inept or is implicitly critical. It may be that 'category e' has less to do with the formal properties of particular films than with the ways in which particular films are read by particular critics. In other words, one may be able to read any films as covertly deconstructing the dominant ideology.

In extract 29, Colin MacCabe outlines the key criticisms of realism and compares literary and cinematic realism. For McCabe, it is the camera that becomes the guarantor of 'truth', so that in the cinema 'seeing is believing'. Whatever characters might say, we are supposed to believe the evidence of our own eyes, or rather to trust that what the camera shows us is the objective truth. In this piece, McCabe also explains some of the issues about the ideological function of realist narratives discussed above, a position which is further clarified by John Hill in extract 30. The passage from Hill not only clarifies these ideas but also demonstrates how they might be applied more concretely in an analysis of British social realist films of the 1950s and 1960s, and particularly the 'social problem' films of this period.

If early work in *Screen* theory tended to emphasise the Althusserian or Marxist influence, later work tended to shift the concentration to psycho-analysis and sexual politics. The next section deals with the relationship between feminism and psychoanalysis within *Screen* theory, but the final two extracts of this section provide a somewhat different approach to psychoanalysis.

The Metz extract (31), for example, introduces three terms which would be important to later feminist work, but which have a quite different meaning within this context: identification, fetishism and voyeurism. For Metz, identification is *not* a matter of identification with particular charac-ters, but rather a question of the spectator's relationship to the film text. In short, viewers identify with the position of the spectator, the point to which all aspects of the film are addressed and at which they become meaningful. In other words, viewers identify with, and hence position themselves within, the addressee of the film text (its hypothetical spectator).

Fetishism therefore involves a particular relationship that the spectator must establish with the film image for it to be pleasurable. Obviously, the film image is really only a play of light upon the screen and as such the image is doubly fictional. It is not only that, in *Speed* (1994), Keanu Reeves is not really a policeman saving a busload of travellers, but that Keanu, the bus and its passengers are not actually present within the movie theatre. However, all cinematic pleasure depends to some extent on a repression of this fact – what is usually called 'suspension of disbelief'. Fetishism is the knowledge of the illusory nature of the film image – its double absence – and the partial suspension of that knowledge, a condition which is best summed up by the phrase 'I know it's only a movie and yet ...'

Voyeurism is therefore the condition within which the spectator relates to the image as a kind of guilty and even perverse pleasure. Just as the voyeur gains a sense of power over his victim by watching without being seen, so the spectator watches images of people and things whose absence means that they cannot respond to or confront the spectator. In addition the spectator watches from a darkened movie theatre so that they are freed not only from the surveillance of those on the screen, but also from other members of the audience. As a result, Metz links the pleasures of spectatorship to a perverse desire for sadistic control over the image.

Despite the fact that Metz draws on Lacanian psychoanalysis, his analysis of film viewing remains very static. However, in the last extract (32), Dayan discusses psychoanalytic approaches to spectatorship that are concerned with spectatorship as a dynamic process. For Lacan, the subject was not only necessarily split but was constantly 'in process'. In other words, the subject is constantly re-produced through its use of language. The syntax of a sentence, for example, not only requires that the subject position itself as either the subject, object, addresser or addressee of the sentence, but also that the subject acts to make sense of the sentence over time: to relate each word to what has come before and to anticipate what will come next. Making sense of a sentence, or any longer linguistic units, is a continual process of interpretation and reinterpretation which not only binds the elements of the sentence together but also creates a sense of the subject's continuity through time.

In much the same way, the watching of the film involves the continual relation of shot to shot and, for Dayan, this process needs to be understood in terms of psychoanalysis. This process, it is argued, not only enables the discourse of the film to present itself as transparent, but also functions to reproduce the subject. Through the act of interpretation, it is argued, the subject stitches together the elements of the film text and is, in turn, stitched together. However, while this offered a far more dynamic account of the relation between the text and the spectator, in which the spectator's subjectivity was not just interpellated by the text but was constantly being reproduced through the activity of interpretation, it tended to remain remote from the analysis of specific texts and spectators.

References

Allen, R. and Gomery, D. (1985). *Film History: Theory and Practice*. New York: McGraw-Hill.

Althusser, L. (1971). 'A Letter on Art in Reply to Andre Daspre'. In *Lenin and Philosophy*. New York: Monthly Review Press, 221–7.

Barthes, R. (1975). *The Pleasure of the Text*. London: Jonathan Cape.

Comolli, J.-L. and Narboni, P. (1971). 'Cinema/Ideology/Criticism'. *Screen* **12**(1): 27–36.

Dayan, D. (1974). 'The Tutor-Code of Classical Cinema'. *Film Quarterly* **28**(1): 22–31.

Hill, J. (1986). *Sex, Class and Realism: British Cinema 1956–63*. London: British Film Institute.

McCabe, C. (1974). 'Realism and the Cinema: Notes on Some Brechtian Theses'. *Screen* **15**(2): 7–27.

Metz, C. (1975). 'The Imaginary Signifier'. *Screen* **16**(2): 14–76.

28 Cinema/ideology/criticism

Jean-Luc Comolli and Paul Narboni

The films

What is a film? On the one hand it is a particular product, manufactured within a given system of economic relations, and involving labour (which appears to the capitalist as money) to produce – a condition to which even 'independent' film makers and the 'new cinema' are subject – assembling a certain number of workers for this purpose (even the director, whether he is Moullet or Oury, is in the last analysis only a film worker). It becomes transformed into a commodity, possessing exchange value, which is realized by the sale of tickets and contracts, and governed by the laws of the market. On the other hand, as a result of being a material product of the system, it is also an ideological product of the system, which in France means capitalism.[1]

No film-maker can, by his own individual efforts, change the economic relations governing the manufacture and distribution of his films. (It cannot be pointed out too often that even film-makers who set out to be 'revolutionary' on the level of message and form cannot effect any swift or radical change in the economic system – deform it, yes, deflect it, but not negate it or seriously upset its structure. [...] Because every film is part of the economic system it is also a part of the ideological system, for 'cinema' and 'art' are branches of ideology. None can escape: somewhere, like pieces in a jigsaw, all have their own allotted place. The system is blind to its own nature, but in spite of that, indeed because of that, when all the pieces are fitted together they give a very clear picture. But this does not mean that every film-maker plays a similar role. Reactions differ.

It is the job of criticism to see where they differ, and slowly, patiently, not expecting any magical transformations to take place at the wave of a slogan, to help change the ideology which conditions them.

A few points, which we shall return to in greater detail later: *every film is political*, inasmuch as it is determined by the ideology which produces it (or within which it is produced, which stems from the same thing). The cinema is all the more thoroughly and completely determined because unlike other arts or ideological systems its very manufacture mobilizes powerful economic forces in a way that the production of literature (which becomes the commodity 'books', does not – though once we reach the level of distribution, publicity and sale, the two are in rather the same position.

Clearly, the cinema 'reproduces' reality: this is what a camera and film stock are for – so says the ideology. But the tools and techniques of film-making are a part of 'reality' themselves, and furthermore 'reality' is nothing but an expression of the prevailing ideology. Seen in this light, the classic theory of cinema that the camera is an impartial instrument which grasps, or rather is impregnated by, the world in its 'concrete reality' is an eminently reactionary one. What the camera in fact registers is the vague, unformulated, untheorized, unthought-out world of the dominant ideology. Cinema is one of the languages through which the world communicates itself to itself. They constitute its ideology for they reproduce the world as it is experienced when filtered through the ideology. (As Althusser defines it, more precisely: 'Ideologies are perceived-accepted-suffered cultural objects, which work fundamentally on men by a process they do not understand. What men express in their ideologies is not their true relation to their conditions of existence, but how they react to their conditions of existence; which presupposes a real relationship and an imaginary relationship.') So, when we set out to make a film, from the very first shot, we are encumbered by the necessity of reproducing things not as they really are but as they appear when refracted through the ideology. This includes every stage in the process of production: subjects, 'styles', forms, meanings, narrative traditions; all underline the general ideological discourse. The film is ideology presenting itself to itself, talking to itself, learning about itself. Once we realize that it is the nature of the system to turn the cinema into an instrument of ideology, we can see that the film-maker's first task is to show up the cinema's so-called 'depiction of reality'. If he can do so there is a chance that we will be able to disrupt or possibly even sever the connection between the cinema and its ideological function.

The vital distinction between films today is whether they do this or whether they do not.

(a) The first and largest category comprises those films which are imbued through and through with the dominant ideology in pure and unadulterated form, and give no indication that their makers were even aware of the fact. We are not just talking about so-called 'commercial' films. The *majority* of films in all categories are the unconscious instruments of the ideology which produces them. Whether the film is 'commercial' or 'ambitious', 'modern' or 'traditional', whether it is the type that gets shown in art houses, or in smart cinemas, whether it belongs to the 'old' cinema or the 'young' cinema, it is most likely to be a rehash of the same old ideology.

[...] These films totally accept the established system of depicting reality: 'bourgeois realism' and the whole conservative box of tricks: blind faith in 'life', 'humanism', 'common sense' etc. A blissful ignorance that there might be something wrong with this whole concept of 'depiction' appears to have reigned at every stage in their production, so much so, that to us it appears a more accurate gauge of pictures in the 'commercial' category than box-office returns. Nothing in these films jars against the ideology, or the audience's mystification by it. They are very reassuring for audiences for there is no difference between the ideology they meet every day and the ideology on the screen.

(b) A second category is that of films which attack their ideological assimilation on two fronts. Firstly, by direct political action, on the level of the 'signified', ie they deal with a directly political subject. 'Deal with' is here intended in an active sense: they do not just discuss an issue, reiterate it, paraphrase it, but use it to attack the ideology (this presupposes a theoretical activity which is the direct opposite of the ideological one). This act only becomes politically effective if it is linked with a breaking down of the traditional way of depicting reality. [...]

(c) There is another category in which the same double action operates, but 'against the grain'. The content is not explicitly political, but in some way becomes so through the criticism practised on it through its form.[2] For *Cahiers* these films (b and c) constitute the essential in the cinema, and should be the chief subject of the magazine.

(d) Fourth case: those films, increasingly numerous today, which have an explicitly political content [...] but which do not effectively criticize the ideological system in which they are embedded because they unquestioningly adopt its language and its imagery. [...]

(e) Five: films which seem at first sight to belong firmly within the ideology and to be completely under its sway, but which turn out to be so only in an ambiguous manner. For though they start from a non-progressive standpoint, ranging from the frankly reactionary through the conciliatory to the mildly critical, they have been worked upon, and work, in such a real way that there is a noticeable gap, a dislocation, between the starting point and the finished product. [...] The films we are talking about throw up obstacles in the way of the ideology, causing it to swerve and get off course. The cinematic framework lets us see it, but also shows it up and denounces it. Looking at the framework one can see two moments in it: one holding it back within certain limits, one transgressing them. An internal criticism is taking place which cracks the film apart at the seams. If one reads the film obliquely, looking for symptoms; if one looks beyond its apparent formal coherence, one can see that it is riddled with cracks: it is splitting under an internal tension which is simply not there in an ideologically innocuous film. The ideology thus becomes subordinate to the text. It no longer has an independent existence: it is *presented* by the film. This is the case in many Hollywood films for example, which while being completely integrated in the system and the ideology end up by partially dismantling the system from within. We must find out what makes it possible for a film-maker to corrode the ideology by restating it in the terms of his film: if he sees his film simply as a blow in favour of liberalism, it will be recuperated instantly by the ideology; if, on the other hand, he conceives and realizes it on the deeper level of imagery, there is a chance that it will turn out to be more disruptive. Not, of course, that he will be able to break the ideology itself, but simply its reflection in his film. (The films of Ford, Dreyer, Rossellini, for example.)

Our position with regard to this category of films is: that we have absolutely no intention of joining the current witch-hunt against them. They are the mythology of their own myths. They criticize themselves, even if no such intention is written into the script, and it is irrelevant and impertinent to do so for them. All we want to do is to show the process in action.

(f) Films of the 'live cinema' (*cinéma direct*) variety, group one (the larger of the two groups). These are films arising out of political (or, it would probably be more exact to say: social) events or reflections, but which make no clear differentiation between themselves and the non-political cinema because they do not challenge the cinema's traditional, ideologically-conditioned method of 'depiction'.

(g) The other kind of 'live cinema'. Here the director is not satisfied with the idea of the camera 'seeing through appearances', but attacks the basic problem of depiction by giving an active role to the concrete stuff of his film. It then becomes productive of meaning and is not just a passive receptacle for meaning produced outside it (in the ideology) [...]

Critical Function

Such, then, is the field of our critical activity: these films, within the ideology, and their different relations to it. From this precisely defined field spring four functions: (1) in the case of the films in category (a): show what they are blind to; how they are totally determined, moulded, by the ideology; (2) in the case of those in categories (b), (c) and (g), read them on two levels, showing how the films operate critically on the level of signified and signifiers; (3) in the case of those of types (d) and (f), show how the signified (political subject matter) is always weakened, rendered harmless, by the absence of technical/theoretical work on the signifiers; (4) in the case of those in group (e) point out the gap produced between film and ideology by the way the films work, and show how they work.

Notes

1 Capitalist ideology. This term expresses our meaning perfectly, but as we are going to use it without further definition in this article, we should point out that we are not under any illusion that it has some kind of 'abstract essence'. We know that it is historically and socially determined, and that it has multiple forms at any given place and time and varies from historical period to historical period. Like the whole category of 'militant' cinema, which is totally vague and undefined at present. We must (a) rigorously define the function attributed to it, its aims, its side effects (information, arousal, critical reflection, provocation 'which always has *some* effect' ...); (b) define the exact political line governing the making and screening of these films – 'revolutionary' is too much of a blanket term to serve any useful purpose here; and (c) state whether the supporters of militant cinema are in fact proposing a line of action in which the cinema would become the poor relation, in the illusion that the less the cinematic aspect is worked on, the greater the strength and clarity of the 'militant' effect will be. This would be a way of avoiding the contradictions of 'parallel' cinema and getting embroiled in the problem of deciding whether 'underground' films should be included in the category, on the pretext that their relationship to drugs and sex, their preoccupation with form, might possibly establish new relationships between film and audience.

2 This is not a magical doorway out of the system of 'depiction' (which is particularly dominant in the cinema) but rather a rigorous, detailed, large-scale work on this system – what conditions make it possible, what mechanisms render it innocuous. The method is to draw attention to the system, so that it can be seen for what it is, to make it serve one's own ends, condemn itself out of its own mouth. Tactics employed may include 'turning cinematic syntax upside-down' but it cannot be just that. Any old film nowadays can upset the normal chronological order in the interests of looking vaguely 'modern'. But *The Exterminating Angel* and *The Diary of Anna Magdalena Bach* (though we would not wish to set them up as a model) are rigorously chronological without ceasing to be subversive in the way we have been describing, whereas in many a film the mixed-up time sequence simply covers up a basically naturalistic conception. In the same way, perceptual confusion (avowed intent to act on the unconscious mind, changes in the texture of the film, etc) are not sufficient in themselves to get beyond the traditional way of depicting 'reality'. To realize this, one has only to remember the unsuccessful attempts there have been of the 'lettriste' or or new kinds of onomatopoeia. In the one and the other case only the most 'zacum' type to give back its infinity to language by using nonsense words superficial level of language is touched. They create a new code, which operates on the level of the impossible, and has to be rejected on any other, and is therefore not in a position to transgress the normal.

29 Realism and the cinema: notes on some Brechtian theses

Colin MacCabe

[...] A classic realist text may be defined as one in which there is a hierarchy amongst the discourses which compose the text and this hierarchy is defined in terms of an empirical notion of truth. Perhaps the easiest way to understand this is through a reflection on the use of inverted commas within the classic realist novel. While those sections in the text which are contained in inverted commas may cause a certain difficulty for the reader – a certain confusion vis-à-vis what really is the case – this difficulty is abolished by the unspoken (or more accurately the unwritten) prose that surrounds them. In the classical realist novel the narrative prose functions as a metalanguage that can state all the truths in the object language – those words held in inverted commas – and can also explain the relation of this object language to the real. The metalanguage can thereby explain the relation of this object language to the world and the strange methods by which the object languages attempt to express truths which are straightforwardly conveyed in the metalanguage. What I have called an unwritten prose (or a metalanguage) is exactly that language, which while placing other languages between inverted commas and regarding them as certain material expressions which express certain meanings, regards those same meanings as finding transparent expression within the metalanguage itself. Transparent in the sense that the metalanguage is not regarded as material; it is dematerialised to achieve perfect representation – to let the identity of things shine through the window of words. For insofar as the metalanguage is treated itself as material – it, too, can be reinterpreted; new meanings can be found for it in a further metalanguage. [...]

It is this [...] that the unwritten text attempts to *anneal*, to make whole, through denying its own status as writing – as marks of material difference distributed through time and space. Whereas other discourses within the text are considered as material which are open to re-interpretation, the narrative discourse simply allows reality to appear and denies its own status as articulation. This relationship between discourses can be clearly seen in the work of such a writer as George Eliot. In the scene in *Middlemarch* where Mr Brooke goes to visit the Dagley's farm we read two different languages. One is the educated, well-meaning, but not very intelligent discourse of Mr Brooke and the other is the uneducated, violent and very nearly unintelligible discourse of the drunken Dagley. But the whole dialogue is surrounded by a metalanguage, which being unspoken is also unwritten, and which places these discourses in inverted commas and can thus discuss these discourses' relation to truth – a truth which is illuminatingly revealed in the metalanguage. The metalanguage reduces the object languages into a simple division between form and content and extracts the meaningful content from the useless form. One can see this process at work in the following passage which ends the scene:

He [Mr Brooke] had never been insulted on his own land before, and had been inclined to regard himself as a general favourite (we are all apt to do so, when we think of our own amiability more than what other people are likely to want of us). When he had quarrelled with Caleb Garth twelve years before he had thought that the tenants would be pleased at the landlord's taking everything into his own hands.

Some who follow the narrative of this experience may wonder at the midnight darkness of Mr Dagley; but nothing was easier in those times than for a hereditary farmer of his grade to be ignorant, in spite somehow of having a rector in the twin parish who was a gentleman to the backbone, a curate nearer at hand, who preached more learnedly than the rector, a landlord who had gone into everything, especially fine art and social improvement and all the lights of Middlemarch only three miles off.[1]

This passage provides the necessary interpretations for the discourses that we have read earlier in the chapter. Both the discourses of Dagley and Mr Brooke are revealed as springing from two types of ignorance which the metalanguage can expose and reveal. So we have Mr Brooke's attitude to what his tenants thought of him contrasted with the reality which is available through the narrative prose. No discourse is allowed to speak for itself but rather it must be placed in a context which will reduce it to a simple explicable content. And in the claim that the narrative prose has direct access to a final reality we can find the claim of the classic realist novel to present us with the truths of human nature. The ability to reveal the truth about Mr Brooke is the ability that guarantees the generalisations of human nature.

Thus then a first definition of the classic realist text – but does this definition carry over into films where it is certainly less evident where to locate the dominant discourse? It seems to me that it does and in the following fashion. The narrative prose achieves its position of dominance because it is in the position of knowledge and this function of knowledge is taken up in the cinema by the narration of events. Through the knowledge we gain from the narrative we can split the discourses of the various characters from their situation and compare what is said in these discourses with what has been revealed to us through narration. The camera shows us what happens – it tells the truth against which we can measure the discourses. A good example of this classical realist structure is to be found in Pakula's film *Klute*. This film is of particular interest because it was widely praised for its realism on its release. Perhaps even more significantly it tended to be praised for its realistic presentation of the leading woman, Bree (played by Jane Fonda).

In *Klute* the relationship of dominance between discourses is peculiarly accentuated by the fact that the film is interspersed with fragments of Bree talking to her psychiatrist. This subjective discourse can be exactly measured against the reality provided by the unfolding of the story. Thus all her talk of independence is portrayed as finally an illusion as we discover, to no great surprise but to our immense relief, what she really wants is to settle down in the mid-West with John Klute (the detective played by Donald Sutherland) and have a family. The final sequence of the film is particularly telling in this respect. While Klute and Bree pack their bags to leave, the soundtrack records Bree at her last meeting with her psychiatrist. Her own estimation of the situation is that it most probably won't work but the reality of the image ensures us that this is the way it will really be. [...]

The analysis sketched here is obviously very schematic but what, hopefully, it does show is that the structure of the classic realist text can be found in film as well.

[...] The unquestioned nature of the narrative discourse entails that the only problem that reality poses is to go and look and see what *Things* there *are*. The relationship between the reading subject and the real is placed as one of pure specularity. The real is not articulated – it is. These features imply two essential features of the classic realist text:

1 The classic realist text cannot deal with the real as contradictory.
2 In a reciprocal movement the classic realist text ensures the position of the subject in a relation of dominant specularity.

The classic realist text as progressive art

[...] All this by way of explaining that the classic realist text (a heavily 'closed' discourse) cannot deal with the real in its contradictions and that in the same movement it fixes the subject in a point of view from which everything becomes obvious. There is, however, a level of contradiction into which the classic realist text can enter. This is the contradiction between the dominant discourse of the text and the dominant ideological discourses of the time. Thus a classic realist text in which a strike is represented as a just struggle in which oppressed workers attempt to gain some of their rightful wealth would be in contradiction with certain contemporary ideological discourses and as such might be classified as progressive. It is here that subject matter enters into the argument and where we can find the justification for Marx and Engels's praise of Balzac and Lenin's texts on the revolutionary force of Tolstoy's texts which ushered the Russian peasant onto the stage of history. Within contemporary films one could think of the films of Costa-Gavras or such television documentaries as *Cathy Come Home*. What is, however, still impossible for the classic realist text is to offer any perspectives for struggle due to its inability to investigate contradiction. It is thus not surprising that these films tend either to be linked to a social-democratic conception of progress – if we reveal injustices then they will go away – or certain *ouvrieriste* tendencies which tend to see the working class, outside any dialectical movement, as the simple possessors of truth. [...]

Moments of subversion and strategies of subversion

[...] It is clear that the classic realist text, as defined above, guarantees the position of the subject exactly outside any articulation – the whole text works on the concealing of the dominant discourse as articulation – instead the dominant discourse presents itself exactly as the presentation of objects to the reading subject. But within the classic realist text the dominant discourse can be subverted, brought into question – the position of the subject may be rendered problematic. [...] We are relatively fortunate in already possessing this kind of analysis within the cinema in the *Cahiers du Cinéma*'s reading of John Ford's *Young Mr Lincoln*.[2] These *moments* are those elements which escape the control of the dominant discourse in the same way as a neurotic symptom or a verbal slip attest to the lack of control of the conscious subject. They open up another area than that of representation – of subject and object caught in an eternal paralysed fixity – in order to investigate the very movement of articulation and difference – the movement of desire. (It is these moments which have been privileged by Roland Barthes and the *Tel Quel* group over the last few years and which have been theorised through the evaluative concept of text.)[3] Over and above these *moments* of subversion, however, there are what one might call *strategies* of subversion. Instead of a dominant discourse which is transgressed at various crucial moments we can find a systematic refusal of any such dominant discourse. One of the best examples of a cinema which practices certain strategies of subversion are the films of Roberto Rossellini. In *Germany Year Zero*, for example, we can locate a multitude of ways in which the reading subject finds himself without a position from which the film can be regarded. Firstly, and most importantly, the fact that the narrative is not privileged in any way with regard to the characters' discourses. The narrative does not produce for us the knowledge with which we can then judge the truth of those discourses. Rather than the narrative providing us with knowledge – it provides us with various settings.

[...] If the reading subject is not offered any certain mode of entry into what is presented on the screen, he is offered a certain mode of entry to the screen itself. For the facts presented by the camera, if they are not ordered in fixed and final fashion amongst themselves, *are* ordered in themselves. The camera, in Rossellini's films is not articulated as part of the productive process of the film. What it shows is in some sense beyond argument and it is here that Rossellini's films show the traditional realist weakness of being unable to deal with contradiction. In *Viva l'Italia* the glaring omission of the film is the absence of Cavour. It is wrong to attack this omission on purely political grounds for it is an inevitable result of a certain lack of questioning of the camera itself. Garibaldi can be contrasted with Francisco II of Naples because their different conceptions of the world are so specifically tied to different historical eras that the camera can cope with their contradictions within an historical perspective. Here is the way the world is now – there is the way the world was then. But to introduce Cavour would involve a simultaneous contradiction – a class contradiction. At this point the camera itself, as a neutral agent, would become impossible. For it would have to offer two present contradictory articulations of the world and thus reveal its own presence. This cannot happen within a Rossellini film where if we are continually aware of our presence in the cinema (particularly in his historical films) – that presence itself is not questioned in any way. We are not allowed any particular position to read the film but we are allowed the position of a reader – an unproblematic viewer – an eternally human nature working on the material provided by the camera.

A possible way of advancing on Rossellini's practice (there are no obvious films which have marked such an advance although some of Godard's early films might be so considered) would be to develop the possibility of articulating contradiction. Much in the way that James Joyce in *Ulysses* and *Finnegans Wake* investigated the contradictory ways of articulating reality through an investigation of the different forms of language, one could imagine a more radical strategy of subversion than that practised by Rossellini in which the possibilities of the camera would be brought more clearly into play. [...]

A possible category: the revolutionary text

[...] Within the framework I have constructed in this article one could say that the revolutionary artist may practice certain strategies of subversion but must finally content himself with the production of a progressive realist text. The question I want to raise here, and it must be emphasised that it can only be raised, is the possibility of *another* activity which rather than the simple subversion of the subject or the representation of different (and *correct*) identities, would consist of the displacement of the subject within ideology – a different constitution of the subject. [...]

Two films which suggest a way of combating this dominance of the metalanguage, without falling into an agnostic position vis-à-vis all discourses (which would be the extreme of a subversive cinema – intent merely on disrupting any position of the subject) are *Kuhle Wampe* (the film in which Brecht participated) and Godard-Gorin's *Tout Va Bien*. In both films the narrative is in no way privileged as against the characters. Rather the narrative serves simply as the method by which various situations can be articulated together. The emphasis is on the particular scenes and the knowledge that can be gained from them rather than the providing of a knowledge which requires no further activity – which just is there on the screen. [...] *Tout Va Bien* [...] does not provide [...] knowledge ready-made in a dominant discourse but in the contradictions offered, the reader has to produce a meaning for the film (it is quite obvious in films of this sort that the meaning produced will depend on the class-positions of the reader). It is this emphasis on the reader as producer (more obvious in *Tout Va Bien* which is in many ways more Brechtian than *Kuhle Wampe*) which suggests that these films do not just offer a different representation for the subject but a different set of relations to both the fictional material and 'reality'. [...]

A definite category: Reactionary art

[...] One fashionable way of receiving and recuperating Brecht, which has been at work since the beginning of the Cold War, is to see him as a satirist ridiculing his contemporary society and the excesses of capitalism and fascism. This approach negates the productive element in Brecht's work and turns the techniques for the production of alienation effects into pure narcissistic signals of an 'intellectual' work of 'art'. A very typical example of this vulgarisation and de-politicisation of Brecht can be seen in Lindsay Anderson's *O Lucky Man!* An explicitly Brechtian film – the loosely connected scenes are counter-pointed by the Alan Price songs – the film pretends to offer a tableau of England in 1973 much as *Tout Va Bien* attempts to offer a tableau of France in 1972. But whereas in the French film the tableaux are used to reflect the contradictions within the society – the different articulations of reality – in the English film the tableaux are all used to express a stereotyped reality of England which the spectator is invited to enjoy from his superior position. The scenes may seem to be dominant over the reality revealed by the narrative but as the film progresses along its endless development it becomes obvious that the narrative simply confirms the evident truths which are offered to us on the screen. And these truths turn out to be that endless message of the reactionary petit-bourgeois intellectual – that we can do nothing against the relentless and evil progress of society (run as it is by a bunch of omnipotent capitalists with the morality of gangsters) except note our superiority to it. [...]

Notes

1 George Eliot, *Middlemarch*, London 1967, pp 432–433.
2 *Screen* 13 (3) (Autumn 1972).
3 See Roland Barthes 'De l'œuvre au texte' *Revue d'esthétique* 1971 and *Le Plaisir du texte*, Paris 1973.

---

30 Narrative and realism

John Hill

Narrative

A definition of narrative, independent of any particular contents, is suggested by Tzvetan Todorov:

> The minimal complete plot consists in the passage from one equilibrium to another. An 'ideal' narrative begins with a stable situation which is disturbed by some power or force. There results a state of disequilibrium; by the action of a force directed in the opposite direction, the equilibrium is re-established; the second equilibrium is similar to the first, but the two are never identical.[1]

Thus, in the case of the detective story or film, a crime is committed (the disequilibrium), requiring a force directed in the opposite direction (the investigation), resulting in a new equilibrium (the capture of the culprit). Implicit in this requirement of a new equilibrium is the idea of a narrative 'solution'. As Seymour Chatman suggests, there is always a sense, in the traditional narrative, of 'problem-solving', of 'things being worked out in some way'.[2] To this extent, there is a presumption, built into the very structure of conventional narrative, that 'problems' can be overcome, can, indeed, be resolved. It is for this reason that Thomas Elsaesser has suggested a link between an ideology of 'affirmation' and the characteristic conventions of narrativity. As he explains, there is 'a kind of *a priori* optimism located in the very structure of the narrative ... whatever the problem one can do something about it.'[3]

Inevitably, this has effects for the way in which both the social problem film and the films of the 'new wave' are able to deal with their subject-matter. Both loosely conform to the Todorov model. In the social problem film, it is characteristically a crime or 'deviant' action which represents the 'force' which initiates the plot; in the films of the 'new wave', it is more usually a socially or sexually transgressive desire. In both cases, it is in the nature of the conventions of narrative that these 'problems' be overcome. In this very presumption of a solution, so an attitude toward the initial 'problem' is already taken. Thus, in the case of the social problem film, the articulation of the film's 'social problem' into the problem-solving structure of narrative necessarily implies that it too is capable of resolution. Russell Campbell, for example, has observed how the American 'social consciousness' movie may portray negative aspects of American society but only in so far as it then proceeds to assert 'the possibility ... of corrective action' and celebrate 'the system for being flexible and susceptible to amelioration'.[4]

Such an ideological manoeuvre is, however, no accident but, more or less, a consequence of the conventions which have been adopted. For narrative form, of its nature, requires corrective action ('a force directed in the opposite direction') and amelioration ('the second equilibrium'), although this 'amelioration' need not, in itself, depend on the 'corrective action' of social reform. It may also result, as in the case of many British films, from the 'corrective action' of legal constraint and punishment. Either way, it is this need for some sort of narrative resolution which tends to encourage the adoption of socially conservative endings. An alternative account of social problems – say, poverty or juvenile delinquency – might, in fact, stress their intractability, their inability to be resolved, at least within the confines of the present social order. The solution to the problem of poverty, for example, would not be achieved by a tinkering with living standards but would depend on a transformation of the social structure whose constitutive principle is that of inequality. By contrast, the stress on resolution in the social problem film tends to imply the opposite that these problems can indeed be overcome in the absence of wholesale change.

This is, however, a tendency rather than a strictly inevitable consequence of the problem-solving structure of narrative. It is possible, for example, to imagine a narrative in which revolution or radical social change *is* offered as a resolution. What makes this unlikely is not this convention alone but its combination with other characteristics of mainstream narrative cinema. The movement from disequilibrium to a new equilibrium is not, of course, random but patterned in terms of a chain of events which is not simply linear but also causal. One thing does not just happen after another but is *caused* or made to happen. For mainstream narrative cinema, it is typically individual characters who function as the agents of this casuality. As Bordwell and Thompson suggest, 'natural causes (floods, earthquakes) or societal causes (institutions, wars, economic depression) may serve as catalysts or preconditions for the action, but the narrative invariably centres on personal, psychological causes: decisions, choices, and traits of character'.[5]

Thus, in the case of the British films under discussion, it is conventionally the actions or ambitions of an individual which precipitate the plot; the counter-actions of other individuals which provide the 'corrective action' and, thus, the establishment of a new equilibrium. Two main consequences stem from this stress on the individual as agent of causality. One, the 'making of things happen' is seen to derive from the aims and actions of individuals rather than social groups or collectives (or if the group does undertake an action it is usually under the wing of a clearly distinguished individual leader). Second, the origins and explanation of actions and events are seen to result primarily from the features of individual psychology rather than more general social, economic and political relations. It is for this reason that Russell Campbell complains that the social consciousness film concentrates on 'private, personal dramas' at the expense of 'political and social dimensions'.[6] Once again, this is not simply fortuitous, for individualisation, a stress on 'private, personal dramas', is already implicit in the conventions of mainstream narrative.

It is also this stress on the individual which helps confirm the ideology of containment characteristic of the narrative drive towards resolution. For the social problem film does not really deal with social problems in their social aspects at all (i.e. as problems of the social structure) so much as problems of the individual (i.e. his or her personal qualities or attributes). Thus, the responsibility for juvenile delinquency, for example, is attributed to the individual inadequacies of the delinquent (cf. *The Blue Lamp, Violent Playground*) rather than to the inadequacies of the social system itself. The social problem is a problem *for* society, rather than *of* it. And, obviously, if the causes of problems are located in the individual, then, *prima facie*, there is no necessity for a reconstruction of the social order. As a result, the endings characteristic of the social problem film tend to oscillate between one or other of two types, stressing, alternatively, the re-establishment of social order or the achievement of social integration. The latter is generally preferred by the more liberal, social-democratic form of problem film-making, emphasising a capacity for social absorption; the former is more hard-hat and conservative, underscoring the demand for punishment and discipline. Both successfully fulfil the requirement for a narrative resolution; but in neither is the social system itself put into question.

A similar set of issues are raised by the films of the 'new wave'. For despite their determination to represent the working class there is a sense in which the individualising conventions of classic narrativity render this problematic. Class is presented as primarily an individual, rather than collective, experience, a moral, rather than socially and economically structured, condition. As with the social problem film, the stress is on the inter-personal drama rather than the play of social and political forces. Inevitably, this has consequences for the types of resolution the films are then able to offer. Implicit in the structure of the narrative, its movement from one equilibrium to another, its relations of cause and effect, is a requirement for change. But, in so far as the narrative is based upon individual agency, it is characteristic that the endings of such films should rely on individual, rather than social and political, change. As a result, the resolutions characteristic of the working-class films tend to conform to one or other of two main types: the central character either 'opts out' of society or else adapts and adjusts to its demands. Alternative solutions, collective struggle or social upheaval are, in effect, excluded by the conventions upon which the films rely.

Realism

The stress on resolution and the role of the individual does not derive from the conventions of classic narrativity alone, however, but also from those conventions which are characteristic of the fictional film's particular brand of realism. A note of caution is appropriate here. There is probably no critical term with a more unruly and confusing lineage than that of realism. Such has been the diversity of art-works to which it has been applied, or for which it has been claimed, that its continuing use-value as either a descriptive or explanatory concept would often seem to be in question. Amidst this plurality of uses, one consistent implication does appear to survive: that the distinctive characteristic of realism resides in the ambition to, in some way or other, approximate reality, to show 'things as they really are'.[7] While this may be in agreement with a commonsense understanding of the term, it does not, in itself, resolve the critical difficulties. Part of the problem here derives from the very definition of reality itself. As Terry Lovell indicates, one of the main reasons for the diversity in application of the term has been the variation in accounts of the 'real' upon which they have been predicated.[8] What has counted as a valid or satisfactory approximation to reality has depended on the epistemology of the real which has been assumed in the first place.[9] The other part of the difficulty which then arises is that, even with agreement upon what constitutes reality, the sense in which an art-work may be said to approximate reality, or reveal things as they are, still remains problematic. No work can ever simply reveal reality. Realism, no less than any other type of art, depends on conventions, conventions which, in this case, have successfully achieved the status of being accepted as 'realistic'. It is this 'conventionality' of realism which also makes its usage so vulnerable to change. For as the conventions change (either in reaction to previously established conventions or in accordance with new perceptions of what constitutes reality) so too does our sense of what then constitutes realism.

This is quite clearly so of the cinema. Films which were accepted as 'realistic' by one generation often appear 'false' or 'dated' to the next. Thus, the working-class films of the British 'new wave', which initially appeared so striking in their 'realism', now appear 'melodramatic' and 'even hysterical' to at least one modern critic.[10] Indeed, even before the cycle of 'new wave' films came to an end, contemporary reviewers were already claiming that its 'realism' had become 'exhausted'.[11] As Thomas Elsaesser suggests, these films quite rapidly demonstrated a 'fundamental point' about 'realism': 'that it is purely conventional and therefore infinitely "corruptible" through repetition'.[12] If the British social problem and 'new wave' films are still to be regarded as 'realistic', then, it is clearly not in any absolute sense but only on the basis of the specific conventions which they employed and the relationship of these to those other conventions which the films saw themselves as superseding. As Raymond Williams suggests, it is usually a 'revolt' against previous conventions which characterises a 'break towards realism' in the arts.[13] He also distinguishes two types of 'revolt': on the one hand, an 'injection of new content' (new people, new problems, new ideas) but within a basically 'orthodox form'; on the other, an 'invention of new forms' which undermine 'habitual' versions of 'dramatic reality' and thus communicate new, and more fundamental, 'underlying realities'.[14] This is a distinction of relevance to an understanding of the British films. For, primarily, their 'break towards realism' was characterised by an 'injection of new content': new characters (the working-class, juvenile delinquents), new settings (the factory, the housing estate) and new problems (race, homosexuality). Although this was accompanied by a certain degree of stylistic novelty (location shooting, for example), it did not, in any major sense, entail the 'invention of new dramatic forms'. Both groups of film continued to depend on the conventions of narrative (albeit in slightly modified forms) and, indeed, the 'version of dramatic reality' made 'habitual' by the fiction film. The quarrel with earlier films was not so much with *how* they 'revealed reality' as with *what* they 'revealed'. To this extent, what both the new and the old films shared was a common epistemology: that it is basically through observation that the world is to be 'revealed' and understood (rather than, say, through a penetration of these appearances to the 'underlying realities' below).

It is for this reason that Colin MacCabe argues that, for all its local variations, the form of 'classic realism' remains substantially the same for not only the nineteenth-century novel but also the standard fictional output of film and television.[15] What he suggests remains a constant in all of these is not their 'content', but their formal organisation, their hierarchy of discourses, which is itself 'defined in terms of an empirical notion of truth'. This, he suggests, is to be understood in terms of the characteristic form of narration of the 'classic realist' text. MacCabe notes, for example, how the shift from first person narration to a form of impersonal narration in the nineteenth century novel results in a form of apparently anonymous enunciation whereby the 'truth' of what we read is guaranteed by the narrative itself rather than the voice of the author. [...]

What is specific to the 'classic realist' film, rather than the novel, is this articulation of narrative and vision. Like the novel, the 'classic realist' film is apparently 'author less': the events of the narrative do not appear to proceed from anywhere in particular but simply unfold. But, unlike the novel, it is on the basis of what we see, what the camera shows, that the 'truth' of events is 'revealed'. It is in this sense that MacCabe identified the epistemology underlying 'classic realism' as 'empirical': for the knowledge which the 'classic realist' film delivers is founded, fundamentally, on sight: 'the unquestioned nature of the narrative discourse entails that the only problem that reality poses is to go and look and see what Things there are'.[16] His definition of 'realism', in this respect, does not depend on the 'mimetic accuracy', or, more properly, the 'diegetic plausibility', of what is shown, only on this dependency on the visible.[17] *The Sound of Music* (to take one of MacCabe's examples) is by this token as much an example of 'classic realism' as *Saturday Night and Sunday Morning*. It is also in this sense that it may be argued that, for all their novelty (particularly of subject-matter), the social problem film and those of the 'new wave' still remained attached to the basic conventions of 'realism', the 'habitual' versions of 'dramatic reality', made familiar by the mainstream fiction film.

The effect of this basic continuity in form, however, was a restriction on the type of knowledge of social 'realities' which these films could then provide. Knowledge of social and political relations, for example, does not derive from any simple observation of what is visible but also from an understanding of what is, in effect, invisible. It is partly for this reason that MacCabe complains that 'classic realism' is 'fundamentally inimical to the production of political knowledge'.[18] Christine Gledhill sums up the argument: cinematic 'realism' is dependent upon an 'ideological' proposition that 'reality equals what we can see, that perception equals cognition'. As a result, 'those material socio-economic forces which, though not immediately perceptible in phenomenal appearances, are responsible for their production' are, in effect, denied.[19] To take an example, it is possible to show how the poor live on the screen. It is rather more difficult, if not impossible, while remaining within the conventions of 'realism' to demonstrate how such poverty is the effect of a particular economic system or socially structured pattern of inequality. The mechanics of capitalism or distribution of wealth are not 'Things' which can be seen, except in their effects (e.g. disparate life-styles). As a result, the characteristic understanding of events provided by 'realism' will, of necessity, tend towards the personal, rather than the socio-political. In the case of *Days of Hope*, for example, it was an adoption of the form of realism which effectively militated against an explication of the social and economic forces leading to the collapse of the General Strike. The film's formal logic (with its dependency on the visible and hence the inter-personal) inevitably led towards conspiracy theory, the attribution of the strike's failure to the betrayal of trade union leaders. [...] It is also in this sense that the suppression of 'social and political dimensions' and corresponding concentration on 'private, personal dramas', already indicated as a characteristic of the social problem film and the working-class 'realism' of the 'new wave', does not derive from the individualising conventions of narrative alone but also from this emphasis on sight and dependency upon an epistemology of the visible.

MacCabe's observations do not apply solely to the kind of knowledge which 'classic realism' can deliver, however, but also to its form. The 'truth' provided by the narrative discourse, he argues, also guarantees a position to the spectator from which 'the material is dominated' and 'everything becomes obvious'.[20] It is in this sense, he goes on to argue, 'the classic realist text cannot deal with the real as contradictory'. It may expose contradictions but these are nonetheless contradictions which have already been resolved. What 'classic realism' cannot do is produce 'a contradiction which remains unresolved and is thus left for the reader (i.e. spectator) to resolve and act out'.[21] It is for this reason that the attitude of the social problem film so often appears to be comforting rather than disturbing. It exposes a social problem but only in a way in which it has been 'resolved' and the spectator is assured of his/her 'mastery' of it. The problem does not remain problematic and therefore up to the spectator to 'resolve and act out'. Inevitably, this has the effect of bolstering the films' tendencies towards socially conservative 'solutions'. It is not just the 'content' of the film which reassures an audience that the problem is 'under control' but also the way in which it is presented whereby the problem is now, in effect, put 'under the control' of the spectator.

There are, of course, problem films which adopt more liberal or reformist 'solutions' but even here the capacity to initiate social change, of the kind they would like, remains limited. *Victim*, for example, reveals the injustice of the law against homosexuals. But while the spectator is confirmed in a position from which he/she knows the law to be wrong they are, at the same time, denied any perspective for change. The film remains allied (in MacCabe's terms) to a social-democratic notion of progress: that the production of knowledge of injustices is sufficient in itself for wrongs to be somehow righted.[22]

Tensions in the text

The discussion so far has depended upon a relative degree of abstraction. It has avoided dwelling on the detail of individual films in favour of a consideration of more general, or ideal-typical, tendencies. In practice, the workings of individual films are more complex. Individual narratives, for example, are usually less neat and tidy than the general model suggests. The movement from one equilibrium to another, in this respect, is never simply achieved but has to be worked through and worked for. In the process, there is always the possibility that the problem, force or threat which has set the plot in motion may defy or outrun the movement towards a resolution. As Stephen Neale suggests, 'a definitive equilibrium, a condition of total plenitude, is always an impossibility'.[23] This is often taken to be the case in 'film noir', for example. As Sylvia Harvey argues, the 'acts of transgression' (the causes of disequilibrium) committed by the film's female characters, and the vitality with which they are endowed, often produce 'an excess of meaning which cannot finally be contained ... narrative resolutions cannot recuperate their subversive significance'.[24] Or, as Annette Kuhn puts it, there is 'an excess of narrative disruption over resolution'.[25] In the same way, the 'acts of transgression' characteristic of the social problem film and those of the 'new wave' may also prove too 'excessive' to be contained by the logic of repression implicit in the film's resolutions. The exhibition of active female sexuality in films like *I Believe in You, Cage of Gold* and *That Kind of Girl*, and of active male sexuality in a film like *Saturday Night and Sunday Morning*, to some extent remains defiant of the 'solutions' which the films are attempting to impose.

A sign of this 'stress' can often be detected in the endings themselves. The ending may itself appear 'excessive' or 'overloaded', as if in indication of the difficulty it is having in tying up all the narrative elements (e.g. *The Gentle Gunman, Spare the Rod*), or it may be inadequately integrated into the film's chain of causality, so that it appears either 'imposed' or peremptory (e.g. *Flame in the Streets, Beat Girl*). [...]

Notes

1 Tzvetan Todorov, *The Poetics of Prose*, Oxford, Basil Blackwell, 1977, p.111.
2 Seymour Chatman, *Story and Discourse: Narrative Structure in Fiction and Film*, Cornell, Cornell University Press, 1980, p.48.
3 Thomas Elsaesser, 'The Pathos of Failure: American Films in the 70s' in *Monogram*, October 1975, p.14.
4 Russell Campbell, 'The Ideology of the Social Consciousness Movie: Three Films by Darryl F. Zanuck', in *Quarterly Review of Film Studies*, vol. 3, no. 1, Winter 1978, p.60.
5 David Bordwell and Kristin Thompson, *Film Art*, London, Addison-Wesley, 1980, p.58.
6 Campbell, 'The Ideology of the Social Consciousness Movie', p.57.
7 Raymond Williams, quoted in Terry Lovell, *Pictures of Reality: Aesthetics, Politics and Pleasure*, London, British Film Institute, 1980, p.65.
8 Lovell, *Pictures of Reality*, p.65.
9 It is for this reason that even modernists such as Brecht and Joyce have been conceived of as realists. See, for example, Dannan Grant, *Realism*, London, Methuen, 1970, Chapter 1.
10 Robert Phillip Kolker, *The Altering Eye*, New York, Oxford University Press, 1983, p.90.
11 See review by Patrick Gibbs in *Daily Telegraph*, 9 February 1963.
12 Thomas Elsaesser, 'Between Style and Ideology' in *Monogram*, no.3, 1972, p.5.
13 'Recent English Drama' in Boris Ford (ed.), *The Pelican Guide to English Literature 7: The Modern Age*, Harmondsworth, Penguin, 1970.
14 Ibid, p.497–9.
15 Colin MacCabe, 'Realism and the Cinema: Notes on some Brechtian Theses' in *Screen*, vol. 15, no.2, Summer 1974.
16 Ibid, p.12.

17 As Maltby suggests, the primary aesthetic end of mainstream narrative cinema is 'that of convincing the audience that the story being told is a plausible fiction (and) is, in that sense, real'. See Maltby, *Harmless Entertainment*, p.205.

18 Colin MacCabe, 'Days of Hope and the Politics of the past' in Claire Johnston (ed.), *History Production Memory*, Edinburgh '77 Magazine, no.2, Edinburgh Festival 1977, p.17.

19 Christine Gledhill, 'Recent Developments in Feminist Criticism' in *Quarterly Review* of *Film Studies*, vol.3, no.4, 1978, p.464.

20 MacCabe, 'Days of Hope A Response to Colin McArthur' in *Screen*, vol.17, no.1, Spring 1976, p.100. See also MacCabe, 'Realism and the Cinema', p.16.

21 MacCabe, 'A Response to Colin McArthur', p.100.

22 MacCabe, 'Realism and the Cinema', p.16.

23 Stephen Neale, *Genre*, London, British Film Institute, 1980, p.20.

24 'Woman's Place: The Absent Family of Film Noir' in E. Ann Kaplan (ed.), *Women in Film Noir*, London, British Film Institute, 1978, p.33.

25 Annette Kuhn, *Women's Pictures*, London, Routledge & Kegan Paul, 1982, p.35.

31 The imaginary signifier

Christian Metz

[...] Let me insist once again, the cinematic institution is not just the cinema industry (which works to fill cinemas, not to empty them), it is also the mental machinery – another industry – which spectators 'accustomed to the cinema' have internalised historically and which has adapted them to the consumption of films. [...] The second machine, i.e. the social regulation of the spectator's metapsychology, like the first, has as its function to set up good object relations with films if at all possible; here too the 'bad film' is a failure of the institution: the cinema is attended out of desire, not reluctance, in the hope that the film will please, not that it will displease. [...]

In a social system in which the spectator is not forced physically to go to the cinema but in which it is still important that he should go so that the money he pays for his admission makes it possible to shoot other films and thus ensures the auto-reproduction of the institution – and it is the specific characteristic of every true institution that it takes charge of the mechanisms of its own perpetuation – there is no other solution than to set up arrangements whose aim and effect is to give the spectator the 'spontaneous' desire to visit the cinema and pay for his ticket. The outer machine (the cinema as industry) and the inner machine (the spectator's psychology) are not just metaphorically related, the latter a facsimile of the former, 'internalising' it as a reversed mould, a receptive hollow of identical form, but also metonymically related as complementary segments: the 'desire to go to the cinema' is a kind of reflection shaped by the film industry, but it is also a real link in the chain of the overall mechanism of that industry. [...]

Perception, imaginary

The cinema's signifier is *perceptual* (visual and auditory). So is that of literature, since the written chain has to be *read*, but it involves a more restricted perceptual register: only graphemes, writing. So too are those of painting, sculpture, architecture, photography, but still within limits, and different ones; absence of auditory perception, absence in the visual itself of certain important dimensions such as time and movement [...] Music's signifier is perceptual as well, but, like the others, less 'extensive' than that of the cinema: here it is vision which is absent, and even in the auditory, extended speech (except in song). What first strikes one then is that the cinema is *more perceptual*, if the phrase is allowable, than many other means of expression; it mobilises a larger number of the axes of perception. [...]

Nevertheless, this as it were numerical 'superiority' disappears if the cinema is compared with the theatre, the opera and other spectacles of the same type. The latter too involve sight and hearing simultaneously, linguistic audition and non-linguistic audition, movement, real temporal progression. Their difference from the cinema lies elsewhere: they do not consist of *images*, the perceptions they offer to the eye and the ear are inscribed in a true space (not a photographed one), the same one as that occupied by the public during the performance; everything the audience hear and see is actively produced in their presence, by human beings or props which are themselves present. This is not the problem of fiction but that of the definitional characteristics of the signifier: whether or no the theatrical play mimes a fable, its *action*, if need be mimetic, is still managed by real persons evolving in real time and space, *on the same stage or 'scene' as the public*. The 'other scene', which is precisely not so called, is the cinematic screen (closer to fantasy from the outset): what unfolds there may, as before, be more or less fictional, but the unfolding itself is fictive: the actor, the 'décor', the words one hears are all absent, everything is *recorded* (as a memory trace which is immediately so, without having been something else before), and this is still true if what is recorded is not a 'story' and does not aim for the fictional illusion proper. For it is the signifier itself, and as a whole, that is recorded, that is absence: a little rolled up perforated strip which 'contains' vast landscapes, fixed battles, the melting of the ice on the River Neva, and whole life-times, and yet can be enclosed in the familiar round metal tin, of modest dimensions, clear proof that it does not 'really' contain all that. [...]

Thus the cinema, 'more perceptual' than certain arts according to the list of its sensory registers, is also 'less perceptual' than others once the status of these perceptions is envisaged rather than their number or diversity: for its perceptions are all in a sense 'false'. Or rather, the activity of perception in it is real (the cinema is not a fantasy), but the perceived is not really the object, it is its shade, its phantom, its double, its *replica* in a new kind of mirror. – It will be said that literature, after all, is itself only made of replicas (written words, presenting absent objects). But at least it does not present them to us with all the really perceived detail that the screen does (giving more and taking the same, i.e. taking more). – The unique position of the cinema lies in this dual character of its signifier: unaccustomed perceptual wealth, but unusually profoundly stamped with unreality, from its very beginning. More that the other arts, or in a more unique way, the cinema involves us in the imaginary: it drums up all perception, but to switch it immediately over into its own absence, which is nonetheless the only signifier present.

The all-perceiving subject

Thus film is like the mirror. But it differs from the primordial mirror in one essential point: although, as in the latter, everything may come to be projected, there is one thing, and one thing only that is never reflected in it: the spectator's own body. In a certain emplacement, the mirror suddenly becomes clear glass. [...]

Thus, what *makes possible* the spectator's absence from the screen – or rather the intelligible unfolding of the film despite that absence – is the fact that the spectator has already known the experience of the mirror (of the true mirror), and is thus able to constitute a world of objects without having first to recognise himself within it. In this respect, the cinema is already on the side of the symbolic (which is only to be expected): the spectator know that objects exist, that he himself exists as a subject, that he becomes an object for others: he knows himself and he knows his like: it is no longer necessary that this similarity be literally *depicted* for him on the screen, as it was in the mirror of his childhood. Like every other broadly 'secondary' activity, the practice of the cinema presupposes that the primitive undifferentiation of the ego and the non-ego has been overcome.

But *with what*, then, does the spectator identify during the projection of the film? For he certainly has to identify: identification in its primal form has ceased to be a current necessity for him, but – on pain of the film becoming incomprehensible, considerably more incomprehensible than the most incomprehensible films – he continues to depend in the cinema on that permanent play of identification without which there would be no social life (thus, the simplest conversation presupposes the alternation of the *I* and the *you*, hence the aptitude of the two interlocutors for a mutual and reversible identification). [...]

Obviously the spectator has the opportunity to identify with the *character* of the fiction. But there still has to be one. This is thus only valid for the narrative-representational film, and not for the psychoanalytic constitution of the signifier of the cinema as such. The spectator can also identify with the *actor*, in more or less 'afictional' films in which the latter is represented as an actor, not a character, but is still offered thereby as a human being (as a perceived human being) and thus allows identification. However this factor (even added to the previous one and thus covering a very large number of films) cannot suffice. It only designates secondary identification in certain of its forms (secondary in the cinematic process itself, since in any other sense all identification except that of the mirror can be regarded as secondary). [...]

The spectator is absent from the screen: contrary to the child in the mirror, he cannot identify with himself as an object, but only with some objects which are there without him. In this sense the screen is not a mirror. This time the perceived is entirely on the side of the object, and there is no longer any equivalent of the own image, of that unique mix of perceived and subject (of other and I) which was precisely the figure necessary to disengage the one from the other. At the cinema, it is always the other who is on the screen; as for me, I am there to look at him. I take no part in the perceived, on the contrary, I am *all-perceiving*. All-perceiving as one says all-powerful (this is the famous gift of 'ubiquity' the film makes its spectator); all-perceiving, too, because I am entirely on the side of the perceiving instance: absent from the screen, but certainly present in the auditorium, a great eye and ear without which the perceived would have no one to perceive it, the *constitutive* instance, in other words, of the cinema signifier (it is I who make the film). [...]

In the cinema the *subject's knowledge* takes a very precise form without which no film would be possible. This knowledge is dual (but unique). I know I am perceiving something imaginary (and that is why its absurdities, even if they are extreme, do not seriously disturb me), and I know that it is I who am perceiving it. This second knowledge divides in turn: I know that I am really perceiving, that my sense organs are physically affected, that I am not fantasising, that the fourth wall of the auditorium (the screen) is really different from the other three, that there is a projector facing it (and thus it is not I who am projecting, or at least not all alone) – and I also know that it is I who am perceiving all this, that this perceived-imaginary material is deposited in me as if on a second screen, that it is in me that it forms up into an organised sequence, that therefore I am myself the place where this really perceived imaginary accedes to the symbolic by its inauguration as the signifier of a certain type of institutionalised social activity called the 'cinema'.

In other words, the spectator *identifies with himself*, with himself as a pure act of perception (as wakefulness, alertness): as condition of possibility of the perceived and hence as a kind of transcendental subject, anterior to every *there is*. [...]

The passion for perceiving

Cinema practice is only possible through the perceptual passions: the desire to see (= scopic drive, scopophilia, voyeurism), acting alone in the art of the silent film, the desire to hear which has been added to it in the sound cinema [...]

What defines the specifically cinematic *scopic regime* is not so much the distance kept, the 'keeping' itself (first figure of the lack, common to all voyeurism), as the absence of the object seen. Here the cinema is profoundly different from the theatre as also from more intimate voyeuristic activities with a specifically erotic aim [...] In the theatre, as in domestic voyeurism, the passive actor (the one seen), simply because he is bodily present, because he does not go away, is presumed to consent, to cooperate deliberately. It may be that he really does, as exhibitionists in the clinical sense do, or as, in a sublimated fashion, does that oft noted triumphant exhibitionism characteristic of theatrical acting, counterposed even by Bazin to cinematic representation. [...]

In the theatre, actors and spectators are present at the same time and in the same location, hence present one to another, as the two protagonists of an authentic perverse couple. But in the cinema, the actor was present when the spectator was not (= shooting), and the spectator is present when the actor is no longer (= projection): a failure to meet of the voyeur and the exhibitionist whose approaches no longer coincide (they have 'missed' one another). The cinema's voyeurism must (of necessity) do without any very clear mark of consent on the part of the object. [...]

Thus deprived of rehabilitatory agreement, of a real or supposed consensus with the other (which was also the Other, for it had the status of a sanction on the plane of the symbolic), cinematic voyeurism, *unauthorised* scopophilia, is from the outset more strongly established than that of the theatre in direct line from the primal scene. Certain precise features of the institution contribute to this affinity: the obscurity surrounding the onlooker, the aperture of the screen with its inevitable keyhole effect. But the affinity is more profound. It lies first in the spectator's solitude in the cinema: those attending a cinematic projection do not, as in the theatre, constitute a true 'audience', a temporary collectivity; they are an accumulation of individuals who, despite appearances, more closely resemble the fragmented group of readers of a novel. It lies on the other hand in the fact that the filmic spectacle, the object seen, is more radically ignorant of its spectator, since he is not there, than the theatrical spectacle can ever be. A third factor, closely linked to the other two, also plays a part: the *segregation of spaces* that characterises a cinema performance and not a theatrical one. The 'stage' and the auditorium are no longer two polar selections made in a single space; the space of the film, represented by the screen, is utterly heterogeneous, it no longer communicates with that of the auditorium: one is real, the other perspective: a stronger break than any line of footlights. For its spectator the film unfolds in that simultaneously quite close and definitively inaccessible 'elsewhere' in which the child *sees* the gambols of the parental couple, who are similarly ignorant of it and leave it alone, a pure onlooker whose participation is inconceivable. [...]

Disavowal, fetishism

As can be seen, the cinema has a number of roots in the unconscious and in the great movements illuminated by psychoanalysis, but they can all be traced back to the specific characteristics of the institutionalised signifier, I have gone a little way in tracing some of these roots, that of mirror identification, that of voyeurism and exhibitionism. There is also a third, that of fetishism. [...]

As for the fetish itself, in its cinematic manifestations, who could fail to see that it consists fundamentally of the equipment of the cinema (= its 'technique'), or of the cinema as a whole as equipment and as technique, for fiction films and others? It is no accident that in the cinema some cameramen, some directors, some critics, some spectators demonstrate a real 'fetishism of technique', often noted or denounced as such ('fetishism' is taken here in its ordinary sense, which is rather loose but does contain within it the analytical sense that I shall attempt to disengage). The fetish proper, like the apparatus of the cinema, is a *prop*, the prop that disavows a lack and in doing so affirms it without wishing to. A prop, too, which is as it were *deposited* on the body of the object; a prop, which is the penis, since it negates its absence, and hence a partial object that makes the whole object loveable and desirable. The fetish is also the point of departure for specialised practices, and as is well known, desire in its modalities is the more 'technical' the more it is perverse.

Thus with respect to the desired body – to the body of desire rather – the fetish is in the same position as the technical equipment of the cinema with respect to the cinema as a whole. A fetish, the cinema as a technical performance, as prowess, as an *exploit*, an exploit that underlines and denounces the lack on which the whole arrangement is based (the absence of the object, replaced by its reflection), an exploit which consists at the same time of making this absence forgotten. The cinema fetishist is the person who is enchanted at what the machine is capable of, at the *theatre of shadows* as such. For the establishment of his full potency for cinematic enjoyment (*jouissance*) he must think at every moment (and above all *simultaneously*) of the force of presence the film has and of the absence on which this force is constructed.[1] He must constantly compare the result with the means set to work (and hence pay attention to the technique), for his pleasure lodges in the gap between the two. Of course, this attitude appears most clearly in the 'connoisseur', the cinephile, but it also occurs, as a partial component of cinematic pleasure, in those who just go to the cinema: if they do go it is partly in order to be carried away by the film (or the fiction, if there is one), but also in order to *appreciate* as such the machinery that is carrying them away: they will say, precisely when they have been carried away, that the film was a 'good' one, that it was 'well made' (the same thing is said of a harmonious body).

It is clear that fetishism, in the cinema as elsewhere, is closely linked to the good object. The function of the fetish is to restore the latter, threatened in its 'goodness' (in Melanie Klein's sense) by the terrifying discovery of the lack. Thanks to the fetish, which covers the wound and itself becomes erotogenic, the object as a whole can become desirable again without excessive fear. In a similar way, the whole cinematic institution is as it were *recovered* by a thin and omni-present garment, a stimulating prop through which it is consumed: the ensemble of its equipment and its tricks – and not just the celluloid strip, the 'pellicule' or 'little skin' which has been rightly mentioned in this connection (Roger Dadoun: ' "King Kong": du monstre comme dé-monstration,' *Littérature* n 8, December 1972, p 109; Octave Mannoni: *Clefs pour l'imaginaire*, op cit, p 180) – of the equipment which *needs* the lack in order to stand out in it by contrast, but which only affirms it insofar as it ensures that it is forgotten, and which lastly (its third twist) needs it not to be forgotten nonetheless, for fear that at the same stroke the fact that it caused it to be forgotten will itself be forgotten. [...]

Note

1   I have studied this phenomenon at slightly greater length in 'Trucage et cinéma' in *Essais sur la signification au cinéma*, tome II, Klincksieck, Paris 1972, pp 173–92.

32 The tutor-code of classical cinema

Daniel Dayan

Semiology deals with film in two ways. On the one hand it studies the level of fiction, that is, the organization of film content. On the other hand, it studies the problem of 'film language', the level of enunciation. Structuralist critics such as Barthes and the *Cahiers du Cinéma* of '*Young Mr. Lincoln*' have shown that the level of fiction is organized into a language of sorts, a mythical organization through which ideology is produced and expressed. Equally important, however, and far less studied, is filmic enunciation, the system that negotiates the viewer's access to the film – the system that 'speaks' the fiction. This study argues that this level is itself far from ideology-free. It does not merely convey neutrally the ideology of the fictional level. As we will see, it is built so as to mask the ideological origin and nature of cinematographic statements. Fundamentally, the enunciation system analyzed below – the system of the *suture* – functions as a 'tutor-code'. It speaks the codes on which the fiction depends. It is the necessary intermediary between them and us. The system of the suture is to classical cinema what verbal language is to literature. Linguistic studies stop when one reaches the level of the sentence. In the same way, the system analyzed below leads only from the shot to the cinematographic statement. Beyond the statement, the level of enunciation stops. The level of fiction begins. [...]

The role of the imaginary in the utilization of language points to an entire realm of inadequacy, indeed absence, in traditional accounts of language. Saussure merely repressed or avoided the problem of the role of the subject in language utilization. The subject is eliminated from the whole field of Saussurian linguistics. This elimination commands the famous oppositions between code and message, paradigm and syntagm, language system and speech. In each case, Saussure grants linguistic relevance to one of the terms and denies it to the other. (The syntagm term is not eliminated, but is put under the paradigms of syntagms, i.e., syntax). In this way, Saussure distinguishes a deep level of linguistic structures from a superficial one where these structures empirically manifest themselves. The superficial level belongs to the domain of subjectivity, that is, to psychology. 'The language system equals language less speech.' Speech, however, represents the utilization of language. The entity which Saussure defines is language less its utilization. In the converse way, traditional psychology ignores language by defining though as prior to it. Despite this mutual exclusion, however, the world of the subject and the universe of language do meet. The subject speaks, understands what he is told, reads, etc.

To be complete, the structuralist discourse must explain the relationship language/subject. [...] The imaginary is an essential constituent in the functioning of language. What is its role in *other* semiotic systems? Semiotic systems do not follow the same patterns. Each makes a specific use of the imaginary; that is, each confers a distinctive function upon the subject. We move now from the role of the subject in language use to the role of the subject in classical painting and in classical cinema. Here the writings of Jean-Pierre Oudart, Jean-Louis Schefer, and others will serve as a guide in establishing the foundations of our inquiry.[1] [...]

The functioning of semiotic systems such as painting and cinema [...] clearly manifests a direct dependency upon ideology and history. Cinema and painting are historical products of human activity. If their functioning assigns certain roles to the imaginary, one must consider these roles as resulting from choices (conscious or unconscious) and seek to determine the rationale of such choices. Oudart therefore asks a double question: What is the semiological functioning of the classical painting? Why did the classical painters develop it?

Oudart advances the following answers. (1) Classical figurative painting is a discourse. This discourse is produced according to figurative codes. These codes are directly produced by ideology and are therefore subjected to historical transformations. (2) This discourse defines in advance the role of the subject, and therefore pre-determines the reading of the painting. The imaginary (the subject) is used by the painting to mask the presence of the figurative codes. Functioning without being perceived, the codes reinforce the ideology which they embody while the painting produces 'an impression of reality' (*effet-de-réel*). This invisible functioning of the figurative codes can be defined as a 'naturalization': the impression of reality produced testifies that the figurative codes are 'natural' (instead of being ideological products). It imposes as 'truth' the vision of the world entertained by a certain class. (3) This exploitation of the imaginary, this utilization of the subject is made possible by the presence of a system which Oudart calls 'representation'. This system englobes the painting, the subject, and their relationship upon which it exerts a tight control.

Oudart's position here is largely influenced by Schefer's *Scénographie d'un tableau*. For Schefer, the image of an object must be understood to be the pretext that the painter uses to illustrate the system through which he translates ideology into perceptual schemes. The object represented is a 'pretext' for the painting as a 'text' to be produced. The object hides the painting's textuality by preventing the viewer from focusing on it. However, the text of the painting is totally offered to view. It is, as it were, hidden *outside* the object. It is here but we do not see it. We see through it to the imaginary object. Ideology is hidden in our very eyes.

How this codification and its hiding process work Oudart explains by analyzing *Las Meninas* by Velasquez.[2] In this painting, members of the court and the painter himself look out at the spectator. By virtue of a mirror in the back of the room (depicted at the center of the painting), we see what they are looking at: the king and queen, whose portrait Velasquez is painting. Foucault calls this the representation of classical representation, because the spectator – usually invisible – is here inscribed into the painting itself. Thus the painting represents its own functioning, but in a paradoxical, contradictory way. The painter is staring at *us*, the spectators who pass in front of the canvas; but the mirror reflects only one, unchanging thing, the royal couple. Through this contradiction, the system of 'representation' points toward its own functioning. In cinematographic terms, the mirror represents the reverse shot of the painting. In theatrical terms, the painting represents the stage while the mirror represents its audience. Oudart concludes that the text of the painting must not be reduced to its visible part; it does not stop where the canvas stops. The text of the painting is a system which Oudart defines as a 'double-stage'. On one stage, the show is enacted; on the other, the spectator looks at it. In classical representation, the visible is only the first part of a system which always includes an invisible second part (the 'reverse shot'). [...]

Reading the signifiers of the presence of the subject, the spectator occupies this place. His own subjectivity fills the empty spot predefined by the painting. Lacan stresses the unifying function of the imaginary, through which the act of reading is made possible. The representational painting is *already unified*. The painting proposes not only itself, but its own reading. The spectator's imaginary can only coincide with the painting's built-in subjectivity. The receptive freedom of the spectator is reduced to the minimum – he has to accept or reject the painting as a whole. This has important consequences, ideologically speaking.

When I occupy the place of the subject, the codes which led me to occupy this place become invisible to me. The signifiers of the presence of the subject disappear from my consciousness because they are the signifiers of my presence. What I perceive is their signified: myself. If I want to understand the painting and not just be instrumental in it as a catalyst to its ideological operation, I must avoid the empirical relationship it imposes on me. To understand the ideology which the painting conveys, I must avoid providing my own imaginary as a support for that ideology. I must refuse that identification which the painting so imperiously proposes to me.

Oudart stresses that the initial relationship between a subject and any ideological object is set up by ideology as a trap which prevents any real knowledge concerning the object. This trap is built upon the properties of the imaginary and must be deconstructed through a critique of these properties. On this critique depends the possibility of a real knowledge. Oudart's study of classical painting provides the analyst of cinema with two important tools for such a critique: the concept of a double-stage and the concept of the entrapment of the subject.

We note first that the filmic image considered in isolation, the single frame or the perfectly static shot, is (for purposes of our analysis) equivalent to the classical painting. Its codes, even though 'analogic' rather than figurative, are organized by the system of representation: it is an image designed and organized not merely as an object that is seen, but as the glance of a subject. Can there be a cinematography not based upon the system of representation? This is an interesting and important question which cannot be explored here. It would seem that there has not been such a cinematography. Certainly the classical narrative cinema, which is our present concern, is founded upon the representation system. The case for blanket assimilation of cinema to the system of representation is most strongly put by Jean-Louis Baudry, who argues that the perceptual system and ideology of representation are built into the cinematographic apparatus itself.[3] Camera lenses organize their visual field according to the laws of perspective, which thereby operate to render it as the perception of a subject. Baudry traces this system to the sixteenth and seventeenth centuries, during which the lens technology which still governs photography and cinematography was developed.

Of course cinema cannot be reduced to its still frames and the semiotic system of cinema cannot be reduced to the systems of painting or of photography. Indeed, the cinematic succession of images threatens to interrupt or even to expose and to deconstruct the representation system which commands static paintings or photos.

For its succession of shots is, by that very system, a succession of views. The viewer's identification with the subjective function proposed by the painting or photograph is broken again and again during the viewing of a film. Thus cinema regularly and systematically raises the question which is exceptional in painting *(Las Meninas):* 'Who is watching this?' The point of attack of Oudart's analysis is precisely here – what happens to the spectator-image relation by virtue of the shot-changes peculiar to cinema?

The ideological question is hardly less important than the semiological one and, indeed, is indispensable to its solution. From the standpoint of the imaginary and of ideology, the problem is that cinema threatens to expose its own functioning as a semiotic system, as well as that of painting and photography. If cinema consists in a series of shots which have been produced, selected, and ordered in a certain way, then these operations will serve, project, and realize a certain ideological position. The viewer's question, cued by the system of representation itself – 'Who is watching this?' and 'Who is ordering these images?' – tends, however, to expose this ideological operation and its mechanics. Thus the viewer will be aware (1) of the cinematographic system for producing ideology and (2) therefore of specific ideological messages produced by this system. We know that ideology cannot work in this way. It must hide its operations, 'naturalizing' its functioning and its messages in some way. Specifically, the cinematographic system for producing ideology must be hidden and the relation of the filmic message to this system must be hidden. As with classical painting, the code must be hidden by the message. The message must appear to be complete in itself, coherent and readable entirely on its own terms. In order to do this, the filmic message must account *within itself* for those elements of the code which it seeks to hide – changes of shot and, above all, what lies behind these changes, the questions 'Who is viewing this?' and 'Who is ordering these images?' and 'For what purpose are they doing so?' In this way, the viewer's attention will be restricted to the message itself and the codes will not be noticed. That system by which the filmic message provides answers to the viewer's questions – imaginary answers – is the object of Oudart's analysis.

Narrative cinema presents itself as a 'subjective' cinema. Oudart refers here not to avant-garde experiments with subjective cameras, but to the vast majority of fiction films. These films propose images which are subtly designated and intuitively perceived as corresponding to the point of view of one character or another. The point of view varies. There are also moments when the image does not represent anyone's point of view; but in the classical narrative cinema, these are relatively exceptional. Soon enough, the image is reasserted as somebody's point of view. In this cinema, the image is only 'objective' or 'impersonal' during the intervals between its acting as the actors' glances. Structurally, this cinema passes constantly from the personal to the impersonal form. Note, however, that when this cinema adopts the personal form, it does so somewhat obliquely, rather like novelistic descriptions which use 'he' rather than 'I' for descriptions of the central character's experience. According to Oudart, this obliqueness is typical of the narrative cinema: it gives the impression of being subjective while never or almost never being strictly so. When the camera *does* occupy the very place of a protagonist, the normal functioning of the film is impeded. Here Oudart agrees with traditional film grammars. Unlike them, however, Oudart can justify this taboo, by showing that this necessary obliquity of the camera is part of a coherent system. This system is that of the suture. It has the function of transforming a vision or seeing of the film into a reading of it. It introduces the film (irreducible to its frames) into the realm of signification.

Oudart contrasts the seeing and the reading of a film by comparing the experiences associated with each. To *see* the film is *not* to perceive the frame, the camera angle and distance, etc. The space between planes or objects on the screen is perceived as real, hence the viewer may perceive himself (in relation to this space) as fluidity, expansion, elasticity.

When the viewer discovers the frame – the first step in reading the film – the triumph of his former *possession* of the image fades out. The viewer discovers that the camera is hiding things, and therefore distrusts it and the frame itself, which he now understands to be arbitrary. He wonders why the frame is what it is. This radically transforms his mode of participation – the unreal space between characters and/or objects is no longer perceived as pleasurable. It is now the space which separates the camera from the characters. The latter have lost their quality of presence. Space puts them between parentheses so as to assert its own presence. The spectator discovers that his possession of space was only partial, illusory. He feels dispossessed of what he is prevented from seeing. He discovers that he is only authorized to see what happens to be in the axis of the glance of another spectator, who is ghostly or absent. This ghost, who rules over the frame and robs the spectator of his pleasure, Oudart proposes to call 'the absent-one' (*l'absent*).

The description above is not contingent or impressionistic – the experiences outlined are the effects of a system. The system of the absent-one distinguishes cinematography, a system producing meaning, from any impressed strip of film (mere footage). This system depends, like that of classical painting, upon the fundamental opposition between two fields: (1) what I see on the screen, (2) that complementary field which can be defined as the place from which the absent-one is looking. Thus: to any filmic field defined by the camera corresponds *another* field from which an absence emanates.

So far we have remained at the level of the shot. Oudart now considers that common cinematographic utterance which is composed of a shot and a reverse shot. In the first, the missing field imposes itself upon our consciousness under the form of the absent-one who is looking at what we see. In the second shot, the reverse shot of the first, the missing field is abolished by the presence of somebody or something occupying the absent-one's field. The reverse shot represents the fictional owner of the glance corresponding to shot one.

This shot/reverse shot system orders the experience of the viewer in this way. The spectator's pleasure, dependent upon his identification with the visual field, is interrupted when he perceives the frame. From this perception he infers the presence of the absent-one and that other field from which the absent-one is looking. Shot two reveals a character who is presented as the owner of the glance corresponding to shot one. That is, the character in shot two occupies the place of the absent-one corresponding to shot one. This character retrospectively transforms the absence emanating from shot one's other stage into a presence.

What happens in *systemic* terms is this: the absent-one of shot one is an element of the code that is attracted into the message by means of shot two. When shot two replaces shot one, the absent-one is transferred from the level of enunciation to the level of fiction. As a result of this, the code effectively disappears and the ideological effect of the film is thereby secured. The code, which *produces* an imaginary, ideological effect, is hidden by the message. Unable to see the workings of the code, the spectator is at its mercy. His imaginary is sealed into the film; the spectator thus absorbs an ideological effect without being aware of it, as in the very different system of classical painting. [...]

Within this system, the meaning of a shot depends on the next shot. At the level of the signifier, the absent-one continually destroys the balance of a filmic statement by making it the incomplete part of a whole yet to come. On the contrary, at the level of the signified, the effect of the suture system is a retroactive one. The character presented in shot two does not replace the absent-one corresponding to shot two, but the absent-one corresponding to shot one. The suture is always chronologically posterior to the corresponding shot; i.e., when we finally know what the other field was, the filmic field is no longer on the screen. The meaning of a shot is given retrospectively, it does not meet the shot on the screen, but only in the memory of the spectator. [...]

The absent-one is masked, replaced by a character, hence the real origin of the image – the conditions of its production represented by the absent-one – is replaced with a false origin and this false origin is situated inside the fiction. The cinematographic level fools the spectator by connecting him to the fictional level rather than to the filmic level.

But the difference between the two origins of the image is not only that one (filmic) is true and the other (fictional) false. The true origin represents the cause of the image. The false origin suppresses that cause and does not offer anything in exchange. The character whose glance takes possession of the image did not produce it. He is only somebody who sees, a spectator. The image therefore exists independently. It has no cause. It is.

In other terms, it is its own cause. By means of the suture, the film-discourse presents itself as a product without a producer, a discourse without an origin. It speaks. Who speaks? Things speak for themselves and of course, they tell the truth. Classical cinema establishes itself as the ventriloquist of ideology.

Notes

1 See Jean-Louis Schefer, *Scènographie d'un tableau* (Paris: Seuil, 1969); and articles by Jean-Pierre Oudart, 'La Suture, I and II,' *Cahiers du Cinéma*, Nos. 211 and 212 (April and May, 1969), 'Travail, Lecture, Jouissance,' *Cahiers du Cinéma*, No. 222 (with S. Daney – July 1970), 'Un discours en defaut,' *Cahiers du Cinéma*, No. 232 (Oct. 1971).
2 Oudart borrows here from ch. 1 of Michel Foucault's *The Order of Things* (London: Tavistock, 1970).
3 Jean-Louis Baudry, 'Ideological Effects of the Basic Cinematographic Apparatus', *Cinéthique* **7–8**.

SECTION SEVEN

SCREEN THEORY II: PSYCHOANALYSIS, FEMINISM AND FILM

The use of psychoanalytical concepts by feminist film critics and theorists has proved to be one of the more productive interventions into film studies in recent years. From the 1970s onwards, feminist psychoanalytical work has generated complex responses to and readings of both commercial and avant-garde cinemas, with particular emphasis on the function of the gaze and the role of the female spectator. Some of this work – notably Laura Mulvey's 'Visual Pleasure and Narrative Cinema' – has now acquired a canonical status in film studies, with the result that the conjunction between feminist film theory and psychoanalysis is often taken for granted. The impression that this particular alliance of ideas and intellectual practices was in some way 'natural' and inevitable is a misleading one, however, and fails to take account of the way in which this development in feminist film theory was both surprising and controversial.

Feminist film theory's turn to psychoanalysis needs to be seen in the context of a more general taking up of psychoanalysis elsewhere in film theory in the 1970s, but it also relates to and is itself an expression of a feminist reinterpretation of psychoanalytical ideas especially evident in British intellectual culture in the 1970s (notable examples of which include Juliet Mitchell's 1974 book *Psychoanalysis and Feminism* and the journal *m/f*). A particular problem that pro-psychoanalysis feminist theorists had to negotiate was that psychoanalysis itself had come to be seen in much feminist work as a patriarchal discourse, a means of monitoring and controlling the activities and identities of women and of 'naturalizing' their oppression in a patriarchal society. A reinterpretation of Freud's ideas involved transforming them from an authoritative normative discourse which forcefully designated gendered identities for women and men to a more open exploration of the processes by which particular identities are achieved, with an accompanying sense of all the difficulties and possibilities for resistance involved in these processes. As far as feminist film theory of the 1970s was concerned, it also involved an engagement with semiotics, the psychoanalytical work of Jacques Lacan and Louis Althusser's work on ideology (see Sections Three, Four and Six). The resulting heady intellectual brew constituted an ambitious attempt to relate the ways in which cinema constructed gendered identity on a psychological level with social and ideological formations of gender. Much of this work was part of a broader intellectual project to link together Freudian and Marxist ideas and thereby produce a historical-materialist theory of human subjectivity, although at the same time feminist psycho-analytical film theory had its own history and its own set of problematics; in particular, it grappled with the application of what often appeared to be male-centred or phallocentric ideas within feminist contexts.

Much of the feminist work on cinema that took place before the turn to psychoanalysis was preoccupied with questions of realism. Feminist critics identified particular stereotypical representations of women in movies and found them more or less adequate (usually less adequate) as expressions of the lived experience of women. (Haskell (1975) and Rosen (1973) are probably the best-known examples of this approach). Pam Cook and Claire Johnston's 1973 piece 'The Place of Women in the Cinema of Raoul Walsh' can be seen, in part at least, as a reaction against this way of thinking about the representation of women. It purposefully takes as its centre a film, *The Revolt of Mamie Stover*, which seems to offer a 'positive' image of a strong, independent woman and then, via a consideration of the way in which this woman is filmed and her role in the narrative, argues that her independence is compromised by its visual phallic qualities and fully contained by the processes of narrative. In other words, Cook and Johnston read the film symptomatically and figuratively rather than liter-ally. In doing this, they deploy some classical Freudian terms – such as fetishism – alongside Lacanian terms such as the Symbolic and the Imaginary, as well as drawing from structural anthropology in their account of the way in which women operate as objects of exchange. To a certain extent, Cook and Johnston's approach, like much psychoanalytical work in this period, can be seen as having elements of bricolage about it in its assemblage of ideas from a range of intellectual sources. Problems sometimes arise from the joining together of concepts not initially meant for the purpose for which they are being used; indeed this problem is endemic in a psychoanalytical approach which by its very nature draws upon discourses which were not necessarily designed with cinema in mind. Cook and Johnston's article is best viewed in this respect as a trying out of ideas in an attempt to find a new way of seeing and thinking about film in a feminist context.

Particularly significant, so far as later work in this area is concerned, is their discussion of the relation of women to notions of lack and castration. Much psychoanalytical theory from Freud onwards has tended to view the woman's difference from the man in terms of lack and castration; i.e. her lacking a penis. The penis itself becomes here, somewhat arbitrarily, a signifier of authority, while the woman is figured as something less than a man, as herself lacking something. Feminist-psychoanalytical work has engaged with and interrogated this very obviously phallocentric model of gendered identity and sexual difference; particular attention has been paid to the ways in which patriarchal institutions and practices seek to identify women in terms of lack and inferiority. Cinema – and especially popular and Hollywood cinema – often features in this work as an institution which promotes and relies upon notions of female lack, both in the way films organize their narratives (which often turn out to be investigations of female difference) and in the ways that women are represented visually. Cook and Johnston's account of *The Revolt of Mamie Stover* (1956) is exemplary in its discussion of how the film's *mise-en-scène* and narrative structure work 'to encase Jane Russell/Mamie within the symbolic order, the Law of the Father'. In retrospect, some of their claims about Mamie seem unduly pessimistic; later feminist accounts of the femme fatale in film noir would be more willing to engage with the ambiguities apparent in another figure of female strength and independence (Kaplan 1978). The equation the article appears to make between the Symbolic Order, in Lacanian terms the realm of subjectivity constituted via the acquisition of language, and patriarchy can also be seen as potentially obscuring a sense of patriarchy in terms of its historical and social specificities.

Some of the issues discussed in Cook and Johnston are recast within a discussion of cinema spectatorship in Laura Mulvey's 'Visual Pleasure and Narrative Cinema'. To say that this 1975 article has been influential on feminist film theory would be something of an understatement. It is hard to think of any other area of film studies where one publication has played such a significant role in defining both the sort of issues that are being addressed and the terms used to discuss these. Seen in this way, Mulvey's article is interesting as much for the work it generates as it is for its own insights into women and film.

Unlike Cook and Johnston, who concentrate on a small group of films, Mulvey identifies mainstream cinema itself as an institution that subordinates and objectifies the female via its coordination of looks: the look of the camera, of the spectator and of characters within films. What Mulvey outlines is an economy of the male gaze, where the male spectator, identifying with the male hero/ego ideal, gains pleasure from an eroticised, objectifying gaze at the woman. But as this woman, the source of this visual pleasure, lacks a penis, the male gaze at the female body also raises the possibility of castration for the male, a threat that – according to Mulvey – mainstream cinema manages and contains either via fetishism (the disavowal of castration through endowing another object or body part with phallic significance – associated by Mulvey with the films of Sternberg) or voyeurism (often involving the sadistic punishment of the female body – associated by Mulvey with the work of Alfred Hitchcock).

For Mulvey, female characters in film only exist in terms of their to-be-looked-at-ness; they are objectified by a male gaze and also represent the threat of castration for the male. (This would even be the case with apparently independent women like Mamie Stover, whose independence is revealed by analysis to be more illusory than real.) As far as female spectators are concerned, the situation seems even more hopeless, for, in Mulvey's model, female spectators are denied the gaze and do not have images of active women with which to identify. The only solution apparently is for women to reject mainstream cinema entirely and turn to avant-garde productions.

This rather stern conclusion, and an accompanying suspicion of pleasure, is only one of the issues to which later theorists (including Mulvey herself) have responded. It is a historical fact that women have formed an important part – in some instances the major part – of the audience for commercial entertainment films. In the light of what Mulvey has to say in 'Visual Pleasure and Narrative Cinema', what is one to make of their spectatorship and the possibilities for female spectatorship generally? And is it always the fate of women to be seen in terms of lack and castration? The self-regulating, self-perpetuating model of the cinematic institution offered by Mulvey, while certainly having a clarity about it, also causes problems inasmuch as it appears incapable of incorporating any sense of historical change or process, or of finding spaces within mainstream narrative cinema for resistance to its operations (hence Mulvey's tactic of refusing this type of cinema entirely).

Mary Ann Doane's 'Film and the Masquerade: Theorizing the Female Spectator' engages with the problematic of female spectatorship as defined by Mulvey. In seeking to find a space for the female film spectator, Doane refers to the possibility – suggested by Mulvey herself in her own commentary on 'Visual Pleasure and Narrative Cinema' – of a transvestite spectatorship where women could temporarily occupy male spectatorial positions (Mulvey 1989). For Doane, however, the idea of the masquerade provides a more interesting way of thinking about female spectatorship. As first formulated by Joan Riviere, the masquerade refers to the performativity of femininity, the way in which a female's flaunting of femininity, producing femininity as an excess, can potentially destabilize patriarchal assumptions about what women 'really' are. In Doane's words, 'Womanliness is a mask which can be worn or removed. The masquerade's resistance to patriarchal positioning would therefore lie in its denial of the production of femininity as closeness, as presence-to-itself, as, precisely, imagistic.' Doane's argument draws upon Mulvey's claim that the voyeurism and fetishism that characterize a male spectatorial position are dependent on a sense of distance from the image. With reference to Freud's 'Some Psychological Consequences of the Anatomical Distinction Between the Sexes', Doane suggests that the female's passage into the realm of knowledge produces a difficulty in establishing the distance from the image necessary to produce a spectatorial position of voyeurism. The role of the masquerade in this respect is that, as Doane puts it, it 'simulates' the distance necessary for a form of female spectatorship to take place.

Doane's work represents an attempt to think feminist psychoanalytical film theory out of a corner, for if one wants to engage with cinema, and especially mainstream cinema, rather than reject it, an account of active female spectatorship is required. Certainly the formulation of the masquerade as a model of spectatorship does valuably open up a theorized space for female agency within the model of gendered spectatorship offered by 'Visual Pleasure and Narrative Cinema'. At the same time, some problems emerge. The extent to which Doane's ideas are meant to relate to actual, historically situated female audiences is not clear. Indeed, a general feature of much psychoanalytical work is its tendency to consider the spectator, female and male, solely in terms of the viewing positions or positions of intelligibility offered by both individual films and cinema itself as an institution. Questions to do with the more localized, socially-specific and heterogeneous responses generated by particular audiences do not seem readily posable within the psychoanalytical method. Another general feature of psychoanalytical work apparent in Doane's argument is the privileging of a male/female binary opposition – expressed via her discussion of 'female' and 'male' spectators – which forecloses on possible considerations of other forms of difference (to do with class, race, nationality and sexual orientation – see Section Nine). Doane is one of a number of feminist critics who have gone on to consider the significance of non-sexual difference in terms both of textual analysis and of spectatorship. The extent to which this new work can be sustained within a psychoanalytical approach remains to be seen.

To a certain extent, Carol Clover's 'Her Body, Himself (from Clover's book *Men, Women and Chainsaws*) is a return to some of the issues addressed in Cook and Johnston's 'The Place of Women in the Films of Raoul Walsh'. Both articles consider the way films represent strong, apparently independent women – Mamie Stover in Cook and Johnston, the slasher film's Final Girl in Clover – and how this independence can ultimately be seen as answering to male desires and anxieties. Where Clover's work is different is in its focus on spectatorship, and male spectatorship in particular. Clover provocatively chooses as her location for images of female strength and resourcefulness the American slasher film, a horror cycle which in the late 1970s and early 1980s was heavily criticized (and protested against) by feminists for its depiction of violence against women. While the trajectory of Clover's analysis returns us to the idea of the masculine 'Final Girl' as a transvestite figure, on the way she has considered more forcefully than Cook and Johnston the possibility of cross-gender identification and a male masochistic relation to events on the screen. She relates this masochism to the male adolescent audience for the slasher (thereby acknowledging differences within masculinity which other psychoanalytical accounts have been reluctant to concede) and also considers horror itself as a 'feminizing' experience so far as its predominantly male audience is concerned. Elsewhere in her book *Men, Women and Chainsaws: Gender in the Modern Horror Film*, Clover argues that it is the fact that horror is a low cultural form that permits it to offer what in effect are deviant or illicit male spectatorial positions; she also suggests that after the slasher cycle some of these practices seep upwards into more mainstream entertainment films.

Clover offers here a more heterogeneous model of cinema spectatorship than that found in previous psychoanalytical accounts. As far as she is concerned, there are different types of film and different types of spectatorship (including different types of male spectatorship), with the development of these part of a broader historical process. One still finds in Clover a version of the male/female binary opposition as well as a fascination with the gaze, but any sense of cinema as an institution that authoritatively identifies men and women in particular ways has receded to the margins of her argument.

In retrospect, it is sometimes easy to underestimate the radical break in feminist film writing represented by the intervention of psychoanalytical thought in the 1970s. What emerges is a systematic consideration of cinema as a particular institution which constructs conditions and positions of spectatorship in ways which reiterate, and arguably reinforce, formations of masculinity and femininity. This way of thinking about film has been extremely influential, especially in its focus on the issue of female spectatorship. In addition, the sophistication apparent in the analysis of particular films, with a concern with the figurative as well as the literal and an awareness of narrative process, has moved feminist analysis decisively beyond the simple consideration of whether a particular image is 'true' or not. However, as a number of feminist critics have pointed out, the relation of this model of cinema to the lived experience of women has sometimes not been clear. At its most crude, the psychoanalytical approach can lead to an ahistorical, essentialist understanding of gender in which 'woman' is by definition relegated to a realm of non-representable Otherness. In its sophisticated outputs – such as those reprinted here – the universalizing, essentialist pull of some Freudian and Lacanian language is still a problem with which critics and theorists have had to struggle. Ultimately, what one finds here is a developing critical sense of both the benefits and the limitations of the psychoanalytical method as it relates to the feminist inquiry into cinema.

References

Clover, C. (1992). *Men, Women and Chainsaws: Gender in the Modern Horror Film*. London: British Film Institute.

Cook, P. and Johnston, C. (1974), 'The Place of Women in the Cinema of Raoul Walsh'. In P. Hardy (ed.), *Raoul Walsh*. Edinburgh: Edinburgh Film Festival, 93–110.

Doane, M. A. (1982). 'Film and the Masquerade: Theorizing the Female Spectator'. *Screen* **23**(3–4): 74–87.

Haskell, M. (1975). *From Reverence to Rape: The Treatment of Women in the Movies*. London: New English Library.

Kaplan, E. A. (ed.) (1978). *Women in Film Noir*. London: British Film Institute.

Mulvey, L. (1975). 'Visual Pleasure and Narrative Cinema'. *Screen* **16**(3): 6–18.

—— (1989). 'Afterthoughts on "Visual Pleasure and Narrative Cinema" Inspired by King Vidor's *Duel in the Sun*'. In *Visual and Other Pleasures*. Basingstoke: Macmillan, 29–38.

Rosen, M. (1973), *Popcorn Venus*. New York: Coward, McCann & Geoghegan.

33 The place of woman in the cinema of Raoul Walsh

Pam Cook and Claire Johnston

[...] Between 1956 and 1957 Raoul Walsh made three films which centre around the social, cultural and sexual definition of women. At first sight, the role of woman within these films appears a 'positive' one; they display a great independence of spirit, and contrast sharply with the apparent 'weakness' of the male protagonists. The first film in this cycle depicts a woman occupying the central function in the narrative; the Jane Russell vehicle, *The Revolt of Mamie Stover*, tells the story of a bar-room hostess's attempts to buck the system and acquire wealth and social status within patriarchy. *The King and Four Queens* made the same year depicts five women who hide out in a burnt-out ghost town to guard hidden gold. *Band of Angels*, made the following year, tells the story of a Southern heiress who suddenly finds herself sold into slavery at the time of the American Civil War. Walsh prefigured the problematic of the independent woman before this period, most notably in a series of films he made in the 1940's, some of which starred the actress Ida Lupino who later became one of the few women filmmakers to work in Hollywood: *They Drive By Night, High Sierra* and *The Man I Love*. However, undoubtedly the most useful films for providing a reference point for this cycle are *Manpower* (1941) and *The Bowery* (1933); in these films, Walsh celebrates the ethic of the all-male group, and outlines the role which women are designated to play within it. Walsh depicts the male hero as being trapped and pinned down by some hidden event in his past. In order to become the Subject of Desire he must test the Law through transgression. To gain self-knowledge and to give meaning to memories of the past, he is impelled towards the primal scene and to the acceptance of a symbolic castration. For the male hero the female protagonist becomes an agent within the text of the film whereby his hidden secret can be brought to light, for it is in woman that his 'lack' is located. She represents at one and the same time the distant memory of maternal plenitude and the fetishized object of his phantasy of castration – a phallic replacement and thus a threat. In *Manpower* Walsh depicts an all-male universe verging on infantilism – the camaraderie of the fire-fighters from the 'Ministry of Power and Light'. Sexual relationships and female sexuality are repressed within the film, and Marlene Dietrich is depicted as only having an existence within the discourse of men: she is 'spoken', she does not speak. As an object of exchange between men, a sign oscillating between the images of prostitutes and mother-figure, she represents the means by which men express their relationships with each other, the means through which they come to understand themselves and each other. *The Bowery* presents a similar all-male society, this time based totally on internal all male rivalry; within this highly ritualised system the women ('the skirts') assume the function of symbols of this rivalry. Whatever the 'positive' attributes assigned to them through characterization, woman as sign remains a function, a token of exchange in this patriarchal order. [...]

In her book *Psychoanalysis and Feminism* Juliet Mitchell, citing Lévi-Strauss, characterises a system where women are objects for exchange as essentially a communications system.

'The act of exchange holds a society together: the rules of kinship (like those of language to which they are near-allied) are the society. Whatever the nature of the society – patriarchal, matrilineal, patrilineal etc. – it is always men who exchange women. Women thus become the equivalent of a sign which is being communicated'.

In Walsh's oeuvre, woman is not only a sign in a system of exchange, but an empty sign: (the major exception in this respect is Mamie Stover who seeks to transform her status as object for exchange precisely by compounding a highly articulated, fetishized image for herself). The male protagonist's castration fears, his search for self-knowledge all converge on woman: it is in her that he is finally faced with the recognition of 'lack'. Woman is therefore the locus of emptiness: she is a sign which is defined negatively: something that is missing which must be located so that the narcissistic aim of the male protagonist can be achieved. The narrative structure of *Band of Angels* is particularly interesting in the light of this model. The first half of the story is concerned with events in Manty/Yvonne de Carlo's life which reduce her from the position of a lady to that of a slave to be auctioned in the slave market. Almost exactly half way through the story – at the 'centre' of the film – Clark Gable appears and takes possession of her: from that moment the unfolding of his 'dark secret' takes precedence. It becomes clear that Manty/Yvonne de Carlo's story was merely a device to bring into play the background (the slave trade, crumbling Southern Capitalism) against which the 'real' drama is to take place. Manty/Yvonne de Carlo is created in Clark Gable's image: half black and half white, she signifies the lost secret which must be found in order to resolve the relationship between Clark Gable and Sidney Poitier – the 'naturalisation' of the slave trade.

One of the most interesting aspects of this *mise-en-scene* of exchange in which woman as sign is located, is the way Walsh relates it directly and explicitly to the circulation of money within the text of the film. Marx states that under Capitalism the exchange value of commodities is their inherent monetary property and that in turn money achieves a social existence quite apart from all commodities and their natural mode of existence. The circulation of money and its abstraction as a sign in a system of exchange serves as a mirror image for woman as sign in a system of exchange. However, in Walsh's universe, women do not have access to the circulation of money: Mamie Stover's attempt to gain access to it takes place at a time of national emergency, the bombing of Pearl Harbor, when all the men are away fighting – it is described as 'theft'. As a system, the circulation of money embodies phallic power and the right of possession; it is a system by which women are controlled. In *Band of Angels* Manty/Yvonne de Carlo is reduced to a chattel and exchanged for money on the slave market; she is exchanged for money because of her father's 'dark secret' and because of his debt. In *The King and Four Queens* the women guard the gold but they cannot gain access to it directly. Its phallic power lies hidden in the grave of a dead husband, surrounded by sterility and devastation. Clark Gable gains access to it by asserting his right of possession by means of tossing a gold coin in the air and shooting a bullet through the middle of it, a trick which the absent males of the family all knew: the mark of the right of possession. The ticket system in *The Revolt of Mamie Stover* takes the analogy between money and women one stage further: men buy tickets at 'The Bungalow' and at the same time they buy an image of woman. It is the symbolic expression of the right men have to control women within their imaginary system. This link between money and phallic power assumes its most striking image in Walsh's oeuvre when Jane Russell/Mamie, having accumulated considerable savings as a bar hostess in Pearl Harbor, declares her love for Richard Egan/Jimmy by asking him if she can place these savings in his safety deposit box at the bank: 'there's nothing closer between friends than money'. Recognising the significance of such a proposition, he refuses.

The Revolt of Mamie Stover is the only one of these films in which the female protagonist represents the central organising principle of the text. As the adventuress *par excellence* she is impelled to test and transgress the Law in the same way that all Walsh's heroes do: she would seem to function at first sight in a similar way to her male counterpart, the adventurer, within the narrative structure. But as the film reveals, her relationship to the Law is radically different. Her drive is not to test and transgress the Law as a means towards understanding a hidden secret within her past, but to transgress the forms of representation governing the classic cinema itself, which imprison her forever within an image. As the credits of the film appear on the screen, Jane Russell looks into the camera with defiance, before turning her back on America and walking off to a new life in Pearl Harbor. This look, itself a transgression of one of the classic rules of cinematography (i.e. 'don't look into the camera'!) serves as a reference point for what is to follow. Asserting herself as the subject rather than the object of desire, this look into the camera represents a reaching out beyond the diegetic space of the film and the myths of representation which entrap her. The central contradiction of her situation is that she can only attempt to assert herself as subject through the exploitation of a fetishized image of woman to be exchanged within the circulation of money; her independence and her desire for social and economic status all hinge on this objectification. The forms of representation generated by the classic cinema – the myths of woman as pin-up, vamp, 'Mississippi Cinderella' – are the only means by which she can achieve the objective of becoming the subject rather than the object of desire. The futility of this enterprise is highlighted at the end of the film when she returns once more to America in a similar sequence of shots; this time she no longer looks towards the camera, but remains trapped within the diegetic space which the film has allotted to her.

The film opens with a long-shot of a neon-lit city at night. Red letters appear on the screen telling us the time and place: SAN FRANCISCO 1941. *The Revolt of Mamie Stover* was made in 1956 – the story is therefore set within the living memory/history of the spectator. This title is the first indication that the film will reactivate the memory of an anxiogenic situation: the traumatic moment of the attack on Pearl Harbor and the entry of the United States into the Second World War. Simultaneously, on the sound band, sleazy night-club music swells up (clip-joints, predatory prostitution, female sexuality exchanged for money at a time when the country, its male population and its financial resources are about to be put at risk). A police car (one of the many representations of the Law in the film), its siren wailing insistently over the music (a further indication of imminent danger), drives fast onto a dock-side where a ship is waiting. As it draws up alongside the ship, a female figure carrying a coat and a small suitcase gets out of the car and appears to turn back to look at the city from which she has obviously been expelled in a hurry. Jane Russell then looks straight into the camera (see above).

Up to this point the text has been multiply coded to signify danger/threat. The threat is closely associated with sexuality – besides the music, the red letters on the screen indicate red for danger and red for sex. Paul Willemen has pointed out that the 'look' in *Pursued* is a threatening object: the *Cahiers de Cinema* analysis of *Young Mr. Lincoln* also delineates Henry Fonda/Lincoln's 'castrating stare' as having the same threatening significance. Besides this threatening 'look,' Jane Russell has other dangerous connotations: qualities of aggression, of preying on the male to attain her own ends. Her 'look' – repeated many times during the film, directed towards men and explicitly described at one point as 'come hither' – doubly marks her as signifier of threat. In the absence of the male, the female might 'take his place': at the moment of Jane Russell's 'look' at the camera, the spectator is directly confronted with the image of that threat. The fact that this image has been expelled from a previous situation is also important: Jane Russell actually represents the repudiated idea: she *is* that idea. Thus the threat is simultaneously recognised and recuperated: the female cannot 'take the place' of the male; she can only be 'in his place' – his mirror-image – the 'you' which is the 'I' in another place.

This moment of dual fascination between the spectator and Jane Russell is broken by the intervention of a third organising principle representing the narrative, as the titles in red letters 'Jane Russell Richard Egan' appear over the female figure. The title has the effect of immediately distancing the spectator: it reminds him of the symbolic role of the narrative by locating Jane Russell as an imaginary figure. In psychoanalytic terms the concept 'imaginary' is more complex than the word would immediately seem to imply. It is a concept central to the Lacanian formulation of the 'mirror stage' in which the 'other' is apprehended as the 'other which is me', i.e. my mirror image. In the imaginary relationship the other is seen in terms of resemblance to oneself. As an imaginary figure in the text of the film Jane Russell's 'masculine' attributes are emphasised: square jaw, broad shoulders, narrow hips, swinging, almost swashbuckling walk – 'phallic' attributes which are echoed and re-echoed in the text; for example, in her aggressive language (she tells a wolf-whistling soldier to 'go mend your rifle, soldier': when Richard Egan/Jimmy fights Michael Pate/Atkins at the Country Club she shouts 'give him one for me, Jimmy'. The girls at 'the Bungalow' hail her as 'Abe Lincoln Stover'). Jane Russell/Mamie is the imaginary *counterpart* of the absent spectator and the absent subject of the text: the mirror-image they have mutually constructed and in whom both images converge and overlap.

Again, borrowing from Lacan, the function of the 'Symbolic' is to intervene in the imaginary situation and to integrate the subject into the Symbolic Order (which is ultimately the Law, the Name of the Father). The narrative of *The Revolt of Mamie Stover* in that it presents a particular model of the world historically, culturally and ideologically overdetermined, could be said to perform a symbolic function for the absent spectator. The anxiety-generating displacement Jane Russell/Mamie appears to threaten the narrative at certain points. For example, after having promised to marry Richard Egan/Jimmy, give up her job at 'The Bungalow' and become 'exclusively his', and having taken his ring in a symbolic exchange which is 'almost like the real thing' and 'makes it legal', Jane Russell/Mamie leaves her man at the army camp and returns to 'The Bungalow' to resign. However, she is persuaded by Agnes Moorhead/Bertha Parchman to continue working there, now that Michael Pate/Atkins has gone (been expelled), for a bigger share of the profits and more power. Richard Egan/Jimmy is absent, so he won't know. His absence is important: it recalls another sequence earlier in the narrative which shows in a quick succession of shots Richard Egan/Jimmy and the army away at war while Jane Russell/Mamie is at the same moment buying up all the available property on the island, becoming 'Sto-Mame Company Incorporated' with Uncle Sam as her biggest tenant. Jane Russell/Mamie makes her biggest strides in the absence of men: she threatens to take over the power of exchange. By promising to marry and give it all up, she is reintegrated into an order where she no longer represents that threat. Richard Egan/Jimmy can be seen as the representative of the absent spectator and absent subject of the discourse in this structure: they are mutual constructors of the text – he is a writer who is constantly trying to write Jane Russell/Mamie's story for her. When Jane Russell/Mamie goes back to work at 'The Bungalow' she in effect negates his image of her in favour of an image which suggests destruction and purging – 'Flaming Mamie' – and becomes again a threatening displacement, reproduced and enlarged 7 foot high. When Richard Egan/Jimmy is confronted with this threatening image at the army camp, when a soldier shows him a photograph of her, a bomb drops and he is wounded. In the face of this renewed threat he returns to 'The Bungalow' and in his final speech to Jane Russell/Mamie repudiates her as his imaginary counterpart; the narcissistic fascination with her is ended; he realises he can no longer control her image.

The symbolic level of the narrative in maintaining its order in the face of a threat is reasserted in the final sequence where the policeman at the dockside re-echoes Richard Egan/Jimmy's words of rejection: 'Nothing's changed, Mamie. You aren't welcome here'. Jane Russell/Mamie replies that she is going home to Leesburg, Mississippi (this is what Richard Egan/Jimmy was always telling her she must do). When the policeman remarks that she does not seem to have done too well, she replies: 'If I told you I had made a fortune and given it all away, would you believe me?' When he says 'No', she replies 'I thought so'. This exchange contains a final assertion that the protagonist cannot write her own story: she is a signifier, an object of exchange in a play of desire between the absent subject and object of the discourse. She remains 'spoken': she does not speak. The final rhetorical question seals her defeat.

On the plane of the image, the symbolic order is maintained by an incessant production within the text, of images for and of Jane Russell/Mamie from which she is unable to escape, and with which she complies though a *mise-en-scene* of exchange. In order to become the subject of desire, she is compelled to be the object of desire, and the images she 'chooses' remain locked within the myths of representation governed by patriarchy. This *mise-en-scene* of exchange is initiated by her expulsion by the police at the dockside – the image of predatory whore is established. This image is elaborated during the next scene when the ship's steward tells Richard Egan/Jimmy about her reputation as sexual predator ('she ain't no lady'). Mamie interrupts the conversation, and realising that Richard Egan/Jimmy as a scriptwriter in Hollywood is interested in her, she suggests he should write and buy her story – the hard-luck story of a 'Mississippi Cinderella'. Growing emotional involvement with him leads her to reject the idea of being 'written' in favour of 'writing' her own story, and to seek out an image more consistent with the wealthy 'hilltop' milieu of which Richard Egan/Jimmy is part, epitomised by Jimmy's girl-friend ('Miss Hilltop'). Jane Russell/Mamie asks Richard Egan/Jimmy to 'dress her up and teach her how to behave'; he refuses. Their relationship from then on is characterised as one of transgression: they 'dance without tickets' at the country club, away from the 'four don'ts' of 'The Bungalow'. For her image as a performer and hostess at 'The Bungalow' Jane Russell/Mamie has dyed her hair red and has assumed the name of 'Flaming Mamie' ('Mamie's not beer or whisky, she's champagne only'). The image of 'Flaming Mamie' is at one and the same time an assertion and a negation of female sexuality; sexually arousing ('fellas who try to resist, should hire a psychiatrist' intones the song) but at the same time the locus of sexual taboo ('Keep the eyes on the hands' she says in another number – they tell the story). It is at 'The Bungalow' that the ticket system formalises this *mise-en-scene* of exchange; men literally buy an image for a predetermined period of time. (It is this concept of exchange of images which Jane Russell/Mamie finally discards when she throws the ticket away as she leaves the boat at the end of the film). Reduced once again to the image of common prostitute when they go dancing at the country club and having decided to stay at 'The Bungalow' in spite of Richard Egan/Jimmy, she finally assumes the iconography of the pin-up, with the 'come hither' look; an image emptied of all personality or individuality; an image based on the effects of pure gesture. This image was prefigured in an extraordinary sequence at the beach when Jane Russell/Mamie jumps up from the sand where she has been sitting with Richard Egan/Jimmy in order to take a swim. As she does so, she turns back to look at him and her image becomes frozen into the vacant grin of a bathing suit advertisement. Talking about money, Jane Russell/Mamie describes herself at one point as a 'have not'; this recurrent imbrication of images, the telling of story within story which the film generates through a *mise-en-scene* of exchange serves to repress the idea of female sexuality and to encase Jane Russell/Mamie within the symbolic order, the Law of the Father. [...]

---

34 Visual pleasure and narrative cinema

Laura Mulvey

I. Introduction

A. *A political use of psychoanalysis*

This paper intends to use psychoanalysis to discover where and how the fascination of film is reinforced by pre-existing patterns of fascination already at work within the individual subject and the social formations that have moulded him. It takes as starting point the way film reflects, reveals and even plays on the straight, socially established interpretation of sexual difference which controls images, erotic ways of looking and spectacle. It is helpful to understand what the cinema has been, how its magic has worked in the past, while attempting a theory and a practice which will challenge this cinema of the past. Psychoanalytic theory is thus appropriated here as a political weapon, demonstrating the way the unconscious of patriarchal society has structured film form.

The paradox of phallocentrism in all its manifestations is that it depends on the image of the castrated woman to give order and meaning to its world. An idea of woman stands as lynch pin to the system: it is her lack that produces the phallus as a symbolic presence, it is her desire to make good the lack that the phallus signifies. Recent writing in *Screen* about psychoanalysis and the cinema has not sufficiently brought out the importance of the representation of the female form in a symbolic order in which, in the last resort, it speaks castration and nothing else. To summarise briefly: the function of woman in forming the patriarchal unconscious is twofold, she first symbolises the castration threat by her real absence of a penis and second thereby raises her child into the symbolic. Once this has been achieved, her meaning in the process is at an end, it does not last into the world of law and language except as a memory, which oscillates between memory of maternal plenitude and memory of lack. Both are posited on nature (or on anatomy in Freud's famous phrase). Woman's desire is subjected to her image as bearer of the bleeding wound, she can exist only in relation to castration and cannot transcend it. She turns her child into the signifier of her own desire to possess a penis (the condition, she imagines, of entry into the symbolic). Either she must gracefully give way to the word, the Name of the Father and the Law, or else struggle to keep her child down with her in the half-light of the imaginary. Woman then stands in patriarchal culture as signifier for the male other, bound by a symbolic order in which man can live out his phantasies and obsessions through linguistic command by imposing them on the silent image of woman still tied to her place as bearer of meaning, not maker of meaning.

There is an obvious interest in this analysis for feminists, a beauty in its exact rendering of the frustration experienced under the phallocentric order. It gets us nearer to the roots of our oppression, it brings an articulation of the problem closer, it faces us with the ultimate challenge: how to fight the unconscious structured like a language (formed critically at the moment of arrival of language) while still caught within the language of the patriarchy. There is no way in which we can produce an alternative out of the blue, but we can begin to make a break by examining patriarchy with the tools it provides, of which psychoanalysis is not the only but an important one. We are still separated by a great gap from important issues for the female unconscious which are scarcely relevant to phallocentric theory: the sexing of the female infant and her relationship to the symbolic, the sexually mature woman as non-mother, maternity outside the signification of the phallus, the vagina. But, at this point, psychoanalytic theory as it now stands can at least advance our understanding of the status quo, of the patriarchal order in which we are caught.

B. Destruction of pleasure as a radical weapon

As an advanced representation system, the cinema poses questions of the ways the unconscious (formed by the dominant order) structures ways of seeing and pleasure in looking. Cinema has changed over the last few decades. It is no longer the monolithic system based on large capital investment exemplified at its best by Hollywood in the 1930's, 1940's and 1950's. Technological advances (16mm, etc.) have changed the economic conditions of cinematic production, which can now be artisanal as well as capitalist. Thus it has been possible for an alternative cinema to develop. However self-conscious and ironic Hollywood managed to be, it always restricted itself to a formal mise-en-scène reflecting the dominant ideological concept of the cinema. The alternative cinema provides a space for a cinema to be born which is radical in both a political and an aesthetic sense and challenges the basic assumptions of the mainstream film. This is not to reject the latter moralistically, but to highlight the ways in which its formal preoccupations reflect the psychical obsessions of the society which produced it, and, further, to stress that the alternative cinema must start specifically by reacting against these obsessions and assumptions. A politically and aesthetically avant-garde cinema is now possible, but it can still only exist as a counterpoint.

The magic of the Hollywood style at its best (and of all the cinema which fell within its sphere of influence) arose, not exclusively, but in one important aspect, from its skilled and satisfying manipulation of visual pleasure. Unchallenged, mainstream film coded the erotic into the language of the dominant patriarchal order. In the highly developed Hollywood cinema it was only through these codes that the alienated subject, torn in his imaginary memory by a sense of loss, by the terror of potential lack in phantasy, came near to finding a glimpse of satisfaction: through its formal beauty and its play on his own formative obsessions. This article will discuss the interweaving of that erotic pleasure in film, its meaning, and in particular the central place of the image of woman. It is said that analysing pleasure, or beauty, destroys it. That is the intention of this article. The satisfaction and reinforcement of the ego that represent the high point of film history hitherto must be attacked. Not in favour of a reconstructed new pleasure, which cannot exist in the abstract, nor of intellectualised unpleasure, but to make way for a total negation of the ease and plenitude of the narrative fiction film. The alternative is the thrill that comes from leaving the past behind without rejecting it, transcending outworn or oppressive forms, or daring to break with normal pleasurable expectations in order to conceive a new language of desire.

II. Pleasure in looking/fascination with the human form

A. The cinema offers a number of possible pleasures. One is scopophilia. There are circumstances in which looking itself is a source of pleasure, just as, in the reverse formation, there is pleasure in being looked at. Originally, in his *Three Essays on Sexuality*, Freud isolated scopophilia as one of the component instincts of sexuality which exist as drives quite independently of the erotogenic zones. At this point he associated scopophilia with taking other people as objects, subjecting them to a controlling and curious gaze. His particular examples centre around the voyeuristic activities of children, their desire to see and make sure of the private and the forbidden (curiosity about other people's genital and bodily functions, about the presence or absence of the penis and, retrospectively, about the primal scene). In this analysis scopophilia is essentially active. (Later, in *Instincts and Their Vicissitudes*, Freud developed his theory of scopophilia further, attaching it initially to pre-genital autoeroticism, after which the pleasure of the look is transferred to others by analogy. There is a close working here of the relationship between the active instinct and its further development in a narcissistic form.) Although the instinct is modified by other factors, in particular the constitution of the ego, it continues to exist as the erotic basis for pleasure in looking at another person as object. At the extreme, it can become fixated into a perversion, producing obsessive voyeurs and Peeping Toms whose only sexual satisfaction can come from watching, in an active controlling sense, an objectified other.

At first glance, the cinema would seem to be remote from the undercover world of the surreptitious observation of an unknowing and unwilling victim. What is seen on the screen is so manifestly shown. But the mass of mainstream film, and the conventions within which it has consciously evolved, portray a hermetically sealed world which unwinds magically, indifferent to the presence of the audience, producing for them a sense of separation and playing on their voyeuristic phantasy. Moreover, the extreme contrast between the darkness in the auditorium (which also isolates the spectators from one another) and the brilliance of the shifting patterns of light and shade on the screen helps to promote the illusion of voyeuristic separation. Although the film is really being shown, is there to be seen, conditions of screening and narrative conventions give the spectator an illusion of looking in on a private world. Among other things, the position of the spectators in the cinema is blatantly one of repression of their exhibitionism and projection of the repressed desire onto the performer.

B. The cinema satisfies a primordial wish for pleasurable looking, but it also goes further, developing scopophilia in its narcissistic aspect. The conventions of mainstream film focus attention on the human form. Scale, space, stories are all anthropomorphic. Here, curiosity and the wish to look intermingle with a fascination with likeness and recognition: the human face, the human body, the relationship between the human form and its surroundings, the visible presence of the person in the world. Jacques Lacan has described how the moment when a child recognises its own image in the mirror is crucial for the constitution of the ego. Several aspects of this analysis are relevant here. The mirror phase occurs at a time when the child's physical ambitions outstrip his motor capacity, with the result that his recognition of himself is joyous in that he imagines his mirror image to be more complete, more perfect than he experiences his own body. Recognition is thus overlaid with misrecognition: the image recognised is conceived as the reflected body of the self, but its misrecognition as superior projects this body outside itself as an ideal ego, the alienated subject, which, re-introjected as an ego ideal, gives rise to the future generation of identification with others. This mirror moment predates language for the child.

Important for this article is the fact that it is an image that constitutes the matrix of the imaginary, of recognition/misrecognition and identification, and hence of the first articulation of the I, of subjectivity. This is a moment when an older fascination with looking (at the mother's face, for an obvious example) collides with the initial inklings of self-awareness. Hence it is the birth of the long love affair/despair between image and self-image which has found such intensity of expression in film and such joyous recognition in the cinema audience. Quite apart from the extraneous similarities between screen and mirror (the framing of the human form in its surroundings, for instance), the cinema has structures of fascination strong enough to allow temporary loss of ego while simultaneously reinforcing the ego. The sense of forgetting the world as the ego has subsequently come to perceive it (I forgot who I am and where I was) is nostalgically reminiscent of that pre-subjective moment of image recognition. At the same time the cinema has distinguished itself in the production of ego ideals as expressed in particular in the star system, the stars centring both screen presence and screen story as they act out a complex process of likeness and difference (the glamorous impersonates the ordinary).

C. Sections II. A and B have set out two contradictory aspects of the pleasurable structures of looking in the conventional cinematic situation. The first, scopophilic, arises from pleasure in using another person as an object of sexual stimulation through sight. The second, developed through narcissism and the constitution of the ego, comes from identification with the image seen. Thus, in film terms, one implies a separation of the erotic identity of the subject from the object on the screen (active scopophilia), the other demands identification of the ego with the object on the screen through the spectator's fascination with and recognition of his like. The first is a function of the sexual instincts, the second of ego libido. This dichotomy was crucial for Freud. Although he saw the two as interacting and overlaying each other, the tension between instinctual drives and self-preservation continues to be a dramatic polarisation in terms of pleasure. Both are formative structures, mechanisms not meaning. In themselves they have no signification, they have to be attached to an idealisation. Both pursue aims in indifference to perceptual reality, creating the imagised, eroticised concept of the world that forms the perception of the subject and makes a mockery of empirical objectivity.

During its history, the cinema seems to have evolved a particular illusion of reality in which this contradiction between libido and ego has found a beautifully complementary phantasy world. In *reality* the phantasy world of the screen is subject to the law which produces it. Sexual instincts and identification processes have a meaning within the symbolic order which articulates desire. Desire, born with language, allows the possibility of transcending the instinctual and the imaginary, but its point of reference continually returns to the traumatic moment of its birth: the castration complex. Hence the look, pleasurable in form, can be threatening in content, and it is woman as representation/image that crystallises this paradox.

III. Woman as image, man as bearer of the look

A. In a world ordered by sexual imbalance, pleasure in looking has been split between active/male and passive/female. The determining male gaze projects its phantasy onto the female figure, which is styled accordingly. In their traditional exhibitionist role women are simultaneously looked at and displayed, with their appearance coded for strong visual and erotic impact so that they can be said to connote *to-be-looked-at-ness*. Woman displayed as sexual object is the leitmotif of erotic spectacle: from pin-ups to stripe-tease, from Ziegfeld to Busby Berkeley, she holds the look, plays to and signifies male desire. Mainstream film neatly combined spectacle and narrative. (Note, however, how in the musical song-and-dance numbers break the flow of the diegesis.) The presence of woman is an indispensable element of spectacle in normal narrative film, yet her visual presence tends to work against the development of a story line, to freeze the flow of action in moments of erotic contemplation. This alien presence then has to be integrated into cohesion with the narrative. As Budd Boetticher has put it:

> What counts is what the heroine provokes, or rather what she represents. She is the one, or rather the love or fear she inspires in the hero, or else the concern he feels for her, who makes him act the way he does. In herself the woman has not the slightest importance.

(A recent tendency in narrative film has been to dispense with this problem altogether; hence the development of what Molly Haskell has called the 'buddy movie', in which the active homosexual eroticism of the central male figures can carry the story without distraction.) Traditionally, the woman displayed has functioned on two levels: as erotic object for the characters within the screen story, and as erotic object for the spectator within the auditorium, with a shifting tension between the looks on either side of the screen. For instance, the device of the show-girl allows the two looks to be unified technically without any apparent break in the diegesis. A woman performs within the narrative, the gaze of the spectator and that of the male characters in the film are neatly combined without breaking narrative verisimilitude. For a moment the sexual impact of the performing woman takes the film into a no-man's-land outside its own time and space. Thus Marilyn Monroe's first appearance in *The River of No Return* and Lauren Bacall's songs in *To Have and Have Not*. Similarly, conventional close-ups of legs (Dietrich, for instance) or a face (Garbo) integrate into the narrative a different mode of eroticism. One part of a fragmented body destroys the Renaissance space, the illusion of depth demanded by the narrative, it gives flatness, the quality of a cut-out or icon rather than verisimilitude to the screen.

B. An active/passive heterosexual division of labour has similarly controlled narrative structure. According to the principles of the ruling ideology and the psychical structures that back it up, the male figure cannot bear the burden of sexual objectification. Man is reluctant to gaze at his exhibitionist like. Hence the split between spectacle and narrative supports the man's role as the active one of forwarding the story, making things happen. The man controls the film phantasy and also emerges as the representative of power in a further sense: as the bearer of the look of the spectator, transferring it behind the screen to neutralise the extradiegetic tendencies represented by woman as spectacle. This is made possible through the processes set in motion by structuring the film around a main controlling figure with whom the spectator can identify. As the spectator identifies with the main male protagonist, he projects his look onto that of his like, his screen surrogate, so that the power of the male protagonist as he controls events coincides with the active power of the erotic look, both giving a satisfying sense of omnipotence. A male movie star's glamorous characteristics are thus not those of the erotic object of the gaze, but those of the more perfect, more complete, more powerful ideal ego conceived in the original moment of recognition in front of the mirror. The character in the story can make things happen and control events better than the subject/spectator, just as the image in the mirror was more in control of motor coordination. In contrast to woman as icon, the active male figure (the ego ideal of the identification process) demands a three-dimensional space corresponding to that of the mirror recognition, in which the alienated subject internalised his own representation of this imaginary existence. He is a figure in a landscape. Here the function of film is to reproduce as accurately as possible the so-called natural conditions of human perception. Camera technology (as exemplified by deep focus in particular) and camera movements (determined by the action of the protagonist), combined with invisible editing (demanded by realism), all tend to blur the limits of screen space. The male protagonist is free to command the stage, a stage of spatial illusion in which he articulates the look and creates the action.

C.1. Sections III. A and B have set out a tension between a mode of representation of woman in film and conventions surrounding the diegesis. Each is associated with a look: that of the spectator in direct scopophilic contact with the female form displayed for his enjoyment (connoting male phantasy) and that of the spectator fascinated with the image of his like set in an illusion of natural space, and through him gaining control and possession of the woman within the diegesis. (This tension and the shift from one pole to the other can structure a single text. Thus both in *Only Angels Have Wings* and in *To Have and Have Not*, the film opens with the woman as object of the combined gaze of spectator and all the male protagonists in the film. She is isolated, glamorous, on display, sexualised. But as the narrative progresses she falls in love with the main male protagonist and becomes his property, losing her outward glamorous characteristics, her generalised sexuality, her show-girl connotations; her eroticism is subjected to the male star alone. By means of identification with him, through participation in his power, the spectator can indirectly possess her too.)

   But in psychoanalytic terms, the female figure poses a deeper problem. She also connotes something that the look continually circles around but disavows: her lack of a penis, implying a threat of castration and hence unpleasure. Ultimately, the meaning of woman is sexual difference, the absence of the penis as visually ascertainable, the material evidence on which is based the castration complex essential for the organisation of entrance to the symbolic order and the law of the father. Thus the woman as icon, displayed for the gaze and enjoyment of men, the active controllers of the look, always threatens to evoke the anxiety it originally signified. The male unconscious has two avenues of escape from this castration anxiety: preoccupation with the re-enactment of the original trauma (investigating the woman, demystifying her mystery), counterbalanced by the devaluation, punishment or saving of the guilty object (an avenue typified by the concerns of the *film noir*); or else complete disavowal of castration by the substitution of a fetish object or turning the represented figure itself into a fetish so that it becomes reassuring rather than dangerous (hence over-valuation, the cult of the female star). This second avenue, fetishistic scopophilia, builds up the physical beauty of the object, transforming it into something satisfying in itself. The first avenue, voyeurism, on the contrary, has associations with sadism: pleasure lies in ascertaining guilt (immediately associated with castration), asserting control and subjecting the guilty person through punishment or forgiveness. This sadistic side fits in well with narrative. Sadism demands a story, depends on making something happen, forcing a change in another person, a battle of will and strength, victory/ defeat, all occurring in a linear time with a beginning and an end. Fetishistic scopophilia, on the other hand, can exist outside linear time as the erotic instinct is focussed on the look alone. These contradictions and ambiguities can be illustrated more simply by using works by Hitchcock and Sternberg, both of whom take the look almost as the content or subject matter of many of their films. Hitchcock is the more complex, as he uses both mechanisms. Sternberg's work, on the other hand, provides many pure examples of fetishistic scopophilia.

C.2. It is well known that Sternberg once said he would welcome his films being projected upside down so that story and character involvement would not interfere with the spectator's undiluted appreciation of the screen image. This statement is revealing but ingenuous. Ingenuous in that his films do demand that the figure of the woman (Dietrich, in the cycle of films with her, as the ultimate example) should be identifiable. But revealing in that it emphasises the fact that for him the pictorial space enclosed by the frame is paramount rather than narrative or identification processes. While Hitchcock goes into the investigative side of voyeurism, Sternberg produces the ultimate fetish, taking it to the point where the powerful look of the male protagonist (characteristic of traditional narrative film) is broken in favour of the image in direct erotic rapport with the spectator. The beauty of the woman as object and the screen space coalesce; she is no longer the bearer of guilt but a perfect product, whose body, stylised and fragmented by close-ups, is the content of the film and the direct recipient of the spectator's look. Sternberg plays down the illusion of screen depth; his screen tends to be one-dimensional, as light and shade, lace, steam, foliage, net, streamers, etc, reduce the visual field. There is little or no mediation of the look through the eyes of the main male protagonist. On the contrary, shadowy presences like La Bessière in *Morocco* act as surrogates for the director, detached as they are from audience identification. Despite Sternberg's insistence that his stories are irrelevant, it is significant that they are concerned with situation, not suspense, and cyclical rather than linear time, while plot complications revolve around misunderstanding rather than conflict. The most important absence is that of the controlling male gaze within the screen scene. The high point of emotional drama in the most typical Dietrich films, her supreme moments of erotic meaning, take place in the absence of the man she loves in the fiction. There are other witnesses, other spectators watching her on the screen, their gaze is one with, not standing in for, that of the audience. At the end of *Morocco*, Tom Brown has already disappeared into the desert when Amy Jolly kicks off her gold sandals and walks after him. At the end of *Dishonoured*, Kranau is indifferent to the fate of Magda. In both cases, the erotic impact, sanctified by death, is displayed as a spectacle for the audience. The male hero misunderstands and, above all, does not see.

In Hitchcock, by contrast, the male hero does see precisely what the audience sees. However, in the films I shall discuss here, he takes fascination with an image through scopophilic eroticism as the subject of the film. Moreover, in these cases the hero portrays the contradictions and tensions experienced by the spectator. In *Vertigo* in particular, but also in *Marnie* and *Rear Window*, the look is central to the plot, oscillating between voyeurism and fetishistic fascination. As a twist, a further manipulation of the normal viewing process, which in some sense reveals it, Hitchcock uses the process of identification normally associated with ideological correctness and the recognition of established morality and shows up its perverted side. Hitchcock has never concealed his interest in voyeurism, cinematic and non-cinematic. His heroes are exemplary of the symbolic order and the law – a policeman (*Vertigo*), a dominant male possessing money and power (*Marnie*) – but their erotic drives lead them into compromised situations. The power to subject another person to the will sadistically or to the gaze voyeuristically is turned onto the woman as the object of both. Power is backed by a certainty of legal right and the established guilt of the woman (evoking castration, psychoanalytically speaking). True perversion is barely concealed under a shallow mask of ideological correctness – the man is on the right side of the law, the woman on the wrong. Hitchcock's skilful use of identification processes and liberal use of subjective camera from the point of view of the male protagonist draw the spectators deeply into his position, making them share his uneasy gaze. The audience is absorbed into a voyeuristic situation within the screen scene and diegesis which parodies his own in the cinema. In his analysis of *Rear Window*, Douchet takes the film as a metaphor for the cinema. Jeffries is the audience, the events in the apartment block opposite correspond to the screen. As he watches, an erotic dimension is added to his look, a central image to the drama. His girlfriend Lisa had been of little sexual interest to him, more or less a drag, so long as she remained on the spectator side. When she crosses the barrier between his room and the block opposite, their relationship is re-born erotically. He does not merely watch her through his lens, as a distant meaningful image, he also sees her as a guilty intruder exposed by a dangerous man threatening her with punishment, and thus finally saves her. Lisa's exhibitionism has already been established by her obsessive interest in dress and style, in being a passive image of visual perfection; Jeffries's voyeurism and activity have also been established through his work as a photo-journalist, a maker of stories and captor of images. However, his enforced inactivity, binding him to his seat as a spectator, puts him squarely in the phantasy position of the cinema audience.

In *Vertigo*, subjective camera predominates. Apart from one flash-back from Judy's point of view, the narrative is woven around what Scottie sees or fails to see. The audience follows the growth of his erotic obsession and subsequent despair precisely from his point of view. Scottie's voyeurism is blatant: he falls in love with a woman he follows and spies on without speaking to. Its sadistic side is equally blatant: he has chosen (and freely chosen, for he had been a successful lawyer) to be a policeman, with all the attendant possibilities of pursuit and investigation. As a result, he follows, watches and falls in love with a perfect image of female beauty and mystery. Once he actually confronts her, his erotic drive is to break her down and force her to tell by persistent cross-questioning. Then, in the second part of the film, he re-enacts his obsessive involvement with the image he loved to watch secretly. He reconstructs Judy as Madeleine, forces her to conform in every detail to the actual physical appearance of his fetish. Her exhibitionism, her masochism, make her an ideal passive counterpart to Scottie's active sadistic voyeurism. She knows her part is to perform, and only by playing it through and then replaying it can she keep Scottie's erotic interest. But in the repetition he does break her down and succeeds in exposing her guilt. His curiosity wins through and she is punished. In *Vertigo*, erotic involvement with the look is disorientating: the spectator's fascination is turned against him as the narrative carries him through and entwines him with the processes that he is himself exercising. The Hitchcock hero here is firmly placed within the symbolic order, in narrative terms. He has all the attributes of the patriarchal superego. Hence the spectator, lulled into a false sense of security by the apparent legality of his surrogate, sees through his look and finds himself exposed as complicit, caught in the moral ambiguity of looking. Far from being simply an aside on the perversion of the police, *Vertigo* focuses on the implications of the active/looking, passive/looked-at split in terms of sexual difference and the power of the male symbolic encapsulated in the hero. Marnie, too, performs for Mark Rutland's gaze and masquerades as the perfect to-be-looked-at image. He, too, is on the side of the law until, drawn in by obsession with her guilt, her secret, he longs to see her in the act of committing a crime, make her confess and thus save her. So he, too, becomes complicit as he acts out the implications of his power. He controls money and words, he can have his cake and eat it.

IV. Summary

The psychoanalytic background that has been discussed in this article is relevant to the pleasure and unpleasure offered by traditional narrative film. The scopophilic instinct (pleasure in looking at another person as an erotic object), and, in contradistinction, ego libido (forming identification processes) act as formations, mechanisms, which this cinema has played on. The image of woman as (passive) raw material for the (active) gaze of man takes the argument a step further into the structure of representation, adding a further layer demanded by the ideology of the patriarchal order as it is worked out in its favourite cinematic form – illusionistic narrative film. The argument returns again to the psychoanalytic background in that woman as representation signifies castration, inducing voyeuristic or fetishistic mechanisms to circumvent her threat. None of these interacting layers is intrinsic to film, but it is only in the film form that they can reach a perfect and beautiful contradiction, thanks to the possibility in the cinema of shifting the emphasis of the look. It is the place of the look that defines cinema, the possibility of varying it and exposing it. This is what makes cinema quite different in its voyeuristic potential from, say, strip-tease, theatre, shows, etc. Going far beyond highlighting a woman's to-be-looked-at-ness, cinema builds the way she is to be looked at into the spectacle itself. Playing on the tension between film as controlling the dimension of time (editing, narrative) and film as controlling the dimension of space (changes in distance, editing), cinematic codes create a gaze, a world, and an object, thereby producing an illusion cut to the measure of desire. It is these cinematic codes and their relationship to formative external structures that must be broken down before mainstream film and the pleasure it provides can be challenged.

To begin with (as an ending), the voyeuristic-scopophilic look that is a crucial part of traditional filmic pleasure can itself be broken down. There are three different looks associated with cinema: that of the camera as it records the profilmic event, that of the audience as it watches the final product, and that of the characters at each other within the screen illusion. The conventions of narrative film deny the first two and subordinate them to the third, the conscious aim being always to eliminate intrusive camera presence and prevent a distancing awareness in the audience. Without these two absences (the material existence of the recording process, the critical reading of the spectator), fictional drama cannot achieve reality, obviousness and truth. Nevertheless, as this article has argued, the structure of looking in narrative fiction film contains a contradiction in its own premises: the female image as a castration threat constantly endangers the unity of the diegesis and bursts through the world of illusion as an intrusive, static, one-dimensional fetish. Thus the two looks materially present in time and space are obsessively subordinated to the neurotic needs of the male ego. The camera becomes the mechanism for producing an illusion of Renaissance space, flowing movements compatible with the human eye, an ideology of representation that revolves around the perception of the subject: the camera's look is disavowed in order to create a convincing world in which the spectator's surrogate can perform with verisimilitude. Simultaneously, the look of the audience is denied an intrinsic force: as soon as fetishistic representation of the female image threatens to break the spell of illusion, and the erotic image on the screen appears directly (without mediation) to the spectator, the fact of fetishisation, concealing as it does castration fear, freezes the look, fixates the spectator and prevents him from achieving any distance from the image in front of him.

This complex interaction of looks is specific to film. The first blow against the monolithic accumulation of traditional film conventions (already undertaken by radical film-makers) is to free the look of the camera into its materiality in time and space and the look of the audience into dialectics, passionate detachment. There is no doubt that this destroys the satisfaction, pleasure and privilege of the 'invisible guest', and highlights how film has depended on voyeuristic active/passive mechanisms. Women, whose image has continually been stolen and used for this end, cannot view the decline of the traditional film form with anything much more than sentimental regret.

35 Film and the masquerade: theorizing the female spectator

Mary Ann Doane

[...] The cinematic apparatus inherits a theory of the image which is not conceived outside of sexual specifications. And historically, there has always been a certain imbrication of the cinematic image and the representation of the woman. The woman's relation to the camera and the scopic regime is quite different from that of the male. As Noël Burch points out, the early silent cinema, through its insistent inscription of scenarios of voyeurism, conceives of its spectator's viewing pleasure in terms of that of the Peeping Tom, behind the screen, reduplicating the spectator's position in relation to the woman as screen.[1] Spectatorial desire, in contemporary film theory, is generally delineated as either voyeurism or fetishism, as precisely a pleasure in seeing what is prohibited in relation to the female body. The image orchestrates a gaze, a limit, and its pleasurable transgression. The woman's beauty, her very desirability, becomes a function of certain practices of imaging – framing, lighting, camera movement, angle. She is thus, as Laura Mulvey has pointed out, more closely associated with the surface of the image than its illusory depths, its constructed three-dimensional space which the man is destined to inhabit and hence control.[2] In *Now Voyager* (1942), for instance, a single image signals the momentous transformation of the Bette Davis character from ugly spinster aunt to glamorous single woman. Charles Affron describes the specifically cinematic aspect of this operation as a 'stroke of genius':

> The radical shadow bisecting the face in white/dark/white strata creates a visual phenom-enon quite distinct from the makeup transformation of lipstick and plucked eyebrows .... This shot does not reveal what we commonly call acting, especially after the most recent exhibition of that activity, but the sense of face belongs to a plastique pertinent to the camera. The viewer is allowed a different perceptual referent, a chance to come down from the nerve-jarring, first sequence and to use his eyes anew.[3]

A 'plastique pertinent to the camera' constitutes the woman not only as the image of desire but as the desirous image – one which the devoted cinéphile can cherish and embrace. To 'have' the cinema is, in some sense, to 'have' the woman. But *Now Voyager* is, in Affron's terms, a 'tear-jerker', in others, a 'woman's picture', i.e. a film purportedly produced for a female audience. What, then, of the female spec-tator? What can one say about her desire in relation to this process of imaging? It would seem that what the cinematic institution has in common with Freud's gesture is the eviction of the female spectator from a discourse purportedly about her (the cinema, psychoanalysis) – one which, in fact, narrativizes her again and again.

[...] Theories of female spectatorship are thus rare, and when they are produced, seem inevitably to confront certain blockages in conceptualization. The difficul-ties in thinking female spectatorship demand consideration. After all, even if it is admitted that the woman is frequently the object of the voyeuristic or fetishistic gaze in the cinema, what is there to prevent her from reversing the relation and appropriating the gaze for her own pleasure? Precisely the fact that the reversal itself remains locked within the same logic. The male striptease, the gigolo – both inevitably signify the mechanism of reversal itself, constituting themselves as aberrations whose acknowledgment simply reinforces the dominant system of aligning sexual difference with a subject/object dichotomy. And an essential attribute of that dominant system is the matching of male subjectivity with the agency of the look.

The supportive binary opposition at work here is not only that utilized by Laura Mulvey – an opposition between passivity and activity, but perhaps more importantly, an opposition between proximity and distance in relation to the image. It is in this sense that the very logic behind the structure of the gaze demands a sexual division. While the distance between image and signified (or even referent) is theorized as minimal, if not non-existent, that between the film and the spectator must be maintained, even measured. One need only think of Noël Burch's mapping of spectatorship as a perfect distance from the screen (two times the width of the image) – a point in space from which the filmic discourse is most accessible.[4]

But the most explicit representation of this opposition between proximity and distance is contained in Christian Metz's analysis of voyeuristic desire in terms of a kind of social hierarchy of the senses: 'It is no accident that the main socially acceptable arts are based on the senses at a distance, and that those which depend on the senses of contact are often regarded as "minor" arts (= culinary arts, art of perfumes, etc.).'[5] The voyeur, according to Metz, must maintain a distance between himself and the image – the cinéphile *needs* the gap which represents for him the very distance between desire and its object. In this sense, voyeurism is theorized as a type of meta-desire:

> If it is true of all desire that it depends on the infinite pursuit of its absent object, voyeuristic desire, along with certain forms of sadism, is the only desire whose principle of distance symbolically and spatially evokes this fundamental rent.[6]

Yet even this status as meta-desire does not fully characterize the cinema for it is a feature shared by other arts as well (painting, theater, opera, etc.). Metz thus adds another reinscription of this necessary distance. What specifies the cinema is a further re-duplication of the lack which prompts desire. The cinema is characterized by an illusory sensory plenitude (there is 'so much to see') and yet haunted by the absence of those very objects which are there to be seen. Absence is an absolute and irrecoverable distance. In other words, Noël Burch is quite right in aligning spectatorial desire with a certain spatial configuration. The viewer must not sit either too close or too far from the screen. The result of both would be the same – he would lose the image of his desire.

It is precisely this opposition between proximity and distance, control of the image and its loss, which locates the possibilities of spectatorship within the problematic of sexual difference. For the female spectator there is a certain overpresence of the image – she *is* the image. Given the closeness of this relationship, the female spectator's desire can be described only in terms of a kind of narcissism – the female look demands a becoming. It thus appears to negate the very distance or gap specified by Metz and Burch as the essential precondition for voyeurism. From this perspective, it is important to note the constant recurrence of the motif of proximity in feminist theories (especially those labeled 'new French feminisms') which purport to describe a feminine specificity. For Luce Irigaray, female anatomy is readable as a constant relation of the self to itself, as an autoeroticism based on the embrace of the two lips which allow the woman to touch herself without mediation. Furthermore, the very notion of property, and hence possession of something which can be constituted as other, is antithetical to the woman: '*Nearness* however, is not foreign to woman, a nearness so close that any identification of one or the other, and therefore any form of property, is impossible. Woman enjoys a closeness with the other that is *so near she cannot possess it any more than she can possess herself.'*[7] Or, in the case of female madness or delirium, '... women do not manage to articulate their madness: they suffer it directly in their body....'[8] The distance necessary to detach the signifiers of madness from the body in the construction of even a discourse which exceeds the boundaries of sense is lacking. In the words of Hélène Cixous, 'More so than men who are coaxed toward social success, toward sublimation, women are body.'[9]

This theme of the overwhelming presence-to-itself of the female body is elaborated by Sarah Kofman and Michèle Montrelay as well. Kofman describes how Freudian psychoanalysis outlines a scenario whereby the subject's passage from the mother to the father is simultaneous with a passage from the senses to reason, nostalgia for the mother henceforth signifying a longing for a different positioning in relation to the sensory or the somatic, and the degree of civilization measured by the very distance from the body.[10] Similarly, Montrelay argues that while the male has the possibility of displacing the first object of desire (the mother), the female must become that object of desire:

> Recovering herself as maternal body (and also as phallus), the woman can no longer repress, 'lose', the first stake of representation.... From now on, anxiety, tied to the presence of this body, can only be insistent, continuous. This body, so close, which she has to occupy, is an object in excess which must be 'lost', that is to say, repressed, in order to be symbolized.[11]

This body so close, so excessive, prevents the woman from assuming a position similar to the man's in relation to signifying systems. For she is haunted by the loss of a loss, the lack of that lack so essential for the realization of the ideals of semiotic systems.

Female specificity is thus theorized in terms of spatial proximity. In opposition to this 'closeness' to the body, a spatial distance in the male's relation to his body rapidly becomes a temporal distance in the service of knowledge. This is presented quite explicitly in Freud's analysis of the construction of the 'subject supposed to know.' The knowledge involved here is a knowledge of sexual difference as it is organized in relation to the structure of the look, turning on the visibility of the penis. For the little girl in Freud's description seeing and knowing are simultaneous – there is no temporal gap between them. In 'Some Psychological Consequences of the Anatomical Distinction Between the Sexes.' Freud claims that the girl, upon seeing the penis for the first time, 'makes her judgement and her decision in a flash. She has seen it and knows that she is without it and wants to have it.'[12] In the lecture on 'Femininity' Freud repeats this gesture, merging perception and intellection: 'They [girls] at once notice the difference and, it must be admitted, its significance too.'[13]

The little boy, on the other hand, does not share this immediacy of understanding. When he first sees the woman's genitals he 'begins by showing irresolution and lack of interest; he sees nothing or disowns what he has seen, he softens it down or looks about for expedients for bringing it into line with his expectations.'[14] A second event, the threat of castration, is necessary to prompt a rereading of the image, endowing it with a meaning in relation to the boy's own subjectivity. It is in the distance between the look and the threat that the boy's relation to knowledge of sexual difference is formulated. The boy, unlike the girl in Freud's description, is capable of a re-vision of earlier events, a retrospective understanding which invests the events with a significance which is in no way linked to an immediacy of sight. This gap between the visible and the knowable, the very possibility of disowning what is seen, prepares the ground for fetishism. In a sense, the male spectator is destined to be a fetishist, balancing knowledge and belief.

The female, on the other hand, must find it extremely difficult, if not impossible, to assume the position of fetishist. That body which is so close continually reminds her of the castration which cannot be 'fetishized away'. The lack of a distance between seeing and understanding, the mode of judging 'in a flash', is conducive to what might be termed an 'over-identification' with the image. The association of tears and 'wet wasted afternoons' (in Molly Haskell's words)[15] with genres specified as feminine (the soap opera, the 'woman's picture') points very precisely to this type of over-identification, this abolition of a distance, in short, this inability to fetishize. The woman is constructed differently in relation to processes of looking. For Irigaray, this dichotomy between distance and proximity is described as the fact that:

> The masculine can partly look at itself, speculate about itself, represent itself and describe itself for what it is, whilst the feminine can try to speak to itself through a new language, but cannot describe itself from outside or in formal terms, except by identifying itself with the masculine, thus by losing itself.[16]

Irigaray goes even further: the woman always has a problematic relation to the visible, to form, to structures of seeing. She is much more comfortable with, closer to, the sense of touch.

The pervasiveness, in theories of the feminine, of descriptions of such a claustrophobic closeness, a deficiency in relation to structures of seeing and the visible, must clearly have consequences for attempts to theorize female spectatorship. And, in fact, the result is a tendency to view the female spectator as the site of an oscillation between a feminine position and a masculine position, invoking the metaphor of the transvestite. Given the structures of cinematic narrative, the woman who identifies with a female character must adopt a passive or masochistic position, while identification with the active hero necessarily entails an acceptance of what Laura Mulvey refers to as a certain 'masculinization' of spectatorship.

> ... as desire is given cultural materiality in a text, for women (from childhood onwards) trans-sex identification is a *habit* that very easily becomes *second Nature*. However, this Nature does not sit easily and shifts restlessly in its borrowed transvestite clothes.[17]

The transvestite wears clothes which signify a different sexuality, a sexuality which, for the woman, allows a mastery over the image and the very possibility of attaching the gaze to desire. Clothes make the man, as they say. Perhaps this explains the ease with which women can slip into male clothing. As both Freud and Cixous point out, the woman seems to be *more* bisexual than the man. A scene from Cukor's *Adam's*

Rib (1949) graphically demonstrates this ease of female transvestism. As Katharine Hepburn asks the jury to imagine the sex role reversal of the three major characters involved in the case, there are three dissolves linking each of the characters successively to shots in which they are dressed in the clothes of the opposite sex. What characterizes the sequence is the marked facility of the transformation of the two women into men in contradistinction to a certain resistance in the case of the man. The acceptability of the female reversal is quite distinctly opposed to the male reversal which seems capable of representation only in terms of farce. Male transvestism is an occasion for laughter; female transvestism only another occasion for desire.

Thus, while the male is locked into sexual identity, the female can at least pretend that she is other – in fact, sexual mobility would seem to be a distinguishing feature of femininity in its cultural construction. Hence, transvestism would be fully recuperable. The idea seems to be this: it is understandable that women would want to be men, for everyone wants to be elsewhere than in the feminine position. What is not understandable within the given terms is why a woman might flaunt her femininity, produce herself as an excess of femininity, in other words, foreground the masquerade. Masquerade is not as recuperable as transvestism precisely because it constitutes an acknowledgment that it is femininity itself which is constructed as mask – as the decorative layer which conceals a non-identity. For Joan Riviere, the first to theorize the concept, the masquerade of femininity is a kind of reaction-formation against the woman's trans-sex identification, her transvestism. After assuming the position of the subject of discourse rather than its object, the intellectual woman whom Riviere analyzes felt compelled to compensate for this theft of masculinity by overdoing the gestures of feminine flirtation.

> Womanliness therefore could be assumed and worn as a mask, both to hide the possession of masculinity and to avert the reprisals expected if she was found to possess it – much as a thief will turn out his pockets and ask to be searched to prove that he has not the stolen goods. The reader may now ask how I define womanliness or where I draw the line between genuine womanliness and the 'masquerade.' My suggestion is not, however, that there is any such difference; whether radical or superficial, they are the same thing.[18]

The masquerade, in flaunting femininity, holds it at a distance. Womanliness is a mask which can be worn or removed. The masquerade's resistance to patriarchal positioning would therefore lie in its denial of the production of femininity as closeness, as presence-to-itself, as, precisely, imagistic. The transvestite adopts the sexuality of the other – the woman becomes a man in order to attain the necessary distance from the image. Masquerade, on the other hand, involves a realignment of femininity, the recovery, or more accurately, simulation, of the missing gap or distance. To masquerade is to manufacture a lack in the form of a certain distance between oneself and one's image. If, as Moustafa Safouan points out, 'to wish to include in oneself as an object the cause of the desire of the Other is a formula for the structure of hysteria',[19] then masquerade is anti-hysterical for it works to effect a separation between the cause of desire and oneself. In Montrelay's words, 'the woman uses her own body as a disguise'.[20]

The very fact that we can speak of a woman 'using' her sex or 'using' her body for particular gains is highly significant – it is not that a man cannot use his body in this way but that he doesn't have to. The masquerade doubles representation; it is constituted by a hyperbolization of the accoutrements of femininity. *A propos* of a recent performance by Marlene Dietrich, Silvia Bovenschen claims, '... we are watching a woman demonstrate the representation of a woman's body.'[21] This type of masquerade, an excess of femininity, is aligned with the *femme fatale* and, as Montrelay explains, is necessarily regarded by men as evil incarnate: 'It is this evil which scandalizes whenever woman plays out her sex in order to evade the word and the law. Each time she subverts a law or a word which relies on the predominantly masculine structure of the look.'[22] By destabilizing the image, the masquerade confounds this masculine structure of the look. It effects a defamiliarization of female iconography. Nevertheless, the preceding account simply specifies masquerade as a type of representation which carries a threat, disarticulating male systems of viewing. Yet, it specifies nothing with respect to female spectatorship. What might it mean to masquerade as spectator? To assume the mask in order to see in a different way?

[...] The first scene in *Now Voyager* depicts the Bette Davis character as repressed, unattractive, and undesirable or, in her own words, as the spinster aunt of the family ('Every family has one'). She has heavy eyebrows, keeps her hair bound tightly in a bun, and wears glasses, a drab dress, and heavy shoes. By the time of the shot signaling her transformation into beauty, the glasses have disappeared, along with the other signifiers of unattractiveness. Between these two moments there is a scene in which the doctor who cures her actually confiscates her glasses (as a part of the cure). The woman who wears glasses constitutes one of the most intense visual clichés of the cinema. The image is a heavily marked condensation of motifs concerned with repressed sexuality, knowledge, visibility and vision, intellectuality, and desire. The woman with glasses signifies simultaneously intellectuality and undesirability; but the moment she removes her glasses (a moment which, it seems, must almost always be *shown* and which is itself linked with a certain sensual quality), she is transformed into spectacle, the very picture of desire. Now, it must be remembered that the cliché is a heavily loaded moment of signification, a social knot of meaning. It is characterized by an effect of ease and naturalness. Yet, the cliché has a binding power so strong that it indicates a precise moment of ideological danger or threat – in this case, the woman's appropriation of the gaze. Glasses worn by a woman in the cinema do not generally signify a deficiency in seeing but an active looking, or even simply the fact of seeing as opposed to being seen. The intellectual woman looks and analyzes, and in usurping the gaze she poses a threat to an entire system of representation. It is as if the woman had forcefully moved to the other side of the specular. The overdetermination of the image of the woman with glasses, its status as a cliché, is a crucial aspect of the cinematic alignment of structures of seeing and being seen with sexual difference. The cliché, in assuming an immediacy of understanding, acts as a mechanism for the naturalization of sexual difference.

But the figure of the woman with glasses is only an extreme moment of a more generalized logic. There is always a certain excessiveness, a difficulty associated with women who appropriate the gaze, who insist upon looking. Linda Williams has demonstrated how, in the genre of the horror film, the woman's active looking is

ultimately punished. And what she sees, the monster, is only a mirror of herself –
both woman and monster are freakish in their difference – defined by either 'too
much' or 'too little'.[23] Just as the dominant narrative cinema repetitively inscribes
scenarios of voyeurism, internalizing or narrativizing the film-spectator relationship
(in films like *Psycho* [1960], *Rear Window* [1954], *Peeping Tom* [1960]), taboos in
seeing are insistently formulated in relation to the female spectator as well. The man
with binoculars is countered by the woman with glasses. The gaze must be dissoci-
ated from mastery. In *Leave Her to Heaven* (John Stahl, 1945), the female protagonist's (Gene Tierney's) excessive desire and overpossessiveness are signaled from
the very beginning of the film by her intense and sustained stare at the major male
character, a stranger she first encounters on a train. The discomfort her look causes
is graphically depicted. The Gene Tierney character is ultimately revealed to be the
epitome of evil – killing her husband's crippled younger brother, her unborn child,
and ultimately herself in an attempt to brand her cousin as a murderess in order to
ensure her husband's future fidelity. In *Humoresque* (Jean Negulesco, 1946), Joan
Crawford's problematic status is a result of her continual attempts to assume the
position of spectator – fixing John Garfield with her gaze. Her transformation from
spectator to spectacle is signified repetitively by the gesture of removing her glasses.
Rosa, the character played by Bette Davis in *Beyond the Forest* (King Vidor, 1949)
walks to the station every day simply to *watch* the train departing for Chicago. Her
fascination with the train is a fascination with its phallic power to transport her to
'another place'. This character is also specified as having a 'good eye' – she can
shoot, both pool and guns. In all three films the woman is constructed as the site of
an excessive and dangerous desire. This desire mobilizes extreme efforts of containment and unveils the sadistic aspect of narrative. In all three films the woman dies.
As Claire Johnston points out, death is the 'location of all impossible signs',[24] and
the films demonstrate that the woman as subject of the gaze is clearly an impossible
sign. There is a perverse rewriting of this logic of the gaze in *Dark Victory* (Edmund
Goulding, 1939), where the woman's story achieves heroic and tragic proportions
not only in blindness, but in a blindness which mimes sight – when the woman
pretends to be able to see. [...]

Notes

1 See Noël Burch's film, *Correction Please, or How We Got Into Pictures,* Great Britain,
   1979.
2 Laura Mulvey, 'Visual Pleasure and Narrative Cinema', *Screen* **16** (3) (Autumn 1975):
   12–13.
3 Charles Affron, *Star Acting: Gish, Garbo, Davis* (New York: E.P. Dutton, 1977) 281–82.
4 Noël Burch, *Theory of Film Practice*, trans. Helen R. Lane (New York: Praeger, 1973) 35.
5 Christian Metz, 'The Imaginary Signifier', *Screen* **16**(2) (Summer 1975): 60.
6 Metz 61.
7 Luce Irigaray, *This Sex Which Is Not One*, trans. Catherine Porter with Carolyn Burke
   (Ithaca: Cornell UP, 1985) 31.
8 Luce Irigaray, 'Women's Exile', *Ideology and Consciousness* **1** (May 1977): 74.
9 Hélène Cixous, 'The Laugh of the Medusa', *New French Feminisms*, ed. Elaine Marks
   and Isabelle de Courtivron (Amherst: U of Massachusetts P, 1980) 257.
10 Sarah Kofman, 'Ex: The Woman's Enigma', *Enclitic* **4** (2) (Fall 1980): 20.

11 Michèle Montrelay, 'Inquiry into Femininity', *m/f* **1** (1978): 91–92.

12 Freud, 'Some Psychological Consequences of the Anatomical Distinction Between the Sexes', *Sexuality and the Psychology of Love*, ed. Philip Rieff (New York: Collier, 1963) 187–88.

13 Sigmund Freud, 'Femininity', *The Standard Edition of the Complete Psychological Works of Sigmund Freud*, vol. 22, ed. James Strachey (London: Hogarth and the Institute of Psychoanalysis, 1964) 125.

14 Freud, 'Some Psychological Consequences ...' 187.

15 Molly Haskell, *From Reverence to Rape* (Baltimore: Penguin, 1974) 154.

16 Irigaray, 'Women's Exile' 65.

17 Laura Mulvey, 'Afterthoughts on "Visual Pleasure and Narrative Cinema" inspired by *Duel in the Sun*', *Framework* **6** (15–17) (Summer 1981): 13.

18 Joan Riviere, 'Womanliness as a Masquerade', *Psychoanalysis and Female Sexuality*, ed. Hendrik M. Ruitenbeek (New Haven: College and UP, 1966) 213. The essay was originally published in *The International Journal of Psychoanalysis* 10 (1929).

19 Moustafa Safouan, 'Is the Oedipus Complex Universal?', *m/f* **5–6** (1981): 84–85.

20 Montrelay 93.

21 Silvia Bovenschen, 'Is There a Feminine Aesthetic?', *New German Critique* **10** (Winter 1977): 129.

22 Montrelay 93.

23 Linda Williams, 'When the Woman Looks ...,' in *Re-vision: Essays in Feminist Film Criticism*, ed. Mary Ann Doane, Patricia Mellencamp and Linda Williams (Frederick, MD: U Publications of America and the American Film Institute, 1984).

24 Claire Johnston, 'Femininity and the Masquerade: Anne of the Indies', in *Jacques Tourneur* (London: British Film Institute, 1975) 40.

36 Her body, himself

Carol J. Clover

[...] On the face of it, the relation between the sexes in slasher films could hardly be clearer. The killer is with few exceptions recognizably human and distinctly male; his fury is unmistakably sexual in both roots and expression; his victims are mostly women, often sexually free and always young and beautiful. Just how essential this victim is to horror is suggested by her historical durability. If the killer has over time been variously figured as shark, fog, gorilla, birds, and slime, the victim is eternally and prototypically the damsel. Cinema hardly invented the pattern. It has simply given visual expression to the abiding proposition that, in Poe's famous formulation, the death of a beautiful woman is the 'most poetical topic in the world.'[1] As horror director Dario Argento puts it, 'I like women, especially beautiful ones. If they have a good face and figure, I would much prefer to watch them being murdered than an ugly girl or man.'[2] Brian De Palma elaborates: 'Women in peril work better in the suspense genre. It all goes back to the *Perils of Pauline*.... If you have a haunted house and you have a woman walking around with a candelabrum, you fear more for her than you would for a husky man.'[3] Or Hitchcock, during the filming of *The Birds*: 'I always believe in following the advice of the playwright Sardou. He said, "Torture the women!" The trouble today is that we don't torture women enough.'[4] What the directors do not say, but show, is that 'Pauline' is at her very most effective in a state of undress, borne down upon by a blatantly phallic murderer, even gurgling orgasmically as she dies. The case could be made that the slasher films available at a given neighborhood video rental outlet recommend themselves to censorship under the Dworkin–MacKinnon guidelines at least as readily as do the hard-core films the next section over, at which that legislation aimed; for if some of the victims are men, the argument goes, most are women, and the women are brutalized in ways that come too close to real life for comfort. But what this line of reasoning does not take into account is the figure of the Final Girl. Because slashers lie for all practical purposes beyond the purview of legitimate criticism, and to the extent that they have been reviewed at all have been reviewed on an individual basis, the phenomenon of the female victim-hero has scarcely been acknowledged.

It is, of course, 'on the face of it' that most of the public discussion of film takes place – from the Dworkin–MacKinnon legislation to Siskel and Ebert's reviews to our own talks with friends on leaving the movie house. Underlying that discussion is the assumption that the sexes are what they seem; that screen males represent the Male and screen females the Female; that this identification along gender lines authorizes impulses toward violence in males and encourages impulses toward victimization in females. In part because of the massive authority cinema by nature accords the image, even academic film criticism has been slow – slower than literary criticism – to get beyond appearances. Film may not appropriate the mind's eye, but it certainly encroaches on it; the gender characteristics of a screen figure are a visible and audible given for the duration of the film. To the extent that the possibility of cross-gender identification has been entertained, it has been that of the female with the male. Thus some critics have wondered whether the female viewer, faced with the screen image of a masochistic/narcissistic female, might not rather elect to 'betray her sex and identify with the masculine point of view'. The reverse question – whether men might not also, on occasion, elect to betray their sex and identify with screen females – has scarcely been asked, presumably on the assumption that men's interests are well served by the traditional patterns of cinematic representation. For there is the matter of the 'male gaze'. As E. Ann Kaplan sums it up, 'within the film text itself, men gaze at women, who become objects of the gaze; the spectator, in turn, is made to identify with this male gaze, and to objectify the woman on the screen; and the camera's original 'gaze' comes into play in the very act of filming.'[5] But if it is so that all of us, male and female alike, are by these processes 'made to' identify with men and 'against' women, how are we then to explain the appeal to a largely male audience of a film genre that features a female victim-hero? The slasher film brings us squarely up against fundamental questions of film analysis: where does the literal end and the figurative begin? how do the two levels interact and what is the significance of the interaction? and to which, in arriving at a political judgment (as we are inclined to do in the case of low horror and pornography in particular), do we assign priority?

A figurative or functional analysis of the slasher begins with the processes of point of view and identification. The male viewer seeking a male character, even a vicious one, with whom to identify in a sustained way has little to hang onto in the standard example. On the good side, the only viable candidates are the boyfriends or school-mates of the girls. They are for the most part marginal, undeveloped characters. More to the point, they tend to die early in the film. If the traditional horror plot gave the male spectator a last-minute hero with whom to identify thereby 'indulging his vanity as protector of the helpless female',[6] the slasher eliminates or attenuates that role beyond any such function; indeed, would-be rescuers are not infrequently blown away for their trouble, leaving the girl to fight her own fight. Policemen, fathers, and sheriffs appear only long enough to demonstrate risible incomprehen-sion and incompetence. On the bad side, there is the killer. The killer is often unseen or barely glimpsed, during the first part of the film, and what we do see, when we finally get a good look, hardly invites immediate or conscious empathy. He is commonly masked, fat, deformed, or dressed as a woman. Or 'he' *is* a woman: woe to the viewer of *Friday the Thirteenth I* who identifies with the male killer only to discover, in the film's final sequences, that he was not a man at all but a middle-aged mother. In either case, the killer is himself eventually killed or otherwise evacuated from the narrative. No male character of any stature lives to tell the tale.

The one character of stature who does live to tell the tale is in fact the Final Girl. She is introduced at the beginning and is the only character to be developed in any psychological detail. We understand immediately from the attention paid it that hers is the main story line. She is intelligent, watchful, levelheaded; the first char-acter to sense something amiss and the only one to deduce from the accumulating evidence the pattern and extent of the threat; the only one, in other words, whose perspective approaches our own privileged understanding of the situation. We register her horror as she stumbles on the corpses of her friends. Her momentary paralysis in the face of death duplicates those moments of the universal nightmare experience – in which she is the undisputed 'I' – on which horror frankly trades. When she downs the killer, we are triumphant. She is by any measure the slasher film's hero. This is not to say that our attachment to her is exclusive and unremit-ting, only that it adds up, and that in the closing sequence (which can be quite prolonged) it is very close to absolute.

An analysis of the camerawork bears this out. Much is made of the use of the I-camera to represent the killer's point of view. In these passages – they are usually few and brief, but striking – we see through his eyes and (on the soundtrack) hear his breathing and heartbeat. His and our vision is partly obscured by the bushes or window blinds in the foreground. By such means we are forced, the logic goes, to identify with the killer. In fact, however, the relation between camera point of view and the processes of viewer identification is poorly understood; the fact that Steven Spielberg can stage an attack in *Jaws* from the shark's point of view (underwater, rushing upward toward the swimmer's flailing legs) or Hitchcock an attack in *The Birds* from the bird-eye perspective (from the sky, as they gather to swoop down on the streets of Bodega) would seem to suggest either that the viewer's identificatory powers are unbelievably elastic or that point-of-view shots can sometimes be pro forma. It has also been suggested that the hand-held or similarly unanchored first-person camera works as much to destabilize as to stabilize identification. [...] For the moment, let us accept this equation: point of view = identification. We are linked, in this way, with the killer in the early part of the film, usually before we have seen him directly and before we have come to know the Final Girl in any detail. Our closeness to him wanes as our closeness to the Final Girl waxes – a shift underwritten by story line as well as camera position. By the end, point of view is hers: we are in the closet with her, watching with her eyes the knife blade pierce the door; in the room with her as the killer breaks through the window and grabs at her; in the car with her as the killer stabs through the convertible top, and so on. And with her, we become if not the killer of the killer then the agent of his expulsion from the narrative vision. If, during the film's course, we shifted our sympathies back and forth and dealt them out to other characters along the way, we belong in the end to the Final Girl; there is no alternative. [...]

Audience response ratifies this design. Observers unanimously stress the readiness of the 'live' audience to switch sympathies in midstream, siding now with the killer and now, and finally, with the Final Girl. As Schoell, whose book on shocker films wrestles with its own monster, 'the feminists', puts it:

> Social critics make much of the fact that male audience members cheer on the misogynous misfits in these movies as they rape, plunder, and murder their screaming, writhing female victims. Since these same critics walk out of the moviehouse in disgust long before the movie is over, they don't realize that these same men cheer on (with renewed enthusiasm, in fact) the heroines, who are often as strong, sexy, and independent as the [earlier] victims, as they blow away the killer with a shotgun or get him between the eyes with a machete. All of these men are said to be identifying with the maniac, but they enjoy *his* death throes the most of all, and applaud the heroine with admiration.[7]

What filmmakers seem to know better than film critics is that gender is less a wall than a permeable membrane.

No one who has read 'Red Riding Hood' to a small boy or attended a viewing of, say, *Deliverance* (an all-male story that women find as gripping as men do) – or, more recently, *Alien* and *Aliens*, with whose space-age female Rambo, herself a Final Girl, male viewers seem to engage with ease – can doubt the phenomenon of cross-gender identification. This fluidity of engaged perspective is in keeping with the universal claims of the psychoanalytic model: the threat function and the victim function coexist in the same unconscious, regardless of anatomical sex. But why, if viewers can identify across gender lines and if the root experience of horror is sex blind, are the screen sexes not interchangeable? Why not more and better female killers, and why (in light of the maleness of the majority audience) not Pauls as well as Paulines? The fact that horror film so stubbornly figures the killer as male and the principal as female would seem to suggest that representation itself is at issue – that the sensation of bodily fright derives not exclusively from repressed content, as Freud insisted, but also from the bodily manifestations of that content.

Nor is the gender of the principals as straightforward as it first seems. The killer's phallic purpose, as he thrusts his drill or knife into the trembling bodies of young women, is unmistakable. At the same time, however, his masculinity is severely qualified: he ranges from the virginal or sexually inert to the transvestite or transsexual, and is spiritually divided ('the mother half of his mind') or even equipped with vulva and vagina. Although the killer of *God Told Me To* is represented and taken as a male in the film text, he is revealed, by the doctor who delivered him, to have been sexually ambiguous from birth: 'I truly could not tell whether that child was male or female; it was as if the sexual gender had not been determined ... as if it were being developed.' In this respect, slasher killers have much in common with the monsters of classic horror – monsters who, in Linda Williams's formulation, represent not just 'an eruption of the normally repressed animal sexual energy of the civilized male' but also the 'power and potency of a *non-phallic* sexuality'. To the extent that the monster is constructed as feminine, the horror film thus expresses female desire only to show how monstrous it is.[8] The intention is manifest in *Aliens*, in which the Final Girl, Ripley, is pitted in the climactic scene against the most terrifying 'alien' of all: an egg-laying Mother.

Decidedly 'intrauterine' in quality is the Terrible Place, dark and often damp, in which the killer lives or lurks and whence he stages his most terrifying attacks. 'It often happens', Freud wrote, 'that neurotic men declare that they feel there is something uncanny about the female genital organs. This *unheimlich* place, however, is an entrance to the former *Heim* [home] of all human beings, to the place where each of us lived once upon a time and in the beginning.... In this case too then, the *unheimlich* is what once was *heimisch*, familiar; the prefix *"un"* [un–] is the token of repression.'[9] It is the exceptional film that does not mark as significant the moment that the killer leaps out of the dark recesses of a corridor or cavern at the trespassing victim, usually the Final Girl. Long after the other particulars have faded, the viewer will remember the images of Amy assaulted from the dark halls of a morgue (*He Knows You're Alone*), or Melanie trapped in the attic as the savage birds close in (*The Birds*). In such scenes of convergence the Other is at its bisexual mightiest, the victim at her tiniest, and the component of sadomasochism at its most blatant.

The gender of the Final Girl is likewise compromised from the outset by her masculine interests, her inevitable sexual reluctance, her apartness from other girls, sometimes her name. At the level of the cinematic apparatus, her unfemininity is signaled clearly by her exercise of the 'active investigating gaze' normally reserved for males and punished in females when they assume it themselves; tentatively at first and then aggressively, the Final Girl looks *for* the killer, even tracking him to his forest hut or his underground labyrinth, and then *at* him, therewith bringing him, often for the first time, into our vision as well. When, in the final scene, she stops screaming, faces the killer, and reaches for the knife (sledge hammer, scalpel, gun, machete, hanger, knitting needle, chain saw), she addresses the monster on his own terms. To the critics' objection that *Halloween* in effect punished female sexuality, director John Carpenter responded: 'They [the critics] completely missed the boat there, I think. Because if you turn it around, the one girl who is the most sexually uptight just keeps stabbing this guy with a long knife. She's the most sexually frustrated. She's the one that killed him. Not because she's a virgin, but because all that repressed energy starts coming out. She uses all those phallic symbols on the guy.... She and the killer have a certain link: sexual repression.'[10] For all its perversity, Carpenter's remark does underscore the sense of affinity, even recognition, that attends the final encounter. But the 'certain link' that puts killer and Final Girl on terms, at least briefly, is more than 'sexual repression'. It is also a shared masculinity, materialized in 'all those phallic symbols' – and it is also a shared femininity, materialized in what comes next (and what Carpenter, perhaps significantly, fails to mention): the castration, literal or symbolic, of the killer at her hands. The Final Girl has not just manned herself; she specifically unmans an oppressor whose masculinity was in question to begin with. By the time the drama has played itself out, darkness yields to light (typically as day breaks) and the close quarters of the barn (closet, elevator, attic, basement) give way to the open expanse of the yard (field, road, lakescape, cliff). With the Final Girl's appropriation of 'all those phallic symbols' comes the dispelling of the 'uterine' threat as well. Consider [...] the paradigmatic ending of *Texas Chain Saw II*. From the underground labyrinth, murky and bloody, in which she faced saw, knife, and hammer, Stretch escapes through a culvert into the open air. She clambers up the jutting rock and with a chain saw takes her stand. When her last assailant comes at her, she slashes open his lower abdomen – the sexual symbolism is all too clear – and flings him off the cliff. Again, the final scene shows her in extreme long shot, standing on the ledge of a pinnacle, drenched in sunlight, buzzing chain saw held overhead.

The tale would indeed seem to be one of sex and parents. The patently erotic threat is easily seen as the materialized projection of the viewer's own incestuous fears and desires. It is this disabling cathexis to one's parents that must be killed and rekilled in the service of sexual autonomy. When the Final Girl stands at last in the light of day with the knife in her hand, she has delivered herself into the adult world. Carpenter's equation of the Final Girl with the killer has more than a grain of truth. The killers of *Psycho, The Eyes of Laura Mars, Friday the Thirteenth II-VI*, and *Cruising*, among others, are explicitly figured as sons in the psychosexual grip of their mothers (or fathers, in the case of *Cruising*). The difference is between past and present and between failure and success. The Final Girl enacts in the present, and successfully, the parenticidal struggle that the killer himself enacted unsuccessfully in his own past – a past that constitutes the film's backstory. She is what the killer once was; he is what she could become should she fail in her battle for sexual selfhood. 'You got the choice, boy,' says the tyrannical father of Leatherface in *Texas Chain Saw II*, 'sex or the saw; you never know about sex, but the saw – the saw is the family'.

The tale is no less one of maleness. If the experience of childhood can be – is perhaps ideally – enacted in female form, the breaking away requires the assumption of the phallus. The helpless child is gendered feminine; the autonomous adult or subject is gendered masculine; the passage from childhood to adulthood entails a shift from feminine to masculine. It is the male killer's tragedy that his incipient femininity is not reversed but completed (castration) and the Final Girl's victory that her incipient masculinity is not thwarted but realized (phallicization). When De Palma says that female frailty is a predicate of the suspense genre, he proposes, in effect, that the lack of the phallus, for Lacan the privileged signifier of the symbolic order, is itself simply horrifying, at least in the mind of the male observer. Where pornography (the argument goes) resolves that lack through a process of fetishization that allows a breast or leg or whole body to stand in for the missing member, the slasher film resolves it either through eliminating the woman (earlier victims) or reconstituting her as masculine (Final Girl). The moment at which the Final Girl is effectively phallicized is the moment that the plot halts and horror ceases. Day breaks, and the community returns to its normal order.

Casting psychoanalytic verities in female form has a venerable cinematic history. Ingmar Bergman, for one, has made a career of it. One immediate practical advantage, by now presumably unconscious on the part of makers as well as viewers, has to do with a preestablished cinematic 'language' for capturing the moves and moods of the female body and face. The cinematic gaze, we are told, is male, and just as that gaze 'knows' how to fetishize the female form in pornography (in a way that it does not 'know' how to fetishize the male form), so it 'knows', in horror, how to track a woman ascending a staircase in a scary house and how to study her face from an angle above as she first hears the killer's footfall. A set of conventions we now take for granted simply 'sees' males and females differently.

To this cinematic habit may be added the broader range of emotional expression traditionally allowed women. Angry displays of force may belong to the male, but crying, cowering, screaming, fainting, trembling, begging for mercy belong to the female. Abject terror, in short, is gendered feminine, and the more concerned a given film is with that condition – and it is the essence of modern horror – the more likely the femaleness of the victim. It is no accident that male victims in slasher films are killed swiftly or offscreen, and that prolonged struggles, in which the victim has time to contemplate her imminent destruction, inevitably figure females. Only when one encounters the rare expression of abject terror on the part of a male (as in *I Spit on Your Grave*) does one apprehend the full extent of the cinematic double standard in such matters.

It is also the case that gender displacement can provide a kind of identificatory buffer, an emotional remove that permits the majority audience to explore taboo subjects in the relative safety of vicariousness. Just as Bergman came to realize that he could explore castration anxiety more freely via depictions of hurt female bodies (witness the genital mutilation of Karin in *Cries and Whispers*), so the makers of slasher films seem to know that sadomasochistic incest fantasies sit more easily with the male viewer when the visible player is female. It is one thing for that viewer to hear the psychiatrist intone at the end of *Psycho* that Norman as a boy (in the back-story) was abnormally attached to his mother; it would be quite another to see that attachment dramatized in the present, to experience in nightmare form the elabora-tion of Norman's (the viewer's own) fears and desires. If the former is playable in male form, the latter, it seems, is not.

The Final Girl is, on reflection, a congenial double for the adolescent male. She is feminine enough to act out in a gratifying way, a way unapproved for adult males, the terrors and masochistic pleasures of the underlying fantasy, but not so feminine as to disturb the structures of male competence and sexuality. The question then arises whether the Final Girls of slasher films – Stretch, Stevie, Marti, Will, Terry, Laurie, and Ripley – are not boyish for the same reason that female 'victims' in Victorian flagellation literature – 'Georgy', 'Willy' – are boyish: because they are transformed males. The transformation, Steven Marcus writes, 'is itself both a defense against and a disavowal of the fantasy it is simultaneously expressing – namely, that a *boy* is being beaten – that is, loved – by another man'.[11] What is repre-sented as male-on-female violence, in short, is figuratively speaking male-on-male sex. For Marcus, the literary picture of flagellation, in which *girls* are beaten, is utterly belied by the descriptions (in *My Secret Life*) of real-life episodes in which the persons being beaten are not girls at all but 'gentlemen' dressed in women's clothes ('He had a woman's dress on tucked up to his waist, showing his naked rump and thighs.... On his head was a woman's cap tied carefully round his face to hide whiskers') and whipped by prostitutes. Reality, Marcus writes, 'puts the literature of flagellation out of the running ... by showing how that literature is a completely distorted and idealized version of what actually happen'.[12] Applied to the slasher film, this logic reads the femaleness of the Final Girl (at least up to the point of her transformation) and indeed of the woman victims in general as only apparent, the artifact of heterosexual deflection. It may be through the female body that the body of the audience is sensationalized, but the sensation is an entirely male affair.

At least one director, Hitchcock, explicitly located thrill in the equation victim = audience. So we judge from his marginal jottings in the shooting instructions for the shower scene in *Psycho*: 'The slashing. An impression of a knife slashing, as if tearing at the very screen, ripping the film.'[13] Not just the body of Marion is to be ruptured, but also the body on the other side of the film and screen: our witnessing body. As Marion is to Norman, the audience of *Psycho* is to Hitchcock; as the audiences of horror film in general are to the directors of those films, female is to male. Hitchcock's 'torture the women' then means, simply, torture the audience. De Palma's remarks about female frailty ('Women in peril work better in the suspense genre.... you fear more for her than you would for a husky man') likewise contemplate a male-on-'female' relationship between director and viewer. Cinefantastic horror, in short, succeeds in incorporating its spectators as 'feminine' and then violating that body – which recoils, shudders, cries out collectively – in ways otherwise imaginable, for males, only in nightmare. The equation is nowhere more plainly put than in David Cronenberg's *Videodrome*. Here the threat is a mind-destroying video signal; the victims, television viewers. Despite the (male) hero's efforts to defend his mental and physical integrity, a deep, vagina-like gash appears on his lower abdomen. Says the media conspirator as he thrusts a videocassette into the victim's gaping wound, 'You must open yourself completely to this.'

If the slasher film is 'on the face of it' a genre with at least a strong female presence, it is in these figurative readings a thoroughly male exercise, one that finally has very little to do with femaleness and very much to do with phallocentrism. Figuratively seen, the Final Girl is a male surrogate in things oedipal, a homoerotic stand-in, the audience incorporate; to the extent she means 'girl' at all, it is only for purposes of signifying male lack, and even that meaning is nullified in the final scenes. Our initial question – how to square a female victim-hero with a largely male audience – is not so much answered as it is obviated in these readings. The Final Girl is (apparently) female not despite the maleness of the audience, but precisely because of it. The discourse is wholly masculine, and females figure in it only insofar as they 'read' some aspect of male experience. To applaud the Final Girl as a feminist development, as some reviews of *Aliens* have done with Ripley, is, in light of her figurative meaning, a particularly grotesque expression of wishful thinking. She is simply an agreed-upon fiction and the male viewer's use of her as a vehicle for his own sadomasochistic fantasies an act of perhaps timeless dishonesty.

Notes

1 Edgar Allan Poe, 'The Philosophy of Composition', p. 55.
2 Argento as quoted in Schoell, *Stay Out of the Shower*, p. 54.
3 De Palma as quoted in ibid., p. 41.

4 Hitchcock as quoted in Spoto, *The Dark Side of Genius*, p. 483.
5 Silvia Bovenschen, 'Is There a Feminine Aesthetic?', p. 114; E. Ann Kaplan, *Women and Film*, p. 15. See also Mary Ann Doane, 'Misrecognition and Identity'.
6 Wood, 'Beauty Bests the Beast,' p. 64.
7 Schoell, *Stay Out of the Shower*, p. 55. Two points in this paragraph deserve emending. One is the suggestion that rape is common in these films; it is in fact virtually absent, by definition. The other is the characterization of the Final Girl as 'sexy.' She may be attractive (though typically less so than her friends), but she is with few exceptions sexually inactive.
8 Linda Williams, 'When the Woman Looks,' p.90.
9 Sigmund Freud, 'The "Uncanny",' p. 245.
10 John Carpenter interviewed by Todd McCarthy, 'Trick or Treat.'
11 Steven Marcus, *The Other Victorians*, pp. 260–61.
12 Ibid., pp. 125–27.
13 As quoted by Spoto, *The Dark Side of Genius*, p. 431.

Works cited

Boveschen, Silvia. 'Is There a Feminine Aesthetic?' *New German Critique* 10 (1977): 444–69.
Doane, Mary Ann. 'Misrecognition and Identity.' *Ciné-Tracts* 11 (1980): 25–32.
Doane, Mary Ann, Patricia Mellencamp, and Linda Williams, eds. In *Re-Vision: Essays in Feminist Film Criticism*. American Film Institute Monograph Series, 3. Frederick, Md.: University Publications of America, 1984.
Freud, Sigmund. 'The "Uncanny" ' (1919). *The Standard Edition of the Complete Psychological Works of Sigmund Freud*. Translated by James Strachey. London: Hogarth Press, 1986, 17: 219–52.
Kaplan, E. Ann. *Women and Film: Both Sides of the Camera*. London: Methuen, 1983.
McCarthy, Todd 'Trick or Treat'. *Film Comment* 16 (1980): 17–24.
Marcus, Steven. *The Other Victorians: A Study of Sexuality and Pornography in Mid-Nineteenth-Century England*. New York: Basic Books, 1964.
Poe, Edgar Allan. 'The Philosophy of Composition.' In *Great Short Works of Edgar Allan Poe*, edited by G. R. Thompson. New York: Literary Classics of the United States, 1970.
Schoell, William. *Stay Out of the Shower: Twenty-five Years of Shocker Films Beginning with Psycho*. New York: Dembner, 1985.
Spoto, Donald. *The Dark Side of Genius: The Life of Alfred Hitchcock*. New York: Ballantine, 1983.
Williams, Linda. 'When the Woman Looks.' In *Re-Vision: Essays in Feminist Film Criticism*, edited by Mary Ann Doane, Patricia Mellencamp, and Linda Williams.
Wood, Robin. 'Beauty Bests the Beast.' *American Film* 8 (1983): 63–65.

SECTION EIGHT
CULTURAL STUDIES

While film studies and cultural studies have frequently been overlapping fields, the relationship between the two has been complex. Approaches from film studies were appropriated by cultural analysts in the 1960s and 1970s in an attempt to analyse and theorize culture, but cultural studies also drew on other theoretical influences which produced a critique of many of the key approaches in film studies. In more recent years, the direction of influence has changed and insights from cultural studies have often informed recent transformations in film studies. Furthermore, critics such as Richard Dyer, Jackie Stacey, Nicholas Garnham and Jane Gaines seen in other sections have all analysed film in ways that are informed by some of the central assumptions of cultural studies.

As film studies was consolidated as a discipline in the 1960s, it was given coherence by a unifying object – film – and given legitimacy by treating film as culture in terms of aesthetics, in a manner borrowed from the study of art and literature. However, cultural studies has always been less easy to classify: its 'object' of study – 'culture' – has been a keenly contested term within cultural studies and, crucially, the area of study aimed to break down the equation between culture and aesthetics (or questions of artistic value). Furthermore, cultural studies not only is interdisciplinary but also has been anti-disciplinary: for example, critics such as Richard Johnson (1986) would claim that many disciplines are required to understand the complexities of culture. For these reasons, among many others, it would be a mistake to claim that there was a single cultural studies approach to film. Nonetheless, approaches generated within cultural studies have contributed to film studies, and critics working within this field have often had common concerns.

While in many instances film studies has been primarily concerned with the film text, cultural studies has also explored the significance of these texts in relationship to the wider cultural contexts which these texts mediate. If, as Raymond Williams argues, cultural analysis is concerned with 'the study of the relationship between elements in a whole way of life' (1981: 47), the mechanisms of film texts cannot be isolated from the conditions of their production and consumption in specific historical and geographical contexts. As Graeme Turner argues, 'Film is a social practice for its makers and its audience; in its narratives and meanings we can locate evidence of the ways in which our culture makes sense of itself' (1988: xiv–v). For example, in extract 37, we see how films in specific historical contexts and consumed by historically situated audiences inform the ways in which national cultural identities are made and remade. Likewise, extract 40 examines how cinema negotiates wider transformations in feminine identities.

The extracts in the section aim to give a flavour of some of the key themes and approaches through which cultural studies has contributed to the study of film, and demonstrate how questions generated within cultural studies have frequently expanded the 'object' of film studies. What the extracts share is an interest in how cultural values, meanings and identities are made, negotiated and remade in historically situated power relations. As will become clear, this also involves questioning how particular cultural values have informed the development of film studies itself. By examining 'the social creation of "standards", "values" and "taste" ' (Morris 1997: 43), it becomes possible to examine the processes by which different 'canons' of 'legitimate' cinema have been formed within film studies.

Extract 37, from Iain Chambers's *Border Dialogues*, picks up on some of these themes and illustrates how American popular forms such as cinema have often been seen as a 'threat' to British cultural standards and traditions. In the process, Chambers problematizes the idea of 'national cultures' and 'national cinemas' and their relationship to lived cultural identities and experience. In the 1940s and 1950s, for example, American movies offered British working-class audiences alternative ways of making sense of the world to those offered by a British cinema which frequently reproduced assumptions about the relationships between classes in the UK. Films and their audiences, therefore, are engaged in struggles over what it means to be British. Furthermore, Chambers argues, the modes of mechanical reproduction upon which technologies such as cinema are based also problematizes notions of national identity: whereas mass culture theorists believed that cinema might erode national boundaries by producing a homogeneous mass culture, Chambers suggests that through the consumption of American cinema, British audiences might have forged 'alternative' ways to be British.

However, the extract from Chambers also employs the work of Antonio Gramsci in analysing cinema. Gramsci's work was very influential in the formation of cultural studies, and offers an alternative way of understanding power relations to that proposed by *Screen* theory. Although many critics agreed that people were not simply free to produce their own culture 'outside' of a capitalist system of unequal power relations, they also found that the model of ideological domination proposed by Marxist structuralism offered a rather mechanical model of cultural reproduction, leaving little room to explore change or struggle. Gramsci argued that in order to generate consent to their rule, the ruling groups or power blocs needed to establish and maintain moral and intellectual leadership in a process that Gramsci called 'hegemony'. In Chambers's words, from such a perspective 'the exercise of power becomes a profoundly cultural affair. In the wide ranging and continual struggle over "making sense" as, for example, in cinema, the hegemonic view seeks to install itself as the consensual vision, as what it is "right", as the perspective that makes most sense' (1990: 44). From such a perspective, films can be thought of as proposing a means of 'making sense' in a particular historical context and, in the case that Chambers discusses, sometimes 'foreign' influences – such as the Hollywood films watched in the UK in the 1940s and 1950s – might offer British audiences an 'alternative' way of making sense of their conditions in contrast to the hegemonic cultural tradition in Britain. Such a point of view also suggests that audiences, far from simply taking up a spectating position inscribed in the film text, may be actively involved in negotiating the meaning of film texts.

Extract 38 addresses this issue far more explicitly. In 'Texts, Readers, Subjects', David Morley demonstrates how insights from within media and cultural studies provided the grounds for a critique of *Screen* theory's model of the relationship between text and subject (see Sections Six and Seven). Morley notes how *Screen* theory leads to a position in which the text has a relatively 'fixed' meaning. This means that the audience is conceived of as a passive 'effect' of the mechanisms of the text. Drawing on the work of Volosinov, Morley argues that texts are 'polysemic' or capable of generating a range of meanings. This relates to Volosinov's insights about the 'multi-accentuality' of the sign: if different voices can inflect signs in different ways, they need no longer be thought of as 'fixed' but instead as a site of struggle. Drawing on Hall (1980), Morley also argues that, while texts are organized in such a way as to construct or propose 'preferred' or 'dominant' readings, different audiences may negotiate or reject these readings.

Such a view offers a radically different approach to audiences to that offered by *Screen* theory, which tends to assume that 'the' meaning of a text can be deduced through textual analysis and that this same meaning is passively reproduced in the audiences that consume the text. As Morley argues, *Screen* theorists 'isolate the encounter of text and reader from all social and historical structures and all other texts'. Instead, Morley conceives of audiences as readers of texts not simply as 'the subject of the text' but also as 'social subjects' who have 'a history'. From such a position, 'The meaning(s) of a text will also be constructed differently depending on the discourses (knowledges, prejudices, resistances) *brought to bear on the text by the reader.*' It is important to note here that Morley is not claiming that a text is capable of generating an infinite range of readings, nor is he arguing that readers make individual readings of a text: as 'social subjects', the knowledges, competences and discourses which readers bring to the text will, to some extent, be shaped by the social groups to which they belong.

This position had a radical impact on media studies, but it also threatens to open up a whole new range of questions in film studies and direct critics away from the text as the focus of analysis, instead turning attention to the relationship between texts and audiences. It also suggests more sociological research methods such as ethnography, which are capable of discovering the meanings that audiences bring to their practices. In this way, research into the relationships between texts and audiences brings into play cultural studies' concern with investigating 'particular ways of using "culture", of what is available *as* culture to people inhabiting particular social contexts, and of people's ways of *making* culture' (Morris 1997: 43). This indicates that texts must be located within a wider historical context and in relation to the 'lived culture' of the period.

The readings that audiences produce from film texts does not exhaust the study of the consumption of films and the relationships between text and lived experience. Extract 39 is based on Marie Gillespie's ethnographic research with South Asian families in the UK and examines how both film texts and technologies for viewing films (in particular, the VCR) are appropriated and put to use in specific domestic contexts. Gillespie offers a way of understanding the complex relationships between consumption and 'the production of meaning in everyday life' (Moores 1993: 3). Her work illustrates how different contexts of consumption, in specific historical and geographical contexts, can transform the 'social and cultural uses of viewing experiences'. For example, watching Hindi films in the domestic context in the UK is a 'social ritual' which not only aims to sustain ideas of family through collective consumption but also is used by parents to educate children about 'traditional' values. For these families, new communications technologies are used to found new rituals to respond to the experience of displacement. In this way, films 'are seen by parents as useful agents of cultural continuity and as contributing to the (re)-formation of cultural identity'. Such work is a far cry from the isolated encounter between text and spectator in a darkened cinema presented by *Screen* theory (see Section Six).

However, it would be wrong to equate the impact of cultural and media studies on film studies with simply raising questions about the consumption of films. For example, in extract 40 Charlotte Brunsdon demonstrates how the construction of femininity in *Pretty Woman* is not simply a product of universal psychic processes (see Section VII) but instead a product of profoundly historical transformations in discourses of femininity in the 1970s and 1980s. She analyses the film text in relation to wider historical shifts in femininity to understand how the film, and its reception by critics, can be seen as a site of struggle over the meaning of femininity. Brunsdon also challenges the opposition between the feminist and the feminine 'other woman' which characterizes much feminist film studies by demonstrating how contemporary femininities are, in different ways, informed by feminism.

In Extract 41, Barbara Klinger engages with historical poetics and, in particular, the ideas informing historical reception studies (see Section Five). In many ways Klinger's argument is underpinned by Raymond Williams's work, as she shows how the study of film as culture is the study of the relationships between elements in a whole way of life. She uses these ideas to problematize what is at stake in historical research which aims to resituate films within the historical contexts in which they were produced and consumed. Whereas many critics have attempted to read films in terms of *the* ideology of a particular historical period, Klinger argues that texts are the product of, and must be situated in relation to, multiple discourses and ideologies. Therefore, she argues, texts do not simply reproduce *an* ideology but instead multiple, and often contradictory, ideologies. In this way, she points not only to the 'multi-accentuality' of film texts but also to the complexity of the historical milieu out of which they are formed and in which they are then consumed and reworked.

If there have been relatively few attempts to carry out audience studies of contemporary films, understanding past audiences for past films obviously presents different problems. While reception studies has attempted to reconstruct how viewing positions might be the product of a particular discourse, Klinger argues that this neglects the ways in which, as Morley has pointed out, the viewer is a product of multiple discourses and social locations. Therefore, she argues, it is necessary to provide 'a sense of what the historical prospects were for viewing at a given moment in time by illuminating the meanings made available within that moment.'

In conclusion, it can be seen that cultural studies has attempted to drag film studies away from a concentration on the text to resituate texts within 'a circuit of ... production, circulation and consumption' (Johnson 1986: 284). Nonetheless, it has been argued (in particular, by political economists) that cultural studies has frequently marginalised questions about the economic conditions within which cultural production takes place, and has overemphasized the freedom of the consumer to produce meaning. However, this position tends to underestimate the ways in which many studies of consumption acknowledge 'physical and symbolic "resource constraints" ' (Moores 1993: 140). It can also end up reaffirming the importance of production over the analysis of texts and consumption practices, rather than seeing each of these as integral to an understanding of a 'circuit of culture'.

References

Brunsdon, C. (1997). *Screen Tastes: Soap Operas to Satellite Dishes*. London: Routledge.

Chambers, I. (1990). *Border Dialogues: Journeys in Postmodernity*. London: Routledge.

Gillespie, M. (1989). 'Technology and Tradition: Audio-Visual Culture among South Asian Families in West London'. *Cultural Studies* 3(2): 227–39.

Hall, S. (1980). Encoding/Decoding'. In S. Hall et al. (eds.), *Culture, Media, Language*. London: Unwin Hyman, 128–38.

Johnson, R. (1986). 'The Story So Far: And Further Transformations?' In D. Punter (ed.), *Introduction to Contemporary Cultural Studies*. Harlow: Longman, 277–313.

Klinger, B. (1997). 'Film History Terminable and Interminable: Recovering the Past in Reception Studies'. *Screen* 38:2. 107–29.

Morley, D. (1980). 'Texts, Readers, Subjects'. In S. Hall et al. (eds.), *Culture, Media, Language*. London: Hutchinson Publishing Group, 163–73.

Moores, S. (1993). *Interpreting Audiences: The Ethnography of Media Consumption*. London: Sage.

Morris, M. (1997). 'A Question of Cultural Studies'. In A. McRobbie (ed.), *Back to Reality? Social Experience and Cultural Studies*. Manchester: Manchester University Press, 36–57.

Turner, G. (1988). *Film as Social Practice*. London: Routledge.

Williams, R. (1981). 'The Analysis of Culture'. In T. Bennett, G. Martin, C. Mercer and J. Woollacott (eds.), *Culture, Ideology and Social Process: A Reader*. London: Batsford, 43–52.

37 Gramsci goes to Hollywood

Iain Chambers

Let us look at this idea of a popular, native tradition from another angle. While in the 1930s and 1940s individual British films often encountered substantial success, the wider attempt at creating a 'national cinema' was spectacularly unsuccessful in contesting the overwhelming presence of American films. Successful British actors and actresses in post-war Britain, for example James Mason, Greer Garson, David Niven, Stewart Granger and Jean Simmons invariably went to Hollywood to continue their careers, as did Alfred Hitchcock – frustrated by the limits of the British film industry.

It is also often argued that the Ealing comedies of the late 1940s and early 1950s, by concentrating on everyday popular culture and characters, offered an important contrast to the middle- and upper-class heroes and mores of British cinema and official versions of 'Englishness'. Viewing them today I am tempted to suggest that what they largely offered was a popular view of 'Britishness': the other side of the consensus, the subaltern world and values of the street community, the pub, the Coronation cup, fading sepia photographs on the parlour mantelpiece, the virtues of working and sticking together. It could be argued that this jocular and soft-edged version of lower-and working-class living represented a paternalistic and largely uncontested reproduction of the existing sense of Britain and its 'people'.

In this sense, American films of the period – whether it is the gangster or the private eye film set in the naked city, images of independent women taking control of their lives, the symbolic violence of the Western, the surrealist fantasy of the musical, or the fear generated by the novelty and uncertainty over modern technology in science fiction films, or just simply individuals taking their chances in the modern world – offered far more daring visions. The willingness of such films, particularly in the 1940s and 1950s, to deal with the more complex and problematic world of crime, corruption, passions and violence suggests that their popularity also had something to do with them being more adequate vehicles for contemporary emotions and expression than the insular universe of British cinema. They promised a more 'open' world which was simultaneously richer and more 'real', for in it you can certainly be defeated, be destroyed, and discover that modern life is indeed corrupt, but you can simultaneously discover yourself to be less oppressed and restricted by your immediate culture and circumstances.

That 'America' became a favourite metaphor among British intellectuals for all that was wrong in the modern world clearly had much to do with the primacy of the United States in the world economy and a subsequent sense of bitterness on the part of British commentators in registering this particular loss of native power. But the real change lay elsewhere, although it was hardly appreciated at the time. It was the dramatically altered reality of cultural production itself in the epoch of mechanical (soon to become electronic) reproduction that was destined, through photography, recorded music, cinema and television, to set the terms for a common language that would constitute what today can be considered as a revolution in perception, æsthetics, meaning and culture.[1]

Against the then prevalent idea of the unilateral growth of a monoculture under the homogenizing impact of the mass media we can today recognize how earlier forms, identities and languages return in different fragments, memories and traces to take up residence in the discontinuous present and there open it up to further possi-bilities. In this manner, uncertain and ambiguous dialogues with locally-placed but increasingly globally connected futures are kept open, leading to a corresponding shift in cultural emphasis and sense. It was the American economy that initially dominated this transformation, but inside a set of languages provided by the mass media and increasingly experienced in 'our common inheritance – where the wide world impinges whether you wish it or not', other traces, accents and dialects would find voice and the opportunity to transmit it across this shared network.[2]

What would eventually lead to the extensive remaking of the very sense and possibilities of 'culture' was, however, largely obscured in the native rush to defend local 'traditions' from 'Americanization', foreign invasion and alien change. In this conservationist mood, where it was intellectuals who defined and prescribed what was 'right' for the 'people', there can be discerned both the confident Arnoldian sense of cultural authority and, in its parochialism, a profound refusal of modernism which ultimately ignored its wider and democratic potential. With this I do not want to suggest that the post-war popular culture of the United States was inherently more democratic, but, against the narrow traditions and austere institutions of British life, it certainly represented a more extensive and imaginative sense of the possible.

There were, of course, changes going on inside British culture in this period. Internal dissent was manifest in the new realism of the 'angry young men' and their rebellious 'kitchen sink dramas', together with a spate of working-class novels and their transformation into film: *The Loneliness of the Long Distance Runner; Saturday Night and Sunday Morning; Billy Liar; This Sporting Life*. But this 'new realism', and its gritty language of native, male revolt, only offered, in its often misogynist rebellion against domesticity, the other, sullen and subaltern, side of a tradition, rarely a way of breaking its mould. While it proposed a series of decidedly un-showbiz faces in Albert Finney, Tom Courtney and Richard Harris, the possi-bility of radically different cultural perspectives and possibilities continued to come from outside Britain.

Here we could compare two films: *The Wild One*, an American film on Californian motorbike gangs starring Marlon Brando that was released in 1953 but initially banned in Britain, and the local version of male rebellion, *Saturday Night and Sunday Morning* that appeared eight years later. The latter is an evocative rendi-tion of working-class life, rebellion and culture, steeped in Hoggartian detail. Its pace, handling of character, language and narrative devices, constitute a 'good film'. *The Wild One*, by contrast, is thin, its acting almost hammy, the story virtually non-existent, the drama predictable. Yet if *Saturday Night and Sunday Morning* with its careful recreation of time place and custom is a 'good film', *The Wild One* belongs to the world of myth: like the motorbike riders who come and go to 'nowhere', it has the power to symbolize everywhere, *an atopia*, a contemporary opening and chance. While *Saturday Night and Sunday Morning* is a text whose richness and detail confirms a native way of life, *The Wild One* suggests another, largely unknown one.

This is a sharp verdict, and the story, with all of its particular pleasures and possibilities of course, does not conclude here. To justify it we perhaps need to remind ourselves, given the prominent role it has played in recent British Marxism and cultural analyses, of the link between cultural hegemony and common sense developed more than half a century ago ago by the Italian Marxist Antonio Gramsci in his *Quaderni del Carcere*.[3] Of particular relevance here are Gramsci's notes on 'popular literature' and 'Americanism and Fordism'. In both he castigates native intellectuals for failing to establish a dialogue with the popular mass culture of the day. In the second set of notes he identifies in the 'intellectual' and 'moral' resistance to 'Americanism' the defensive refusal of a 'possible new order' represented by the emerging forms of American industrial production and its mass culture. Untroubled by 'tradition', 'Americanism' threatened to sweep away the passive and sedimented character of European 'tradition' and 'civilization'.

For Gramsci, the question was not so much whether there existed in America a new civilization or culture that was now invading Europe, but that the weight of the American economy and its methods of production were destined to shift 'the antiquated social-economic axes' of the old world and transform the material bases of European culture. Sooner or later, and pretty soon in Gramsci's own estimate, this would lead 'to the forced birth of a new civilization'. It is therefore perhaps worth while underlining that the oft-quoted Gramscian concept of the 'national-popular', and its project for a radical and political sense of culture did not exclude commercial or American inspired forms.

To this remarkably open reading of 'Americanization' there is to be added the well-known Gramscian elaboration of 'hegemony'. With the concept of *egemonia* the simple idea of the direct ideological domination and manipulation of subaltern social forces by a ruling class is replaced with the proposition that ideological domination – the everyday acceptance of the world and its existing relations of power and social relations – is not imposed from 'above', but established across the shifting fields of relations that constitute a shared 'consensus'. This consensus has to be continually constructed and produced inside the different fields of public representation and social life; it involves not merely political but also 'intellectual and moral leadership'. In other words, the exercise of power becomes a decentred and profoundly cultural affair. In the wide ranging and continual struggle over 'making sense' as, for example, in cinema, the hegemonic view seeks to install itself as the consensual vision, as what is 'right', as the perspective that most makes sense. It seeks to be accepted as 'common sense'. Clearly a regard for 'tradition', which is, above all, a cultural construction, where what is 'right' and 'makes sense' is preserved in historical memory and identified with the fate of the community, with a social group or class, and, ultimately with the nation, has much to do with the formation of a native 'common sense' and a historical cultural bloc.

In Gramsci's elaboration we can perhaps appreciate how, even in their languages of dissent, popular forms that look to tradition for their 'authority over perceptions of reality' can unconsciously participate in the complex reproduction of a cultural conservatism, the status quo and a particular hegemony.[4] It is in such contexts, that 'foreign' influences, as Gramsci himself pointed out, can provide a radical alternative.[5] In Britain by the 1950s, 'America' and all it seemingly stood for – consumerism, modernism, youth, the 'new', the refusal of tradition – could, and did, represent a more significant challenge to a native cultural hegemony than more local forms of opposition based on more traditional affiliations. [...]

Notes

1 The momentous cultural impact of 'mechanical reproduction' on our overall sense of the modern world had, of course, been established by Walter Benjamin in 1936 in his famous essay, 'The work of art in the age of mechanical reproduction'. Many of us are still exploring the implications of what Benjamin said and suggested there.
2 The quote on our common inheritance comes from Graham Swift, *Waterland* (London: Picador, 1984), p. 16.
3 A. Gramsci, *Prison Notebooks* (London: Lawrence & Wishart, 1971). *Quaderni del Carcere* (Turin: Einaudi, 1975), pp. 2139–81.
4 The quote comes from Zygmunt Bauman's reflections on the nature and effects of historical memory in the first chapter of his *Memories of Class* (London: Routledge & Kegan Paul, 1982).
5 Gramsci's own example was that of the popularity of foreign authors in popular reading habits in Italy. He suggested that this reflected the absence of Italian intellectuals from the formation of an Italian national popular culture; they had failed to respond, to be 'organic', to such popular tastes.

---

38 Texts, readers, subjects

David Morley

One major problem with the dominant theoretical position advanced by *Screen* is that it operates with what Neale has characterized as an 'abstract text-subject relationship'.[1] The subject is not conceived as already constituted in other discursive formations and social relations. Also, it is treated in relation to only one text at a time (or, alternatively, all texts are assumed to function according to the rules of a single 'classic realist text'). This is then explicated by reference to the universal, primary psychoanalytic processes (Oedipus complex, 'mirror phase', castration complex and its resolution and so on), through which, according to Lacan's reading of Freud, 'the subject' is constituted. The text is understood as reproducing or replaying this primary positioning, which is the foundation of any reading.

Now, apart from the difficulty of trying to explain a specific instance of the text/reader relationship in terms of a universalist theory of the formation of subjects-in-general, this proposition also serves to isolate the encounter of text and reader from all social and historical structures *and* from other texts. To conceptualize the moment of reading/viewing in this way is to ignore the constant intervention of other texts and discourses, which *also* position 'the subject'. At the moment of textual encounter other discourses are always in play besides those of the particular text in focus – discourses which depend on other discursive formations, brought into play through 'the subject's' placing in other practices – cultural, educational, institutional. And these other discourses will set some of the terms in which any particular text is engaged and evaluated. 'Screen theory' may be assumed to justify its neglect of the interplay of other discourses on the text/reader encounter by virtue of its assumption that all texts depend on the same set of subject positions, constituted in the formation of the subject, and therefore that they need be accorded no other distinctive effectivity of their own. Here, however, we wish to put in question this assumption that all specific discursive effects can be reduced to, and explained by, the functioning of a single, universal set of psychic mechanisms.

Pêcheux has provided us with the useful and important concept of *interdiscourse*.[2] As explicated by Woods, he argues that:

> The constitution of subjects is always specific in respect of each subject ... and this can be conceived of in terms of a single, original (and mythic) interpellation – the entry into language and the symbolic – which constitutes a *space* wherein a complex of continually interpellated subject forms interrelate, each subject form being a determinate formation of discursive processes. *The discursive subject is therefore an interdiscourse, the product of the effects of discursive practices traversing the subject throughout its history.* [...]

The concept of contradictory interpellations can be employed to clarify and modify the sociological approach of Parkin and others,[3] who refer to workers who grant legitimacy to a 'dominant ideology' in the abstract but inhabit a 'negotiated' or 'situationally defined' ideology at the level of concrete practice. That is, it can be used to clarify the problem of contradictory ideological positions, and specifically forms of corporate or sectional class-consciousness, without recourse to the premises of 'false consciousness'. Parkin refers to this evidence as showing 'split levels of consciousness'. However, if we introduce the concept of interpellation, we get rid of the presumption that there is a prescribed, unitary, homogeneous form of class-consciousness. This allows us to specify the articulation of different, contradictory subject positions or interpellations, to which the same individual worker (a contradictory subject, traversed by different discursive practices) is 'hailed': for example, he/she can be interpellated as 'national subject' by the television discourses of the dominant news media, but as 'class/sectional' subject by the discourses of his/her trade union organization or co-workers. In this approach the relative dominance of these contradictory interpellations and the political practices with which they are articulated are not given elsewhere (for instance, at the level of the formation of the subject) but vary with the conjuncture in which the subject is interpellated. [...]

By 'interdiscourse' Pêcheux appears to mean the complex of discursive formations in any society which provide already available subject positions (the 'preconstructed') as a necessary category of their functioning. It is clear that the concept of inter-discourse transforms the relation of one text/one subject to that of a multiplicity of texts/subjects relations, in which encounters can be understood not in isolation but only in the moments of their combination.

A further consideration, not taken into account in 'screen theory', is that subjects have histories. If it is correct to speak not of text/subject but of texts/subjects relations with reference to the present, it must also be the case that past interpellations affect present ones. While these traditional and institutionalized 'traces' (to use Gramsci's term) cannot in themselves determine present interpellations, they do constitute the well established elements of the interdiscourse and frame successive new encounters. [...]

Since 'screen theory' does not make any distinction between how the subject is constituted as a 'space' and specific interpellations, it deduces 'subjects' from the subject positions offered by the text and identifies the two. Thus the 'classic realist text' recapitulates, in its particular discursive strategies, the positions in which the subject has been constituted by the 'primary' processes. There is a fixed identity and perfect reciprocity between these two structures, which in 'screen theory' are, in effect, one and the same structure. The 'realist text' is therefore not so much 'read' as simply 'consumed/appropriated' straight, via the only possible positions available to the reader – those reinscribed by the text. This forecloses the question of reading as itself a moment in the production of meaning. In the 'screen theory' account this moment is doubly determined – by the primary subject positions which inscribe the subject in a relation of empiricist to knowledge/language and by those positions as they are reinscribed in the text through the strategies of realism.[4] Since these are posed as very general mechanisms, 'screen theory' is not required to address either the possibility of different, historically specific 'realisms' or the possibility of an inscribed realist reading being refused.[5] Readers here appear merely as the bearers or puppets of their unconscious positionings, reduplicated in the structure of the realist discourse (singular). But this runs counter to two of the most important advances previously established by structural linguistics: the essentially polysemic nature of signs and sign-based discourses, and the interrogative/expansive nature of all readings. In many ways 'screen theory', which insists on the 'productivity of the text', undermines that concept by defining the 'realist text' as a mere replay of positions established elsewhere.

In contradiction to this argument, we would still want to retain some of the ideas expressed through the concept of 'preferred readings'. This suggests that a text of the dominant discourse *does* privilege or prefer a certain reading. We might now expand this to say that such texts privilege a certain reading in part by inscribing certain preferred discursive positions from which its discourse appears 'natural', transparently aligned to 'the real' and credible. However, this cannot be the *only* reading inscribed in the text, and it certainly cannot be the only reading which different readers can make of it. The theory of the polysemic nature of discourse must hold to the possibility of establishing an articulation between the 'encoding' and 'decoding' circuits, but it should not adopt a position of a 'necessary correspon-dence' or identity between them. Vološinov[6] insists that it is the 'multi-accentuality of the sign' which makes it possible for discourse to become an 'arena of struggle'. What we may call the 'reality effect' is not the product of the required reduplication of the empiricist subject in the discourse of realism but the effect of an achieved alignment between subjects and texts which the discourse itself accomplishes. 'The ruling class tries to impart a supraclass, eternal character to the ideological sign, to extinguish or drive inward the struggle between social value judgements which occurs in it, to make the sign uniaccentual.'[7]

Even in the case of the 'classic realist text', the subject positions inscribed by the text, as a condition of its intelligibility, may be inhabited differently by subjects who, in the past (as the result of interpellations by other texts/discourses/institutions) or in the present, are already positioned in an interdiscursive space. It does not follow that because the reader has 'taken the position' most fully inscribed in the text, sufficient for the text to be intelligible, he/she will, for that reason alone, subscribe to the ideological problematic of that text. The text may be contradicted by the subject's position(s) in relation to other texts, problematics, institutions, discursive formations. This means that we must establish a distinction between inhabiting inscribed subject positions, adopting an ideological problematic and making a dominant reading of a text. We cannot, then, assume that one text inscribes a required subject, but only that specific text/subject relations will depend, in part, on the subject positions given by a multiplicity of texts that produce (and have produced) contradictory 'subjectivities' which then act on and against each other within 'the space of the subject'. [...]

'Screen theory' constantly elides the concrete individual; his/her constitution as a 'subject-for-discourse', and the discursive subject positions constituted by specific discursive practices and operations. These need to be kept analytically distinct, otherwise we will fail to understand the relation subjects/texts within the terms of a 'no necessary correspondence'. Of course, specific combinations – for example, between specific problematics and specific modes of address – may exist historically as well secured, dominant or recurring patterns in particular conjunctures in definite social formations. These may be fixed in place by the institutionalization of practices within a particular site or apparatus (for example, Hollywood cinema). Nevertheless, even these correspondences are not 'eternal' or universal. They have been secured. One can point to the practices and mechanisms which secure them and which reproduce them, in place, in one text after another. Unless one is to accept that there is no ideology but the dominant ideology, which is always in its appointed place, this 'naturalized' correspondence must constantly be deconstructed and shown to be a historically concrete relation. It follows from this argument that there must be different 'realisms', not a single 'classic realist text' to which all realist texts can be assimilated. And there is no *necessary* correspondence between these realisms and a particular ideological problematic.

Individuals, subjects, 'subjects'

In an important contribution Paul Willemen has identified an unjustified conflation, in a great deal of 'screen theory', between the *subject of the text* and the *social subject*. He argues:

> There remains an *unbridgeable gap between 'real' readers/authors and 'inscribed' ones, constructed and marked in and by the text*. Real readers are subjects in history, living in social formations, rather than mere subjects of a single text. The two types of subject are not commensurate. But for the purposes of formalism, real readers are supposed to coincide with the constructed readers.[8]

Hardy, Johnston and Willemen also mark the distinction between the 'inscribed reader of the text' and the 'social subject who is invited to take up this position'.[9] More recently Christine Gledhill has opened up this question of the psychoanalytic and the historical 'subject';[10] in response Claire Johnston, who retains a firm base in the psychoanalytic framework, has also called for

> a move away from a notion of the text as an autonomous object of study and towards the more complex question of subjectivity seen in historical/social terms. Feminist film practice can no longer be seen simply in terms of the effectivity of a system of representation, but rather as a production of and by subjects already in social practices, which always involve heterogeneous and often contradictory positions in ideologies.[11]

In their earlier paper Hardy, Johnston and Willemen proposed a model of 'interlocking' subjectivities', caught up in a network of symbolic systems, in which the social subject

> always exceeds the subject implied by the text because he/she is also placed by a heterogeneity of other cultural systems and is never coextensive with the subject placed by a single fragment (i.e. one film) of the overall cultural text.[12]

The subjects implied/implicated by the text are thus always already subject within different social practices in determinate social formations – not simply subjects in 'the symbolic' in general. They are constituted by specific, historical forms of sociality:

> this subject, at its most abstract and impersonal, is itself in history: the discourses ... determining the terms of its play, change according to the relations of force of competing discourses intersecting in the plane of the subject in history, the individual's location in ideology at a particular moment and place in the social formation.[13]

[...] the meaning produced by the encounter of text and subject cannot be read off straight from its 'textual characteristics' or its discursive strategies. We also need to take into account what Neale describes as 'the use to which a particular text is put, its function within a particular conjuncture, in particular institutional spaces, and in relation to particular audiences'.[14] A text should, also, not be considered in isolation from the historical conditions of its production and consumption – its insertion into a context of discourses in struggle, in discursive formations cohering into different strands of ideology and establishing new condensations between them; also its position in the field of articulation secured between the discursive and economic/political practices. Both the text and the subject are constituted in the space of the interdiscursive; and both are traversed and intersected by contradictory discourses – contradictions which arise not only from the subject positions which these different discourses propose, but also from the conjuncture and institutional sites in which they are articulated and transformed.

The meaning(s) of a text will also be constructed differently depending on the discourses (knowledges, prejudices, resistances) *brought to bear on the text by the reader*. One crucial factor delimiting this will be the repertoire of discourses at the disposal of different audiences. Willemen notes that

> individuals do have different relations to sets of discourses, in that their position in the social formation, their positioning in the real, will determine which sets of discourses a given subject is likely to encounter and in what ways it will do so.[15]

Willemen here returns to the agenda – but now from a position within 'the discursive' – a set of questions about the relations between the social position of 'the reader' and discursive formations. These questions, in a more 'sociological' form, were at the centre of Bernstein's early work and that of Bourdieu and Baudelot and Establet.[16] Their disappearance from the discussion is, no doubt, attributable to that general critique of 'sociological approaches' common in 'screen theory'. Though basically correct, this has sometimes been taken to extreme lengths, where the mere ascription of the qualifier 'sociological' is enough to consign a text so stigmatized to the scrap-heap of theory.[17] Bernstein did invite criticisms by the overly deterministic way in which the relation between class and language was posed in his early work. The position was extensively criticized, and there has been some modification on his part since then.[18] The terms of the argument can be extensively faulted. But the questions addressed are not without their 'rational core'. Willemen argues that 'the real determines to a large extent the encounter of/with discourses'.[19] Neale observes that 'audiences are determined economically, politically and ideologically'.[20] The basic problem with the sociological formulations is that they presumed a too simple, one-to-one correspondence between social structure and discourse: they treated language as ascribed by and inscribed in class position. Thus, as Ellis remarked, 'it is assumed that the census of employment category carries with it both political and ideological reflections'.[21] This position cannot be defended or sustained. It is based on a too simple notion of how classes are constituted, and on the ascription of fixed ideologies to whole classes. There is no conception of signifying practices, their relative autonomy and specific effects.

The weaknesses in the position need not be elaborated at length. Class is not a unitary category with effective determination at the level of the economic only. There is no simple alignment between the economic, the political and the ideological in the constitution of classes. Classes do not have fixed, ascribed or unitary world views. In Poulantzas's phrase, they do not carry their world views around like number plates on their backs.[22] Laclau argues that even 'ideological elements, taken in isolation, have no necessary class connotation and this connotation is only the result of the articulation of those elements in a concrete ideological discourse'[23] and the articulation of these discourses with class practices in specific conjectures.

Much the same problems beset Parkin's formulations, which on other grounds were highly suggestive.[24] Parkin's dominant, negotiated and oppositional 'meaning systems' provided a useful point of departure for early work on 'decoding'.[25] But his framework, too, can be faulted on the grounds outlined above. Simply, he proposed that a given section of the audience 'either shares, partly shares or does not share the dominant code in which messages are transmitted'. He related these fairly unproblematically to class position, defined in a sociological manner. This formulation was useful in the preliminary work of establishing, in a hypothetical-deductive manner, the presence of different and variable 'decoding' positions. (These, of course, then required further refinement and concrete exemplification.) Now the definition of a range of possible 'decoding' positions is *not* undermined by the objections advanced earlier. What *is* undermined is the simple ascription of these positions to classes as such or, alternatively, the deduction of them from socio-economic positions in some *prior* manner. Parkin did himself identify the category of 'negotiated code', the amplification of which has potentially fruitful uses in the analysis of sectional or corporate class-consciousness. He also identified the possibility of 'contradictory' meaning systems. But he did not take this finding, which undermined the ascriptive nature of his basic framework, far enough. In fact, there are no simple meaning systems but a multiplicity of discourses at play in a social formation. These discourses have varied sources of origin – they cannot be attributed to classes as such. There is no unproblematic link between classes and meaning systems. Different discursive positions need to be analysed in terms of their linguistic and discursive characteristics and effects.

However, the essentialism and class-reductionism which tends to characterize this position has generally been countered by its simple opposite or inversion: the premise, in essence, of an absolute autonomy, and the assumption that any relationship between discursive formations and class formations must be, by definition, 'reductionist'. This is not acceptable either. The problem can only be resolved if we are able to think through the full implications of two apparently contradictory propositions: first, discourses cannot be explained by or reduced to classes, defined exclusively at the level of the economic; second, nevertheless, 'audiences *are* determined economically, politically and ideologically'. The first proposition suggests that classes, understood economically, will not always be found 'in place' in their proper discursive position. The second proposition, however, insists that the economic and political constitution of classes will have some real effectivity for the distribution of discourses to groups of agents. (We deal here exclusively with the question of the reduction of discourses to classes. But it must be remembered that other structures and relations – for example, those of gender and patriarchal relations, which are not reducible to economic class – will also have a structuring effect on the distribution of discourses.)

In short, the relation classes/meaning systems has to be fundamentally reworked by taking into account the full effectivity of the discourse level. Discursive formations intervene between 'classes' and 'languages'. They intervene in such a way as to prevent or forestall any attempt to read the level of the operation of language back in any simple or reductive way to economic classes. Thus we cannot deduce which discursive frameworks will be mobilized in particular reader/text encounters from the level of the socio-economic position of the 'readers'. But position in the social structure may be seen to have a structuring and limiting effect on the *repertoire* of discursive or 'decoding' strategies available to different sectors of an audience. They will have an effect on the pattern of the distribution of discursive repertoires. What is more, the key elements of the social structure which delimit the range of competences in particular audiences may not be referable in any exclusive way to 'class' understood in the economic sense. The key sites for the distribution of discursive sets and competences are probably – following some of the leads of Bernstein and Bourdieu – the family and the school – or, as Althusser (following Gramsci) argued, the *family–school couplet*.[26] This is the key institutional site or articulation for the distribution of 'cultural capital', in Bourdieu's terms. Other formations – for example, gender and immediate social context or cultural milieu – may also have a formative and structuring effect, not only on which specific discourses will be in play in any specific text/reader encounter, but also in defining *the range and the repertoire of performance codes*. The distribution of the discourses of the media and other cultural apparatuses will also have a structuring effect on the differentiated discursive competences of socially structured audiences.

This proposition now requires to be elaborated at a more concrete level. But the direction in which further work must proceed is already clear. In effect, what is required is to work through more fully the consequences of the argument that the discourses mobilized by 'readers' in relation to any 'text' cannot be treated as the effect of a direct relation between 'discourses' and 'the real'. It must be analysed, instead, in terms of the effects of social relations and structures (the extra-discursive) on the structuring of *the discursive space* – that is, of the 'inter-discourse'. These structured relations cannot produce 'a reading' (and no other) in any specific instance. But they do exercise a limit on (that is, they 'determine') the formation of the discursive space, which in turn has a determinate effect on the practice of readings at the level of particular text-reader encounters. This approach undermines any notion of the automatic or 'unquestioned performance of the subject by the text' – an approach which merely replaces a sociological determinism by a textual one. It provides the theoretical space in which the subject may be placed in some relation to the signifying chain other than that of a 'regulated process'.

Notes

1   Steve Neale, 'Propaganda', in *Screen*, vol. **18** no. 3 (Autumn 1977).
2   M. Pêcheux, *Analyse Automatique du Discours* (Paris: Dunod 1969) and *Les Vérités de la Palice* (Paris: Maspero 1975). Cf. Roger Woods, 'Discourse analysis: the work of Marcel Pêcheux', in *Ideology and Consciousness*, no. **22** (Autumn 1977).
3   Frank Parkin, *Class Inequality and Political Order* (Macgibbon and Kee 1971).
4   See, for example, Colin McCabe, 'Realism and the cinema', in *Screen*, vol. **15**, no. 2 (Summer 1974), and 'Realism and pleasure', in *Screen*, vol. **17**, no. 3 (Autumn 1976).
5   For critiques or variants of the dominant *Screen* position on 'realism' see, *inter alia*, Christine Gledhill, 'Whose choice?', in *Screen Education*, vol. **24** (Autumn 1977); Tony Stevens, 'Reading the realist film', in *Screen Education*, vol. **26** (Spring 1978); and Dick Hebdige and Geoff Hurd, 'Reading and realism', in *Screen Education*, vol. **28** (Autumn 1978).
6   V.N. Vološinov, *Marxism and the Philosophy of Language* (New York: The Seminar Press 1973).
7   *ibid.*, p. 23.
8   Paul Willemen, 'Subjectivity under siege', in *Screen*, vol. **19**, no. 1 (Spring 1978), p. 48.
9   P. Hardy, C. Johnston and P. Willemen, in papers from the Edinburgh Television Event, *Edinburgh 1976* (British Film Institute 1976).
10 Christine Gledhill, 'Recent developments in film criticism', in *Quarterly Review of Film Studies*, vol. **3**, no. 4 (Fall 1978).
11 Claire Johnston, 'The subject of feminist film: theory/practice', in *Edinburgh Television Papers* (1979).
12 Hardy, Johnston, Willemen, in *Edinburgh 1976*.
13 Willemen, 'Subjectivity under siege', pp. 63–4.
14 Neale, 'Propaganda', pp. 39–40.
15 Willemen, 'Subjectivity under siege', pp. 66–7.

16 Basil Bernstein, *Class, Codes and Control* (Paladin 1973); Pierre Bourdieu and J.C. Passerson, *Reproduction* (Sage 1977); C. Baudelot and R. Establet, *L'ecole Capitaliste en France* (Paris: Maspero 1971). For an elaboration of this connection, see David Morley, 'Reconceptualizing the media audience', CCCS Stencilled Paper no. 9.

17 See the way this charge is levelled in Ros Coward's 'Class, culture and the social formation', in *Screen*, vol. **18**, no. 1 (Spring 1977). See also the reply, I. Chambers, J. Clarke, I. Connell, L. Curti, S. Hall and T. Jefferson in *Screen*, vol. **18**, no. 4 (Winter 1977/8).

18 For a critique, see Rosen, *Language and Class* (Bristol: Falling Wall Press 1972). For some Bernstein reformulations, see the 1973 'Postscript' to *Class, Codes and Control*, vol. 1; and his 'Classification and framing of educational knowledge'.

19 Willemen, 'Subjectivity under siege'.

20 Neale, 'Propaganda'.

21 John Ellis, 'The institution of the cinema', *Edinburgh Magazine* (1977).

22 Nicos Poulantzas, *Political Power and Social Classes* (Sheed and Ward, New Left Books 1971).

23 Laclau, *Politics and Ideology in Marxist Theory* (New Left Books 1977).

24 Parkin, *Class Inequality and Political Order*.

25 See S. Hall, 'Encoding/decoding', pp. 128–38 above; and Morley, 'Reconceptualizing the media audience'.

26 Louis Althusser, 'Ideology and Ideological State Apparatuses', in *Lenin and Philosophy and Other Essays* (New Left Books 1971).

39 Technology and tradition: audio-visual culture among South Asian families in West London

Marie Gillespie

This ethnographic account is based on research among south Asian families in Southall, Middlesex.[1] Southall is a 'town', formerly an autonomous London borough, with a population of some 65,000. Its demographic majority is of south Asian origin, predominantly of Sikh religion, but divided along cross-cutting cleavages of national, regional, religious, and caste heritage.

The study evolved over seven years of teaching in two Southall high schools where the popularity of 'Indian' films was evident; and yet various manifestations of resistance to its pleasures seemed to signify a great deal more than mere expressions of taste or preference.

The extensive use of the VCR at home to view 'Indian'[2] films represents a powerful means for grandparents and parents to maintain links with their country of origin. Second-generation children, however, born and educated in Britain, position themselves and are positioned rather differently in relation to notions of 'Asian' and 'British' culture. The legitimation of state racism in postwar Britain has been secured in an important way around particular ideological constructions of south Asian cultures, especially their marriage and family systems. For long, these have been seen to be based on archaic and traditional customs and practices and are presented as an 'alien threat' to the 'British way of life'. But in much of the literature produced by the 'Race Relations Industry' it is 'culture-clash' and inter-generational conflict, low self-esteem and negative self-image, rather than racism, that, paradoxically, have been identified as both 'the problem' and 'the cause'.[3]

Such dominant assumptions went unchallenged as young Asian voices were usually excluded or marginalized from debates which concerned them. This paper therefore is an attempt to re-present 'their voices', concentrating on their interpretations of popular Indian films and the themes and issues arising from their viewing experiences and which they find salient.

The ethnographic data are based on interviews carried out with young people predominantly of Panjabi origin and aged 15–18. A set of basic questions was used to spark off each interview. When do you watch? What do you watch? With whom do you watch? Who chooses what you watch in which situations? The wide range of methodological issues which the study raises will not be dealt with here [...]

Indian cinema in Southall: from public pleasure to private leisure

The first 'Indian' films were shown in Southall in 1953 in hired halls and then in three local cinemas. During the 1960s and 1970s the cinema provided the principal weekend leisure activity in Southall and represented an occasion for families and friends to get together; the social event of the week.

In 1978, when VCRs came on the market, many families were quick to seize the opportunity to extend their choice and control over viewing in the home. Many Asian communities obtained them as early as 1978/9 before most other households in Britain. It is now estimated that between 40 and 50 per cent of households in Britain now own or rent a VCR but in Southall the figure is held to be 80 per cent.[4]

Most shops rent popular Hindi (also known as 'Bombay') films and although films in Panjabi and Urdu are also obtainable from shops they lack the broad-based appeal of the popular Hindi movie. In fact the Bombay film has gained something of a cultural hegemony in south Asia and among many 'Asian' settlers across the world. To understand this one has to look to the specific evolution of the popular Hindi genre which, in order to appeal to a mass audience, had to produce films which would cross the linguistic, religious, and regional differences that exist within India, as indeed within Southall.

Many of the films combine a catholicity or universality of appeal with a careful handling of regional and religious differences. A distinctive form of Bombay Hindi, characterized by a certain 'linguistic openness' has evolved which makes most films accessible also to speakers of other south Asian languages. The distinctive visual style, often foregrounded over dialogue, combines with successive modes of spectacle, action and emotion which facilitates cross-cultural understanding.[5] In the light of this we can understand the huge uptake of Hindi films on cassette among the diverse linguistic groups in Southall.

With the arrival of video, the adventure, romance, and drama of the Bombay film was to be enjoyed in domestic privacy. A small piece of home technology brought the cinema hall into the home, or so it appeared. A lot was gained but much was lost.

The weekly outing became a thing of the past as the cinemas closed and the big screen image shrunk into the TV box and entered the flow of everyday life in the living room.

In Southall the rapid expansion of the home video market needs to be considered not only as providing an extension to an already important and dynamic film culture but also very much a response on the part of a black community to life in Britain. Southall, like many other black communities, has come into existence in the first instance as a result of racist immigration and housing policies. Such communities have developed as 'sanctuaries' against the racism they experience.[6] The exclusion and marginalization of many people in Southall from mainstream British society, coupled with the failure to provide adequate leisure/culture facilities, has (like among the *Gastarbeiter* (guest worker) Turkish community in West Germany) contributed to the development of an important home video culture.

But the consequences of a decade of video use are perceived in contradictory ways by the youth of Southall. Many young people feel that the VCR has served further to isolate the community from mainstream British society. It is also seen to have specific effects on the lives of women: 'The video has isolated the community even more. They might as well be in India, especially the women.' Others see it as a liberating pleasure, especially for females: 'Some girls can't get out of the house that much so they can get a film and keep themselves occupied within the four walls of the house. It's an advantage for them.'

Such contradictory evaluations need to be seen in the contexts in which they originate.

Domestic viewing contexts

During the course of the study it became possible to construct a broad typology of contexts and associated texts. For the purpose of this account I shall concentrate on weekend family viewing because this situation was so frequently and consistently discussed by all interviewees, and due to the importance given to it within this cultural context.[7]

The VCR is used predominantly at the weekend in most families. Viewing 'Indian' films on video is the principal, regular family leisure activity. Weekend family gatherings around the TV set is a social ritual repeated in many families. The VCR and TV screen become the focus and locus of interaction. Notions of togetherness and communality are stressed: 'It's probably the only time in the week that we are all together so when we're watching a film at least we're all together.'

This togetherness is by no means that of passive viewers: 'No one is silent, we're all talking through the film about what's happening here and there and generally having a chat ... it sort of brings you closer together.'

The weaving of conversation through the narrative is facilitated by an impressive familiarity with films brought about by repeated viewings. The episodic structure of films which moves the spectator through the different modes of spectacle, song and dance, drama, action, and affect also provides natural breaks for talk, emotion and reflection.

With such large family gatherings the question of power and control over viewing becomes important. The interviews highlight the way in which parents actively set and maintain viewing rules which govern viewing patterns and modes of parent-child interaction.

While the father is usually seen to determine when children are allowed access to the screen by his absence or presence in the home, the mother is perceived as exercising a greater degree of power and control over the choice of what is watched. This was a significant pattern across the interviews, emphasizing the important role mothers play in socializing their children in the domestic context. It also makes clear that the relationship between family power structures and family viewing patterns is not one of simple correspondence.

There are also clear differences in the attentiveness and in the degree of salience of Indian films to various family members, which are obscured by the simple observation that the family all watched the same programme.[8] Many young people say they sit with parents and view parts of the films just to please them or that their parents encourage or even 'force' them to watch.

As gender differences are important to understand parental control over viewing they are also a significant factor in understanding young people's viewing preferences and behaviour. Boys tend to experience greater freedom in deciding how they use their leisure time and spend more time engaged in activities outside the home. In contrast, girls are usually socialized to remain within the domestic realm and often participate in strong and supportive female cultures in the home where the viewing of Indian films on video frequently plays an important role. This explains to some extent the generally greater engagement with popular Hindi videos on the part of most girls interviewed. In one interview two boys rather begrudgingly claim: 'It doesn't hurt to watch an Indian film with the parents.' 'No, it kills you.'

In spite of this repeatedly expressed reluctance the way in which the screen can serve social interaction in the family tends to override individual preferences and return young people to the family situation. One boy commented to the general agreement of the group: 'Well we don't usually stay in another room while they're watching, if you've got something to yourself, you isolate yourself don't you?' It is clear that what might be seen on the one hand as 'enforced' or 'reluctant' viewing can take on pleasurable connotations where the emphasis is on 'being together'. Parents do not have much time for leisure due to long working hours and shift work, so the time when the family is together around the TV set is often much appreciated by all concerned.

Conversely, the family audience is frequently fragmented by English and American films: 'When it's Indian films it's all of us together but when it's English films it's just me and my brother.' This fragmentation is partly due to the texts of English and American films themselves. Given parental reservations about the language, sensuality, and references to sexuality, young people may often prefer to view them on their own to escape parental censure or vigilance.

You may now have the impression that the avid consumption of VCR films falls into two neat categories. While Hindi films tend to be viewed in large family gatherings and to be celebrated by intense social interaction, British and American films tend to be consumed on their own in a more or less assertive circumvention of parental control and preferences. While viewing patterns tend indeed to correspond to this dichotomy, young people's viewing of Hindi films raises further ethnographic questions about perceptions of 'Indianness' and Britain or India and 'Britishness'. (...)

Social and cultural uses of viewing experiences

The final part of this account concerns the social and cultural uses of viewing experiences, broadening the scope beyond that of contemporary popular Hindi films to include the full range of films viewed.

For the older members of the community, nostalgia is a key element in the pleasure experienced through film. In one particularly moving account by a man in his 70s, tears welled in his eyes as he recounted: 'When we see black-and-white films it reminds us of our childhood, our school days, our school mates, of what we were thinking, of what we did do, of our heroes ... and I tell you this gives us great pleasure.' The films would appear to act as a form of collective popular memory and some parents are able to convey a sense of their past in India to their children.

With the emergence of second-generation children parents and grand-parents have found new uses for films. These uses are primarily defined in terms of linguistic, religious, and socio-cultural learning. In viewing Indian films together many families are enabled to come together on a 'shared' linguistic basis. Both parents and children see this as a major advantage of watching films: 'They help children get a hold of the language.'

For many children the films provide one of the rare opportunities, outside communication in the family and community, to hear that language used and legitimated: 'They can hear and see how the language is used and should be used'. One boy put it more directly: 'They teach not only the language but how "to be" in an Indian environment.' The notion of language as transmitter of culture is prevalent among parents: 'If the children don't speak the language they lose their culture. Language is a potent symbol of collective identity and often the site of fierce loyalties and emotional power. In the context of a society which constructs linguistic difference as a problem rather than as a tool, the desire to defend and maintain one's linguistic heritage becomes strong.

In a community faced with religious distinctiveness and at times division, it is not surprising that cultural identity is often construed as being based not only on linguistic but also on religious continuity. 'Religious' or mythological films are also watched for devotional purposes, particularly by Hindu families, and often integrated with daily acts of worship: 'When we start fasting we always watch these films, sometimes five times a day ... you kind of pray to God at the same time you know'.

The films are also used as a form of religious education: 'They help parents teach their children about the Holy Books like the *Ramayana*, the *Mahabharat*, and the *Bhaghavat Gita*. It's the tradition in families to tell the young children the stories but some families don't have the time and so there are children who don't know who is Rama.' In some families viewing devotional films has come to replace reading the holy books. Certainly, the video is seen as a great advantage in familiarizing children with parables and religious stories, largely due to the widespread illiteracy of second- and third-generation children in their mother tongue. Not only are the religious and moral values inherent in the films an important aspect of viewing but the visual representation of the deity plays an extremely important symbolic role in the devotional and ritual acts of worship. This relates to the importance of popular forms of religious iconography in Indian society.

Parents use the films to talk about religious festivals: 'Here we can never really celebrate festivals like Holi which involves the whole village and people smearing each other's faces with colour. No one does that here but when you watch you can really appreciate what it's like in India. Here the kids just know about the fireworks but they don't know the real basic thing about why, they don't know about the religious aspects of the festivals.'

Young people and their parents use the films to negotiate, argue, and agree about a wider range of customs, traditions, values, and beliefs. Together, they often enjoy films which encourage discussion: 'films which bring out the contradictions in families, the arranged marriage system, the caste or class system'. The films function as tools for eliciting attitudes and views on salient themes; family affairs and problems, romance, courtship, and marriage were often discussed. There is a recurrent recognition of the 'influence' and value of the films in the lives of girls in particular. There are frequent references to the 'meanings, the really deep meanings, which reflect the way we think, it's just so ... so ... so I don't know, so influential'.

It would appear that Hindi films can serve to legitimate a particular view of the world and at the same time to open up contradictions within it. So while young people sometimes use films to deconstruct 'traditional culture' many parents use them to foster certain 'traditional' attitudes, values and beliefs in their children. Films are expected to have both an entertainment and a didactic function and are seen by parents as useful agents of cultural continuity and as contributing to the (re)-formation of cultural identity.

Various degrees of scepticism are registered among the boys about parents' attempts to 'artifically maintain a culture' through film: 'Parents want their children to maintain certain religious values, beliefs and customs but that doesn't mean that Indian films are necessarily going to educate them in that way. They may well do the opposite ... I think the moral standards in most recent films is pretty appalling.' But clear distinctions are made between religion and a sense of cultural identity and whilst firmly upholding the Sikh faith one boy claims: 'Parents use the films to represent their culture to their children but that will not work because those are not my roots, that place [India] has nothing to do with me anymore.'

Many parents lament what they see as a process of progressive 'cultural loss' in each generation of children. Looking to the past they attempt to re-create 'traditional culture'. Meanwhile young people, with eyes to the future, are busy re-creating something 'new'. The striving after cultural continuity and the negotiation of cultural identity are thus inescapably dialectical processes and they must, moreover, be seen in the widest possible context. The notion of viewing as a social activity which takes place in families needs to be extended to include more detailed explorations of the wider social, cultural, and ideological contexts and uses of the VCR.

What is clear is that for the young people interviewed a sense of ethnic, national, and cultural identity does not displace or dominate the equally lived and formed identities based on age, gender, peer group, and neighbourhood. Static notions of culture are extremely disabling as are absolutist views of black-and-white cultures as fixed, mutually impermeable expressions of 'racial' or national identity. Notions of national culture with unique customs and practices understood as 'pure' homogenous nationality need to be challenged.

One is reminded in this context of the arguments put forward by Benedict Anderson (1983) about the use of cultural artefacts in constructing 'imagined communities' based on notions of nation and nationness. The 'imagined communities', constructed and created through the viewing of films on VCR may link Asian communities across the world. However, these communities, with their origins in history and experience, are not fixed but change, develop and combine, and are in turn redispersed in historic processes.

If cultural practices are detached from their origins they can be used to found and extend new patterns of communication which can give rise to new common identities. Perhaps most of all this study provides a contemporary example of how 'traditional' ties are created and recreated out of present rather than past conditions.

Notes

1 This paper is based on a dissertation submitted for MA Film and Television Studies for Education, University of London Institute of Education, 1987.

2 The term 'Indian' film is used most commonly by interviewees but distinctions between films are also drawn according to language (i.e. Hindi, Panjabi, and Urdu) as well as genre.

3 See, for example, Ballard (1979) and Community Relations Commission (1979), and for a critique of such perspectives see Parmar (1981).

4 This estimated figure is based on surveys carried out in three Southall schools.

5 Lutze (1985).

6 Gundara (1986).

7 Other contexts documented in the research included siblings viewing together in the home, viewing with friends/peers, women/girls-only groups, women solo viewing and male-only viewing.

8 For further accounts of family contexts of viewing see, for example, Morley (1986); Simpson (1987).

References

Anderson, Benedict (1983). *Imagined Communities*. London: Verso.

Ballard, Catherine (1979). 'Conflict, continuity and change: second generation Asians', in V. Saifullah Khan (ed.) *Minority Families in Britain*. London: Macmillan.

Community Relations Commission (1979). *Between Two Cultures: A Study of the Relationship between Generations in the Asian Community*. London: Community Relations Commission.

Gundara, Jagdish (1986). 'Education in a multicultural society', in Gundara *et al.* (eds) *Racism, Diversity and Education*. London: Hodder & Stoughton.

Lutze (1985). 'From Bharata to Bombay: change and continuity in Hindi film aesthetics', in B. Pfleiderer (ed.) *The Hindi Film: Agent and Re-Agent of Cultural Change*. Manohar: 7.

Morley, David (1986) *Cultural Power and Domestic Leisure*. London: Comedia.

Parmar, Pratibha (1981) 'Young Asian women: a critique of the pathological approach'. *Multi-Racial Education*, 10(1).

Simpson, Philip (ed.) (1987) *Parents Talking*. London: Comedia.

40 Post-feminism and shopping films

Charlotte Brunsdon

Working Girl (directed by Mike Nichols, 1987) and *Pretty Woman* (Garry Marshall, 1990) were immensely successful and popular films. *Pretty Woman* transformed Julia Roberts to a major star, doomed for ever to strive to repeat the success of the 'shopping sequence'.[1] *Working Girl* was seen as a return to form for director Mike Nichols,[2] while Melanie Griffith's performance was widely regarded as one of her best although there was some complaint about her 'squeaky voice'.[3] Responses to Sigourney Weaver's Katherine in the same film were a little more muted, as most critics recognised that this character somehow bore the brunt of the film, most explicitly in the repeated reference to her 'bony ass' at the end.[4] Both films were aimed at, and enjoyed by, a female audience. A clear signifier of this was the concern within each with dress and the performance of feminity. They were girls' films. However, this address, as I will discuss below, was more complex than that of, for example, the 'independent woman' group of 1970s films [...]. There is here a different kind of bodily display, a different kind of catering to reluctant husbands and boyfriends who might be in the audience. Nevertheless, both films were clearly recognised as feminine in their concerns and newspaper reviewers were quick to point out the re-telling of *Cinderella* in these women's pictures for the late twentieth century.[5]

Both films have proved troubling to feminist critics in ways that are reminiscent of the mixed feminist response to the 'independent woman' cycle of the 1970s (*Alice Doesn't Live Here Anymore* (directed by Martin Scorsese, 1974), *Unmarried Woman* (directed by Paul Mazursky, 1978), *Julia* (directed by Fred Zinneman, 1977). Then the trouble lay in the way in which these films were some kind of response to – even, in some cases, dramatisations of – feminist demands, but they were not movement-originated and they were also, unavoidably, Hollywood films. So although they might have core narratives about women finding themselves, there was constant feminist criticism of the type of women involved (white, middle-class), the focus on the individual and the relative case of their quests for meaning, and, most problematic of all, a man. Those films were criticised both for their lack of realism and for their generic origins in melodrama, romance and the woman's picture. In short, for what we could call their Hollywoodness. Concepts frequently invoked in discussion of this cycle were 'recuperation' and 'inoculation', both of which imply a model in which feminist ideology and demands exist outside dominant structures such as Hollywood and are rendered innocuous when mobilised by Hollywood in its constant search for novelty and new audiences.[6]

With *Working Girl* and *Pretty Woman* the trouble is articulated slightly differently, for each film has been seen as symptomatic of a 'backlash' against feminism, or in some ways representative of a 'post-feminist' era. So while to a large extent the realist feminist critique would still apply – these are still white girls' stories focused on an individual's search for what turns out to be a man – these have not been the terms of critique. These films have not been criticised for distorting or rendering safe feminist critique, but rather for bypassing, ignoring or attacking feminism.[7] Thus US feminist comment on *Pretty Woman*:

> The immensely popular film *Pretty Woman* is emblematic of the post feminist genre. A glitzy reworking of the classic Cinderella tale, *Pretty Woman* offers yet another backlash dystopia; a world where women are whores with warm hearts of gold and men are rich corporate raiders with organs in need of thawing by those self-same hearts.

> (Walters 1995: 126)

[...] Feminist discourse, I would suggest, is profoundly structuring of each of these films, as it is of a range of 1980s and 1990s media representations. However, while these films could not have been imagined without the particular history of 1970s western feminism, it is the disavowal of this formation which is most evident. I want here to look at each film in detail to show how it is formed by, but also disavows, feminism. This project demands an engagement with the notion of 'post-feminism', a greatly contested term within feminist critical work. I want to suggest that 'post-feminism' has considerable purchase in any approach to this type of material, not least because of the way in which it attributes an historical specificity to the women's movement of the late 1960s and 1970s. It is a useful term historically because it does allow us to point to certain representational and discursive changes in the period since the 1970s. At the same time, I will argue a more orthodox feminist position – although I will only touch on this latter point as it is more readily available – and suggest that 'post-feminism' is a profoundly ahistorical concept, and in that sense misleading and not useful to the feminist political project.

Underlying both arguments and the choice of films is a desire to juxtapose two terms, 'post-feminism' and 'shopping'. My hypothesis here – of course not mine alone – is that something happens in the 1980s in the conjunction (in the West) of the new social movements, with their stress on the claiming and reclaiming of identities, and the expansion of leisure shopping and consumption. To trace this conjunction just in relation to feminism – and I should stress that I don't think it happens only in relation to women and feminism[8] – we can initially refer to a useful periodisation of feminism made by Michèle Barrett and Anne Phillips in the introduction to their collection *Destabilizing Theory* (1992).

Barrett and Phillips suggest that a distinction can be made, in western feminism, between what they call '1970s' modernist feminism and 1990s post-modern feminism. The labels of 1970s and 1990s are offered in their account as convenient shorthand with some temporal reference, and I will follow their example. They suggest that the well-known differences within 1970s feminism in understanding women's subordination concealed considerable agreement that it was possible to specify a cause of women's oppression. Although there was great disagreement about what it was, there was consensus that this cause could be found at the level of social structure, be that characterised as patriarchy or capitalism. The term for women's subordination was unquestionably that of 'oppression', and, analytically, the sex/gender distinction was talismanic. In this context, it is conventional femininity that is seen as particularly problematic (Barrett and Phillips 1992: 2–3).

Postmodern 1990s feminism, in contrast, in their argument, is a humbler, less universalistic and much less unified current. Challenged both internally and externally on the differences between women, and most particularly on issues of sexuality, racism and ethnocentrism, 1970s feminism was forced to recognise its particularity and the inadequacy of the concentration on class and gender alone. A range of positions and practices contested the axiomatic quality of the sex/gender distinction, which became much trickier to maintain. Postmodernism and poststructuralism offered theoretical challenges of a different order. That is, 1970s feminism was, in the 1980s and 1990s, challenged on both political and theoretical grounds. Or, to put it another way, 1990s feminism itself is post-1970s feminism in ways that are not simply chronological. 1970s feminism produced a particular inflection of the category 'woman' through which identity political mobilization could take place. 1990s feminism deconstructs this category, while still arguing for its salience.

Barrett and Phillips are mainly concerned to highlight differences between 1970s and 1990s feminism in relation to theory, politics and feminist intellectual work, while being insistent that they are not offering a simple progress model. I want to address their periodisation in relation to feminist ideas about consumption and identity. With all the necessary caveats about broad generalisation, it seems possible to make some clear distinctions. 1970s feminism, which in both Britain and the USA arose partly out of the New Left and the Civil Rights and anti-war movement, and generally involved women with access to higher education (although of quite mixed class origin) was anti-consumption, often in a quite puritanical manner, across the range of goods (houses, clothes, make-up and high art such as opera). Ideas of identity, which often draw on 'anti-repression' theories, were marked by notions of sincerity, expression, truth-telling. 1990s feminism, in contrast, partly through the 1980s feminist defence of 'women's genres' such as fashion, soap opera and women's magazines, is permissive and even enthusiastic about consumption. Wearing lipstick is no longer wicked, and notions of identity have moved away from a rational/moral axis and are much more profoundly informed by ideas of performance, style and desire.[9]

Barrett and Phillips carefully avoid 'post-feminism'. Their project is to think changes in feminism in relation to other posts, such as postmodernism and poststructuralism, and indeed their periodisation is, essentially, a distinction between a modernist 1970s feminism and a postmodern 1990s feminism. The changing concerns round consumption and identity that I have sketched can be satisfactorily mapped across this distinction. However, the rediscovery of the pleasures of feminine consumption associated with post-modern feminism are also congruent with what is popularly formulated as post-feminism. By this I intend to designate a journalistic or popular periodisation in which 'women's lib' is somehow over in the mid-1980s (Walters 1995 offers one account but she understands post-feminism simply as backlash). The reference is usually to a series of popular cultural representations which are both dependent on but transcendent or dismissive of the impulses and images of 1970s feminism. Women's and girls' magazines themselves are an interesting site here, as suggested by both McRobbie (1996) and Winship (1985), while cable networks like *Lifetime* (see Feuer 1994), or British television shows like *Absolutely Fabulous* and *The Girlie Show* all offer post-feminist versions of femininity. That is, I would propose the necessity of marking and recognising a qualitative shift in the repertoire of anglophone popular femininities from (approximately) the early 1980s. The reasons for these changes are extremely complex, and include punk as much as women's liberation, changing patterns of employment as well as AIDS, but the point here is that they are labelled and recognised within the popular media in which they appear as being 'post-feminist'.[10] The privileged site for academic discussion of this type of image has been, repeatedly, Madonna (see Schwitchenberg 1993, hooks 1992 and Ang 1995b) but I would suggest that both *Working Girl* and, in a different way, *Pretty Woman* offer exemplary instances of post-feminist women characters.

The key point in this popular story is that the post-feminist woman has a different relation to femininity than either the pre-feminist or the feminist woman. As a persona in the public sphere, the post-feminist woman is also not necessarily 'white', which I think is the case, historically, with the persona '1970s feminist' – which of course is not to say that only white women were or are feminists. Precisely because this postmodern girl is a figure partly constructed through a relation to consumption, the positionality is more available. She is in this sense much more like the postmodern feminist, for she is neither trapped in femininity (pre-feminist), nor rejecting of it (feminist). She can use it. However, although this may mean apparently inhabiting a very similar terrain to the pre-feminist woman, who manipulates her appearance to get her man, the post-feminist woman also has ideas about her life and being in control which clearly come from feminism. She may manipulate her appearance, but she doesn't just do it to get a man on the old terms. She wants it all. The Melanie Griffith character in *Working Girl* wants a career *and* Harrison Ford. The Julia Roberts character in *Pretty Woman* won't settle for being kept as Edward's (Richard Gere) 'beck and call girl'. She demands a proper rescue by her prince and 'the whole fairytale'. When she has this promise (implicitly, marriage), 'she'll rescue him right back'. Exactly to the extent that this persona is constituted through a desire to make it individually, it is a persona that can be accommodated within familiar (if historically masculine) western narratives of individual success. The key narrative trope for this figure in 1980s Hollywood cinema – the site of both the inscription and the remaking of femininity – is shopping and trying on clothes. Post-feminist woman can try on identities and adopt them, as we have seen in a range of films, from *Desperately Seeking Susan* (directed by Susan Seidelman, 1985) to *Clueless* (Amy Heckerling, 1995). Now I am not suggesting that in the authentic 'outside' of politics in the 1980s there was a considerable transformation in radical thinking about identity which wicked Hollywood recuperates as shopping and identity swapping. For I would want to argue against this separation of an authentic outside and realm of representation. Instead, I am suggesting that, despite 1970s feminism, Jane Gaines's observation that 'it is the woman's story that is told in dress' (1990: 181) is still true. However, the woman's relation to costume in the 1980s and 1990s is slightly different, as is the understanding of femininity. What in current critical theory is called the performativity of gender, always an element in the common sense of women's magazines, is currently much more widely available in the popular media. *Working Girl* and *Pretty Woman* are two films in which the performance of femininity was much foregrounded – to the evident enjoyment of huge audiences, but considerable ambivalence from feminist critics. [...]

The explicitness of the reference to *Cinderella* in *Pretty Woman* has tempted some critics to see this film as a reversion to a pre-feminist narrative. But just as the reference to *Cinderella* is contemporary and self-conscious, so is the invocation of the romance genre and the construction of the heroine. Kit (Laura San Giacomo), Vivian's best friend, tries to answer the question. 'But who does it work for?' and, after searching through their mutual acquaintance, comes up with the only answer, 'Cinderfuckingrella'. Similarly, the film is framed with a street voice from Hollywood Boulevard, opening with 'Welcome to Hollywood, everybody comes to Hollywood, land of dreams, some dreams come true, some don't, but keep on dreaming'. This is a film that is at pains to point out that its fantasy is a similar one. Its heroine, too, seems familiar. She is part whore with the heart of gold, part Eliza Doolittle. But she is also post-feminist in the sense I am suggesting the term is useful. For Vivian has a vocabulary of self and attitude towards her profession which are historically specific. Hilary Radnor (1993) has very usefully shown the way in which Vivian belongs both in the post-1960s history of the single girl – a story in which Helen Gurley Brown figures prominently – and in the even longer history of the heroine's role in the marriage plot. In my analysis of *An Unmarried Woman* I suggested that the 1970s figure of the independent woman was formed in the contradiction of the demand to be both desirable and desiring [...]. Radnor, discussing Vivian, suggests that the single girl is subject to a double injunction:

> the single girl must represent desire for the masculine subject while simultaneously acting as the agent of her own desire – must re-enact the specular image of consumer desire and yet assume agency and autonomy in the context of her own wishes. (Radnor 1993: 66)

I think the particular configuration of desirable/desiring that we find in these 1980s films is a key element in the popular perception of them as post-feminist. In this popular image 'feminist' would thus signify only 'desiring' and, by implication, the repudiation of the necessity for the feminine subject to also be desirable. And it is shopping and dressing up which makes one desirable.

Pretty Woman is very knowing about its retrenchments, simultaneously informed by feminism and disavowing this formation. Thus the narrative scenario, although deeply indebted to the screen history of the whore with the heart of gold, would be unimaginable without second-wave feminist perspectives on sex-work. *Klute* (directed by Allan J. Pakula, 1971) and *McCabe and Mrs Miller* (directed by Robert Altman, 1971), with Bree Daniels (Jane Fonda) and Constance Miller (Julie Christie), introduced that generation of independent women for whom prostitution is a job like any other, and the best paid one to which they have access. For Kit and Vivian working on the street is a dull necessity, a way of paying the rent. The film uses these post-feminist attitudes – notably explored in films like Jan Worth's *Taking a Part* (1979) or Lizzie Borden's *Working Girls* (1986) – to disavow any voyeurism associated with this particular way of paying the rent, indeed to legitimate a scrutiny of Vivian's preparation for work, and to show both Vivian and Kit displaying themselves for trade. Thus in an ego-boosting session on Hollywood Boulevard Kit and Vivian chant what is clearly a feminist derived mantra: 'We say who, we say where, we say how much', affirming both their own control and their independence from a pimp.

One of the concerns of this film, as with *Working Girl*, is the performance and masquerade of a class-specific femininity. In each film the heroine has to labour to carry off the performance of the right sort of femininity. Tess has to go speech class, Vivian has learn about the tines of forks. However, while the narrative of the film would suggest that it is in Vivian's act as Edward's hired companion that we would find the primary locus of pretence and disguise, in fact the reverse is true. So although Vivian's masquerade as Edward's classy latest is threatened with exposure by Edward's lawyer, through performance and *mise-en-scène* we learn that Vivian's real masquerade is as a hooker. That is, although Vivian is working as a prostitute for most of the film, the dominant presentation of her is as naturally not-a-hooker. It is the blonde wig and the cheap tarty dress which turn out to be the real disguise. This is achieved through a variety of devices and narrative contrasts, the most significant of which are Vivian's attitude to money and the contrast between her and her friend Kit.

Pretty Woman offers itself as being up front about the importance of money in contemporary US society. One of the few distinguishable comments in the early part of the pre-credit sequence, a party for Edward (Richard Gere) thrown by his lawyer, is 'It's all about money', knowingly offered to the audience when the screen is still dark. This film, the strategy suggests, is a film which is all about money which knows it's all about money. The promise, of course, is that this type of self-consciousness about money and Hollywood might be prompted by other values, but in fact the film *is* all about money and the appreciation of its value. Thus the first moment of rapport between Edward and Vivian is when she proves herself a tough bargainer, saying 'I never joke about money'.

Similarly, Vivian is initially differentiated from her friend Kit through their attitudes to money. Despite working as a hooker on Sunset Boulevard, Vivian is shown to be a nice girl with housewife potential because she saves the rent. That she has to keep it in the lavatory cistern is what she later calls 'just geography'. It is Kit who is essentially of the street, foolishly blowing the secret rent stash on drugs. The essential straightness of the Julia Roberts character, one of the key elements of the characterisation, is first established as she wails at Kit: 'You spent the rent money on drugs ...'

Edward, at the other end of the money spectrum, is shown to have no real sense of what money means, particularly to those who have less than himself. He doesn't understand the value in which he deals. At the beginning of the film he commandeers his host's new car with no recognition of its value to Philip – a well-documented fictional characteristic of the very rich – and then cannot drive it. It is Vivian who recognises its value as a car, not just for the money it means but for its mechanical properties. She can drive it with the skill and appreciation it demands. That is, although on the streets Vivian is shown to have an instinctive or natural appreciation of the accoutrements of great riches which bypasses their financial cost, and goes straight to their heart, be it a fifth gear or an aria. So we have here the basic division of qualities through which the romance will work: she has no money but a sense of value, whereas he has lots of money but doesn't always understand what things mean. The image offered for this is his penthouse suite (the best) with a balcony that he can't use because he's afraid of heights. She appreciates what he's got – and she will eventually rescue him, show him how to appreciate it too.

To be able to do this plausibly – even in a film which self-consciously nominates itself as a fairy tale – Vivian's quality has to shine through her street apparel. This is managed in a range of ways in the film: the Roberts performance, responses of other characters and a series of texts and tests. It is the mutually confirming affirmation of Vivian's great value through each of these which contributes to the righteous outcome. Vivian gets her prince because she deserves him, as we learn throughout the film. Hilary Radnor points to Vivian's character-revealing encounters with texts such as *The Lucy Show* and *La Traviata*. Liking *Lucy* reveals an ordinary American down-home innocence, while being moved by *La Traviata*, as the film labours to point out, reveals that Vivian has a 'soul'. Similarly, both the really rich (James Morse/Ralph Bellamy), and those who cater to them (Bernard the hotel manager/Hector Elizondo) recognise her quality. Morse leads her into eating hors d'oeuvres with her fingers when she is confused about cutlery, while Bernard makes possible her first dress purchase as well as helping her with her table manners. The Roberts performance is complicated by the widely disseminated knowledge that a body double was used for key scenes, particularly the opening sequence of getting dressed. Radnor offers an excellent discussion of the use of the body double within her general argument that Vivian's progress in the film is from object of voyeuristic gaze to object of a fetishistic gaze. Here I would merely point to the way in which it is the body double scenes, particularly the use of sub-pornographic codes in the opening, which point to the ambitions of the film's address. I observed earlier that the address of these post-feminist films was more complex than that of the 1970s independent woman films. There is an attempt to offer pleasures within what are generically women's films, to viewers occupying a conventionally masculine posi-tion. [...] In *Pretty Woman* Vivian's profession is used to legitimate close-ups on body and underwear in the early part of the film. The fact that it is the body double in these scenes offers a rather literal rendition of the difficulty of this double address to a lusting and an identifying audience. One actress alone, even Julia Roberts, cannot or will not meet the contradictory demands of femininity. More generally we are cued to read the performance – the mixture of bravado, vulnerability, street smarts and innocence – through the extract from *Breakfast at Tiffany's* which is shown on television in the hotel room. Roberts manages to project sincerity through a certain unpredictability in her timing. Edward says he finds her surprising, and he also tells her repeatedly to stop fidgeting. Her performance emphasises these two elements: a certain nerviness which is repeatedly transformed by a smile or a tableau of her beauty. Roberts never leads a scene with her wide, dazzling smile, instead only offering it as a revelation as she tosses the hair from her face or slowly turns round. Similarly, there is an occasional awkwardness in her deployment of her limbs, as if her long legs are sometimes a little outside her control. These are signi-fiers of a non-manipulative sexuality, a guarantee that, even though Vivian works as a prostitute, she is unconscious of the power of her beauty. She just naturally sits down for breakfast the first morning, firstly on the edge of one of the dishes and then on a chair with her knee peeking through her white towelling dressing-gown while she hungrily and unselfconsciously tears into a croissant. She might be a hooker outside, but she's clean inside.

Vivian, as she tells Edward while offering him a selection of condoms, is 'a safety girl'. She works the street, but, as the film is at pains to point out, she flosses her teeth. Vivian's profession makes it narratively impossible for there to be a with-holding of sex – as she puts it herself, 'I'm a sure thing'. However, romantic narra-tive demands a withholding, and this is achieved through the displacement of the customary narrative importance of intercourse to 'kissing on the mouth'. This device allows Vivian to remain pure while working as a prostitute, and also allows a proper romantic courtship working up to the night when they really 'do it'. Here she is crucially contrasted with Kit, whose destiny, we know, is like that of Skinny Marie. Kit will never leave the street – her fate sealed in her readiness to party, her incontinence with drugs. Kit spends the rent money – she betrays her room-mate. She is not really a bourgeois housewife in waiting – she would not 'clean up good'. And she doesn't seem to have the 'non-street' normal clothes that Vivian is revealed to possess in the last scene. It is Kit's destiny which gives the poignancy to their farewell.

However it is the prerequisites of the clean-up, the clothes purchased in the shop-ping trip on Rodeo Drive, which have provided a central focus for fans and critics. Radner argues that Vivian becomes 'pretty' only when she starts shopping. Certainly this is when the title song first appears. However, I have tried to suggest that Vivian is shown to be already 'pretty' *before* she gets the accoutrements of expensive femininity. It is only because, as I have discussed at length, Vivian is *already*, naturally, underneath 'not-a-hooker' that she *can* clean up good. In this the film can be usefully contrasted with *Now Voyager*, which also has a transformation of a central female character. Charlotte (Bette Davis) too cleans up good, but in her case she moves not from street-femininity to penthouse-femininity but from non-sexual spinster aunt to desirable sexual and maternal woman. The plucking of eyebrows, the weight loss and the hair cut are the essentials here – in conjunction with psychiatric help and an originally loaned new wardrobe and identity. As several critics have commented, *Now Voyager* reveals the labour of femininity, the difficulty of successfully inhabiting this contradictory position (see for example, Maria LaPlace, 1987). In that sense *Now Voyager* has been read to reveal the constructedness of femininity. In contrast *Pretty Woman* while showing the trans-formation achieved through the series of expensive outfits and offering what can only be described as a triumphant shopping binge, implicitly uses a natural model of femininity. In the shopping trip Edward's credit card buys for Vivian what she already deserves. She naturally deserves it, for the reasons discussed, but, just to make sure, she narratively deserves it as well because of her humiliation the previous day when the snooty shop assistants refused to serve her. Just like Tess, Vivian proves a successful shape-changer, a righteous inheritor of one of the new 1980s 'public' femininities, to use Radner's term.

Jennifer Wicke, in an acerbic recent article, argues for the significance of 'the celebrity zone' as 'the public sphere where feminism is negotiated, where it is now in most active cultural play' (Wicke 1994: 757). She proposes the category 'celebrity feminism' as a significant media category, arguing that a woman with a profile in the public sphere will be assimilated to this category. Wicke argues, that the familiar binary division of feminism into 'movement' and 'academic' is near-useless, and that the domain of celebrity feminism demands engagement, for this is the most significant contemporary site for the generation of meanings round femi-nism. She argues that a range of US figures are best understood within the celebrity feminist zone – Camille Paglia, Oprah Winfrey, Whoopi Goldberg, Catherine McKinnon, Naomi Wolf and Judith Butler – and engages with the different politics associated with each. But what she is most insistent about is that celebrity feminism cannot be dismissed in the name of some real authentic feminism which is 'elsewhere'. I want to use a comment she makes about Naomi Wolf to approach my conclusion to this essay. Wicke writes, 'However problematic, some form of feminist discourse is occurring within Wolfian celebrity space' (1994: 765). I think the same could be said of these two films. However problematic, some form of feminist discourse is occurring within these women's films for the 1990s. Julia Hallam has shown how *Working Girl* was widely recognised as engaging with feminism, generating a whole series of articles that were not film-specific about women in the workplace, the glass ceiling, etc. (Hallam 1994). Hilary Radnor has argued that *Pretty Woman* marks a specifically 1990s reconfiguration of the marriage plot and that the film attempts to 'imagine a fantasy in which a woman always receives a just return for her investment without relinquishing her right to the pursuit of happiness' (Radnor 1993: 75). That is, both these writers can be understood to argue that something to do with feminism is happening in these films. I have suggested that the term 'post-feminist', routinely rejected by feminist critics, *is* useful in an approach to these films as it marks the considerable distance that we find here, in popular representation, from popular representation of 1970s feminism. If the 'independent woman' of the 1970s cycle marked a response to the women's movement – and the new female audience – of that period, this figure has all but disappeared by the mid-1980s. Instead, we have a new kind of girly heroine who, while formed in the wake of 1970s feminism, disavows this formation. But the post-feminist girly is only one of the Hollywood cast of post-feminist characters. As we have seen in *Working Girl*, we also have monster-career woman, and, in another genre, as Carol Clover (1992) suggests, we also find what she calls 'the final girl'. Feminist critics have tended to be more attracted by less girly characters such as Thelma and Louise (see, for example, Sharon Willis 1993), but I have argued that something to do with feminism is going on in this girly space. For the disavowal of 1970s feminist formation does not, in some ways, seem important. Why should 1970s feminism have a copyright on feminism? As Angela McRobbie (1996) has argued in another context, the old vocabularies of 1970s feminism are not adequate to the experience of young women growing up today. That is, I would argue that the very currency of the term *post-feminism* needs addressing, and that it is quite useful if used in an historically specific sense to mark changes in popularly available understandings of femininity and a woman's place that are generally recognised as occurring in the 1980s. These changes may also have a very particular generational resonance. The story of 1970s feminism can be seen in some ways as the story of the baby boomer generation, growing up between the pills and AIDS.[11] However, in its very historical specificity, 'post-feminism', it is also not useful at all in two different ways. Firstly, it is not useful if it installs 1970s feminism as the site of 'true' feminism, from which lipstick-wearers and shoppers are excluded. Here I think the arguments that Jennifer Wicke makes about celebrity feminism are extremely pertinent, for she suggests that it behoves us (those who think of themselves as feminists) to recognise the changed context of debate on feminist-related issues. The second reason to oppose the use of post-feminism is that it reduces all feminisms, and their long histories, to that one

1970s movement. In this, it is a profoundly ahistorical concept, recognising only one moment and form of feminism. In that sense, as Nancy Fraser (1992) has observed, the time to speak of post-feminism will be when we can legitimately speak of post-patriarchy.
Review 21: 25–46.

Notes

1   I am grateful to Ginette Vincendeau and Ellen Seiter for comments on this essay. Julia Roberts's next film, *Sleeping with the Enemy*, has an equivalent trying-on-hats sequence.

2   For example, in the London reviews, Phillip French observed, 'Directed by Mike Nichols from a screenplay by Kevin Wade, the highly enjoyable *Working Girl is Wall Street* remade in the style of a 1930s screwball comedy, and something of a cross between Nichols' blue-chip fantasy *The Graduate* and his blue-collar tragedy *Silkwood*' ('Marnie grows up', *Sunday Telegraph*, 2 April 1989: 41). Margaret Walters wrote in *The Listener*, 'Mike Nichols hasn't made a movie this good since *The Graduate* (1967) or *Carnal Knowledge* (1971)' ('The office copier', *The Listener*, 6 April 1989: 41). Pauline Kael offered the most substantial negative review of the film in *The New Yorker*, 9 January 1989: 80–1.

3   For example, Melanie Griffith was described as 'bimbo-voiced' by Derek Malcolm ('Working the system for all it's worth', *The Guardian*, 30 March 1989: 25), while Lorraine Gamman referred to her 'squeaky little girl voice' (review in *Spare Rib* 200 (April 1989): 31–2).

4   Elizabeth Traube has the most extended discussion of the 'bony ass' insult, with reference to a script scene cut from the movie (Traube 1992: 113).

5   *Cinderella* was mentioned in many reviews of both films. Examples include: Sue Heal in the British newspaper *Today*, 'Take Cinderella in thigh-length boots, a pinch of Pygmalion and mix in the glossy air of corporate greed and you have *Pretty Woman*' (11 May 1990: 20) and Amy Taubin in *The Village Voice*, 'Cinderella with the niceties of royal blood replaced with the not-yet-fallen-dollar' (*Film Special*, December 190: 11).

6   See part (iii) of *Films for Women* (Brunsdon 1986b) for documentation of feminist responses to 1970s films. Lesage (1982) writes on *An Unmarried Woman* as an example of 'hegemonic female fantasy'.

7   The substantial exceptions here are Taubin (1990), Hallam (1994) and Radnor (1993). Hallam and Radnor, which I discuss at more length below, are however, both concerned with what is different about these films in their relation to femininity and feminism. Thus the general point remains true – it is just that Taubin, Hallam and Radnor don't write off the films – and indeed, as I do, seem to quite enjoy them.

8   Frank Mort, in his *Cultures of Consumption* (1996), traces the complex articulation of masculinities and consumption in this period.

9   Jane Gaines, introducing a 1990 feminist collection on fashion, gives an extremely evocative account of these shifts, including a mention of a group called 'Lesbians for Lipstick' (1990a: 5–6).

10 Teresa de Lauretis (1990a) discusses *Black Widow* (directed by Bob Rafelson, 1987) as exemplifying 'the narrative images and trajectories typical of the woman's film in the age of post-feminism'. My own interest here is in rather more girly films and heroines. Walters (1995: 116–42) discusses *Pretty Woman* within a more general context of post-feminism but understands what she calls 'popular post-feminism' as simply negative.

11 John Updike, discussing the difficulty of writing about sex in the 1990s, points to this periodisation: 'One of the things that interested me was that the mid-Seventies were a kind of window of sexual opportunity between the invention of the pill and the onset of Aids' (John Updike interviewed by Mark Lawson, 'Sex and the rabbit man', *Independent on Sunday Magazine*, 27 February 1993: 33–6, p. 36). There are objective reasons why sexual experimentation – as used for example in *An Unmarried Woman* – is a 1970s, rather than a 1990s, metaphor for female self-discovery.

References

Barrett, M., and Phillips, A. (1992), 'Introduction', in Barrett and Phillips (eds), *Destabilizing Theory*. Cambridge: Polity.

Clover, C. (1992), *Men, Women and Chainsaws*. London: British Film Institute.

Feuer, J. (1994), 'Feminism on Lifetime: Yuppie TV for the Nineties', *Camera Obscura* 33–4: 13–45.

Fraser, N. (1992), 'The Uses and Abuses of French Discourse Theories for Feminist Politics', *Theory, Culture and Society* 9(1): 51–72.

Gaines, J. (1990), 'Costume and Narrative: How Dress Tells the Womn's Story', in J. Gaines and C. Herzog (eds), *Fabrications: Costume and the Female Body*. New York and London: Routledge.

Hallam, J. (1994), '*Working Girl*: A Woman's Film for the Eighties', in S. Mills (ed.), *Gendering the Reader*. Hemel Hempstead: Harvester.

LaPlace, M. (1987), 'Producing and Consuming the Woman's Film: Discursive Struggle in *Now Voyager*', in C. Gledhill (ed.), *Home Is Where the Heart Is*. London: British Film Institute.

McRobbie, A. (1996), 'Body, Space and Capitalism', paper presented to 'Dialogue with Cultural Studies' Conference, Tokyo University, March 1996.

Walters, S. (1995), *Material Girls*. Berkeley and Los Angeles: University of California Press.

Wicke, J. (1994), 'Celebrity Material: Materialist Feminism and the Culture of Celebrity', *South Atlantic Quarterly* 93(4): 751–78.

Winship, J. (1985), ' "A Girl Needs to Get Streetwise": Magazines for the 1980s', *Feminist Review* 21:25–46

41 Film history terminable and interminable: recovering the past in reception studies

Barbara Klinger

In the early 1980s, Tony Bennett called for a revolution in literary study, in which one would no longer just study the text, but 'everything which has been written *about* it, everything which has been collected on it, becomes attached to it – like shells on a rock by the seashore forming a whole incrustation'.[1] In these oceanic terms, the text's meaning would not be a function of its own internal system, but a function of what John Frow would later refer to as the text's 'multiple historicities': 'the contradictory modes of its social inscription' synchronically, as well as its 'serial reinscriptions' diachronically.[2] Not all scholars, however, have shared this enthusiasm for radically historicizing literary enterprise by taking extended voyages through textual pasts. Antony Easthope, for example, has questioned the very feasibility of achieving such a grand materialist vision of literary production. He argues that 'texts cannot be adequately analysed in relation to a definition of a particular social and historical context' because they 'exceed that context not only diachronically, always temporally going beyond a given reading, but also synchronically, always available to *another* reading at the same time, even in the supposedly "original" moment when they were first produced'.[3] There is, then, something so elusively excessive about the historical that we can never sufficiently grasp its relation to textuality.

Implicated within this scholarly disagreement is an area of research in media studies particularly devoted to the historical excavation of meaning. As Bennett and others redefined the object of literary analysis from the text to the intertext – the network of discourses, social institutions, and historical conditions surrounding a work – they helped inspire the development of historical reception studies in film. Those engaged in reception studies typically examine a network of relationships between a film or filmic element (such as a star), adjacent intertextual fields such as censorship, exhibition practices, star publicity and reviews, and the dominant or alternative ideologies of society at a particular time. Such contextual analysis hopes to reveal the intimate impact of discursive and social situations on cinematic meaning, while elaborating the particularities of cinema's existence under different historical regimes from the silent era to the present.

I would like to contemplate an issue raised by Bennett's and Easthope's polarized views of the text/history couplet, specifically as it applies to this kind of film research. The issue has to do with the potential for reception studies to recover adequately a film's past, to reconstruct fully a film's relation to social and historical processes. Can researchers uncover 'everything' which has been written about a film? Can they exhaust the factors involved in the relation between film and history, providing a comprehensive view of the rich contexts that once brought a film to life and gave it meaning for a variety of spectators? Can they, as one scholar exhorts them to do, ask how mass media events 'correspond to the massive data of their origin', so that these events can be 'seized' in their 'totality'?[4] If not, is the entire enterprise of historical research into film meaning jeopardized, because it can only ever offer partial and therefore historically inadequate views of textual pasts? Totality is of course the utopian goal of those critics seeking 'multiple historicities', and a target of those who advocate doubt. In this sense, the issue of comprehensiveness lingers at the borders of historical reception studies as both a promise and a threat.

In addition, many philosophers of history would have grave suspicions about any historian claiming comprehensiveness, seeing it as a failure to exercise what Paul Ricoeur refers to as 'epistemological prudence' in historical explanation.[5] This prudence is made necessary, at the very least, by the scholar's recognition of the interpretive element present in all historical writing and of the always fragmentary and incomplete nature of the historical record itself. Even so, as I will argue, exhaustiveness, while impossible to achieve, is necessary as an ideal goal for historical research. Its impossibility should not lead, as in the case of Easthope, to its dismissal: that would be the rough equivalent of saying because we cannot know all of outer space we should stop our investigations. Rather more in the spirit of Fernand Braudel's concept of *histoire totale*, we can acknowledge both the unattainability of such a history and the benefits of its pursuit.[6]

In a total history, the analyst studies complex interactive environments or levels of society involved in the production of a particular event, effecting a historical synthesis, an integrated picture of synchronic as well as diachronic change. In Foucauldian terms, total history appears as the general episteme of an archaeological stratum which would include the system of relations between heterogeneous forms of discourse in that stratum. A Marxist gloss defines total history as a 'dialectical history of ceaseless interaction among the political, economic, and cultural, as a result of which the whole society is ultimately transformed'.[7] Whatever the specific permutation, the grand view behind a *histoire totale* has several valuable functions for film history. Embodying a scholarly aim rather than an absolutely achievable reality, the concept promises to press historians' enquiries beyond established frontiers, broadening the scope of their enterprise, and continually refining their historical methods and perspectives. What David Bordwell refers to in other contexts as a 'a totalized view' of history suggests that recovering the past is eminently tied not only to the discovery of documents of yore, but to reflection upon how best to engage thoroughly with that past.[8] In addition, pursuing this idea in the context of film studies provides the occasion for imagining what a cinematic version of *histoire totale* might comprise, creating a panaromic view of the contexts most associated with cinema's social and historical conditions of existence, and returning us to the question of what exactly is at stake in materialist approaches to textuality.

Before considering the details of a cinematic *histoire totale* for a dominant kind of filmmaking – the classical Hollywood cinema – I would like to examine briefly how such an enterprise necessarily reorients some existing tendencies of research in reception studies. Keeping in mind that the historians I mentioned never set out to produce a synthetic social picture, a more global view of a film's reception history raises several questions about the parameters of contemporary contextual research.

The first question pertains to the selection and use of the external discourses the researcher includes in a case study. Some scholars, such as Mike Budd and Maria LaPlace, mobilize a number of different extrafilmic fields to interrogate cinema's relation to its historical context – respectively advertising, censorship, and reviews for *The Cabinet of Dr Caligari* (Robert Wiene, 1919); and star discourse, conventions of women's fiction, and consumerism for *Now, Voyager* (Irving Rapper, 1942).[9] The hermeneutic importance of this position becomes clear when we weigh the implications of the 'single discourse' approach to reception. Studying a film's connection to a single external field, such as reviews, is obviously not enough to portray exhaustively the elements involved in a film's social circulation. Such a study can tell us how that field produced meaning for the film and give us a partial view of its discursive surround.[10] But at the same time, and perhaps less obviously, it can result in an insufficient depiction of film's relationship to its social context, with consequences for how we hypothesize cinema's historical and ideological meaning.

This point finds illustration in Mary Beth Haralovich's commentary on *All That Heaven Allows* (Douglas Sirk, 1955) in which she initially speculates that its mise-en-scene be understood against the 'external social fact of suburbia in the 1950s'. She sees the film as participating in social consciousness about housing and its role in the social order, particularly in its expressive mise-en-scene, which acts poten- tially to resist 'idealist discourses about the qualities of suburban liveability'. But aware that a single historical frame is insufficient, she suggests further investigating the film's production, the state of domestic architecture, consumerism at the time, and other factors necessary to a more complete social history.[11] And, indeed, if one were to look at the industry's production strategies for the style of the film, and reviewers' reception of it against consumerism and other historical tides, one would find that *All That Heaven Allows* was planned and received largely as a support for consumer culture and the affluent climate of the 1950s. The point here is that if the researcher rests with discussing a film's connection to a particular contextual frame, she/he may assess its historical role and ideology too hastily. In this case, such haste might produce a monolithic view of *All That Heaven Allows* as subversive of 1950s domestic ideology by focusing too narrowly on the relation of its self-reflexive mise-en-scene to discourses on housing at the time. By neglecting to consider how the mise-en-scene is situated within broader discursive activities, the researcher's assessment of the film's ideology would be premature.

By contrast, a totalized view provides a sense, not of *the* ideology the text had in historical context, but its *many* ideologies. By placing a film within multifarious inter- textual and historical frames – the elements that define its situation in a complex discursive and social milieu – the film's variable, even contradictory, ideological meanings come into focus. There is then a desired *Rashomon*-like effect in totalized reception studies, where the researcher uncovers different historical 'truths' about a film as she/he analyses how it has been deployed within past social relations. A total- ized view necessarily addresses the competing voices involved in a particular film's public signification as a means of attempting to describe its full historicity. It thus avoids arriving at premature, partial, ideological identities for films, that result from imposing a unity between a film and its historical moment at the expense of consid- ering the intricate untidiness of this relationship.

Another tendency in historical reception studies forecloses the impulse towards a cinematic *histoire totale* in a different way. Here, the researcher stays too close to home. 'Home' happens to be the film industry, the environment with the closest ties to the film text and the one that has long been of interest to historians. On occasion, reception studies focused on the industry fail to raise the question of how the indus- trial context connects to surrounding social and historical processes. Part of this provincialism results from the debt reception studies owes to the 'new' revisionist film history: the former has been revolutionized by the latter's interest in displacing secondary and anecdotal forms of history with primary documentation, archival research and other historiographical tools of evidence and verification. The new film history has concentrated particularly on industry practices, including modes of production and exhibition, film style and technology. But, as Miriam Hansen has pointed out, this concentration has led at times to a 'self-imposed abstinency ... with regard to the social and cultural dynamics of cinematic consumption, with discourses of experience and ideology'.[12]

We can see a distinction between historical accounts emphasizing the industrial and those exploring connections to external social and historical discourses in Lea

Jacobs's and Annette Kuhn's respective works on film censorship. Jacobs analyses how the operation of censorship affected the style and narrative of the 'fallen woman' cycle of the woman's film from the late 1920s and the 1940s. She illuminates the intricate business of censorship as it attempts to regulate sexual difference in this significant subgenre, but does not extend her analysis to consider its positioning within larger social processes. Kuhn, taking a different tack, contextualizes her discussion of censorship or early British cinema by discussing the eugenics movement, sexology, wartime Britain, and broader conceptions of cinema in the public sphere.[13] The two authors clearly have different objectives. But for a totalized view, questions of history must extend beyond the industry to engage in a potentially vast system of interconnections, from the film and its immediate industrial context to social and historical developments.

Besides addressing the problems of single discourses and industrial preoccupations, this view demands a diachronic dimension. Almost all film historians are 'stuck in synchrony', focusing on the conjuncture in which films initially appeared to reveal their original circumstances of production, exhibition and reception. Reception studies scholars almost exclusively come to terms with a film's meaning by considering the impact that its original conditions had on its social significance. Research into origins, while all-consuming, can ultimately lapse into a kind of historicism that sidesteps the big meaning question: that is, the radical flux of meaning brought on by changing social and historical horizons over time. Studies of reception can synchronically excavate texts without necessarily speculating on how this context helps reconceive the process of meaning-production – how the act of historicizing challenges notions about the stability of textual meaning. At an extreme, textual exegesis is replaced by historical exegesis. *Now, Voyager* is no longer, via psychoanalytic close readings, a visual essay on sexual difference figuring the potentially liberatory enunciation of woman's desire, but, via historical analysis, a reappropriation of discourses of consumerism as liberatory for women in the 1940s.[14]

Without question, historical reception studies has a strong interpretive dimension: the chief arena for the discovery of meaning and significance has in a sense been displaced from text to context.[15] But, as Janet Staiger writes, the prime objective of materialist approaches is not simply to secure new contextualized meanings for texts, but to attempt a 'historical *explanation* of the event of interpreting a text' by tracing the 'range of [interpretive] strategies available in particular social formations'.[16] Once one makes this meta-interpretive move, questions of value, continuously at the heart of interpretive enterprise, become themselves contextualized. That is, the aesthetic or political value of a film is no longer a matter of its intrinsic characteristics, but of the way those characteristics are deployed by various intertextual and historical forces. A danger of synchronic research is that researchers can find themselves attempting to settle a film's historical meaning, much like a standard interpretation would fix its textual meaning. Ideally, reception theory influenced by cultural and historical materialism analyses, rather, the discontinuities and differences characterizing the uses of a particular film within and beyond its initial appearance. This is not to say that the film in question has no definite historical meanings; simply that what appears to be definite at one moment will be subject to penetrating alterations with the ascendancy of new cultural eras.

Diachronic research is especially important to reception studies, then, because it forces consideration of a film's fluid, changeable and volatile relation to history. These qualifiers are essential for realizing the historicity of meaning beyond origins, and for giving authority to all of the semiotic intrigues surrounding films during the course of their social and historical circulation. The issue of diachrony thus advances the film/culture relation well beyond even 'the massive data of its origins', addressing how that relation is remade continuously through diverse institutions and historical circumstances over the decades subsequent to initial release dates.

The diachronic dimension of Charles Maland's work on Charlie Chaplin, for example, explains how conditions upon the rerelease of this director's films in the 1960s and 1970s helped restore his artistic reputation and star persona, after all of the previous negative publicity stemming from his controversial radicalism and marital mishaps. The changing, more self-critical, political climate of the 1960s and 1970s, combined with auteurism and other transformations in film reviewing and criticism, helped rewrite Chaplin and his films, emphasizing his victimization by Cold War zealots, his artistic genius and his comic persona over his 'Communism' and disastrous relationships. These combined historical factors thus resulted in a new canonization of his works.[17]

A cinematic *histoire totale* thus presses against the boundaries of historical reception study by asking at least that researchers analyse public combat over film meaning rather than unities, historicize their enquiries beyond industrial practices, and pursue diachronic meanings not only to better represent the text's social circulation, but to engage fully with the impact historical context has on meaning. It now remains to ask: what might a cinematic version of *histoire totale* look like?

Before getting to the heart of the matter, a few words about the parameters of this account are in order. Because classical Hollywood cinema has been centre stage for a great deal of work in historical reception studies, my discussion here will pertain primarily to this kind of film. I will address the contextual factors involved in negotiating the meaning of films made in Hollywood roughly between 1917 and 1960 – the so-called classical period in US filmmaking. Though the model I propose may have application to other modes of production (such as documentary and avant-garde film), other national cinemas and visual communications media (such as television), I do not suggest that a total history for one particular kind of filmmaking, no matter how dominant, somehow comprehensively represents others.[18]

I have divided a total history for this kind of film into two large categories: the synchronic and diachronic. The more specific subdivisions under the synchronic are organized in a progressively outward-bound direction, beginning with those areas most closely associated with the production of a film ('cinematic practices'), moving to those technically outside the industry, but closely affiliated with a film's appearance ('intertextual zones'), and ending with social and historical contexts circulating through and around its borders. As we shall see, while each of these areas still apply, the peculiarities of the diachronic dimension dictate a slightly different organization.

These subdivisions are so labelled to maintain familiar distinctions between contextual areas typically explored by researchers. I do not mean to deny the intertextuality and discursivity of all that surrounds the film, as well as the film itself: but for the purposes of clarity in discussion, I wish to avoid collapsing everything contextual into a single, chaotic identity. These three subdivisions – cinematic practices, intertextual zones, and social and historical contexts – depict a geographic space which suggests the intricate situations in which cinema exists historically. Of course, not all of these regions may be equally important to each film analysed. The researcher attempts to discover which regions seem particularly applicable to reconstructing the vital relations which comprise the contexts in which particular films are produced and received.

In addition, the nature of interrelations between various areas is deeply interactive. The film in question, for example, is not just *acted upon* by external forces, it in turn can affect and transform the contextual activities which surround it – as, for example, when controversy over a film's censorship results in changes in censorship codes or public debate about the regulation of media content. Similarly, the relations between an aspect of cinematic practice, such as film style or exhibition, to intertextual zones and historical contexts are not to be understood as ultimately separable, but as fluid and reciprocal: for example, the lushness of 1950s Technicolor melodramatic mise-en-scene in Hollywood is linked intertextually to decors shown in *Better Homes and Gardens* within the overall spectacle of postwar consumer culture.[19] In this example, intertexts and history penetrate the films' visuals at the same time as those visuals continue to construct a utopian vision of consumption. By imagining such reciprocity between areas, we can see historically how film and its contexts act as participants in the discursive fray of which they are a part.

A reception history aimed at a totalized view, then, would ask how the factors within these general areas helped reconstruct the historical conditions of existence for a film at the moment of its first and subsequent releases. However, researchers in reception are not primarily interested in these conditions *per se*, as some film historians might be. Rather, those pursuing issues of reception interrogate such contextual elements to understand how they helped negotiate the film's social meanings and public reception, attempting to pinpoint the meanings in circulation at a given historical moment.

It is important to point out that the viewer in this semantic geography is everywhere and nowhere, neither the product nor the subject of one particular discourse.[20] The viewer does not exist in one stable location in relation to the flux of historical meanings around a film, and therefore cannot be placed conveniently at the centre, the periphery or some other 'niche' within this interaction. Thus, a total history does not tell us (except in the case of empirical research on fans and spectators) how specific individuals responded to films: it cannot generally 'pin' the viewer down as subject to a series of discursive manoeuvres. Instead, it provides a sense of what the historical prospects were for viewing at a given time by illuminating the meanings made available within that moment. A totalized perspective thus depicts how social forces invite viewers to assume positions, giving us a range of possible influences on spectatorship, without securing an embodied viewer. As a result, this depiction is not 'subject free', but underpinned by the assumption that social discourses recruit and depend on social subjects to support them.

Below is a schematic account of the more specific factors that enter into a total history for the classical Hollywood cinema. Many of these have been individually identified as relevant to understanding the historicity of the cinema. Taken together, they begin to provide a sense of the magnitude of a total reception history of a film. [...]

Notes

1 Tony Bennett, quoting Pierre Macherey, in 'Text and social process: the case of James Bond', *Screen Education*, no. 41 (1982), p. 3.

2 John Frow, *Marxism and Literary History* (Cambridge, MA: Harvard University Press, 1986), pp. 187–8.

3 Anthony Easthope, *Literary Into Cultural Studies* (London: Routledge, 1991), p. 113.

4 Traian Stoianovich, *French Historical Method: the Annales Paradigm* (Ithaca: Cornell University Press, 1976), p. 216.

5 Paul Ricoeur, *The Contribution of French Historiography to the Theory of History* (Oxford: Clarendon Press, 1980), p. 19.

6 Braudel writes that his work covering the fifteenth to the eighteenth centuries 'does not claim to have depicted all material life throughout the whole complex world.... What it offers is an attempt to see all these scenes as a whole.... If not to see everything, at least to locate everything, and on the requisite grand scale'. Fernand Braudel, *Capitalism and Material Life, 1400–1800*, trans. Miriam Kochan (London: Weidenfeld and Nicolson, 1967), pp. 441–2.

7 Robert Mandrou, quoted in Stoianovich, *French Historical Method*, p. 112.

8 David Bordwell, 'Our dream cinema: western historiography and the Japanese film', *Film Reader*, no 4 (1979), p. 58. I use Bordwell's phrase 'totalized view' because of its suggestiveness for my analysis, while acknowledging that our perspectives on the relations between film and culture differ.

9 Mike Budd, 'The moments of Caligari', in Mike Budd (ed), *The Cabinet of Dr Caligari* (New Brunswick: Rutgers University Press, 1990), pp. 7–119; Maria LaPlace, 'Producing and consuming the woman's film: discursive struggle in *Now, Voyager*', in Christine Gledhill (ed). *Home Is Where the Heart Is* (London British Film Institute, 1987), pp. 138–66.

10 I am indebted to Dana Polan for coining the apt phrase 'discursive surround' as a means of describing film's contextual situation.

11 May Beth Haralovich, 'Film history and social history', *Wide Angle*, vol. **8** no. 2 (1986), pp. 12–13.

12 Miriam Hansen, *Babel and Babylon: Spectatorship in American Silent Film* (Cambridge, MA: Harvard University Press, 1991), p. 5.

13 Lea Jacobs, *The Wages of Sin: Censorship and the Fallen Woman Film, 1928–1942* (Madison: University of Wisconsin Press, 1991); Annette Kuhn, *Cinema, Censorship, and Sexuality, 1909–1925* (London: Routledge, 1988)

14 Lea Jacobs, '*Now, Voyager*: some problems of enunciation and sexual difference', *Camera Obscura*, no. **7** (1981), pp. 89–104; LaPlace, 'Producing and consuming the woman's film'.

15 See Jonathan Culler on this point in *Framing the Sign: Criticism and Its Institutions* (Norman: University of Oklahoma Press, 1988), p. 148.

16 Janet Staiger, *Interpreting Films: Studies in the Historical Reception of American Cinema* (Princeton: Princeton University Press, 1992), pp. 80–81.

17 Charles Maland, *Chaplin and American Culture: the Evolution of a Star Image* (Princeton: Princeton University Press, 1989), especially pp. 317–60. See also Robert Kapsis's evolutionary treatment of Hitchcock in *Hitchcock: the Making of a Reputation* (Chicago: University of Chicago Press, 1992).

18 Some examples of work in reception studies on other models of production include: Juan Suarez, *Bike Boys, Drag Queens, and Superstars: Avant-Garde, Mass Culture, and Gay Identities in the 1960s Underground Cinema* (Bloomington: Indiana University Press, 1996); and Lauren Rabinovitz, *Points of Resistance: Women, Power, and Politics in the New York Avant-Garde Cinema, 1943–1971* (Urbana: University of Illinois Press, 1991). In the area of other national cinemas, see Annette Kuhn, *Cinema, Censorship, and Sexuality*, Kyoko Hirano, *Mr Smith Goes to Tokyo Under the American Occupation, 1945–1952* (Washington: Smithsonian Institution Press, 1992) and Jostein Gripsrud and Kathrine Skretting (eds), *History of Moving Images: Reports from a Norwegian Project* (Oslo: Research Council of Norway, 1994). Since television and film are such different media, I could not simply equate the two. However, reception studies in film have much to learn from similar enquiries in television studies.

19 Barbara Klinger, *Melodrama and Meaning: History, Culture, and the Films of Douglas Sirk* (Bloomington: Indiana University Press, 1994), pp. 57–68.

20 See Michel Foucault's discussion of subjectivity in relation to discursivity in *The Archaeology of Knowledge*, trans. A.M. Sheridan Smith (New York: Pantheon Books, 1972), p. 200. Foucault does not wish to exclude the problem of the subject, but to 'define the positions and functions that the subject could occupy in the diversity of discourse'.

SECTION NINE
THEORIZING DIFFERENCE(S)

Of all the sections in this book, this is probably the most diverse in terms of the critical and theoretical traditions from which it draws. While some of the work included here is broadly feminist in character, there are also articles that consider race as a key issue and others that operate from gay and lesbian perspectives; there are accounts of representation as well as accounts of spectatorship. When one looks at the articles themselves, one finds that the quality that most links them together is a desire to explore questions which are not readily posable within the critical and methodological traditions from which they derive. In particular they all focus on and seek to problematize the notion of difference as it has previously been formulated in film theory. Since the 1970s, difference in this context has often meant sexual difference, with this expressed as a mutually defining opposition between male and female (see Section Seven). Numerous theoretical accounts of both representation and spectatorship can be characterized by the way in which they adhere to and depend upon the idea that the human race is divided into two fundamental groups – women and men. As powerful and productive as the idea of sexual difference has undoubtedly been, it has sometimes obscured other differences which not only divide up but actively construct the category of 'human' – differences to do with, for example, race, class, national identity, sexual orientation.

This does not mean that these other differences have been ignored in film studies – far from it. Explorations of each of the differences cited above have formed an important part of academic work on film and have substantially benefited our understanding of cinema. At the same time, however, much of this work, not unlike the work on sexual difference, has tended to prioritize one particular difference – be it class or race or sexual orientation – over others. This in turn has often involved setting up further binary oppositions – white/black, for example, or gay/straight or sometimes gay/lesbian. Of course, it is perfectly understandable and legitimate for particular groups to focus on an investigation of that difference which relates most closely to and in part defines their own identity, especially when, as is often the case in this area, that identity does not significantly register in the dominant culture. Binary oppositions are especially useful in this respect inasmuch as they can dramatize a feeling of belonging as well as a sense of exclusion and marginality – *they* have power and *we* don't; *they* are central and *we* are on the edge.

The articles collected here explore some of the limitations and problems

involved in thinking of difference in this way. They offer a sense of identities as constituted in the interplay of differences rather than via binary
oppositions, and they discuss the ways in which differences to do with
race, class, nationality and gender can interact with and cut across each
other within historically and socially specific formations and contexts.
They show us, if we need showing, that we are all many things, not just
men or women but also and at the same time white/black, straight/gay,
working/middle-class as well as mothers/fathers, brothers/sisters, daugh-
ters/sons, etc. At the same time, they retain from earlier work on identity
and difference the need to think of notions of identity in terms of power
and ideology.

Robert Stam and Louise Spence's 'Colonialism, Racism and
Representation: An Introduction' is a wide-ranging article which focuses
primarily on third world cinema but which does not rely on any absolute
either/or division between the western world and the third world. It
includes, amongst other things, discussions of the stereotypical representation of blacks in North American cinema and the representation of racial
difference in Brazilian cinema as well as an account of *The Battle of Algiers*,
a 1966 film directed by an Italian about French colonial rule in Algeria. As
with other anti-racist work, the article reconfigures racial difference so that
the oppressed race, the object of racism, is no longer seen in terms of
Otherness, as that which is designated as Other, as not-Us, by a more
powerful race, but instead is viewed in terms of difference (or, to be more
specific, differences). A space is thereby opened up both for resistance to
definitions and identities imposed by others and for self-identification. The
article's international scope further problematizes any simplistic division
between whiteness and blackness.

The approach adopted by Stam and Spence to racial stereotypes is
similar to that adopted by 1970s feminist work on 'woman as image' in
film. Both tend not to evaluate stereotypical representations, negative and
positive, in terms of how these might relate to some pre-existing reality but
are instead more interested in the cinematic and cultural contexts within
which these stereotypes operate. Hence Stam and Spence's discussion of
point-of-view structures as well as their comparison between North
American and Brazilian images of 'blackness'. One outcome of this is the
undermining of any sense of American or Eurocentric whiteness as the
centre or norm against which other races are simply marked as Other.
Significant in this respect are Stam and Spence's references to instances
of an ironic reversibility where whiteness itself is presented in terms of
Otherness and thereby denaturalized, its limitations revealed for all to see.
In particular, they refer to Jean Rouch's *Petit à Petit* (1970), in which
Parisians are made the objects of an African anthropological study, and, in
more detail, *The Battle of Algiers*, where the white European colonialists
are via various cinematic means rendered an unnatural, alien presence in
the Algerian landscape. Much is made of the scene in *The Battle of Algiers*
where some Algerian women dress up as Europeans in order to plant
bombs. The idea of European whiteness as a costume or disguise that can

be put on and then removed by non-European non-whites clearly throws into disarray any notion of there being fixed, visible divisions between races.

In 'White Privilege and Looking Relations: Race and Gender in Feminist Film Theory', Jane Gaines discusses some of the problems involved in applying feminist-psychoanalytical methods (see Section Seven) to inter-preting images of black women. Gaines's concern that the feminist move-ment has sometimes privileged white middle-class perspectives of female experience over other perspectives, thereby rendering other femininities invisible, is not a new one in feminist criticism. A key feature of feminism is its ability to link women through the identification of shared experiences, yet, as Christine Gledhill has pointed out,

> a feminist theory and cultural practice that seeks practical political effectivity must be able to take account of the intersections of gender with class and racial difference among others. In political terms, it would seem essential to have recourse to some form of recognition through which women can identify with themselves as women and as an oppressed group, yet at the same time relate this to their class experience. (Gledhill 1984: 35)

Gaines's particular concern is with the model of film spectatorship offered by Laura Mulvey in her influential article 'Visual Pleasure and Narrative Cinema' (see extract 34). Mulvey's argument that mainstream cinema is based on a male spectatorial gaze at the female is disputed by Gaines, who points out that in historical terms whites have often been freer to gaze than blacks; because of this, racial difference intervenes into and disrupts Mulvey's model of male voyeurism and fetishism.

Gaines's analysis of the Diana Ross star vehicle *Mahogany* (1975) demonstrates the ways in which racial, gendered and class identity inter-sect with and play off each other, with much of this organized around the Diana Ross character herself – a black, working-class woman whose uncertainty about her identity is largely what the film is about. Gaines argues that *Mahogany*'s coordination of these differences is such that racial and class difference are in the course of the narrative subordinated to sexual difference to the extent that the film seems to invite a psycho-analytical reading (although the traces of class and race remain visible throughout). Like other feminist critics, Gaines worries about what she sees as the universalizing quality of some psychoanalytical thought, and in her article she stresses the need to relate the 'reading positions' constructed by film to the social experience of women, black and white. This is especially important with a film like *Mahogany* which, on a certain level, seems to misrepresent itself in its various attempts to deflect atten-tion away from the class and racial difference upon which its narrative relies.

In 'Feminism, "The Boyz", and Other Matters Regarding the Male', Robyn Wiegman retains the emphasis on the need to think beyond a binary male/female opposition when considering what she refers to as the race/gender nexus. As Wiegman herself puts it, 'the binary description of social positioning betrays the compounded production of identity and difference, their mutual and contradictory inscription not only across the social body but at the specific corporeal sites where the meanings of categories of identity are literally and metaphorically imposed.' Where Wiegman differs from Gaines is in her focus on the representation of black males; she is also less concerned than Gaines with the psychoanalytical method. Instead she locates a particular set of images of black men – drawn from 1990s 'New Jack Cinema' – within a representational history of North American black masculinity, and argues that this history is to a certain extent characterized by a mobility of categorization so that black masculinity has been designated as both 'feminine' and 'hypermasculine'. She also addresses some of the ways in which this mobility, and an associated play of racial and sexual differences, has featured in both racist fantasies and black political struggle. What emerges from Wiegman's article is a sense of images and stereotypes being constantly reworked by different groups within specific contexts.

This sensitivity to the tension between racial and gendered categories means that Wiegman can deal sympathetically with *Boyz N the Hood* (1991), a film which in its systematic privileging of the father figure over the mother could easily be read in patriarchal and even misogynist terms. Wiegman presents a convincing account of the ways in which the film attempts, not entirely successfully, to modify particular models of black male identity. Perhaps surprisingly, given its feminist perspective, the article spends little time discussing the film's female characters (who are fairly marginal in any event) and refers only in passing to the paucity of black women film-makers in US cinema; its usefulness for feminism arguably resides instead in its discussion of masculinity as a set of fractured identities, divided in this instance by race (and class as well, although the article tends to subsume this into racial difference). Patriarchal power and authority are seen as dispersed unevenly across a range of historical and social contexts, and patriarchy itself is accordingly figured as less monolithic, more open to critical interrogation.

In 'There's Something Queer Here', Alexander Doty discusses some of the complexities of difference from a queer perspective. For Doty, 'queerness' refers to the idea that gendered and sexual identity is more fluid and multi-faceted than previously supposed, and that while terms such as 'straight', 'gay' and 'lesbian' should still be seen as important markers of identity, the actual formation of identities, understood here as a process of identification and desire, does not necessarily respect any fixed categorical borders. Doty focuses in particular on Hollywood cinema, which he sees, along with other elements of mass culture, as offering a potentially 'queer' spectatorship to all its audiences, affording them the opportunity to contra-identify, in effect to put a distance between their socially defined selves and their spectatorial identity. To a certain extent, this is the model sometimes used for gay and lesbian spectatorship within a mainstream cinema that seems either indifferent or actively hostile towards same-sex desire. Doty's inclusion of straight-identified audiences in the process of contra-identification suggests that cinema can offer pleasures which else-where would be deemed illicit, and that this can potentially lead to a bene-ficial destabilization of fixed gender identity. However, there is also an implication that gay/lesbian audiences are more attuned to this 'queer' quality, and that their experience of it is accordingly more intense than that of a straight audience.

Doty is insistent that this queer quality is apparent both in the production and in the consumption of films rather than just being the product of an audience reading 'against the grain'. He cites the significant gay produc-tion input into both the musical and horror genres as evidence of a queer aesthetic at work within Hollywood itself; perhaps more importantly, he offers a sense of the entertainment process itself as involving an opening up of and play with identificatory possibilities that has a destabilizing queer quality to it. At the same time, he is concerned that queerness should not simply be seen as a space where straight and non-straight freely meet; for one thing, gay and lesbian identities (and spectatorial positions) tend to be formed under conditions that are considerably more oppressive than those experienced by straights (although more could have been made in his analysis of the ways in which other forms of difference – racial and class – impact upon the formation of identities). In fact, the readings of specific films offered by Doty tend to be gay/lesbian-specific in their detail; and the specific ways in which straight-identified audiences might partici-pate in this queer experience are not discussed at any length. Seen in this way, Doty's work sets an agenda for future critical activity. Its ideas about the complexities of audience response to entertainment cinema, and espe-cially the possibility of there being disparities or gaps between social iden-tities and spectatorial positions, certainly merits further discussion.

Tamsin Wilton's 'On Not Being Lady Macbeth: Some (troubled) Thoughts on Lesbian Spectatorship' has much in common with Doty's article. Both stress the potential mobility of spectatorship and the possi-bility of the spectator identifying with that which is different from her/himself as well as that which is similar. However, as the title of her article indicates, Wilton concentrates on a particular sector of the audience rather than thinking about audiences in general. Like Gaines, she takes issue with the psychoanalytical model of spectatorship offered by Laura Mulvey's 'Visual Pleasure and Narrative Cinema'; for Wilton, such a model renders the very idea of lesbianism – let alone lesbian spectatorship – diffi-cult, if not impossible, to conceptualize, and because of this another way of thinking about spectatorial identity and pleasure is required. Wilton's starting-point, then, is not the theoretical question of whether a lesbian spectatorship can actually exist but rather the fact of lesbian spec-tators and their pleasures which needs to be explained. In doing this, Wilton's article, like Doty's, takes on an unashamedly autobiographical air as she discusses *Strictly Ballroom* (1992), a film which she as a lesbian very much enjoyed but which, as far as its representation of same-sex desire goes, 'sucks' (to use Wilton's term). The apparent paradox of

Wilton's spectatorial pleasure is resolved through a sense of the ways in which she can step away from her lesbian identity, can go on 'queer holiday' as she puts it, and participate in the pleasure of a straight fantasy. Arguably this is facilitated in the case of *Strictly Ballroom* by that film's campness (or assimilated camp), its repeated injunctions to its audiences not to take it too seriously. This temporary abandonment of self is somewhat different from the 'reading against the grain' process sometimes discussed as the principal reading strategy for socially subordinated groups, although importantly Wilton stresses that this 'escape' is staged in the context of social oppression. In this respect, Wilton's version of a queer response to movies is less utopian and less inclusive than the version set out by Doty.

It is difficult to provide a neat cohesive conclusion to this section. As already indicated, the work is too disparate and varied for that. Certainly there is agreement here that thinking of identity in terms of binary oppositions (and especially an opposition between male and female) is not really adequate any more, and that account needs to be taken of the interaction of a range of differences in the formation of particular socially and historically specific identities. This has implications for an understanding of the ways that films operate in representational terms as well as the ways in which they are experienced by audiences. Identities emerge in this respect as sets of processes subject to constant negotiation and renegotiation within specific historical situations. The mobile spectatorship discussed by a number of the articles included here is by no means a free spectatorship, marked and limited as it always is by social relations of power, but its existence does at the very least recognize the possibility of individuals and groups intervening in and effecting the formations of identity. Ultimately the complex and sometimes surprising ways in which categories of difference interact can be seen to produce not just positions of power and subordination but also positions of uncertainty and resistance.

References

Doty, A. (1993). 'There's Something Queer Here', in A. Doty, *Making Things Perfectly Queer*. Minneapolis and London: University of Minnesota Press.

Gaines, J. (1988). 'White Privilege and Looking Relations: Race and Gender in Feminist Film Theory'. *Screen* (4): **29** 12–27.

Gledhill, C. (1984). 'Developments in Film Criticism', in M. A. Doane, P. Mellencamp and L. Williams (eds), *Revision: Essays in Feminist Film Criticism*. Frederick, MD: University Publications of America, 18–48.

Stam, R. and Spence, L. (1983), 'Colonialism, Racism and Representation: An Introduction'. *Screen* (2): 2–20.

Wiegman, R. (1993). 'Feminism, "The Boyz", and Other Matters Regarding the Male'. In S. Cohan and I.R. Hark (eds.), *Screening the Male: Exploring Masculinities in Hollywood Cinema*. London: Routledge, 173–193.

Wilton, T. (1995). 'On Not Being Lady Macbeth: Some (Troubled) Thoughts on Lesbian Spectatorship'. In T. Wilton (ed.), *Immortal Invisible: Lesbians and the Moving Image*. London: Routledge, 143–162.

42 Colonialism, racism and representation: An Introduction

Robert Stam and Louise Spence

[...] We should begin ... with some preliminary definitions. What do we mean by 'colonialism', 'the Third World' and 'racism'? By colonialism, we refer to the process by which the European powers (including the United States) reached a position of economic, military, political and cultural domination in much of Asia, Africa and Latin America. This process, which can be traced at least as far back as the 'voyages of discovery' and which had as its corollary the institution of the slave trade, reached its apogee between 1900 and the end of World War I (at which point Europe had colonised roughly 85% of the earth) and began to be reversed only with the disintegration of the European colonial empires after World War II.

The definition of the 'Third World' flows logically out of this prior definition of colonialism, for the 'Third World' refers to the historical victims of this process – to the colonised, neo-colonised or de-colonised nations of the world whose economic and political structures have been shaped and deformed within the colonial process. The colonial relation has to do with *structural* domination rather than with crude economic ('the poor'), racial ('the non-white'), cultural ('the backward') or geographical categories.

Racism, finally, although not limited to the colonial situation (anti-semitism being a case in point), has historically been both an ally and a product of the colonisation process. It is hardly accidental that the most obvious victims of racism are those whose identity was forged within the colonial process: blacks in the United States, Asians and West Indians in Great Britain, Arab workers in France, all of whom share an oppressive situation and the status of second-class citizens. We will define racism, borrowing from Albert Memmi, as 'the generalized and final assigning of values to real or imaginary differences, to the accuser's benefit and at his victim's expense, in order to justify the former's own privilege or aggression'.[1] Memmi's definition has the advantage of calling attention to the *uses* to which racism is put. Just as the logic of sexism leads to rape, so the logic of racism leads to violence and exploitation. Racism, for Memmi, is almost always a rationale for an already existing or contemplated oppression. Without ignoring the accumulated prejudices and cultural attitudes which prepared the way for racism, there is a sense in which it can be argued that racism comes 'in the wake' of concrete oppressions. Amerindians were called 'beasts' and 'cannibals' *because* white Europeans were slaughtering them and expropriating their land; blacks were slandered as 'lazy' *because* the United States had seized half of their territory; and the colonised were ridiculed as lacking in culture and history *because* colonialism, in the name of profit, was destroying the basis of that culture and the memory of that history.

The same Renaissance humanism which gave birth to the code of perspective – subsequently incorporated, as Baudry points out, into the camera itself – also gave birth to the 'rights of man'. Europe constructed its self-image on the backs of its equally constructed Other – the 'savage', the 'cannibal' – much as phallocentrism sees its self-flattering image in the mirror of woman defined as lack. And just as the camera might therefore be said to inscribe certain features of bourgeois humanism, so the cinematic and televisual apparatuses, taken in their most inclusive sense, might be said to inscribe certain features of European colonialism. The magic carpet provided by these apparatuses flies us around the globe and makes us, by virtue of our subject position, its audio-visual masters. It produces us as subjects, trans-forming us into armchair conquistadores, affirming our sense of power while making the inhabitants of the Third World objects of spectacle for the First World's voyeuristic gaze.

Colonialist representation did not begin with the cinema; it is rooted in a vast colonial intertext, a widely disseminated set of discursive practices. Long before the first racist images appeared on the film screens of Europe and North America, the process of colonialist image-making, and resistance to that process, resonated through Western literature. Colonialist historians, speaking for the 'winners' of history, exalted the colonial enterprise, at bottom little more than a gigantic act of pillage whereby whole continents were bled of their human and material resources, as a philanthropic 'civilising mission' motivated by a desire to push back the fron-tiers of ignorance, disease and tyranny. Daniel Defoe glorified colonialism in *Robinson Crusoe* (1719), a novel whose 'hero' becomes wealthy through the slave trade and through Brazilian sugar mills, and whose first thought, upon seeing human footprints after years of solitude, is to 'get (him) a servant'.

Other European writers responded in more complex and ambiguous ways. The French philosopher Montaigne, writing at the end of the sixteenth century, suggested in 'Des Cannibales' that the Amerindian cannibalising of dead enemy warriors paled in horror when compared to the internecine warfare and torture prac-ticed by European Christians in the name of a religion of love. Shakespeare has Caliban in *The Tempest*, whose name forms an anagram of 'cannibal', curse the European Prospero for having robbed him of his island: 'for I am all the subjects that you have/which first was mine own king'. (Aimé Césaire had to alter Shakespeare's character but slightly, in his 1969 version, to turn him into the anti-colonialist mili-tant Caliban X.[2]) And Jonathan Swift, a century later in *Gulliver's Travels* (1726) portrays colonialism in satirical images that in some ways anticipate Herzog's *Aguirre*:

> A crew of pyrates are driven by a storm they know not whither; at length a Boy discovers Land from the Topmast; they go on shore to rob and plunder; they see an harmless people, are entertained with kindness, they give the country a new name, they take formal posses-sion of it for the king, they set up a rotten plank or a stone for a memorial, they murder two or three dozen of the natives, bring away a couple more by force for a sample, return home and get their Pardon.... And this execrable crew of butchers employed in so pious an expe-dition, is a modern colony sent to convert and civilise an idolatrous and barbarous people.[3]

The struggle over images continues, within literature, into the period of the begin-nings of the cinema. Conrad's *Heart of Darkness* (1902), published but a few years after the first Lumière screenings, describes colonialism in Africa as 'just robbery with violence, aggravated murder on a grand scale' and emphasises its racist underpinnings. 'The conquest of the earth, which mostly means the taking it away from those who have a different complexion or slightly flatter noses than ourselves,' Conrad has his narrator say, 'is not a pretty thing when you look into it too much.'[4][...]

Much of the work on racism in the cinema, like early work on the representation of women, has stressed the issue of the 'positive image'. This reductionism, though not wrong, is inadequate and fraught with methodological dangers. The exact nature of 'positive', first of all, is somewhat relative: black incarnations of patience and gradualism, for example, have always been more pleasing to whites than to blacks. A cinema dominated by positive images, characterised by a bending-over-back-wards-not-to-be-racist attitude, might ultimately betray a lack of confidence in the group portrayed, which usually itself has no illusions concerning its own perfection. ('Just because you're black don't make you right,' one black brother tells another in *Ashes and Embers*, directed by Haile Gerima.) A cinema in which all black actors resembled Sidney Poitier might be as serious a cause for alarm as one in which they all resembled Stepin Fetchit.

We should be equally suspicious of a naive integrationism which simply inserts new heroes and heroines, this time drawn from the ranks of the oppressed, into the old functional roles that were themselves oppressive, much as colonialism invited a few assimilated 'natives' to join the club of the 'elite'. A film like *Shaft* (1971) simply substitutes black heroes into the actantial slot normally filled by white ones, in order to flatter the fantasies of a certain (largely male) sector of the black audience. *Guess Who's Coming to Dinner* (directed by Stanley Kramer, 1967), as its title suggests, invites an elite black into the club of the truly human, but always on white terms. Other films, such as *In the Heat of the Night* (1967), *Pressure Point* (1962), or the television series *Mod Squad*, place black characters in the role of law-enforcers. The ideological function of such images is not dissimilar to that pointed out in Barthes' famous analysis of the *Paris Match* cover which shows a black soldier in French uniform, eyes upraised, saluting what we presume to be the French flag. All citizens, regardless of their colour, can serve law and order, and the black soldier's zeal in serving the established law is the best answer to critics, black and white, of that society. The television series *Roots*, finally, exploited positive images in what was ultimately a cooptive version of Afro-American history. The series' subtitle, 'the saga of an American family', reflects an emphasis on the European-style nuclear family (retrospectively projected onto Kunta's life in Africa) in a film which casts blacks as just another immigrant group making its way toward freedom and prosperity in democratic America.

The complementary preoccupation to the search for positive images, the exposure of negative images or stereotypes, entails similar methodological problems. The positing and recognition of these stereotypes has been immensely useful, enabling us to detect structural patterns of prejudice in what had formerly seemed random phenomena. The exclusive preoccupation with images, however, whether positive or negative, can lead both to the privileging of characterological concerns (to the detriment of other important considerations) and also to a kind of essentialism, as the critic reduces a complex diversity of portrayals to a limited set of reified stereotypes. Behind every black child performer, from Farina to Gary Coleman, the critic discerns a 'pickaninny', behind every sexually attractive black actor a 'buck' and behind every attractive black actress a 'whore'. Such reductionist simplifications run the risk of reproducing the very racism they were initially designed to combat.

The analysis of stereotypes must also take cultural specificity into account. Many North American black stereotypes are not entirely congruent with those of Brazil, also a multi-ethnic New World society with a large black population. While there are analogies in the stereotypical images thrown up by the two cultures – the 'mammy' is certainly a close relation to the '*mae preta*' (black Mother), there are disparities as well. Brazilian historian Emilia Viotti da Costa argues, for instance, that the 'sambo' figure never existed, as reality or stereotype, in Brazilian colonial society.[5] The themes of the 'tragic mulatto' and 'passing for white', similarly, find little echo in the Brazilian context. Since the Brazilian racial spectrum is not binary (black *or* white) but nuances its shades across a wide variety of racial descriptive terms, and since Brazil, while in many ways oppressive to blacks, has never been a rigidly *segregated* society, no figure exactly corresponds to the North American 'tragic mulatto', schizophrenically torn between two radically separate social worlds.

An ethnocentric vision rooted in North American cultural patterns can lead, similarly, to the 'racialising', or the introjection of racial themes into, filmic situations which Brazilians themselves would not perceive as racially connoted. *Deus e Diabo na Terra do Sol (God and the Devil in the Land of the Sun*, directed by Glauber Rocha, 1964) was mistranslated into English as *Black God, White Devil*, suggesting a racial dichotomy not emphasised either in the original title or in the film itself. The humour of *Macunaíma* (1969), similarly, depends on an awareness of Brazilian cultural codes. Two sequences in which the title character turns from black to white, for example, occasionally misread as racist by North Americans, are in fact sardonic comments on Brazil's putative 'racial democracy'.

A comprehensive methodology must pay attention to the *mediations* which intervene between 'reality' and representation. Its emphasis should be on narrative structure, genre conventions, and cinematic style rather than on perfect correctness of representation or fidelity to an original 'real' model or prototype. We must beware of mistakes in which the criteria appropriate to one genre are applied to another. A search for positive images in *Macunaíma*, for example, would be fundamentally misguided, for that film belongs to a carnivalesque genre favouring what Mikhail Bakhtin calls 'grotesque realism'. Virtually all the film's characters are two-dimensional grotesques rather than rounded three-dimensional characters, and the grotesquerie is democratically distributed among all the races, while the most archly grotesque characters are the white industrialist cannibal and his ghoulish spouse. Satirical or parodic films, in the same way, may be less concerned with constructing positive images than with challenging the stereotypical expectations an audience may bring to a film. *Blazing Saddles* lampoons a whole range of ethnic prejudices, mocking audience expectations by having the whites sing 'Ole Man River' while the blacks sing 'I Get No Kick from Champagne'. [...]

One mediation specific to cinema is spectator positioning. The paradigmatic filmic encounters of whites and Indians in the western, as Tom Engelhardt points out, typically involve images of encirclement. The attitude toward the Indian is premised on exteriority. The besieged wagon train or fort is the focus of our attention and sympathy, and from this centre our familiars sally out against unknown attackers characterised by inexplicable customs and irrational hostility: 'In essence, the viewer is forced behind the barrel of a repeating rifle and it is from that position, through its gun sights, that he [sic] receives a picture history of western colonialism and imperialism.'[6] The possibility of sympathetic identifications with the Indians is simply ruled out by the point-of-view conventions. The spectator is unwittingly sutured into a colonialist perspective.

A film like *The Wild Geese* (directed by Andrew McLaglen, 1978) inherits the conventions of anti-Indian westerns and extends them to Africa. This glorification of the role of white mercenaries in Africa makes the mercenaries, played by popular heroic actors Richard Burton, Richard Harris and Roger Moore, the central focus of our sympathy. Even the gamblers and opportunists among them, recruited from the flotsam and jetsam of British society, are rendered as sympathetic, lively and humorous. Killing Africans *en masse*, the film implies, fosters camaraderie and somehow brings out their latent humanity. White Europe's right to determine Africa's political destiny, like the white American right to Indian land in the western, is simply assumed throughout the film.

In *The Wild Geese*, the imagery of encirclement is used against black Africans, as the spectator, positioned behind the sight of mercenary machine guns, sees them fall in their hundreds. One of the crucial innovations of *Battle of Algiers* (directed by Gillo Pontecorvo, 1966) was to invert this imagery of encirclement and exploit the identificatory mechanisms of cinema on behalf of the colonised rather than the coloniser. Algerians, traditionally represented in cinema as shadowy figures, picturesquely backward at best and hostile and menacing at worst, are here treated with respect, dignified by close-ups, shown as speaking subjects rather than as manipulable objects. While never caricaturing the French, the film exposes the oppressive logic of colonialism and consistently fosters our complicity with the Algerians. It is through Algerian eyes, for example, that we witness a condemned Algerian's walk to his execution. It is from *within* the casbah that we see and hear the French troops and helicopters. This time it is the colonised who are encircled and menaced and with whom we identify.

One sequence, in which three Algerian women dress in European style in order to pass the French checkpoints and plant bombs in the European sector, is particularly effective in controverting traditional patterns of identification. Many critics, impressed with the film-makers' honesty in showing that the FLN committed terrorist acts against civilians, lauded this sequence for its 'objectivity'. (Objectivity, as Fanon pointed out, almost always works against the colonised.) But that *Battle of Algiers* shows such acts is ultimately less important than *how* it shows them; the signified of the diegesis (terrorist actions) is less important than the mode of address and the positioning of the spectator. The film makes us want the women to complete their task, not necessarily out of political sympathy but through the mechanisms of cinematic identification: scale (close shots individualise the three women); off-screen sound (we hear the sexist comments as if from the women's aural perspective); and especially point-of-view editing. By the time the women plant the bombs, our identification is so complete that we are not terribly disturbed by a series of close shots of the bombs' potential victims. Close-ups of one of the women alternate with close-ups of French people in a cafe, the eyeline matches suggesting that she is contemplating the suffering her bomb will cause. But while we might think her cruel for taking innocent life, we are placed within her perspective and admire her for having the courage to perform what has been presented as a dangerous and noble mission.

Other narrative and cinematic strategies are deployed in this sequence to solicit support for the three women. The narrative placement of the sequence itself presents their action as the fulfilment of the FLN promise, made in the previous sequence, to respond to the French terror bombing of the casbah. Everything here contributes to the impression that the bombing will be an expression of the rage of an entire people rather than the will of a fanatical minority. It is constructed, therefore, not as an individual emotional explosion but as a considered political task undertaken with reluctance by an organised group. The sequence consequently challenges the image of anti-colonialist guerrillas as terrorist fanatics lacking respect for human life. Unlike the Western mass media, which usually restrict their definition of 'terror' to anti-establishment violence – state repression and government-sanctioned aerial bombings are not included in the definition – *Battle of Algiers* presents anti-colonialist terror as a response to colonialist violence. We are dealing here with what might be called the political dimension of syntagmatic organisation; while the First World media usually present colonial repression as a response to 'leftist subversion', *Battle of Algiers* inverts the sequencing. Indeed, examining the film as a whole, we might say that Pontecorvo 'highjacks' the techniques of mass-media reportage – hand-held cameras, frequent zooms, long lenses – to express a political point of view rarely encountered in establishment-controlled media.

The *mise-en-scène*, too, creates a non-sexist and anti-colonialist variant on the classic cinematic *topos*: women dressing in front of a mirror. The lighting highlights the powerful dignity of the womens' faces as they remove their veils, cut their hair and apply make-up so as to look European. The mirror here is not the instrument of *vanitas*, but a revolutionary tool. The women regard themselves, without coyness, as if they were putting on a new identity with which they do not feel entirely comfortable. They perform their task in a disciplined manner and without vindictive remarks about their future victims.

The film also highlights the larger social dimension of the drama in which the women are involved. The colonial world, writes Fanon, is a world cut in two: 'In the colonies it is the policeman and the soldier who are the official instituted go-betweens, the spokesmen of the settler and his rule of oppression.'[7] The background imagery, readable thanks to the depth of field, show that the French have imposed their regime by what amounts to military occupation. The French are in uniform, the Algerians in civilian dress. The casbah is the Algerian's home; for the French it is an outpost on a frontier. The barbed wire and checkpoints remind us of other occupations, thus eliciting our sympathy for a struggle against a foreign occupant. The proairetic 'code of actions', meanwhile, shows the soldiers treating the Algerians with racist scorn and suspicion, while they greet the Europeans with a friendly 'bonjour'. They misperceive the three women as French and flirtatious when in fact they are Algerian and revolutionary. Their sexism, furthermore, prevents them from seeing women, generally, as potential revolutionaries. In the negative dialectic of oppression, the slave (the colonised, the black, the woman) knows the mind of the master better than the master knows the mind of the slave.

Western attitudes toward non-Western peoples are also played on here. Hassiba is first seen in traditional Arab costume, her face covered by a veil. So dressed, she is a reminder of Arab women in other films who function as a sign of the exotic. But as the sequence progresses, we become increasingly close to the three women, though paradoxically, we become close to them only as they strip themselves of their safsaris, their veils, and their hair. They transform themselves into Europeans, people with whom the cinema more conventionally allows the audience to identify. At the same time, we are made aware of the absurdity of a system in which people warrant respect only if they look and act like Europeans. The French colonialist myth of 'assimilation', the idea that select Algerians could be first-class French citizens, is demystified. Algerians can assimilate, it is suggested, but only at the price of shedding everything that is characteristically Algerian about them – their religion, their clothes, their language.

If *Battle of Algiers* exploits conventional identification mechanisms on behalf of a group traditionally denied them, other films critique colonialism and colonialist point-of-view conventions in a more ironic mode. *Petit à Petit* (directed by Jean Rouch, 1969) inverts the hierarchy often assumed within the discipline of anthropology, the academic offspring of colonialism, by having the African protagonist Damouré 'do anthropology' among the strange tribe known as the Parisians, interrogating them about their folkways. Europe, usually the bearer of the anthropological gaze, is here subjected to the questioning regard of the other. *How Tasty Was My Little Frenchman* (directed by Nelson Pereira dos Santos, 1971), meanwhile, updates Montaigne by persuading us to sympathise with Tupinamba cannibals. The film plays ironically on the traditional identification with European heroes by placing the camera, initially, on American shores, so that the Amerindian discovers the European rather than the reverse. By the final shot, which shows the Frenchman's Tupinamba lover dining on him while manifesting no emotion beyond ordinary culinary pleasure, our 'natural' identification with the coloniser has been so completely subverted that we are quite indifferent to his fate.

The question of point of view is crucial then, but it is also more complex than might at first appear. The granting of point-of-view shots to the oppressed does not guarantee a non-colonialist perspective, any more than Hitchcock's granting of subjective shots to the female protagonist of *Marnie* inoculates that film from what is ultimately a patriarchal and infantilising discourse. The arch-racist *The Birth of a Nation* grants Gus, the sexually aggressive black man, a number of subjective shots as he admires little Flora. The racism in such a case may be said to be displaced from the code of editing onto the code of character construction, here inflected by the projection of white sexual paranoia onto the black male, in the case of Gus, and of patriarchal chivalry (tinged perhaps with authorial desire), in the case of Flora. The Brazilian film *João Negrinho* (directed by Oswaldo Censoni, 1954) is entirely structured around the perspective of its focal character, an elderly ex-slave. The film apparently presents all events from João's point of view so as to elicit total sympathy, yet what the film elicits sympathy *for* is in fact a paternalistic vision in which 'good' blacks are to leave their destiny in the hands of well-intentioned whites. [...]

Notes

1 Albert Memmi, *Dominated Man*, Boston, Beacon Press, 1968, p. 186.
2 See Aimé Césaire, *Une Tempête*, Paris, Seuil, 1969.
3 Jonathan Swift, *Gulliver's Travels*, New York, Random House, 1958, p. 241.
4 Joseph Conrad, *Heart of Darkness*, New York: New American Library, 1950, p. 69.
5 See Emilia Viotti da Costa, 'Slave Images and Realities', in *Comparative Perspectives on Slavery in New World Plantation Societies*, New York, New York Academy of Sciences, 1977.
6 Tom Engelhardt, 'Ambush at Kamikaze Pass', *Bulletin of Concerned Asian Scholars*, Winter-Spring 1971, vol. **3**, no. 1.
7 Frantz Fanon, *The Wretched of the Earth*, New York, Grove Press, 1968 p. 38.

43 White privilege and looking relations: race and gender in feminist film theory

Jane Gaines

[...] What I want to do here is to show how a theory of the text and its spectator, based on the psychoanalytic concept of sexual difference, is unequipped to deal with a film which is about racial difference and sexuality. The Diana Ross star-vehicle *Mahogany* (directed by Berry Gordy, 1975) immediately suggests a psychoanalytic approach because the narrative is organised around the connections between voyeurism and photographic acts, and because it exemplifies the classical cinema which has been so fully theorised in Lacanian terms. But as I will argue, the psychoanalytic model works to block out considerations which assume a different configuration, so that, for instance, the Freudian-Lacanian scenario can eclipse the scenario of race-gender relations in Afro-American history, since the two accounts of sexuality are fundamentally incongruous. The danger here is that when we use a psychoanalytic model to explain black family relations, we force an erroneous universalisation and inadvertently reaffirm white middle-class norms. [...]

[...] In *Mahogany*, her follow-up to *Lady Sings The Blues*, Diana Ross plays an aspiring fashion designer who dreams of pulling herself up and out of her Chicago South Side neighbourhood by means of a high-powered career. During the day, Tracy Chambers is assistant to the modelling supervisor for a large department store. At night she attends design school, where the instructor reprimands her for sketching a cocktail dress instead of completing the assignment, the first suggestion of the exotic irrelevance of her fantasy career. She loses her job, but the famous fashion photographer Sean McEvoy (Anthony Perkins) discovers her as a model and whisks her off to Rome. There, Tracy finally realises her ambition to become a designer, when a wealthy Italian admirer gives her a business of her own. After the grand show unveiling her first collection of clothes, she returns to Chicago and is reunited with community organiser Brian Walker (Billy Dee Williams), whose political career is a counterpoint to Tracy's modelling career.

With its long fashion photography montage sequences temporarily interrupting the narrative, *Mahogany* invites a reading based on the alternation between narrative and woman-as-spectacle as theorised by Laura Mulvey in 'Visual Pleasure and Narrative Cinema'. To the allure of pure spectacle these sequences add the fascination of masquerade and transformation. Effected with wigs and make-up colours, the transformations are a play on and against 'darkness'; Diana Ross is a high-tech Egyptian queen, a pale mediaeval princess, a turbaned Asiatic, a body-painted blue nymph. As her body colour is powdered over or washed out in bright light, and as her long-haired wigs blow around her face, she becomes suddenly 'white'.

Contemporary motion pictures never seem to exhaust the narrative possibilities associated with the camera-as-deadly-weapon metaphor; *Mahogany* adds to this the sadomasochistic connotations of high fashion photography with reference to the mid-seventies work of Guy Bourdin and Helmut Newton, linked to the tradition of 'attraction by shock'.[1] The montage sequences chronicling Tracy's career, from perfume ads to high fashion magazine covers, equate the photographic act with humiliation and violation. Camera zoom and freeze-frame effects translate directly into aggression, as in the sequence in which Sean pushes Tracy into a fountain and her dripping image solidifies into an Italian Revlon advertisement. Finally, the motif of stopping-the-action-as-aggression is equated with the supreme violation: attempted murder. Pressing his favourite model to her expressive limits, Sean drives her off an expressway ramp. Since this brutality escalates after the scene in which he fails with Tracy in bed, the film represents her punishment as a direct consequence of his impotence.

With its classic castration threat scenario, its connection between voyeurism and sadism, and its reference to fetishisation – as seen in Sean's photographic shrine to the models he has abused – *Mahogany* is the perfect complement to a psychoanalytic analysis of classical Hollywood's visual pleasure. The film further provides material for such an analysis by producing its own 'proof' that there is only an incremental difference between voyeurism (fashion photography) and sadism (murder). The black and white photographic blow-ups of Tracy salvaged from the death car seem undeniable evidence of the fine line between looking and killing, or, held at another angle, between advertising imagery and pornography.

This, then, is to suggest the kind of evidence in the film which would support an analysis of it as patriarchal discourse, in its use of the female image as fetish to assuage castration anxiety, and through its rich offering of views to please the male spectator. There's even an inescapable suggestion of voyeurism as pathology, since the gaze is that of the actor whose star persona is fatally haunted by the protagonist of *Psycho*. To explain the ideological function of the film in terms of the construction of male pleasure, however, is to 'aid and abet' the film's other ideological project. In following the line of analysis I have outlined, one is apt to step into an ideological signifying trap set up by the chain of meanings that lead away from seeing the film in terms of racial conflict. Because there are so many connotative paths – photographer exploits model, madman assaults woman, voyeur attempts murder – we may not immediately see white man as aggressor against black woman. Other strategies encourage the viewer to forget or not notice racial issues. For instance, the narrative removes Tracy from racially polarised Chicago to Rome, where the brown Afro-American woman with Caucasian features is added to the collection of a photographer who names his subjects after prized objects or their qualities. Losing her black community identity, Tracy becomes Mahogany, acquiring the darkness, richness and value the name connotes; that is, her blackness becomes commodified.

Mahogany functions ideologically for black viewers in the traditional Marxist sense, that is, in the way the film obscures the class nature of social antagonisms. This has certain implications for working-class black viewers, who would gain most from seeing the relationship between race, gender and class oppression. Further, *Mahogany* has the same trouble with representing black femaleness that the wider culture has had historically; a black female is either all woman and tinted black, or mostly black and scarcely woman. These two expectations correspond with the two worlds and two struggles which structure the film: the struggle over the sexual objectification of Tracy's body in the face of commercial exploitation, and the struggle of the black community in the face of class exploitation. But the film identifies this antagonism as the hostility between fashion and politics, embodied respectively by Tracy and Brian, and it is through them that it organises conflict and, eventually, reconciliation. Intensifying this conflict between characters, the film contrasts 'politics' and 'fashion' in one daring homage to the aesthetic of 'attraction by shock'; Sean arranges his models symmetrically on the back stairwell of a run-down Chicago apartment building and uses the confused tenants and street people as props. Flamboyant excess, the residue of capital, is juxtaposed with a kind of dumb-founded poverty. For a moment, the scene figures the synthesis of gender, class and race, but the political glimpse is fleeting. Forced together as a consequence of the avant-garde's socially irresponsible quest for a new outrage, the political antagonisms are suspended – temporarily immobilised as the subjects pose.

The connection between gender, class and race oppression is also denied as the ghetto photography session's analogy between commercial exploitation and race/class exploitation merely registers on the screen as visual incongruity. Visual discrepancy, which, as I have argued, is used for aesthetic effect, also makes it difficult to grasp the confluence of race, class and gender oppression in the image of Tracy Chambers. The character's class background magically becomes decor in the film – it neither radicalises her nor drags her down; instead it sets her off. Diana Ross is alternately weighed down by the glamour iconography of commercial modelling or stripped to a black body. But the *haute couture* iconography ultimately dominates the film. Since race is decorative and class does not reveal itself to the eye, Tracy can only be seen as exploited in terms of her role as a model.

If the film plays down race, it does not do so just to accommodate white audiences. In worshipping the success of the black cult star and combining this with Diana Ross's own dream-come-true – a chance to design all of the costumes in her own film – *Mahogany* hawks the philosophy of black enterprise and social aspiration. Here it does not matter where you come from, what you should be asking yourself, in the words of the theme song, is 'Where are you going, do you know?' Race, then, should be seen as any other obstacle – to be transcended through diligent work and dedication to a goal. Supporting the film's self-help philosophy is the related story of Diana Ross's 'discovery' as a skinny teenager singing in a Baptist Church in

Detroit. With *Mahogany*, Motown president and founder Berry Gordy (who fired Tony Richardson and took over the film's direction) helps Diana Ross to make something of herself again, just as he helped so many aspiring recording artists, by coaching them in money management and social decorum in his talent school.

The phenomenon of Motown Industries is less a comment on the popularity of the self-help philosophy than a verification of the discrepancy between the opportunity formula and the social existence of black Americans. Ironically, black capitalism's one big success thrives on the impossibility of black enterprise: soul entertainment as compensation and release sells because capitalism cannot deliver well-being to all. Black music and performance, despite the homogenisation of the original forms, represents a utopian aspiration for black Americans, as well as for white suburbanites. Simon Frith describes the need supplied by rock fantasy:

> Black music had a radical, rebellious edge: it carried a sense of possibility denied in the labor market; it suggested a comradeship, a sensuality, a grace and joy and energy lacking in work ... the power of rock fantasy rests, precisely on utopianism.[2]

Given that popular culture can accommodate the possibility of both containment and resistance in what Stuart Hall calls its 'double movement', I want to turn to the ways *Mahogany* can be seen to move in the other direction.[3]

Racial conflict looms or recedes in this film rather like the perceptual trick in which, depending on the angle of view, one swirling pattern or the other pops out at the viewer. Some perceptual ambiguity, for instance, is built into the confrontation between black and white, as in the scene in which Sean lures Brian into a struggle over an unloaded weapon. The outcome, in which Sean, characterised as a harmless eccentric, manipulates Brian into pulling the trigger, could be read as confirming the racist conception that blacks who possess street reflexes are murderous aggressors. *Ebony* magazine, the black equivalent of *Life* magazine in the US, however, features a promotional still of the scene (representing Brian holding a gun over Sean), with a caption describing how Brian is tricked but still wins the fight.[4] Just as viewers choose the winners of such ambiguous conflicts, they may also choose to inhabit 'looking' structures. [...] Certainly more work needs to be done with the positioning of the audience around the category of race, considering, for instance, the social prohibitions against the black man's sexual glance, the interracial intermingling of male 'looks', and other visual taboos related to sanctions against interracial sexuality, but these are beyond the scope of this article.

One of the original tenets of contemporary feminist film theory – that the (male) spectator possesses the female indirectly through the eyes of the male protagonist (his screen surrogate) – is problematised here by the less privileged black male gaze. Racial hierarchies of access to the female image also relate to other scenarios which are unknown by psychoanalytic categories. Considering the racial categories which psychoanalysis does not recognise, then, we see that the white male photographer monopolises the classic patriarchal look controlling the view of the female body, and that the black male protagonist's look is either repudiated or frustrated. The sumptuous image of Diana Ross is made available to the spectator via the white male character (Sean) but *not* through the look of the black male character (Brian). In the sequence in which Tracy and Brian first meet outside her apartment building, his 'look' is renounced. In each of the three shots of Tracy from Brian's point of view, she turns from him, walking out of his sight and away from the sound of his voice as he shouts at her through a megaphone. The relationship between the male and female protagonists is negotiated around Brian's bullhorn, emblem of his charismatic black leadership, through which he tries to reach both the black woman and his constituents. Both visual and audio control is thus denied the black male, and the failure of his voice is consistently associated with Tracy's publicity image in the white world. The discovery by Brian's aides of the Mahogany advertisement for Revlon in *Newsweek* coincides with the report that the Gallup polls show the black candidate trailing in the election. Later, the film cuts from the *Harper's Bazaar* cover featuring Mahogany to Brian's limping campaign where the sound of his voice magnified through a microphone is intermittently drowned out by a passing train as he makes his futile pitch to white factory workers. The manifest goal of the film, the reconciliation of the black heterosexual couple, is thwarted by the commercial appropriation of her image, but, in addition, its highly-mediated form threatens the black political struggle.

[...] Quite simply, then, there are structures relevant to any interpretation of *Mahogany* which override the patriarchal scenario feminists have theorised as formally determining. From Afro-American history, we should recall the white male's appropriation of the black woman's body which weakened the black male and undermined the community. From Afro-American literature, we should also consider the scenario of the talented and beautiful mulatta who 'passes' in white culture, but decides to return to black society. The mulatta suggests the rich possibilities of a theory of black female representation which takes account of 'passing' as an eroticising alternation and a peculiar play on difference, as well as a sign of the double consciousness of those women who can be seen as either black or white at the same time as they may see themselves as both races at once. Further, we need to reconsider the woman's picture narrative convention – the career renounced in favour of the man – in the context of black history. Tracy's choice recapitulates black aspiration and the white middle class model which equates stable family life with respectability, but her decision is significantly different from the white heroine's capitulation since it favours black community cooperation over acceptance by white society. Finally, one of the most difficult questions raised by Afro-American history and literature has to do with interracial heterosexuality and sexual 'looking'. *Mahogany* suggests that, since a black male character is not allowed the position of control occupied by a white male character, race could be a factor in the construction of cinematic language. More work on looking and racial taboos might determine whether or not mainstream cinema can offer the male spectator the pleasure of looking at a white female character via the gaze of a black male character. Framing the question of male privilege and viewing pleasure as the 'right to look' may help us to rethink film theory along more materialist lines, considering, for instance, how some groups have historically had the licence to 'look' openly while other groups have 'looked' illicitly. In other words, does the psychoanalytic model allow us to consider the prohibitions against homosexuality and miscegenation?

  Feminists who use psychoanalytic theory have been careful to point out that 'looking' positions do not correlate with social groups, and that ideological posi-

tioning is placement in a representational system which has no one-to-one correspondence with social experience. This, of course, keeps the levels of the social
ensemble hopelessly separate. While I would not want to argue that form is ideologically neutral, I would suggest that we have overemphasised the ideological function
of 'signifying practice' at the expense of considering other ideological implications
of the conflicting meanings in the text. Or, as Terry Lovell puts it:

> ... while interpretation depends on analysis of the work's signifying practice, assessment of
> its meanings from the point of view of its validity, or of its ideology, depends on compar-
> ison between those structures of meaning and their object of reference, through the media-
> tion of another type of discourse.[5]

The impetus behind Marxist criticism, whether we want to admit it or not, is to make
comparisons between social reality as we live it and ideology as it does not correspond to that reality. This we attempt to do knowing full well (having learned from
post-structuralism), the futility of looking for real relations which are completely
outside ideology in either the present or in history. And we probably need to turn this
critique on the emerging notion of the 'days of slavery' as the key to black female
sexuality, in order to avoid the temptation of using it as some searing truth which,
held up to the bloated discourses of patriarchy, had the power to make them finally
groan and shrivel.

 Thus, while I am still willing to argue, as I did in the earlier version of this
article, that we can see the *Mahogany* narrative as a metaphor of the search for
black female sexuality, I see something else in hindsight. I would describe this as
the temptation in an emerging black feminist criticism, much like an earlier
tendency in lesbian criticism, to place sexuality safely out of patriarchal bounds
by declaring it outside culture, by furtively hiding it in subcultural enclaves where
it can remain 'its essential self', protected from the meaning-making mainstream
culture. *Mahogany*, then, is finally about the mythical existence of something
elusive yet potent. We know it through what white men do to secure it, and what
black men are without it. It is the ultimate object of desire to the photographer-
connoisseur of women who dies trying to record its 'trace' on film. It is known by
degree – whatever is most wild and enigmatic, whatever cannot be conquered or
subdued – the last frontier of female sexuality. Although it is undetectable to the
advertising men who can only analyse physical attributes, it is immediately
perceptible to a lesbian (Gavina herself, the owner of the Italian advertising
agency), who uses it to promote the most intangible and subjective of commodities – perfume.[6] Contrary to the suggestion that black female sexuality might still
remain in excess of culture, and hence unfathomed and uncodified, it is worked
over again and again in mainstream culture because of its apparent elusiveness,
and in this context it is rather like bottled scent which is often thought to convey its
essence to everyone but the person wearing it.

 To return to my main point, as feminists have theorised women's sexuality, they
have universalised from the particular experience of white women, thus effecting
what Hortense Spillers has called a 'deadly metonymy'.[7] While white feminists
theorise the female image in terms of objectification, fetishisation and symbolic
absence, their black counterparts describe the body as the site of symbolic resist-

ance and the 'paradox of non-being', a reference to the period in Afro-American history when black female did not signify 'woman'.[8] What strikes me still in this comparison is the stubbornness of the terms of feminist discourse analysis which has not been able to deal, for instance, with what it has meant historically to be designated as not-human, and how black women, whose bodies were legally not their own, fought against treatment based on this determination. Further, feminist analysis of culture as patriarchal cannot conceive of any connection between the female image and class or racial exploitation which includes the male. Historically, black men and women, although not equally endangered, have been simultaneously implicated in incidents of interracial brutality. During two different periods of Afro-American history, sexual assault, '... symbolic of the effort to conquer the resistance the black woman could unloose', was a warning to the entire black community[9] If, as feminists have argued, women's sexuality evokes an unconscious terror in men, then black women's sexuality represents a special threat to white patriarchy; the possibility of its eruption stands for the aspirations of the black race as a whole.

My frustration with the feminist voice that insists on change *at the level of language* is that this position can only deal with the historical situation described above by turning it into discourse, and even as I write this, acutely aware as I am of the theoretical prohibitions against mixing representational issues with historical ones, I feel the pressure to transpose people's struggles into more discursively manageable terms. However, a theory of ideology which separates the levels of the social formation, in such a way that it is not only inappropriate but theoretically impossible to introduce the category of history into the analysis, cannot be justified with Marxism. This has been argued elsewhere by others, among them Stuart Hall, who finds the 'universalist tendency' found in both Freud and Lacan responsible for this impossibility. The incompatibility between Marxism and psychoanalytic theory is insurmountable at this time, he argues, because 'the concepts elaborated by Freud (and reworked by Lacan) cannot, *in their in-general and universalist form*, enter the theoretical space of historical materialism'.[10] In discussions within feminist film theory, it has often seemed the other way round – that historical materialism could not enter the space theorised by discourse analysis drawing on psychoanalytic concepts. Sealed off as it is (in theory), this analysis may not comprehend the category of the real historical subject, but its use will always have implications *for* that subject.

Notes

1 Nancy Hall-Duncan, *The History of Fashion Photography*, New York, Alpine Books, 1979, p. 196.
2 Simon Frith, *Sound Effects*, New York Pantheon, 1981, p. 264.
3 Stuart Hall, 'Notes on Deconstructing "The Popular" ', in *People's History and Socialist Theory*, p. 228.
4 'Spectacular New Film for Diana Ross: "Mahogany" ', *Ebony*, October, 1975, p. 146.
5 Terry Lovell, *Pictures of Reality*, London, British Film Institute, 1980, p. 90.
6 Richard Dyer, 'Mahogany', in Charlotte Brunsdon (ed), *Films for Women*, London, British Film Institute, 1986, p. 135, suggested this first about Gavina.

7 Hortense J Spillers, 'Interstices: A Small Drama of Words', in Vance, *Pleasure and Danger*, p. 78.

8 Ibid, p. 77.

9 Angela Davis, 'The Black Woman's Role in the Community of Slaves', *The Black Scholar*, December 1971 p. 11.

10 Stuart Hall, 'Debate: Psychology, Ideology and the Human Subject', *Ideology and Consciousness*, October 1977, pp. 118–19.

44 Feminism, 'The Boyz', and other matters regarding the male

Robyn Wiegman

When *Newsweek* featured the street smart hero of blaxploitation films, John Shaft, on its cover in October, 1972, it was marking a new era for Hollywood cinema: 'All over the country', the cover story exclaimed, ' "bad-ass niggers" are collecting dues with a vengeance – and, if you don't believe it, just head downtown for a movie' (October 23, 1972: 74). By the end of the decade, however, African American male stars were increasingly finding themselves the twilight figures in interracial male bonding films, and the high hopes of black cinema in the 1970s seemed at an end. But now, *Newsweek* is heralding another revolution. 'With 19 films this year', it asserts, 'Hollywood fades to black' (June 10, 1991: 50).[1] And as anyone knows who has gone screening, the primary images issuing from these new films concern the historical complexity and contemporary conditions affecting the African American male, whose high rates of poverty, incarceration, and early death have coalesced in the startling appellation: 'an endangered species' (Gibbs 1988). At risk for extinction are several generations, and although cinema can certainly not be collapsed into a naive 'real,' these new films take quite seriously and self-consciously their representational role as modeling a future for today's young black men.

How do we understand the historical emergence of this 'New Jack Cinema', as *Newsweek* (June 10, 1991: 51) calls it, and what kinds of critical discourse can negotiate the political demands implicit in their narrative production? I ask these questions from an avowedly feminist position, foregrounding my political interests not in order to supplant the radical racial content and context of this cinematic production, but to approach, once again, the compelling critical issue of representation and what has been called, reductively and problematically, multicultural difference. It is perhaps no accident that the critical language in cinema studies surrounding issues of gender, race, class, and/or sexuality so clearly and easily betrays the asymmetry of cultural relations – reiterating 'difference' without the positivity of a critical analysis into its logical underpinnings, most often white, heterosexual, bourgeois, and male. But already, right here, we confront the political and theoretical difficulty of the whole difference dilemma, where the paradigms available for our articulation of the multiplicity of social subjectivity and (dis)empowerment too often fail to comprehend their inherent complexity. Simply positing the primary terms of each binary configuration does not make possible the many instances in which social positioning straddles the strict duality of oppressor/oppressed, where rights and privileges may be accorded along one particular axis but are circumvented and violently denied along others. Most importantly, the binary description of social positioning betrays the compounded production of identity and difference, their mutual and contradictory inscription not only across the social body, but at the specific corporeal sites where the meanings of categories of identity are literally and metaphorically imposed.

It is this situation, in which social positioning is often at odds within itself, that attends the cultural location of and tensions surrounding the category of identity defined as the African American male. For in his relation of sameness to the masculine and in his threatening difference to the primacy of white racial supremacy, the African American male is stranded between the competing – and at times overdetermining – logics of race and gender. Denied full admittance to the patriarchal province of the masculine through the social scripting of blackness as innate depravity, and occupying a position of enhanced status through masculine privilege in relation to black women, the African American male challenges our understanding of cultural identity and (dis)empowerment based on singular notions of inclusion and exclusion. The simultaneity of his position – to be at once inside and outside the definitional domains of hierarchical empowerment – demonstrates the difficulty of maintaining unified and disengaged readings of the structure and function of race, class, sexuality, and/or gender. Instead, we are impelled toward thinking of new ways to approach not simply relations of identity and difference but, most crucially, their embodied asymmetries as well. In doing so, various complexities within the race/gender nexus, in particular, can be revealed. [...]

It is within this context that I want to read the emergence of the new black cinema of the 1990s, where we can approach some of the complexities of the race/gender nexus by understanding how the deployment of the discourse of sexual difference has functioned historically as the governing framework for representational productions of the African American male. For it is in the oscillation between feminization (buffoonish Uncle Tom) and hypermasculinization (well-endowed rapist) that the contradictory social positioning of the black male has been negotiated, providing the means for disavowing his sameness to the masculine on one hand, while marking his masculinity as racially produced excess on the other. Importantly, where the logic of white supremacy and the white masculine's pre-eminent cultural positionality are overtly secured in each of these scenarios, the relationship between the feminine and the black masculine is just as thoroughly opposed. In casting the feminine as either an internalized, effete consciousness or the externalized emblem of the black male's sexual threat, the discourse of sexual difference inscribes the relationship between the black masculine and the feminine (of any racial designation) as coterminous, in metaphor or material practice, with psychic dissolution and death. Not surprisingly, such an inscription engenders a political context of distrust, alienation, and paralysis, making affiliations across categories of identity and difference difficult to envision, let alone to articulate and sustain.

While the oscillation between feminization and hypermasculinization varies according to the specific economic, social, and political contexts defining the cultural terrain, it is possible nonetheless to mark the historical arrival of the mythology of the phallicized black rapist as engendered by African American emancipation in the late nineteenth century. Here, the minstrel figuration of the African American male as Sambo, Tambo, Bones, Uncle Remus, and Jim Crow is joined by a new, highly stylized disciplinary representation: the myth of the black male rapist, defiler of white womanhood. Through the guise of an aggressive, hyperphallic masculinity, the symbolic feminization of the black male that characterizes the popular consumptive sphere is exchanged for a discursive scenario that begets literal castration. As Trudier Harris discusses, reconstruction signals a transition in the cultural meaning of lynch law, marking not only its articulation as a racially coded formulation, but defining that formulation as the symbolic linkage between lynching, castration, and an assumed black male sexual predilection for white women. In casting the white male as defender of white female sexuality, the economic crisis wrought by the transformation from slavery to freedom is translated into gendered terms, offering the dominant culture a powerful means through which not only black men but the entire black population could be recontained as innately, if no longer legally, inferior. As Richard Wright would later depict in *Native Son*, even the acusation of rape serves as 'that death before death came' (1966: 214), a death whose frequent culmination in lynchings and castrations literalized the equation between the black male and the feminine.

Given this relationship between the male body and cultural power, and the historical features of black male representation as sexual and gendered, it is no coincidence that Black Power discourses would turn to the figuration of sexual difference as the means for making claims to black male empowerment in the 1960s. In 'Initial Reactions on the Assassination of Malcolm X', Eldridge Cleaver epitomizes the rhetorical method of depicting the struggle for Black Power: 'We shall have our manhood. We shall have it or the earth will be leveled by our attempts to gain it' (Cleaver 1968: 66). Such attempts to 'heal the wound of my Castration', as Cleaver writes, are necessary to right the deep wrong inflicted on black men through slavery and cultural dispossession, where '[a]cross the naked abyss of negated masculinity ... I feel a deep, terrifying hurt, the pain of humiliation ... and a compelling challenge to redeem my conquered manhood' (Cleaver 1968: 188–9). By defining the politics of race within a metaphorics of phallic power as a counter to cultural articulations of black male inferiority, Black Power rhetoric reiterates the parameters of black male representation provided by the discourse of sexual difference, simultaneously marking the political and economic as part of a naturalized realm of gender. Such a formulation significantly participates in the broader cultural articulation of racial exploitation and oppression as a problem within the structure of masculine relations themselves.

It is perhaps obvious that such images of an aggressively violent black male who poses a physical threat to 'white civilization' nourishes the cultural fascination with and fantasy of black male castration in the nineteenth century and our own. But while the scenario of seemingly unprovoked black violence is certainly not new, its proliferation since the dawning of Civil Rights and Black Power provides a context in which African American political activity can be defined and contained within the parameters of a socially delinquent, if not pre-eminently dangerous, masculinity. That African American writers and political theorists in the 1960s and 1970s – not only Cleaver, but Amiri Baraka, Ishmael Reed, and Malcolm X – each reiterated at one time the metaphorics of a threatening phallic power attests to the powerful deployment of sexual difference in US culture more generally, and provides the framework for understanding the emergence of Shaft, Superfly, Hammer, Willie Dynamite, Black Belt Jones, and other exceedingly masculine figures in the cinema of the 1970s. The oscillation between feminization and masculinization described here not only marks the oppositional logic of sexual difference that underlies African American male representation for the past two centuries, but specifies the discursive context in which any discussion of contemporary black male cinema must be made.

It is my contention, in fact, that many of the recent films by black male directors seek to subvert and deny in various ways the paradigmatic exchange of activity for objectification, on the one hand, while struggling for a more culturally productive black masculinity on the other. John Singleton's *Boyz N the Hood* (1991) is a case in point, not only because of the narrative's concern for the life-threatening contours of black masculinity, but also because of the attention it has received for purportedly instigating audience violence (see *Newsweek*, July 29, 1991: 48). By displacing the socio-political issues surrounding black masculinity – issues that *Boyz N the Hood*, for one, is at pains to reveal – on to the panic-image of irrational black violence, the logic of white supremacy exchanges the complexities of contemporary US culture for the alternatively terrorizing and appealing phantasm of massive violence and death. But in wrenching the scenario of black masculinity from the more easily consumable images of incipient feminization and one-dimensional criminality, *Boyz N the Hood* grapples quite seriously – if not always satisfactorily – with the contradictions embedded in the black male's social positioning, offering an interesting negotiation of the historical (con)text of black male representation in US cinema and culture.

For feminists schooled in conventional film theory, the kinds of issues I will be highlighting in *Boyz N the Hood*, particularly its political agenda toward a mediated masculinity, might seem to displace the film's overt signs of sexism: its reliance on objectifying language, as well as cinematography, for defining and characterizing women; its binary inscription of masculine and feminine as oppositional personal and cultural encodements; and its figuration of male separatism as part of, and at times precondition to, a black nationalist aesthetic. Clearly, the failure of motherhood and the championing of the black father characterize the oppositional and hierarchical logic of sexual difference that governs the film, providing the terms through which the contemporary crisis of black masculinity is being both challenged and defined. But to point to these representational effects without the historicizing gesture that seeks to place them in the broader context of US cultural production not only reifies their political deployment, but risks the inscription of a feminist analysis inattentive to the multiplicity and overdetermining construction of race and gender. For this reason, while I do not want to dismiss the film's use of certain conventional means for affirming the primacy of the masculine. I also do not want to understand that masculine as simply coterminous with patriarchy itself. For it is patriarchy as well as white supremacy that must be held accountable for the prevailing conditions of destruction and disenfranchisement attending African American men.

Boyz N the Hood specifically highlights this destruction in its opening sequence with two full screen statements: first, 'One out of every 21 Black American males will be murdered ... [and then] Most will die at the hands of another Black male', followed by the camera's rapid focus on a Stop sign. In this half minute, the film delivers its most immediate context and its most overt message, and in doing so establishes a significatory framework through which those who contribute to this cultural undoing are targeted as the primary audience. For a black male to kill another black male, the film posits, is tantamount to killing oneself. But more importantly, it is to act out, to its logical extreme, the desire of white supremacy. Where Spike Lee's *Do the Right Thing* (1989) made cross-racial violence its primary concern, *Boyz* draws its most daring critique of power and the internalized processes of annihilation by foregrounding the trajectories of racism within members of the black community itself. An especially powerful example of this is the presentation of a black male Los Angeles police officer, whose desire to rid the streets of 'niggers' reveals his own sadistic pleasure in the harassment, torture, and destruction of other black men. To counter this kind of black male abandonment of one another, the film offers the primary characters, Furious Styles (Larry Fishburne) and his son, Tre (Cuba Gooding Jr.), whose relationship forges a paradigm of inter-generational bonding that functions in the film's narrative as the means for translating the past and present into a different future for young black men. Locating the significance and impact of white supremacy in broad strokes, the film's primary focus is thus on the structures of discipline turned inward by the African American subject, whose defense against racism is often, paradoxically, a reiterative devaluation of black life.

Defined as a classic coming of age story, *Boyz* moves between the philosophical underpinnings of Furious's approach to teaching his son 'how to be a man' and the codes of masculinity ushered in on the streets. With a mix of neo-nationalist and safe sex rhetoric, Furious wants his son to know 'any fool with a dick can make a baby but only a real man can raise his kids.' His nationalism is highlighted at various, often didactic moments in the film where the link between responsibility and reproduction is set within the overarching context of violence, drugs, and alcohol abuse. In pointing out the significance of gun shops and liquor stores 'on ever corner' in African American neighborhoods, Furious explains to a group of onlookers (in a speech with scenic overtones of a sermon-on-the-mount): 'They want us to kill ourselves ... The best way to kill a people is to destroy their ability to reproduce themselves.' The focus on the question of sex and reproduction throughout the film – and its relation to economic and cultural survival – provides an important rearticulation of what the narrative posits as the prevailing mythos of masculinity, where guns, women, and offspring circulate in a psychological and social nexus of increasingly ineffectual, indeed murderous, machismo. Here, the distance from the black cinema of the 1970s is at its most forceful, as the terrain of sexuality takes on a seriousness that implicitly critiques the iconography of masculine prowess epitomized by Shaft and his various characterological reincarnations. In Singleton's cinematic world, the super phallic imago of black masculinity is too often a self-fulfilling fantasy of a genocidal white supremacy.

The tension between phallicism and a mediated black masculinity is played out in the competing characterizations of young black men in the Styles's neighbourhood, from the troubled Doughboy (Ice Cube) who spends his youth in and out of reform school, to his brother Ricky (Morris Chestnut), a teenage father who is on course for a football scholarship to the University of Southern California, to the more peripheral figures, Monster, Dooky, and the wheel-chair-bound Chris, all participants in Doughboy's raucous circle. Doughboy is, of these players, most central to the narrative, for it is in his story that the primary failure of the masculine eventually emerges as the precondition not only for his own death, but for the revenge slayings he performs on three other young black men. On one level, the narrative too simplistically marks this failure as the absence of the black father (an issue I will return to), as in Furious's early explanation of his strictness to Tre: 'I'm trying to teach you to be responsible. Your little friends across the street, they don't have nobody to show them how to do that. We'll see how they turn out.' But at other discursive levels, the failure of the masculine is more complex, as the scene leading to Doughboy's first arrest for theft indicates. Here, the boys (Doughboy, Ricky, Tre, and Chris) are examining the corpse of a black male murdered and dumped behind an abandoned building when they become targets for harassment by a group of older males. In trying to defend his friends, Doughboy is knocked to the ground, kicked, and left muttering, 'I wish I could kill that mother-fucker.' It is at this point that he decides to go to a nearby store, though he is clearly equipped with no money. By the time we see him again, he is under arrest for shoplifting.

I read Doughboy's response to this scenario within the double context of his ineffectuality and humiliation at the hands of other black men, and as part of the seemingly reduced significatory value of black male life in general. That this humiliation and physical assault is accompanied by the defunct gaze of the culturally abject dead body links Doughboy's transgressive performance to the tableau of racial expenditure that not only organizes but defines the subjective and social contours of contemporary African American culture in the film. His 'criminality' in this and subsequent scenes is part of a performative masculinity whose overdetermination can be envied only in so far as one can ignore its deeper psychological vacuity. This vacuity is evinced in Doughboy's final words of the film, when the deaths of those who killed his brother subtend his now even more intense alienation. In thinking about a local television discussion of increasing world violence, Doughboy notes the absence of any mention of his brother's murder; instead 'They showed all these foreign places ... Either they don't know ... or don't care what's going on in the Hood', he says. 'The shit just goes on and on. The next thing you know somebody'll try to smoke me. Don't matter though. We all have to go sometime.' Doughboy's resignation is the final performative strategy, and its cyclical undoing becomes manifest in an ensuing frame when we are told that 'two weeks later' Doughboy, too, meets his end at the hands of another black male.

But rather than close the film on this moment, Singleton offers the trajectory of Tre's life – his exodus from the Hood to attend Morehouse College – as the future-sustaining alternative, an alternative made possible by the presence of Furious as guide and mentor to his son. This emphasis, as I have mentioned above, is at times disturbingly simple because of the way it posits African American fatherhood as a necessary compensation for the inadequacies of the mother. The very narrative ploy that sanctions Tre's removal from his mother's home in the early moments of the film pivots on her lack: 'I can't teach him how to be a man,' she says to Furious, 'that's your job.' And Ricky and Doughboy's mother is represented as so discriminatory in her love that even Doughboy admits at the end, 'I ain't got no brother, got no mother neither. She loved that boy more than she loved me.' But *Boyz N the Hood* does offer a contradictory reading to this overarching motif when Tre's mother, Reva, historicizes Furious's role: 'Of course you took in your son ... and you taught him what he needed to be a man ... What you did is no different than what mothers have been doing since the beginning of time ... Don't think you're special.' While this speech does not have the authoritative weight of a developed characterization to carry off a more lasting narrative effect, it does provide a telling rupture of the filmic text, drawing in Furious's model masculinity from its often antiseptic and prophetic orbit, and figuring such masculinity as *within* and not opposed to the parameters of the maternal feminine. It is at such a moment that sexual difference and its historical relationship to race in US culture emerge as multi-layered, complex in their interconnections.

Perhaps the film's most sustained and successful tracing of the contradictions and difficulties within the masculine occurs in its depiction of Tre, a contemplative, still virginal young man whose negotiation of the pitfalls of black masculinity is significantly linked to his relationship with women. One of the few characters who does not routinely refer to women with the slang, 'bitch,' Tre not only evinces the tension I have discussed above between phallicism and a mediated masculinity, but embodies that tension in the contradiction between his sexual anxieties and his own falsified self-representation. This contradiction is made apparent in a scene between Furious and Tre where the possibilities for the traditional cinematic scene of masculine bonding across the body of woman are seemingly served up for the purpose of being subverted. When Furious asks his son if 'you got some pussy yet?' Tre concocts an elaborate story of affirmation, one that highlights his sexual performance and appeal. But Tre has misinterpreted the intent of Furious's question, presenting his prowess while Furious is far more concerned about the issue of birth control. The moment of disclosure, this manufactured image of woman as the sexualized object of masculine desire, is thus denied its ability to function as the pretext for closer masculine bonds. In response to Tre's assertion that she was on the pill, Furious reinforces his central lesson: 'If a girl tells you she's on the pill, use something anyway. Pill ain't going to keep your dick from falling off.' The issue of masculine responsibility for sexuality transforms the scene of male bonding into internal discord, and the significance of the body of woman disappears in its inability to fortify relations among men.

In addition, the cinematic construction of Tre's story of sexual bliss highlights the traditionality of this masculine scenario of union as a self-serving production. As Tre unravels his narrative, we are offered a seeming re-enactment of the encounter, from the moment the woman appears (with appropriate jeers and competition among Tre and his friends) to their subsequent sexual consummation at her house the next day. But as Tre tells the story and the woman begins to speak, it is his voice that issues from her mouth, marking in a rather interesting way the very denial of female subjectivity that Tre's narrative itself enacts. In this regard, Singleton's approach to the sexual conquest scenes feature both the significance of sexual confirmation within the mythos of masculine bonds while demonstrating their appropriate contours. In denying the woman the seeming authenticity of her own voice, these scenes reveal their own narrative reliance on a masculine point of view that constructs and defines the parameters of sexual desire. That such a construction is a wholesale fabrication – and that its effect leads to discord and not affirmation within masculine relations – demonstrates one of the particular power aspects of the negotiatory politics of *Boyz N the Hood* and its rearticulation of black masculinity.

For Tre, in fact, the narrative of sexual assertion emerges as a scene of betrayal, a guilt-inducing production that forces him to examine his own fears about sexuality more generally. When his teenage friend who is already a father, Ricky, inquires about his sexual inexperience, Tre admits, 'I was afraid ... of being a daddy.' This fear is legitimized throughout the film, and the end of Tre's virginity is heralded not as a conquest of the masculine over the feminine but as the act of a self-conscious and responsible sexual subject. Indeed, the entire dimensions of masculinity as conquering imposition – whether in terms of sexuality or its metaphoric extension, life on the streets – are reconfigured in *Boyz N the Hood*, enabling an articulation of black masculinity that moves, albeit uneasily, in less than polarized ways within the discursive contours of race and sexual difference. Most importantly perhaps, the film challenges the binary figuration of the black masculine as feminization on one hand or hypermasculinization on the other, seeking a way beyond the representational impasse that oversees the political, economic, and sexual containment of black men. While the political agenda of *Boyz N the Hood* is often undermined, as I have discussed, by its representational effect, the questing gesture toward a different figuration doubles back on the earlier and much heralded black cinema of the 1970s, finding 'manhood' a more complicated and contradictory domain.

That the tenaciousness of such a masculine quest often lends itself rather quickly to feminist suspicion is beyond question. But the political imperative guiding this essay necessitates that we not dismiss, on that basis alone, the significance and implications of this cinema for excavations of the contextual history of race and sexual difference in US culture. I am rejecting, in other words, the notion that because they focus on issues of masculinity, contemporary films by black male directors are simply reinscriptions of the dominant patriarchal organization of US culture – as if attention to the field of masculine relations is in itself either inherently anti-feminist or transhistorically and essentially misogynist. Such a rejection is necessary, I believe, even as we may recognize and lament the startling absence of African American female film-makers, as well as the paucity of scripts concerned with issues affecting most specifically black women. But to posit this absence or paucity as the result of the seeming success of black men in contemporary film is to forge a one-dimensional oppositionality whereby gender becomes the primary figuration of social relations, discounting once again the significance of differences among men in historical, political, and economic ways. These differences provide the broad cultural context through which the narrative of *Boyz N the Hood* in particular is made, establishing the racial dimensions of a competitive masculine order that routinely invests in the destruction of African American men.

While the film's desire to forge a different masculinity, to recognize the framework of masculine relations that underlie race in the US without eschewing the masculine altogether, does not invoke a post-gender utopian feminist vision, its significance lies in foregrounding this specific configuration of race and gender. For it is here that the crisis of race within feminism will continue to visit itself, posing crucial questions about the relationship between the masculine and patriarchal organization that we are as yet unable to adequately understand or answer. What does become clear, within this kind of historicizing discussion of race and sexual difference, is that any simple collapse of issues of the masculine into patriarchal organization sacrifices the very materiality of race and gender in US culture today. It is in this light that I wish to end by reiterating my own political desire in crafting this paper, which is not to appropriate black male cinema for feminism but to place the dilemma of feminism squarely within the discursive field of black masculinity. This means that one does not simply produce a context in which African American male representations are measured in terms of the political standards of feminism, but that their representations provide an important (though not the only) public moment through which the entire domain of sexual difference can be rethought in the cultural context of white racial supremacy. In negotiating this increasingly public moment of black masculine critique, feminism confronts itself precisely where it has been convinced it did not or could not exist, making possible a universe of political alliance no longer reducible to the monolithic laws of gender.

Note

1   Among the films, Mario Van Peebles, *New Jack City* (1991): John Singleton, *Boyz N the Hood* (1991); Spike Lee, *Mo' Better Blues* (1990) and *Jungle Fever* (1991); Matty Rich, *Straight Out of Brooklyn* (1991); Charles Burnett, *To Sleep with Anger* (1990); Robert Townsend, *The Five Heartbeats* (1991); Joseph Vasquez, *Hangin' With the Homeboys* (1991); Ernest Dickerson, *Juice* (1991); Bill Duke, *A Rage in Harlem* (1991); Kevin Hooks, *Go Natalie* (1991); and Charles Lane, *True Identity* (1991).

References

Cleaver, E. (1968) *Soul on Ice*, New York: Dell.
Gibbs, J. T. ed. (1988) *Young, Black and Male in America: an Endangered Species*, Dover, MA: Auburn House Publishing Company.
Harris, T. (1984) *Exorcising Blackness: Historical and Literary Lynching and Burning Rituals*, Bloomington: Indiana University Press.
Wright, R. (1940; rpt 1966) *Native Son*, New York: Harper and Row.

45 There's something queer here

Alexander Doty

[...] I would like to propose 'queerness' as a mass culture reception practice that is shared by all sorts of people in varying degrees of consistency and intensity. Before proceeding, however, I will need to discuss – even defend – my use of 'queer' in such phrases as 'queer positions', 'queer readers', 'queer readings', and 'queer discourses'. In working through my thoughts on gay and lesbian cultural history, I found that while I used 'gay' to describe particulars of men's culture, and 'lesbian' to describe particulars of women's culture, I was hard-pressed to find a term to describe a cultural common ground between lesbians and gays as well as other nonstraights – a term representing unity as well as suggesting diversity. For certain historical and political reasons, 'queer' suggested itself as such a term. As Adele Morrison said in an OUT/LOOK interview: 'Queer is not an "instead of", it's an "inclusive of". I'd never want to lose the terms that specifically identify me.'[1]

Currently, the word 'gay' doesn't consistently have the same gender-unifying quality it may once have possessed. And since I'm interested in discussing aspects of cultural identification as well as of sexual desire, 'homosexual' will not do either. I agree with those who do not find the word 'homosexual' an appropriate synonym for both 'gay' and 'lesbian', as these latter terms are constructions that concern more than who you sleep with – although the objects of sexual desires are certainly central to expressions of lesbian and gay cultural identities. I also wanted to find a term with some ambiguity, a term that would describe a wide range of impulses and cultural expressions, including space for describing and expressing bisexual, transsexual, and straight queerness. While we acknowledge that homosexuals as well as heterosexuals can operate or mediate from within straight cultural spaces and positions – after all, most of us grew up learning the rules of straight culture – we have paid less attention to the proposition that basically heterocentrist texts can contain queer elements, and basically heterosexual, straight-identifying people can experience queer moments. And these people should be encouraged to examine and express these moments *as* queer, not as moments of 'homosexual panic', or temporary confusion, or as unfortunate, shameful, or sinful lapses in judgment or taste to be ignored, repressed, condemned, or somehow explained away within and by straight cultural politics – or even within and by gay or lesbian discourses.

My uses of the terms 'queer readings', 'queer discourses', and 'queer positions', then, are attempts to account for the existence and expression of a wide range of positions within culture that are 'queer' or non-, anti-, or contra-straight. I am using the term 'queer' to mark a flexible space for the expression of all aspects of non- (anti-, contra-) straight cultural production and reception. As such, this cultural 'queer space' recognizes the possibility that various and fluctuating queer positions might be occupied whenever *anyone* produces or responds to culture. In this sense, the use of the term 'queer' to discuss reception takes up the standard binary opposition of 'queer' and 'nonqueer' (or 'straight') while questioning its viability, at least in cultural studies, because, as noted earlier, the queer often operates within the nonqueer, as the nonqueer does within the queer (whether in reception, texts, or producers). The queer readings of mass culture I am concerned with in this essay will be those readings articulating positions *within* queer discourses. That is, these readings seem to be expressions of queer perspectives on mass culture from the inside, rather than descriptions of how 'they' (gays and/or lesbians, usually) respond to, use, or are depicted in mass culture.

When a colleague heard I had begun using the word 'queer' in my cultural studies work, she asked if I did so in order to 'nostalgically' recapture and reassert the 'romance' of the culturally marginal in the face of trends within straight capitalist societies to co-opt or contain aspects of queer cultures. I had, in fact, intended something quite different. By using 'queer', I want to recapture and reassert a militant sense of difference that views the erotically 'marginal' as both (in bell hooks's words) a consciously chosen 'site of resistance' and a 'location of radical openness and possibility'.[2] And I want to suggest that within cultural production and reception, queer erotics are already part of culture's erotic center, both as a necessary construct by which to define the heterosexual and the straight (as 'not queer'), and as a position that can be and is occupied in various ways by otherwise heterosexual and straight-identifying people.

But in another sense recapturing and reasserting a certain nostalgia and romance is part of my project here. For through playfully occupying various queer positions in relation to the fantasy/dream elements involved in cultural production and reception, we (whether straight-, gay-, lesbian-, or bi-identifying) are offered spaces to express a range of erotic desire frequently linked in Western cultures to nostalgic and romantic adult conceptions of childhood. Unfortunately, these moments of erotic complexity are usually explained away as part of the 'regressive' work of mass media, whereby we are tricked into certain 'unacceptable' and 'immature' responses as passive subjects. But when cultural texts encourage straight-identified audience members to express a less-censored range of queer desire and pleasure than is possible in daily life, this 'regression' has positive gender- and sexuality-destabilizing effects. [...]

Clearly we need more popular and academic mass culture work that carefully considers feminine gay and other gendered queer reception practices, as well as those of even less-analyzed queer readership positions formed around the nexus of race and sexuality, or class and sexuality, or ethnicity and sexuality, or some combination of gender/race/class/ethnicity and sexuality. These studies would offer valuable evidence of precisely how and where specific complex constructions of queerness can and do reveal themselves in the uses of mass culture, as well as revealing how and where that mass culture comes to influence and reinforce the process of queer identity formation.

One of the earliest attempts at such a study of queers and mass culture was a series of interviews with nine lesbians conducted by Judy Whitaker in 1981 for *Jump Cut*, 'Hollywood Transformed.' These interviews touched upon a number of issues surrounding lesbian identity, including gender identification. Although careful to label these interviews 'biographical sketches, not sociological or psychological studies', Whitaker does make some comments suggesting the potential for such studies:

> Of the nine women who were interviewed, at least six said they identified at some time with male characters. Often the explanation is that men had the interesting active roles. Does this mean that these lesbians want to be like men? That would be a specious conclusion. None of the women who identified with male characters were 'in love' with the characters' girl friends. All of the interviewees were 'in love' at some time with actresses, but they did not identify with or want to be the male suitors of those actresses. While the context of the discussion is film, what these women are really talking about is their lives.... Transformation and positive self-image are dominant themes in what they have to say. Hollywood is transcended.[3]

After reading these interviews, there might be some question about how fully the straight ideologies Hollywood narratives encourage are 'transcended' by these lesbian readers' uses of mainstream films, for as two of the interviewees remark, 'We're so starved, we go see anything because something is better than nothing,' and 'It's a compromise. It's a given degree of alienation.'[4] This sense of queer readings of mass culture as involving a measure of 'compromise' and 'alienation' contributes to the complexity of queer articulations of mass culture reception. For the pathos of feeling like a mass culture hanger-on is often related to the processes by which queers (and straights who find themselves queerly positioned) internalize straight culture's homophobic and heterocentrist attitudes and later reproduce them in their own queer responses to film and other mass culture forms.

Even so, traditional narrative films such as *Sylvia Scarlett, Gentlemen Prefer Blondes, Trapeze, To Live and Die in L.A., Internal Affairs*, and *Thelma and Louise*, which are ostensibly addressed to straight audiences, often have greater potential for encouraging a wider range of queer responses than such clearly lesbian- and gay-addressed films as *Scorpio Rising, Home Movies, Women I Love*, and *Loads*.[5] The intense tensions and pleasures generated by the woman-woman and man-man aspects within the narratives of the former group of films create a space of sexual instability that already queerly positioned viewers can connect with in various ways, and within which straights might be likely to recognize and express their queer impulses. For example, gays might find a form of queer pleasure in the alternately tender and boisterous rapport between Lorelei/Marilyn Monroe and Dorothy/Jane Russell in *Gentlemen Prefer Blondes*, or in the exhilarating woman-bonding of the title characters in *Thelma and Louise*. Or lesbians and straights could queerly respond to the erotic elements in the relationships between the major male characters in *Trapeze, To Live and Die in L.A.*, or *Internal Affairs*. And any viewer might feel a sexually ambiguous attraction – is it gay, lesbian, bisexual, or straight? – to the image of Katharine Hepburn dressed as a young man in *Sylvia Scarlett*.

Of course, these queer positions and readings can become modified or can change over time, as people, cultures, and politics change. In my own case, as a white gay male who internalized dominant culture's definitions of myself as 'like a woman' in a traditional 1950s and 1960s understanding of who 'a woman' and what 'femininity' was supposed to be, my pleasure in *Gentlemen Prefer Blondes* initially worked itself out through a classic gay process of identifying, alternately, with Monroe and Russell; thereby experiencing vicarious if temporary empowerment through their use of sexual allure to attract men – including the entire American Olympic team. Reassessing the feminine aspects of my gay sexual identity sometime in the 1970s (after Stonewall and my coming out), I returned to the film and discovered my response was now less rooted in the fantasy of being Monroe or Russell and gaining sexual access to men, than in the pleasure of Russell being the 'gentleman' who preferred blonde Monroe, who looked out for her best interests, who protected her against men, and who enjoyed performing with her. This queer pleasure in a lesbian text has been abetted by extratextual information I have read, or was told, about Russell's solicitous and supportive offscreen behavior toward Monroe while making the film. But along with these elements of queer reading that developed from the interaction of my feminine gay identity, my knowledge of extratextual behind-the-scenes gossip, and the text itself, I also take a great deal of direct gay erotic pleasure in the 'Is There Anyone Here for Love?' number, enjoying its blatantly homo-historic and erotic ancient Greek Olympics mise-en-scène (including Russell's large column earrings), while admiring Russell's panache and good humor as she sings, strides, and strokes her way through a sea of half-naked male dancer-athletes. I no longer feel the need to mediate my sexual desires through her.

In 1985, Al La Valley suggested that this type of movement – from negotiating gay sexual desire through strong women stars to directly expressing desire for male images on screen – was becoming increasingly evident in gay culture, although certain forms of identification with women through gay connections with 'the feminine' continue:

> One might have expected Stonewall to make star cults outmoded among gays. In a sense it did: The natural-man discourse, with its strong political and social vision and its sense of a fulfilled and open self, has supplanted both the aesthetic and campy discourses.... A delirious absorption in the stars is now something associated with pre-Stonewall gays or drag queens, yet neither gay openness nor the new machismo has completely abolished the cults. New figures are added regularly: Diana Ross, Donna Summer, Jennifer Holliday from the world of music, for example. There's a newer, more open gay following for male stars: Richard Gere, Christopher Reeve [and, to update, Mel Gibson], even teen hunks like Matt Dillon [Christopher Atkins, Johnny Depp, Jason Priestley and Luke Perry].[6]

One could also add performers such as Bette Midler, Patti LaBelle, and Madonna to La Valley's list of women performers. While ambivalent about her motives ('Is she the Queen of Queers.... Or is she just milking us for shock value?'), Michael Musto's *Outweek* article 'Immaculate Connection' suggests that Madonna is queer culture's post-Stonewall Judy Garland:

> By now, we finally seem willing to release Judy Garland from her afterlife responsibility of being our quintessential icon. And in the land of the living, career stagnation has robbed Diana [Ross], Liza [Minnelli], and Barbra [Streisand] of their chances, while Donna [Summer] thumped the bible on our heads in a way that made it bounce back into her face. That leaves Madonna as Queer Queen, and she merits the title as someone who isn't afraid to offend straight America if it does the rest of us some good.[7]

Musto finds Madonna 'unlike past icons' as she's 'not a vulnerable toy'; this indicates to him the need to reexamine gay culture's enthusiasms for women stars with greater attention to how shifting historic (and perhaps generational) contexts alter the meanings and uses of these stars for particular groups of gay men.[8]

Examining how and where these gay cults of women stars work in relation to what LaValley saw in the mid-1980s as the 'newer, more openly gay following for male stars' would also make for fascinating cultural history. Certainly there have been 'homosexual' followings for male personalities in mass culture since the late nineteenth century, with performers and actors – Sandow the muscleman, Edwin Booth – vying with gay enthusiasms for opera divas and actresses such as Jenny Lind and Lillian Russell. Along these lines, one could queerly combine star studies with genre studies in order to analyze the gay appreciation of women musical performers, and the musical's 'feminine' or 'effeminized' aesthetic, camp, and

emotive genre characteristics (spectacularized decor and costuming, intricate choreography, and singing about romantic yearning and fulfillment), with reference to the
more hidden cultural history of gay erotics centered around men in musicals.

In film, this erotic history would perhaps begin with Ramon Navarro (himself
gay) stripped down to sing 'Pagan Love Song' in *The Pagan*. Beyond this, a gay
beefcake musical history would include Gene Kelly (whose ass was always on
display in carefully tailored pants); numbers like 'Is There Anyone Here for Love?'
(*Gentlemen Prefer Blondes*) and 'Y.M.C.A.' (*Can't Stop the Music*) that feature
men in gym shorts, swimsuits (Esther Williams musicals are especially spectacular
in this regard), military (especially sailor) uniforms, and pseudo-native or pseudo-
classical (Greek and Roman) outfits; films such as *Athena* (bodybuilders), *Seven
Brides for Seven Brothers* (Western Levis, flannel, and leather men), *West Side
Story* (Hispanic and Anglo t-shirted and blue-jeaned delinquents, including a butch
girl); Elvis Presley films (and those of other 'teen girl' pop and rock music idols –
Frank Sinatra, Ricky Nelson, Fabian, Cliff Richard, the Beatles, and so on); and the
films of John Travolta (*Saturday Night Fever, Grease, Staying Alive*), Patrick
Swayze (*Dirty Dancing*), and Mikhail Baryshnikov, who in *The Turning Point and
White Nights* provided the impetus for many gays to be more vocal about their
'lowbrow' sexual pleasure in supposedly high-cultural male bodies. If television,
music video, and concert performers and texts were added to this hardly exhaustive
list, it would include David Bowie, Morrissey, David Cassidy, Tom Jones, and
Marky Mark, among many others, and videos such as *Cherish, Express Yourself*,
and *Justify My Love* (all performed by Madonna), *Being Boring* (The Pet Shop
Boys), *Love Will Never Do Without You* (Janet Jackson), *Just Tell Me That You Want
Me* (Kim Wilde), and *Rico Suave* (Gerardo), along with a number of heavy-metal
videos featuring long-haired lead singers in a variety of skintight and artfully
opened or ripped clothes.[9]

I can't leave this discussion of gay erotics and musicals without a few more
words about Gene Kelly's 'male trio' musicals, such as *On the Town, Take Me Out
to the Ball Game*, and *It's Always Fair Weather*.[10] Clad in sailor uniforms, baseball
uniforms, and Army uniforms, the male trios in these films are composed of two
conventionally sexy men (Kelly and Frank Sinatra in the first two films, Kelly and
Dan Dailey in the last) and a comic, less attractive 'buffer' (Jules Munshin in the
first two, Michael Kidd in the last) who is meant to diffuse the sexual energy generated between the two male leads when they sing and dance together. Other Kelly
films – *Singin' in the Rain, An American in Paris*, and *Anchors Aweigh* – resort to
the more conventional heterosexual(izing) narrative device of using a woman to
mediate and diffuse male-male erotics.[11] But whether in the form of a third man or
an ingenue, these devices fail to fully heterosexualize the relationship between
Kelly and his male costars. In *Singin' in the Rain*, for example, I can't help but read
Donald O'Connor maniacally unleashing his physical energy to entertain Kelly
during the 'Make 'Em Laugh' number as anything but a case of overwrought,
displaced gay desire.

Kelly himself jokingly refers to the queer erotics of his image and his many buddy
musicals in *That's Entertainment!*, when he reveals the answer to the often-asked
question, 'Who was your favorite dancing partner ... Cyd Charisse, Leslie Caron,
Rita Hayworth, Vera-Ellen?,' by showing a clip of the dance he did with Fred Astaire

('The Babbit and the Bromide') in *Ziegfeld Follies*. 'It's the only time we danced together,' Kelly remarks over the clip, 'but I'd change my name to Ginger if we could do it again.' As it turned out, Kelly and Astaire did 'do it again' in *That's Entertainment 2*, and their reunion as a dancing couple became the focus of much of the film's publicity campaign, as had been the case when Astaire reunited with Ginger Rogers in *The Barkleys of Broadway*.[12]

While there has been at the very least a general, if often clichéd, cultural connection made between gays and musicals, lesbian work within the genre has been less acknowledged. However, the evidence of lesbian viewing practices – in articles such as 'Hollywood Transformed,' in videos such as *Dry Kisses Only* (1990, Jane Cottis and Kaucyila Brooke) and *Grapefruit* (1989, Cecilia Dougherty), and in informal discussions (mention *Calamity Jane* to a group of thirty- to forty-something American lesbians) – suggests that lesbian viewers have always negotiated their own culturally specific readings and pleasures within the genre.[13] Although it never uses the word 'lesbian', Lucie Arbuthnot and Gail Seneca's 1982 article 'Pre-text and Text in *Gentlemen Prefer Blondes*' is perhaps the best-known lesbian-positioned piece on the musical. While couched in homosocial rhetoric, this analysis of the authors' pleasures in the film focuses upon Lorelei/Monroe's and Dorothy/Russell's connection to each other through looks, touch, and words ('lovey', 'honey', 'sister', 'dear'). Noting that a 'typical characteristic of [the] movie musical genre is that there are two leads, a man and a woman, who sing and dance together, and eventually become romantically involved,' Seneca and Arbuthnot recognize that in *Gentlemen Prefer Blondes* 'it is Monroe and Russell who sing – and even harmonize, adding another layer to the metaphor – and dance as a team.'[14] Since the men in the film are 'never given a musical role', the authors conclude 'the pre-text of heterosexual romance is so thin that it scarcely threatens the text of female friendship.'[15]

One note hints at a possible butch-femme reading of the Russell/Monroe relationship, centered upon Russell's forthright stride and stance: 'The Russell character also adopts a "masculine" stride and stance. More often, Monroe plays the "lady" to Russell's manly moves. For example, Russell opens doors for Monroe; Monroe sinks into Russell's strong frame, allowing Russell to hold her protectively.'[16] Released in 1953, during the height of traditional butch-femme role-playing in American urban lesbian culture, *Gentlemen Prefer Blondes* could well have been read and enjoyed by lesbians at the time with reference to this particular social-psychological paradigm for understanding and expressing their sexual identity. The film continues to be read along these lines by some lesbians as well as by other queerly positioned viewers. Overall, Seneca and Arbuthnot's analysis of *Gentlemen Prefer Blondes* qualifies as a lesbian reading, as it discusses the film and the musical genre so as to 're-vision ... connections with women' by focusing upon the pleasures of and between women on the screen and women in the audience, rather than on 'the ways in which the film affords pleasure, or denies pleasure, to men'.[17]

Working with the various suggestive comments in this article and considering actual and potential lesbian readings of other musicals can lead to a consideration of other pairs and trios of song-and-dance women performers (often related as sisters in the narratives), certain strong solo women film and video musical stars (Eleanor Powell, Esther Williams, Carmen Miranda, Lena Horne, Eartha Kitt, Doris Day,

Julie Andrews, Tina Turner, Madonna), and musical numbers performed by groups of women, with little or no participation by men. Of particular interest in this latter category are those often-reviled Busby Berkeley musical spectacles, which appear in a different light if one considers lesbians (and other queers) as spectators, rather than straight men. I'm thinking here especially of numbers like 'The Lady in the Tutti-Frutti Hat' in *The Gang's All Here*, where Carmen Miranda triggers an all-woman group masturbation fantasia involving banana dildos and foot fetishism; 'Dames' in *Dames*, where women sleep, bathe, dress, and seek employment together – some pause to acknowledge the camera as bearer of the voyeuristic (straight) male gaze, only to prohibit this gaze by using powder puffs, atomizer sprays, and other objects to cover the lens; 'The Polka-Dot Ballet' in *The Gang's All Here*, where androgynized women in tights rhythmically move neon hoops and large dots in unison, then melt into a vivid, hallucinogenically colored vaginal opening initially inhabited by Alice Faye's head surrounded by shiny cloth; 'Spin a Little Web of Dreams' in *Fashions of 1934*, where a seamstress falls asleep and 'spins a little web of dreams' about a group of seminude women amid giant undulating ostrich-feather fans who, at one point, create a tableau called 'Venus with Her Galley Slaves'; and parts of many other numbers (the two women sharing an upper berth on the Niagara Limited who cynically comment upon marriage in *42nd Street*'s 'Shuffle Off to Buffalo', for example).[18]

Since this discussion of queer positions and queer readings seems to have worked itself out so far largely as a discussion of musical stars and the musical genre, I might add here that of the articles and books written about film musicals only the revised edition of Jane Feuer's *Hollywood Musicals* goes beyond a passing remark in considering the ways in which this genre has been the product of gay film workers, or how the ways in which musicals are viewed and later talked about have been influenced by gay and lesbian reception practices.[19] From most accounts of the musical, it is a genre whose celebration of heterosexual romance must always be read straight. The same seems to be the case with those other film genres typically linked to gays, lesbians, and bisexuals: the horror/fantasy film and the melodrama. While there has been a rich history of queers producing and reading these genres, surprisingly little has been done to formally express this cultural history. There has been more queer work done in and on the horror film: vampire pieces by Richard Dyer, Bonnie Zimmerman, and Sue-Ellen Case; Bruna Fionda, Polly Gladwin, Isiling Mack-Nataf's lesbian vampire film *The Mark of Lilith* (1986); Amy Goldstein's vampire musical film *Because the Dawn* (1988); a sequence in *Dry Kisses Only* that provides a lesbian take on vampire films; an article by Martin F. Norden on sexuality in *The Bride of Frankenstein*; and some pieces on *The Rocky Horror Picture Show* (although most are not written from a queer position), to cite a few examples.[20]

But there is still much left unexamined beyond the level of conversation. Carl Dreyer's lesbophobic 'classic' *Vampyr* could use a thorough queer reading, as could Tod Browning's *Dracula* – which opens with a coach ride through Transylvania in the company of a superstitious Christian straight couple, a suit-and-tie lesbian couple, and a feminine gay man, who will quickly become the bisexual Count Dracula's vampirized servant. Subsequent events in the film include a straight woman who becomes a child molester known as 'The Woman in White' after the count vampirizes her. It is also amazing that gay horror director James Whale has yet to receive full-scale queer auteurist consideration for films such as *Frankenstein* (the idea of men making the 'perfect' man), *The Bride of Frankenstein* (gay Dr. Praetorius; queer Henry Frankenstein; the erotics between the blind man, the monster, and Jesus on the cross; the overall campy atmosphere), *The Old Dark House* (a gay and lesbian brother and sister; a 103-year-old man in the attic who is actually a woman), and *The Invisible Man* (effete, mad genius Claude Rains spurns his fiancée, becomes invisible, tries to find a male partner in crime, and becomes *visible* only after he is killed by the police).[21] Beyond queer readings of specific films and directors, it would also be important to consider how the central conventions of horror and melodrama actually encourage queer positioning as they exploit the spectacle of heterosexual romance, straight domesticity, and traditional gender roles gone awry. In a sense, then, *everyone's* pleasure in these genres is 'perverse', is queer, as much of it takes place within the space of the contra-heterosexual and the contra-straight.

Just how much everyone's pleasures in mass culture are part of this contra-straight, rather than strictly antistraight, space – just how *queer* our responses to cultural texts are so much of the time – is what I'd finally like this chapter to suggest. Queer positions, queer readings, and queer pleasures are part of a reception space that stands simultaneously beside and within that created by heterosexual and straight positions. These positions, readings and pleasures also suggest that what happens in cultural reception goes beyond the traditional opposition of homo and hetero, as queer reception is often a place beyond the audience's conscious 'real-life' definition of their sexual identities and cultural positions – often, but not always, beyond such sexual identities and identity politics, that is. For in all my enthusiasm for breaking down rigid concepts of sexuality through the example of mass culture reception, I don't want to suggest that there is a queer utopia that unproblematically and apolitically unites straights and queers (or even all queers) in some mass culture reception area in the sky. Queer reception doesn't stand outside personal and cultural histories; it is part of the articulation of these histories. This is why, politically, queer reception (and production) practices can include everything from the reactionary to the radical to the indeterminate, as with the audience for (as well as the producers of) 'queercore' publications, who individually and collectively often seem to combine reactionary and radical attitudes.

What queer reception often does, however, is stand outside the relatively clear-cut and essentializing categories of sexual identity under which most people function. You might identify yourself as a lesbian or a straight woman yet queerly experience the gay erotics of male buddy films such as *Red River* and *Butch Cassidy and the Sundance Kid*; or maybe as a gay man your cultlike devotion to *Laverne and Shirley, Kate and Allie*, or *The Golden Girls* has less to do with straight-defined cross-gender identification than with your queer enjoyment in how these series are crucially concerned with articulating the loving relationships between women.[22] Queer readings aren't 'alternative' readings, wishful or willful misreadings, or 'reading too much into things' readings. They result from the recognition and articulation of the complex range of queerness that has been in popular culture texts and their audiences all along.

Notes

1   Adele Morrison as quoted in 'Queer', Steve Cosson, OUT/LOOK **11** (Winter 1991): 21.
2   bell hooks, 'Choosing the Margins as a Space of Radical Openness', *Yearning: Race. Gender, and Cultural Politics* (Boston: South End Press, 1990), 153.
3   Judy Whitaker, 'Hollywood Transformed', *Jump Cut* **24/25** (1981): 33.
4   Ibid., 34.
5   Films mentioned in this section: *Sylvia Scarlett* (1936, RKO, George Cukor), *Gentlemen Prefer Blondes* (1953, Twentieth Century-Fox, Howard Hawks), *Trapeze* (1956, United Artists, Carol Reed), *To Live and Die in L.A.* (1985, New Century, William Friedkin), *Internal Affairs* (1990, Paramount, Mike Figgis), *Thelma and Louise* (1991, MGM, Ridley Scott), *Scorpio Rising* (1962–63, Kenneth Anger), *Home Movies* (1972, Jan Oxenberg), *Women I Love* (1976, Barbara Hammer), *Loads* (1980, Curt McDowell).
6   Al LaValley, 'The Great Escape', *American Film* **10**, no. **6** (April 1985): 71.
7   Michael Musto, 'Immaculate Connection', *Outweek* **90** (March 20, 1991): 35–36.
8   Ibid., 36.
9   Films mentioned in this section: *The Pagan* (1929, MGM, W. S. Van Dyke), *Athena* (1954, MGM, Richard Thorpe), *Seven Brides for Seven Brothers* (1954, MGM, Stanley Donen), *West Side Story* (1961, United Artists, Robert Wise and Jerome Robbins), *Saturday Night Fever* (1977, Paramount, John Badham), *Grease* (1980, Paramount, Randall Kleiser), *Staying Alive* (1984, Paramount, Sylvester Stallone), *Dirty Dancing* (1987, Vestron, Emile Ardolino), *The Turning Point* (1977, Twentieth Century-Fox, Herbert Ross), *White Nights* (1987, Paramount, Taylor Hackford).
10   Films cited: *On the Town* (1950, MGM, Gene Kelly and Stanley Donen), *Take Me Out to the Ball Game* (1949, MGM, Busby Berkeley), *It's Always Fair Weather* (1955, MGM, Gene Kelly and Stanley Donen).
11   Films cited: *Singin' in the Rain* (1952, MGM, Gene Kelly and Stanley Donen), *An American in Paris* (1951, MGM, Vincente Minnelli), *Anchors Aweigh* (1945, MGM, George Sidney).
12   Films cited: *That's Entertainment!* (1974, MGM, Jack Haley, Jr.), *Ziegfeld Follies* (1946, MGM, Vincente Minnelli), *That's Entertainment 2* (1976, MGM, Gene Kelly), *The Barkleys of Broadway* (1949, MGM, Charles Walters).
13   Film cited: *Calamity Jane* (1953, Warners, David Butler).
14   Lucie Arbuthnot and Gail Seneca, 'Pre-text and Text in *Gentlemen Prefer Blondes*', *Film Reader* **5** (1982): 20. This essay is reprinted in *Issues in Feminist Film Criticism*, ed. Patricia Erens (Bloomington and Indianapolis: Indiana University Press, 1990), 112–25.
15   Arbuthnot and Seneca, 'Pre-text and Text', 21.
16   Ibid., 23.
17   Ibid., 21.
18   Films mentioned in this section: *The Gang's All Here* (1943, Twentieth Century-Fox, Busby Berkeley), *Dames* (1934, Warners, Ray Enright), *Fashions of 1934* (1934, Warners, William Dieterle), *42nd Street* (1933, Warners, Lloyd Bacon).
19   Feuer's 'Gay Readings of Musicals' section in *Hollywood Musicals* (London: BFI/Macmillan) concentrates on gay male production and reception of musicals.
20   Articles mentioned in this section: Richard Dyer, 'Children of the Night: Vampirism as Homosexuality, Homosexuality as Vampirism', *Sweet Dreams: Sexuality, Gender and Popular Fiction*, ed. Susannah Radstone (London: Lawrence and Wishart, 1988), 47–72; Bonnie Zimmerman, '*Daughters of Darkness*: Lesbian Vampires', *Jump Cut* **24/25** (1981): 23–24; Sue-Ellen Case, 'Tracking the Vampire', *differences* **3**, no. 2

(Summer 1991): 1–20; Martin F. Norden, 'Sexual References in James Whale's *Bride of Frankenstein*', *Eros in the Mind's Eye: Sexuality and the Fantastic in Art and Film*, ed. Donald Palumbo (New York: Greenwood Press, 1986), 141–50; Elizabeth Reba Weise, 'Bisexuality, *The Rocky Horror Picture Show*, and Me', *Bi Any Other Name: Bisexual People Speak Out*, ed. Loraine Hutchins and Lani Kaahumanu (Boston: Alyson, 1991), 134–39.

21 Films mentioned in this section: *Vampyr* (1931, Gloria Film, Carl Theodore Dreyer), *Dracula* (1931, Universal, Tod Browning), *Frankenstein* (1931, Universal, James Whale), *The Bride of Frankenstein* (1935, Universal, James Whale), *The Old Dark House* (1932, Universal, James Whale), *The Invisible Man* (1933, Universal, James Whale).

22 Films and television series mentioned in this section: *Red River* (1948, United Artists, Howard Hawks), *Butch Cassidy and the Sundance Kid* (1969, Twentieth Century-Fox, George Roy Hill), *Laverne and Shirley* (1976–83, ABC), *Kate and Allie* (1984–90, CBS), *The Golden Girls* (1985–92, NBC).

46 On not being Lady Macbeth: some (troubled) thoughts on lesbian spectatorship

Tamsin Wilton

Film theory, including much from feminist and queer perspectives, has come to be dominated by a psychoanalytic paradigm that itself is dominated by a highly restrictive binarism whereby masculine/feminine are not only understood as the definitional polarities of gender but also coopted unproblematically as the exemplary paradigm for understanding sexual desire, pleasure and identity. Film theory is not unique in this, rather it is merely obedient to the hegemonic paradigm which has structured mainstream thinking about both gender and the erotic since Freud (and indeed, on and off since Plato). It also reflects [...] what has tended to happen in film itself, whereby a pop-Freudian paradigm has profoundly influenced film-making. This obedience to the paradigm has presented difficulties for those who would claim a place for women as spectators rather than as spectacle of film, for, within the psychoanalytic paradigm, agency (and this includes ownership of the gaze), is masculine. Feminist film theory has tied itself up in increasingly baroque knots trying to establish a coherent and radical theory of female cinema spectatorship and of female identification as part of that spectatorship within the terms of this binarism (Stacey 1994). For lesbian film theory, there is the added problem that psychoanalytic binarism has no place for lesbian desire.

Issues of identification and spectatorship remain moot within and between competing theories of film and audience, and are of course especially problematic for a lesbian viewer, for only a tiny proportion of films construct a lesbian viewing position or enable lesbians to enjoy uncomplicated identification with either onscreen character or voyeuristic camera. Indeed, if Laura Mulvey is to be believed, it is impossible for any woman to get pleasure from a mainstream narrative film without temporarily unsexing herself in order to carry out what is understood to be an intrinsically male set of behaviours, *à la* Lady Macbeth (Mulvey 1981). Yet lesbians still go to the movies and still get pleasure from watching films. Because it has no place within film theory, and because it is largely excluded from authorial intent or textual construct, this is a pleasure which many lesbian film critics have described as being somehow 'against the grain' (Florence 1993), a reading disobedient to intended address. Some critics have even gone so far as to suggest that queer consumers (and producers) of culture are so accustomed to self-consciously inhabiting contradictory viewing/reading positions as to make us preeminently skilled deconstructionists, subtle cynics about the various performative gender/sex roles which the less sophisticated still assume to be somehow natural or real (Dyer 1991; Traub 1991). As Dyer puts it:

> In this perspective both authorship and being lesbian/gay become a kind of performance, something we all do but only with the terms, the discourses, available to us, and whose relationship to the imputed self doing the performing cannot be taken as read. This may be a characteristically gay (I hesitate to claim lesbian/gay) perception, since for us performance is an everyday issue. (Dyer 1991, p. 188)

The notion of camp is of use here, and Dyer's hesitation to do violence to the question of gender marks a significant difference between lesbians and gay men with regard to camp. Queer theorists have mounted a resounding (and I think successful) challenge to Susan Sontag's interpretation of camp as apolitical and assimilationist/assimilated (see the essays collected in Meyer 1994), and insist rather on its political and its specifically queer status. Camp is understood within this queer paradigm to be rooted in gay men's lack of access to the machinery of representation (which is cultural reproduction). For Cynthia Morrill,

> Camp discourse is the epiphenomenon of the queer subject's proscription in the dominant order; it is an effect of homophobia ... Camp results from the uncanny experience of looking into a nonreflective mirror and falling outside of the essentialized ontology of heterosexuality, a queer experience indeed. (Morrill 1994, p. 119)

Furthermore, it is claimed that, because gay men have been obliged by the homophobic elision of sexuality and gender identity to pay critical attention to gender, camp has emerged as a radical paradigm within which gender becomes artificial and open to deconstruction: 'To some extent, Camp originates in a gay male perception that gender is, if not quite arbitrary, certainly not biologically determined or natural, but rather that gender is socially constructed, artificial, and performed (and thus open to being consciously deformed)' (Kleinhans 1994, p. 188). This may be the case, but camp is a concept which is itself clearly gender-specific and hence problematic for lesbians. Gay men may lack access to the machinery of representation *qua* gay, they certainly do not *qua* men. It is the execrated sexuality 'gay' which finds no reflection in the mirror of cultural production, *not* the privileged gender 'man'. Camp is less a product of lack of access to the machinery of representation and more a product of *compromised* access to that machinery. It is the lesbian who, vampire-like, must look in vain for her reflection in the glass, invisible by reason of the desire that her gender makes impossible. It is the lesbian who, more than any other sexed and gendered subject, cannot be successfully incorporated into the body of psychoanalytic film theory, and it is the question of lesbian spectatorship, and specifically of lesbian identification within that spectating, that I am concerned with here. [...]

[...] *Strictly Ballroom* (1992) was hailed by *Gay Times* as: 'Beautifully constructed, emotionally involving and a riot of sheer camp.... a thoroughly satisfying movie – a glorious mix of tears and laughter' (Burton 1993). In case you missed it this Australian-made film, a 'surprise international hit' of 1992, tells the story of how the handsome Scott brings a dash of authentic passion to the ersatz posturings of the ballroom dancing competition circuit, by scavenging on the Spanish heritage of his ugly-duckling partner, Fran. Camping it up to the hilt in a riotous blizzard of Frocks and 1950s pastiche, the film struck me as being a softened up, less cynical and decidedly less queer version of *Hairspray* (1988). It is, of course, not authentic (i.e., queer) camp. Rather it is vestigial or assimilated camp, evidence of what Margaret Thompson Drewal (1994) calls the 'camp trace'. In postmodernity, subcultural codes and vernaculars are constantly incorporated into the body of mainstream culture, witness Madonna's assimilation of S/M. 'The media world's cannibalization of subcultures' as Chuck Kleinhans puts it, 'is a structural feature of the culture industry' (1994, p. 187), and *Strictly Ballroom* is a good example of this cannibalism.[1]

The main theme is a familiar one: white kid from alienated, artificial, colonialist culture goes out and steals some authenticity from another, less civilized, immigrant/oppressed culture and brings back the booty. His peers are at first scandalized, but what he brings back calls to something buried in them beneath the thin veneer of that civilization, and narrative closure is attained when their alienation (seen as the inevitable price of civilization) is breached and their lives enriched by this enforced contact with authenticity. This may only be accomplished by breaking through (not breaking down) the social barriers between (in this case) white Australian and Spanish Australian culture, a task which takes the form of transforming Fran: reforming her immigrant poverty, ugliness and nonconformity into a predictable docility to the prevailing white Australian standards of female beauty.

From a lesbian point of view – especially a lesbian feminist point of view – the film sucks. Fran is introduced as a beginner with *no partner*, when in fact she is partnered by a (fat) woman. During one of the diegetic moments of crisis, we see her, transformation temporarily suspended, back in beginners with 'no partner', whirling miserably around the floor with the fat woman again. The message is almost farcically anti-lesbian: to have a female partner *means* to be unattractive to men (both women are presented as ugly when they are dancing together) and *means* 'really' to have no partner at all. In addition what Scott needs to learn from the authentic Spanish dancing lessons Fran's parents give him is not merely passion but passionate heterosexual masculinity. What would Freud have to say about the scenes where Fran's father teaches him the steps of the male dancer, where her mother stands in for Fran and teaches Scott how to dance properly with a woman, or where mother's dancing dress is handed on to Fran to enable her to dance with Scott!

Ironically, the hidden text of this gay cult film is profoundly anti-gay. Heterosexuality is clearly in crisis on the ballroom dancing circuit, with male/female partnerships disintegrating faster than you can say 'passa doble'. The suggestion made by the film is that this crisis in heterosexuality is due to the artifice and alienation of the postmodern world, where authentic manliness and womanliness are no longer passed on through the generations. What saves Scott and Fran is that they are privileged to have access to real, genuine, 100 per cent authentic traditional heterosexuality, as represented by Fran's immigrant Spanish family where the men and the woman know their places and are content. We are being seduced back to basics.

In order to reach this place of safety for heterosexuality and as heterosexuals, both Fran and Scott must be rescued from the alternative. Scott is quite clearly at risk of homosexuality, simply because he is a dancer. In addition, his father is a hen-pecked failure – nurturing a dangerous secret from his inadequate dancing past – and hence not in a position to initiate his son into the mysteries of virility. Fran is quite overtly saved from lesbianism – a salvation symbolically represented by the ritualistic removal of her glasses by Scott. Mary Ann Doane has suggested that the clichéd transformation of the female ugly duckling by ritualistic removal of the glasses represents a cinematic defence against female usurpation of the gaze, and the agency that comes with it:

> Glasses worn by a woman in the cinema do not generally signify a deficiency in seeing but an active looking, or simply the fact of seeing as opposed to being seen. The intellectual woman looks and analyses, and in usurping the gaze she poses a threat to the entire system of representation. It is as if the woman had forcefully moved to the other side of the specular. (Doane 1992, p. 236)

In Fran's case, the usurped gaze threatens to be doubly dangerous, because the implied object of her bespectacled gaze is her female dancing partner. Strange things are done to the cinematic gaze when it associates with Fran. That female partner, whom we see quite clearly, is rendered invisible, nonexistent, by the script. Although we *see* a woman, we *hear* that Fran has *no* partner. Interestingly, hearing takes precedence over seeing *while Fran is wearing her glasses*. Once Scott removes her glasses, she becomes more dependent on his guidance, and much more active in looking. Stripped of the means to see clearly, she gazes long and increasingly lovingly into his face. A disobedient lesbian reading which springs to mind is that she only fancies Scott once she can't see clearly.

As an apology for white colonialism and an active 'promoter' of heterosexuality, it is clear that the universally positive gay response to *Strictly Ballroom* must have to do with something other than its narrative content. The attractions of Paul Mercurio, who plays Scott, loomed large in the promotion of the film, with his suitably confrontational face gazing directly at you from the publicity poster. Certainly the film offers him as object of desire as much as or perhaps more than Tara Morice (Fran), and it is hardly surprising that, given the hegemonic status of the *male* sexually desiring gaze, any object of desire of whatever gender should be assumed to be an object of desire for men. The film was promoted with full page adverts in *Gay Times*, in which context Mercurio became a sexual product alongside porn star Jeff Stryker and the Foto Fantasy Guys.

But I am not a gay man, and found myself unable to take either Fran or Scott seriously as objects of desire, despite having Scott's moderate amount of chest hair looming at me from the screen and being privileged witness to the despectacling of Fran. Yet I thoroughly enjoyed the film, as did many of my lesbian friends, weeping and laughing in all the right places and telling other dykes that they simply had to see it. Why? [...]

[...] There was no hard work involved in my engagement with *Strictly Ballroom*. The film is a clever pastiche, giving off very clear messages that you are not *supposed* to take it seriously, any more than you are supposed to regard candyfloss as food or Mills & Boon as literature. The terms of engagement set by the film are that you should 'simply' abandon yourself to the pleasurable superficialities of the sensuous experience it offers. German and Germanist scholars, not least Heidi Schlüpmann, have resurrected *Zerstreuung*, a word current in Weimar Germany meaning 'abandoning oneself to pure appearances, to the 'dazzle', renouncing concern with meaning' (Schlüpmann, cited in Dyer 1992, p. 9), and it is a useful word to sum up the process by which I got great pleasure from *Strictly Ballroom*. For the 'dazzle' of the film is delightful and very well done; the self-consciously clichéd romantic narrative preempts cynicism, and the colour and sparkle of the world it depicts seduce the eye.

But that leaves open the question as to why *Zerstreuung* should be in and of itself pleasurable. I am forced to conclude that the pleasure I took from *Strictly Ballroom* lay simply in my queer-chameleon ability to adopt an alien reading position for the night. This ability to spectate/consume from multiple positions is becoming a given in lesbian cultural criticism. There is a tendency to assume that such a change of position is necessary for pleasurable lesbian consumption of all cultural products, and indeed, for lesbian cultural production: '[we can all] read from more than one position (what other explanation is there for lesbian enjoyment of mainstream novels?) and write multifaceted texts' (Lewis 1992, p. 20). But my (guilty) pleasure in *Strictly Ballroom* lay in being able to *set aside entirely* my lesbian reading position and have a rest from it. As 'who I am', namely a queer feminist with a critique of racism, I could not possibly have sat through the film without considerable discomfort. But far from 'not sit[ting] easily and shift[ing] restlessly in [my] borrowed transvestite clothes', as Mulvey insists all women must at the cinema (Mulvey 1981, p. 33), I revelled in my successful temporary escape from my social and political position.

There is an influential sociology of escapism (Cohen and Taylor 1974) which characterizes cinema (among other sites) as a 'free area' wherein the fantasies which maintain sanity may flourish, safely contained. It is this perspective which much Freudian/Lacanian-inspired film theory seems to me to lack. The question is not, which sex position does a woman (or a man, or a lesbian) have to occupy in order to get pleasure from film, but what pleasures are to be gained from that positioning itself? Mulvey admits that the fantasy of control offered by identification with a male protagonist may present women with something denied to them in their 'real' lives: 'She may find herself secretly, unconsciously almost, enjoying the freedom of action and control over the diegetic world that identification with a hero provides' (Mulvey 1981, p. 29). I think that a less complex set of pleasures is at issue, one which does not depend for its success on identification with onscreen characters but on the degree to which the film facilitates the viewer relinquishing her 'self', escaping for a while from identity.

This isn't a new idea. Peter Wells, the New Zealand writer and film-maker who wrote and codirected *Desperate Remedies* (1993), told Rose Collis that the film was 'trying to reconnect with that extreme world which, on one level, doesn't have anything to do with reality, but does answer the need to pop into another life' (Collis 1994); and 'escapism' has long been recognized as a desirable feature of 'entertainment' (Dyer 1992). Of course, some political commentators believe the power of escapist fantasy to be a dangerous drug, the sugar on the pill of capitalism/patriarchy/homophobia. This may well be true, although some sociologists have suggested that political radicalism itself is merely a different kind of strategy for escaping an intolerable existence (Cohen and Taylor 1974). What remains to be asked is, what is to be gained by sitting in a darkened room and 'popping into another life'?

This is where I want to pull back once more from the screen, glittering seductively with frocks and jocks from the Pan-Pacific ballroom dancing finals, and pan around to me, sitting in the dark, face turned obediently up to the screen, lesbian feminist self switched off for the duration. What is going on? [...]

Watching a film is clearly hard work for the lesbian spectator. To read much lesbian film theory is to understand lesbian spectatorship as a constant struggle to insist on and locate 'lesbian' as a reading/viewing position. This is in itself a mightly battle, in the teeth of Freudian/Lacanian film theory which sets up a rigidly (one might say, anxiously) gendered polarity whereby the unstable, multiple inflections of genders, sexualities and desires are mercilessly beaten into the square hole of heterosexuality (see Dyer 1992, pp. 4–5, or Stacey 1994, for sensible deflations of psychoanalytic film theory). The lesbian spectator is forced to defend herself against a plethora of fantastic phallocentric assumptions that psychoanalysis has bred, and that have become influential even within feminism. Thus, for example, Teresa de Lauretis is obliged to rescue lesbian desire from Julia Kristeva's declaration that:

> Lesbian loves comprise the delightful arena of a neutralized, filtered libido, devoid of the erotic cutting edge of masculine sexuality. Light touches, caresses, barely distinct images fading one into the other, growing dim or veiled without bright flashes into the mellowness of a dissolution, a liquefaction, a merger. (cited in de Lauretis 1991, p. 253)

As a lesbian reader I chuckle and ask myself *who* she has been having lesbian sex with, and what recreational drugs were involved at the time. I also recognize, as does de Lauretis, that ignorance and silence about lesbian sexuality is so utter that non-lesbians reading Kristeva will have no doubt that she is speaking the truth, and will be grateful for having their own phallocentrism reassured and their anxiety about lesbians assuaged. Public speech about lesbians (and film is in this category) is thus an automatic source of anxiety for lesbians, who fear having to defend themselves against misrepresentation.

In addition, the elision of sexuality and gender makes it almost impossible for any film theory informed by psychoanalysis to make sense of lesbians. Jackie Stacey is right when she calls for an untangling of the two:

This insistence upon a gendered dualism of sexual desire maps homosexuality on to an assumed antithesis of masculinity and femininity. Such an assumption precludes a description of homosexual positioning.... In arguing for a more complex model of cinema spectatorship, I am suggesting that we need to separate gender identity from sexuality, too often conflated in the name of sexual difference. (Stacey 1992, p. 249)

Unless the separation that Stacey advocates occurs, the unfortunate lesbian viewer is doomed in film theory to ricochet back and forth between 'castrated male' and 'fetishized phallic female', existing only as an antidote to male anxiety, a salve for the cruellest cut of all. Having spent so much time and energy fighting the windmills of penis envy, castration anxiety, etc. (themselves a form of cultural misrepresentation), insisting that 'a lass (is) not a lack' (Doane 1992, p. 230), there is little left to expend on the business of watching.

What we are watching also presents us with a struggle. Saturated as it is in patriarchal, heterosexist signs, codes and ideologies, privileging as it does the sexual and erotic as sites of scopophilic pleasure, film by and large obliges its lesbian spectators to engage with an undiluted reflection of mainstream cultural hostility to lesbian existence. Either there are no lesbians, or, if there are, they must bear the burden of representing the whole class 'lesbian'. As Sander Gilman notes in the context of race: 'the representation of individuals implies the creation of some greater class or classes to which the individual is seen to belong' (Gilman 1992, p. 171). Any onscreen lesbian must meet the demands of every other lesbian looking at her that she represent *their* lesbianness. Clearly this can only end in tears.

There is, further, the social as opposed to the theoretical business of being a lesbian. For all the (interesting, valid and useful) challenges posed by social construction theory to the 'reality' of a lesbian identity, the materialities of lesbian oppression continue. Even social construction theory does not propose that 'lesbian' is any less real than any other social category, and as such, 'women' who identify as 'lesbian' inhabit a particular set of interstices among social notions of gender, desire, deviance, criminality, sin, naturalness, etc. It is a complex positioning, but what it boils down to is oppression. As a lesbian sitting in a cinema I bring personal and social narratives of oppression – both material and ideological – along with me. When called upon, [...] I make use of that set of narratives to construct engagement strategies with which to make meaning of the film; such is the nature of the cinematic contract. But the delight of spectating *Strictly Ballroom* lies precisely in the film's persuasive invitation to set all that aside, to step out of the tight and beleaguered social space which, as a lesbian, I inhabit as a matter of course. Is this perhaps the simple solution to the appeal of escapist fantasy cinema for gay men? Can the success of such films as *The Wizard of Oz* or *Strictly Ballroom* in the gay milieu be due not to the production side of the cinematic contract, but to the consumption side?

If we understand the cultural product which is the 'meaning' of films to occur [...] at the meniscus between production (determined by and expressive of specific social and economic relations of power) and consumption (equally determined by and expressive of such relations), then the relative significance of the social factors impacting upon production and consumption will determine the success or otherwise of the reception of a particular film by a particular social group. When the weight of homophobia (or racism, or sexism/misogyny) is present as a determining factor on the consumption side of the contract, the business of simple escapism takes on added significance. To be able to sit in the dark, temporarily released from one's own performative obligations, and be allowed to take unproblematic pleasure in the joys, sorrows and fantasies of the wider culture, is like going on queer holiday; an experience that partakes of the painful and poignant illusion of stepping out of the (cold, dark) margins and being included within society for a change. [...]

Note

1   In contrast, Stewart Main and Peter Well's queer-produced film *Desperate Remedies* (1993) is authentic camp, making hay not only with the codification systems of heterosex, but with heterosexuality itself, something that *Strictly Ballroom* conspicuously refuses to do.

References

Burton, P. (1993) Review of *Strictly Ballroom*, in *Gay Times*, July 1993.

Cohen, S. and Taylor, L. (1974) *Escape Attempts: The Theory and Practice of Resistance to Everyday Life*, Harmondsworth, Penguin; new edition, London: Routledge, 1994.

Collis, R. (1994) 'Peter Wells: Throwing Naturalism Aside', in *Gay Times*, January 1994.

de Lauretis, T. (1991) 'Film and the Visible', in Bad Object-Choices (eds), *How Do I Look? Queer Film and Video*, Seattle: Bay Press.

Doane, M. A. (1992) 'Film and the Masquerade: Theorising the Female Spectator', in M. Merck *et al.* (eds), *The Sexual Subject: A Screen Reader in Sexuality*, London: Routledge.

Drewal, M. Thompson (1994) 'The Camp Trace in Corporate America: Liberace and the Rockettes and Radio City Music Hall', in M. Meyer (ed.), *The Politics and Poetics of Camp*, London: Routledge.

Dyer, R. (1991) 'Believing in Fairies: The Author and the Homosexual', in D. Fuss (ed.), *Inside/Out: Lesbian Theories, Gay Theories*, London: Routledge.

—— (1992) *Only Entertainment*, London: Routledge.

Florence, P. (1993) 'Lesbian Cinema, Women's Cinema', in G. Griffin (ed.), *Outwrite: Lesbianism and Popular Culture*, London: Pluto Press.

Gilman, S. L. (1992) 'Black Bodies, White Bodies: Towards an Iconography of Female Sexuality in Late Nineteenth Century Art, Medicine and Literature', in J. Donald and A. Rattansi (eds), *'Race', Culture and Difference*, London: Sage.

Kleinhans, C. (1994) 'Taking Out the Trash: Camp and the Politics of Parody', in M. Meyer (ed.), *The Politics and Poetics of Camp*, London: Routledge.

Lewis, R. (1992) 'The Death of the Author and the Resurrection of the Dyke', in S. Munt (ed.), *New Lesbian Criticism: Literary and Cultural Readings*, Hemel Hempstead: Harvester Wheatsheaf.

Meyer, M. (ed.) (1994) *The Politics and Poetics of Camp*, London: Routledge.

Morrill, C. (1994) 'Revamping the Gay Sensibility: Queer Camp and Dyke Noir', in M. Meyer (ed.), (1994) *The Politics and Poetics of Camp*, London: Routledge.

Mulvey, L. (1981) 'Afterthoughts on "Visual Pleasure and Narrative Cinema" inspired by King Vidor's *Duel in the Sun* (1946)', in L. Mulvey (1989) *Visual and Other Pleasures*, London: Macmillan.

Stacey, J. (1992) 'Desperately Seeking Difference', in M. Merck *et al.* (eds), *The Sexual Subject: A Screen Reader in Sexuality*, London: Routledge.

—— (1994) *Star Gazing: Hollywood Cinema and Female Spectatorship*, London: Routledge.

Traub, V. (1991) 'The Ambiguities of "Lesbian" Viewing Pleasure: The (Dis)articulations of *Black Widow*', in J. Epstein and K. Straub (eds), *Body Guards: The Cultural Politics of Gender Ambiguity*, London: Routledge.

INDEX